Fundamentals of Java Programming for Information Systems

AF761082

Jeremy D. Ezell

James Madison University

Prospect Press

Copyright © 2024 Prospect Press. All rights reserved.

No part of this publication may be reproduced, stored in a retrieval system, or transmitted in any form or by any means, electronic, mechanical, photocopying, recording, scanning, or otherwise, except as permitted under Sections 107 or 108 of the 1976 United States Copyright Act, without the prior written permission of the Publisher. Requests to the Publisher for permission should be addressed to the Permissions Department, Prospect Press, 47 Prospect Parkway, Burlington, VT 05401, or emailed to Beth.golub@prospectpressvt.com.

Founded in 2014, Prospect Press serves the academic discipline of Information Systems by publishing essential and innovative textbooks across the curriculum, including introductory, emerging, and upper-level courses. Based in Burlington, Vermont, Prospect Press distributes titles worldwide. We welcome new authors to send proposals or inquiries to Beth.golub@ProspectPressVT.com.

Oracle, Java, MySQL, and NetSuite are registered trademarks of Oracle and/or its affiliates. Other names may be trademarks of their respective owners.

Editor: Beth Lang Golub
Assistant Editor: Dave Williams
Production Management: Scribe Inc.
Cover Design: Annie Clark

eTextbook:
Edition 1.0
ISBN: 978-1-958303-04-7
Available from Redshelf and VitalSource

Printed Paperback:
Edition 1.0
ISBN: 978-1-958303-05-4
Available from Redshelf

For more information, visit https://www.prospectpressvt.com/textbooks/ezell-java

To Mom,
who stressed the importance of learning early

To Nikki,
who offered encouragement and support through long hours of writing

To Bobby,
who once asked "OK, but what can you do *with it?" regarding programming*

To Spencer,
whose many successes I look up to every day and who cheers me on

To every single student
who thought success in learning programming was beyond them

Contents

The six companion chapters are included in the eTextbook only. For those using the paperback version, PDFs of the companion chapters can be freely downloaded from the title's website at https://www.prospectpressvt.com/textbooks/ezell-java. Scroll to the red horizontal menu bar, then click on "Student Resources."

Preface

About the Text

Welcome to *Fundamentals of Java Programming for Information Systems*. This textbook explores programming concepts in the Java language with a specific focus on solving real-world business problems through an information systems (IS) development lens. Application development examples throughout this textbook include business-oriented and information systems–related examples in management, finance, economics, and accounting.

The vast majority of programming textbooks, including those covering the Java language, include a range of topics far wider than those typically needed in a business-oriented programming course. This often results in the following:

- Instructors using a textbook containing topical material far in excess of what is taught or needed for their course
- Often complex course schedules where students have to be guided around topics, problems, and chapters that are not used or immediately relevant, causing a disjointed learning experience
- Programming concepts that are "muddied" with topics and examples that, while rigorous, are not directly applicable to a business-oriented curriculum, adding to students' difficulty in learning
- Considerable additional work needed on the part of the instructor to develop materials, programming assignments, exam and quiz questions, and larger projects that allow for a direct application to business problems

This textbook takes an information systems–focused approach to programming in the Java language with topics, problems, and materials that are both rigorous in their quality and relevant in their business focus. Instructors will find chapter topics, code examples, learning problems, and programming assignments that are ready to use within an information systems curriculum, needing minimal revision compared to the contents of alternative programming textbooks.

Target Audience

This textbook has been designed for Java programming courses at the undergraduate or graduate levels within an information systems or business curriculum. No prior programming experience is needed by the student. Instructors teaching information systems or business courses will find this textbook relevant and valuable for use in the following:

- One-semester courses covering fundamentals of business application development using the Java language
- One-semester intermediate business application development courses using the Java language for students who have studied another language in a prior course
- Two-semester courses covering Java language fundamentals (first course) followed by intermediate and advanced topics in Java programming (second course)

Instructors teaching basic and intermediate programming courses in other curriculums such as engineering and computer science will find this textbook useful as well. Coverage of Java language topics is rigorous and thorough, making this textbook valuable in any programming course experience.

Key Features of the Textbook

Information Systems and Business Focus

This textbook was written with a ground-up focus on adding value to the programming learning efforts of information systems students using the Java language. This approach keeps in mind that information systems students may have little to no prior undergraduate experience with computer science topics and, typically, will leverage software development alongside other skill sets in their careers. Rigor and relevance are two overarching themes that guided the development of the text: rigor in the high-quality and up-to-date discussions of contemporary programming and object-oriented development concepts and relevance through the business- and information systems–oriented problems and scenarios that these programming topics are grounded within. Students will find topics, discussions, examples, and challenging problems throughout this textbook that are directly relevant to their information systems curriculums, particularly if they will experience a systems development and implementation capstone before graduation.

A selection of business-oriented programming examples include business-appropriate output and report formatting; application of business rules; employee retirement investment status calculation; password checking and adherence to security rules; processing of highly structured textual and numeric data; user interface considerations during systems development in both console- and GUI-based contexts; Java language features and impact on systems development in a team context; usage of classes to represent real-world entities in information systems and usage of state to capture entity characteristics; processing and management of employee rosters, customer queues, and related data; and integration of a database into an information systems application in a contemporary retail business context, among others.

Textbook-Spanning Opening Scenario

A textbook-spanning opening scenario grounds each chapter's discussion of the Java programming language squarely within an information systems context. The scenario describes the reader's experience as a member of a contemporary development team implementing a prototype information system for a family-owned regional grocery chain. At the start of each chapter, the opening scenario describes a problem or situation occurring in the development efforts that can be resolved by the reader's study of the chapter's Java language topics. In many chapters, short programming examples describe or walk through the solution to smaller problems faced by the team member in that chapter's scenario. Supplementary chapter sections, titled "Opening Scenario Applications" (for chapters 8, 9, 11, and 12 as well as for all companion chapters), are provided on the Instructor Resources site and cover extended development of application functionality described in the opening scenario within the scope of that chapter's syntax topics. By the end of the textbook, students will have developed the logic ("back-end"), GUI ("front-end"), and extensive database integration of a functional Java-based information system prototype.

Bloom's Taxonomy–Based Self-Assessment Opportunities

At the end of each chapter section are quick problems that allow students to easily practice Java language concepts and test their understanding of the material. At the end of each chapter are short discussion questions giving the student the opportunity to remember, understand, and apply their knowledge. Additionally, students have the opportunity to further assess their learning at the end of each chapter through terminology matching, find-the-error code listings, think-about-it discussion questions, and short and full program assignments. Grounded in Bloom's taxonomy of learning, each successive set of end-of-chapter problems moves the student higher up in the learning framework from remembering/understanding to evaluating/creating in the short and full programming problems. Discussions of topics and examples throughout the textbook additionally build upon the prior ones, helping students move from simple memorization to the ability to apply Java language features in new and ever more complex problem scenarios.

Dual-Focus Approach: Demonstration and Discussion

In order to maximize students' learning and comfort with the material, a dual-focus approach to the Java language has been taken. In many programming textbooks, topics are demonstrated but not discussed in sufficient detail. In other situations, topics are discussed but not appropriately demonstrated to a satisfactory degree. Both of these situations can cause frustration for the student. Throughout the textbook, a balanced approach has been sought to rectify this: Java language syntax and contemporary programming topics are demonstrated with code examples highlighted with iconography. Students who prefer to "jump right in" can quickly find the examples and begin practicing various Java syntax. Students who have prior programming experience in other languages may also prefer this faster approach. For students who prefer to read and consider a topic first before writing code, a substantive discussion accompanies most Java topics to allow for the detailed study of the language features, particularly as they connect to a business- and information systems–oriented context. Discussions are kept as concise as possible without diminishing the coverage of the topic, and the language is light, informal, and positive in its encouragement of student learning.

Integrated Best Practices

Throughout the chapters, best practices have been sprinkled across both discussions and code examples. Optimal uses of Java syntax in numerous scenarios have been demonstrated and discussed. Common pitfalls encountered by students first learning the Java language, common errors and why they occur, and how to best avoid these have all been highlighted throughout the text (e.g., data-type incompatibilities, unexpected expression behaviors, text comparisons, unexpected logic behaviors, common errors encountered with the processing of arrays, issues with instantiated object references, and many more). Chapter 10 ("Exceptions, Good Practice, and Professional Java") is dedicated to the coverage of many contemporary best practices in development with the Java language. The chapter explores the uses of exception handling in Java to mitigate runtime errors to increase application resilience to issues. Additionally, chapter 10 covers several other contemporary development best practices, such as class security and privilege management; optimal naming of variables, methods, and classes; masking of sensitive and often legally private information in business scenarios; and proper commenting and documentation of code.

Hybrid Objects Approach

The flexibility of this textbook's chapters, which benefits instructors in course development, was another focus from the ground up. As many instructors have a time preference for the introduction of class and object concepts to students in a Java programming course, this textbook attempts to strike a balance. For instructors who prefer an "objects-early" approach, chapter 2 ("Using Object-Oriented Java") covers the terminology, nature, and behavior of Java classes and objects in their usage. This gives students the opportunity to become familiar with class and object concepts that they will encounter in successive chapters, enhancing learning and understanding. Alternatively, for instructors who prefer an "objects-later" approach, discussions of Java topics in chapters 3 through 7 do not require students to have worked through chapter 2 first. This allows the instructor to move coverage of chapter 2 to immediately precede work in chapter 8 ("Object-Oriented Programming with Java Classes") if they wish or to leave chapter 2 as optional reading for students.

Flexibility of Chapter Sequences

This textbook's chapters have been developed to maximize instructors' flexibility in the topic coverage sequence while developing their courses. Instructors can choose to work through the textbook's core chapters in their included order or move chapters around to adapt to their curriculum's needs more flexibly. For example, chapter 2 can be covered earlier or later depending on the instructor's object preference. Companion chapter 3 ("Recursion") can be taught following chapter 6 ("Methods") to help students gain a proficiency in the usage of methods in Java. Companion chapter 5 ("Java `Collections` Framework") can be covered following chapter 7 ("Working with Data in Arrays") to help students gain a thorough understanding of using highly structured data sequences in Java. For instructors who teach GUI development in their courses, chapter 11 ("Creating Java User Interfaces with JavaFX") can be taught using the newer JavaFX GUI library, or companion chapter 1 ("Creating Java User Interfaces with Swing") can be used instead for instructors who have experience with and prefer the Swing library. Problem scenarios discussed in each chapter's continuing opening scenario are kept modular in nature. Coverage of chapters out of their included order will not disrupt students' understanding of how Java language topics fit within the larger information systems development effort described in the scenario.

Chapter Elements

At the **beginning of each chapter**, you will find the following:

- A "What You Will Learn in This Chapter" section that discusses the relevance of that chapter's topics to contemporary programming and the benefits to the student's eventual career in information systems
- A **list of skills** in Java programming the student will possess after working through the chapter's material
- An "Opening Scenario" that relates that chapter's learning topics to a real-world information systems development effort that spans the textbook's chapters

Within each chapter section, certain topics are highlighted with the following:

"Information Systems": Highlights certain Java programming topics that are directly relevant to challenges or situations that students might face in their information systems careers.

"Core Concept": Highlights the core idea or key point to remember for certain Java programming topics.

"Think": Highlights Java programming concepts that require some thought or consideration on the part of the student, approaches that may change from case to case.

"Quick Syntax": Highlights a code example demonstrating a key chapter concept. Useful for students who want to explore example code quickly and review the discussion of the topic later.

At the **end of each section**, you will find the following:

- A "Summary Points" section that reviews the key chapter concepts
- A "Quick Problems" section that consists of a mix of both small programming tasks allowing the student to quickly test their knowledge of section topics and short discussion questions that help the student test their understanding and application of Java programming topics

At the **end of each chapter**, you will find the following:

- A "Summary" section that recaps the topics discussed in the chapter, their further relevance to students in the information systems profession, and their relationship to topics yet to come in the textbook.
- "Terminology" questions that give the student practice in remembering and understanding chapter terms and definitions.
- "Find the Error" problems that allow the student an opportunity to test their understanding of the chapter's Java language syntax topics and to apply their knowledge to new code situations.
- "Think about It" problems that will allow the student to apply their understanding of chapter topics and analyze connections between both topics in the chapter and those that have been covered in prior chapters.
- "Short Syntax Problems" that give the student practice in applying the chapter's Java language topics to small programming assignments.
- "Full Problems" that describe larger Java programming scenarios and require the student to analyze the needs of the application, evaluate the business problem as described to determine the extent and scope of the development efforts, and create an application that solves the business problem at hand. These larger programming assignments can easily be adapted to serve as teamwork assignments, giving students the opportunity to plan, delegate, and combine work on a complex information system development and implementation task.

Overview of the Textbook

The core chapters of the textbook can be divided into two main parts:

- Part 1: Java Language Basics
- Part 2: Intermediate Java Concepts

In part 1, the basic syntax, characteristics, and behavior of the Java programming language are explored. Chapter 0 ("Basics of Java Programming") covers the overarching basics of a Java program: where code execution begins, the parts of a Java program, declaring and using variables, basics and details of data types, and interacting with the output console. Chapter 1 ("Putting Data to Work with Operators") describes the arithmetic, logical, and boolean operators commonly used in the Java language, their outcomes, and the precedence of their execution. Since Java is an object-oriented programming language, chapter 2 ("Using Object-Oriented Java") covers the object-oriented terminology and behavior of the language, exploring the usage of classes in the Java library. Chapter 3 ("Strings and Text Formatting") explores topics in the usage, manipulation, and formatting of text data in Java through the use of the `String` class. Chapter 4 ("Decision Logic and Code Flow") covers the nature of logic and code flow in Java using the `if` and `switch` statements. Chapter 5 ("Loops, Loops, Loops, Loops . . .") explores the usage of looping statements in Java through the `for`, `while`, and `do…while` statements. Chapter 6 ("Methods") introduces methods and Java's pass-by-value nature and discusses best practices regarding parameters, return types, and reducing code repetition. Chapter 7 ("Working with Data in Arrays") introduces the nature, usage, and manipulation of array data structures in Java, exploring topics regarding both single- and multidimensional arrays.

In part 2 of the text, more intermediate Java language concepts are explored. In chapter 8 ("Object-Oriented Programming with Java Classes"), students are introduced to user-defined data types in Java through the definition and instantiation of Java classes. Chapter 9 ("Class Inheritance and Polymorphism") topics regarding the extension of classes and the polymorphic behavior of class objects are discussed. Chapter 10 ("Exceptions, Good Practice, and Professional Java") walks the student through handling errors and logic exceptions programmatically and discusses some common best practices in the Java language. In chapter 11 ("Creating Java User Interfaces with JavaFX"), students are introduced to graphical user interface development in Java via the JavaFX library. In chapter 12 ("Java Applications and Database Integration"), students explore the integration of both console and GUI Java applications with an Oracle® database.

Textbook Appendices

- Appendix A ("Java Development Kit, Java IDEs, Oracle DB Setup, Debugging, and jShell") contains the following: instructions for installing the latest Java Development Kit (JDK); instructions for how to compile and run a Java program using a simple text editor and command/terminal window; overviews of the popular Java integrated development environments (IDEs) such as Apache NetBeans, Eclipse, and jGRASP; how to identify and understand common syntax and logic errors flagged by contemporary IDEs and how to use debugging tools such as those in NetBeans to explore error causes; instructions for installing and using the latest Oracle Express database software; and an overview of how to use `jShell` as an additional learning tool for students to run and test small snippets of Java code.
- Appendix B ("Operator Precedence and Working with Java Expressions") details operator precedence in Java and demonstrates its impact on the execution of expressions through several examples.
- Appendix C ("Working with ASCII Character Codes") details the ASCII character codes and how to use and manipulate character logic in various business-oriented scenarios.

Textbook Companion Chapters

To strengthen the relevance of the textbook to contemporary business-oriented application development scenarios and increase the usefulness and flexibility of the text for instructors developing programming courses, six companion chapters have been included. These six companion chapters are included in the eTextbook only. Users of the paperback can freely access these chapters at the Student Companion Site.

- Companion chapter 1 ("Creating Java User Interfaces with Swing") introduces students to GUI development in the Java language using the Swing library for those instructors who prefer it instead of the more recent JavaFX.
- Companion chapter 2 ("File I/O in Java") explores the interaction between Java applications and external data files (reading and writing data). Instructors may find this chapter a companion to chapter 12.
- Companion chapter 3 ("Recursion") covers the use of recursion to solve many business-oriented, real-world problems in simple, efficient ways. Instructors may find this chapter a great follow-up to chapter 6.
- Companion chapter 4 ("Abstract Classes, Interfaces, and Generics") is the first of the three advanced object-oriented chapters and covers the nature, development, and usage of abstract Java classes and Java interfaces; their benefits; and the usage of generic-type methods and classes.

- Companion chapter 5 ("Java `Collections` Framework") explores many of the classes in the Java Collections framework, including stacks, queues, sets, iterators, and the map class and its variations.
- Companion chapter 6 ("Multithreading and Parallel Programming"), the last of the three advanced object-oriented concept chapters, introduces multithreaded and parallel programming in the Java language, using the `Thread` and `Runnable` classes as well as the more sophisticated concurrency API Java library.

Figure P.1 details the suggested dependencies between the core and companion chapters in the textbook.

Development Tools

There are many IDE software tools available for instructors to choose from to pair with this textbook. Appendix A details the use of a text editor and command line to run Java programs as well as three of the more popular IDEs: Eclipse, NetBeans, and jGRASP. Where relevant, NetBeans is used in this textbook to highlight various language examples and IDE tools but is not required. Java code examples throughout the book use the Java Development Kit 17 (Java 17 SE). Later versions of Java released after the publication of this textbook are compatible with its code examples.

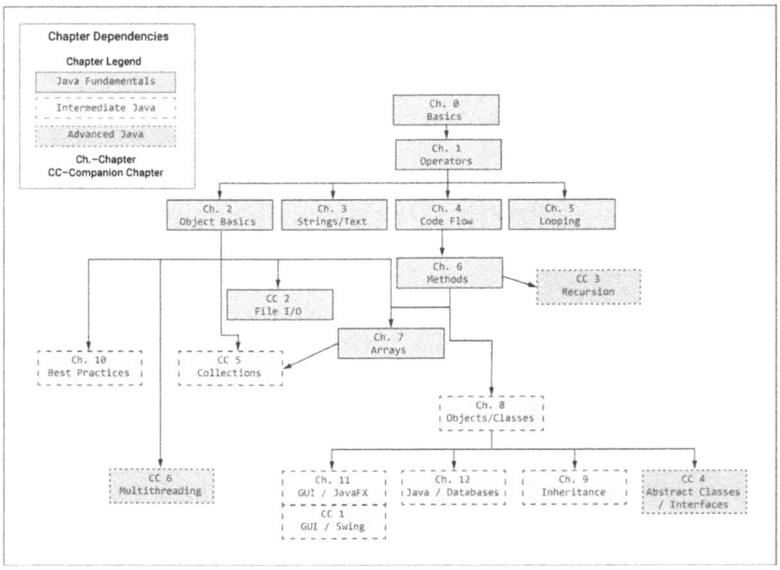

Figure P.1. Suggested Dependencies between Core and Companion Textbook Chapters

Instructor Resources

Instructor resources for this textbook include the following:

- Example Java applications and, where relevant, data files in `.zip` format that can be provided to students for in-class use, practice, and exploration.
- PowerPoint slides for all textbook chapters.
- A test bank that includes multiple-choice questions not printed in the textbook itself.
- An instructor guide that contains suggested answers to both "Short Syntax Problems" and "Full Problems" assignments as well as answers to "Terminology" and "Find the Error" problems.
- "Opening Scenario Application" supplementary chapter sections, where students are guided through extended development of functionality for the "Opening Scenario" information system. Each supplementary section's development efforts are focused on using the syntax topics described in the accompanying chapter. Instructors may distribute these "Opening Scenario Applications" to students as desired.
- Suggested sequences for one- and two-semester courses focusing on Java in an information systems curriculum.

To access the Instructor Resources:

- Visit **https://www.prospectpressvt.com/textbooks/ezell-java**.
- Scroll down to the horizontal red menu bar.
- Click on **Instructor Resources**.
- Click on the yellow button titled **Resources Login**.
- Click on **Instructor Resource Access Form**, and fill it out. Only verified faculty will receive access information.

Student Resources

Student resources for this textbook include the following:

- Six companion chapters for optional use. These are included in the eTextbook. Students using paperbacks may freely download the companion chapters.
- Video demonstrations of selected chapter topics and problems will be located here, organized by chapter.

To access the student resources, do the following:

- Visit **https://www.prospectpressvt.com/textbooks/ezell-java**.
- Scroll down to the horizontal red menu bar.
- Click on **Student Resources**.

Acknowledgments

Teaching programming concepts is often a difficult task. Learning them can often be similarly difficult. The author has found that an active and multifaceted pedagogical approach is needed to help both the teacher and the learner interact with programming concepts successfully. A successful approach as adopted by the author is not developed overnight and is influenced through interactions with valuable colleagues and supportive family members over the years. I could not have been successful in the efforts involved with this textbook without the love, support, and continued encouragement of my wife, Nicole. Among those most influential in the academic community, the author would like to acknowledge Diane Lending, Mike Mitri, Jeff May, Tom Dillon, Luis Novoa, Carey Cole, Shawn Lough, Amy Connolly, Ben Larson, Jeff Clark, Steven Morris, Jim Clark, Bob Bradley, and Emery Gathers. Each of them has been influential in shaping the author's approach to programming topics in the classroom, subsequently influencing the learning approach contained in this book. Influential colleagues in the practitioner community include Mark Bondurant, Dustin Miles, Shane McDaniel, Marshall Sparkman, and Jason Nelms, among many others.

The author would also like to offer his sincere thanks and immense gratitude to those academic colleagues who took time out of their busy schedules to review the textbook manuscript. All of them offered very valuable suggestions, a great number of which have been incorporated into this textbook. Thank you to the following:

Deepak Agrawal, Morgan Stanley
Karen Aguar, PhD, University of Georgia
Dr. Mohammed Ali, Prince George's Community College
Sarbani Banerjee, PhD, SUNY Buffalo State College
Michael Choi, University of Illinois at Chicago
Steven J. Clayden, PhD, CISSP, Arizona State University Polytechnic Campus
Dr. Ramakrishna Dantu, California State University, Sacramento
Subramanyam Dantu, Sr. Software Engineer
Neelam Dwivedi, PhD, Carnegie Mellon University
Dr. Zarreen Farooqi, University of Akron
Jim Gerland, Adjunct Professor, Computer Information Systems, Buffalo State College
Ashish M. Gulati, Arizona State University
Yousra Javed, Illinois State University
Kelli J. Kleindorfer, Des Moines Area Community College
Christopher Kreider, Christopher Newport University
Dr. Mary Lebens, Galvanize Inc.
Gilliean Lee, Lander University
Doug Lundquist, University of Illinois at Chicago
Douglas B. Malcolm, Kennesaw State University
Dr. Lauren Mayhew, York County Community College
Ava Meredith, Seattle Central College
Nick Murphy, Kennesaw State University

Professor Sarhan Musa, Prairie View A&M University
Louis Ngamassi, PhD, Prairie View A&M University
Delmer William Nicholson Jr., Clermont College, University of Cincinnati
Parag Pendharkar, Penn State Harrisburg
Kathryn L. Schultz, SUNY Cobleskill
Cara Tang, PhD, Portland Community College
John Whitehouse, MSIS, Penn State Harrisburg
Yu Zhang, East-West University

The author would further like to acknowledge Prospect Press president and editor Beth Lang Golub, who skillfully guided this project from manuscript proposal all the way to the finished textbook. Thank you for your insights, leadership, and eager support. Also, a huge thanks to Andy Golub for his design and insights, Dave Williams for his constant editorial and organizing support, and Anne Clark for her aesthetic brilliance in the visualization of the many charts and images found throughout this textbook.

About the Author

Jeremy D. Ezell is an associate professor of computer information systems and business analytics at the College of Business at James Madison University. He holds a PhD in information systems management from Auburn University, a master's in information systems from Middle Tennessee State University, and a bachelor's in computer science from the University of Tennessee, Martin. He teaches intermediate Java application development, leads instruction for the information systems development and implementation integrative capstone course, and has taught executive leadership in information systems at the graduate level.

His academic research interests include organizational dynamic capabilities, IT innovation mindfulness and adoption, absorptive capacity, data quality, requirements elicitation, and information systems pedagogy. He has coauthored work in several journals, including the *Journal of Information Systems Education*, the *International Journal of Production Economics*, *Technometrics*, and *Computers and Industrial Engineering*, among others. He lives in Harrisonburg, Virginia, with his wife, Nicole, and their adopted rescue dog, Caylee.

PART 1

Java Language Basics

Chapter 0

Basics of Java Programming

What You Will Learn in This Chapter

This chapter covers fundamental aspects of the Java programming language. Understanding the basic structure and contents of an executable Java program and learning Java syntax basics are a must. This chapter compares and contrasts Java with other programming languages in how its code is compiled and executed. The basic rules for Java's syntax will also be examined. This chapter will additionally detail the basic variable data types available in Java, how they are used to store data, and how they interact with one another. Finally, how to print to the console as well as the important task of how to capture and process user-input data will be covered.

Specifically, this chapter will help you do the following:

1. Understand and describe the parts of a basic Java main class application and describe the general purpose of each
2. Understand and use commenting syntax in your application
3. Understand and describe what happens when a Java program is compiled and describe the similarities and differences between Java and other languages in both compilation and execution
4. Describe some of the major benefits of the use of the Java programming language over other languages
5. Understand, describe, and differentiate between many basic syntax rules in Java
6. Describe the differences and similarities between the Java primitive data types
7. Understand and be able to use the `.println()` method to print output to the Java console and how to incorporate the values of variables in that output
8. Understand and be able to use the `Scanner` class to create a `Scanner` variable and invoke various `Scanner` class methods to read and process data entered using the keyboard.

Opening Scenario

Graduation seems like just yesterday. Where did the last four years go? You sit at your new desk mere feet from those of your new colleagues at ConsultCorp and wonder where the time went to. Looking up at your information systems (IS) degree on the wall above your desk, you think back to all the great classes, classmates, and faculty members you encountered in your IS program. "Systems analysis, development, database, project management—whew!" you think as you look at your name on the degree parchment. "A lot to remember."

It is your first day after the two-week orientation program at ConsultCorp. Your orientation coordinator noted how "well prepared" and "knowledgeable" you are, beyond that of your fellow new hires. "Probably because of where you studied IS," she said. "I've heard great things about that program!" You are excited to jump into the first consulting project ConsultCorp has assigned you. After grabbing a breakfast beverage, you head to the meeting room for the 9 a.m. all-hands with the rest of your project team.

Your project manager begins with a concerning description of your team's client: "They're a fairly large mom-and-pop-style grocery store. Several locations. Hundreds of employees. They are running disparate, per-location, and unconnected point-of-sale systems; nothing is integrated; and spreadsheets are used a lot. I was afraid to ask if these were on actual paper.

They have reached the point where their manual methods are preventing them from growing. Their data is a mess. They don't have the funds to purchase an expensive new system or pay for a subscription service. They're hearing whispers of a national chain eying their region. They need a new, unified sales and store management system, built at low cost and built fast. It is our job to assess their processes and requirements. Once we know that, we can prototype a system for them using a Java front end and logic. If we don't scare them off, we'll build it out the rest of the way."

You think back again to your IS classes: "I had Python, not Java . . ." You have heard that they are different languages, designed for different outcomes and with differing syntaxes. Though you are a little concerned about learning an entirely new programming language, an excitement wells up within you. "They use Java a lot here at ConsultCorp. If I want to grow my career, I've got to learn it." Drawing on that excitement, you walk out of the meeting room with a renewed energy. "Time to jump in headfirst and start with the basics . . ."

0.1 Your First Java Program

The code examples and instructions found in this chapter and throughout the book are compatible with any of the Java Integrated Development Environment (IDE) software that you use or your instructor may have you use. The most commonly used Java IDEs are Eclipse (most popular out there), Apache NetBeans, and jGRASP, among others. Appendix A gives you a quick tour of these three IDEs as well as quick instructions on creating your first Java project and main class application within each. Your instructor may demonstrate these steps during lecture as well, with separate, specific instructions.

After you have created a new project and package folder (we will cover packages in Java later), create a new Java main class file in your package with the name "`FirstJavaApp`." Note that the created file is named "`FirstJavaApp.java`." Java source code files will end with the "`.java`" extension, with a few exceptions. Some IDEs will create only a blank Java file, while others will create a Java file with the class and `main()` method already defined but empty. Examine yours to see how much code the IDE has written for you. In the following listing, note the code in bold, which you should add to your program as shown. This code will print a message to the console when the application is executed.

Full Program 0.1

```
/*
Author: That's You!
Purpose: My first Java application.
*/
public class FirstJavaApp {
    public static void main(String[] args) {
        // (Output): Print to output
        System.out.println("Hello from my Java App!");
    }
}
```

Exploring Your First Program

There are a few parts of this first program that may be initially confusing. There are several concepts later in the book that should be covered first, so what follows are "trust your author" moments for some of the syntax. But for the rest of the code, you can gain a basic understanding of Java program concepts right from the start. Figure 0.1 highlights some of the more important parts of your first Java code.

Some of the more important parts of this code listing to understand are as follows:

- **Access modifier** `public`
  The keyword `public` is an **access modifier** for the **class**. Think of it as the security setting for the class.
- **Keyword** `class`

Java is a class-based language. All Java programs consist of classes. The contents of a class, known as its **definition**, will fall in between the beginning and ending curly braces ({ and }), which are the start and end of the **code block** for the class. Code blocks can **nest** within others (as seen in the example above, with the other pair of curly braces inside the `class` code block). A common error is to accidentally delete or omit a beginning or ending curly brace.

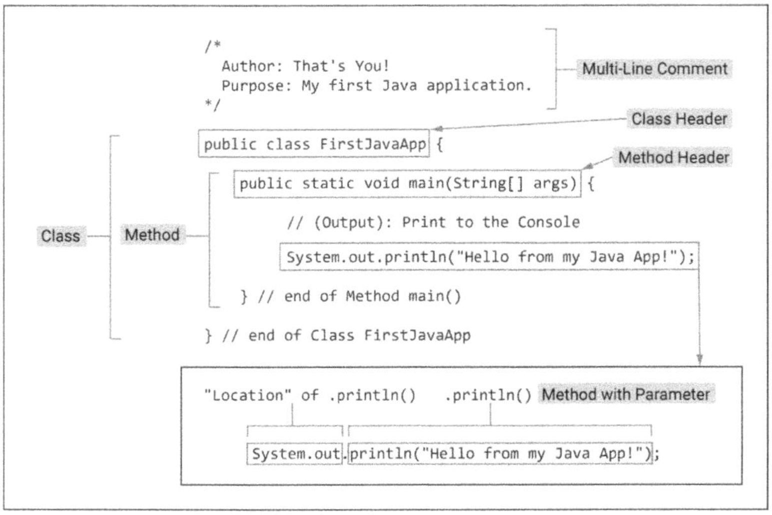

Figure 0.1. Overall Structure of a Java Main Class Program and Details of Print Statement

- **Name of the application class and `.java` file `FirstJavaApp`**
  Both the Java file and the class inside have the same name. As a **rule**, Java requires that the `class` inside a `.java` file be named the same as the name of the file it is contained within.
- **Access and nonaccess modifiers and return type `public static void`**
  In addition to the `public` access modifier, `static` (nonaccess modifier) and `void` deal with instantiation and return type concepts, respectively, that will be discussed later in the textbook.
- **Header of starting application method `main(String[] args)`**
  This defines a **method** called `main()`. The first line of code within method `main()` is the starting point for your application. A method will have a code block defined with curly braces, similar to classes. The line of code

  ```
  public static void main(String[] args)
  ```

  makes up the **method header** for the method. The header, along with the code within the curly braces / code block of a method, makes up the **definition** for the method, and the code in that block can only run if its method is **invoked** (i.e., called).
- **Nature of the `main()` method**
  When your Java program runs, the `main()` method of your class will be invoked automatically, and starting with the first line of code within the `main()` method's code block, your program's code will execute line by line. The `String[] args` part of the method header looks strange but is a single-method **parameter**: an **array** of **String** values referenced by the variable name **args**. This part of the program is rarely, if ever, changed.
- **Code comments**
  Good programming involves good documentation. You should always strive to document your program with **comment** lines to clarify the functionality of your code. Comments in a Java program do not execute. *Remember:* you might write your code, but if you work in a collaborative/team setting, others may be reading and performing maintenance upon or updating your code. It is a good idea to comment **sufficiently yet not too extensively**. Not every single line of code needs a comment!
  - **Multiline comment:** This consists of starting and ending multiline comment symbols: /* and */. If you have experience in other programming languages, you will find similar multiline comment symbols/usage in those as well. As you can see in this first program, the author has placed their name and the program's purpose at the top of the Java source file. Again, it is usually good programming practice to include a descriptive header like this at the top of all your source files.

- **Single comment:** This will consist of double slashes: `//`. Anything on that same line that follows these will be considered by the Java compiler to be a nonexecutable comment. Alternatively, you can use the multiline comment symbols on a single line as well `/* In a manner similar to this */`.

  Most commonly, you will see a single comment line placed at the end of a line of code (after the semicolon):

```
int myAge = 109;  // Starting value for myAge variable
```

- **Analysis of the single line of code within the `main()` method**

```
System.out.println("Hello from my Java App!");
```

  - Our program really only consists of one single executable line of code (code that runs). This line of code will print the phrase in quotation marks to the **console output** (usually at the bottom of your IDE's user interface). If you are running your program from the command line, then you will see the output in the same command-line window you compile and run your program from.
  - The quotation marks are used to enclose a `String` (note the capital *S* for this data type's name). In this line of code, a `String` **literal** is used, which is a text value not stored inside a **variable** but "literally" placed where it is used. This `String` literal is the one and only parameter for the method being called/invoked here.
  - **Invocation of `PrintStream` method `.println()`**

    This is the name of a method being invoked. You can call it "print line," since it does two things: prints the value of its parameter (the value or variable between the opening/closing parentheses) to the output console and appends a **new-line** character to the end of this output. This will cause any output that occurs after this line to print on the next line down (like hitting the Enter key in your favorite word processing program).
  - **Class `System` and `PrintStream` object `System.out`**

    `System` is the name of a class that is defined for every Java program by default. The word "`out`" represents a variable that belongs to the `System` class (this is not entirely correct terminology, but for now, it is the best way to think about this without getting completely confused). The period, or **dot notation**, represents a hierarchical structure between them. The word "`out`" is part of `System`, so that is typed as "`System.out`." The `.println()` method is associated with the "`out`" object (again, not entirely correct language but will be clarified later).
  - Notice the capital *S* for "`System`," which is a great way to recognize a class name (a capital letter at the start of the name). To invoke `.println()`, you must specify its location (`System.out`) and its name (`.println()`) and **pass** a `String` parameter to it in the parentheses.
  - At the end of the `.println()` invocation/call, there is a semicolon (;). Normal lines of executable Java code must end with a semicolon to indicate the end of that statement and the start of the next. This rule does not apply to things like **class headers** and **method headers** and to ending curly braces. Examine this first Java application's code closely and take note of all the times that a semicolon was used (answer: just one time).

When this first Java application executes, the following prints to the output console:

```
Hello from my Java App!
```

Depending on which IDE you use, you may see more output (or not) in the console. If you do, look for the above to see your application's actual output.

Understanding the Nature of Java and Java Applications

How Java programs run: Most programming languages that you will encounter will have their code either **interpreted** or **compiled** in order to create an executable program. A programming language could have either occur, and the nuances of this discussion are beyond the scope of this text. For the most part, any language you work in will fall under one or the other scenario. Interpreted languages generally have the benefit of **platform independence**. What this means is that once you write a program in an interpreted language, it can be "run" on any hardware and operating system combo where software has been developed that can understand its syntax. The key here is that some groups or organizations (or even individuals) have purposefully written software for each and every hardware/operating system platform where they want programs written in the interpreted language to run. But once each separate platform has that ability, developers working in the language only have to write their program once, and then it will run on all those separate platforms without issue. The contrast to this is **compiled** languages. In these types of languages, code compilation targets a specific hardware/operating system platform. For example, an application written in a compiled language might need to be compiled for your desktop, then work may need to be done (possibly involving a completely separate code version with substantial code rewriting) to recompile it for your smartphone, then all that work may need to be done again so that it will run on a tablet platform.

Why is there a difference at all? Why aren't all programming languages just interpreted, and then that's the end of the story? For creators of programming languages, there are trade-offs between each approach. Generally, interpreted languages are **portable** but **slower** than compiled languages. That generalizability increases the processing needed in order to execute programs written in these languages. Think of this a little like scope creep: there is one more translation step that has to be completed between the code and actual code execution. On the other side, compiled languages tend to produce programs that execute **faster** but are **limited** to the platform they were targeted for. The reason for this is the opposite of interpreted languages: all the "work" to get a program to run on a platform is done up front, then all the program has to do is just run when placed on the targeted system. Again, this is a vast simplification of this discussion, and going into more detail is beyond the scope of this text.

How does Java fit into all this? **Java is known primarily as an interpreted language**, but compilation does occur occasionally when your Java program executes. How? First, your Java code is converted into an intermediary language known as **bytecode**. When you "compile" your Java programs, the Oracle® binary program **javac** (the Java compiler, which is an executable program) converts your code into bytecode. Figure 0.2 shows what this intermediate, machine-readable version of your first Java program looks like.

The Java Virtual Machine: Next, software known as the Oracle HotSpot Java Virtual Machine (or JVM for short) has been created for each and every hardware/operating system platform where Java programs are intended to execute. The JVM is like NASA's mission control: it handles the interpretation of your Java code into the hardware/platform-specific **machine language** that the targeted platform understands—in other words, the "language" the CPU on that device can speak. This is why Java is primarily known as an interpreted language: the JVM interprets bytecode into machine code on each and every hardware system for which a JVM has been created. The **portability** characteristic of Java comes into play here as well: once you write a Java program, you can run it on any platform that has a JVM installed without having to change any of your code. Write once, run anywhere. Figure 0.3 shows this portability of compiled Java programs. The JVM also has built into it something known as the Just-in-Time compiler, which puts Java into categories of both interpreted and compiled. How does it work? Certain lines of code in your program that are executed most often (i.e., a loop; see chapter 5) may be converted from interpreted bytecode to machine-specific compiled statements automatically by the JVM. Oracle has implemented this feature for speed and code execution efficiency. Java as a programming language has the best of both worlds.

```
/*
Author: That's You!
Purpose: My first Java application.
*/
import java.util.*;

public class FirstJavaApp {
    public static void main(String[] args) {
        // (Output): Print to the Console
        System.out.printIn("Hello from my Java App!");
 }
}
```

```
Compiled from "FirstlavaApp.java"
public class Chapter0Pkg.FirstJavaApp {
  public ChapterOPkg.FirstJavaApp();
    Code:
       0: aload O
       1: invokespecial    #1           // Method java/lang/Object."<init>":()V
       4: return

  public static void main(java.lang.String[]);
    Code:
       O: getstatic        #7           // Field java/lang/System.out:Ljava/io/PrintStream;
       3: Idc              #13          // String Hello from my Java App!
       5: invokevirtual    #15          // Method java/io/PrintStream.println:(Ljava/lang/String;)V
       8: return
}
```

Figure 0.2. Your First Java Program Compiled into Computer-Friendly Bytecode

The Java Development Kit—or the JDK, as it is called—contains all the tools and Java library packages needed in order to write and compile your programs.

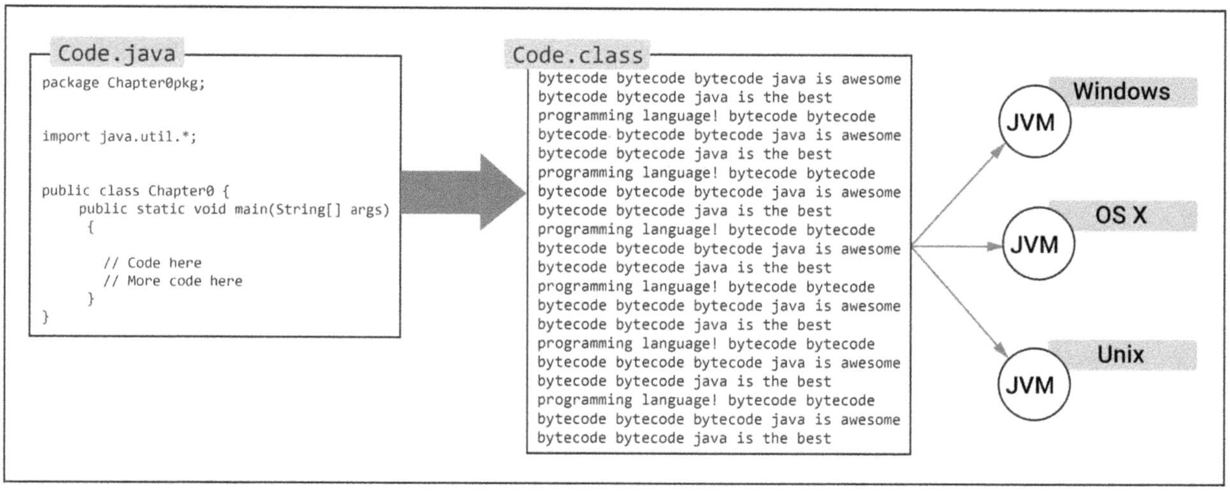

Figure 0.3. Java Code Is Compiled into Bytecode, Which the JVM Implementation on Various Computing Platforms Can Run

Oracle's JDK for its Java Standard Edition (SE) is free for personal, nonbusiness use, and the company also supports and participates in the OpenJDK project, a completely-free-for-most-all-uses version of the proprietary JDK. For the purposes of your studies in this text, there are no major differences between the two in terms of syntax or major language functionality. Once a program is compiled, the JRE contains the tools needed to run them, and this includes launching the JVM "program" on your computer and then allowing it to run your Java program (this is a simplified explanation, but again, details are beyond the scope of this work).

Earlier, you coded and executed `FirstJavaApp.java`. When the `javac` program compiles your code, it creates a `.class` file ("dot class file"), usually in the same directory as your `.java` file and with the same name. Most IDEs then run your program by calling the main Java binary `java` program and using just the name of the public class that was found inside of your `.java` file. For example, with the Java program earlier, you could manually execute the program (see appendix A for further details) on the command line by typing out the following command:

```
java FirstJavaApp
```

The `java` binary will look for a `.class` file with the name "`FirstJavaApp`," which contains your program from earlier, converted into bytecode, and then will launch the JVM and execute your program. Most Java IDEs perform this step automatically when you run your application within them.

Understanding Basic Java Syntax

Overall Java program structure: Before diving into syntax details, first you should understand the overall structure of a Java program, where things should generally go, and in what order:

Figure 0.4 should look similar to the code listing for the Java program from earlier, with a few new things. This is a stand-alone, executable Java program. You will see a slightly different structure in chapter 8, which discusses user-defined Java classes. Some important program parts to highlight:

- **Package statement:** Every Java code listing will generally start with a package listing: What package does this Java file belong to? Packages serve to group together Java files that have something in common.
- **Import statement:** Import statements are often needed to define data types/classes that are not included by default with each Java program. Your program can have zero, one, or many import statements based on what parts of the Java library you need to "teach" your program to be aware of.

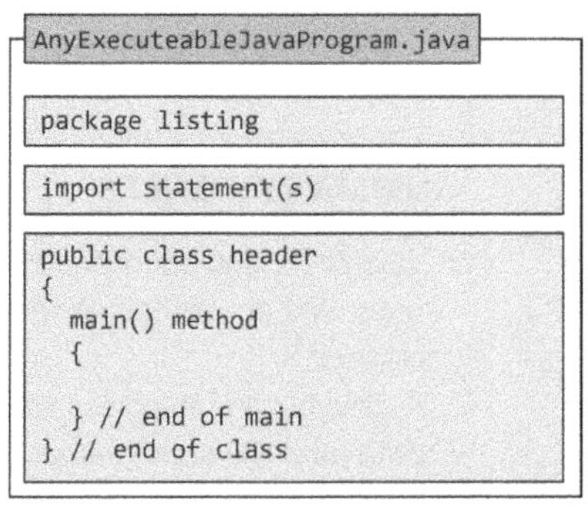

Figure 0.4. General Structure of an Executable Java Program

- **The Java `class`:** Finally, your Java program will need one `public class` within the file. As you will see later, your file can have several classes **defined** within, but **only one of those can be given the public access modifier.** This is a hard-and-fast Java syntax rule; otherwise, the **javac** compiler will throw an error. The name of the class must match **exactly** the name of the physical file it is defined within. Inside this is the `main()` method, which is the "starting line" for code execution in your program.
- **Syntax rules and guidelines:** Some of the syntax structures discussed here are thought of more as "industry standards" than hard-and-fast rules that you must abide by. Other programmers will expect your code to follow many of these guidelines, and most are considered good practice:
  - **Curly braces (rule):**

    {

    Classes and methods in Java must begin and end with an opening and closing curly brace symbol, respectively. Recall that this forms a code block attached to the class and/or method.

    }
  - **Curly braces (guideline):** How can curly braces be both a rule and a guideline? For some syntax statements (apart from class and method headers), you are not required to use curly braces if you do not need them. For selection statement headers (chapter 4) and loop headers (chapter 5), you are not required to enclose code associated with those headers in curly braces **if you only have one line of code.**
  - **Semicolon (rule):** For a single, stand-alone line of code, a semicolon is required as the terminating character on that line (even if the line of code stretches over multiple actual text lines). Notice in your first Java program earlier, the line of code that calls to `.println()` ends in a semicolon; So does that sentence; So did that one; For code like class and method blocks as well as selection statement and loop blocks, you **do not** have to end them with a semicolon. Again, notice in your first Java program earlier that the closing curly braces do not end with a semicolon. **The misuse of the semicolon is the most common error that beginning Java programmers (and old, forgetful textbook authors) make.** Think of the semicolon as a stop sign—processing for that line of code ends at the semicolon.
  - **Tabbing and spacing (guideline):** As an information systems professional, keep in mind that business-appropriate, well-formatted work is an important step in communicating effectively. Indeed, all visualizations depend heavily on their clarity, intuitiveness, and concise presentation. The same goes for code and code listings. Messy, unformatted, untabbed, and poorly aligned code will be difficult to read and hard to understand clearly. Keep your code neat, aligned, and professional in appearance.
  - **Commenting (guideline but should be a rule . . .):** In the same spirit as the previous point, commenting your code is vitally important to both you and others who might read your code. As an information systems professional, you will most definitely work alongside others in a corporate setting on team-based projects. They will look at your code and you at theirs. Commenting your code should be **sufficient but not excessive** in order to bring clarity to parts of your logic that might be confusing at first. Not every line of code needs a comment. How do you know how many comments you need? Easy: put yourself in the shoes of another person looking at **your** code for the first time. What sections of code need commenting in order to help another person understand them better?

SUMMARY POINTS

- Java is a class-based language. All Java programs are contained within and use classes.
- A Java file and the class within that file must both have the same name.
- Java code is organized in a block style, meaning its classes, methods, and some control structures enclose code in opening and closing curly braces, forming "blocks" of code.
- When the `main()` method is present in a Java class, the class is considered to be executable (i.e., it can be run).
- The first line of code in the `main()` method block is the starting point for code execution.

- In Java, a semicolon is required to terminate a single, stand-alone line of code. For code syntax that has a code block (with curly braces) associated with it, a semicolon would not be used at the end of that block but would be used on the lines of code within that block.
- Java code is first compiled into bytecode, which is then primarily interpreted and executed by the Java Virtual Machine. Frequently executed code may be compiled just-in-time by the JVM into code specific to the platform the application is running on to increase efficiency.
- Java has many advantages over other languages, including portability, security, ease of learning and use, and the benefits of its object-oriented nature.

QUICK PROBLEMS

1. **Coding:** Change the code printing example from earlier so that it prints your name and your age to the console. For example, "`Name: Your Name, Age: 103`."
2. **Think:** What would happen if you left the double quotation marks off the String value being printed within the `.println()` method?
3. **Coding:** Change the code printing example from earlier and have it print your initials to the console. Print each initial on its own line of console output. (*Hint:* Invoke `.println()` three times.) Have each initial print five spaces farther to the right than the last. (*Hint:* Use spaces within the quotation marks.) For example,

```
A
     R
          T
```

0.2 Data Types and Variables

Variable basics: Almost every programming language provides the use of **variables** to store data in memory while programs are running. Creating a variable in your program reserves a tiny space in the computer's memory (or more specifically, in the JVM's memory area) to store numbers, text, and so on. You can also change the value of a variable and store the results of calculations in them as well. Figure 0.5 shows two examples of variables, `aVariable` and `aReference`, and the way they are stored in memory.

A discussion of variables goes hand-in-hand with a discussion of **data types.** In Java, you **declare** a variable and assign it a data type. The data type of a variable defines how that tiny space in memory that you reserved will be **configured** and lets the JVM know what **kind of data** you will store in the space. Should the tiny space be configured to store a number? To store text? Something else? Consider the **amount** of memory needed for each type of data you want to store in it. Java has been developed so that some variables take up more memory per variable than others, and this is simply due to the nature of the data to be stored in those variables. A full discussion of the size, in bytes, of each variable data type is beyond the scope of this chapter.

There are eight basic variable data types that you will work with in Java. These are commonly called **primitive** data types because they are simple "buckets" that hold data, and they have no other actions that they are capable of. They are just buckets of data. In figure 0.5, the variable "`aVariable`" is declared with the primitive data type `int`, acting simply as a bucket for the numeric data "47" stored within. Table 0.1 details the eight primitive data types in Java and covers some important information for each.

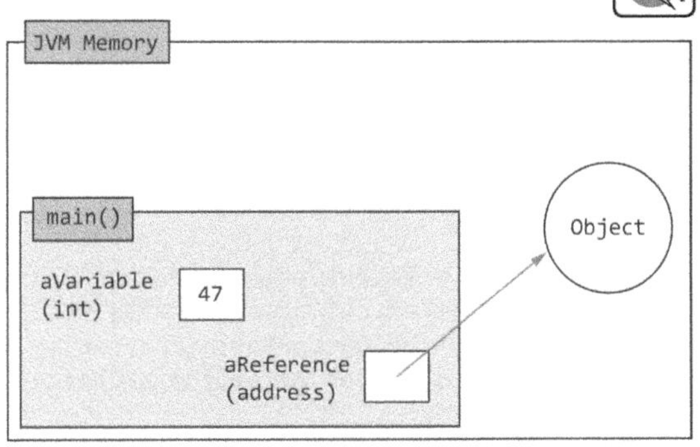

Figure 0.5. Primitive and Complex Variables in Memory

Some things to keep in mind regarding a few of the data types in table 0.1:

- The `int` data type is probably the one most familiar to you if you have used any other programming language at all. This is a regular whole number. An `int` uses a 32-bit

Table 0.1. The Eight Java Primitive Data Types with Examples

Type	Syntax	Data type's "default" value	Range of data type's possible values
Boolean	`boolean`	`false`	`true` or `false`
Byte	`byte`	`0`	-128 to 127
Short	`short`	`0`	-32,768 to 32,767
Integer	`int`	`0`	-2^{31} to $(2^{31} - 1)$
Long integer	`long`	`0L` or `0`	-2^{63} to $(2^{63} - 1)$
Floating-point number	`float`	`0.0f`	6–7 decimal places
Double precision number	`double`	`0.0d` or `0.0`	15–16 decimal places
Character	`char`	`''` (empty)	0 to 65,535 or `'\u0000'` to `'\uffff'`

memory space, whereas a long uses a 64-bit memory space. An `int` can store a big whole number, and a `long` can store an even larger whole number.

- The data types `float` and `double` are used to store a number that has **decimal data.** A `double` can store more decimal data than a `float` can, and the **usage of the `double` is more common.** Notice that for `float` and `double`, a **literal character** can be added after the value as a command to let Java know that this is not just a plain old `int`. The Java compiler will not complain, however, if you leave the `d` off the end of a double, but it is good practice to use it (guideline). The compiler **will** complain, however, if you leave the `f` off the end of a float value (rule). The character data type uses single quotes to enclose a single character. What you see in the table above is the minimum and maximum range of the number and hexadecimal equivalents of what can be stored in a `char` variable.
- Normally, a single character is enclosed in single quotes, like `'j'` or `'J'`. In Java, every character has its own ASCII Unicode character number assigned to it (like a map of characters to numbers; see appendix C), so for the char, you can use the number of a character if you wish, but it is more common to store just a character.

Usage of some of the primitive data types can be seen by modifying the example Java application from earlier (changes noted in **bold**):

Full Program 0.2

```
public class FirstJavaApp {
    public static void main(String[] args) {

        // (Output): Print to the Console
        System.out.println("Hello from my Java App!");

        int authorAge = 98;
        double valueOfPi = 3.141595653589793d;
        char aLetter = 'A';
        boolean passClass = true;

        System.out.println(authorAge);
        System.out.println(valueOfPi);
        System.out.println(aLetter);
        System.out.println(passClass);

    }
}
```

When you run the updated program, it will produce the following output to the console:

```
Hello from my Java App!
98
3.141595653589793
A
true
```

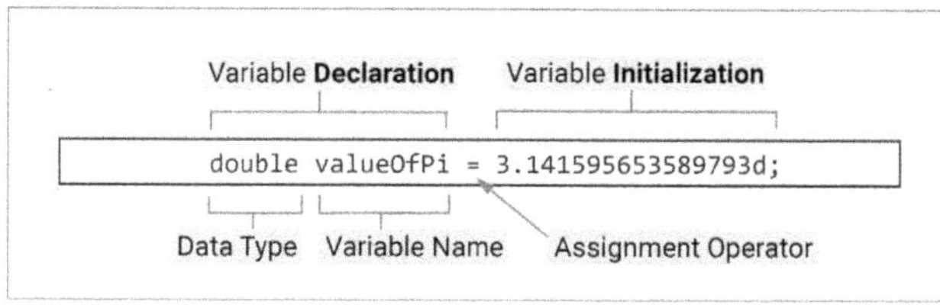

Figure 0.6. Diagram of Variable Declaration and Initialization

Notice how all fifteen decimal places of precision were used for the `double` to store as much of the value of pi as possible. You can use up to fifteen places or fewer if you need to. Also notice that to print out the values that were **stored within** the variables, the variables are used as parameters in the `.println()` method call. Java knows that you want to print what is **inside** the variables and extracts a copy of the variable's contents for you.

Declaration and initialization of variables: Figure 0.6 highlights an example of the syntax used to create variables in Java and to copy data into them.

There are really two parts to this process, as you can see in the diagram: variable declaration and variable initialization. These two parts do not have to occur at the same time. In Java, you can (and frequently will) do something like the following:

Code Snippet 0.1

```
double valueOfPi;
//
//
// . . . several milliseconds later

valueOfPi = 3.141595653589793d;
```

Notice that the initialization (the first filling of a variable with data) can occur anytime **after** the declaration of a variable has occurred. Think about the reverse: Can you pour water into a glass if you do not have a glass? No! The glass must exist first, then the water can be poured in. You have to declare (create) the variable first, then you can "pour" the data into it. It is helpful to think of (primitive data-type) variables as "buckets" that store data.

Notice the role of the equal sign, called the **assignment operator** in Java language. In Java, **assignment is very different from testing equality**. As a general rule of thumb, whenever you see the assignment operator, think of "the results on the right" of the equal sign as **always flowing / being copied** into the "variables on the left" of the equal sign. Figure 0.7 shows the directionality of data copying.

The reverse of this does **not** work—you cannot copy a variable declaration into a literal value:

Code Snippet 0.2

```
3.141595653589793d = double valueOfPi; // NOPE!
3.14 = valueOfPi;  // Still more NOPE!
```

Primitive versus "complex" data types: The eight primitive data types discussed earlier are not the only data types possible in Java. There are actually **two** categories of data types possible in the language: **primitive** and **class** data types. You will frequently see the latter described as "complex" data types throughout this text. In industry- and Java-related literature, complex data types are also known as "**reference**" types. Variables with a complex data type can store a reference (i.e., address) of an object in memory (you can see this in figure 0.5). A class in Java defines a complex data type for variables, giving those variables capabilities beyond those of primitive data-type variables.

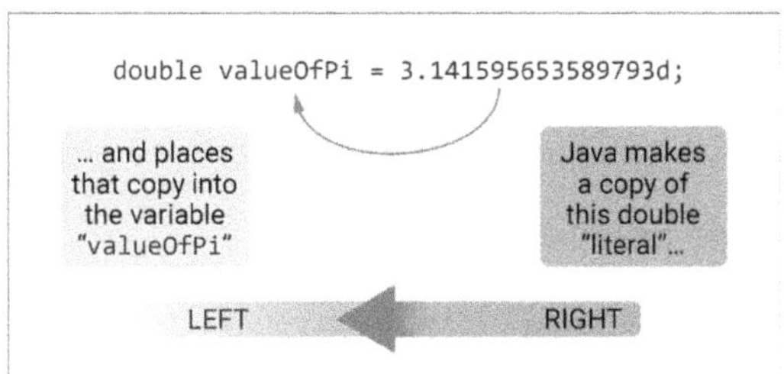

Figure 0.7. How the Assignment Operator Works for Primitive Data-Type Variables and Literals

Whereas a primitive is simply that, a primitive (it can only store data, and that is it), a class data type can **both store data and do something with it (carry out actions)**. Classes can do much more than that, as you will see later in this textbook. While there are only eight primitive data types in Java, there can be an unlimited number of complex data types. Later in the textbook, when you learn to create and use your own classes (user-defined classes), you will actually **be creating your own brand-new data types**.

Table 0.2. Listing of Both Primitive and Class Data Types in Java

Primitive data types	Class data types
`boolean`	`String`
`byte`	`Scanner`
`short`	*And many, many more*
`int`	*Also any classes that you create*
`long`	
`float`	
`double`	
`char`	

How can you tell the data types apart? Or how can you tell variables that have complex data type declarations apart from those that have primitive ones? Here is a great rule of thumb: **If the data type is capitalized, then it is a class/complex/reference data type.** If the data type starts with a lowercase letter, then it is a primitive data type. Listed in table 0.2 are two class data types, `String` and `Scanner`. You will see examples of both of these in the next section. In figure 0.5, you can see how complex data-type variables are stored in memory a little differently than primitive ones. This difference will be explored in detail later in the textbook.

Rules on data types and variable assignment: At this point, a few more syntax rules can be added to the prior list:

- **Assignment operator (rule)**: When the assignment operator is used, you must have something on both the left and the right side of it. Recall that the data on the right will "flow" or be copied into something (a variable, etc.) on the left.
- **Assignment operators do not work in method parameters (rule)**: You cannot use an assignment operator inside the parameter parentheses of a method. Assign a value to a variable before you use the variable as a method's parameter. For example, the following would throw an error when you tried to compile the program (and probably before, depending on the IDE you use):

Code Snippet 0.3

```
int aVariable;
someMethod(aVariable = 5); // NOPE!
someMethod(int anotherVar = 78); // Not going to work.
```

- **Java is a type-strict language (rule):** By nature, Java is a type-strict programming language. What does this mean? Well, it is a grumpy language: it sits on its front porch and frowns at different data types that try to share data, especially if the data types are fairly different (Java is not socially awkward: it just knows the memory copy operations will not work properly). For example, you cannot copy the data from a `double` into an `int` like so:

Code Snippet 0.4

```
double taxRate = 5.6d;
int simpleRate = taxRate; // Incompatible Types Error
```

Since a `double` just simply takes up more space in memory, you will not be able to copy the contents of a `double` into an `int` without losing some data. Java prevents this. There are cases where the reverse is true: a variable whose data type takes up **less space in memory** can be copied into a variable whose data type takes up more space. Java calls this an "up-conversion" of one data type into another. For example, the following is allowed:

Code Snippet 0.5

```
int simpleRate = 5;
double taxRate = simpleRate; // Stores 5.0d in "taxRate"
long bigTaxRate = simpleRate; // Stores 5 in "bigTaxRate";
```

Formally, this is known as **type promotion** (just like getting a raise, but there's no money involved here, sadly).

Numeric data types are somewhat compatible, like `int` and `double`, for example. Consider the following:

Code Snippet 0.6

```
int GPA = 3.5;
```

The compiler will allow this but it will "chop off" the decimal data in an attempt to fit the data within the `int`. The student just lost half a GPA point, since only three will be stored within the GPA variable. Be careful of the type of variable you try to initialize or assign a value to. Notice that the amount of data **narrows** as you go from a double to an `int` and **widens** as you go from `int` to double. If you have to narrow your data like this, it is better to use a cast operator:

Code Snippet 0.7

```
int measurement = (int)43.2; // cast
```

- **Variable declaration (rule):** When declaring a variable, the **data type** must be written first, followed by the **variable name.** The use of the assignment operator and an initialization value can then follow this if desired.
- **How to name variables in Java (rule):** There are some hard-and-fast rules for variable naming in Java programs. These are the following:
  - Variable names must begin with a letter or a $ symbol. Since Java version 9, the underscore symbol is **not** allowed as the first character of a variable name.
  - A variable name cannot begin with a number but can include them.
  - A variable name can be relatively unlimited in length. (Try not to use the entire contents of *War and Peace* to name a single variable.)
  - A variable cannot contain any spaces.
  - There are certain words, called **reserved keywords** in Java, that you cannot use as a variable name. Some of these include but are not limited to `public`, `package`, `void`, `class`, and others.
- **Variable naming convention and style (guideline):** Many Java programmers will name their variables using "camel-style notation," where the first word in a variable name is lowercase, and each successive word in the variable is capitalized. For example, the variable from before called "`bigTaxRate`" follows this naming style. Think carefully about your variable names, as they will serve as part of the **documentation** of your program. Both you and others who may view and try to understand your code later will thank you for intuitive names. Variable names like `a` and `sV` are OK but discouraged because they can make understanding what is going on in your program harder to understand.
- **Variables have to be declared before use (rule):** You have to formally declare a variable before you can use it. Java requires a formal data type and variable name, either in the same line as you perform the variable's initialization or prior to storing a value in the variable in a later line of code.
- **Two or more variables cannot have the same name (rule):** Once you have declared a variable by a name, Java partitions a space in memory (sized appropriately for the variable data type) and uses the variable name as a label/map to that space in memory (see figure 0.5). After this, you cannot in the same code block declare another variable **with the same name.** Once you have declared a variable, simply use it from then on. Once the car is built, hop in and take it for a test-drive! You do not need to rebuild the car each time you want to drive it. Exceptions to this that involve same-name variables in scope contexts will be discussed later in the textbook.
- **Declaring multiple variables at one time (rule):** As you get more comfortable with Java, you may want to save keystrokes by declaring multiple variables **of the same data type** at the same time. You can do so by listing the data type **once** and then using commas and assignment operators to divide out the various separate variables. The following is a good example:

Code Snippet 0.8

```
// These are ok.
int varOne = 5, varTwo = 10, varThree = 15;
double taxRateToday, taxRateTomorrow, taxRateForever = 6.55d;

// This is not allowed - you cannot mix data types:
int firstNum, char aLetter;
```

Note that in this example, `taxRateToday` and `taxRateTomorrow` are declared but **not initialized**, and you will have to give them values before you can use them.

SUMMARY POINTS

- Variables are common to most all programming languages. Each variable represents a label associated with a small area of computer memory where an application can temporarily store data while it executes.
- In Java there are eight different primitive data types, and each can store a specific type and amount of data.
- Variables in Java that have smaller-memory-sized data types can have their contents copied to variables that are larger in the amount of memory they reserve, though the reverse of this (larger into smaller variables) is not directly allowed.
- The assignment operator copies data from the right to the left. Whatever value is on the right of the assignment operator will have a copy made, and that copy is placed into the target variable on the left.
- The primitive data types in Java differ from the class data types in that primitives can generally only store data, whereas variables of the various class data types can both store data and perform actions with/upon that data. This makes class data types "complex."
- Once a variable has been declared/created, there is no need to redeclare it to use it. Simply use it from that point until the end of the program (or the end of scope).

QUICK PROBLEMS

1. **Coding:** Write a small Java program where you store your name in a `String` variable and your age in an `int` variable. Print each to the console on its own line.
2. **Think:** Why does placing the variable value on the right of the assignment operator and the name of the variable on the left make more sense than the reverse?
3. **Coding:** Create a small Java program, and within the `main()` method's curly braces, type the following code (which contains a second, inner set of curly braces):

```
{
    int aNumber = 45;
}

System.out.println(aNumber);
```

Do any errors appear with this code? How does the rule about not redeclaring a variable within the same code block relate to this example where a variable is used outside the code block it was declared in?

0.3 Printing to Console Output

Details on the `.println()` method: As shown in figure 0.8, you have been able to print to the output console using the `.println()` method. Notice one important fact about this method: you have been able to use pretty much any data-type variable, along with a text, inside of its parentheses as a **method parameter** and print it all to the console. So the method `.println()` seems to be pretty flexible in terms of what values can be **passed to it** through its parameter. Most commonly, text values are passed to the `.println()` method. In Java, text and phrases are represented by the `String` data type. Notice the capitalization: this means that `String` is a class data type (i.e., "complex").

Notice that in the following example, declaring and initializing a `String` looks very similar to that for primitive data types:

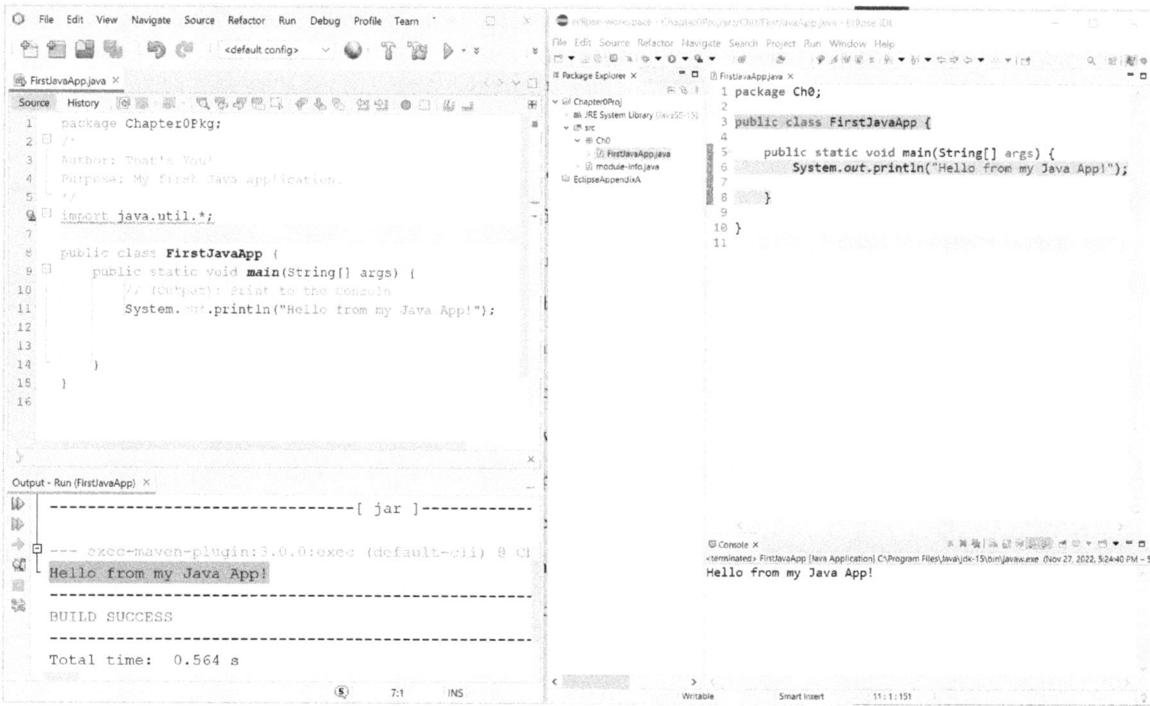

Figure 0.8. Output Area in Apache NetBeans (Left) and in Eclipse (Right)

Code Snippet 0.9

```
String myName = "Sarah Mickelson";
String copyOfMyName = myName;
```

So even though a `String` is a class data type, it can be created **in a similar manner as a primitive data type.** Oracle has done this as a convenience to developers working in the language. A variable of the `String` class can more formally be created like so:

Code Snippet 0.10

```
String myName = new String("Bob Javastone");
```

The stuff on the right side of the assignment operator includes a lot more than just the value that is copied from right to left with a primitive variable declaration and initialization. Later chapters will detail what is happening here. Both of these approaches to `String` creation are perfectly OK.

Concatenation: In Java, `String` variable values can be built using concatenation where the programmer "glues" together other `String` values (literals or variables). To do this, the addition operator in Java performs a second job: as a concatenation operator. (It even gets two paychecks. Ask it. It is proud of the hard work it does.) The following code demonstrates concatenation:

Code Snippet 0.11

```
String aPhrase = "Hello there" + " ";
String secondPhrase = "students";
String fullPhrase = aPhrase + secondPhrase;
System.out.println(fullPhrase);
```

When you compile and execute this code (as part of a complete Java program), the console output will be

```
Hello there students
```

For `String` concatenation to work, **there must be a `String` value on one or both sides of the addition operator.** Otherwise, Java might try to use it to add two numbers (its normal job), or it may perform a gapless concatenation of the two values. You can use this rule to concatenate primitive data-type variables with a `String` as well:

Code Snippet 0.12

```
int aValue = 56;
String anotherPhrase = "I wished for $";
String fullWish = anotherPhrase + aValue;
System.out.println(fullWish);
```

The console output for this would look like the following:

```
I wished for $56
```

Since the method `.println()` can take a `String` value as its method parameter, you can also perform concatenation and output building within the `.println()` parameter itself, inline style. You can do something like the following very easily:

Code Snippet 0.13

```
int firstAge = 20;
int secondAge = 45;
System.out.println("The parent's age was: " + secondAge
        + " and their child was aged: " + firstAge);
```

Notice that the last line of code is split across two actual editor lines in the IDE. Java does not mind this at all, since blank spaces are ignored by the Java compiler outside of `String` literal values.

The output for this would look like this:

```
The parent's age was: 45 and their child was aged: 20
```

Using concatenation effectively is key to developing professional, business-appropriate output that displays neatly. Notice a space placed at the end of the `String` literals so that the output would not run together like this:

```
The parent's age was:45and their child was aged:20
```

SUMMARY POINTS

- The dot notation allows us to access resources or methods that are part of a class data-type variable or in a class itself.
- The `.println()` method is a method found within a variable called "`out`," which itself is part of the class "`System`." Invoking `.println()` involves the use of the dot notation to describe the fully qualified location of where the method is defined: `System.out.println()`
- The `.println()` method receives the data it will print to the console through its parentheses, known as the parameter list. `.println()` only accepts one parameter, a `String`.
- Concatenation allows us to build a `String` one part at a time and further allows us to include the value of variables in a `String`, especially useful for printing information to the console.
- Concatenation works with the char data type as well. You can concatenate several `char` variable values into a `String`.

QUICK PROBLEMS

1. **Coding:** In a small Java program, concatenate your first and second name together within a `String` variable, including a space between the two names. Then pass this variable to the `.println()` method and print it to the console.
2. **Think:** How will Java interpret a variable name that has a space in it?
3. **Coding:** Write a small Java program that has two numbers stored in `int` variables. Print these to the console using concatenation in one single line. Then print their sum to the console using the addition operator.

0.4 Capturing User Input from the Console

Modern applications allow users to interact with them through the typing in of data (in addition to other UI interactions discussed later in the textbook). Most IDEs allow for interaction via data entry within **the same console that the output has been printed to.**

The `Scanner` class: In a Java program, an easy way to capture user input is by using a `Scanner` class variable (i.e., a variable you've created and declared with the data type "`Scanner`"). Basic Java programs do not know what the `Scanner` class is. An `import` statement is used to "teach" Java applications what the `Scanner` class is and how to use it.

Create a new Java application called "`AddThreeNumbers`" to practice the use of `Scanner`. You can create a new Java main class file in your chapter 0 project if you wish or create an entirely new Java project with a new Java main class file within. Either will ultimately produce the file "`AddThreeNumbers.java`," which looks like the following:

Full Program 0.3

```
package Chapter0Pkg;  // Your package may be differently named

public class AddThreeNumbers {

    public static void main(String[] args) {

        // Empty program.

    }
}
```

After the package line, import the `Scanner` class. This will **define the** class and make your Java application aware of its existence and nature. Add the following import statement after your "package" line:

Code Snippet 0.14

```
import java.util.Scanner;
```

Java groups together related classes in package folders. Sometimes, these packages themselves can be grouped within other packages and so on hierarchically. This provides a very organized structure to the JDK. If you see an import statement with "`java`" at the beginning, a class (or classes) from the official Java API (application programming interface) library is (are) being imported. Notice that the only capitalized word in that import statement is "`Scanner`." This means that "`java`" is a top-level package, and "`util`" is a package within that top level (i.e., a subpackage). Notice also that the dot notation is used to "drill down" into each level and the level below that, until the needed class is reached. Many IDEs will give you live views of the contents of the packages as you write an import statement, which will help.

Alternatively, you could have written the statement like this:

Code Snippet 0.15

```
import java.util.*;
```

The use of an asterisk tells Java to import **all** the classes that are within that package but **not** the classes in any subpackages. In this line of code, all the classes in the package `util` are imported, including `Scanner`. Either way is fine. Conversely, the following would **not** successfully import the `Scanner` class:

Code Snippet 0.16

```
import java.*;
```

Only classes in the top-level package would be imported, and all classes in all subpackages would be ignored. If you need subpackage classes, you will have to add additional import statements to your code.

In the `main()` method, a variable of the `Scanner` class can be declared and initialized like so:

Code Snippet 0.17

```
Scanner keyboardIn = new Scanner(System.in);
```

Notice that the variable name is `keyboardIn`. Remember that variable names are up to you; there are no required variable names. The data type for this variable is `Scanner`. The initialization on the right side of the assignment operator creates an instance object of the `Scanner` class, which can listen to keyboard input via an `InputStream` data-type object (the "`System.in`" part). For now, whenever you need a `Scanner` variable to read in user data from the console, type this line of code and simply change the variable name. Recall too that once you create any variable, you can use it without having to re-create it later in your program. The same goes for the `Scanner` variable. Once it is created, you can use the same one over and over each time you need keyboard input captured in your `main()` method's code.

Using a Scanner class variable for input: The purpose of this program is to add up three numbers. Listing out a basic series of steps that are needed in order to accomplish this might look like the following:

1. Create a `Scanner` variable.
2. Prompt the user, and ask them very nicely to type in three numbers.
3. Create three numeric variables that will store the numbers that the user types in.
4. Read in the three numbers from the console, and store them in the three variables.
5. Add them up, and store the sum in another variable.
6. Print the results to the console.

As your programs grow more and more complex, it might be a good idea to get into the habit of planning out the steps for your logic (your instructor may require this from you first before you write any code). Mixing plain language with Java syntax in your listing plan is known as **pseudocode**.

In order to read data from the console using a `Scanner` class variable, you can use various methods of the `Scanner` class. As you will see later in the textbook, since the `Scanner` class variable is "complex," the data reading methods should be invoked **upon the variable itself**, since it will be doing the gathering. The variable performs the gathering of the data from the keyboard, and the method invoked determines how to format the value that is retrieved from the keyboard.

Here is the full listing for this user-data-reading Java program:

Full Program 0.4

```
package Chapter0Pkg; // Your package may be differently named

import java.util.Scanner;

public class AddThreeNumbers {

    public static void main(String[] args) {

        Scanner keyboardIn = new Scanner(System.in);

        int firstNumber = 0;
        int secondNumber = 0;
        int thirdNumber = 0;

        int theSum = 0;

        System.out.println("Please enter three numbers as ## ## ##:");

        firstNumber = keyboardIn.nextInt();
        secondNumber = keyboardIn.nextInt();
        thirdNumber = keyboardIn.nextInt();

        theSum = firstNumber + secondNumber + thirdNumber;
```

```
        System.out.println("The sum is: " + theSum);
    }
}
```

Notice that the user is asked to type in three numbers, each separated by a **space**, and then finish the input with the **Enter** key on the keyboard to allow the program to move on. On the next three lines of code, a method of the `Scanner` class called `.nextInt()` is invoked upon that variable. This method tells the `Scanner` variable how to go and gather the data **and** determines in what data format the data will be retrieved. Notice the assignment operator as well. Remember, stuff on the right is copied over into something on the left. So here, the `.nextInt()` method gathers the first number typed in, formats it as an `int`, then copies that `int` over to the variable that is on the left side of the assignment operator (`firstNumber` in the first line and so on).

Run your program, and enter any three numbers, hitting Enter to generate the sum. For example, here is what the console will look like after one execution where three numbers are entered:

```
Please enter three numbers as ## ## ##:
5 10 15
The sum is: 30
```

Alternatively, you could have written the code for the prompting and reading in like so:

Code Snippet 0.18

```
. . .
System.out.println("Please enter the first number: ");
firstNumber = keyboardIn.nextInt();

System.out.println("Please enter the second number: ");
secondNumber = keyboardIn.nextInt();

System.out.println("Please enter the third number: ");
thirdNumber = keyboardIn.nextInt();
. . .
```

Here the application prompts for and receives each number, one at a time. Figure 0.9 shows how this program looks in Apache NetBeans. Notice that the user types their data and then presses the Enter key on their keyboard right in the output console in most IDEs (Apache, Eclipse, etc.) or at the terminal if you are running your Java program from a command prompt.

You should consider the input behavior of each application as you design and test them. The experience of how keyboard inputs are entered by the user can and will differ from situation to situation. The first approach earlier works because many of the `Scanner` class's "next" methods will **ignore blank space characters** and only focus on **actual data**. There are several different input methods within the `Scanner` class that you can use, and the most commonly used of them are covered in table 0.3.

Table 0.3. Most Commonly Used Scanner Class Console Input Methods

Input task	`Scanner` method	Ignores blank space?
Read in an `int`	`.nextInt()`	Yes
Read in a `double`	`.nextDouble()`	Yes
Read in a single word or letter	`.next()`	Yes
Read in an entire phrase	`.nextLine()`	No (captures blanks and text all)

You may have noticed that no parameter value is used with the `.nextInt()` method. There are some versions of these `Scanner` class methods that have parameters, but for now the zero-parameter versions will work just fine for this program's needs.

For numeric data to be read in from the console, a great rule of thumb is to **choose the Scanner method based on the target data type you need to capture**. Earlier, `int` values were required, and `int` variables were needed to store the captured values within. Because `int` is the target data type to capture from the keyboard, a `Scanner` method is needed that

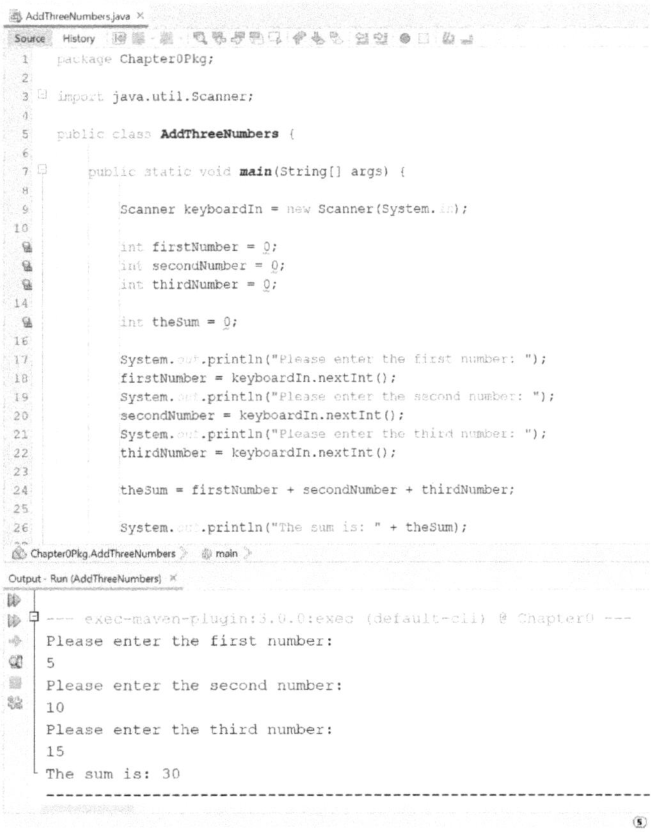

Figure 0.9. Accepting Keyboard Input via the Output Console in Apache NetBeans

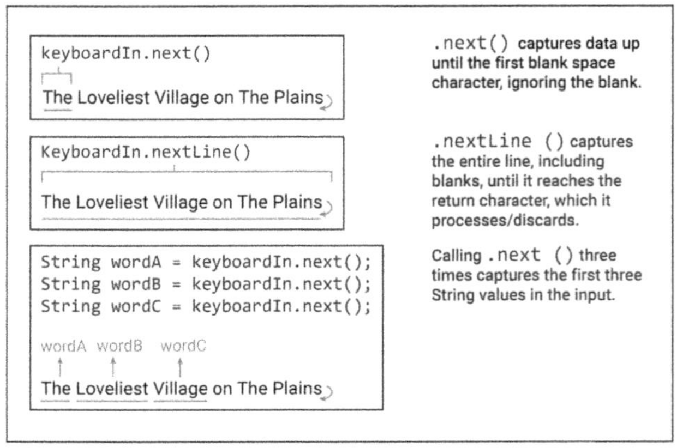

Figure 0.10. Capturing String Input from the Console

will read in and **format the incoming data as an** `int` before it copies it over to the variable. The `.nextInt()` method is most appropriate in this situation. For a `double` or a `long` variable, either the `.nextDouble()` or the `.nextLong()` `Scanner` methods could be used, respectively.

For text, both the `.next()` and the `.nextLine()` methods are very useful, as shown in figure 0.10. The former can read in a single word at a time as typed in, like this:

Code Snippet 0.19

```
System.out.println("Please enter your first and second name:");
String firstName = keyboardIn.next();
String secondName = keyboardIn.next();
```

Or you can read in the entire name as one single `String` (which would include the blank space character typed between them):

Code Snippet 0.20

```
System.out.println("Please enter your full name:");
String fullName = keyboardIn.nextLine();
```

Understanding how to read in basic numeric and text data from the console and use it in your program gets you off to a very solid start in Java programming. Try running the full program above and practice the various text input methods of the `Scanner` class detailed here before moving on.

SUMMARY POINTS

- The `Scanner` class, a complex class data type, allows for the capture of user-entered input data from the console, among many other uses.
- Java programs are not initially aware of the `Scanner` class and are not able to use it. Java programmers first have to use the `import` statement to "teach" a program about the class and enable its usage in code.
- Variables with a class data type are declared and initialized a little differently from primitive data-type variables. The "new" keyword is used along with a constructor for the class.
- To use the `Scanner` class, you first have to create a variable whose data type is `Scanner`, then invoke methods of the `Scanner` class to read in user-entered input. The method used is chosen based on the data type it reads in and matched to the data type you ask the user to enter.

QUICK PROBLEMS

1. **Coding:** Write a small Java program that prompts the user to enter any three letters. Concatenate each letter into a `String` variable, and print that variable back out to the console.
2. **Think:** When would it be useful to use the `.nextLine()` method of the `Scanner` class versus the `.next()` method? When would `.next()` be more useful?
3. **Coding:** Write a small Java program that will prompt the user to enter three numbers on the keyboard, subtracting the numbers as they are entered (second from the first, then the third from that difference). Print the result of the calculation (even if it is negative). Use the subtraction operator ("`-`") to perform the subtractions.

Summary

In this chapter, you have learned the very basics of creating, coding, and running your first Java program. You have learned about the basic structure of a Java program and the minimum structure that is needed. You have learned many basic syntax rules, some that are unique to Java and some that are not, and you have learned about several of the benefits of using the Java language. You have learned how Java is both similar to and different from other programming languages and how this enables the benefits discussed. You have, importantly, explored the eight basic "primitive" data types built into the Java language and how they enable you to store data in memory. You have additionally learned how to output information to the console and how to read in, store, and use data entered by the user as inputs, bringing your learning in this chapter full circle. In the next chapter, you will explore how to put data to work and examine the uses and powerful capabilities of the various Java operators.

Practice Problems

Terminology

Match the following terms from the chapter with their most appropriate definition:

1. z	a. Creation of a variable and assignment of a name/label to the reserved space in memory.
2. `main()`	b. The input data for a method, placed in between the method's parentheses.
3. Console	c. Symbol used to indicate the end of a single line of code. Not used at the end of a block.
4. Class	d. Area of output for Java programs in development environments, either in the command line or in the GUI for a Java IDE.
5. Platform independence	e. A numeric value not contained within a variable used directly in Java code.
6. Bytecode	f. Words used for various parts of the Java syntax that cannot be used as variable names by developers.

7. Java Virtual Machine	g. The automatic up-conversion by Java of a smaller data type to a larger one during assignment or usage in an expression.
8. Java development kit	h. Command used to "teach" your application about various classes in the Java library.
9. Semicolon	i. Set of binaries and libraries provided with Java to assist with application development, debugging, testing, and deployment.
10. Variable	j. A quasi-code listing of the parts and logical sequence of an intended program in a conversational style, a useful planning tool.
11. Data type	k. A technique for building String values one part at a time, useful for incorporating values of variables into text output.
12. Declaration	l. The building "block" of Java and found throughout the language. These are also complex data types in Java.
13. Initialization	m. Software developed by Oracle that executes Java programs on various hardware/software computing platforms.
14. Literal	n. A benefit of the Java language enabled by versions of the JVM on various hardware/software platforms.
15. Reserved keywords	o. The first assignment of a value to a newly created variable; can happen at the time of variable creation or afterward.
16. Type promotion	p. A space in memory reserved by the programmer to temporarily store data. The name represents a label that "points" to that reserved memory.
17. Method parameter	q. An intermediate language that Java code is compiled into by the Java compiler; is interpreted and/or compiled by the JVM when a Java program executes.
18. Concatenation	r. An area of code enclosed by curly braces that denotes code associated with a structure in a Java application. Classes, methods, and other control structures in Java are associated with them.
19. Pseudocode	s. A defined way in which data will be sized and stored in memory and assigned to a newly declared variable.
20. Import	t. The starting point for code execution in a Java stand-alone program. The first line of code in its code block is the first line of developer code executed in a Java program.

Find the Error

In each of the following problems, carefully examine the code given, and determine the error(s)/issue(s) with each. Keep in mind, the error(s) could be syntax (code) or logic (intended outcome) based or both!

1.

```
aNumber int = 45.4d;
float anotherNumber = 45.4;
```

2.

```
firstNumber = 65;
firstNumber = secondNumber;
int secondNumber = 100;
int firstNumber = 0;
```

3.

```
int 4Digits = 3456;
int 5Digits = 65445;
System.out.println("4 Digits: " + 3456);
```

4.

```
double weightInPounds = 5.4d;
System.out.println("Weight: " + WeightInPounds);
```

5.

```
scanner readInput = new scanner(System.in);
System.out.println("Please enter your age: ");
int userAge = .nextInt();
```

6.

```
double salaryAmount = int employeeTenure;
salaryAmount = 56000.50d;
employeeTenure = 15;
int totalPaid = salaryAmount * employeeTenure; // multiply
Systemoutprintln("Total Salary Paid: " + totalPaid);
```

7.

```
double costOfProduct = 6.34d;
System.out.println("Cost of Product " + costPerOz);
```

8.

```
scanner readInput = new scanner(System.in);
System.out.println("Please enter your age: ");
int userAge = .nextInt();
```

9.

```
// Think about this one. . .
System.out.println("Welcome to Three Numbers Sum!");
Scanner readIn = new Scanner(System.in);
int numOne = readIn.nextInt();
int numTwo = readIn.nextInt();
int numThree = readIn.nextInt();
int total = numOne + numTwo + numThree;
System.out.println("The sum is: " + total);
```

10.

```
// Think about this one. . .
System.out.println("Enter your name, age, and today's temperature:");
Scanner input = new Scanner(System.in);
System.out.println("Name: " + input.nextInt()
     + ", age: " + input.nextInt()
     + ", Daily Temp: " + input.nextInt());
```

Think about It

1. What are the basic parts of a Java application? Where does code execution start in a stand-alone Java application?
2. What is the purpose of a code block? How can you easily determine which part(s) of your program are enclosed in a code block?
3. What are the two ways to place a comment in a Java program? What purpose does commenting serve in a Java code listing?
4. What is the purpose of the Java Virtual Machine (JVM)? How does your Java application use the JVM?
5. How is Java both an interpreted and a compiled programming language? What benefits does this bring to the language over others?
6. What does "platform independence" mean, and why is it a benefit for Java?
7. What does an import statement do, and why is it needed for some Java applications?
8. What is a semicolon used for, and when do you use it? When would you not use it?
9. What does it mean for Java to be a "type-strict" programming language? How does this impact your use of variables?
10. What is the difference between a variable and a literal?
11. How is the creation of a `Scanner` class variable different from the creation of a variable of any of the primitive data types?
12. Why is it a good idea to prompt for user input before attempting to read it in your application?

Short Syntax Problems

1. Create three variables: one for a person's age, one for their height in feet (include decimals), and one for the first character of their first name. Store any values you wish in these, then print them to the console using the `.println()` method.
2. Create three `int` variables at the same time (on the same line), and store the value "5" in them.
3. Create an `int` variable and a `double` variable, and store any value you wish in them. Copy the value of the `int` variable into the double, then print the value stored in the double. What prints?
4. Create three `char` data-type variables, and place your initials into each (use `x` if you do not have a middle name). Create a String variable, and concatenate the three char variables into it. Print out the contents of the String to the console.
5. Create two `int` variables, and place whatever values into them you wish. Create a third `int` variable called "`temp`." Using "`temp`," swap the values in the first two variables without deleting/losing either of them. For example, if the variables held "10" and "20," they would now hold "20" and "10," respectively.

Full Problems

1. Write a Java program that prompts the user to enter the phrase "Java!" at the console but one character at a time (separated by a space or return key). Capture each character. Print the characters back to the console in the reverse order they were captured (do not use a loop structure for this problem).
2. Write a Java program that prompts the user to enter their name, their job title, their salary, and their years on the job. Output the captured information back to the console in a conversational style, like so:

```
Our employee NAME has worked as a
JOBTITLE for #YEARS and earns$ #####.##
per year in Salary and bonuses.
```

3. Write a full Java program that will prompt for and allow a user to enter the full information for an employee of an organization. The program will gather the following information:
   a. The employee name (first and second name)
   b. The employee's badge ID (no letters, just numbers in the badge ID)
   c. The employee's salary (with decimal information)
   d. The employee's address (think about breaking this out into street, city, state, and zip for a US address—or customize it to your locality)
   e. The employee's email address

   Once this information is gathered, print the information out to the console in a business-professional manner. Use concatenation when needed. Be sure to use the appropriate methods of the `Scanner` class as needed for each data type of input. Use a dollar sign to precede any monetary amounts.
4. Write a full Java program that will prompt the user to enter the first name and second name of three separate people. Capture the names from the console. Output the names in the following manner:
   a. The names will be entered in "first name second name" format (no punctuation needed).
   b. The names will be printed in the reverse order they were gathered in. If persons A, B, and C are entered in that order, then print out C's information, then B's, and finally A's.
   c. The names will be printed in "`Second Name, First Name`" style. Print a comma as well.
   d. Print each name on a separate line of output.
5. Write a full Java program that will do the following:
   a. Prompt the user to enter the full name of a student. Capture and store that name.
   b. Prompt the user to enter five test scores for the student in order from highest to lowest. Capture each one.
   c. Print to the console the name of the student, and print their highest test score, the lowest, and the sum of all five scores ("total points earned").

Chapter 1

Putting Data to Work with Operators

What You Will Learn in This Chapter

Operators are a syntax common to most contemporary programming languages, including Java. They are symbolic commands that allow us to manipulate, compare, process, and alter data. Operators in programming languages can differ from one another in both their usage and their purpose. They are indispensable tools in any language and make up the basic foundation of the processing stage of any software system. You will explore many of the more commonly used operators in the language as you continue to learn the basics of the Java language.

Specifically, this chapter will help you do the following:

1. Understand and describe what an operator is in general, the broad categories of its types, and the purpose of its usage across programming languages, including Java
2. Understand and describe the differences between unary and binary operator types
3. Understand the concept of operator outcomes and how to use them for the various types of Java operators
4. Understand, describe, and use the Java implementations of arithmetic, relational, and boolean logic operators
5. Understand and describe the purpose and use of the Java operator precedence chart and how it can help describe the expected behavior of a Java expression

Opening Scenario

Your project team colleague for the mom-and-pop grocery store client relates to you how the on-site requirements-gathering visit went: "They have a lot of business rules. A lot. Round two of the requirements meeting happens Monday. I never thought a small business doing things manually could have so many rules. Coupons, savings club, inventory levels and stock reordering, daily pricing, holidays, employee work hours, and vacation rules—and we are just scratching the surface." It sounds like they made a lot of progress on the first visit. As you listen, pseudocode starts racing through your mind: comparison of hours, pricing, boolean status of customer shopping club status, and so on. The logic to implement their business rules will be nuanced. "We have a lot to think about, and we have to get it right. Every business rule must work every time. And every rule will impact their revenues and profits both. We have to get it right the first time and understand every possible outcome their new system will have to deduce."

You have made progress as well. As the project team divides up into subtasks to prepare for the prototype build, you have been paired with several colleagues and crash-coursing on the basics of the Java language. As you listen to the variety and complexity of the initially elicited business rules for the client, that feeling of progress starts to slip away. "I still have a lot to learn; understanding how to process formulas and perform logic comparisons in Java will be a must," you think as you listen. "Every language does it slightly differently. I'll have to understand how the operators in **this** language work precisely." Your experience with prior languages, though, gives you confidence that learning how Java handles logical and boolean operators will not be hugely difficult. For what you feel will not be the last time, you decide to dig in and study the nuances of operators in the Java language. "The client's confidence in the prototype could shatter if it outputs decisions that are not in line with what they expect, so I have to get this right . . ."

1.1 Understanding Operators

Operators in programming languages: What is an operator exactly? To put it simply, an operator in most programming languages is a **single symbol** or a **pair of symbols**, generally not a letter or number, that carries out some task. For a programming language and the software built from it to be useful, the ability to store and manipulate data in memory is critical. Operators provide the basis for this ability. In the information systems field, recall how data flows into a system and is processed in some way and then how an output of some manner is (typically) produced. Java programs (for now) are much smaller than a full system. Even so, operators give us the ability to perform data processing and manipulation of the "information" flowing through programs.

Why operators are needed: Take a moment and look up from this textbook at the space or area where you are currently sitting. Notice the number of things in your area (pieces of furniture, decor, people, squirrels, robots, etc.). Digital devices like computer systems are not able to count "at a glance" like humans can. Computing systems must process data **one chunk at a time** in a very sequential, in-order kind of way. Now digital devices can do this much faster than people can, but the processing is still sequential; they would have to start with the first squirrel, count it, then move on to the next, and so on. Recall that an operator is a syntax symbol that performs some action or command with data. The operator instructs the software as to **how** to process data and in what **order** and **how to handle the results** afterward. Remember too that the computer cannot read your mind (yet!). You have to be very specific and tell it exactly what to do with exactly what data. This is what operators allow us to do.

Types of operators: Unary and binary operators are the most common types of operators in most programming languages—unary, coming from the Latin word meaning "one," and binary, from the Latin word meaning "two."[*,†] Java also has a **ternary** ("three") operator that involves three pieces of data. **Unary** operators will only manipulate one "chunk" of data, this chunk commonly known as an **operand.** This means that only one value is involved in the operation by the operator. In Java, you will typically see the unary operator "attached" to the value or variable it is manipulating with no space between the operator symbol and the variable/value involved in the operation (see figure 1.1). An example of a unary operator with its operand would be as follows:

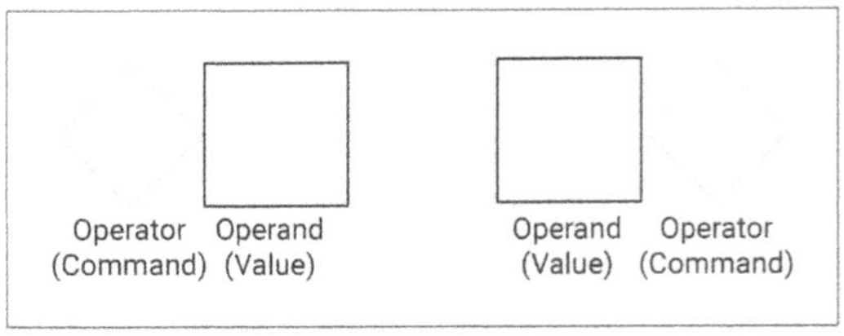

Figure 1.1. Two Ways to Use a Unary Operator

Code Snippet 1.1

```
int aNum = 5;
int anotherNum = aNum++;  // "++" is a Unary operator
```

In Java, **binary** operators are used frequently. For example, the assignment operator is a binary operator. Think about it: using the terms operator and operand from above, the assignment operator has two **things** on both sides of it: a value to the right to be copied into the variable on the left. The assignment operation, or the task of copying a value from one variable/literal to another variable, involves an operand on the right and an operand on the left. It is a binary operator in the sense that it requires two values/variables/"things" to perform its task (see figure 1.2). With a binary operator, having a space in between the operands and the operator will not affect its operation (i.e., the syntax will understand which operands are involved with the operator you are trying to use). The operand on the right is commonly called the **right operand**, and the one on the left is the **left operand.** Recall your use of the addition operator, which is also a binary operator:

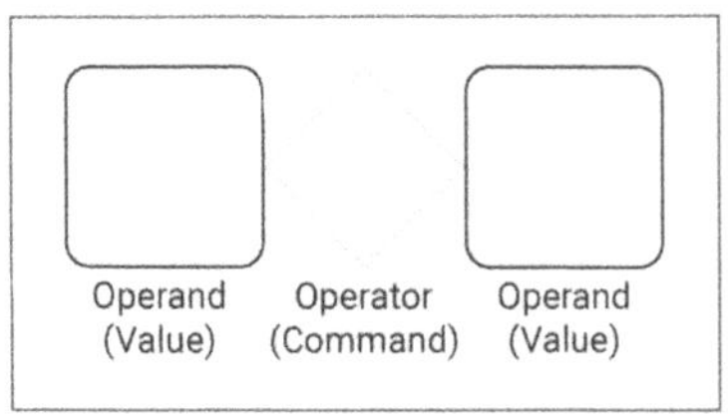

Figure 1.2. Structure of Usage for a Binary Operator

---

[*] https://www.etymonline.com/word/binary.

[†] https://www.etymonline.com/word/unary.

Code Snippet 1.2

```
int aThirdNumber = 10 + 4; // Binary Operators + and =
```

Operators and outcomes: Operators also produce a result as the last step of the operation they perform, known as an **outcome.** The outcome of the operation is what makes operators useful to us. For example, a binary operator might be used to compare two values. The outcome of that comparison would be the result to be stored and used at a later point in the code. In some cases, an operator performs a math operation on the two values. Its outcome would be the result of that operation.

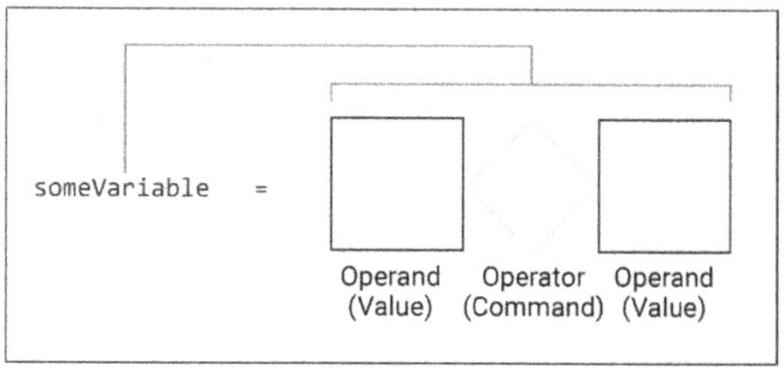

Figure 1.3. The Outcome of a Binary Operator Being Copied into a Variable Using the Assignment Operator

Operators and execution order: When you use the assignment operator, data is copied from right to left. If you use a binary operator on the right-hand side as shown in figure 1.3, this adds an additional command to the expression. That operator's command must finish first, **then** the assignment/copy can occur from the right to the left. Typically, the common usage of a binary operator is to capture and use its outcome. The common usage of a unary operator is to change or manipulate some singular value. This is not always the case but is the most common scenario you will encounter.

SUMMARY POINTS

- Operators in Java consist of a single symbol or a pair of symbols grouped together without a space.
- Operators help instruct a program as to how and in what order numeric or other values should be processed and in what manner based on the operators chosen and their purpose.
- There are three categories of operators in Java: unary (single operand), binary (two operands), and ternary (three operands). The unary and binary are the more commonly used operators in most programming languages, Java included.
- A unary operator only has one operand, or "chunk" of data, it will operate/act upon. Some unary operators will behave differently depending on whether the operator is placed to the left or the right side of the operand.
- A binary operator will have two operands: a left and a right operand. A space in between these is optional and will not impact their usage.
- Most operands in a Java expression are processed from left to right. Some, like the assignment operator, process from right to left.
- An operator, when it has finished its task, will produce an outcome. This is a value it "returns" or that replaces it and the operand(s) in the expression. Different operators will have different outcomes, many of which are useful for code logic.

QUICK PROBLEMS

1. **Coding:** Write a small Java program that adds five numbers of your choice together. After printing the sum, print to the screen the number of operators and operands that were involved in the calculation.
2. **Think:** Do you think it is possible for an operator in Java to **not** have an outcome? Why or why not?
3. **Think:** Think about the coding problem above (quick problem #1) where you added five numbers together. How many outcomes were there? How does this relate to the number of operators needed to complete the calculation?

1.2 Arithmetic Operators

Among the commonly used binary operators in Java, the **arithmetic** operators form the base of most numeric expressions you will write: add, subtract, multiply, and divide. The versions of these operators found in Java are typically the same in most modern programming languages. Their usage is usually very straightforward. Table 1.1 below lists them along with the **modulo** operator (for finding remainders). These are not all the arithmetic operators found in Java but the ones that you will most commonly use. You have already used some of these previously.

Table 1.1. Basic Arithmetic Operators

Operator name	Operator
Addition	+
Subtraction	-
Multiplication	*
Division	/
Modulo	%

The following code snippet shows these operators in use. Notice how these binary arithmetic operators are used and how they execute: First, the two variables on the right side of the assignment operator are used in the command; they're added, subtracted, multiplied, or divided, or the remainder is found. **Then** the outcome of that operation/command is copied into the target variable on the left of the assignment operator. "The stuff on the right always executes first" is a good rule of thumb to keep in mind for now:

Code Snippet 1.3

```
int firstNum = 5;
int secondNum = 10;
int thirdNum = 15;
int fourthNum = 3;

int varA = firstNum + secondNum;  // outcome is 15
int varB = firstNum - secondNum;  // outcome is -5
int varC = firstNum * secondNum;  // outcome is 50
int varD = thirdNum / firstNum;   // outcome is 3
int varE = secondNum % fourthNum; // outcome is 1
```

It is very important to understand the order of execution in these statements, as you will write more complicated expressions later on. Figure 1.4 shows the order of execution, with the sum outcome copied into `varA`.

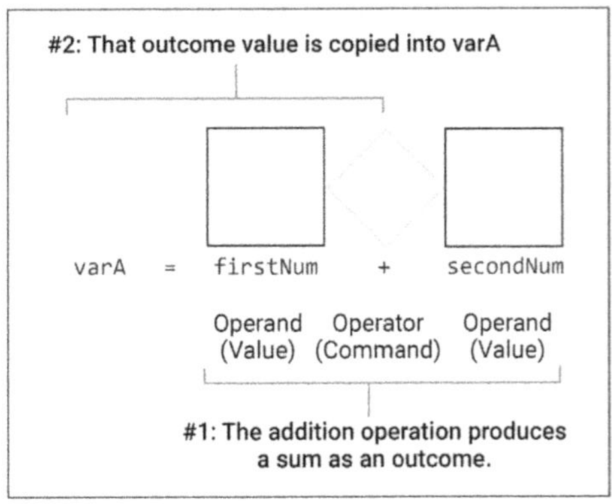

Figure 1.4. Processing Order for an Expression with Two Binary Operators

Notice that the modulo operator, the `%` (percent) symbol, produces the remainder of the division of the left operand by the value contained in the right operand. Remember, an operand can be a value (literal or from a method return), a variable, or the return from a method (discussed later in the textbook). In the code example's last expression, the value within `secondNum` is divided by that within `fourthNum`, producing a result of `3` with a `1` remainder. It is the remainder produced as the outcome by the modulo operator. The modulo operator can cleverly be used to discover if a number is odd or even (use this trick and impress your friends at the next Java party you host!). For example,

Code Snippet 1.4

```
int oddNumber = 13;
int evenNumber = 8;

System.out.println("Even (0) or Odd (1): " + oddNumber % 2);
System.out.println("Even (0) or Odd (1): " + evenNumber % 2);
```

When you run this code, the following output occurs:

```
Even (0) or Odd (1): 1
Even (0) or Odd (1): 0
```

This is useful when the program is running, and variables are receiving values that you are not aware of beforehand. Examples include user input from the keyboard, reading in data from an external data source, and so on. There are many times when determining the even/odd nature of a number can be useful in programming.

Using multiple binary arithmetic operators in one expression: The arithmetic operators are useful because you can combine them within a single expression to perform whatever math you need. For example,

Code Snippet 1.5

```
int sumAll = firstNum + secondNum + thirdNum + fourthNum;
```

Remember that when an assignment operator is involved, data flows from the right to the left. In this case, there are three addition operators on the right side of the assignment operator. Java will process each one at a time, from the left to the right (see appendix B for the processing order of Java operators). Once the full right-hand sum is obtained, that outcome will **then** be copied into the `sumAll` variable on the left. Figure 1.5 shows how this expression is processed step-by-step.

Java will use the first addition operator and its two operands (values on the left and right) and perform the first addition. The outcome from this addition, fifteen, becomes the left operand for the next addition operator to the right, and so on.

```
                 5          10          15          3
int sumAll = firstNum + secondNum + thirdNum + fourthNum;
int sumAll =          15            + thirdNum + fourthNum;
int sumAll =                  30                + fourthNum;
int sumAll =                        33                    ;
```

Figure 1.5. Processing Order for Multiple Operators in an Expression

Incrementing and decrementing: Computing systems are sequential, repetitive, and step-by-step in the way they process data and execute logic. **Incrementing** (i.e., increasing a value sequentially) and **decrementing** (i.e., decreasing a value sequentially) are two ideas that are central to the nature of systems. Earlier when you counted the items and people (and robots) nearby, you unknowingly kept a counter in your head and increased it by one each time you found an instance of something. Computers operate the same way—counting values that meet some threshold or a number of objects in memory or using incrementation to keep track of how many times a segment of code has looped and executed. Computers are very good at this sort of stuff, and programmers can leverage this nature to their advantage.

In Java, the unary increment and decrement operators allow us to increase or decrease by one, respectively, the numeric value of a variable. Additionally, in Java, you can use the increment and decrement operators in two different yet useful ways. You can increment the value of a variable **before** its value is used in an expression, known as a **pre-increment** ("prefix" form—something "before") operation. Alternatively, you can alter a variable's value **after** that value has been used in an expression, known as a **post-increment** ("postfix" form—something "after") operation. The increment operator is two addition operators ("++") placed together and placed immediately to the left of a variable with no space (pre-increment) or immediately to the right with no space (post-increment). The same goes for decrementing, with the use of the **pre-decrement** and **post-decrement** operators, and the use of two subtraction operators ("--"). These are unary operators, so their usage would look like the following example. Notice that the values of both variables in each expression **after all processing is done** are listed in the comment beside each line:

Code Snippet 1.6

```
int aVar = 5;
int aSecondVar = aVar++;      // aSecondVar = 5, aVar = 6;
int varF = ++firstNum + 5;    // varF = 11, firstNum = 6
int varG = secondNum-- + 6;   // varG = 16, secondNum = 9
```

Figure 1.6 compares how the pre- and post-increment operators affect the values of the `aVar` and `aSecondVar` variables.

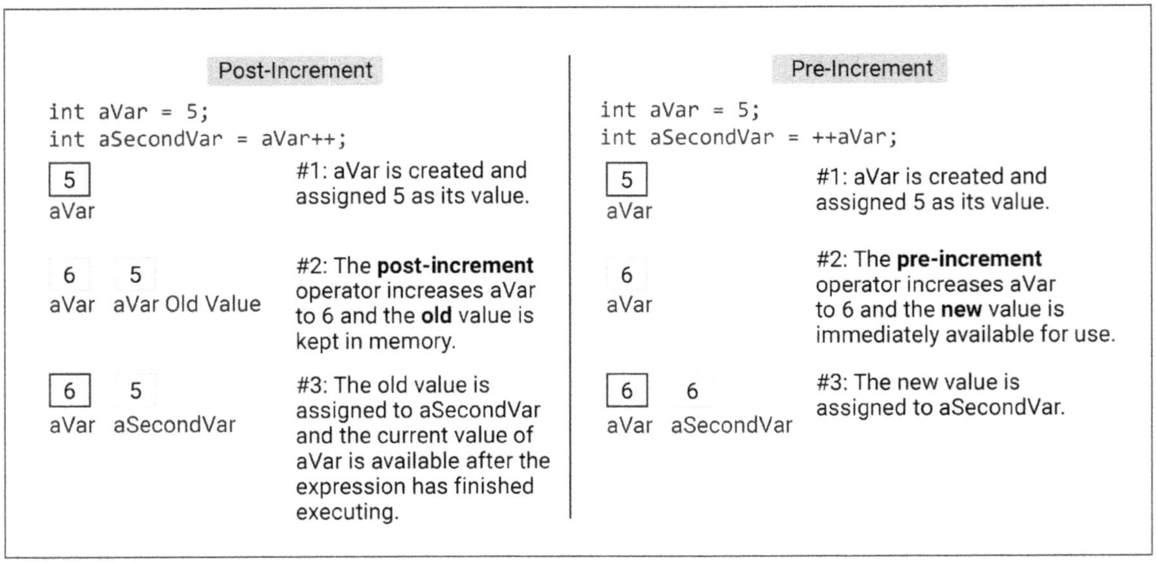

Figure 1.6. Comparison of Post-increment and Pre-increment Operators

Understanding how Java processes the pre- and post-increment and pre- and post-decrement operators can be a little tricky at first. Table 1.2 helps summarize their usage:

Table 1.2. Simplified Summary of Unary Increment Operators and Their Usages

Operator	Usage	Meaning
Pre-increment	`++someVariable`	"Increase the variable's value by one, then use the **new larger value** in the expression."
Post-increment	`someVariable++`	"Increase the variable's value by one, <u>but</u> use the **old, smaller value** in the expression."
Pre-decrement	`--someVariable`	"Decrease the variable's value by one, then use the **new lower value** in the expression."
Post-decrement	`someVariable--`	"Decrease the variable's value by one, <u>but</u> use the **old, larger value** in the expression."

In each case, the value of the variable `someVariable` is either incremented or decremented by one. Depending on whether you use the prefix or postfix version of the operator determines **which** value is used in the expression where the operator is found, the old value or new value. With the postfix versions, the variable is changed but the value of the variable before it was changed was used. Take a look at this slightly trickier example (assume that the changes to `firstNum` and `secondNum` earlier did not occur, and `firstNum`'s value coming into this line of code is still 5 and `secondNum`'s is still 10):

Code Snippet 1.7

```
int varH = ++firstNum + secondNum-- + 3;    // Tricky!
```

What is the value of `varH` after this line of code is done? It will help to think about this statement in stages:

- Eventually, the final outcome (i.e., value) from the right will be copied to the variable on the left.
- Of the stuff on the right, processing occurs from left to right.
- A pre-increment operator is present. First, increase `firstNum`'s value to `6` and <u>use that new value in the expression</u>.
- A post-decrement operator is also used. Decrease the value of `secondNum` to `9`, **but** <u>use the old value of</u> `10` for `secondNum` in the expression.

To help understand the outcomes of the increment/decrement operators, consider this version of the expression with the final values substituted manually (in bold):

Code Snippet 1.8

```
int varH = 6 + 10 + 3;    // Not so tricky - varH is 19!
```

Promotion and type casting: As an information systems professional, your primary concern will most likely be with business-oriented systems and software and the precise data manipulation and reporting that comes along with them. Think about a particular example that may cause some concern in the business world: You and six other friends have opened up a lemonade stand just off campus, and you have raked in $489 of profit in one day! Now it is time to divide that profit among the seven partners. So you decide to write a small program to find out how much of a share of the profit everyone gets:

Code Snippet 1.9

```
int amountOfProfit = 489;
int numberOfPartners = 7;
double profitPerPartner = amountOfProfit / numberOfPartners;

System.out.println("Profit per Partner: " + profitPerPartner);
```

When you run this small program, the following outputs:

```
Profit per Partner: 69.0
```

Sounds pretty good! But when a fellow partner who minored in finance uses her calculator to double-check your math, she comes up with the figure `69.8571428571`. Everyone realizes that they will miss out on their `.8571428571` cents! What happened?

Notice that the code divided an `int` data type by an `int` data type. Numeric binary operators in Java will take on the **largest/widest data type** of their two operands. In this case, you have an `int` for both, so the result, the outcome, is an `int` with no decimal data at all. This is a behavior called **promotion**, and it can come in handy if you know how to use it. How can you fix this code? There are two ways:

- **First correction approach:** Change your code so that one of the two operands is a `double`. A `double` is a larger data type (takes up more memory) than an `int`, so Java will promote the outcome of the operand to a `double`, preserving the decimal data (change in bold):

Code Snippet 1.10

```
double amountOfProfit = 489.0;
int numberOfPartners = 7;
double profitPerPartner = amountOfProfit / numberOfPartners;

System.out.println("Profit per Partner: " + profitPerPartner);
```

When run, this code now yields the following output:

```
Profit per Partner: 69.85714285714286
```

- **Second correction approach:** You can use a **cast operator** to force one variable to **be interpreted** as another data type. These are also commonly called "type cast" operators. Keep in mind that even when casting a variable or value on the right of an expression, the target variable you are copying on the left must be of equal or larger "size." You still cannot put a `double` outcome into an `int` variable. It only works for target variable data types the same or larger in memory size. So you could change (in bold) your code like so:

Code Snippet 1.11

```
int amountOfProfit = 489;
int numberOfPartners = 7;
double profitPerPartner = (double)amountOfProfit / numberOfPartners;

System.out.println("Profit per Partner: " + profitPerPartner);
```

The cast operator is a simple, valid type name (any of the primitives + any defined complex type that you will see later on in this book) enclosed in parentheses and **always to the left** of the variable you are casting as. This does **not** change the value of the variable at all or permanently change its type. A cast is like putting on a costume mask: you ask the variable to "pretend" to be another type just for this expression. After the expression is done, the variable goes back to its old data type. The change above yields the same result:

```
Profit per Partner: 69.85714285714286
```

There are other promotion rules in Java that you can research that could be useful later in your Java studies.[*]

Taking the assignment operator further: The old programming maxim of "doing more with less code" is always a worthwhile goal for anyone who writes software. Java provides convenient shorthand ways of writing commonly needed arithmetic expressions. These are called the **arithmetic compound operators**. Some call these "augmented assignment operators," but that is not even close to the correct name for them (professional Java programmers are already writing angry letters to your author, to be sure!). These provide a shorter, convenient syntax for common mathematical expressions. For example,

Code Snippet 1.12

```
int newVar = 0;
newVar += firstNum;  // newVar = newVar + firstNum;
```

Here you have two different operators paired together (technically, this is a **single** binary operator). First, the two operands `newVar` and `firstNum` are added together. Then the assignment operator is processed, and its two operands are `newVar` and the outcome of the addition operation. The sum is stored in the variable on the left, `newVar`. Table 1.3 details all the arithmetic compound operators and how they are used:

Table 1.3. Listing and Summary of the Common Arithmetic Compound Operators

Arithmetic compound operator	Example usage	Meaning
+=	`varA += varB`	"Add `varA` to `varB`, and store the sum in `varA` (overwrites `varA`'s value)."
-=	`varA -= varB`	"Subtract `varB` from `varA`, and store the difference in `varA` (overwrites `varA`'s value)."
*=	`varA *= varB`	"Multiply `varA` by `varB`, and store the product in `varA` (overwrites `varA`'s value)."
/=	`varA /= varB`	"Divide `varA` by `varB`, and store the quotient in `varA` (overwrites `varA`'s value)."
%=	`varA %= varB`	"Calculate the remainder obtained by dividing `varA` by `varB`, and store the remainder in `varA` (overwrites `varA`'s value)."

SUMMARY POINTS

- The arithmetic operators in Java allow us to perform simple math in Java expressions. Most of these operators are binary in nature, meaning they need a left and right operand to perform the mathematical task.
- The modulo operator produces as an outcome the remainder of dividing the left operand by the value in the right operand. Modulo can be useful in determining if a variable has an odd or even numeric value stored within also.
- The increment and decrement operators will increase or decrease the value of a numeric variable by one, respectively. These are unary operators that are placed to the left (prefix) or right (postfix) of a variable. This placement will change whether or not the new value or the old

[*] https://docs.oracle.com/javase/specs/jls/se7/html/jls-5.html.

one is used in the expression the operator is found within.
- In an expression, if there is a mix of numeric data types used with an arithmetic operand, Java will promote the outcome of the operator to the larger data type.
- A cast operator can also be used to temporarily force a variable to be interpreted as a different data type other than the one it was declared with, useful when ensuring the accurate processing of an expression.
- The arithmetic compound operators allow programmers to perform math and assign outcomes to a variable in a much more succinct syntax manner, saving keystrokes and in some cases increasing computational efficiency.

QUICK PROBLEMS

1. **Coding:** Write a small Java program that divides any large number (larger than one thousand) by any smaller one (smaller than fifteen). Print to the screen both the quotient (the result of the division) and the remainder.
2. **Think:** Can you use both the pre- and post-increment operators on the same variable, at the same time, in the following manner?

   ```
   int someVar = ++anotherInt++;
   ```

   Why or why not?
3. **Coding:** Write a small Java program that instructs the user to enter two numbers with decimals, with one number's decimal larger than `.5` and another's less than `.5` (e.g., `15.7` and `1.2`). Capture both as `double` data types using the appropriate `Scanner` class method, then cast them both as `int` values. Print them back to the screen. What are the results? Why did they print the way they did?

1.3 Operators That Compare Values

In an object-oriented language like Java, comparisons of equality and relation to one another can get tricky. Comparison of objects differs greatly from the comparison of, say, two primitive variables. Any modern program will need to not only store data but also perform math upon that data and possibly compare the data to one another. Is `studentA`'s GPA higher than that of `studentB`? Did that employee's salary reach a threshold that puts them into a higher (or lower) tax bracket? The comparison of data values will underlie the implementation of many business rules you will encounter in your career.

Figure 1.7. Some Java Operators Compare Values like Scales Compare Weights
Source: "Money Scales" by Images_of_Money is licensed under CC BY 2.0, https://www.flickr.com/photos/59937401@N07/5857910508.

Operators that examine equality: The **equality binary operator** simply compares two values and tests for their exact equality. It produces a `boolean` **true** or **false** outcome value that can be used in decision-making logic later. For example,

Code Snippet 1.13

```
boolean equalityResult = false; // init value
int varLarger = 150;
int varSmaller = 56;

equalityResult = varLarger == varSmaller;

System.out.println("Are they equal? " + equalityResult);
```

When this code executes, the following will appear in the output:

```
Are they equal? false
```

Typically, programmers will use parentheses to isolate the test for equality and make the code a bit easier to understand (we will discuss how parentheses impact an expression later):

Code Snippet 1.14

```
equalityResult = (varLarger == varSmaller);
```

Notice how the ending parentheses go **before** the semicolon. The parentheses only encapsulate part of the expression, while the semicolon applies to the whole line of code.

The **not equal to** operator examines if two values differ at all. For example,

Code Snippet 1.15

```
boolean equalityResult = false; // init value
int varLarger = 150;
int varSmaller = 56;

equalityResult = varLarger != varSmaller;

System.out.println("Are they not equal? " + equalityResult);
```

The output from this code when executed would look like this:

```
Are they not equal? true
```

Difference between the assignment and equality operator: The difference between the assignment and equality operator in Java is highly important to note. In some programming languages, the assignment operator acts as the equality operator also. In Java, this is **not the case.** The assignment operator (=) always copies the value from the right into a target variable on the left and **will never return a boolean or allow you to compare values.** In fact, the outcome from the assignment operator is the value itself that was copied. The equality operator (==) is specifically tasked with value comparison and boolean outcome (`true` or `false`). It is a common mistake to confuse the two or simply type one equal sign where two are needed. Be careful!

Operators that perform relative comparisons: More than just equality can be determined. **Relational binary operators** allow for the comparison of values beyond equality: Is a number larger or smaller than another? Is one variable's value equal to or smaller than another variable's value? It is typically a good idea to store the `boolean` outcome of relational operators in a variable, but it is not required. Table 1.4 lists the relational operators commonly used in Java programs.

Note the following code example that demonstrates the use of some of these relational operators:

Table 1.4. Relational Operators in Java

Relational operator	Summary
>=	Greater than or equal to
<=	Less than or equal to
>	Strictly greater than (no equality)
<	Strictly less than (no equality)

Code Snippet 1.16

```
int varLarger = 150;
int varSmaller = 56;
. . .
boolean largerOrEqual = varLarger >= varSmaller;
System.out.println(largerOrEqual);
boolean isLarger = varSmaller > varLarger;
System.out.println(isLarger);
System.out.println(varSmaller < varLarger);
```

And the output when this code executes:

```
true
false
true
```

Notice that the outcome of the relational operation can simply be used as the input parameter for a method, such as `.println()`, or a variable storing their outcomes can be used as well.

Operators that perform `Boolean` comparisons: Business rules that you encounter in your career as an information systems professional will rarely be as simple as examining two GPAs or salaries. In real life, decision logic can be quite complex. Take the following elicited business rule as an example: "If the employee is between twenty-one and sixty-five years old; and if the employee's status is 1 for full time; and if the employee is not located in Florida (state == 14), California (state == 21), or Texas (state == 29); and if the employee has worked for five years or more . . ." You could examine these with one single expression at a time, one part at a time. But this would become tedious and awkward. Luckily, like most programming languages, Java provides boolean operators that allow us to perform boolean logic and examine more than one relationship between values at a time, which makes a task like this easier. Table 1.5 has the list of boolean operators that you will commonly use:

Table 1.5. More Commonly Used Boolean Logic Operators in Java

<table>
<tr><th>Operator</th><th>Name</th><th>Result</th></tr>
<tr><td>&</td><td>AND</td><td>If both operands evaluate to true, this operator returns true.</td></tr>
<tr><td>|</td><td>OR</td><td>If one or the other of the operands evaluate to true, this operator returns true.</td></tr>
<tr><td>!</td><td>NOT</td><td>This operator returns the reverse of the operand's boolean value (unary operator).</td></tr>
<tr><td>^</td><td>XOR</td><td>If one and only one of the two operands is true, this operator returns true.</td></tr>
<tr><td>&&</td><td>Short circuit AND</td><td>If both operands are true, this operand returns true. If the left operand is false, the right is never evaluated.</td></tr>
<tr><td>||</td><td>Short circuit OR</td><td>If one or the other operand is true, this operand returns true. If the left operand is true, the right is never evaluated.</td></tr>
</table>

All of these boolean operators are binary except for the NOT operator, which is unary and is always placed on the immediate left side of the value being "flipped" temporarily. Remember the cast operators from earlier? NOT is similar to these in that it does not change the value of the variable it's operating on; it just temporarily "masks" it.

The XOR ("exclusive OR") operator will only allow one or the other of its two operands to be `true` in order to produce a `true` outcome. If both are `true` or both are `false`, it returns `false`. The "short circuit" operators are useful, especially when the right operand may be an invocation to a resource-intensive method (database read/write operation, network communication, hard drive operation, etc.). These are handy when the right operand depends heavily on the left operand (they are not independent of each other). Consider the following partial statement with only the decision rule shown: "If the business has not declared bankruptcy **AND** if their dividend is less than 2%, then . . ." Businesses usually will not pay a dividend if they have declared bankruptcy. So the boolean test on the right heavily depends on the left one being true. If the left is false, there's no need to check for the one on the right.

Notice that for the short circuit AND, if the left operand is **false**, then the right is never even evaluated, since the result of the AND will be **false**. Similarly for the short circuit OR, if the left is **true**, then the right operand is not evaluated, since the result of the OR will be **true**.

Some examples of boolean operators in use are as follows:

Code Snippet 1.17

```
boolean leftOperand = true;
boolean rightOperand = false;

System.out.println(leftOperand & rightOperand);
System.out.println(leftOperand | rightOperand);
System.out.println(leftOperand ^ rightOperand);
```

And the output when this code executes:

```
false
true
true
```

Typically, the boolean logic operators evaluate the outcomes of relational operators in expressions. Consider the business rule scenario from earlier: relational operators and boolean operators can be used together like this:

Code Snippet 1.18

```
int employeeAge = 34;

boolean ageCheck = (employeeAge >= 21) & (employeeAge <= 65);
```

Parentheses are used to keep each relational comparison clean and separate, making the code more readable and easier to troubleshoot (if needed). Notice as well that the outcome of each relational operator becomes the operands for the boolean operator. Parentheses have the further effect here of **ensuring that each relational part of the expression executes first**. Both relational operations are processed first, then the boolean operation is processed. Finally, the results of that boolean operation are copied into the `boolean` variable `ageCheck`.

Checking for both the full-time status of the employee and their state residency status is simplified using the OR operator. Notice that the organization in the business scenario earlier has conveniently mapped each state to a number in their system. This is a common technique to make the logic easier:

Code Snippet 1.19

```
int employeeStatus = 1;
int employeeState = 37;

boolean employmentCheck = (employeeStatus == 1);
boolean stateCheck = (
        (employeeState == 14) ||
        (employeeState == 21) ||
        (employeeState == 29));
```

The first check for employee status is relatively straightforward: use the equality operator to test if the contents of the variable `employeeStatus` are equal to the value of `1`. The second check is a bit more involved. The entire boolean logic test for state residency has been wrapped in parentheses. You are not required to do this syntax-wise, but it makes for more readable code. Next, the short circuit OR boolean operator is used. If the employee is a resident of Florida (`employeeState == 14`), then they immediately fall into the category of belonging to one of these states, and there is no need to check the others. Notice that each state test is wrapped in parentheses as well to keep things neat and tidy (and logically isolated). As your expressions get more complex, it is a good idea to use parentheses to force the tests to process in the order and arrangement you require.

Finally, you can test for the duration of employment. The business rule is testing for five years or more of employment with the organization:

Code Snippet 1.20

```
int employmentDuration = 7;
boolean careerCheck = (employmentDuration >= 5);
```

Since the elicited business rule specifically states "five years or more," you should use the greater-than or equal-to relational operator to check for this possibility. Again, the `true` or `false` value is stored in a boolean variable.

Finally, test whether or not the employee meets the overall qualification for this business rule and print the results of your findings to the user:

Code Snippet 1.21

```
boolean ruleQualify = (ageCheck && employmentCheck
          && (!stateCheck)
          && careerCheck);

System.out.println("Age Qualify?: " + ageCheck);
System.out.println("Employment Qualify?: " + employmentCheck);
System.out.println("Resident of Excluded States?: " + stateCheck);
System.out.println("Tenure Length Sufficient?: " + careerCheck);
System.out.println("Overall Qualify?: " + ruleQualify);
```

The test for the overall rule and the filling of the variable `ruleQualify` are the trickiest parts of this and need a bit of explanation. Think about what it will take to say that an employee qualifies for this business rule: they must be in an allowed age range (`true`); they must be a full-time employee (`true`); they must not be a resident of an excluded state (`false`); and they must have worked for the company five years or more (`true`). The test employee in the earlier example meets all of these rules. Testing for these conditions is straightforward:

- The AND operator (both normal and short circuit) will return `true` if both left and right operands are `true`. Checking for the ones that **should** be `true` is easy (age, employment status, and tenure).
- If the employee is not a resident of one of the three excluded states, that variable will be false. How do you include a potential false variable in this statement? Here is where the NOT operator comes in handy: if they are not a resident of an excluded state, that test will return `false`. You can use the NOT operator to flip the `false` to a `true`, ensuring the chain of AND operators results in a final `true` value.

Here is the output for the test values above:

```
Age Qualify?: true
Employment Qualify?: true
Resident of Excluded States?: false
Tenure Length Sufficient?: true
Overall Qualify?: true
```

What if the employee is a resident of Florida? How would that change things? Here is the output for that scenario, with new results in bold (you can test this yourself: change the `employeeState` variable's initialization to fourteen in your code as you are following along):

```
Age Qualify?: true
Employment Qualify?: true
Resident of Excluded States?: true
Tenure Length Sufficient?: true
Overall Qualify?: false
```

As you can see, both the boolean and the relational operators can be used to perform some complex tests to adhere to organizational business rules in software systems. There are a few things to note here. Normally in a system, values would not be directly compared. For example, you would not compare `employeeState` directly to the number fourteen (`int` literal). This value would most likely be stored in a variable somewhere or in some other data structure, or it may even come from a database. Also, the characteristics of the employee themselves may be coming from the same (database, user input, external data file, etc.). There are better ways to test if a variable contains one of multiple values, which will be explored later in the textbook.

SUMMARY POINTS

- The relational category of operators allows for tests of equality or nonequality between values or the comparison of variable values and relational determinations such as larger or smaller.
- The equality operator performs a test of exact equivalence between numeric values. The nonequality operator tests for nonequivalence in numeric values.
- The assignment operator and the equality operator perform two completely separate tasks and are represented by two separate symbols. A common mistake is to confuse the usage of the two.
- The relational operators compare numeric values, whether they are less than, equal to, or larger than one another.
- The boolean logic operators are commonly used to compare boolean outcomes from relational operators. Mostly binary in nature, boolean logic operators require a boolean value on both the left and the right operands. These boolean values could come from a relational operator expression or from other sources, such as the return type from a method invocation.
- The "short circuit" boolean logic operators will not process the right operand if the left is evaluated and its value is found to make the

right's unnecessary to be checked. This occurs in cases where the value of the right operand is directly dependent on the value of the left.

- The NOT operator does not change the value of the variable it operates upon but temporarily reverses the found boolean value for the duration of the expression processing. The operator's outcome is the reverse of the boolean value of the variable it is operating upon.
- Parentheses are often used to enclose or "wrap" relational statements in an expression where boolean logic operators are used to keep code organized and readable and to make expression processing predictable and understandable.

QUICK PROBLEMS

1. **Coding:** Write a small Java program that prompts the user to enter two numbers. Use the equality operator and print back to the console the result of the comparison of these two numbers.
2. **Think:** Imagine someone asks you to count numbers (0, 1, 2, 3, etc.) upward in value while your numbers are `<= 50`. Now imagine they ask you to do the same but while your numbers are `< 50`. How are the two situations different?
3. **Coding:** Write a small Java program that will prompt the user to enter four `boolean` values and store each in four separate `boolean` variables. Using `boolean` operators and the four `boolean` variables, print "`true`" to the console if and only if all four variables contain "`false`." (*Note:* Do not use any `if` statements to complete this task.)

1.4 Operator Precedence

Do not confuse Java's **operator precedence** with the mathematical order of operations you may have learned elsewhere in your studies. Though they are similar in their goal of helping bring order to the processing of a statement, they are not the same, and Java's operator precedence behaves differently. In Java, operator precedence means that as an expression is processed (this is the "stuff" on the right side of the assignment operator), the outcomes of some operators will be produced earlier than those of others. Task precedence can be seen all around you. For example, think of the home under construction in figure 1.8: you cannot build the roof of the home until the floors and walls are done. Some tasks are completed first.

Figure 1.8. Precedence—Some Tasks Are Completed First
Source: "New Home Construction" by Great Valley Center is licensed under CC BY 2.0, https://www.flickr.com/photos/95391240@N00/38286807.

You can find Oracle's full operator precedence chart online, and you should eventually become familiar with it.* For now, Oracle's listing is simplified and summarized in table 1.6. Operators that are listed **closer to the top** of the table are processed and executed **earlier/sooner** than those below them. Those **near the bottom** of the table are processed **later/last** after the others above them. Labels have been provided for some operators in the table (note that the symbol is the operator itself, and for some, a label in quotes is provided to name the operator).

From a glance at the chart, you should already notice a few things. Remember earlier that a business rule for an organization was tested using an expression. Notice in the chart that the relational operators are higher in precedence than the logical boolean operators. This means that they are processed before the boolean logic operators are. Remember the following line of code from earlier:

Code Snippet 1.22

```
boolean ageCheck = employeeAge >= 21 & employeeAge <= 65;
```

* https://docs.oracle.com/javase/tutorial/java/nutsandbolts/operators.html.

Table 1.6. Summary of Operator Precedence for Selected Operators

Precedence/order	Operator category	Specific operators (with description)
Higher/earlier	Ordering and invocation	`( ) [ ] .`
	Postfix/postoperators	Post-increment and post-decrement
	Prefix/preoperators	Pre-increment and pre-decrement
	Higher math	`* / %`
	Lower math	`+ -`
	Relational	`>= <= > <`
	Equality	`== !=`
	Boolean logical	`&`
	Boolean logical	`^`
	Boolean logical	`|`
	Boolean logical	`&&`
	Boolean logical	`||`
	Ternary	`? :`
Lower/later	Assignment	Assignment operator and arithmetic compound operators

Though the earlier parentheses have been removed, this will still execute just fine. As Java processes the expression on the right side from left to right, it will process the relational operators first. Since all relational operators are equivalent to one another in terms of precedence (they are on the same level in the precedence chart), Java will process operators of equal precedence from left to right, in that order. After the first "pass" of processing, the expression is the equivalent of the following:

Code Snippet 1.23

```
boolean ageCheck = true & false;
```

Since the relational operators were higher in precedence, they were processed first and their outcomes determined. Now the AND operator is lower in precedence, so it goes next:

Code Snippet 1.24

```
boolean ageCheck = false;
```

Finally, since the assignment operator is pretty much at the bottom of the precedence chart, it goes last. Remember that Java processes these from right to left and copies the value from the right into the variable on the left.

Think about a math expression like the following:

Code Snippet 1.25

```
int firstNum = 5;
int secondNum = 10;
int fourthNum = 3;

int result = firstNum + secondNum * fourthNum;
```

What will be the resulting value? Use the operator precedence chart to help. Higher-level math, like multiplication, has earlier processing precedence than addition. So the multiplication would be performed first:

Code Snippet 1.26

```
int result = firstNum + 30;
```

Then the addition:

Code Snippet 1.27

```
int result = 35;
```

You have seen the use of parentheses in this chapter, especially when processing the business rule. They are at the very top of the operator precedence chart and are processed before everything else. The power of parentheses comes in their ability to force sections of expressions to execute before others, overriding the operator precedence chart. For example, let's change the math expression as follows:

Code Snippet 1.28

```
int result = (firstNum + secondNum) * fourthNum;
```

The addition operation has been elevated higher in precedence by wrapping its operands within parentheses, causing it to execute first:

Code Snippet 1.29

```
int result = 15 * fourthNum;
```

And now the multiplication can occur:

Code Snippet 1.30

```
int result = 45;
```

Notice that the value of the result is now different! When you use parentheses to change the operator precedence in an expression, you change the way the expression is evaluated. This can change (and has in this case) the outcome of the expression. Parentheses can be very helpful in bringing order to a chaotic or complex expression. Use them carefully, as they can be a negative and cause things to not work as intended (a **logic error**) if used carelessly.

SUMMARY POINTS

- Like in many other programming languages with operators, Java implements operator precedence in order to help programmers structure expressions in a way such that their processing will be predictable and useful, not to mention accurate.
- In an expression, operators with a higher level of precedence will be evaluated by Java earlier than those with a lower level of precedence.
- Operators that have the same level of precedence will be evaluated by Java in order from left to right, except for the assignment operator, which is always evaluated from right to left.
- Parentheses are in fact operators (a pair of them) that enclose a part of an expression, and they are at the highest level of operator precedence. Parentheses can often be used to force parts of an expression to be evaluated earlier than other parts, regardless of the precedence level of the operators found within the parentheses and in other parts of the expression.

QUICK PROBLEMS

1. **Coding:** Write a small Java program that prompts the user for their age, their height in inches, and the year of their vehicle (19XX or 20XX). Use boolean operators to ensure that "true" is returned if, first, the age is greater than twenty and the height is less than ninety inches or if the year of the vehicle is earlier than 2002. (*Note:* Do not use an `if` statement for this problem.)

2. **Think:** Why does it make sense that the assignment operator is one of the lowest in terms of precedence in Java?
3. **Coding:** Write a small Java program that has a fairly long formula (at least four operands) that combines the multiplication and addition of numbers. Place parentheses around two pairs of operands, and print the results to the console. Then duplicate the formula and move the parentheses around two other pairs. How does the result change? Why did this change (or no change) occur?

Summary

Operators in Java, like in most programming languages, allow programmers to leverage the values stored in variables and values retrieved from other sources (like databases or user input) and compose some powerful expressions and logic. As information systems professionals, you understand that the processing phase of data flow through a system is where data is manipulated, changed, grouped, associated, and structured. Operators help form the foundation of all the data-processing tasks in any single software application or information system. They are an indispensable tool to have in your mental programming "toolbox," and the practice you put in with them will pay off big dividends later on. Experienced programmers know that thorough knowledge of operators helps write not only powerful data processive code but also succinct and more efficient code as well. In the next chapter, you will explore the basics of how thoroughly object oriented a language Java is and the syntax needed to leverage the powerful tools and commands built into the language. Since Java is a class-based language, you will find class usage and method invocation used throughout the language right alongside the basic syntax you have learned so far and will learn in the next few chapters. Keep going; you are doing great!

Practice Problems

Terminology

Match the following terms from the chapter with their most appropriate definition:

1. Operator	a. The order in which Java processes operators within an expression, with some operators processed before others.
2. Outcome	b. Operator that produces the remainder of the left operand divided by the right.
3. Unary	c. Type of operator that compares the size and/or equality of the values of the left and right operands.
4. Binary	d. From the Latin meaning "two"; describes a category of operators with two operands.
5. Operand	e. A behavior where Java will temporarily up-convert a variable with a lower data type to the highest data type found in an expression.
6. Modulo operator	f. A type of operator that compares two operands for identical values.
7. Operator precedence	g. Describing the position to the right of a unary operator in relation to the operand it acts upon. Placed after the operand.
8. Increment operator	h. A type of operator that assesses the values of two boolean data-type operands. These operands could be variables or outcomes from a relational expression.
9. Decrement operator	i. A symbol in a programming language reserved for the carrying out of data manipulation commands such as math, comparison, or boolean logic.
10. Prefix	j. Describing the position to the left of a unary operator in relation to the operand it acts upon. Placed before the operand.
11. Postfix	k. A type of operator that performs simple mathematical operations upon the operands it is associated with.

12. Data-type promotion	l. From the Latin meaning "one"; describes a category of operators with only one operand.
13. Type cast	m. Describes the result produced by an operand after it has finished executing its action.
14. Arithmetic compound operator	n. A type of operator that increases the value of a numeric variable by one.
15. Equality operator	o. The data or value that is evaluated or acted upon by an operator. Operands can have one, two, or three of these.
16. Relational operator	p. The forcing of Java to temporarily interpret the data type of a variable as another data type.
17. Boolean logic operator	q. A type of operator that decreases the value of a numeric variable by one.

Find the Error

In each of the following problems, carefully examine the code given, and determine the error(s)/issue(s) with each. Keep in mind, the error(s) could be syntax (code) or logic (intended outcome) based or both!

1.

```
int regularNumber = 5;
++regularNumber++;
System.out.println(regularNumber);
```

2.

```
boolean theResult = 5 + 3 * 2;
```

3.

```
int aNum = 0;

5 * 2 = aNum;
```

4.

```
Int numberOfEmployees = 23;
double payRate = 23.45d;
int totalPay = numberOfEmployees * payRate;
```

5.

```
int aNum = 10;
int bNum += aNum += 45;
```

6.

```
Scanner readIn = new Scanner(System.in);
System.out.println("Please enter two numbers: ");
int aNum = readIn.next();
int bNum = readIn.next();
int larger = (aNum > bNum);
System.out.println("Is the first number larger?" + larger);
```

7.

```
// Check if an age is between 20 and 40 years inclusive:
int theAge = 23;
boolean rangeCheck = (theAge >= 20) | (theAge <= 40);
```

8.

```
// Check to see if a person's age is not less than 30 or their
// salary is greater than $50,000 a year, but not both.
int associateAge = 34;
double associateSalary = 65000d;
boolean ruleCheck =
 (associateAge < 30) | (associateSalary >= 50000);
```

9.

```
// Check to see if a salary amount is between $15 and $25 an hour:
double theSalary = 16.78d;
boolean rangeCheck = (theSalary <= 25) && (theSalary => 15);
```

10.

```
// If a person is not an employee (status == 0), skip
// the other checks. Otherwise, process them.
// Think about it!
int associateStatus = 0;
int associateDepartment = 4;
int associateTenure = 13;
boolean ruleCheck = (associateStatus == 1) &
 (associateDepartment > 2) | (associateTenure > 10);
```

Think about It

1. What does an operator do in a programming language like Java?
2. What is the purpose of operands? How does an operator interact with them?
3. What are the two common types of operators? What is the major difference between these two types?
4. What is the difference between the pre- and post-increment operators? Between the pre- and post-decrement operators?
5. What is the main difference between the division and modulo operators?
6. How does an assignment operator differ from most other Java operators?
7. What happens if you use multiple instances of the same operator in the same expression?
8. What happens if you use multiple different operators in the same expression? How does Java process the expression?
9. What is data type promotion? Why is it useful in the context of business software?
10. How does data casting differ from data type promotion?
11. How does the use of an arithmetic compound operator in an expression differ from an expression with normal operators?
12. How does the assignment operator differ from the equality operator?
13. How can you use the relational operators to check for exclusivity versus inclusivity of a number in a range of numbers?
14. When would a short circuit AND operator return a "false" as an outcome?
15. When would a short circuit OR operator return a "true" as an outcome?
16. How can parentheses alter the normal precedence of operators in a Java expression?

Short Syntax Problems

1. Create four variables with a `double` data type. Write an expression that uses the multiplication, addition, and modulo operators. Use parentheses to ensure that the addition occurs first, the modulo second, and the multiplication third. Store the result of the expression in a fifth variable with a `double` data type.
2. Create an `int` variable, and initialize it with any value you wish. Use the pre-increment operator to increase the value of that variable four times. Print the value of the variable to the console.
3. Create an `int` variable, and initialize it with any value you wish. Use the compound arithmetic addition operator to increase the value of the variable four times. Print the value of the variable to the console.
4. Create an `int` variable to prompt the user to enter a value between one hundred and one thousand, and store that value in the variable. Use both relational and boolean logic operators to test if the entered value of the variable is within that range, exclusive. Store the result of the logical test in a boolean variable, and print that variable's value to the console.
5. Create an `int` variable, and initialize it with a value between one hundred and one thousand. Use both relational and boolean logic operators to test if the value of the variable is **not** within that range / outside that range, inclusive. Store the result of the logical test in a boolean variable, and print that variable's value to the console.

Full Problems

1. Write a full Java program that determines if a student is eligible for an academic scholarship. Your program should prompt for and test the following information (using relational operators to evaluate `true` or `false` for each):
   a. Prompt for the student's high school GPA. The GPA should be between 3.0 and 4.0.
   b. Prompt for the student's honor roll level. The honor roll level should be in the range of 1 to 4.
   c. Prompt for the student's aptitude test score. The score should be greater than 800 but less than 1500.
   d. The scholarship has a hardship rule: if the student's aptitude test score is greater than 1400 and their honor roll level is greater than 3, then their GPA can be greater than 2.7, and they will still qualify for the scholarship.
   e. Do not use a decision structure like `if` or `switch` for this assignment.

   Print the information entered back out to the screen, then print the results of the scholarship determination for the user. Use only the syntax covered up to chapter 1 to accomplish this problem.
2. Write a full Java program that determines if an individual is in a "high" or "low" tax bracket. Prompt for, store, and use the following information:
   a. The individual's full name
   b. Their yearly salary
   c. Their age
   d. Their marital status (1 for "yes" and 0 for "no")
   e. Their employment status (1 for "yes" and 0 for "no")

   The elicited rules for calculating the taxes owed are as follows:
   a. If an individual has a salary greater than $100K, is not married, and is employed, they fall in the higher tax bracket, and your program should print "true."
   b. Otherwise, print "false." Use only the syntax up until chapter 1 to accomplish this problem.
3. Write a full Java program that will prompt the user to enter five `int` numbers:
   a. Store each entered number in a variable.
   b. For each pair of variables, compare the sizes. In separate bool variables, store true if the earlier number is less than or equal to the later number.
   c. Use boolean operators to determine if all five numbers were entered in numeric order (from smallest to largest). Print the results of this determination (`true` or `false`) to the console with a message.
4. Write some logic that will determine the status of a customer for the mom-and-pop grocery store. Prompt the user to enter information on the customer. Create any variables needed, and choose the appropriate data type for each. The client's business rules for customer status are as follows:
   a. Customer can become a member of the savings club if they
      i. have been a customer for 120+ days (can enter "0" for new customers).
      ii. have purchased at least $500 from the store (can enter "0.0" for no purchases).
      iii. do not already have a member of their household who is a savings club member (consider a `boolean` value here, and have the user enter "true" if this rule holds and "false" otherwise).
      iv. have an email address
   b. Customer can additionally be a member of the supersavings club if they
      i. are fifty-five years of age or older.
5. An academic client has asked you to write a small Java program that will determine if numbers entered by a user are prime numbers (numbers that can only be cleanly divided by themselves and one. Five would be a prime number, while six is not, etc.). They have asked for the program to do the following:
   a. Prompt the user to enter seven numbers.
   b. For each number, determine if the number is prime or not. Print this to the console with the entered number.
   c. At the end of the program, print the quantities of numbers that were prime and the quantities that were not.

Chapter 2

Using Object-Oriented Java

What You Will Learn in This Chapter

Before diving too deeply into the syntax and topics of the Java language, it will be beneficial to understand the object-oriented (OO) nature of Java at a high level. If you have not worked extensively with an OO-based programming language before, the syntax might seem strange. Many of the critically useful tools in Java are implemented as classes. OO concepts impact almost everything you will do and learn in the Java language.

Specifically, this chapter will help you do the following:

1. Differentiate between an object and a regular variable
2. Understand the nature of a class in Java, its purpose, and how it impacts the creation of objects
3. Understand the purpose of the "new" operator and the constructor method(s) of classes and the relationship these have with objects
4. Understand the nature and purpose of data fields and be able to describe the difference between static and instance data fields of a class
5. Understand the nature and purpose of class methods and be able to describe the difference between static and instance methods of a class
6. Describe the nature of a reference variable and how it differs from a variable declared with a primitive data type
7. Describe the purpose and usage of many of the static methods of the `Math` class and how their static nature impacts how they are used

Opening Scenario

"It is an object-oriented language, so some of the syntax is going to look strange," a colleague on your mom-and-pop grocery store system project team states. "Every language does it a little differently." You have spent the last few days learning the basics of the Java programming language. The class-based structure seems straightforward, though you are unsure of what a "class" is just yet. The syntax for variables and expressions using operators seems fairly straightforward as well. Already, the code for several of the major business rules the project team is eliciting from the client is forming in your mind. These do not seem problematic.

"As we start building the prototype out, the object-oriented nature of the language will really help us scale and ensure parts of the system can easily interact with one another, and it allows for a disconnected development style, each team of developers and analysts working on their own parts, connecting them later." You nod in agreement: the system will grow so large that perfecting your knowledge of objects and classes in Java will be a must. You think back to your coursework prior to your current position. There was some discussion of objects in Python but not an in-depth study. You've seen code in languages in C# and C++ that use classes and objects that seemed fairly straightforward, but you didn't have a solid grasp. Already in your study of the basics of Java, you've encountered terms such as "constructors," "instance methods," and "static."

As you have previewed some other topics in Java, you have noticed a heavy use of objects and interactions between them. You decide that first, it will be helpful to gain an understanding of how to use objects in Java and all the terminology and meaning around them. This will allow you to make your way through the increasingly sophisticated programming techniques. Hopefully, this will give you a good foundation to later learn how to **create** classes and their objects. Your colleague agrees this is a good plan. "We will be building a lot of custom classes for our system. Modeling entities in our system will be a must with classes, at the least. Building and using classes will allow us to delegate the development efficiently as well. Understanding how objects and classes work is a must!" You agree and once again decide to dive into this topic to push your Java knowledge further . . .

2.1 Understanding Java's Object-Oriented Nature

Java's object-oriented nature: Java is an object-oriented, class-based language. It was one of the earliest object-oriented programming languages that became broadly popular. What does it really mean for a programming language to be "object oriented"? To understand this, think of instead what it means for a language to **not** be object oriented. Keep in mind that a "procedural" style of programming generally means that code is relatively linear and straightforward in nature. Consider the following pseudocode as a procedural example:

```
start
variable A = 10
variable B = 20
variable C = add A and B
print C to screen
end
```

Code executes in a straight listing from start to finish. Primitive data types dominate, and "objects" are few, if present at all. The program executes in a script-like fashion (just a set of simple, sequential instructions). In Java, even a straightforward procedural code listing must execute within a class. Java fully embraces the OO development paradigm.

A **class** represents code that gives the JVM instructions for creating **objects**, defining their **data** characteristics, and delineating the **actions** associated with them. Everything in Java is **class** based, except for the primitive data types (and even these have classes that can "wrap" around them as will be discussed later in the textbook). The class defines what the object's internal structure will look like, the data it will store, and how it can be interacted with through Java code syntax. Recall that a primitive data type is very simple: it just contains data, like a bucket contains water. That is pretty much all it can do. Compared to these, a variable with a class data type is often called "complex" because it can hold data of varying data types and is capable of performing actions. In Java, classes are what enable Java's object-oriented nature.

Objects in Java are variables with complex data types created using a class as their template. Object-oriented programming techniques in Java enable the creation of contemporary, sophisticated applications. You will learn all about *defining and creating* classes in chapter 8. This introductory chapter is focused simply on how to *use classes* and their objects. You will encounter classes throughout the Java language and see object-oriented concepts everywhere in the syntax. Learning how to use and interact with classes and objects will help you understand the nature and usefulness of the rest of the Java language and libraries.

The benefits of Java classes: Classes give programmers the ability to specify exactly what kinds of data future objects will contain, the manner and steps needed for creating those objects, and the actions/behavior they will be capable of. As future information systems professionals, this should pique your interest. This ability to bundle data and actions together within objects empowers the programmer to build ever larger programs with increasing complexity but with less complex code. Primitive data type variables are useful only up to a certain point: they can hold data but not do anything with it. Additional logic must be written to interact with them. On the other hand, objects can have logic "baked in" and invoked with very simple syntax. The programmer (you!) only needs to write a few lines of code to potentially have an object execute a great deal of the programmed logic associated with it. The data and the code that can interact with that data are bundled together and accessed through one convenient digital package!

By creating a class, the Java developer creates a template (i.e., blueprint) by which objects can be created using that template. A class can define the following regarding objects:

- The class name also acts as the data type for the object.
- The class acts as a blueprint for objects that will be created with it as their data type. Code written in the class specifies the quantity, names, and data types of variables stored within objects created using that class's actions. Variables defined by a class that will be stored inside objects of the class are called **data fields** and are sometimes called **member variables.** You can see these variables stored within the "class object" in figure 2.1.
- Within a class, certain **member methods** can be defined. In the future, these member methods of the class will be invokable upon objects that were created using the class as their blueprint. You can see where these are defined in the class definition file (CDF) in figure 2.1.
- Classes are not required to define variables inside their objects, but the developers of these classes have the *option* of doing so.
- For some classes, the variables and methods defined by them will be associated with the overall class *itself* and not associated with *future objects* of the class.

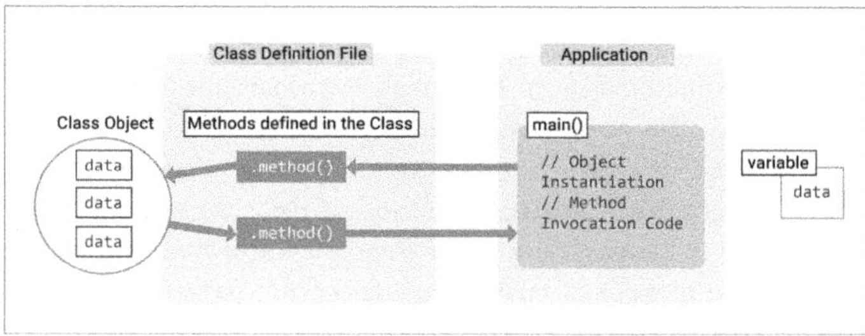

Figure 2.1. Comparing a Class Object to a Primitive Data-Type Variable

Recall the application example where a `Scanner` class variable is created and one of its methods invoked to read an `int` from the keyboard:

Full Program 2.1

```
import java.util.*;

public class Ch2ScannerExample {

    public static void main(String[] args) {
        Scanner keyboardIn = new Scanner(System.in);
        int someNumber = keyboardIn.nextInt();
        System.out.println("Entered Number: " + someNumber);
    }
}
```

Some things to note about this code example and classes in Java:

- The code needed to create the `Scanner` variable is different from, say, that of an `int`. Particularly, the initialization on the right-hand side of the assignment operator is what is different from that of an `int`. Notice in the second line, the value captured by the `nextInt()` method is stored in an `int` variable called `someNumber`. The `int` variable called `someNumber` has a primitive data type, but the `Scanner` object called `keyboardIn` has a class (i.e., complex) data type.
- The operator `new` creates a `Scanner` class object. Notice that `new` is not used for primitive data types like `int`.
- Objects of a class are created via **instantiation.** The code written within the class guides the process by which its new objects are instantiated.
- Instantiated objects of a class are initialized (i.e., given initial values) by calling the **constructor** method of a class.
- The actions that `Scanner` objects are capable of are the member methods of the class. The code for these actions is defined in the `Scanner` class itself. For example, the method `.nextInt()` is defined within `Scanner` and contains code that, when invoked upon a `Scanner` object, performs some activity. In this case, the activity is the reading of data from the console, formatting the data as an `int`, and returning that data back to the calling code so it can be copied by the assignment operator. The code you write to invoke the method is the calling code.

- A variable that is declared using a complex, class-based data type is typically called a **reference variable.** In the example, the `Scanner` variable `keyboardIn` is a reference variable.

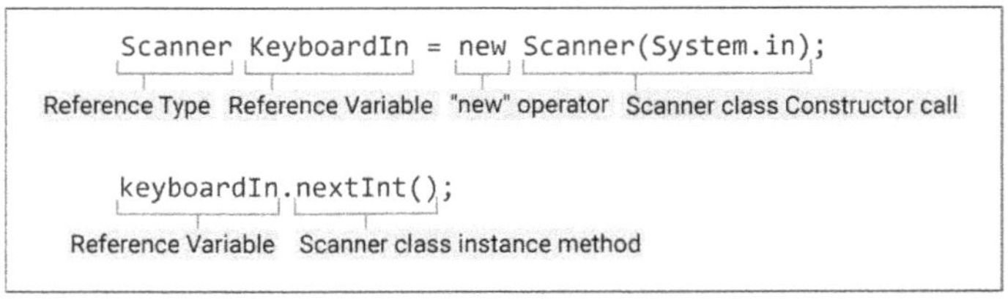

Figure 2.2. The Object-Oriented Nature of a Scanner Object Creation and Usage

Figure 2.2 diagrams two lines of code from the example. Though only two lines, there is a lot going on. Figure 2.2 also shows most (but not all) of the ways classes and objects can be used in Java: using the new operator, invoking a class's constructor, invoking a method of the class on one of its instance objects, and so on. Notice that you do not have to know how to write the code for Java classes in order to use them. *Learning the syntax of how to use Java classes is the focus of the remainder of this chapter.*

SUMMARY POINTS

- A class can be thought of as a set of instructions that defines how new instance objects of a class should be created, what data they should contain, and what actions are possible by them and upon them.
- An object is a bundle of both data and the actions possible with that data, all in one variable.
- A constructor is a special method of a class whose purpose is to initialize the data within an instance object. The constructor is only ever called once per new instance object and never again afterward on that object.
- The data fields of a class define the variable data types and quantity of variables that will be both stored within instance objects of a class and associated with the class in general.
- The member methods defined in a class detail the methods that are invokable upon instance objects of the class and upon the class itself.

QUICK PROBLEMS

1. **Coding:** In a small Java program, declare (but do not initialize) a Scanner variable called "`inputA`." Then both declare and initialize a second Scanner variable called "`inputB`." Set `inputA` equal to `inputB`, and then use `inputA` to read in keyboard input. What happens?
2. **Think:** How is a class data-type object similar to a primitive data-type variable? How is it different?
3. **Think:** How is a class different from a class data-type object?

2.2 Class Constructors and Instance Objects

To understand how to *use* objects in Java, you first have to understand how they are created and initialized. With primitive data type variables (`int`, `double`, `float`, etc.), initialization is much simpler: the final value resulting on the right of the assignment operator is copied left into the newly created variable:

Code Snippet 2.1

```
int authorsAge = 120; // Declaration and Initialization
```

"Final value resulting" because the value on the right could be the result of an expression, or a method call, or a combination of both. For example,

Code Snippet 2.2

```
ageMultiply = keyboardIn.nextInt();
int authorsRealAge = (((12 * ageMultiply) + 6) - 2); // Old Person!
```

Initialization of complex variables such as objects is not as simple. Objects are "complex" due to both the actions associated with them and the ability to hold multiple data types. Complexity! Initializing a newly created object involves invoking the **constructor method** for the class that the complex object "belongs" to. This relationship between an object and its class will be further clarified ahead.

The "official" definition for a constructor method is as follows: **the constructor is a class method whose primary job is to initialize a newly created instance object of that class.** There is a lot to deconstruct in that statement (pun intended). In information systems, real-world "things" or "entities" are often re-created within a digital system. People are often represented with digital records in a database—so are cars, houses, job positions, consumer electronics, and so on. For each of these "instances" of real-world things, various attributes are stored in database tables: age, cost, size, salary amount, battery storage capability, and many other attributes. Real-world entities not only possess these attributes but also can perform actions. Application logic can be written that re-creates many of these actions and draws on the data in the database tables to complement and fulfill the purpose of these actions (e.g., representing a trip in a vehicle, storing the distance, the amount of fuel used, the time, etc. for the trip). A class simplifies this entity representation by allowing the developer to bundle data within and associate actions with an object that can be used in code.

Example—class `Person`: In order to understand how a class works and is used, the code for a highly simplified Java class called **Person** is listed here.

Before you look at the code example, please keep the following in mind:

- The purpose of this chapter is to help you understand how to **use** classes and objects, **not necessarily how to create them**. This chapter **will not** explain the whys and whats of the `Person` class code or how to create your own classes. Chapter 8 is given that job.
- Notice that class `Person` has been listed **after** the full listing for `PersonApp`, which contains the `main()` method. You can re-create this code by doing the following:
  - creating a new Java main class application called `PersonApp`
  - below the last curly brace in that class, typing the `Person` class code listing
- Notice that the `PersonApp` class has "`public`" in front of it, while "`class Person`" **does not**. This is OK and correct. In this example, there are **two** classes in the same Java file `PersonApp.java`.

The full code for the application `PersonApp.java` containing the example class is as follows:

Full Program 2.2

```
package chapter2pkg;
import java.util.*;  // For Scanner
// "Primary" class for the file
public class PersonApp {

    public static void main(String[] args) {

        // Application and Example Code Goes Here

    } // End of main()

} // End of application class PersonApp


// Very simplified example class
// Definition also inside PersonApp.java
class Person{

    // Instance Data Fields
    // (Variables inside the object)
    // Each Person object will have
    //  their own copy of each.
    String name;
```

```
    int age;
    int heightInInches;
    String profession;
    String hobby;

    // Private data fields
    private double personSalary;

    // Static Data Fields
    // (Variables for the entire class)
    static int totalPersonCount;

    // Constructor with parameters
    Person(String pName, int pAge, int pHeight,
            String pProf, String pHobby)
    {
        name = pName;
        age = pAge;
        heightInInches = pHeight;
        profession = pProf;
        hobby = pHobby;

        // Increment the static variable
        // each time a Person is instantiated
        totalPersonCount++;
    }

    // Instance Method
    // Invoke upon Person objects
    String stateName()
    {
        return name;
    }

    // Instance Method
    // Invoke upon Person objects
    String reportAge()
    {
        return "My age is" + age;
    }

    // Instance Method
    // Invoke upon Person objects
    void changeAge(int newAge)
    {
        age = newAge;
    }

    // Static Method
    // Invoke upon the Class Person itself
    static String reportTotalPersonCount()
    {
        return "There has been" + totalPersonCount + "  Person
         object created";

    }

} // End of Class Person Definition
```

Each object of the `Person` class will represent some real-world "person." Data about that person will be stored within each `Person` object. Each `Person` object will be capable of doing something, of performing some action, due to methods defined within the `Person` class code.

Figure 2.3. `Person` Instance Objects Enjoying a Nice Day
Source: "People" by ThisParticularGreg is licensed under CC BY-SA 2.0, https://www.flickr.com/photos/41084935@N00/362937046.

Instance objects: Can you think of what it means to be a person **in general**? Consider figure 2.3, which shows many **instances** of individual people. Characteristics like being alive and being able to think, talk, walk (barring any physical restrictions), eat, see a movie, get a job, and so on might come to mind. Now can you think of any **specific** people? You can probably think of specific family members, friends, loved ones, coworkers, costudents, faculty, and many others right away.

If you understand the difference between a person in general and a specific person, you can understand the difference between a **class** and an **instance object**. In addition to being a data type, a class is a definition of what data its future objects, its instance objects, should contain and how they should act. Think of it like a contract: the class's objects will follow the contract, and developers can read the contract to understand what those objects will contain within them and how they can behave. Importantly, the class can tell you how your code should *interact* with other objects and code. Figure 2.4 shows a blueprint for a car as well as a specific car actually built from that blueprint. A class is the blueprint for an instance object. The `new` operator builds the object based on the class's instructions. The **constructor method** initializes that newly created instance object of a class and fills it with data.

Methods: Methods can be called, or **invoked**, by using their name along with parentheses. The parentheses allow one or more pieces of data to be passed into the method for use, each piece being called a parameter (when defined in the class) or an argument (when used during invocation). Methods enable the developer to call a "chunk" of code listing that is located somewhere else in the application. Methods are useful because the code defined within them only has to be written once and can then be called from multiple places. Chapter 6 will walk you through a full tour of how to create Java methods and their benefits as well as uses.

The constructor is a method of a class that has the job of initializing a newly created instance object of a class. Each and every new instance object of a class will have one of the constructors of its class invoked upon it at the very beginning. After this, the constructor is not needed again for that one particular object. Does a constructor method have an appropriate analogy to a real-world person in this example? Think back to the analogy of a new car in figure 2.4 and the assembly line it was built on. Once the assembler has built the new car (new operator), it rolls down the line and is painted (constructor method). The constructor initializes newly created instance objects by setting their characteristics (known as their "state"). Nothing stops the car from being repainted later on, but the first, initializing paint job only happens once per new car.

Take a moment and consider what data the `Person` class instance objects should contain and what actions they should be capable of. Table 2.1 summarizes some of the methods and variables that are defined in the `Person` class code listing from earlier.

Each `Person` object will contain ("know") its own `name`, `age`, `heightInInches`, `profession`, and favorite `hobby`. If you want to digitally represent real-world people in an information system, you can do so reasonably well with this class. Each `Person` object will also be able to report their `name`, `age`, `profession`, `hobby`, and height converted to feet. Also, notice that one of the actions allows us to change the `age` of any `Person` object.

Figure 2.4. Blueprint for a Vehicle and the Instance Object Created from That Blueprint
Sources: "Porsche 914 Roadster Blueprint" by nickmix011 is licensed under CC BY 2.0, https://www.flickr.com/photos/123638374@N08/14184697490; "Porsche 914_swap-1" by wbaiv is licensed under CC BY-SA 2.0, https://www.flickr.com/photos/9998127@N06/8776357061.

Table 2.1. Summary of the Parts of the Person Class	
Class Person	
Attributes or characteristics to store as internal variables	*Actions that each Person object should be capable of (Class methods)*
name age heightInInches profession hobby	.stateName() .reportAge() .changeAge()

As they grow older, you will need to regularly change their age. As a Java developer, you will be able to glance at these two major areas for **any** existing Java class and understand what data instance objects of that class can store and what the class's objects are capable of doing.

Constructor methods: Recall that a constructor is a method of a class that initializes an already newly created instance object of a class. For a Person instance object, you can create **and** initialize a new instance object with the following line of application code (placed in main() for PersonApp):

Code Snippet 2.3

```
// In the PersonApp main() method:
Person personA = new Person("JulieSmith", 21, 71, "Student", "Soccer");
```

This code looks very similar to the code that creates a Scanner class variable. On the right, notice the name of the class used with parentheses, which contain data values (i.e., arguments). This is the constructor invocation. A constructor has the same name as the class and has parentheses where data can be passed into the constructor method. Remember that the constructor's job is to initialize the newly created instance object. The Person class's constructor receives data from the application (i.e., the arguments in the parentheses) and passes them **into** the newly created instance object. After the constructor has finished its job, personA will have an age of twenty-one, a heightInInches of seventy-one, and so on. The constructor is initializing the instance object personA by passing the constructor parameter data into the object. Figure 2.5 shows how this data flows into the new instance object.

Keep this rule in mind: the constructor can only be invoked one time per each new instance object. Once a class's constructor has initialized one of its objects, that object can never have the constructor called upon it ever again. Each new instance object will have its class's constructor invoked upon it one and only one time.

The **new** operator is used on the left of the constructor and creates the new instance object. The constructor **does not** itself create the object; it only initializes it. Additionally, the only data the constructor can place into the object are the types and quantity of data defined by the class itself for that constructor. Java will always follow the defined plan specified in the class when it creates the instance objects of that class and executes the class's methods, constructor included.

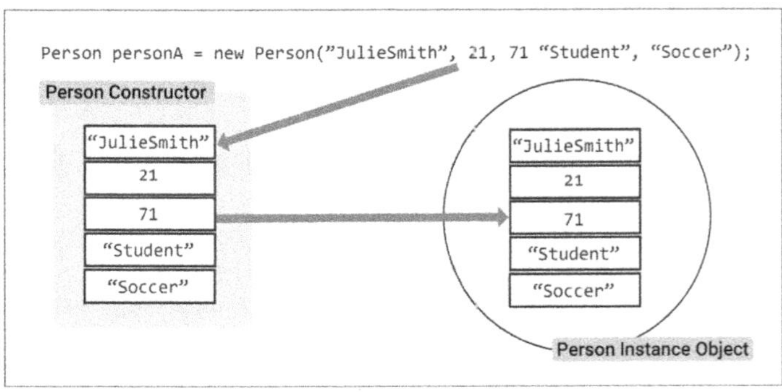

Figure 2.5. Initialization of Person Object by Constructor Method

SUMMARY POINTS

- A class can be thought of as a data type. Variables given a class data type are thought of as "complex" variables.
- The primary job of the constructor is to initialize the data fields of an instance object and to perform any other work needed for instance object initialization.
- The constructor does not create the instance object. This is performed by the "new" operator, which uses the class itself as instructions on how to do so. The constructor acts upon the newly created instance object to initialize it.
- Methods of a class can be invoked upon instance objects of a class or upon the class itself, depending on how they are defined in the class. The constructor is a special method of a class that can only be invoked at the moment of instance object creation.
- Like any method, a constructor can have zero, one, or many input parameters. The constructor can use the data in its parameters to initialize the instance object.

QUICK PROBLEMS

1. **Coding:** In a small Java program, create a `String` variable (you may have to look back to prior chapters or research in Oracle's documentation) using its constructor, passing the value for the `String` via the constructor parentheses. Create a second String using the more straightforward initialization you have seen previously. Finally, set the first `String` equal to the second, then print it to the console. What value prints? Why?
2. **Think:** What should happen to the data inside a class object if no data is passed to it via its constructor (an "empty" constructor)? For example, if a `Person` object was created "empty," what should its internal variables store? Who decides this?
3. **Coding:** Implement the `PersonApp` and `Person` classes as instructed in section 2.2 (if you have not already). Create two new `Person` instance objects in your `main()` method of `PersonApp`. For the first, keep the constructor parentheses blank, and run your program. For the second, include only an `age`. In both cases, what happens?

2.3 Instance and Static Data Fields of Classes

Understanding the dot (.) operator: In Java, the "dot" operator (a period, "`.`") is used to gain access to resources that are associated with both a class in general and its instance objects. Usage of the dot operator in different contexts means different things. Oracle refers to the dot operator as an "intervening" operator, meaning that it usually is found between two words or statements in the Java syntax. You will find it "attached" to variable and method names instead of being spaced out, as you would in the case of the assignment (`varA = varB`) or math operators (`4 + 7`).

You can use the dot operator on instance objects to gain access to the data stored inside those objects or to invoke class methods upon instance objects of a class. The defined characteristics of a class will either enable or prevent the use of the dot operator in various class-related situations. In the example class `Person` from earlier in this chapter, all data and methods are accessible by using the dot operator. In addition to the dot operator allowing access, also think of it as representing a **hierarchical** nature to the things stored inside of an instance object.

To understand this, consider the instructions that a friend may give you to find their favorite flavor of sports drink in a grocery store: "Go to the supermarket, go to the beverages section, go to aisle 7, look on the second

Figure 2.6. Arrangement of Inventory in a Grocery Store
Source: "Grocery Store" by IAN RANSLEY DESIGN + ILLUSTRATION is licensed under CC BY 2.0, https://www.flickr.com/photos/11154980@N04/10538892236.

shelf from the top, look to the left, grab a Ripple drink; it's great!" Notice how the instructions start more **general** and then move to the specific. If you were to use dot notation to represent these instructions in a "Java" class–like style, you could do so conceptually like this:

```
SuperMarket.Beverages.Aisle7.Shelf2.RippleDrink003.Grab();
```

Notice that the grabbing of the drink looks like an action (in **bold**), represented by methods in classes. The rest is a hierarchical, nested style of describing exactly where the Ripple drink is at. The dot notation when used with the data inside a class instance object mimics this same hierarchical nature: whatever is on the right can be found **inside** the something on the left of the dot notation or accessed via it. Conceptually, it looks like this:

```
SomeObject.InternalDataField = someValueToAssign;
```

Using a `Person` object as an example,

Code Snippet 2.4

```
Person somePerson = new Person();
somePerson.age = 21;
```

When the dot notation is used with methods of a class, the concept is a little different. Here, things are **sequential**: the object on the left of the dot notation invokes the action (i.e., method) that is to the right of the dot notation back upon it. Using the same `Person` object, an example of this would be the following:

Code Snippet 2.5

```
String personage = somePerson.reportAge();
```

In both cases, you are acting upon a specific instance object of a class by either accessing something inside the object or invoking a `Person` class method to act upon the object.

Accessing data fields of an instance object: Data fields that are stored inside an instance object of a class are known as **instance data fields.** Remember that instance objects are built according to the class, or the "plan" for what those objects will contain and how they will behave. Recall from table 2.1 above, a `Person` instance object will have an `age`, `name`, `heightInInches`, `profession`, and `hobby` all stored within it. Since this is what the class defines for all objects created from it, **each and every** `Person` object that is created will have its **own copy** of these data fields within it. These data fields are inside each **instance.** For example, if there are one hundred `Person` objects in your program, then each `Person` instance object will have its own unique `age` instance data field. This means that if you change one object's `age` data field, it does not automatically change the `age` within another object.

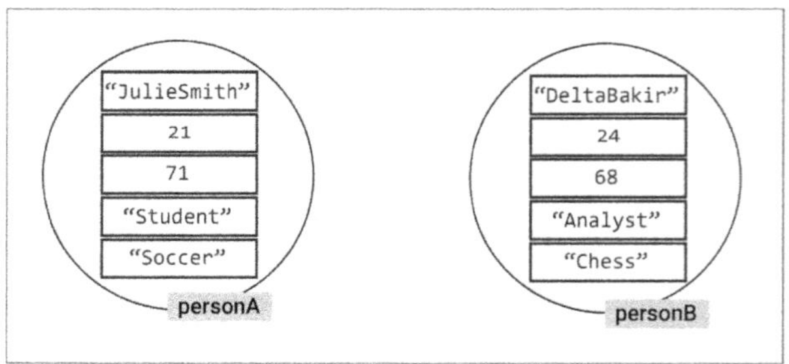

Figure 2.7. Instance Objects Each Have Their Own Copy of Instance Data Fields Bundled Inside

Recall the `personA` instance object from earlier. Consider the following full application code that uses the `Person` class (the listing for which is omitted here but found earlier in the chapter). Note the new code added in **bold**:

Code Snippet 2.6

```
import java.util.*;  // For Scanner

public class PersonApp {
    public static void main(String[] args) {

        Person personA = new Person("JulieSmith",21,71,"Student","Soccer");


        // Retrieve the Person's age:
```

```
        int tempAge = personA.age;
        System.out.println("personA's age is: " + tempAge);
        // or
        System.out.println("personA's age is: " + personA.age);


        System.out.println("personA's name is: " + personA.name);
        System.out.println("personA's age is: " + personA.age);
        System.out.println("They are " + personA.heightInInches + " in tall");
        System.out.println("Their job: " + personA.profession);
        System.out.println("Favorite Hobby: " + personA.hobby);

    } // End of main()
} // End of application class PersonApp

// Person class from earlier omitted here for brevity. . .
```

If you wanted to retrieve the value of the "age" data field within this object and make a copy of that value into a simple variable, write code like this:

Code Snippet 2.7

```
int tempAge = personA.age;
```

Notice that the code on the right has to finish first before anything is copied into `tempAge`. Since you are accessing a data field, the dot notation acts in a **hierarchical** manner: within the `personA` object, find the `age` data field, and copy its value to the left into the `tempAge` integer variable. What if you wanted to print this to the console using `.println()`? Note the needed line of code:

Code Snippet 2.8

```
System.out.println("personA's age is: " + personA.age);
```

The same hierarchical action occurs here. First, the value in the age data field of the `personA` object is copied, and that copied value is concatenated to the `String`. Then the new larger `String` is printed to the **console**:

```
personA's age is: 21
```

Alternatively, you can print the `age` in this manner:

Code Snippet 2.9

```
int tempAge = personA.age;
System.out.println("personA's age is:" + tempAge);
```

Notice too that the earlier code example prints all details of the `Person` object like so:

Code Snippet 2.10

```
System.out.println("personA's name is: " + personA.name);
System.out.println("Their age is:" + personA.age);
System.out.println("They are" + personA.heightInInches + " tall");
System.out.println("Their job is:" + personA.profession);
System.out.println("Their favorite hobby is:" + personA.hobby);
```

Static data fields of a class: Think about the last time you went to a party or gathering. Have you ever tried to quickly count how many people were in the room or space you were in? Think about what type of data the count of the number of people in a room can be characterized as. Is the quantity of people in a room a characteristic of any one person in particular? No! It is an overall count, some **general** characteristics of people overall. Instance data fields and how these are pieces of data that are tied/associated with single, specific instance objects of a class have been discussed. The **static data field** of a class is similar in nature to the total count of people in a room: it is not about a particular instance object, but it is a characteristic or data value that is associated with **the entire class** overall. A static data field is called "static" because of the following:

- No matter how many instance objects of a class are created, only **one copy** of each static data field in a class is ever created.
- No matter how many instance objects of a class are **deleted/destroyed**, the same single copy of a class's static data fields remains in memory. Its existence doesn't depend on any one instance object of a class in particular.

Static data fields of a class are not impacted directly by the creation and destruction of class instance objects! Table 2.1 from earlier can be addended to define a **static data field** for class `Person`:

Table 2.2. Expanding the Example `Person` Class by Adding a Static Data Field

<table>
<tr><td colspan="2">Class <code>Person</code></td></tr>
<tr><td colspan="2">Static data fields (only one of these will ever exist in your application, and this data field applies to the entire class overall)
<code>totalPersonCount</code></td></tr>
<tr><td>Instance data fields (each instance object has its own copy of all of these)</td><td>Instance actions that each <code>Person</code> object should be capable of (Class methods)</td></tr>
<tr><td><code>name</code>
<code>age</code>
<code>heightInInches</code>
<code>profession</code>
<code>hobby</code></td><td><code>.stateName()</code>
<code>.reportAge()</code>
<code>.changeAge()</code></td></tr>
</table>

You can imagine the static data field as a variable stored on behalf of the overall class and not for any one instance object of that class. Also consider the static data field's name, `totalPersonCount`. This is, apparently, a variable that will represent a fact about the overall usage of the class in total: how many `Person` instance objects exist in the application. Since this variable is stored for the overall class, the usage of the dot (.) operator is a little different. To access this **static** variable, the dot notation is used on the *class name itself*, since this is a variable *concerning the entire class* and its use in the application:

Code Snippet 2.11

```
int tempCount = Person.totalPersonCount;
```

You can read this as "take the value of the static data field `totalPersonCount` from class `Person` and copy that value into the `tempCount` variable on the left." Of course, the same usage applies if you wanted to print this directly to the console:

Code Snippet 2.12

```
System.out.println("Total Person objects created:"
    + Person.totalPersonCount);
```

The dot notation is used throughout the Java API library, with many classes and their objects. You will see it used throughout this textbook as well where needed in the Java syntax.

SUMMARY POINTS

- The dot operator in Java gives the programmer access to the resources that are associated with classes and their instance objects, among other uses.
- Instance data fields are defined by the class but declared and created in each and every instance object of the class that is created. Each instance object has its own unique copy of any and all instance data fields defined by the class.
- Static data fields are variables associated with the overall class itself. There will only ever be one copy of a static data field created when a class is used, no matter how many instance objects there are.
- The data fields stored inside an instance object can be accessed by using the dot operator on the instance object's reference variable and those associated with the class by using the operator on the class name itself.

QUICK PROBLEMS

1. **Coding:** Implement the `PersonApp` and `Person` classes as instructed in section 2.2 (if you have not done so already). In `main()`, create two `Person` objects as shown in section 2.2 using the correct constructor and parentheses values. Change the value of the `age` data field variable on the first `Person` object by setting it equal to a new `int` value. Then print the age data field variable for the second of the `Person` objects and print its age to the console. What prints?
2. **Think:** How are instance data fields for class objects similar to individual characteristics of people?
3. **Coding:** Implement the `PersonApp` and `Person` classes as instructed in section 2.2 (if you have not done so already). In `main()`, create a `Person` object as shown in section 2.2 using the correct constructor and parentheses values. Using the dot notation, print the values for all the `Person` object's data fields (internal variables) to the console in a statement-like manner. For example, "(name) is of age (age) and . . ."

2.4 Instance and Static Methods of a Class

Instance methods of a class: Similar to instance and static data fields, instance and static **methods** of a class have different uses and different results depending on which one you use. **Instance** methods of a class are used to perform an action upon an instance object or have that object itself perform some action, possibly using the data stored within it. Keep in mind that a method is a **chunk of code** located elsewhere in your application, and that code only needs to be written once. Invoking methods allows you to call that same chunk of code over and over without the need for unnecessary duplication.

Consider the `Person` class and the methods/actions listed in table 2.2 for this class. Those listed are **instance methods**, invocable upon **instance objects** of the class. These methods can only be called by using the dot notation (.) on a class's instance object. You are not able to call them in a stand-alone fashion. For example, the following two lines of code would not work:

Code Snippet 2.13

```
String ageStatement = "";
ageStatement =  reportAge(); // Will not work.
ageStatement = .reportAge(); // Ditto
```

Think about why these two lines of code will not work. You want the age of a `Person`, but **whose age? Which `Person` object's age?** Reasonably, you want the age of **one `Person` in particular.** If you were to use the instantiated `personA` object above ("an instance object of class `Person`"), then you need to invoke the `.reportAge()` method specifically upon the `personA` object to get a statement of the `age` data field from that object in particular:

Code Snippet 2.14

```
String ageStatement = "";
ageStatement = personA.reportAge();
```

This code instructs `personA` object to report **its own age**. Notice that on the left of the assignment operator is a `String` variable `ageStatement`. The data type that `.reportAge()` "returns back" is a `String`. Methods have **return data types**, or just "return types" for short. Even methods that return nothing have a return type (of `void`). The instance method `.reportAge()` returns back a statement containing the `age` of `personA`. The returned value can be used like so in your application:

Code Snippet 2.15

```
System.out.println(personA.reportAge());
```

The console output for this line of code would be the following:

```
My age is 21
```

Logically, if you invoke `.reportAge()` on `personA`, then only the `age` and statement for `personA` will be "returned back" from the call to the method. You would not receive `personB`'s or `personC`'s information and so on. Instance methods only work on the instance object they are invoked upon.

Static methods of a class: In table 2.2 a static data field `totalPersonCount` was added to the description of the `Person` class. This static data field keeps track of a characteristic regarding the entire class overall. In a similar fashion, notice the **static class method** present in the `Person` class that will return back data or perform some action with data that is general to the overall class itself. You will also occasionally see static methods used to allow an action or activity to occur among two or more instance objects of a class (i.e., comparing two objects). Static methods in Java are often considered "utility" methods, tool methods, and so on. You will see static class methods used in many different ways. In table 2.3, the summary of class `Person` is expanded to include a static class method that returns back a statement containing the value of the static data field `totalPersonCount`:

Table 2.3. Adding a Static Class Method to the `Person` Class Example

Class person	
Static data fields *(only one of these will ever exist, and this data field applies to the entire class overall)* `totalPersonCount`	
Static class methods *(these methods are invoked upon the class name itself)* `.reportTotalPersonCount()`	
Instance data fields *(each instance object has its own copy of all of these):*	**Instance actions** *that* **each** `Person` *object should be capable of (Class methods)*

`name`
`age`
`heightInInches`
`profession`
`hobby`
	`.stateName()`
	`.reportAge()`
	`.changeAge(int newAge)`

This static class method can be invoked using the dot notation on the class name itself, similar to the invocation for a static data field:

Code Snippet 2.16

```
System.out.println(Person.reportTotalPersonCount());
```

Notice that the innermost method, the static class method, will execute first. It returns back a `String` value that is then passed as the input parameter for the `.println()` method. Something similar to the following could print to the **console** (again, it would if this were not an imaginary class):

```
There has been 1 Person object created
```

Both the static data field `totalPersonCount` and the static method `.reportTotalPersonCount()` are directly accessible by developers using class `Person`.

Security of class members: As you progress through your learning of the Java syntax, you will find that in some classes, **there are data fields that will not be directly accessible.** In those cases, you will be forced to use a method (either static or instance) whose purpose is to give you that value. For example, consider a data field added to the following `Person` class:

Code Snippet 2.17

```
private double personSalary;
```

The "`private`" **access modifier** prevents direct access to the `personSalary` data field by your application's code. You will encounter several classes in the Java library that have `private` data fields. In these cases, a class method will "gatekeep" access to the private data field. Often, this is to allow application code to read the value of a private data field but prevent the application from changing its value ad hoc or to use business rules to manage any change. For example, a salary would not be a negative number, and a class method could be written to prevent an application from setting a `Person` instance object's `personSalary` data field to a below-zero value.

Usage of instance and static syntax: Keep in mind too that **instance** methods of a class are only invokable upon **instance objects** of that class. You are not able to call an instance method upon the class name itself, like so:

Code Snippet 2.18

```
String nameStatement = Person.stateName(); // Nope
Person.changeAge(); // This will not work either.
```

Think about these two lines of code, and you will understand why they cannot work. In real life, you would ask a **specific person** what their name is. In a database record, you would change the age for a specific record that represents a person. In these two lines of code, the class `Person` itself is being asked to state its name, not a **specific instance object** of class `Person`. The class does not have a name variable, but its instance objects do. Remember the class simply is the **plan** that is followed for building new instance objects of the class. The class also defines what actions the objects and what actions the class itself are capable of performing.

SUMMARY POINTS

- Instance methods of a class are invoked by using the dot operator along with the method's name upon an instance object of a class. Though the class itself defines the method, the methods are associated with, or "callable" upon, its future instance objects.
- Static methods of a class are invoked by using the dot operator upon the class name itself, followed by the name of the static method being called.
- Methods that return back data following their execution have a return type defined. Methods can return back either primitive or complex data types. Methods that return no data will have `void` defined as their return type, meaning that nothing at all is returned.
- Methods can be defined with zero, one, or many input parameters, allowing for programmers to pass data into a method to help perform a task.

QUICK PROBLEMS

1. **Coding:** Implement the `PersonApp` and `Person` classes as instructed in section 2.2 (if you have not done so already). In `main()`, create a `Person` object as shown in section 2.2 using the correct constructor and parentheses values. Using the dot notation, change the value of the `Person` object's `age` data field. Next, use the `.changeAge()` method, and use a new `int` value for the parameter. Finally,

print the value of the `age` data field to the console. What value prints, and why?

2. **Think:** Why is it useful for methods of a class to be able to return back data values about both the class and its instance objects?
3. **Coding:** Implement the `PersonApp` and `Person` classes as instructed in section 2.2 (if you have not done so already). In `main()`, create a `Person` object as shown in section 2.2 using the correct constructor and parentheses values. Using the dot notation, print the `age` data field variable for your `Person` object to the console. Also, use the dot notation to invoke the `.reportAge()` method, and print its result to the console as well. Why did the same value print twice?

2.5 Understanding Complex Variables

The JVM and memory management: The Java Virtual Machine (JVM) does a lot more than interpret, partially compile, and guide the execution of Java bytecode (see the discussion in chapter 0 about the JVM). It manages how and where your program's variables and objects are created. It manages the traffic of methods, their invocation, and their eventual exiting of memory when execution is complete. It also sends the "garbage trucks" out to discard old variables and objects in memory that are no longer used by your application in a process called "garbage collection" (GC). Among major tasks, the management of the creation and location of variables in memory is vitally important.

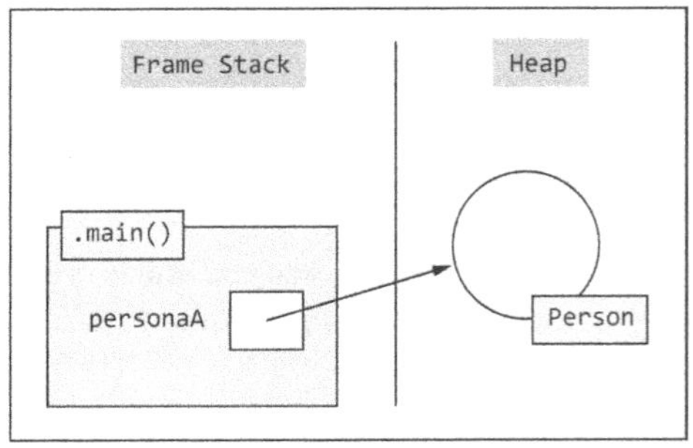

Figure 2.8. Example Contents of the Frame Stack and Heap When One `Person` Object Is Created in `main()`

The frame stack and the heap: The JVM reserves for itself a space in your computer's memory (RAM), and then partitions that space into smaller areas, each with specific purposes. Two of these areas are of importance to us: the JVM frame stack and the heap (sometimes also called the free store). These two areas of memory store the vast majority of variables and objects that will be created and interacted with in Java applications (see figure 2.8).

The frame stack is where the JVM loads methods into memory when you invoke/call them. Any variables that are created inside those methods are created within the allocated area of memory in the frame stack for that method. In Java applications the `main()` method is where code execution begins. The `main()` method is allocated space on the frame stack where all its variables are created and stored. When application execution ends, the area of memory reserved for the frame stack is freed up, and all the variables in that space for that method are deleted.

The word "stack" comes from the idea that areas on the frame stack are allocated for methods **as they are invoked.** The first method is given the first space, and if its code invokes a second, successive method, that one is "stacked" above it, and so on. For example, if you were to invoke a method called `methodA()` from `main()`, and `methodA()` just so happens to invoke `methodB()`, then the frame stack area might look like the visual representation in figure 2.9.

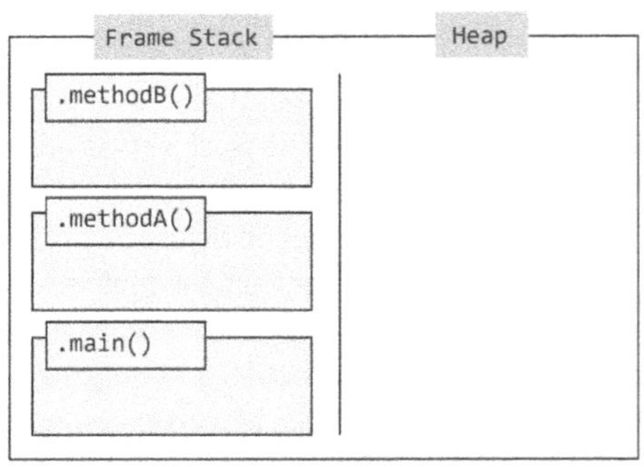

Figure 2.9. Method "Chaining" Shown as Methods Are "Stacked" into the Frame Stack in a Last in, first out (LIFO) Manner as They Are Invoked

The heap is a little less organized, so to speak. It is a free area where **instance objects**, among other objects, are created and stored while they are in use or while the application is running. Consider the creation of both an `int` variable and a `Person` instance object in the `main()` method:

Code Snippet 2.19

```
int varA = 23;
Person personA = new Person(21, 71, "Julie", " Programmer", "Soccer");
```

The frame stack / heap memory areas after this line executes would look like figure 2.10.

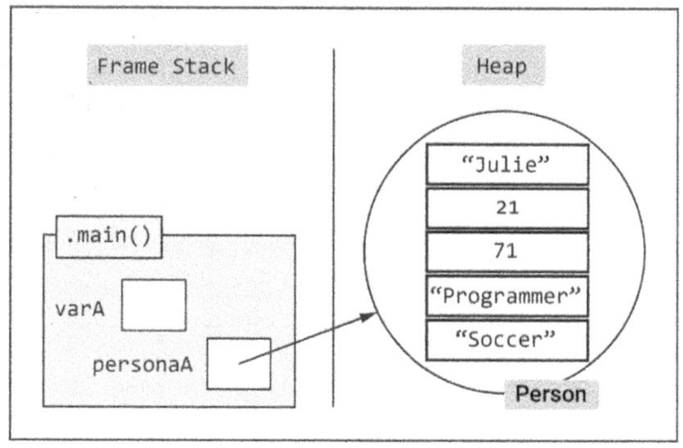

Figure 2.10. Simple Stack and Heap Diagram for the Code Example

Understanding reference variables: Notice the difference in how the variable `varA` is displayed with the way that `personA` is displayed. Visually, the differences between **primitive** and **complex** variables in Java are obvious. Notice that `varA` is essentially just a "bucket" that stores an `int`. The name "`varA`" is a label that corresponds to an actual hardware address in memory where the number twenty-three is stored. Simple variable data types all work this way (essentially). Notice that `personA` has two parts: a variable on the left inside the frame for `main()` and an **object** on the right in the **heap**. Notice also the arrow pointing from the `personA` variable to the object. This variable in `main()` is known as a **reference variable.** In the reference variable `personA`, there is an address stored. This address is the location of the instance object for the `Person` class on the heap. This address is visually represented by the arrow, pointing to the `Person` instance object in the heap.

The reference variable itself is a primitive data type; it holds an address (reference variables only ever hold addresses, **never** any other type of data!). A complex data-type variable in the frame stack can refer to an object on the heap through a reference. Keep in mind that the data for that object is **bundled inside the object itself,** not in the reference variable! Figure 2.10 shows this clearly: the `Person` instance object's data is inside the object, not inside the reference variable `personA`. The reference variable simply points to where the object itself is on the heap. Stored inside the instance object is the object's data.

Lastly, remember that reference variables will always act the same, no matter where they are or what complex data type they have been created with. Whether reference variables are declared in a method, stored on the heap, used as a variable inside of a class instance object, or passed as a method parameter, it does not matter: in all these cases, they are a variable that stores a reference to an instance object.

Remember the following:

- Variables with **simple** data types (`int`, `double`, `float`, etc.) do **not** reference. They are merely a "bucket" that contains the actual data.
- Variables that have a complex data type (`Scanner`, `Person`, etc.) are variables that **store a reference** to **where an instance object of that data type can be found on the heap.** The data **is stored in the object, not in the reference variable.**

SUMMARY POINTS

- The Java Virtual Machine (JVM) manages two areas of memory where the methods, variables, and objects are stored: the frame stack and the heap.
- The frame stack is an area of memory where methods can allocate a space of that memory for their temporary and exclusive use. Methods use their memory "frame" as a place to declare and store local and parameter variables and references to instance objects.
- The heap, also known as the "free store," is where Java creates new instance objects of classes as well as an area where static data fields of classes are stored.
- A reference variable for a class instance object does not store any data of the object at all. Instead, the reference variable stores the address of where the object is located on the heap. All the data fields for that instance object are stored inside it, not in the reference variable. Reference variables will never hold any other kind of data other than a reference address for an instance object.

QUICK PROBLEMS

1. **Coding:** Implement the `PersonApp` and `Person` classes as instructed in section 2.2 (if you have not done so already). In `main()`, create two `Person` objects as shown in section 2.2 using the correct constructor and parentheses values of your choice. Ensure they each have different ages. Next, set the first `Person` object equal to the second in a manner like this:

   ```
   personA = personB;
   ```

   Finally, print the value of the age data field variable for the **first** `Person` object to the console. Which age prints?
2. **Think:** How are reference variables and primitive data-type variables the same? How are they different?
3. **Coding:** Implement the `PersonApp` and `Person` classes as instructed in section 2.2 (if you have not done so already). In `main()`, declare a `Person` reference variable, but do not initialize it (i.e., do not include the assignment operator or anything to the right). Use the dot notation, and set the value of the name of the `Person` to your name. What happens when you run this code?

2.6 Using an Example Class from the Java Library

As you learn more and more about the Java programming language, you will come across the usage of some of the classes that are built into Java. You will also inevitably encounter documentation or descriptions of the major parts of these classes. A major goal of this chapter was to introduce you to the concepts of classes you will encounter and to give you an initial idea of both what they are (and mean) and how they impact the usage of Java classes. In your early Java learning steps, you will use several classes that are included with the Java API (application programming interface).

One habit as the good programming student that you are is to look up the official Oracle Java documentation for classes as you first encounter them.* Also, searches on the web† will produce numerous definitions and examples of how various Java classes are used. As you find this information, you will usually find examples or listings of the class's **constructors, (data) fields,** and **methods.** To summarize some of what has been discussed so far in this chapter, keep these handy rules of thumb in mind for each of these terms as you look up more information on new classes you encounter:

Table 2.4. Parts of Java Classes along with Context of Usage and Brief Definitions of Each

Part of class	Context of usage	Definition
Constructors	Always instance (nonstatic)	The special, one-time-per-instance-object method that initializes an object with data
(Data) fields	Both instance and static types are possible	Variables that are either inside each instance object (instance) or associated with the entire class itself (static)
Member methods	Both instance and static types are possible	Methods of the class that can be invoked upon objects (instance) or upon the class name itself (static)

Discussion of constructors in the Oracle documentation will usually include how many and what types of parameters will be required for constructor invocation. Keep in mind that not all classes are **instantiable** and may just contain mostly static methods to be invoked on the class name itself. Most examples also will demonstrate what data fields are useful and accessible and what methods are available and how to call them (again with any needed parameters).

* https://docs.oracle.com/en/java/javase/14/docs/api/index.html.

† Usually, most students end up looking at examples on https://stackoverflow.com/, but there are other resources!

Practicing Java classes with the `Math` class: It will be helpful to discuss one of the commonly used classes in the Java API, the `Math` class. The official Oracle documentation for this class, as well as many other examples on the web, will show how this class has two data fields (one for *pi* and one for *e*—it is a math class after all!) and several static methods![*] The class has a constructor, but it is not accessible by programmers writing Java applications. The `Math` class **is a noninstantiable class**, as opposed to the `Person` class exampled earlier, which can have objects instantiated from it. Often you will hear classes like `Math` called "utility" classes, since they contain mostly static methods and are noninstantiable. The class itself performs all necessary actions, and objects of `Math` are not needed. Table 2.5 details some of the more commonly used static methods in this class:

Table 2.5. Some of the Common Methods of the Math Class Found in `java.lang`

Method	Description
`static int max (int a, int b)`	Returns a copy of whichever of the two integer parameters `a` or `b` is the larger. If they are equal, that value is returned.
`static int min (int a, int b)`	Returns a copy of whichever of the two integer parameters `a` or `b` is the smaller. If they are equal, that value is returned.
`static double floor(double a)`	Returns the next double value lower than `a` that is numerically the same as a whole number.
`static double ceil(double a)`	Short for "ceiling." Returns the next double value larger than `a` that is numerically the same as a whole number.
`static double pow(double a, double b)`	Returns the value of `a` raised to the `b`th power. For example, 2^2 would be 2 raised to the second power.
`static double random()`	Returns a double that is between 0.0 and 1.0, inclusive (meaning 0.0 or 1.0 themselves are possible returns). A great random number generator. Notice that `.random()` does not require any parameters and will not allow any.

Notice that these `Math` methods have **static** listed with them, meaning that you would invoke these methods by using the class name itself. The `Math` class is part of the `java.lang` package, which is included by default in every Java program, with no need to add an `include` statement to your code. Notice as well that with documentation on classes and their methods, you will often see names given to the parameters of a method. In table 2.5, you can see names like `a` and `b` given. This does not mean you have to use variables with those names when you use these methods. This is simply a labeling convenience in method documentation showing you where arguments should go when the methods are invoked. Any variable that matches the listed data type can be used instead of `a` and/or `b`, along with literal values that match the data type as well.

You should research the `Math` class on your own and explore the many methods and their features/usages and add them to your mental toolbox. Here is an example usage of the `Math` method `.max()`:

Code Snippet 2.20

```
System.out.println(Math.max(10, 20));
```

Since this method is a **static method** of class `Math`, you must invoke it by using the dot notation on the class name itself. The console output after this code executes is the following:

```
20
```

Variables can be used as the arguments for a method invocation like this also. Notice that the **data type** of each variable matches the **required parameter data type** as defined in the class documentation:

* https://docs.oracle.com/en/java/javase/14/docs/api/java.base/java/lang/Math.html.

Code Snippet 2.21

```
int varA = 10;
int varB = 20;
System.out.println(Math.max(varA, varB));
```

Console output:

```
20
```

Example of `.ceil()` with a variable parameter:

Code Snippet 2.22

```
double hourlyRate = 17.85;
double largerAmount = Math.ceil(hourlyRate);
System.out.println(largerAmount);
```

Console output:

```
18.0
```

Example of `.random()` to generate a number between zero and ten (not including ten):

Code Snippet 2.23

```
double randomNumber = Math.random();
System.out.println("The random number is:" + (randomNumber * 10));
```

Console output (the number generated is random, so yours may differ!):

```
The random number is: 1.8387594490969261
```

You can also rewrite this in the following manner and use a **cast operator** to "downgrade" the `double` to an `int` whole number:

Code Snippet 2.24

```
double randomNumber = (Math.random() * 10);
System.out.println("The random number is:" + (int)randomNumber);
```

Console output (the number generated is random so yours may differ!):

```
The random number is: 1
```

SUMMARY POINTS

- The `Math` class in Java is not instantiable, meaning that you cannot create instance objects of this class (usually because its constructor is hidden from the programmer).
- Most of the methods of the `Math` class are defined as static, meaning that they are invoked by using the dot operator on the `Math` class name itself.
- The `.random()` method of the `Math` class returns a double that is between the values `0.0` and `1.0` inclusive. This returned value can be used in many types of expressions and logic.

QUICK PROBLEMS

1. **Coding:** Write a small Java program that prompts the user to enter three `int` values between zero and one hundred. Store these in `int` variables. Using the `Math` class method `.max()`, find the largest of the first two, and store that in another `int` variable. Then compare that largest with the third number, and store the largest of those two in a final `int` variable. Print that value to the console with an appropriate message.
2. **Coding:** Write a small Java program that will generate three random numbers between zero and ten. Use the `(int)` cast operator to convert these to whole numbers. Use the `.min()` method of the `Math` class in a similar fashion as `.max()` in quick problem #1 to find the smallest number generated. Print this value to the console with an appropriate message.

3. **Coding:** Write a small Java program that will generate a random number in the value range of `-10` to `10`. (*Hint:* Subtraction can help here.) Print that value to the console.

Summary

Java is an object-oriented language through and through, and the syntax that leverages its OO nature is found everywhere. Now that you have taken a high-level look at the OO nature of the language, you will see the same syntax throughout the rest of the textbook. This will help with your learning as you encounter code that uses new classes you have not seen yet. Constructors, methods, data fields, reference variables, usage of the dot operator: the syntax for these remains relatively unchanged throughout the rest of the language. At this point in your learning, you do not need to know how to define a class, but when you get to that point, you will be familiar with many of the basics of OO already. Additionally, as an information systems professional, you most likely will not be limited to working in one programming language. The object-oriented concepts discussed in this chapter and throughout this text are applicable to any contemporary object-oriented programming language you might encounter in your career. It is even more important for us to have explored these concepts now. The next chapter will examine the `String` class in detail and explain how these OO concepts can be put to work in leveraging the power of that class for text manipulation.

Practice Problems

Terminology

Match the following terms from the chapter with their most appropriate definition:

1. Class	a. An object created by using its class data type as the instructions for its data fields and the associating of methods with that object as its activities.
2. Object	b. Gives the programmer access to either the data fields or the methods associated with a class and/or its instance objects. Also used for qualifying locations of classes in package import hierarchies.
3. Member method	c. A method invoked by calling it upon the name of the class itself and not upon any of its instance objects.
4. Initialization	d. A variable that each class instance object contains its own unique copy of. These variables are defined by the class the instance object belongs to.
5. Constructor	e. An area of memory managed by the JVM where methods are given space to declare local variables and receive parameter variables for use in code execution.
6. Dot operator	f. A special type of variable that is complex in nature and stored by the JVM in an area of memory separate from most method-local primitives.
7. Instance object	g. A variable that stores only an address of an instance object somewhere in memory. No actual data other than an address is stored in the variable. The object it addresses stores the data instead.
8. Instance data field	h. A data field associated with a class itself, not its instance objects. Usually, this means only one copy of the data field will ever exist.
9. Parameter	i. Set of instructions for the creation of instance objects, what data they will store, and the actions they will be capable of. Serves as a data type for reference variables.
10. New operator	j. A value returned by a method after its execution has finished. The method return is `void` if no data is returned.
11. Static data field	k. An area of memory managed by the JVM where instance objects and other class data fields are kept. Sometimes called the "free store."
12. Static method	l. A value that is passed to a method within its parentheses. The method's code can then use a copy of that value when the method executes.

13. Method return	m. A method defined in the class file as belonging to a class. Could be static or instance in nature.
14. Reference variable	n. A class from which instance objects can be created.
15. Frame stack	o. A Java class that contains mostly static methods useful for numeric calculations and comparisons.
16. Heap	p. A command that instructs Java to follow the instructions in a class to create an instance object of that class data type. The class directs the variables stored within and the actions associated with the object.
17. Instantiable class	q. The activity that involves giving a variable (primitive or complex) a starting value. Does not prevent the variable's value from changing later.
18. Math class	r. A class method whose specific purpose is to initialize all the data fields of newly created instance objects of that class.

Think about It

1. How does object-oriented programming add complexity to the flow of code execution that may not be as present in a more procedural, simpler, more straightforward style of programming?
2. Describe how an object in Java differs from a primitive data-type variable.
3. Describe how a class in Java serves as a data type for variables in the language.
4. How does the initialization of a class object in Java differ from the initialization of a primitive data type variable?
5. What is the purpose of the class constructor method? What makes this method unique when compared to other class methods? How often can this method be called?
6. What is the purpose of parameters in methods of all types? How many parameters must be present in the definition of any method?
7. Describe what an instance object is and how Java knows the steps to create one. What real-world process could you relate instance object creation in Java to?
8. Describe what an instance data field is. How many copies of an instance data field are there at any one time? Where are instance data fields defined? When are they initialized?
9. What purpose does the "`new`" operator serve in Java? How does its activity differ from that of the constructor?
10. What purpose does the dot operator (`.`) serve in Java? How does it let us use classes and their instance objects?
11. In general, what is the difference between resources of a class that are defined as static and those defined as instance? How does the syntax you would write differ between these two?
12. When creating an instance object of a class in Java, what does the assignment operator do during this process?
13. What is stored within a reference variable? How is an instance object related to a reference variable? Where is the instance object's data stored?
14. Describe the areas of memory known as the frame stack and the heap and what the Java Virtual Machine typically stores in each.
15. Since the `Math` class in Java contains mostly static methods, how will this impact your usage of the class in your applications? How can you create instance objects of the `Math` class?

Short Syntax Problems

1. Generate a random number between −10 and 10, including those end values. Print out the result of the number in a statement to the console. Convert the number to an integer using a cast operator.
2. Generate a random number between 0 and 100, and print the number in a statement. Round the number to the next highest number, and convert it to an int using a cast operator.
3. Use the `.pow()` method to calculate 2^8 (two to the eighth power), but only use `.pow()` to raise 2 to the second power each time. *Hint:* Consider method nesting.
4. Generate two random numbers between 0 and 10. Convert as appropriate, and store in int variables. Use the `.max()` method to report which one is larger.
5. Generate two random numbers between 1 and 10. Convert as appropriate, and store in an int. Using

the `.pow()` method, use the `.min()` method to compare the two stored `int` values for the first parameter. Use the `.max()` method to compare the two `int` values for the second parameter. Print the results in a statement to the console.

6. Do a little research about a national lottery, and find out the ranges of numbers that are possible for both its regular values and any special values (i.e., a "supernumber" that increases prize winnings). Write a small Java application that will use `.random()` to produce a "drawing" similar to what the national lottery does, each value randomly chosen in the ranges defined by the rules of that game. Print the results of the drawing to the console.

Full Problems

Full problems #1–#3 require you to implement the `Person` class as instructed in section 2.2 (if you have not already).

1. Create three `Person` objects. Use `Math.random()` to generate a random age (between 1 and 120) and a random height in inches (between 40 and 90) for each of the `Person` objects. Print their names, ages, and heights to the console, along with the total count of `Person` objects as reported by the class itself.
2. Create two `Person` objects, choosing their characteristics as you wish. When done, copy each characteristic (data field value) of the first `Person` object into the second. Print the details of the second in a business-appropriate manner to the console with appropriate labels. For example,

```
Name: ......
Age: ......
```

3. Use two of the `Person` objects from full problem #1, or instantiate two new ones with random ages and heights. Use the `Math.max()` method to compare the age data fields of the two objects. Print the larger of the two to the console.
4. Write a Java application that will calculate the compound interest for an amount of savings a customer initially deposits in a savings account. After eliciting the requirements of the application, you have learned that the formula used by your client for compound interest looks like the following:

   amount = principal * (1 + (interestRate / timesPerYear)) ^ (timesPerYear * numberOfYears)

   Where
   - `principal` is the amount of money the customer initially deposits.
   - `interestRate` is the interest that the account gains in each "compounding period" (i.e., how many times the bank pays interest to the customer).
   - `timesPerYear` is how many times per year the bank pays the customer interest.
   - `numberOfYears` is how long the customer leaves the money in their savings account.

   Prompt your user for all these pieces of information. Use the formulas of the `Math` class to both randomly generate an interest between `0.0` and `1.0` (interest is usually typed in as #.#%, so you may have to convert to the mathematically correct form!), and perform the exponent calculation (noted by the mathematical symbol "^" in the equation). Print the amount in the account to the console with an appropriate message, and round the amount up to the next whole integer.
5. You have been tasked with creating a small Java application that will tutor students in the use of the distance formula (used to find the linear distance between two points on a graph). The distance formula looks something like this:

   distance = $\sqrt{((x_2 - x_1)^2 + (y_2 - y_1)^2)}$

   Each point on a graph consists of an x and y coordinate. The first point would be (x_1,y_1) and the second would be (x_2,y_2).
   - Prompt the user to enter each of these sets of coordinates as `double` values (without any parentheses or other characters).
   - Use the appropriate methods of the `Math` class to calculate the distance, and report it to the user in an appropriate statement to the console.
   - Reprint the user's entered coordinates in the form "(x_1,y_1), (x_2,y_2)."
   - *Hint:* You may have to research other methods of the `Math` class in Oracle's official documentation for one part of the above formula's calculation!

Chapter 3

Strings and Text Formatting

What You Will Learn in This Chapter

For developers learning a new programming language, the ability to use, manipulate, and format text for output is a key skill to acquire. For information systems professionals who work in software development, text manipulation is vitally important. Effective processing of data from sources like databases and the web, displaying business-appropriate output, cleaning data, and improving data quality are activities critical for a successful information system. A large part of the data generated by users that will flow through systems is text based—entered comments, descriptions of product, attribute information for entities in the system, and so on. Being able to use a programming language like Java to process and manipulate text-based data is a must for the contemporary IS professional.

Specifically, this chapter will help you do the following:

1. Understand the basics of the `String` class and know several ways to create and use a `String` variable
2. Understand how to directly compare two `String` variables in multiple ways and leverage the benefits of each method
3. Know how to search a `String` variable and extract substrings to meet your application's data needs
4. Know how to manipulate and alter text values according to your application's needs
5. Know how to format `String` output within certain usage contexts through several highly sophisticated and effective ways

Opening Scenario

The lengthy requirement-elicitation and system-planning phase for the mom-and-pop grocery information system has reached a point where a great deal of the business is now well understood. Your team is ready to start building the prototype. The client has, for many years, used spreadsheets to manually enter much of the business's information, particularly inventory information. Occasionally they have tried to clean up the data, but running the business itself has prevented any substantive work in this area. You recall them saying in a meeting just a few days ago, "We just don't have the time; that's why we reached out to your firm." After looking over an example of some of their spreadsheets, you and the team are not surprised to see that the data is truly a mess! Some names are first name, last name; others are the reverse. Some addresses are in one attribute; others are spread across columns. Some columns are all uppercase characters; others are more normal text. There appears to be no standardization of the data, no rules to govern its structure and upkeep. "They'll eventually want to perform some simple analytics on their data at one point. With data like this, that won't be possible," a teammate comments to you as you take a cursory look through their data.

Before they can load the client's data into a prototype system, it will have to be cleaned and standardized. The team has only briefly talked with the client regarding how they want their data formatted. "You know, standard stuff: capitalized names, addresses, and so on. Just take a look at our spreadsheets, and you'll get the idea," they replied. You are fairly certain this will be a continuing discussion with the client. Ensuring that the new system guides users in entering data "the right way" is relatively easy. Converting and cleaning up the existing historical data will be the hard part and is a must to prevent a hiccup in their operations after they go live. After some thought, you think that a simple Java application, which can apply some text manipulation logic to the customer's old data, might do the trick. You have not worked much with text manipulation in Java but are eager to learn. The team will need this old customer data pretty fast to test out the prototype system as it is being developed. While you will need to understand how logic and decision-making in Java work as well, an understanding of how to process text and manage output is a basic must-have. You will need this foundation before you can write the data-processing logic later on. You decide to dive in and get started with these basics of manipulating and processing text in Java . . .

3.1 "Understanding the `String` Class"

Most programming languages can store and manipulate text (a word, sentence, character, etc.). This is not so much for the computer's sake but more for us people. Working with text is one of the most common activities in **any** programming language. In Java, multicharacter text is stored in a `String` data-type variable, which is **not** one of the eight primitive Java data types (`bool`, `float`, `double`, `byte`, `int`, `char`, `short`, `long`). A `String`'s value is just a sequence of `char` values arranged in a sequential order, as demonstrated in figure 3.1. `String` class objects can be instantiated using the `new` operator and a `String` constructor method, similar to how you have created `Scanner` variables in the past. They can also be initialized similarly to primitive data types by simply using the assignment operator, setting them equal to a string in double quotes. The `String` class defines several useful methods that can act upon individual `String` variables. `String` class methods implement logic for testing the equality of two `String` values; extracting smaller chunks of the text, called "substrings"; converting and formatting `String` values for better-looking output and printing; and many other useful tasks.

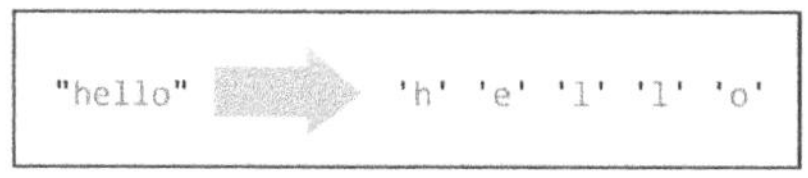

Figure 3.1. A `String` Is Actually a Sequence of `char` Values

Creating and using strings in Java: There are really two main ways to create a `String` object in Java. Either way results in a `String` variable ready for use. Consider the following Java main class application called `WorkingWithStrings.java`, which demonstrates how to create a `String`. The `String` class is part of the automatically imported `java.lang` library, so no imports are needed. For many of the code examples, you can simply type them in as additional code to this application:

Full Program 3.1

```
public class WorkingWithStrings {
    public static void main(String[] args) {

        // Creating a String like you would a primitive data type:
        String myName = "The Author";

        // Creating a String in a fully object-oriented manner:
        String yourName = new String("The Reader");

        // Add more code here as you practice
        //  the concepts in the chapter.

    }
}
```

The initialization of the `myName` variable demonstrates why `String` is often called a "fence-sitting" class: you have a reference type on the left but a `String` literal value on the right. Java provides this `String` creation method as both a convenience and a way to efficiently handle `String` objects in memory. The JVM will often keep a recent history of `String` objects that you create like this and attempt to reuse the literal value on the right to keep memory neat and tidy. The second method is the "fully" object-oriented technique. Here, the `new` operator causes a new `String` object to be created in memory. **Both** versions of `String` creation work well and will not impact your development efforts.

Think back to how you have worked with text so far in this textbook: concatenation between some variable or method return value and some text in a print statement like so:

Code Snippet 3.1

```
double taxAmount = .0725 * 150000;
System.out.println("Taxes Paid on Tesla Vehicle: " + taxAmount);
```

The text placed between quotation marks is a `String` literal value and works the same as any other primitive literal value would: it exists in memory just as it's used and then is discarded. You can create a `String` to store this print and display that to the console as well:

Code Snippet 3.2

```
String paymentStatement = "Taxes Paid on Tesla Vehicle: " + (.0725 * 150000);
System.out.println(paymentStatement);
```

The **console** output for this would look like the following:

```
Taxes Paid on Tesla Vehicle: 10875.0
```

This works the same. Notice the use of the **addition operator** along with a `String`. Since `String` values are so common in Java, the functionality of the addition operator has been expanded when used with them. **Concatenation** occurs when a `String` serves as one operand of the addition operator and a literal value, variable, or numeric return of a method as the other. Stated simply, concatenation simply means the "gluing" together of two things. Notice the expression used to create the string for the variable `paymentStatement`. Parentheses neatly contain and arrange the expression forcing a desired processing order. Though the parentheses are optional in this expression, the multiplication operator would still process first due to its higher precedence.

Consider an expression like the following, where parentheses **are** needed:

Code Snippet 3.3

```
String twoNumbersAdded = "The Sum of 10 and 20 is: " + 10 + 20;
System.out.println(twoNumbersAdded);
```

The console output for this would be the following:

```
The Sum of 10 and 20 is: 1020
```

The addition did not occur! The expression on the right-hand side of the assignment operator is still evaluated from left to right, so the first addition operator is processed. Since there is a `String` literal value on the left (left operand) and a numeric value on the right (an int as the right operand), text concatenation occurs first. Then text concatenation occurs again, since the second addition operator has a `String` as the left operand and a numeric value on the right. Either using parentheses or reordering the expression will resolve this:

Code Snippet 3.4

```
String twoNumbersAdded = "The Sum of 10 and 20 is " + (10 + 20);
String anotherSum = 30 + 40 + " is the sum of 30 and 40";
System.out.println(twoNumbersAdded);
System.out.println(anotherSum);
```

Console output:

```
The Sum of 10 and 20 is 30
70 is the sum of 30 and 40
```

Notice that for the `String twoNumbersAdded`, the careful usage of parentheses operators forces the addition operation to process first. The result of that math expression then becomes the right operand of the first addition operator that has a string value as its left operand. Concatenation then occurs. For the variable `anotherSum`, with expressions processing from left to right, the first addition operator sees a numeric value on both sides of it, so it adds them. That result becomes the left operand for the second addition operator with a `String` value on the right. Text concatenation occurs. In both cases, because `String` is a class, `twoNumbersAdded` and `anotherSum` are **reference** variables that "point" to where in memory the `String` objects are located and give us a way to access them.

String text blocks: In Java SE 13 (as a preview feature) and Java SE 14 (official feature), `String` text blocks were added to the language as a convenient way to use and display longer "blocks" of text on multiple lines of output. To create a text block, you will use three quotation marks on either end of the `String` literal value and a semicolon at the end as you would for a single line of Java code:

Code Snippet 3.5

```
String javaPoem = """
       Mary loved her Java book.
       Its heft was light, you know.
       Everywhere that Mary went,
       her Java book was in tow!
       """;
```

A text block in Java is a convenient way to format a `String` for multiline display and to include any tabbing or "blank spaces" in the text without complicated formatting. If you wanted to display each line of the above poem a little differently, you could hit "Tab" on your keyboard for each row as it is typed in:

Code Snippet 3.6

```
String javaPoem = """
       Mary loved her Java book.
            Its heft was light, you know.
                Everywhere that Mary went,
                    she had her Java book in tow!
       """;
```

The console output would preserve the spacing that starts each line:

```
Mary loved her Java book.
     Its heft was light, you know.
         Everywhere that Mary went,
             she had her Java book in tow!
```

Comparing two strings: Comparing two or more strings for equality or content is a common activity in Java as in most programming languages. For example, comparing a username on a login form with the correct one stored in a database record occurs constantly on digital devices (how many times did you log into some device or app today?). When users create new passwords, often various rules have to be followed for the new password to be accepted as valid (number of characters, special characters, numbers, capitalization, etc.). Programmatic comparison and processing of `String` values accomplish all of the above.

In chapter 1, you practiced using the equality operator (==) to compare two values to determine if they are the same or not, producing a `true` or `false` outcome from that comparison. It is tempting to try to use the equality operator to test if two `String` values are the same. Consider the following example:

Code Snippet 3.7

```
String stringA = "test";
String stringB = "test";
String stringC = new String("test");
String stringD = new String("test");

System.out.println(stringA == stringB);
System.out.println(stringB == stringC);
System.out.println(stringC == stringD);
```

Here is the console output from executing this code:

```
true
false
false
```

Notice the inconsistency of results! It was stated earlier that you can create a `String` in either the "primitive" way or the object-oriented way. Doing so will cause the equality operator to give you different results. Notice that each of the four `String` objects contains the same text value, "`test`." For `stringA` and `stringB`, the equality test seems to work just fine. But when comparing `stringB` and `stringC`, which both have the same value of "`test`," the comparison fails and results in "`false`." Recall also that the JVM handles `String` objects in memory a little differently depending on how they are created (primitive vs. OO). For `stringA` and `stringB`, the equality operator seems to work properly. For the comparison between `stringC` and `stringD`, the **reference addresses of two separate `String` instance objects** are compared instead of the text. Since they are separate instance objects, their memory address locations are not the same. If you use the equality operator, you will have to keep up with which `String` objects are created in one way or the other or with methods and **how** they return `String` values. Exhaustion will quickly set in.

There is a better way: the `String` class has two instance methods that can simplify the comparison of text values in Java.[*] These methods compare the actual text values inside `String` objects and help eliminate inconsistent comparison results. Table 3.1 details these methods:

Table 3.1. `String` Class Methods Used for Comparison

Instance method headers with parameters listed	Description
`boolean equals(String otherString)`	Compares the value of the `String` object the method is invoked upon with the value of the `String` object referenced by the parameter `otherString` (parameter type and name adjusted slightly in this listing)
`boolean equalsIgnoresCase(String otherString)`	Performs the same `String` value comparison as `.equals()` but ignores upper/lowercase differences in the characters of the two strings

A better way to compare two `String` values is as follows:

Code Snippet 3.8

```
String stringA = "test";
String stringB = "test";
String stringC = new String("test");
String stringD = new String("test");

System.out.println(stringA.equalsIgnoreCase(stringB));
System.out.println(stringB.equalsIgnoreCase(stringC));
System.out.println(stringC.equalsIgnoreCase(stringD));
```

And the console output for this would be the following:

```
true
true
true
```

The method `.equalsIgnoresCase()` is an **instance method** of class `String`, meaning it has to be invoked on instance objects of `String`. That is why for `stringA`, for example, the variable name is followed with the **dot notation** and then the name of the instance method to invoke upon it. This method's only parameter is a reference to another `String` instance object (in this case, `stringB` in the first comparison). If you think about the first comparison, you could describe what is happening in a literal sense as follows:

> Upon the instance object of the `String` class referenced by the reference variable `stringA`, invoke the `String` class instance method `.equalsIgnoresCase()`, and pass to that method

[*] The official Oracle documentation for class String can be found at https://docs.oracle.com/javase/9/docs/api/java/lang/String.html.

through its required parameter a reference to the String instance object referenced by variable stringB.

The .equalsIgnoresCase() method is written so that it compares the text values **stored inside** the String objects. It performs the comparison character by character and ignores whether the characters are uppercase or lowercase. For example,

Code Snippet 3.9

```
String stringE = "Java Rocks!";
String stringF = "java rocks!";
System.out.println(stringE.equalsIgnoreCase(stringF));
```

Console output for this code:

```
true
```

This comparison differs in result than if you used just .equals(), which is case sensitive:

Code Snippet 3.10

```
String stringE = "Java Rocks!";
String stringF = "java rocks!";
System.out.println(stringE.equals(stringF));
```

with console output of

```
false
```

SUMMARY POINTS

- String variables in Java are known as "immutable," meaning they cannot be directly changed. Instead, another String object must be set as the String object's reference. Since String is a complex data type (i.e., class), its variables are references to instance objects on the heap.
- The usage and manipulation of text in a Java application are handled at a basic level through the use of the String class to create instance objects that store string values.
- There are two ways to create a String variable: through the use of a String literal value for initialization and in an object-oriented manner through the use of the "new" operator and the String class constructor.
- Concatenation allows the programmer to "glue" two String values together to form a larger String variable or to append a numeric, variable, or method return value to a String to form that larger value.
- In Java, the addition operator also serves as the concatenation operator for String. If either of the two operands used in an expression with an addition operator is a String value, the operand will perform a String concatenation.
- Operator precedence can change the behavior of a concatenation expression. The use of parentheses to change this precedence can resolve any unintended behavior.
- String text blocks allow the programmer to easily create a multiline string that preserves new line breaks and tabbing in each line to display a block of text as the programmer intended.
- Usage of the String class methods .equals() and .equalsIgnoresCase() is strongly recommended instead of using the equality operator, as these methods will compare the actual text values stored in String variables.

QUICK PROBLEMS

1. **Coding:** Create a String and store the word "Java" in it. Compare it to a String literal with the value "java." Print the results of this comparison. Why did this result occur?

2. **Think:** What is occurring when you set one `String` equal to another using the assignment operator? How is this different from primitive data-type variables?

3. **Coding:** Create two `String` variables, and store text in each. Write some code that will effectively swap the two values between the two `Strings`. Did you need to create any new variables to accomplish this?

3.2 Working with Index Notation and Substrings

The term "substring" simply means a smaller part of a text value. Within an information systems context, there are several occasions when you might need to "extract" a substring from a larger string and use it in your logic and processing: breaking an entered name into subparts of first, middle, and last names; building a new user's username according to a business rule (e.g., first three letters of first name, first two letters of last name, and the middle initial); taking a sequence of characters with a predefined pattern and storing it into complex variables/data structures; and many more. The `String` class has two instance methods that focus on substring extraction detailed in table 3.2.

Table 3.2. Versions of the Overloaded `String` Class Method `.substring()`

Instance method header and parameters	Description
`String substring(int beginIndex)`	Extracts the substring from within the `String` object the method is invoked upon starting at the index position parameter `beginIndex` and extending until the end of the `String`
`String substring(int beginIndex, int endIndex)`	Extracts the substring from within the `String` object the method is invoked upon starting at the index position parameter `beginIndex` and until the character at `endIndex - 1`

Index notation: These methods require an `int` parameter called `beginIndex` that tells the method which specific character to begin the extraction with. **Index notation** is a simple way to map out the positions of elements in a sequence of data (characters, numbers, etc.). There are two main concepts with indexes:

- The **first** element in that sequence is always at **index location** `0` (zero).
- The **last** element in a sequence is always at index location `n - 1`, where `n` represents the number of elements in the sequence.

Recall that a `String` is simply a sequence of characters. For example, if you take the text "`Hello there`," the character at index position `0` would be the character `H`, and the last character in the `String` would be the last letter, `e`, at index position `10`. There are eleven characters in total, **including** the blank space character between the two words. The last position in any `String` is always `n - 1`. In this example, the last is at `11 - 1`, or index position `10`. All characters in a `String` variable have an index position. Notice this mapping visually in figure 3.2, where decorative brackets have been added to help distinguish each single character (the brackets are not part of the `String`).

```
[H][e][l][l][o][ ][t][h][e][r][e]
 0  1  2  3  4  5  6  7  8  9  10
```

Figure 3.2. Index Notation Mapping of Characters in a `String` (Brackets Added)

Index notation helps developers map out positions in both `String` variables and other data sequences like arrays (chapter 7). The parameter(s) for the `.substring()` method requires a beginning and/or ending index position for the smaller text chunk you want to extract. The one-parameter version can be used like so:

Code Snippet 3.11

```
String nameWithStructure = "B. Burke";
String anotherName = "L. Anderson";
int lastNamePosition = 3;
System.out.println(nameWithStructure.substring(lastNamePosition));
System.out.println(anotherName.substring(lastNamePosition));
```

The console output for this example would be the following:

```
Burke
Anderson
```

Imagine a business rule that states that employee name records are stored as the first letter of the first name, followed by a period and a space, followed by the last name. Using the first `.substring()` method, which extracts from a beginning index position all the way to the end, keeps things flexible in terms of the variety of last name lengths. According to the business rule, the first letter of the first name would always be at index position `0`, the period at `1`, and the blank space at position `2`. The last name will, according to this organization's data rules, always start at index position `3` in the `String`. The first version of the `.substring()` method starts at **and includes** the character at `beginIndex` and continues extracting characters all the way to the end. Using these same `String` variables, what if you wanted to capture the first initial along with the period? Consider the following:

Code Snippet 3.12

```
String nameWithStructure = "B. Burke";
String anotherName = "L. Anderson";
int lastNamePosition = 3;
System.out.println(
       nameWithStructure.substring(
            0, lastNamePosition - 1));
System.out.println(
anotherName.substring(
0, lastNamePosition - 1));
```

The console output from this would be the following:

```
B.
L.
```

Recall that a `String` always starts at index position `0`. Remember too that the business rule from earlier requires that the first letter initial is always at the very start of the `String`. With this information, you can use `0` as the `beginIndex` parameter for the second version of the method. How was the value for the `endIndex` determined? The client's metadata reveals that the last name in these `String` values starts at `lastNamePosition`, or at index position 3. Since the overloaded version of the `.substring()` method extracts the substring until `endIndex - 1` (the index position **before** `endIndex`'s value), subtract `1` from `lastNamePosition`. Effectively, this will capture characters until `lastNamePosition - 1 - 1`, or position `1` (3 – 1 – 1). The characters at index positions `0` and `1` will be extracted from the name, these characters being the first initial and the period. Notice that the console output confirms this behavior!

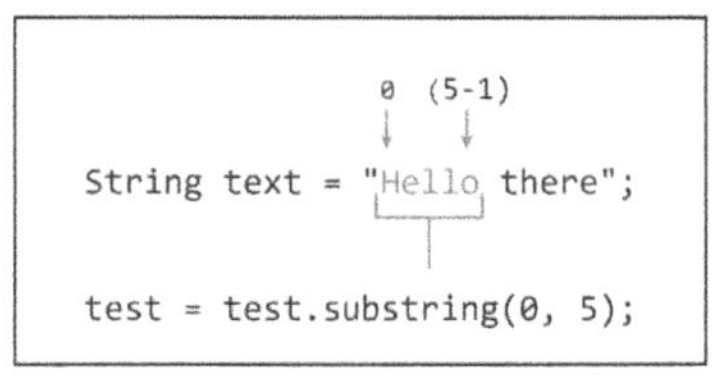

Figure 3.3. Use of the `.substring()` Method with Index Arguments

Academic journals will often list authors of papers in the format of "last name, first initial." Taking several author names and using the `.substring()` method, you can adhere to this author name formatting style as follows (in this example, the blank space character index positions have been "found" for you already):

Code Snippet 3.13

```
String firstAuthor = "Noor Malik";
String secondAuthor = "Sarah Meyerson";

String formattedAuthorOne = firstAuthor.substring(5)
        + ", "
        + firstAuthor.substring(0, 1)
        + ".";

String formattedAuthorTwo = secondAuthor.substring(6)
        + ", "
```

```
        + secondAuthor.substring(0, 1)
        + ".";

System.out.println("Paper Authors: "
        + formattedAuthorOne + ", "
        + formattedAuthorTwo);
```

The console output from this example would be the following:

```
Paper Authors: Malik, N., Meyerson, S.
```

Searching text: In the academic journal author example earlier, the index location for the blank space characters was provided for each. If you were processing several thousand author names in this way, it would be **very tedious** to manually count index positions in each until a blank space is found. Instead, you can let Java do all the hard work of finding these. There are several very useful methods that will search a `String` variable and provide various pieces of information as results. Table 3.3 details two useful methods and their overloads for `String` searches (this is **not** an exhaustive list; explore the documentation for the `String` class to see the other overloaded versions!):

Table 3.3. Some `String` Instance Methods Used for Searching

Instance method header and parameters	Description
`int indexOf(String str)`	Returns the index position of the first occurrence of the `String` str in the `String` the method is invoked upon. If the search string value is not found, the method returns -1.
`int indexOf(String str, int fromIndex)`	Returns the index position of the first occurrence of the `String` str in the `String` the method is invoked on, starting the search at position `fromIndex`. If the search text value is not found, the method returns -1.
`int lastIndexOf(String str)`	Returns the index position of the last occurrence of the `String` str in the `String` the method is invoked upon.
`int lastIndexOf(String str, int fromIndex)`	Returns the index position of the last occurrence of the `String` str in the `String` the method is invoked upon, starting the search backward from the position `fromIndex`.
`boolean contains(String str)`	Returns a true or false if the `String` the method is invoked upon contains the value of the `String` str. Does not indicate position or quantity of occurrence.

The first version of method `.indexOf()` is useful if you know the smaller string value searched for only occurs once in a larger `String`. For example, in the author names, the business data may only keep first and last names, so you can assume that only one blank space character occurs in the string. By using `.indexOf()`, you can find the index position of the blank space in each name `String`:

Code Snippet 3.14

```
String firstAuthor = "Noor Malik";
String secondAuthor = "Sarah Meyerson";
System.out.println(firstAuthor.indexOf(" "));
System.out.println(secondAuthor.indexOf(" "));
```

This would print the following to the console:

```
4
5
```

Here the language does all the hard work of finding the location of the blank spaces. Adapting the prior example makes this name-processing logic a little "smarter":

Code Snippet 3.15

```
String firstAuthor = "Noor Malik";
String secondAuthor = "Sarah Meyerson";
String formattedAuthorOne =
        firstAuthor.substring(firstAuthor.indexOf(" ")+1)
        + ", "
        + firstAuthor.substring(0, 1)
        + ".";

String formattedAuthorTwo =
        secondAuthor.substring(secondAuthor.indexOf(" ")+1)
        + ", "
        + secondAuthor.substring(0, 1)
        + ".";

System.out.println("Paper Authors: "
        + formattedAuthorOne + ", "
        + formattedAuthorTwo);
```

This code produces the same console output as in the earlier example. In order to capture the last name, start the substring at the next position **after** the blank space's position by adding `1` to the `int` result that `.indexOf()` returns back.

Searching and `.substring()` used together: Full words can be searched for within a `String` also. For example, you can find the location of a word and extract the two names from the `String` by nesting method invocations:

Code Snippet 3.16

```
String namePair = "Alora and Emery";
String firstName = namePair.substring(0, namePair.indexOf("and")-1);
String secondName = namePair.substring(namePair.indexOf("and")+4);
System.out.println(firstName + ", " + secondName);
```

In this case, you have foreknowledge that there are two first names in the `String` separated by the word "and" in the middle. The code extracts these two names in the following way:

- The method `.indexOf()` is nested and invoked to search the `String` for the starting position of the word "and" in the variable `namePair`.
- The first name starts at index position 0, so the first call to `.substring()` uses a starting position of 0 in the first parameter.
- The second parameter of the `.substring()` call is the result from the call to `.indexOf()` with `1` subtracted to omit the first blank space.

This will extract the first name "Alora" from the `String`. The second name is extracted as follows:

- First, invoke `.indexOf()` to find the starting position of the word "and" in `namePair`. The value of `4` is added to this to refer to the first character following the blank space that follows "and."
- This call to `.indexOf()` is nested within the call to `.substring()`. Since this is the one-parameter version of the method, it will extract characters all the way to the end of the `String`.

This will extract the second name, "Emery," from the variable `namePair`.

StringIndexOutOfBoundsException: In the name example, you can see an assumption that has been made: that there are actually four more characters in the `String` value following the starting point of the second name. If this assumption is not true, an **index out of bounds** error will be generated on the substring attempt. Consider the following example that attempts to capture all the words in a sentence after the word "and":

Code Snippet 3.17

```
String longString = "trouble if the last word is and";
System.out.println(
        longString.substring(
                longString.indexOf("and") + 4));
```

If you execute this code, you will receive an error message (part of which is displayed here):

```
Exception in thread "main" java.lang.StringIndexOutOfBoundsException
```

Our code attempts to start the substring **beyond** the end of the `String` variable's last index position! This throws a `StringIndexOutOfBoundsException`. Later in the textbook, you will see how to test for this first before the attempt can generate an error.

The other version of `.indexOf()` is useful when the `String` you are searching for occurs multiple times (or you have information that states that it definitely will) in a larger `String`. Again, consider the following example, using the sentence that caused the error above:

Code Snippet 3.18

```
String longString = "trouble if the last word is and";
System.out.println(longString.lastIndexOf(" "));
```

The console output from this would be the following:

```
27
```

This will give you the position of the **last occurrence** of the blank space character that occurs in the string. If you were to use just `.indexOf()`, it would give you only the **first occurrence** of the blank space character. Using clever loop logic you will learn in chapter 5, you can extract each and every word from a `String` through the use of both of these methods and their overloaded versions. The two-parameter version of `.lastIndexOf()` will give you the last occurrence of text present in the `String` **before** the `fromIndex`, like so:

Code Snippet 3.19

```
String longString = "trouble if the last word is and";
System.out.println(
        longString.lastIndexOf(
                " ", longString.lastIndexOf(" ") - 1));
```

Notice that the invocations of these methods are nested. The innermost `.lastIndexOf()` executes first. It will return position `27` from the long `String`. Because you do not want the outermost call to `.lastIndexOf()` to also return the position of that last blank space, subtract `1` from the result so the search looks *behind* the location of that last blank space. The console output from this would be the following:

```
24
```

This is the index position of the second to last blank space character in the `String`. Finally, the `.contains()` method also performs a search, but it merely returns a `bool` value of `true` or `false` if the `String` value being searched for is found at all:

Code Snippet 3.20

```
String listOfNames = "Rainey Oaklee Saanvi Selene";
System.out.println(listOfNames.contains("Saanvi"));
```

The console output for this would be the following:

```
true
```

This method can only tell us if the `String` it is invoked upon simply contains the smaller `String` or not, not the location within or the number of occurrences.

SUMMARY POINTS

- A substring is a smaller, usually extracted part of a larger `String`. The `String` class in Java has several methods for extracting a substring.
- Index notation refers to the "map" of elements in a sequence of data. For a `String`, these elements are the individual characters. Index notation provides a convenient way to assign a position number to each character in a `String`, starting with `0` for the first character and so on.

- The last character in a `String` variable is always at position `n - 1`, where `n` is the number of characters in the `String` value stored within. The first character is always at index position `0`.
- If you attempt to use an index position in a `String` that doesn't exist, then Java will throw a `StringIndexOutOfBounds` error and not complete the operation. This can occur if you attempt to use a location **before** the start of the `String` (a negative index position) or after the **end** of the `String` (a position that is >= `n`).
- Java has several methods for searching a `String` for a text value. The method `.indexOf()` returns an int index position of the location of the start of the first occurrence of the searched-for value. The method `.lastIndexOf()` performs the same task but reports the last position in the `String` of the value. Lastly, the `.contains()` method simply reports if the value is present at all in the `String`, with no information on the value's location.

QUICK PROBLEMS

1. **Coding:** Create a `String`, and take note of how many characters are present in its value. Use the `.substring()` method, and extract the second half of the `String`. Print this extracted substring to the console.
2. **Think:** What will happen if you attempt to start a substring extraction at a larger index position and end it at a smaller one?
3. **Coding:** Create a `String` with the following value: "`java JAVA jAvA java`." Write some code that will extract the middle two "java" words from the `String` and print them to the console.

3.3 Other Useful String Methods

There are many other instance methods that are available to programmers who need to use the `String` class to successfully manipulate text in their Java applications. Table 3.4 lists these with descriptions and examples of usages following (again there are overloaded second versions of these methods that are not listed here; the official Oracle documentation for the `String` class discusses these other versions):

Table 3.4. Other Useful Instance Methods of the `String` Class

Instance method header and parameters	Description
`int length()`	Returns the length of the `String` it is invoked upon.
`char charAt(int index)`	Returns a copy of the character primitive value at the parameter index position of the `String` it is invoked upon.
`String trim()`	Deletes all the blank space characters from the beginning and end of the `String` it is invoked upon. Returns the "cleaned-up" version of the `String`.
`int compareTo(String secondString)`	Returns an int whose value represents a relative comparison, alphabetically and lexicographically, between the parameter `String` and the `String` the method is invoked upon.
`String concat(String secondString)`	Returns a `String` that is the concatenated version of the parameter `String` and the `String` the method is invoked upon. Similar to the work the addition operator does.
`String toUpperCase()`	Returns a `String` where every character in the `String` upon which the method was invoked has been converted to an uppercase version.
`String toLowerCase()`	Returns a `String` where every character in the String upon which the method was invoked has been converted to a lowercase version.

`.length()` method: This method is an easy way to find the length of a `String`. This is the total length, including blank space and any other characters in the `String`:

Code Snippet 3.21

```
String listOfNames = "Rainey Oaklee Saanvi Selene";
System.out.println(listOfNames.length() + " characters long!");
```

Console output:

```
27 characters long!
```

`.charAt()` method: This is a great way to extract a single character from a single position in a `String` without having to overcomplicate your code using `.substring()` when you do not need to (though it is always OK to use it):

Code Snippet 3.22

```
String listOfNames = "Rainey Oaklee Saanvi Selene";
System.out.println(
        listOfNames.charAt(0)
                + " - "
                + listOfNames.charAt(
                        listOfNames.length()-1));
```

With this example, you are gathering the first character (at index position `0`) and the last character (at position `.length() - 1`) and printing both characters in a decorative manner. The console output here would be the following:

```
R - e
```

Remember that because of index notation, the last character is always at position `n - 1`, never at position `n` (if you attempted to extract the character at position n, you would throw a `StringIndexOutOfBoundsException`—there is no character at position `n`!).

`.trim()` method: This method can be handy in helping increase the quality of data by cleaning up extra blank space characters at the beginning and end of a `String`. In this example, the resulting `String` itself is printed with decorative brackets so you can see the cleanup occur:

Code Snippet 3.23

```
String leadingBlanks = "        Hello";
String trailingBlanks = "There        ";
System.out.println("[" + leadingBlanks + " " + trailingBlanks + "]");
leadingBlanks = leadingBlanks.trim();
trailingBlanks = trailingBlanks.trim();
System.out.println("[" + leadingBlanks + " " + trailingBlanks + "]");
```

Here is what will print to the console when this code executes:

```
[        Hello There        ]
[Hello There]
```

The `.trim()` method will remove both leading and trailing blank spaces at the same time if both are present in the same `String`:

Code Snippet 3.24

```
String leadingBlanks = "        Hello";
String trailingBlanks = "There        ";
String fullPhrase = leadingBlanks + " " + trailingBlanks;
System.out.println("[" + fullPhrase + "]");
fullPhrase = fullPhrase.trim();
System.out.println("[" + fullPhrase + "]");
```

Console output would be the following:

```
[        Hello There        ]
[Hello There]
```

`.compareTo()` **method:** This method provides an easy way to compare `String` variables lexicographically (*think:* alphabetically!). This means that the letters, their order in the English alphabet, and their quantity are all compared. The value that is returned can be a little confusing. Stated simply,

- The method will return a value that is **less than zero (negative)** if the invoked-upon `String` precedes the parameter `String` alphabetically.
- The method will return a value that is **greater than zero (positive)** if the invoked-upon `String` follows the parameter `String` alphabetically.
- The method will return **exactly zero** if the two `String` values are exactly the same.

Some examples:

Code Snippet 3.25

```
String wordOne = "bat";
String wordTwo = "batter";
String wordThree = "referee";
System.out.println(wordOne.compareTo(wordTwo));
System.out.println(wordThree.compareTo(wordTwo));
```

The console output for this would be the following:

```
-3
16
```

Notice how in the first comparison of "bat" (invoked-upon `String`) with "batter" (the parameter `String`), the result is `-3`. Less than `0` means that the invoked-upon `String` alphabetically precedes the parameter. For the comparison of "referee" to "batter," the result returned is `16`. Oracle describes `.compareTo()` as providing the "lexicographic" difference in `String` values. To clarify with some examples,

Code Snippet 3.26

```
String wordOne = "bat";
String wordTwo = "bas";
System.out.println(wordOne.compareTo(wordTwo));
```

The output for this would be `1`. Why? Notice that both words are the same number of characters. The `String` `wordOne` ends in `t`, which is one English alphabet letter past "`s`." If you were alphabetically arranging these words in order, a difference of `1` means "`bat`" is the word right in front of "`bas`."

Code Snippet 3.27

```
String wordOne = "arr";
String wordTwo = "atv";
System.out.println(wordOne.compareTo(wordTwo));
```

Here the result is `-2`. Even though the last letters of both words are four English alphabet characters apart, if you were arranging these words in order of spelling, the second letter would determine the order first. Since `r` is two letters behind `t`, `wordOne` would be two places behind `wordTwo`.

Code Snippet 3.28

```
String wordOne = "Zoom";
String wordTwo = "Zoo";
System.out.println(wordOne.compareTo(wordTwo));
```

The output here would be `1`. In this case, "`Zoom`" would alphabetically come right after "`Zoo`," since the first three letters in both words are the same.

These values above or below zero give you a **relative sense** of how strongly a word precedes or follows the other. For logic purposes, a simple check of above or below zero will tell you most of what you need to know about the results of the text comparison. This method is great for sorting lists of names, words, and so on. What about words of the same length and those in which most of the characters are the same? Consider this example:

Code Snippet 3.29

```
String wordOne = "farmed";
String wordTwo = "farmer";
System.out.println(wordOne.compareTo(wordTwo));
```

The output would be the following:

```
-14
```

The only character that differs between these two words is the last one. The letter `d` precedes the letter `r` by quite a bit (fourteen letters), which is indicated by the strongly negative value returned.

`.toUpperCase()` **and** `.toLowerCase()`**:** These methods are fairly self-explanatory: they will produce a version of an invoked-upon `String` that has all characters converted to either uppercase (in the former) or lowercase (in the latter). Keep in mind that these methods will **not** alter an existing `String` but only produce an altered copy of the `String` value. What this means is that the following will not do what you might initially think it will:

Code Snippet 3.30

```
String city = "Greenfield";
city.toUpperCase();
System.out.println(city);
```

Console output:

```
Greenfield
```

Notice that there were no changes made to the `String city` at all. These methods, like other `String` class methods that return a `String` value, return a new `String` version of the invoked-upon `String` that you need to store or use somewhere. You can overwrite the same `String` as follows:

Code Snippet 3.31

```
String city = "Greenfield";
city = city.toUpperCase();
System.out.println(city);
city = city.toLowerCase();
System.out.println(city);
```

Console output:

```
GREENFIELD
greenfield
```

Notice that the result of the method overwrites the same `String` variable in order to see the conversion reflected in that variable. You can also print the return from the methods into `.println()` as you have done with numerous examples already.

SUMMARY POINTS

- Java's `String` class also contains methods that allow for the alteration and manipulation of text values. These methods return an altered copy of the `String` that can then be set as the new object to be referenced by a `String` reference variable, used in another String expression, or printed (among other uses).
- The `String` class method `.length()` will report the number of characters in a `String` as an integer. The index positions for all the characters in that `String` will range from `0` to `length - 1`.
- The method `.compareTo()` will compare `String` variables lexicographically, returning an integer that represents a relative position (negative for preceding, positive for following) of one `String` to another alphabetically.
- Method `.charAt()` returns the single character located at its parameter int index location in the `String`. The programmer must be careful that the intended index position in the `String` exists.

QUICK PROBLEMS

1. **Coding:** Create a `String` with a long sentence or phrase stored within it. Use the `.length()` method and determine the index position of the middle character. Use the `.substring()` method to extract the first half of the `String` using the determined middle position.
2. **Think:** What happens if the length of a `String` is an odd number and you try to determine the middle character? What happens if the length is an even number?
3. **Coding:** Create a small `String` with one to two short words within. Using only the topics learned up until this point, use the `.charAt()` method to capture every second character and concatenate it into a new `String`. Print that `String` value to the console. Avoid any `String IndexOutOfBounds` errors!

3.4 Formatting Strings for Display

Printing to the console is a convenience that allows us to quickly see the results of code and expressions in your applications. Learning how to format `String`-based output **in general** will help you display output in a business-report-appropriate manner. The output may be sent to the console or, later, to a user interface or other destinations. Displaying dates, formatting spacing of strings, determining how many decimals to "round up" to, displaying monetary amounts—these are just a few of the common scenarios professionals in information systems face as they work with data and strive for high-quality data in decision-making contexts.

Using escape sequences: An **escape sequence** is a formatting command that you can place right inside a `String` value itself. When Java attempts to display that `String` (either in the console output or in a GUI element), it will see and process that command according to the command type. The name "escape sequence" basically means that a flag is placed next to a command character, telling it to "escape" from the `String` and allow itself to be processed as a command (instead of another character). Each command involves a slash ("\") and the format command character. Table 3.5 details the escape sequences in the Java language and their usage, listed in descending order of commonality of usage (well, according to this author, anyway!):

Table 3.5. Escape Sequences and Their Usages

Escape sequence	Description
`\n`	Inserts a new-line character (invisible) into the `String`, causing what follows to appear on a separate line of output. Similar to what `.println()` does at the end of printed `String` values.
`\t`	Inserts a tab character and moves the text that follows to the next built-in tab stop position (how far it moves depends on the length of the `String` value behind this command).
`\"`	Inserts a double quote into the `String` as part of the text itself.
`\\`	Inserts a slash into the string. Handy for building file path `String` values.
`\'`	Inserts a single quote into the `String`.
`\b`	Inserts a backspace character that essentially deletes the one character behind it.
`\r`	Inserts a form feed character into the `String`.
`\f`	Inserts a carriage return into the `String`.

The new-line escape sequence is very common, especially when you are formatting multiline output along with concatenated values, method returns, or expression calculations. For example,

Code Snippet 3.32

```
String newLines = "Practice\nyour\nJava\nevery\nday!";
System.out.println(newLines);
```

would produce the console output

```
Practice
your
Java
every
day!
```

A simple addition of the tab escape sequence can demonstrate its usage:

Code Snippet 3.33

```
String newLines = "Practice\n\tyour\nJava\n\tevery\nday!";
System.out.println(newLines);
```

This displays the following:

```
Practice
   your
Java
   every
day!
```

Notice that the tab command comes after the new-line command. The new-line escape sequence is processed, and then the tab command applies to the next line of output. Usage of the others is very similar, as you will see in these examples:

Code Snippet 3.34

```
String compliments = "They described her as a \"Great Programmer\""
        +  " and \"Highly Skilled\"";

System.out.println(compliments);

String filePath = "C:\\Windows\\Program Files\\Java\\";

System.out.println("Java is installed at: " + filePath);

String myName = "theAuthor\b\b\b";
System.out.println(myName);
```

These would display as

```
They described her as a "Great Programmer" and "Highly Skilled"
Java is installed at: C:\Windows\Program Files\Java\
theAut
```

Notice also that the backspace escape sequence inserts actual backspace "keystrokes" into the `String` output, deleting the last three characters (because three backspace escape-sequence commands were inserted). For the `String` variable `filePath`, the slash escape sequence prevents Java from attempting to process the slash as part of the language syntax and instead inserts a slash into the `String` at that position. Escape sequences can be very useful in many scenarios.

Using the static method `.format()`: There are a few **static** methods of the `String` class that are highly useful (remember, static means you invoke the method by calling it upon the name of the class itself, not any of its instance objects). One in particular is the overloaded `.format()` method. This method will apply formatting commands to "chunks" of data that you would like inserted into a `String` that you will eventually print/display. It uses a **format specifier** syntax with various commands and flags, similar to escape sequences.

The method header for the relevant version of `.format()` is

```
static String format(String stringToAlter, Object... argumentsToInsert)
```

The first parameter is a `String` into which data will be inserted (single or multiple) and formatted (i.e., rounded to two decimal places, etc.). The second parameter uses an ellipsis, which basically means that you can place **one or more parameters** after the first. For example, both

Code Snippet 3.35

```
// Three arguments, each would be positions 1, 2, and 3
String newString = String.format(someString, 10.4, "Avery", 105.2);
```

and

Code Snippet 3.36

```
// Using only one argument, it is at position 1
String newString = String.format(someString, 109.2323122);
```

would be valid. You can format and insert into the `String` as many arguments as you need to. The `.format()` method returns the new version of the `String someString` with the data formatted and inserted into it.

Format specifiers: A **format specifier** is a bit more complicated than an escape-sequence command. You can use **one** or **more** format specifiers in a `String` you are using in the `.format()` method. As many as you need. The following shows the basic structure of a format specifier command. For convenience, brackets have been used here to separate out the various "parts" of the command that are optional and can change depending on the formatting command you choose to use. The brackets are **not** part of the command, and you will see them omitted with examples later:

```
%[argument_index_number$][flags][width][.precision]conversionCommand
```

The parts that are **required** for a single format specifier command are the percent sign (`%`) at the start and the `conversionCommand` at the end (both in **bold**). No matter what other optional choices in between these two you include, **you have to include these** for Java to recognize it as a format specifier command. For the other parts,

- The `argument_index_number` is **not** an index notation. It simply allows you to refer to a specific argument that follows in the parameters. If you do not include this, Java assumes that each argument at the end, left to right, corresponds to each format specifier "placeholder" in the string, also left to right inside the string. The first refers to the first, the second to the second, and so on. If you do include this value, you **have** to include the dollar sign (`$`) attached to the number (example to follow).
- The **flags** allow you to do various things, like left- and right-justify text within a certain width/area, show negative numbers in a different way, display large integers in location-/country-specific manners, and so on.
- **Width** allows you to force whatever is displayed to be shown within a certain width of characters. For example, you could make 4.25 display in a space that is always ten characters wide (using blank spaces), even though 4.25 is only four characters wide itself. This helps with formatting and alignment!
- The **precision** flag allows you to force rounding up to a certain number of decimals for floating-point numbers like doubles. Notice the dot (`.`) attached to the word "precision" in the template above. You must include the dot attached to a number for Java to understand you want to use decimal place rounding. The number 101.346223 with a precision flag of "`.2`" would round up to 101.35 when it is inserted into the string.

Some common values for all these options are shown later, and you can examine the official Oracle documentation to learn about more formatting commands.* First is a simple example where a `double` that is rounded to two decimal places is inserted into the `String`:

Code Snippet 3.37

```
String testString = "";
testString = String.format("%.2f", 2.456332d);
System.out.println(testString);
```

This would produce the output

```
2.46
```

* https://docs.oracle.com/javase/9/docs/api/java/util/Formatter.html.

Notice that for the first parameter of the `.format()` method, a `String` literal is used, and there is only **one** format specifier command within. This means only one data argument will be needed as additional parameters for `.format()`. Notice as well that the % is there, and the `f` is the `conversionCommand`: "Convert the incoming argument to a floating-point number." The floating-point conversion command also **rounded up** to the `double` value! The value in the only argument (the second parameter) is converted according to the command type, then it is inserted into the `String` at the **exact** location where the format specifier (*think:* placeholder) is located. It is a useful and efficient syntax. This example can be expanded to show the placeholder nature of these format specifiers:

Code Snippet 3.38

```
String testString =
        "A large cup of coffee costs $%.2f as of yesterday";
testString = String.format(testString, 2.462332d);
System.out.println(testString);
```

This would display the following to the console:

```
A large cup of coffee costs $2.46 as of yesterday
```

Figure 3.4 shows this multistep process of format, insert, and result.

Notice that you can place your text that contains format specifiers into a `String` variable, or you can build it "in-line" as you did in the first example. Java will not mind either way. If you want to control alignment and spacing, think about these examples (notice that a decorative bracket is used in the `String` itself to show you the spacing; the bracket is **not part** of the format specifier command, which is in **bold** in the example):

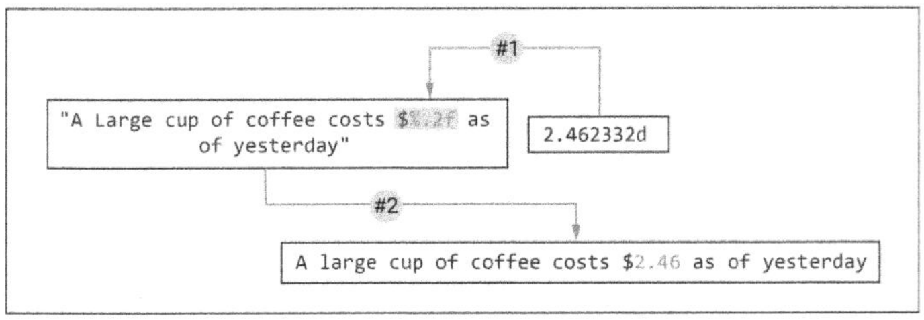

Figure 3.4. Formatting and Inserting a Value into a `String` with a Format Specifier

Code Snippet 3.39

```
String testString = " ";

testString = String.format("[%15.2f]", 2.546223d);
System.out.println(testString);

testString = String.format("[%-15.2f]", 2.546223d);
System.out.println(testString);
```

When these display, the results look like the following:

```
[           2.55]
[2.55           ]
```

Notice how the incoming `double` is formatted as a floating-point (i.e., decimal) value and rounded to two decimal places. The incoming value is forced to display in an area that is **always** fifteen characters wide, no matter how long the value itself is. Notice that with the first format, the value is right-justified by default. A **flag**, the minus sign, is added to the second format example to force a left-justify of the incoming value within the fifteen-character space. This is very useful: you can display values and keep them aligned for a neat-looking report in an information system, no matter the lengths of the numeric values you are displaying! If you divide up the format specifier used in the example into the optional template areas described earlier, they would partition out like so:

```
%[argument_index_number$][flags][width][.precision]conversionCommand
%[    ][-][15][.2]f
```

Notice that the argument index is not used, since there is only one argument (usage of this is optional anyway).

Working with whole numbers is just as easy. Consider the following examples (brackets have been included in these examples so that you can see just where the format specifier command is inserting the data argument; they are not required):

Code Snippet 3.40

```
// Integers

String testString = "";
testString = String.format("[%d]", 316000000);
System.out.println(testString);
testString = String.format("[%,d]", 316000000);
System.out.println(testString);
testString = String.format("[%,20d]", 316000000);
System.out.println(testString);
testString = String.format("[%-,20d]", 316000000);
System.out.println(testString);
Console output for this code:
[316000000]
[316,000,000]
[         316,000,000]
[316,000,000         ]
```

Notice that the comma flag (,) is used to force the integer to display in a locale-specific way, meaning Java takes account of your computer's country/location settings for how whole numbers should be displayed. The conversion command for displaying as an integer is "d."

Using two or more format specifiers in a `String` is relatively straightforward. Consider this example:

Code Snippet 3.41

```
String employee = "Calliope";
int salary = 125000;
double timeWithCompany = 4.3263423;

String display = "%s has worked for %.1f years and makes $%,d a year!";
System.out.println(
        String.format(display, employee, timeWithCompany, salary));
```

This will produce the output

```
Calliope has worked for 4.3 years and makes $125,000 a year!
```

The `String` variable `display` contains text with three format specifiers. When used in the `.format()` method, the variable is included along with three other variables that contain the data to format. As Java processes the format specifiers in the `String`, it uses the first variable (the first argument) as the incoming data that will be formatted and "dropped in place" where the first format specifier is. Same for the second and same for the third.

Displaying the time and date can be tricky in many programming languages. Working with them in your application's logic can be even trickier! But it is important to understand how to both display and use dates and times in your code to ensure you develop a modern and useful application. The `.format()` command allows you to format the display of the value stored in a `LocalDateTime` class object (among others). Include the following import in a Java main class file:

Code Snippet 3.42

```
import java.time.LocalDateTime; // java.time.* would work too
```

After this, some format specifiers for displaying the **current** date and time can be used:

Code Snippet 3.43

```
LocalDateTime ldt = LocalDateTime.now(); // LocalDateTime object
String testString = "";
testString = String.format("%tA, %tB %te %tY", ldt, ldt, ldt, ldt);
System.out.println(testString);
```

The conversion command for date and time conversions starts with a percent sign (as all format specifiers do) and then the letter `t`. This is then followed by a secondary command that lets you grab a certain part of the date/time value (the day, the month, the year, name of the day, name of the month, etc.). If you run this code, it will produce the following output:

```
Sunday, March 7 2021
```

Notice in the example here that the same variable, `ldt`, is used for each and every argument. Since this is a bit repetitive, you can simplify the usage via the `argument_index$` option to tell each format specifier to use the same single argument (an index position followed by the dollar sign):

Code Snippet 3.44

```
testString = String.format("%1$tA, %1$tB %1$te %1$tY", ldt);
```

Use the number `1` followed by the dollar sign to indicate that you want each format specifier to use the variable at parameter index `1`. Mapping out the first of the format specifiers done earlier looks like the following:

```
%[argument_index_number$][flags][width][.precision]conversionCommand
%[1$][ ][ ][  ]tA
```

Notice that you do not have to use the other options if you do not need them. Another shortcut to referring to the same format argument is to tell each successive format specifier after the first to use the argument that **the previous format specifier used**. You can do this by using the less-than symbol (<) as an argument index command. Notice that the first format specifier assumes default order, meaning since it is the first format specifier, it will use the first argument listed at the end. The rest will use the one prior to it and so on:

Code Snippet 3.45

```
testString = String.format("%tA, %<tB %<te %<tY", ldt);
```

This produces the same output as earlier:

```
Sunday, March 7 2021
```

Here are a few more examples of how to display date times in different ways using some built-in "shortcut" format specifier commands that produce preformatted date/time strings that are useful when you are in a hurry:

Code Snippet 3.46

```
LocalDateTime ldt = LocalDateTime.now();
String testString = "";

// HH:MM:SS 24-Hour
testString = String.format("%tT", LocalDateTime.now());
System.out.println(testString);

// HH:MM:SS 12-Hour with AM/PM
testString = String.format("%tr", LocalDateTime.now());
System.out.println(testString);

// YYYY-MM-DD
testString = String.format("%tF", LocalDateTime.now());
System.out.println(testString);
```

These will produce the following console output:

```
12:18:20
12:18:20 PM
2021-03-07
```

In the next few tables, some of the possible values/flags that you can use for each optional part of a format specifier command are listed. Note that each character is in single quotes, but you *will not* include single quotes in a format command:

Table 3.6. More Common Conversion Command Characters Used in Format Specifiers

Conversion character	Description
`'f'`	Formats the incoming argument as a floating-point number (like a double or float).
`'s'` or `'S'`	Formats the incoming argument as a `String`.
`'d'`	Formats the incoming argument like a whole number (int).
`'g'` or `'G'`	Formats the incoming argument as a floating-point number in scientific notation (i.e., 1.22134e+09).
`'t'` or `'T'`	Formats the incoming argument as part of a date/time value. This letter is followed by a second date/time-specific command character.

Table 3.7. Commonly Used Format Specifier Flags

Format specifier flag	Description
`'-'`	Flag for forcing the display of the formatted argument in a left-justified manner. If you do not include this flag, then right-justify is the default display.
`'+'`	Flag for forcing the sign for a numeric value to always be displayed for both negative and positive numbers.
`','`	Flag for forcing the location-specific style for displaying a number to be used.
`'('`	Flag for forcing negative numbers to be displayed in an "accounting" style of parentheses.

Table 3.8. Secondary Conversion Characters Focused on Time and Date Formatting

Conversion characters focused on time (used following the `t` or `T` character)	
`'I '`	Displays the hour in a twelve-hour format
`'H'`	Displays the hour in a twenty-four-hour format
`'M'`	Displays the minutes
`'S'`	Displays the seconds
`'L'`	Displays the milliseconds
`'p'`	Displays "a.m." or "p.m."
`'s'`	Displays the number of seconds that have elapsed since January 1, 1970 (Unix time)
`'Q'`	Displays the number of milliseconds that have elapsed since January 1, 1970 (Unix time)
Conversion characters focused on the date (used following the `t` or `T` character)	
`'B'` or `'b'`	Displays the full month or the abbreviated month (e.g., "August" or "Aug")
`'A'` or `'a'`	Displays the full day of the week or the abbreviated day (e.g., "Friday" or "Fri")
`'Y'` or `'y'`	Displays the year as YYYY or YY
`'m'`	Displays the number equivalent of a month (e.g., May would be `05`)
`'e'` or `'d'`	Displays the day of the month without a leading zero or with a leading zero (e.g., `5` vs. `05`)
`'j'`	Displays what numbered day it is in the year (e.g., `167`)
"Shortcut" conversion characters that produce preformatted date/time strings	
`'r'`	Produces a time string of "HH:MM:SS a.m./p.m."
`'D'`	Produces a date string of "MM/DD/YY"
`'F'`	Produces a more international date string of "YYYY-MM-DD"
`'c'`	Produces a conveniently built full date/time string of "DayName Month DD HH:MM:SS Timezone YYYY"

Final note on the use of `.format()`: The beauty of using the static `.format()` static method of the `String` class is that once you have formatted a `String` value and stored it in a variable, you can display or write that value anywhere, not just the console. You can display the formatted `String` values in labels, text boxes, and other controls in a graphical user interface (GUI). Additionally, formatted `String` values can be stored in a database table or in an external file, transmitted across a network, and so on. Alternatively, a companion method to `.println()` called `.printf()` allows you to print a `String` value using the same formatting commands used throughout this chapter. But `.printf()` only sends the formatted `String` to the console and does not make it otherwise available to your application. Use of `.format()` is the recommended technique.

SUMMARY POINTS

- Escape sequences are simple commands that can alter the structure and, to a lesser extent, the contents of a `String` variable. They "escape" some characters so that these characters are treated as actual characters and not part of the command syntax the language interprets in other contexts.
- The `String` class method `.format()` is static, meaning it must be invoked upon the class `String` name itself and not upon any particular instance object.
- The `.format()` method allows for a much more sophisticated and compact formatting syntax for `String` variables, giving the programmer the ability to format numbers and text, ensure columnar alignment, and easily format the display of dates and times in several convenient ways.

QUICK PROBLEMS

1. **Coding:** Write a small Java program where you divide two double numbers. Print the resulting double value with four decimal places of accuracy to the console.
2. **Think:** Why is it useful to be able to specify the default width/number of columns for a numeric value to print in output? How does this help any output look professional and business appropriate?
3. **Coding:** Write a small Java program that displays **your** current date in the following manner to the console (*Hint:* use the format flags in table 3.8):

```
Today is the 13th day of May in the year
2024
```

Summary

The `String` class in Java is, first and foremost, your first deep look at an instantiable class that contains a mix of instance and static methods. `String` variables form the basic level of text usage and manipulation in the Java language. `String` class methods are useful and diverse and allow for the manipulation and formatting of text output, comparison of text values, and extraction of substrings, among other uses. This examination of the `String` class not only provides a great deal of practice with object-oriented concepts in Java but also highlights the `String` class's nature as a complex data type containing a sequence of data mapped with index notation. It is a great preview of more advanced syntax to come. For information systems professionals, the ability to manipulate text programmatically touches upon areas of data quality, enabling better decision-making and more effective prompting and reporting to the users of implemented systems. Whereas before your experience with manipulation of text data may have been limited to spreadsheets or even tools built by others, you now have the ability to develop your own flexible text-processing routines in the context of the systems you develop. As you progress through the Java syntax, you will come back to the skills learned in this chapter over and over. More intermediate Java language features will make these text manipulation techniques even more useful.

Practice Problems

Terminology

Match the following terms from the chapter with their most appropriate definition:

1. `String` literal	a. A method of mapping out the location of individual elements in a sequence of data stored in complex variables in Java.
2. `String`	b. A technique in Java of creating another method using the same name but differing in some other aspect, usually in the parameters.
3. Substring	c. A `String` class method that reports the index position of a searched String value in a larger String.
4. Concatenation	d. A variable that contains the address of an instance object located on the heap.
5. Text block	e. A type of error that occurs when an index position that does not exist is attempted to be used in a String.
6. Blank space	f. A `String` formatting command that can alter the structure or contents of a String value.
7. `.equals()`	g. A `String` class method that returns the int value of the number of characters in a `String` object's stored value.
8. `.compareTo()`	h. A character that represents a specific formatting command.
9. Reference variable	i. A `String` class method that will remove leading and trailing blank space characters from a `String`.
10. Instance method	j. Data targeted for formatting and to be inserted into a copied `String` value.
11. Index notation	k. A smaller `String` value extracted from a larger one.
12. `.length()`	l. A `String` class method that allows for formatting commands and associated data targeted for formatting to be inserted into a copied `String` value.
13. Method overloading	m. A character that displays visually as an empty space.
14. Method parameter	n. The action of "gluing" together two different string values.
15. `.substring()`	o. A formatting command that changes data external to a `String` according to the specific command used and inserts that formatted value into the String at the command's location.
16. `.contains()`	p. A value that consists of a sequence of characters.
17. Index out of bounds error	q. A type of Java class method that is meant to be invoked upon instance objects of that class.
18. `.indexOf()`	r. A `String` class method that compares the string values stored inside `String` instance objects.
19. `.trim()`	s. A type of `String` variable that maintains new-line and tab characters as typed in when the variable is initialized.
20. Escape sequence	t. A `String` class method that will search an invoked-upon `String` for a parameter `String` value and return a boolean value that reports if the searched value is present in the larger String.
21. Format specifier	u. A `String` class method that compares two string values in a lexicographic manner.
22. Conversion character	v. A Java class that allows for the storage and manipulation of text values.
23. `.format()`	w. A `String` class method that extracts a smaller string value from a larger, invoked-upon `String` object using parameters to determine the range of characters extracted.
24. Format argument	x. A variable or value that is "passed" to a method through its parentheses.

Find the Error

In each of the following problems, carefully examine the code given, and determine the error(s)/issue(s) with each. Keep in mind, the error(s) could be syntax (code) or logic (intended outcome) based or both!

1.

```
// Extracting the word "cat" from the String varA:
String varA = "dog cat bird gerbil hamster chicken";
        System.out.println(varA.substring(varA.indexOf("cat"), 0));
```

2.

```
// Concatenate first and last name:
        String firstName = "Ellison";
        String lastName = "Bexley";
        firstName = lastName;
        System.out.println(firstName);
```

3.

```
// Extracting the word "dog" from the String varA:
        String varA = "dog cat bird gerbil hamster chicken";
        System.out.println(
                varA.substring(
                        varA.indexOf("dog") - varA.length(), 4));
```

4.

```
System.out.println("Stated Nickname: "Bexley", Age: 31");
```

5.

```
System.out.println(
        String.format(
                "Three Versions: [%f][%.2f][%8.2f]",4523.2295));
```

6.

```
System.out.println(
        String.format(
                "Three Versions: [%1$f][%2$.2f][%3$8.2f]",4523.2295));
```

7.

```
// Extracting the word "gerbil" from the String varA:
        String varA = "dog cat bird gerbil hamster chicken";
        System.out.println(
        varA.substring(
                varA.indexOf("gerbil")
                        - varA.indexOf("hamster"),
                          varA.indexOf("hamster")-1));
```

8.

```
// Extracting the numbers 1, 2, and 3 and inserting them
        // into a decorative String
        String varA = "123";
        String newString = varA.substring(varA.indexOf("1"));
        newString += varA.substring(varA.indexOf("2"));
        newString += varA.substring(varA.indexOf("3"));
        System.out.println(newString);
```

9.

```
// Adding the numbers 1, 2, and 3 and storing the sum in a String
        String varA = " " + 1 + 2 + 3;
```

10.

```
// Adding the numbers 1, 2, and 3 and storing the sum in a String
      String varA = "1" + "2" + "3";
```

Think about It

1. How is a `String` variable different from a primitive variable like an integer?
2. How are the two different methods for creating a `String` variable different? How is their result the same and object oriented in both cases?
3. How does the addition operator behave when both operands are a `String`? When one is a `String` and one is a numeric value?
4. How does operator precedence change the behavior of the addition operator when one operand is a `String`?
5. What are the two primary characteristics of a `String` text block that make them useful and unique?
6. Why are escape sequences like new line and tab not needed in a `String` text block variable?
7. Why is the equality operator not a reliable way to compare the values of `String` variables?
8. If you have two `String` variables created in the "object-oriented" method, why does the equality operator fail to perform a comparison of their `String` values? What is being compared instead?
9. Why are two parameters not needed for the `String` class method `.equalsIgnoresCase()`? How is this method properly invoked and used?
10. What are some things you should keep in mind when using the two-parameter version of the `.substring()` method?
11. Describe the primary difference between the `.indexOf()` method and the `.contains()` method.
12. Why do `String IndexOutOfBounds` errors occur? How can you prevent them when using various `String` class methods?
13. Describe a few ways that you can keep data quality high through the usage of various `String` class methods.
14. How are escape-sequence commands similar to format specifiers? How are they different in their primary purpose?
15. Using the floating-point format specifier conversion character, how would you display a double without any rounding and with all decimals?
16. What is the relationship between the quantity of format specifier commands in a `String` and the quantity of data arguments used in the same `.format()` method? Can a variation of this relationship be used in a `.format()` method?

Short Syntax Problems

1. Create a `String` that contains three words separated by blank space characters. Using `String` class methods, extract each word from this `String` (omitting blank spaces), and store each in three separate `String` variables. Print these concatenated with a descriptive statement.
2. Perform the same task as in short syntax problem #1, but include the blank space characters with the first two words. Print each word in a decorative bracket that will show the blank space at the end of the first two words.
3. Create a `String` variable in the "object-oriented" manner (using "`new`" and the constructor for `String`). Create a second `String` variable, and initialize it by setting it equal to the first `String` you created. Convert the second `String` to all uppercase characters, and store it back in the same `String` variable. Finally, print the first `String`. Consider what printed and why.
4. Research the populations of four major cities. Using the `.format()` method and format specifiers, display these populations using your locality's method of displaying large whole numbers, and display them right-justified with enough space for the large numbers. Concatenate the name of the city to the left of the formatted population.
5. Display the current time in a twenty-four-hour format. Precede each value with the full description of the value. For example, "Hour:## Minute:## Second:## [a.m. or p.m.]" Do this without using concatenation and in one single statement.

Full Problems

1. Process a mailing address for a customer of the mom-and-pop grocery store. Prompt the user to enter a full mailing address in the console exactly in this format:

```
###  nameOfRoute streetOrRoute City,
State ZipCode
```

   Assume each address entered will be in this format. Extract each part of the mailing address, and print it to the console in a business-appropriate manner like so:

```
"104 Nolan Ave Fulton, KY 42041"
Route and Type: [Nolan Ave]
Building Number: [104]
City: [Fulton]
State: [KY]
Zip Code: [42041]
```

2. Using a regular `String` variable, type in and store the full first sentence of section 3.1 in this chapter. You can omit punctuation like periods, commas, and parentheses. Perform the following tasks:
   a. Print out the full sentence in all lowercase characters. Begin and end the print with decorative enclosing brackets.
   b. Print out the length of the `String`, and include the label "`Length: ## Characters`," where ## is the length you determined.
   c. Using however many `int` and `String` variables you need, extract and print the last five words in the phrase. Use only the methods learned in chapter 3. Print each word in decorative enclosing brackets as well.
   d. Along with each word (after the first), print out the result of the `.compareTo()` comparison with the one behind it.
3. Store a word in a `String` variable. Using just the methods and techniques learned up until this chapter, perform the following:
   a. Find the length of the `String`.
   b. Starting with the last character, extract every single character in reverse, concatenating it to a new `String`. Create and use whatever `int`, `char`, and `String` variables you need to accomplish this. Decrement the `int` to determine the next character position to extract from.
   c. Once you have built the new `String`, print it along with the original string separated by a colon.
   d. Once you are done, consider the inefficient and repetitive nature of this task. Why is it inefficient and repetitive?
4. Prompt the user to enter a seven-word sentence in the console. Write logic to perform the following:
   a. Starting with the first word in the sentence, extract and copy each word into a String variable.
   b. Use the `.compareTo()` method to compare the first word with the second, and print the results of the method. Compare the second with the third, print the results, and so on for all words in the phrase.
   c. Do not use a loop structure to complete this assignment.
5. Prompt the user to enter a seven-word sentence in the console. Write logic to perform the following:
   a. Starting with the first word in the sentence, copy each word into a String variable (you can use the same one over and over). Print that word to the console along with its length.
   b. Use the `.substring()` method to remove that word from the sentence, shortening the sentence each time. Continue to print each word and its length.
   c. As each word is extracted, keep track of which word is the **longest** in character length and which word is the **shortest** in character length in separate String and int variables. When all words have been extracted, report the longest and shortest words at the end of the output.
   d. Do not use a loop structure to complete this assignment.

Chapter 4

Decision Logic and Code Flow

What You Will Learn in This Chapter

Modern information systems consist of often complicated logic, built around business rules and governmental regulations. Modern systems involve processing user input and historical or real-time data. As this data is processed, evaluation logic will help software make decisions about whether to execute this or that business rule or behave in different ways based on the inputs. As an information systems professional engaged in designing, developing, and building these systems, you will be heavily involved in helping plan software systems that can do all this and more. In this chapter, you will begin to learn how to enable your Java applications to handle increasingly complex decision-making and data-processing behaviors through the use of decision structures.

Specifically, this chapter will help you do the following:

1. Explain how decision structures increase the capabilities of an application and move the flow of code execution to the nonlinear in style
2. Understand the structure of the `if` statement in Java, its typical nature and use, and some common mistakes and logic errors to avoid while using it
3. Understand the behavior of nested `if` statements and how nesting impacts the behavior and results of code execution
4. How to use the `if…else` statement to evaluate and handle a two-case scenario and how the syntax of this statement can be superior to the chaining of `if` decision statements
5. Understand and use the ternary operator to mimic the behavior of basic `if…else` statements to simplify and declutter simple decision-making logic
6. Understand and use the `if…else if` statement to handle cases of three or more outcomes in decision-making scenarios
7. Understand the use and particular benefits of the `switch` statement, what it is and is not capable of, and various ways of changing its behavior to the advantage of your logic
8. Understand the use and benefits of the `switch` expression and the various ways of changing its behavior to the advantage of your logic

Opening Scenario

After some work, you and a team member have loaded the client's example data from spreadsheets into a few database tables. Armed with your knowledge of text manipulation in Java, you have worked out your "battle plan" for cleaning up the client's messy text and numeric data. Looking over several rows of data, you think about how you would go about manually fixing each name, address, number, cell, and so on: "The problem is I need to write the logic to do all this for me; there are thousands of rows in just this sample data!" You note that not every row of data will need data cleaning. Not every column will either. In discussing this with teammates, you express your desire to make this a very "smart" process. "You'll have to pair decision structures with string actions in Java in order to 'automate' this," a teammate responds.

For example, if a name field contains a comma, you might want to restore the proper order of the names; otherwise, no changes are needed to a column. If an address contains "Apt" or "Apartment," you might need two separate address fields for the various parts; otherwise, the address is a singular street address. There are lots of examples like this. Luckily, since the client has provided no set-in-stone formatting rules, you can standardize things in a "reasonable manner" per your project manager. Looking over the messy data, you realize that you will need to use decision statements of "if this, do this; otherwise, do something else" and build many of these types of rules into your data-cleaning logic just to get it ready for prototype testing. "We have to write some software that will help us later write better software," you state. After a while, you realize that combining decision-making structures with your text manipulation skills in Java will be the perfect combo to clean the vast majority of this client data and get it ready for the testing group. Once again, you decide to dive in and learn the nuances of code that can branch and perform different tasks based on evaluations of arithmetic and boolean expressions . . .

4.1 Evaluation Using the `if` Statement

Linear versus nonlinear code flow: Most people have a "daily routine": wake up, dress, maybe eat breakfast, go to the gym, go to work or school, eat lunch, go home, study Java, run errands, eat dinner, wind down for the evening, and then back to sleep at the end of the day. If you really think about it, every day is different: routines change, and detours happen all the time. Is it raining? Better grab an umbrella and maybe drive in or ride public transport instead of walking. Are you hungry? Better eat a snack before heading out. Is there an accident on your normal route? Better take a detour path. Uh-oh, you forgot your umbrella. Better loop back home and grab it then head the same way in. Road is blocked? Now you have to detour again. Daily life is rarely a **linear** or straightforward path. Figure 4.1 shows a winding, branching, diverting river—a good metaphor for our daily lives as our paths change constantly. With each of these examples, something different occurs based on certain facts or evaluations of conditions.

Figure 4.1. Like a Flowing River, Code Execution Can Branch and Divert Using Decision Structures

Source: "Glacier & Runoff Rivers Merge" by Dave Bezaire is licensed under CC BY-SA 2.0, https://www.flickr.com/photos/75988799@N00/3698002133.

Logic written for information systems will often not be linear or straightforward. Modern systems that are responsive to user input and business rules will need to pivot, performing one set of instructions or another. The path of code execution in applications is rarely a sequential procession from first to last. Based on statements of evaluation, code execution might jump around, re-execute several lines of code several times, or skip whole blocks of logic entirely. This is the idea of **code flow** and altering the **path of execution** through your application using evaluation, selection, and control structures. Since business rules and data handling increasingly attempt to capture the complexity of the real world, using control structures that alter code flow in your application can help you process these rules and create information systems that are increasingly effective and useful. Like the river in figure 4.1, your code may branch off and execute differently on each run.

Selection statements: In most programming languages, an expression forming a **boolean** statement can be evaluated, and the result of the evaluation sends code execution off in one direction or another. To understand how selection statements work, think of a river or stream that diverges (thus the "flow" part of "code flow"). In Java, boolean statements are evaluated, usually based on a business rule or relevant logic. The result of the evaluation causes code execution to change. Boolean decision statements are usually evaluating mutually exclusive value scenarios, meaning your code may go down one path or the other but **never both** at the same time. One path is mutually exclusive of the other(s). Code will follow either one path or the other through a section of our code listing. Selection and control statements will allow you to effectively leverage prior chapters' operators and object-oriented techniques.

The `if` statement: The `if` statement is the simplest of the control structures you will encounter in most programming languages, Java included. Figure 4.2 shows the basic structure of the `if` statement. First, notice a few **syntax** characteristics about the `if` statement: there is **no semicolon** at the end of the `if` statement itself.

This is because it is intended to be understood as an "If this, then that, or else something other" type of statement (a **compound statement**—it has multiple parts). The `if` statement performs an evaluation that **resolves** to `true` or `false`. Code execution flows to the logic associated with the `if` statement if the result is `true`. This association usually happens with curly braces right after the `if`, forming a **code block** that only executes when the `if` evaluates to `true`. If there is only one line of executing code needed, then the curly braces are optional. When there are two or more lines of executing code that should be associated with the `if`, then the curly braces are **not** optional! Consider these two scenarios:

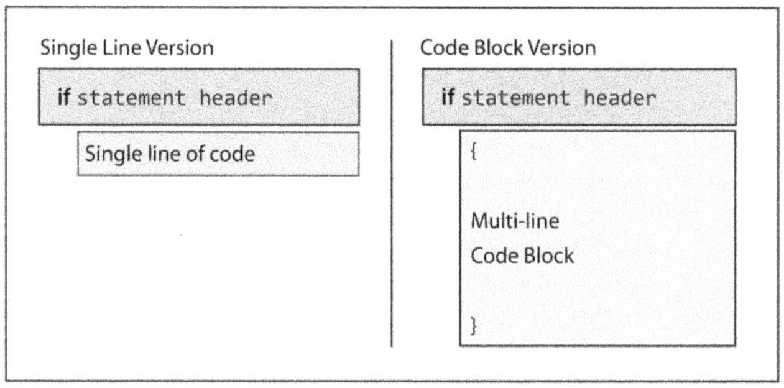

Figure 4.2. Two Versions of the `if` Statement

Code Snippet 4.1

```
int employeeAge = 53;
double rothIRAYearly = 0.0;

if (employeeAge >= 50)
    rothIRAYearly = 7500.0;

if (employeeAge >= 50)
{
    rothIRAYearly = 7500.0;
    System.out.println("Qualifies for Catch-Up Contributions!");
}
```

Recall that a boolean evaluation can be performed using **relational** and **equality** operators. In the example, a particular employee's age is involved in a business rule: if someone is fifty years or older, they can contribute an additional $1,000 a year beyond the normal $6,500 maximum to their Roth IRA retirement savings account. Remember that relational operators **resolve** to `true` or `false`. The `if` statement acts differently based on these resulting values. However simple or complex the `if` statement, eventually it will resolve to `true` or `false`. If it resolves to `true`, the code that is associated with the `if` statement will execute. If `false`, the associated code will be **skipped**. Additionally, note the two occurrences of curly brace usage. If one line of executing code is needed due to the `if` evaluating to `true`, the curly braces can be omitted. If curly braces are included, **all the code** within them will be executed in the case where the `if` statement evaluates to `true`. It is a recommended best practice to always use curly braces even when there is only one line of executing code, like so:

Code Snippet 4.2

```
int employeeAge = 53;
double rothIRAYearly = 0.0;

if (employeeAge >= 50)
{
    rothIRAYearly = 6500.0;
}
```

Notice also the lack of a semicolon at the end of the curly braces. Java can easily distinguish the beginning and end of the code block formed by the curly braces, eliminating the need for a semicolon at the end. Only the statements inside the curly braces need end-of-line semicolons.

The `if` statement can handle increasingly complex evaluation statements. Consider the following expansion of the business-oriented investment logic:

Code Snippet 4.3

```
int employeeAge = 53;
double yearlySalary = 198000.0;
double rothIRAYearly = 0.0;

if ((employeeAge >= 50) & (yearlySalary <= 206000))
{
   rothIRAYearly = 7500.0;
   System.out.println("Catch up Qualified!");
   System.out.println("IRS Approved Income Level!");
}
```

Here a boolean operator is used to compare the `true` or `false` values of both relational statements. If the left-hand relational statement resolves to `true`, and the right-hand relational statement resolves to `true` as well, then the boolean operator itself will resolve to `true`, and that `true` will cause the code in the `if` statement to execute. Notice that parentheses are carefully used to force the inner expressions to evaluate first. The boolean operator then performs its comparison, producing the eventual result the `if` statement evaluates. You can take the logic here one step further: ensure that the employee is **currently** active (and not fired or laid off) before evaluating their other retirement considerations:

Code Snippet 4.4

```
int employeeAge = 53;
boolean employeeActive = false;
double yearlySalary = 198000.0;
double rothIRAYearly = 0.0;

if ((employeeActive == true)
        && ((employeeAge >= 50) & (yearlySalary <= 206000)))
{
   rothIRAYearly = 7500.0;
   System.out.println("Catch up Qualified!");
   System.out.println("IRS Approved Income Level!");
}
```

Notice that in this example, both a **short circuit AND operator** and a "normal" **AND operator** are used to perform certain checks. Notice the careful parings of the parentheses as well. If the employee is not actively employed, the first evaluation, `employeeActive == true`, will evaluate to `false`, causing the short circuit AND operator to not check the rest of the statement. This statement can be simplified by recalling that boolean variables self-resolve to their contained value. For example, if a `bool` contains `false`, then it resolves to `false` without having to compare it to `false` directly. Consider the following:

Code Snippet 4.5

```
int employeeAge = 53;
boolean employeeActive = false;
double yearlySalary = 198000.0;
double rothIRAYearly = 0.0;

if ((employeeActive)
        && ((employeeAge >= 50) & (yearlySalary <= 206000)))
{
   rothIRAYearly = 7500.0;
   System.out.println("Catch up Qualified!");
   System.out.println("IRS Approved Income Level!");
}
```

The equality operator was not needed to compare `employeeActive` to `true`; the `if` statement now evaluates if the `bool` variable contains a `true` value.

The `if` statement can use the return values from method invocations as well. Consider the following example of checking an entered password:

Code Snippet 4.6

```
// Assume Scanner has been correctly imported
Scanner in = new Scanner(System.in);
String password = "";
String correctPass = "javarocks";

System.out.print("Please enter your password: ");
password = in.nextLine();

if (correctPass.equalsIgnoreCase(password))
{
    System.out.println("Password Accepted!");
}
```

And the execution of the program on the console would look like this:

```
Please enter your password:
javarocks
Password Accepted!
```

Method return values will work as long as they return `true` or `false` or if the returned value can be compared to some other value, resulting in a `true` or `false`.

Nested `if` statements: Nest `if` statements when you do not want to perform one comparison unless a prior one has evaluated to `true` or if there is other code that needs to execute along with your second comparison. Take the following example comparing donation amounts:

Code Snippet 4.7

```
// Assume Scanner has been imported
Scanner in = new Scanner(System.in);
double firstDonation = 0.0;
double secondDonation = 0.0;

System.out.println("Enter first donation amount: ");
firstDonation = in.nextDouble();
if (firstDonation >= 1000.0) // Outer if
{
    System.out.println("Enter second donation amount: ");
    secondDonation = in.nextDouble();

    if (secondDonation >= 1000)  // Nested if statement
    {
        System.out.println(
                "The larger donation is: $"
                        + Math.max(firstDonation, secondDonation));
    }
}
```

Executing this code with test values entered might look like this:

```
Enter first donation amount:
1500
Enter second donation amount:
2300
The larger donation is: $2300.0
```

Notice that if the first donation is **less than** $1,000, no prompt occurs, and the code compares the second donation amount. **Conditional execution** occurs when other data-processing steps are not even carried out if earlier conditions are not met. Nested `if` statements are helpful in these scenarios. The above code can be restructured and simplified (thus optimizing it) as follows:

Code Snippet 4.8

```
// Assume Scanner has been imported
Scanner in = new Scanner(System.in);
double firstDonation = 0.0;
double secondDonation = 0.0;

System.out.println("Enter first donation amount: ");
firstDonation = in.nextDouble();
System.out.println("Enter second donation amount: ");
secondDonation = in.nextDouble();

if ((firstDonation >= 1000.0) && (secondDonation >= 1000))
{
    System.out.println(
            "The larger donation is: $"
                    + Math.max(firstDonation, secondDonation));
}
```

The short circuit AND operator is used here. In the situation where `firstDonation` does not contain a value of $1,000 or greater, the second comparison for `secondDonation` is excluded along with the comparison of which value is larger. Nesting `if` statements also works in the cases where there is only one line of code associated with each `if`. Consider the following example:

Code Snippet 4.9

```
double studentGPA = 3.7;
double totalHours = 121;
boolean scholarship = false;

if (studentGPA > 3.0)
    if (totalHours >= 120)
        scholarship = true;
```

Notice that the second `if` statement is the one single line of code associated with the first (since there are no curly braces, this is what Java assumes). The second `if` statement has one line of code: the assignment of `true` to the boolean variable `scholarship`. Both of the `if` statements will need to evaluate to true in order for this assignment to occur. Notice that only the executing line of code has a semicolon at its end. The two `if` statements will **not** have semicolons. This logic can be altered so that two separate comparisons happen if the GPA of the student is at an appropriate level. Consider the following:

Code Snippet 4.10

```
double studentGPA = 3.7;
double totalHours = 121;
boolean scholarship = false;

if (studentGPA > 3.0)
{
    if (totalHours >= 90)
    {
        scholarship = true;
        System.out.println("Eligible!");
    }

    if (scholarship == false)
    {
        System.out.println("Ineligible due to Hours");
    }
}
```

Though somewhat clunky, this code works! Optimally, it would be better to structure this logic more cleanly using an `else` paired with the `if`, which will be discussed later in the chapter.

Avoiding common mistakes using `if` statements: As the sophistication of applications increases, so too does the possibility of logic errors. A **logic error** occurs when the code you have written executes without syntax errors but does not behave in the way that you expected. This can happen due to selection statement logic, assumptions about variable values, issues with your relational and boolean comparison statements, or something else. Logic errors are more frustrating than **syntax errors,** which occur when you have not followed the rules of the Java language or written code in such a way that the Java compiler does not recognize it. Syntax errors are typically obvious, highlighted by your IDE before you even run your program, or they cause the program to halt while running with the compiler, which is doing its best to point out the error. For logic errors, no error messages are displayed. Depending on the complexity of your logic, these errors may be hard to hunt down. Some common logic/syntax errors that occur with `if` statements are the following:

- **Forgetting to use curly braces when they are needed:** This happens when you have more than one line of code that will be executed in the event the if evaluates to true. Consider the following:

Code Snippet 4.11

```
double studentGPA = 3.7;
boolean scholarship = false;

if (studentGPA > 3.0)
    System.out.println("Eligible!");
    scholarship = true;  // Will always execute - error!
```

Notice that the message should print and the `bool` variable will be assigned `true` if the GPA of the student is strictly above 3.0. Remember that Java is a block-style language: tabs and indents **will not** determine what lines of code you want grouped together. Curly braces **must** be used in order to associate both lines of code as the outcome of the `if` statement. The logic issue with this example is that the `bool` variable scholarship will be set to true **regardless** of the value of `studentGPA`. If you have logic later on in your code that depends on the value of the `bool`, it is now in error too. Be careful with your `if` statements and the blocks of code associated with them—use curly braces to ensure no ambiguity in what code executes after an `if` evaluation.

- **Trying to use an assignment or arithmetic expression instead of a comparison:** An `if` statement relies on the statement within its parentheses ultimately resolving to a single true or false value. An expression using assignment is not a valid boolean evaluation expression. Consider the following:

Code Snippet 4.12

```
double studentGPA = 3.7;

if (studentGPA = 3.8)    // Incompatible Types Error
    System.out.println("Great Student!");
```

The assignment operator always returns a copy of the value it is copying from right to left in the expression. Since it returns a double in this case, an incompatible types error occurs, since the if statement expects a boolean value to be resolved within. A simple type may be plaguing the programmer here, and they intended to use the equality operator (==) instead. Keep in mind that the `if` statement's expression must evaluate to true or false eventually. The following attempts at using an arithmetic expression in an `if` statement will not work either:

Code Snippet 4.13

```
int var = 5;
if (var + 4 + 7) // Error: Incompatible Types
{
    // some code
}

if (Math.max(4,var)) // Error: Incompatible Types
{
    // some other code
}
```

Recall the test for an active employee from earlier:

```
if (employeeActive = true) . . . // Incorrect use of assignment
```

since the result of the assignment operator is a copy of the value it sends to the left side of the expression. In this case, the developer has mistakenly used assignment instead of equality. The variable `employeeActive` may contain `false`, but the assignment operator returns `true`. Keep an eye out for mistakes like this!

- **Putting a semicolon at the end of the if statement:** With programming languages like Java that require semicolons as line terminators, muscle memory may cause you to type one at the end of all statements, particularly in places where they are not needed. You **can** put a semicolon at the end of an `if` statement and it will not throw an error. This will, however, change the way the `if` behaves. Code placed after an `if` that has a semicolon will not be associated with the `if` and will be considered a stand-alone line of code. The semicolon will end the `if` statement immediately. Consider the following two examples:

Code Snippet 4.14

```
double studentGPA = 3.7;
boolean scholarship = false;

if (studentGPA > 3.0); // Ends the if statement prematurely
{
    System.out.println("Eligible!");      // Always executes!
    scholarship = true;                   // Always executes!
}

if (scholarship == true); // Ends the if statement prematurely
    scholarship = false;  // Always executes!
```

The presence of the curly braces will have no effect on how these if statements work because of the semicolon at the end of each `if`. Java will consider the line(s) of code after each `if`, in these cases, as stand-alone statements. Additionally, notice that in Java, curly braces can form a code block without it being associated with any decision structures. The `if` statements in this example will still evaluate, but the lines of code after them will **always** execute, regardless of the `if` statements' true or false evaluation. The semicolon breaks the association between the two.

- **Preventing or duplicating code execution through imprecise use of relational operators:** When using relational operators in an if statement, you have to be careful not to accidentally prevent the `if` statement from evaluating to true in certain cases. Consider the following example:

Code Snippet 4.15

```
// Assume the Scanner class has been imported
Scanner in = new Scanner(System.in);
int studentAge = 0;

System.out.println("Please enter the student's age: ");
studentAge = in.nextInt();
if (studentAge > 21)
    System.out.println("Older Student");

if (studentAge < 21)
    System.out.println("Independent Student");
```

What if the user enters the student's age as exactly twenty-one? In this situation, nothing will print to the console. A potential outcome has been excluded by poor use of relational operators. This is a logic error—it would not throw any syntax errors. You might also cause two or more different scenarios to execute if you are not careful with your relational operators and your if statements. Consider this modified `studentAge` example:

Code Snippet 4.16

```
// Assume the Scanner class has been imported
Scanner in = new Scanner(System.in);
int studentAge = 0;

System.out.println("Please enter the student's age: ");
studentAge = in.nextInt();

if (studentAge > 21)
    System.out.println("Older Student");

if (studentAge < 21)
    System.out.println("Independent Student");

if (studentAge < 18)
    System.out.println("Teenage Student");

if (studentAge < 12)
    System.out.println("Child Student");
```

When executed with the following inputs at the console, the following results:

```
Please enter the student's age:
14
Independent Student
Teenage Student
```

Only one category message was intended to print at a time. However, due to the use of less-than relational operators for each category and age input of fourteen, two of the `if` statements evaluated to true and executed their code. Additionally, the "gap" at the age of twenty-one is still present. This can be corrected as follows:

Code Snippet 4.17

```
// Assume the Scanner class has been imported
Scanner in = new Scanner(System.in);
int studentAge = 0;

System.out.println("Please enter the student's age: ");
studentAge = in.nextInt();
if (studentAge >= 21)
    System.out.println("Older Student");

if ((studentAge < 21) & (studentAge >= 18))
    System.out.println("Independent Student");

if ((studentAge < 18) & (studentAge >= 13))
    System.out.println("Teenage Student");

if (studentAge < 13)
    System.out.println("Child Student");
```

The correct classification will now print for the age of fourteen. Each age range has been considered one at a time and in numeric order, keeping the logic clean and clear.

- **Rarely reachable statements:** When nesting `if` statements of any type, be careful how statements are placed in the nested structure. Consider the following, where a `bool` variable is assigned `true` but in an improper location in the logic:

Code Snippet 4.18

```
String jobType = "Dog Stylist";
double salary = 65000.0d;
int yearsWorked = 4;
```

```
boolean dogStylistExperience = false;

if (jobType.equalsIgnoreCase("Dog Stylist"))
{
    if (salary > 10000000.00)
    {
        if (yearsWorked > 1000)
        {
            // Some other code
            // Some more other code
            // Wow that is a lot of code.
            dogStylistExperience = true;
        }
    }
}
```

Notice in this case that the boolean variable "`dogStylistExperience`" should be set if the applicant has ever been a dog stylist. The `salary` and `yearsWorked` (for this business scenario) do not affect whether they have ever worked in a dog salon. The "flag" for this experience was assigned a value deep inside the nested if and within two cases that will almost never be evaluated to true (especially for one thousand years of experience!). This will prevent the `bool` value from ever being properly set and may alter the behavior of logic that occurs later in the application that depends on its value being correctly set. This is an exaggerated scenario, but it can happen in much more subtle and realistic ways. Move the assignment to the boolean closer to where the statement for its being set is evaluated:

Code Snippet 4.19

```
String jobType = "Dog Stylist";
double salary = 65000.00;
int yearsWorked = 4;
boolean dogStylistExperience = false;

if (jobType.equalsIgnoreCase("Dog Stylist"))
{
    dogStylistExperience = true;

    if (salary > 10000000.00)
    {
        if (yearsWorked > 1000)
        {
            // This would be a very experienced stylist!
        }
    }
}
```

SUMMARY POINTS

- A basic `if` statement will evaluate an expression that resolves to `true` or `false` and run its associated code if the expression evaluates to true. Otherwise, the code will not run.
- You can associate a single line of code with an `if` statement by placing it immediately after the statement or multiple lines of code by placing them within a code block following the `if` statement.
- The `if` statement will not use a semicolon at its end, since Java expects one or more lines of code to follow the `if` statement to be executed if it evaluates to true.
- The `if` statement expects its expression to result in a `true` or `false`. Expressions that produce other data types will result in an incompatible types error.

- Relational and boolean operators can be used to create very sophisticated decision logic within an `if` statement.
- Nesting of `if` statements allows a developer to check for a condition prior to testing a second condition. This can help make code and its logic more readable and more easily maintainable, not to mention more sophisticated and capable.
- Failure to carefully set up the decision logic structured by `if` statements can result in a logic error where the application executes but does not behave in the way expected based on its design.

QUICK PROBLEMS

1. **Coding:** Use a chain of `if` statements to calculate the amount of taxes paid for the following "filing single" tax brackets (calculate the amount based on the %): under $10K: 10%; $10K–$40K: 12%; $40K–$87K: 22%; $87K–$100K: 14%.
2. **Think:** How would you cause the calculations in the previous quick problem to change if the filing status were "filing married" versus "filing single"? Can you do this using two if statements?
3. **Coding:** Prompt for a user to enter their birth year, and capture it. Calculate the user's age based on this entry (use the current year in your calculation). If the user is twenty-five years or older, print to the console their car insurance rate as $300. If they are less than twenty-five years old, print to the console that their car insurance rate is $350.

4.2 Expanding the `if` Statement

The `if…else` statement: Up until this point, `if` statements have been "chained" in order to test certain ranges of values or to test for different discrete (i.e., singular) values. The `if…else` statement can perform this chain of tests much more cleanly. As shown in figure 4.3, the `else` block of the statement immediately follows an `if` statement's single line or block of code lines. Consider the investment example from earlier, and notice how the `else` simplifies things:

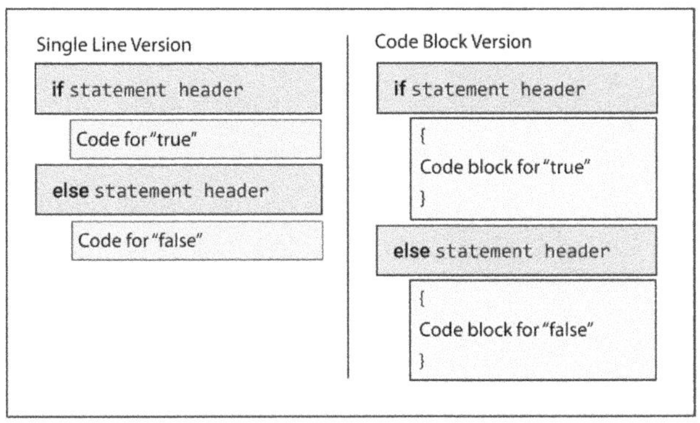

Figure 4.3. Basic Structure of the `if…else` Statement

Code Snippet 4.20

```
int employeeAge = 53;
double yearlySalary = 198000.0;
double rothIRAYearly = 0.0;

if (employeeAge >= 50)
{
    rothIRAYearly = 7500.0;
    System.out.println("Catch-up Eligible!");
}
else
{
    rothIRAYearly = 6500.0;
    System.out.println("Normal Contributions Only!");
}
```

Using an `else` block along with the `if` statement improves the **readability** and **understandability** of code. Intuitively, someone viewing this code would understand that if the employee is at least fifty-three, they can make catch-up contributions to their Roth IRA; otherwise, they make the standard ones. While the chaining `if` statements are valid Java syntax, they can complicate code unnecessarily. The more complicated your code, the more likely logic errors will occur. As information systems professionals who will be tasked with interpreting business rules and often implementing them in code, the `if…else` structure helps with clean implementation of threshold rules like those discussed.

Expanding the example, check first for a qualifying income for age:

Code Snippet 4.21

```
Scanner in = new Scanner(System.in);
int employeeAge = 0;
double yearlySalary = 0.0;
double rothIRAYearly = 0.0;

System.out.println("Please enter the Employee's Age: ");
employeeAge = in.nextInt();
System.out.println("Please enter the Employee's Salary: ");
yearlySalary = in.nextDouble();

if (yearlySalary <= 206000.0)
{
    if (employeeAge >= 50)
    {
        rothIRAYearly = 7500.0;
        System.out.println("Catch-up Qualified!");
    }
    else
    {
        rothIRAYearly = 6500.0;
        System.out.println("Standard Yearly Investment");
    }
}
else
{
    // The employee's salary was too high, execution
    // jumped to here.
    System.out.println("IRS Income Limits Exceeded!");
}
```

Notice the various comparisons in this code. First, the "outermost" `if` statement is evaluated. Is the employee's yearly salary below the business rule threshold? If so, then execution jumps "inside" that `if`, and code execution resumes within its code block. In the case that the outer `if` evaluates its statement to `false`, code execution will move to the `else`, and the code within its block will execute. Only if **both** the employee's salary is low enough and their age high enough will their investment information be set to the higher level. The "inner" and "outer" terminology is often used with nested structures in Java. There is no limit to how deep you can nest if statements. Consider this **very suboptimal** example:

Code Snippet 4.22

```
int studentAge = 15;
String description = "";

if (studentAge > 12)
    if (studentAge > 17)
        if (studentAge > 20)
            if (studentAge > 29)
                description = "Adult Student";
            else
                description = "Young Adult Student";
        else
            description = "Undergrad Category Student";
```

```
        else
            description = "Teenage Student";
    else
        description = "Child-Aged Student";
System.out.println(description);
```

There are `if` statements nested four levels deep. Each successively nested `if` is the "single line of code" associated with its outer. Consider the decision statements carefully: if the student's age is strictly greater than twelve, that means they are thirteen years of age or older and move to the next if within—and so on. If they are seventeen years old or less, the `String` variable `description` is assigned the value "`Teenage Student`" due to the second if statement's block executing.

Recall the student scholarship opportunity example from earlier. You can clean up the logic in this code by clever use of the `if…else` statement:

Code Snippet 4.23

```
double studentGPA = 3.7;
double totalHours = 121;
boolean scholarship = false;

if (studentGPA >= 3.0)
{
    if (totalHours >= 90)
        System.out.println("Qualifies as Candidate!");
    else
        System.out.println("Student not at Senior level");
}
else
    System.out.println("Student GPA too low");
```

Notice the mix and absence of curly braces. If more code is needed in addition to a nested `if…else` statement, you will **need** to use curly braces. When in doubt, include them!

Ternary operator (or how to impress your friends!): The Java syntax provides a more succinct way to express a simple `if…else` statement. Consider the following:

Code Snippet 4.24

```
boolean salesTaxState = true;
double taxRate = 0.0;

if (salesTaxState)
    taxRate = .0975; // Numeric form of 9.75%
else
    taxRate = .0150; // Numeric form of 1.50%
```

Here an `if…else` is used to set a tax rate `double` variable to a specific value based on a business rule. Since this is a very simple logic check and variable assignment, this is simplified by using a **ternary operator.** The ternary operator is the only Java operator that takes three operands. The operator here is both the ? and the : together. Figure 4.4 shows the basics of this operator.

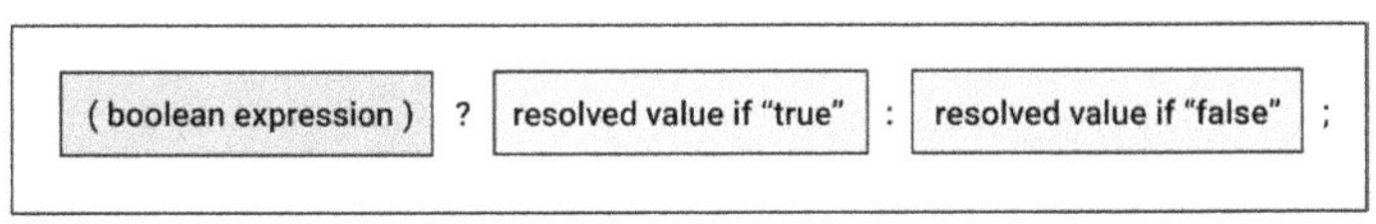

Figure 4.4. The General Structure of the Ternary Operator

The ternary operator works in that the first part must be an expression that resolves to `true` or `false` (this would be the part in the if statement's parentheses). After the ? symbol, the first value is the value that is "returned" by the operator if the expression resolves to `true`. The value after the : symbol will be the value returned if the expression resolves to `false`. The tax rate example can be simplified like so:

Code Snippet 4.25

```
boolean salesTaxState = true;
double taxRate = 0.0;

taxRate = salesTaxState ? .0975 : .0150;
System.out.println(taxRate);
```

When this runs, the value `.0975` will print to the console. Remember that a `bool` variable by itself resolves to its stored value. In long form, this performs the same comparison:

```
taxRate = (salesTaxState == true) ? .0975 : .0150;
```

The values returned by the ternary operator do not have to be the same data type as one another, **but** the variable or method argument that receives the ternary operator's returned value must be able to handle both types. Consider the following:

Code Snippet 4.26

```
int employeeTenure = 12;
System.out.println(employeeTenure >= 15 ? 1500.0 : "No Bonus");
```

Java allows this very succinct logic, but you probably will not write a line of code like this a lot. Notice that this line of code works; since the `.println()` method can print either a `double` or a `String`, it just converts it all to a `String` for console output. You would not want to store the result of a ternary operator statement like this in a data-type variable like a `double`, as the Java compiler would throw an error.

The `if…else if…else` statement: Figure 4.5 shows the general structure of the `if…else if…else` statement, where you can conduct several tests as part of the overall single decision structure.

Consider again the example of student age classification from earlier. Recall that ranges of ages were evaluated. The expanded `if` statement can be used to clean up the decision structure:

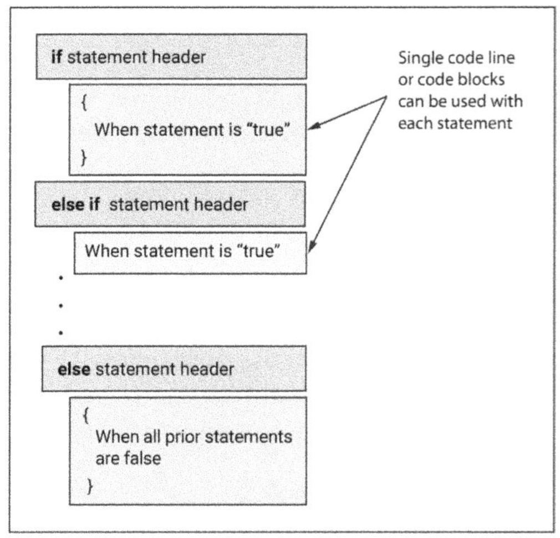

Figure 4.5. Basic Structure of the `if…else if…else` Decision Structure

Code Snippet 4.27

```
Scanner in = new Scanner(System.in);
int studentAge = 0;

System.out.println("Please enter the student's age: ");
studentAge = in.nextInt();

if (studentAge >= 21)
{
    System.out.println("Adult Student");
}
else if ((studentAge < 21) & (studentAge >= 18))
{
    System.out.println("Undergraduate Student");
}
else if ((studentAge < 18) & (studentAge >= 13))
{
    System.out.println("Teenage Student");
}
else
    System.out.println("Child Student");
```

Much cleaner! Notice that in the case where the first `if` fails, Java moves on to the next part of this structure, which is an `else if` statement—another test. That expression is evaluated and resolved, and if it resolves to false, execution moves down the "chain," eventually ending at the `else` block at the end. This last `else` is sometimes called the "default" condition: this condition will be the case when all other conditions are evaluated as `false`. The `else` at the end is optional. As mentioned earlier, ensuring correct relational comparisons will determine this decision structure's accuracy. Discrete singular values can be tested for also, omitting curly braces if only a single line of code is needed with each scenario:

Code Snippet 4.28

```
int userCategory = 2;
String userType = "";

if (userCategory == 1)
    userType = "Normal User";
else if (userCategory == 2)
    userType = "System Manager";
else if (userCategory == 3)
    userType = "Systems Analyst";
else if (userCategory == 4)
    userType = "Admin/Directors";
```

A semicolon is not needed at the end of each `else if` evaluation statement. As already seen, `if` and `if...else` statements can be nested within each `else if` statement if needed.

SUMMARY POINTS

- The `if...else` statement is useful in situations where you face an either-or decision-making scenario with your logic, where code should execute for both the true and the false situations of the expression.
- Like normal if statements, `if...else` statements can be nested to increase the sophistication of your logic and its decision-making ability.
- The else part of the statement will not evaluate the expression. If the if evaluates to false, execution will jump to the else without reevaluating the expression.
- The else part of the statement can also have either one line of code or multiple lines in a code block associated with it.
- The ternary operator is the only dual-operator/three-operand structure in Java. It is useful to replace both a simple `if...else` statement and a single-variable assignment with a one-line ternary operator statement.

QUICK PROBLEMS

1. **Coding:** Implement quick problem #1 from section 4.1 using an `if...else` statement for the "filing single" versus "filing married" tax status.
2. **Think:** In what case(s) would the ternary operator not be a direct replacement for an `if...else` statement?
3. **Coding:** Input the user for two option numbers: "1" if they want to find the maximum of two numbers and "2" if they want to find the minimum. Prompt them for the two numbers to use. Use a ternary operator and appropriate method calls to produce the max or min number based on their choice. Print this returned value to the console.

4.3 `switch` Statement

Though the `if…else` decision structure is useful, even it can become awkward to use in certain situations. Consider a situation with many evaluations: a company pays a bonus only during certain months, and depending on the month, the bonus amount changes:

Code Snippet 4.29

```
String month = "March";
double salaryBonus = 0.0;

if (month.equals("January"))
    salaryBonus = 10.0;
else if (month.equals("February"))
    salaryBonus = 500.0;
else if (month.equals("March"))
    salaryBonus = 2500.0;
else if (month.equals("April"))
    salaryBonus = 10.0;
else if (month.equals("May"))
    salaryBonus = 2500.0;
else if (month.equals("June"))
    salaryBonus = 10.0;
else if (month.equals("July"))
    salaryBonus = 500.0;
else if (month.equals("August"))
    salaryBonus = 10.0;
else if (month.equals("September"))
    salaryBonus = 10.0;
else if (month.equals("October"))
    salaryBonus = 500.0;
else if (month.equals("November"))
    salaryBonus = 4500.0;
else if (month.equals("December"))
    salaryBonus = 4500.0;

System.out.println("Employee Salary Bonus for "
        + month + ": $"
        + salaryBonus);
```

That was as tiring for me to write as it was for you to read! It is a simple `if…else` if structure, with only one comparison being tested in each part. With each evaluation, only one line of code is executed for each `true`. Java provides a decision structure known as a **`switch` statement** that allows us to write this logic in a more succinct and easier-to-read manner. Figure 4.6 shows the general structure of the `switch` statement.

Think of the last time you saw a US judicial trial in a television show or movie or in real life. The defendant is called to the stand to testify. They are evaluated and judged by their peers. A `switch` statement is like a trial: a single value (usually from a variable) is evaluated, and one or more code execution scenarios can occur. The `switch` statement has several characteristics to keep in mind:

- The `switch` will only evaluate the value of one single variable or a single result of an expression.
- Only certain variable data types are allowed in the switch evaluation: `int`, `String`, `char`, `byte`, `short`, and `enum` values. The object-oriented or "wrapper class" versions of some of these primitive data types are allowed as well.

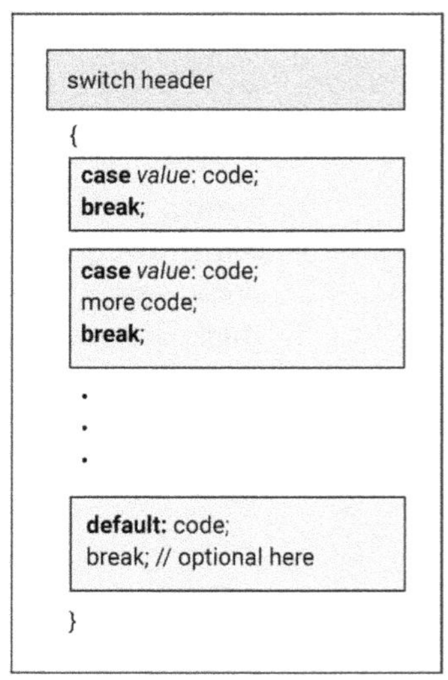

Figure 4.6. Structure of the `switch` Statement

- A `switch` can contain as many case statements as you need as potential outcomes of the evaluated variable having a certain value. You can check as many values as you want!
- The `switch` statement is optimally used for evaluating discrete (i.e., singular) values of a variable. If you want to test for a range of values, it is best to use a normal `if…else` statement.
- The default "case" in a `switch` statement is optional. Use it like you would an else in an `if…else if…else`: it will be the "catchall" for any values of the assessed variable other than the one you are looking for.
- The "case" values your `switch` statement evaluates do not have to be in any order or sequence. You can decide the structure and sequence of the evaluations.
- The break statements in a `switch` are optional as well. If you leave them out, you will change the behavior of the `switch` and the cases it decides to execute.

First, consider a very simple example of a `switch` statement. Check to see if a variable contains the value 1, 2, or 3:

Code Snippet 4.30

```
int variableOnTrial = 2;

switch (variableOnTrial)
{
    case 1: System.out.println("Value was 1!");
    break;

    case 2: System.out.println("Value was 2!");
    break;

    case 3: System.out.println("Value was 3!");
    break;
}
```

Notice that the `switch` statement puts the evaluated variable "on trial" and assesses its value. If the value matches any of the values used in the case statements, then the line of code associated with that case before the break statement will execute. The break statement tells Java to stop executing code and leave the switch after all the code for a particular case is done. This switch statement can also be rewritten using several if statements as well:

Code Snippet 4.31

```
int variableOnTrial = 2;
if (variableOnTrial == 1)
   System.out.println("Value was 1!");
if (variableOnTrial == 2)
   System.out.println("Value was 2!");
if (variableOnTrial == 3)
   System.out.println("Value was 3!");
```

Consider the following example, which determines a bonus amount for years of an employee's service:

Code Snippet 4.32

```
int yearsOfService = 10;
double bonusAmount = 0.0;

switch (yearsOfService)
{
    case 5: bonusAmount = yearsOfService * 1250.0;
        System.out.println("Bonus is: " + bonusAmount);
    break;

    case 10: bonusAmount = yearsOfService * 1850.0;
        System.out.println("Bonus is: " + bonusAmount);
    break;

    case 15: bonusAmount = yearsOfService * 2850.0;
```

```
        System.out.println("Bonus is: " + bonusAmount);
    break;
}
```

For each of the case statements here, there are two associated lines of code to calculate and report the bonus to the console. Again, the break statements tell Java to stop execution of lines of code for a particular case and then leave the `switch` statement entirely. If you leave break statements off some cases, you will cause what is known as **fall-through behavior**, where Java executes all the code for one case and then continues executing the lines of code for the next case as if it were the assessed value of the variable. Fall-through behavior can enhance efficiency if certain cases have similar code or actions that need to accompany them. Consider this example where shipping rates can be roughly determined:

Code Snippet 4.33

```
// Weight has been rounded up to nearest unit
int parcelWeight = 1;
double shippingCost = 5.0;
double totalCost = 0.0;

if (parcelWeight > 0)
{
    switch (parcelWeight)
    {
        case 1:
        case 2:
        case 3: totalCost = (shippingCost * 1);
              break;
        case 4:
        case 5:
        case 6: totalCost = (shippingCost * 2);
                break;

        default: totalCost = (shippingCost * 3);
    }
}
else
{
    System.out.println("Invalid Weight!");
}

System.out.println("Shipping Cost for Customer: $" + totalCost);
```

Notice that for the first two `case` statements, there are no code or `break` statements. How does this work? If the `parcelWeight` is exactly equal to `1` (which it is in this case), then the `switch` statement "falls through" to the second case. Because there is no `break` statement in that case statement, execution falls through again to the third `case`. Now code is encountered and executed, and the `break` is processed. This ends the `switch` and moves execution out and past it. Another clever way to use fall-through behavior is in a summative fashion, where each case adds to some running total. Consider the example of garment manufacturing and sizes with materials costs:

Code Snippet 4.34

```
String shirtSize = "XXL";
double manufactureCost = 0.0;

switch (shirtSize)
{
    case "XXLT":    manufactureCost += 4.00;
    case "XLT":     manufactureCost += 3.00;
    case "XXL":     manufactureCost += 7.00;
    case "XL":      manufactureCost += 5.00;
    case "L":       manufactureCost += 4.00;
```

```
    case "M":         manufactureCost += 3.00;
    case "S":         manufactureCost += 2.00;
}

System.out.println("Shirt Cost: $" + manufactureCost);
```

Look at how fall-through behavior helps us here. None of the cases have break statements. An XXL shirt is larger than all the other sizes under it, so the extra material costs are added at each step as the sizes get larger by "falling through" each case to the next one below it, executing its code, then falling through again. If the shirt were of size "XXLT," then that would incur the highest manufacturing cost.

The original example of the month check can easily be converted to a `switch` statement like so:

Code Snippet 4.35

```
String month = "March";
double salaryBonus = 0.0;

switch (month)
{
    case "January":
    case "April":
    case "June":
    case "August":
    case "September":    salaryBonus = 10.0;
        break;
    case "February":
    case "July":
    case "October": salaryBonus = 500.0;
        break;
    case "March":
    case "May": salaryBonus = 2500.0;
        break;
    default:     salaryBonus = 4500;
}
```

Notice that some months have the same bonus: $10. Fall-through behavior is used for these months so that you only have to write the resulting line of code once. The other months are grouped similarly. November and December are covered under the default case. The basic switch statement can involve very clever and clear logic that would otherwise be tedious and nonintuitive. From an information systems standpoint, if the business rules on the salary amount change for a particular month, it is very easy to modify this logic. This code is much cleaner and easier to understand than a long chain of `if...else` statements.

`Switch` **expressions:** As of Java SE 12, Oracle has worked to upgrade the switch statement in Java to give it features similar to what you might find in other contemporary programming languages.* The `switch` expression can return a value as if it were a method of a class you might invoke or an expression where you perform some math. It uses an arrow operator (`->`) instead of a colon at the end of a `case` statement. This operator indicates the value that should be returned back by the entire `switch` expression. A `switch` expression can easily be used for the salary example from earlier:

Code Snippet 4.36

```
String month = "March";
double salaryBonus = 0.0;

salaryBonus = switch (month)
{
    case "January", "April", "June", "August", "September" -> 10.0;
    case "February", "July", "October" -> 500.0;
    case "March", "May" -> 2500.0;
```

* https://docs.oracle.com/en/java/javase/13/language/switch-expressions.html.

```
    default -> 4500.0;
}; // Do not forget the semicolon here on a switch expression!
```

This example is even better! Notice that instead of fall-through behavior, commas are used to separate out the potential values for each particular case. Each outcome returns a desired value for that outcome. The variable `salaryBonus` is assigned the value that is returned by the `switch` expression. When you use a `switch` expression (instead of a normal `switch`), you **must** include the semicolon after the ending curly brace.

If code execution is needed along with each outcome in a switch expression, the `yield` statement can be used after the outcome's logic. For example,

Code Snippet 4.37

```
String month = "March";
double salaryBonus = 0.0;
String salaryLabel = "";

salaryBonus = switch (month)
{
    case "January", "April", "June", "August", "September":
        salaryLabel = "Low";
        yield 10.0;
    case "February", "July", "October":
        salaryLabel = "Medium";
        yield 500.0;
    case "March", "May":
        salaryLabel = "High";
        yield 2500.0;
    default:
        salaryLabel = "Top";
        yield 4500.0;

}; // Switch expression: semicolon is needed

System.out.println("Employee Bonus Level: "
        + salaryLabel + ", amount: $ "
        + salaryBonus);
```

The command `yield` returns the value and acts like a `break` statement, ending execution of code for that particular case. If you need fall-through behavior like you would on a normal `switch`, use the `yield` style of a switch expression, and group the cases as you would for fall-through like with a normal `switch` statement.

Table 4.1 provides a convenient summary of the decision structures that have been covered in this chapter.

Table 4.1. Summary of Common Decision Structures in Java

Decision structure	# of decisions	# of outcomes	Can nest?	Best used for
`if` (single code line)	One	One	Yes	One line of code outcome, value range test
`if` (code block)	One	One	Yes	Multiple lines of code outcome, value range
`if…else`	One	Two or more	Yes	Testing for a value in two ranges
`if…else if…else`	Multiple	Two or more	Yes	Testing for a value in multiple ranges/scenarios
Ternary operator	One	Two	Yes	Single decision, two outcomes, test a value range
`switch` statement	Multiple	One or more	Yes	Testing for one or more single, discrete values
`switch` expression	Multiple	One or more	Yes	Testing for one or more single, discrete values, return a value in response

SUMMARY POINTS

- The `switch` statement will assess the value of a single variable and execute one or more lines of code based on the case value that matches that variable's value.
- The `switch` statement is efficient at examining single, discrete values. If you need to determine if a value is within a range, the switch can be clunky in handling this. Ranges are better handled with if statements and the use of relational and boolean operators.
- A `switch case` is usually ended with a `break` statement. You can place as many lines of code between the `case` and `break` statements as needed.
- Omitting the `break` statement from a `case` will cause fall-through behavior if that `case` is executed. Fall-through behavior allows execution to continue on to the next `case`, as if it were the selected and assessed variable value.
- Statements such as `switch` can assess `int`, `String`, `char`, `byte`, `short`, and `enum` (i.e., "enumerated") values. They can also assess the object-oriented wrapper class versions of these primitive data types.
- In a `switch`, the `default case` is optional. A `break` statement is not necessarily needed with default, since it is usually placed at the end of the `switch`, though it does not have to be. If placed anywhere else in the `switch` statement, it is recommended to use a `break` with `default`.

QUICK PROBLEMS

1. **Coding:** Use a `switch` statement to assess the value of a `String` that contains the name of a day of the week. If the day is a weekend day ("Saturday" or "Sunday"), print "Weekend!" to the console. Otherwise, print "Weekday" to the console. For an extra challenge, prompt the user to enter this day and convert it to uppercase prior to switch assessment.
2. **Think:** Would it be advisable to use a `switch` to check the value of an integer to see if its value is between 0 and 200, inclusive? Why or why not? Does Java allow you to do this?
3. **Coding:** Use a `switch` statement and fall-through behavior to code the following logic: if an employee has been with the company one, three, or five years, they are awarded a lapel pin; if seven, ten, or twelve years, they are awarded a plaque; if fifteen or twenty years, they are awarded a small silver medal. Print the award the employee receives to the console in a professional statement.

Summary

In this chapter, you have learned how to use the `if` statement and its several variants to your advantage to change the flow of code execution in your application. You have learned how to use this to increase the decision-making capabilities of your application in performing certain simple tasks with data and/or calculations. You have also learned the ins and outs of the `switch` statement and `switch` expression and how these can mimic the behavior of an otherwise complex `if…else` statement. In all these topics, you have additionally learned when each is useful, when each may not work, and some of the common issues and logic errors to be aware of and avoid as you develop software systems. This chapter overall has helped you create "smarter" applications that can process data and make simple decisions based on values that flow through the variables and expressions in your logic. This chapter, along with the next two, really forms the core of your learning how to increase the capabilities of your applications and change their behavior in ways beneficial to the logic, business rules, or system requirements you are attempting to implement. In the next chapter, you will see how to initiate looping behavior in your program, to repeat code, and to handle iterative processing and/or calculations. Again, this will take the alteration of the flow of code execution in applications to the "next level," as the path of execution through the logic becomes more complex. Even so, this will be to the benefit of both the developer and the application and/or system being implemented.

Practice Problems

Terminology

Match the following terms from the chapter with their most appropriate definition:

1. Path of execution	a. Pair of symbols used to enclose a code block, distinguished from parentheses.
2. Mutually exclusive	b. Java decision structure that simplifies the testing of a variable for the presence of single, discrete potential values.
3. If statement	c. A Java statement used in `switch` expression to indicate the value to be returned. Used in the version of the switch expression where multiple lines of code are needed per case scenario.
4. Semicolon	d. Java statement used to execute code in the case of one or the other of two mutually exclusive scenarios being possible. Evaluates an expression to determine which scenario is the case.
5. Compound statement	e. A Java decision structure that additionally returns a data value for use in an expression or to be stored in a variable.
6. Expression resolving	f. Java statement used to execute code in the case of three or more scenarios being present. Expression evaluations can occur with each potential scenario.
7. Code block	g. A logical design where break statements are purposefully omitted from a `switch` statement to change its behavior. Useful to prevent code duplication across switch cases.
8. Syntax error	h. The line-by-line sequence of code processing that occurs in your application. Can be straightforward or complicated/branching.
9. Logic error	i. Java statement that ends execution of code in a code block and causes execution to leave that code block and resume with the next line of code following it.
10. Curly braces	j. The processing of an expression in an order that results in a single value, either numeric, boolean, or another type. Distinguished from a method return type.
11. `if…else` statement	k. An error that occurs because of incorrect syntax. May be noted by either the development IDE or the compiler.
12. If statement nesting	l. Syntax symbol that indicates the end of a single Java line of code or statement/expression.
13. Ternary operator	m. Logic design where one `if` statement is placed within another. Typically consisting of an outer and inner if statement, but additional deeper levels could be present.
14. `if…else if…else`	n. One or more lines of code grouped together and enclosed by curly braces. Normally used to group related lines of code that are associated with various Java statements.
15. Switch statement	o. A condition where two scenarios cannot happen simultaneously. Either one or the other occurs, but never both at the same time.
16. Break statement	p. A Java statement used within a `switch` to represent a potential value of a tested variable and associate one or more lines of code with this scenario.
17. Case statement	q. An expression that consists of two or more parts that will each resolve, then their values will be compared to one another.
18. Fall-through behavior	r. An error that occurs when an application does not behave or produce values as expected when the application was designed. May still compile and execute successfully.
19. Switch expression	s. Symbol used in the return-value-only version of the `switch` expression to indicate the value to be returned by the expression.
20. Yield statement	t. A Java decision statement that tests for a single scenario or value condition. One or more lines of code can be associated with the scenario.
21. Arrow operator	u. Java operator that consists of two operators and three operands. Can be considered a one-line equivalent of a normal `if…else` statement. Returns a value based on the evaluation of an expression.

Find the Error

In each of the following problems, carefully examine the code given, and determine the error(s)/issue(s) with each. Keep in mind, the error(s) could be syntax (code) or logic (intended outcome) based or both!

1.

```
char userCode = 'b';
int userLevel = 0;

if (userCode == 'a');
    userLevel = 1;
if (userCode == 'b');
    userLevel == 2;
if (userCode = 'c');
    userLevel = 3;
if (userCode == 'd');
    userLevel = 4;
```

2.

```
// Business Rule: Password must contain '!' or '#'
// and have a length of greater than 5 characters
String password = "java!rocks#56";
if (password.equals(password.contains('!' || '#')).length() > 5)
    system.out.println("New Password Accepted!");
```

3.

```
int studentAge = 20;
if {studentAge > 18}
(
    System.out.println("Undergrad");
)
else
(
    System.out.printnl("Student Age Category");
)
```

4.

```
int category = 2;
String level = "";

if (category == 1)
    level = "Starter Class";
else
    level = "Intermediate Class";
else if (category == 3);
    level = "Advanced Class";
```

5.

```
boolean trueVar = false;
boolean falseVar = true;

if (!falseVar)
{
    trueVar = !trueVar;
    if (falseVar)
        falseVar = !falseVar;
    else
        trueVar = !trueVar;
}
```

6.

```
double taxRate = 0.0;
int taxBracket = 3;

switch (taxBracket)
{
    case 1: System.out.println("Low Bracket");
    taxRate -> 0.0275;
    break;
    case 2: System.out.println("Middle Bracket");
    taxRate -> 0.0475;
    break;
    case 3: System.out.println("Upper Bracket");
    break;
    taxRate -> 0.0775;
};
```

7.

```
double taxRate = 0.0;
int taxBracket = 3;

taxRate = switch (taxBracket)
{
    case 1 -> System.out.println("Low Bracket");
    taxRate yields 0.0275;
    break;
    case 2 -> System.out.println("Middle Bracket");
    taxRate yields 0.0475;
    break;
    case 3 -> System.out.println("Upper Bracket");
    break;
    taxRate yields 0.0775;
}
```

8.

```
int formulaOption = 2;
int firstNumber = 3;
int secondNumber = 7;

if (formulaOption > 0)
    System.out.println("Add: " + (firstNumber + secondNumber));
else if (formulaOption > 1)
    System.out.println("Subtract: " + (firstNumber - secondNumber));
else if (formulaOption > 2)
    System.out.println("Multiply: " + (firstNumber * secondNumber));
else if (formulaOption > 3 & secondNumber != 0)
    System.out.println("Subtract: " + (firstNumber - secondNumber));
```

9.

```
int numA = 10;
int numB = 20;
boolean findMax = false;
int largerNumber = 0;

true ? max(numA, numB) : min(numA, numB);
```

10.

```
int numA = 10;
int numB = 20;
```

```
boolean findMax = true;
int largerNumber = 0;

switch(findMax ? max(numA, numB) : min(numA, numB))
{
   case true: largerNumber = numA;
   break;
   case false: largerNumber = numB;
   break;
}
```

Think about It

1. Describe how decision structures enable decision-making in our applications. How do they change the path of execution of code? How does this increase the abilities of our applications?
2. What types of expressions can be used in an `if` statement? What types of values can be used in the expressions? Where can those values come from?
3. Why are the two outcomes of an `if…else` statement considered mutually exclusive?
4. Describe how a code block changes the behavior of an `if` statement. What are the benefits of associating a code block with an if statement?
5. How does an `if` statement behave if there is no code block associated with it?
6. How are boolean and relational operators helpful within an `if` statement? Is there a way for an `if` statement to work without using any of these operators within its expression?
7. What is a benefit of nesting `if` statements one within the other? What is a potential negative of doing this? How can you prevent it?
8. Describe the differences between a logic error and a syntax or "runtime" error.
9. What is a great way to determine which type of `if` statement you need to use in your decision-making logic?
10. How is the ternary operator similar to a simple `if…else` statement? What can an `if…else` statement do that a ternary operator cannot?
11. Describe what a switch statement does. How is it similar to an if statement? How is it different?
12. What are the data types for the assessed variable in a `switch` statement? Why do you think that data types like double are not effective in a `switch` statement?
13. Describe the `switch` statement behavior known as "fall-through." How can this work to your advantage in enabling decision-making in your application?
14. What is the main difference between a `switch` statement and `switch` expression? How do you enable multiline code execution in `switch` expression cases?

Short Syntax Problems

1. Write some logic that will test a `String` variable to see if it contains the English alphabet vowels `a`, `e`, `i`, `o`, and `u` (and `y` if you want to). For each vowel, print a message to the console stating that it contained that particular vowel. Add logic to this that will print a message if the `String` contains no vowels at all.
2. Write some logic that will print a custom message to the console depending on the day of the week. Prompt for and have the user type in the current day. For "Friday," print "Weekend is here!" For "Saturday," print "Enjoy your weekend!" For "Sunday," print "Back to work tomorrow!" For all other days of the week, print "Work hard!" Ensure that your logic can handle the user forgetting to capitalize the day of the week.
3. Write some logic that will prompt for the user to enter three pieces of information: their GPA (include decimal information!), their major, and their undergraduate level (freshman, sophomore, junior, or senior). Use this information to determine the amount of scholarship funds they are eligible for. If their GPA is above 3.00, they are eligible for $500; if below, $250. Each undergraduate level adds $100 to this base amount (freshman: $100; senior: $400). Print their information and their total scholarship amount to the console in a message. Be sure to handle both capitalized and noncapitalized undergraduate-level labels.
4. Write some logic that will prompt the user to enter the current month's name (i.e., "May") and whether

or not it is a leap year ("Y" or "y," "N" or "n"). Print a message to the console that states the number of days in the month entered, and account for February if it is currently a leap year.

5. Write some logic that will print a rough "progress bar" to the console using text. For example, a 50% full progress bar (*think:* downloading a file) might look like this: "`[=====     ]`." Notice that it is "half" full (five equal signs out of a possible ten). Prompt the user to enter a percentage as a whole number (i.e., 27). Use a decision structure to print out a progress bar in the following manner by accounting for the following ranges of percentages entered by the user: 0–25%, one-fourth full; 25–50%, one-half full; 50–75%: three-fourths full; 75–100%: progress bar is full. Use only the topics learned up until this chapter to accomplish this.

Full Problems

1. Write a program that will clean up the customer names for the mom-and-pop grocery store. Implement the following:
   a. Prompt the user to enter a customer name in the console. Your application should be able to accept and process customer names in any of the following formats:

   ```
   Second name, First name
   First name Second name
   Second name, Middle initial First name
   ```

   b. Use `String` manipulation and decision structures to format all three possible types of customer name entries from above into the following format: Second name, First name initial. Middle initial. For example, if the user types in "`Sally Customer`" or "`Customer, R. Sally`" or "`Customer, Sally`," your program will handle any of these and print to the console "`Customer, S. R.`" (if the middle initial is provided—omit if not).
2. Write some logic for the mom-and-pop grocery store that will generate a random mailing address for a customer. Use the Math class, String manipulation, and decision structures.
   a. First, generate a random three-digit building/house number, between one and nine for the first digit and between zero and nine for the next two.
   b. Second, randomly pick a location from among three different words: "Blecker," "Garland," and "Mopsick."
   c. Finally, randomly pick a type of location from "Road," "Street," and "Route."
   d. Format the street address in a business-appropriate manner.
   e. Execute your logic a few times, and note the composed addresses.
3. Write a program that will perform various mathematical calculations based on the user typing in and selecting a menu option. Implement the following:
   a. Prompt the user with four menu options, and capture their choice. Use an appropriate decision structure to handle the menu option the user has typed in, and execute the appropriate code.
   b. Menu option 1 will perform a multiplication of two numbers. If the user types in option 1 and hits enter, prompt them for the two numbers, multiply them, then display the results similar to "The product of ## and ## is ####."
   c. Menu option 2 will perform an exponent calculation, a number raised to a power. If the user types in option 2 and hits enter, prompt for the two numbers, and raise the first number to the power of the second. Display the results in a professional way.
   d. Menu option 3 will perform the calculation of an average. If the user types in option 3 and hits enter, prompt them to enter four numbers, and then find the average of those four numbers (sum/quantity). Be careful with conversion to a double! Display the result (with decimal information) in a professional way.
   e. Menu option 4 will display the largest of **four numbers**. If the user types in option 4 and hits enter, prompt them for four numbers, and capture them. Then find the largest of the four numbers. *Hint:* Perform the comparisons two at a time, then compare the larger with the next number. Display the results in a professional way.
4. You and a colleague are developing a small Java application for a client. The program will inform a chemical lab specialist of how many units of a chemical should be added to a manufacturing process that takes five days (Monday through Friday).

Each day for ten hours, the specialist manages the process and adds the appropriate units of the chemical to the process. The amount added each hour is different. If the day is Tuesday or Friday, then the amount changes for several specific hours. This chart has guided the lab specialists in the past:

Hour	Base amount	If Tuesday	If Friday
1	2.00		
2	3.50		Add 3.00
3	1.00		
4	0.50	Add 1.00	
5	3.50		
6	2.00		
7	1.00		
8	1.00	Add 2.00	
9	2.00		
10	2.00		Add 4.00

Write a program that will report to the lab specialist the appropriate information on how many units of the chemical to add based on the above schedule. For example, the specialist would use your program to type in the current day and the hour of that day, and the program would report the number of units. For "Monday" and hour "3," the units of chemical would be reported as "1.00." If the day is "Tuesday" and the hour is "8," the units of chemical would be "3.00"—the base amount plus the amount to add. Use the appropriate decision structure(s) and logic to implement the logic. Keep decimal data as you add and report chemical units to be added! Be careful with the user typing in lowercase versions of the days and handle those efficiently.

5. Write a program that will calculate shipping costs for a package to be shipped to a customer's address. The program will prompt the user to enter all the information discussed in the following business rules:
   a. The width (across), height (tall), and depth (back) of the package are all multiplied to calculate the cubic inches. If the cubic inches is <= 500, the base price is $10.00; if <= 1,000, the base price is $12.00; and if larger than this, it is $20.00
   b. The weight of the package impacts shipping as well: <= 32 ounces adds $3.00 to the price, <= 100 ounces adds $7.00, and heavier than this adds $12.00 to the price.
   c. The distance that the package has to travel impacts the price as well: <= 100 miles adds $5.00 to the price, longer than 100 miles adds $11.00 to the shipping price.
   d. Finally, shipping to certain states adds a surcharge to the costs: California (CA), Oregon (OR), and Idaho (ID) add $2.00 to the cost of the package. Florida (FL) and Maine (ME) add a $3.00 charge. Shipment is not possible to Alaska (AK) and Hawaii (HI) at this time.
   e. Have your program output the cost for each characteristic, and display a total in a business-appropriate manner.
   f. **Extra challenge:** Use your random street address generator from full problem #2 to generate a street address the package is shipping to. Include this in the report.

Chapter 5

Loops, Loops, Loops, Loops . . .

What You Will Learn in This Chapter

In the prior chapter, you learned how to put decision structures in Java to good use implementing decision-making logic. Looping behavior in programming languages, Java included, uses these decision structures and enables repetitive behavior in code logic. Machines, computers, and digital processing devices are extremely good at looping behavior. Using loops in applications offers many benefits, including eliminating tedious programming, simplifying unnecessarily complex logic, and reducing code repetition. Looping in software development involves elegant, concise code that leverages computing power, letting the computer do more of the work. Information systems professionals who are engaged in systems development and implementation efforts through software development will encounter numerous situations where sequential data processing and the ability to invoke repetitive behavior in software are needed. Leveraging looping behavior in any programming language, including Java, is a must. Syntax that invokes looping behavior combined with decision structures to determine the extent and nature of that repetitive behavior enables highly effective logic implementation in software.

Specifically, this chapter will help you do the following:

1. Understand the nature, uses, and benefits of the `for` loop structure, its syntax, and common issues that can occur with its usage
2. Understand the nature, uses, and benefits of nested loop structures—particularly, nested `for` loops—and how these benefit the processing of tabular / highly structured data, among other uses
3. Understand how a `while` loop functions, how its syntax compares with and differs from that of a `for` loop, and some of its common uses
4. Understand the nature and syntax of the `do…while` loop, its unique properties, and some common scenarios for its usage

Opening Scenario

Now that you have become comfortable with text manipulation and decision-making structures along with the code branching they enable, the enormity of the data-cleaning effort unfolds before you. The cleaning efforts will involve some manner of code looping, since your data are in database tables. Each table contains rows and columns, and the cleaning logic will probably involve several "passes" over the data (one loop to fix address issues; another to fix errant spaces in the data; another to fix phone numbers, which are not in a unified format; yet another to fix email address issues; etc.). You have additionally considered performing some simple analyses on the data (summaries, averages, minimums, maximums, clustering of addresses, etc.). This data might be useful to the client or could be a future reporting function, or it could inform the development team where efficiencies and speed could be gained (most common tasks, etc.). You want the rest of the team to be prepared for any issues that could be data related. Your cleaning and analytics code will need to "walk" along the rows and columns of your data, make several passes when needed, and branch off and perform a different set of actions based on expression evaluations. Teaching your code how to effectively repeat tasks and loop will be critical. As you have already learned, computers are not very "smart," and any subtleties in the logic must be carefully considered before writing code. Looping behavior will not be any different. You decide to dive into the Java syntax once again to understand how looping structures are used in the language, when they would work best, and how best to implement them. The ability to build this looping and data-cleaning logic solidly will be useful for you and your colleagues on the team. You feel confident that your cleaning logic will be possible once you have explored looping behavior in the Java language . . .

5.1 Machines Love Loops

Figure 5.1. A Looping Airport Baggage Carousel

Source: "The World's Shortest Baggage Carousel?" by 4nitsirk is licensed under CC BY-SA 2.0, https://www.flickr.com/photos/26223114@N02/36335481110.

Filling bottles of soda (or "pop," depending on where you are from). Stamping out new skillets from sheet metal. Bending metal into links to make a chain (go search for this on your favorite online video service . . . it is mesmerizing!).[*] The sequence of steps that occur when you start your vehicle. The rolling of the dryer over and over again that you watch when you are bored sometimes. Repetitive actions are everywhere in real life. Think about the software that operates the stoplights at the next intersection you drive to. Over and over, day after day, that software will repeat its actions and repeat the same sequence to change the lights in a preprogrammed, purposefully designed way. Decision structures are often in place within software to change its execution depending on varying inputs and business rules. For the most part, machines repeat their instructions and carry out the same actions over and over. We mere mortals are very lucky that machines are great at repetitive tasks, as they save us from having to carry those tasks out.

The software you write can make data-grounded decisions and similarly change code execution based on those decisions. Your software can also perform repetitive actions to process data, carry out a task a certain number of times, or continue to carry out a task until some evaluative result stops the repetition. **Looping behavior**, or code execution repetition, can allow your software to "intelligently" process data or perform tasks, evaluating how long or how many times it should do this before stopping. Many times, you will know before you write any code the exact number of times a repeating action should occur, and other times you will want the repetition to occur until "something changes." Knowledge of how to implement and use loops in code is a powerful skill in the mental toolbox of any programmer.

Designing looping behavior in code will come in handy on many occasions in later chapters as well. Computers will execute looping code the exact same way every time (if decision structures allow). Software can process data through looping behavior much more **accurately**, much **faster**, and with more **endurance** than a person ever could. It is to your benefit to take the time to explore the looping structures that Java syntax provides. Some loop structures will repeat code a **fixed** number of times and others will run a **flexible/variable** number of times based on the evaluation of some boolean expression. Loop structures can be divided into two kinds: one that **tests before looping** and one that **tests after looping**. Sometimes, you will see these called "pretest" and "posttest" loops. Table 5.1 summarizes the major loop structures available in Java.

There are **many** occasions where a developer can leverage looping behavior to their benefit:

- Processing a known or unknown number of records from a database table, stream of internet data, or external data file
- Processing the characters in a name or other type of string value
- Processing a sequence of numbers to perform a mathematical or statistical calculation

Table 5.1. Summary of Loop Structures in Java

	Test before looping	Test after looping
Fixed loop quantity	• `for` loop • Enhanced `for` loop[*]	n/a
Flexible loop quantity	• `while` loop	• `do...while` loop

[*] Covered in chapter 7

[*] https://www.youtube.com/watch?v=iw8we_BWdsw&ab_channel=TechWorldReviews.

- Looping until a user has entered their username/password correctly
- Directing extraction, transformation, and load (ETL) processes to increase data quality and prepare that data from disparate sources for analytics activities.

Information systems professionals have many, many reasons to gain solid skills in leveraging looping behavior to accomplish these and many other vitally important tasks.

SUMMARY POINTS

- Digital systems can perform repetitive behavior much faster and more accurately than any person.
- Most programming languages are capable of looping behavior, repeating the execution of one or more lines of code until a decision forces the repetition to stop.
- Looping behavior in a programming language is very useful in many contexts, especially in IS where user interaction and data processing tasks are often nuanced and complex, involving many repeated steps.
- Looping structures in Java like the `for` loop will evaluate a boolean condition prior to beginning a defined amount of repetition.
- Structures like the `while` and do...`while` loops are more flexible and do not predefine the number of repetitions that will occur.
- The do...`while` loop will always execute the first iteration/loop, only evaluating a boolean statement afterward.

QUICK PROBLEMS

1. **Think:** Consider the following programming task—A bank needs software that will allow a customer to withdraw $10.00 a day from their account until their account balance reaches $0.00. Considering the code you would have to write for this, how many times should the account balance be checked? How does the starting balance impact your answer? What if the customer's balance drops below $10.00?
2. **Think:** Consider a simple interest savings account, where each year, the account earns 2.4% on the current balance. The interest is calculated and added once a year. Jot down the pseudocode for some logic that will prompt the user to enter a starting balance, then loop five years, calculating and adding the interest to the balance each year. Include a print of the final balance at the end.
3. **Think:** Consider the following programming task: A classroom contains five rows of desks, and on each row sit six students. You want to gather the first name of each student and add that to a list using a repetitive loop. Thinking about the code you would have to write for this, how many loops total will there be? How would your code know when to stop looping? How do you handle the situation of an empty seat (student is absent that day?) and when would you check for this? How would your algorithm change if each row contains a different number of seats?

5.2 `for` Loops

The `for` loop is a basic loop structure present in many programming languages. Figure 5.2 shows the basic parts and structure of the `for` loop. Like an `if` statement, the `for` loop can have multiple lines of code enclosed in curly braces following it or a single line of code with curly braces omitted. Unlike the `if` statement, though, the code associated with the `for` loop will be **repeatedly**

```
for (loop-variable;
loop-until condition;
post-iteration action)
    Single line of associated
    repeating code
```

```
for (loop-variable;
loop-until condition;
post-iteration action)
    {
    // Multiple lines of code
    // These will repeat
    }
```

Figure 5.2. Basic Structure of a `for` Loop with Single and Multiple Lines of Associated Code

executed and repeated a fixed number of times depending on how you set up the `for` loop **header** (the statement itself). As the developer, you are able to control exactly how the `for` loop will behave through careful setup of the three main parts of the `for` loop's header. Consider the following basic example that most programmers first practice when learning how to use these types of loops:

Code Snippet 5.1

```
for (int i=0; i<10; i++)
{
    System.out.println("Hello World!"); // Print on separate lines
}
```

When this code runs, it will print the following to the console:

```
Hello World!
Hello World!
Hello World!
Hello World!
Hello World!
Hello World!
Hello World!
Hello World!
Hello World!
Hello World!
```

Go ahead and count how many times the phrase "Hello World!" printed to the console. Your author will wait. Hopefully, you counted ten successive prints. How did the `for` loop as written know to repeat its code exactly ten times? Notice that there are three separate expressions in the `for` loop header. Each expression is separated by a semicolon. Consider each of these expressions in order:

- **Loop variable:** In the `for` loop's header, you can see the code `int i = 0;` as the first expression. This is known as the **loop variable** or sometimes the **loop control variable.** In a `for` loop, this variable helps control the repeating behavior of the `for` loop. If you carefully look at this first part, you might think it looks like a variable declaration and initialization, and you would be right. The loop header can create a control variable that has **scope** for the life of the `for` loop itself. After the loop ends, this variable will be destroyed and unusable outside/after the loop. An `int` called `i` is created that starts with a value of `0` and uses this variable to control how many times the loop repeats its associated code.
- **Loop-until condition:** The next expression in the `for` loop header looks like this: `i < 10;`. This expression in a `for` loop is known as the **loop-until condition**, and it means just what its name implies: continue looping and repeatedly executing your associated code until this expression evaluates to `false`. This is a boolean expression (just like with `if` statements) and can be read as "loop until the value of the loop variable `i` is no longer strictly less than ten." Now you should be able to see how the first and second expressions in the `for` loop header are related: the first specifies the initial value of the loop variable, and the second bases the continued test of looping upon the value of the variable **during each loop iteration.** If at the start of any successive loop, the value of `i` equals `10`, the `for` loop will not continue and will end. This is why the `for` loop is known as a **test-before-looping** structure.
- **After-iteration action:** Finally, the last expression in the `for` loop's header (the only one not ended by a semicolon because it is the last and not needed) is the **after-iteration action.** This is how the `for` loop's control variable **will be changed at the end of each individual loop** (known as a loop **iteration**). This change to the loop variable will eventually cause the loop-until condition to evaluate to `false` (or it should if you have designed it well!), ending the loop. Notice that this last expression is simply the use of the post-increment operator on the control variable: `i++`. Since this is a stand-alone expression within the header, you could use the pre-increment operator, and it would have no effect on the loop's behavior.

To understand the sequence of how the `for` loop operator starts, repeats its code, and ends, examine figure 5.3 carefully, and note the order of events:

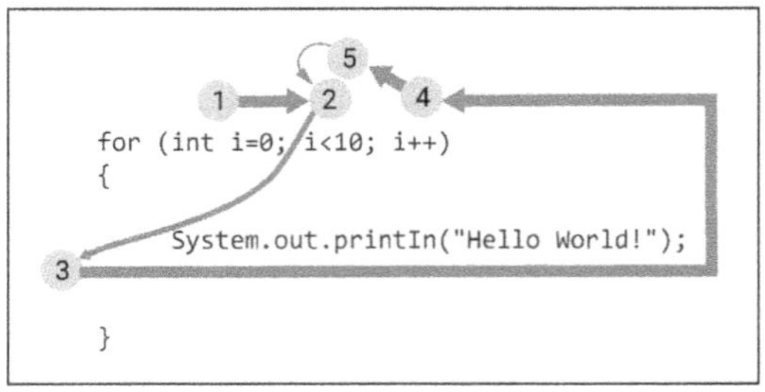

Figure 5.3. Path of `for` Loop Evaluation and Execution in Java

Step 1: The `for` loop begins, and the control variable is declared locally within the `for` loop. The variable is given an initial value.
Step 2: The loop-until condition expression is evaluated, and a true or false is generated. If true, then the `for` loop will execute the code associated with the `for` loop header. If false, the loop will end, and execution will move to the next line of code beyond the `for` loop.
Step 3: The code associated with the `for` loop is executed.
Step 4: When the associated code has executed, the postiteration action will occur. The loop control variable will be incremented by one.
Step 5: The loop-until condition is reevaluated, now with the **new** value of the control variable. Again, if true, the loop will continue at step 3 above. If false, the loop will end.

Notice that it is very important that you carefully consider the starting value of the loop control variable and what boolean expression you use as the loop-until condition. This will, barring any control structures or statements within the `for` loop's code, determine exactly how many loops the for will execute. Here, start `i` at a value of `0` and loop while `i` is less than `10`. That gives us the values `0-9` for the control variable, which is `10` numbers.

The `for` loop in figure 5.3 can be conversationally described as follows: **"For `i` to equal `0`, while `i` is strictly less than `10`, loop and print 'Hello World' to the console each time, incrementing `i` up by `1` at the end of each loop."**

You can make this `for` loop a bit more conventional and use the control variable in the loop code:

Code Snippet 5.2

```
for (int i=0; i<10; i++)
{
    System.out.print(i + " ");
}
```

Here, the `.print()` method is used instead of `.println()`. This method does not append the new line to the end of the console output. This works well, since it prints the results of all the loops on a single line in the console, like so:

```
0 1 2 3 4 5 6 7 8 9
```

In this version of the `for` loop, the value of `i` prints concatenated with a single blank space character. And because this is the code associated with the `for` loop header, this print occurs ten successive times. Interestingly, the value of `i` does reach `10` after the last loop, and this last value is what causes the loop-until condition to evaluate to `false`, forcing the `for` loop to end.

Why use `i` for the name of the loop control variable? You can really use any variable name you wish! Using single-letter names for loop control variables like this one in a `for` loop is a traditional programming practice. Since the variable really only serves one main purpose (to control the loop) and may be used in the loop's code (to be printed, or used in a calculation, or used as an index), keeping the name short reduces clutter and increases code readability. Other programmers will typically spot this common practice and understand the variable's purpose. Though a traditional naming style, it is **not** a Java syntax rule: you can use any nonreserved word name for a loop control variable that you wish.

You can use any starting and ending loop control variable value: Keep in mind that `for` loops are most useful when you **know ahead of time** how many loops you will need. For example, imagine that an external data file has exactly 5,345 student records stored within. In this case, you know that 5,345 loops are needed to read in those records. Here, a `for` loop might be the most useful loop structure. It does not really matter what the starting value is for the loop control variable as long as you set up the loop-until boolean expression so that it ends the loop after X number of iterations. For example, the loop earlier can be rewritten like so:

Code Snippet 5.3

```
for (int i=46; i<56; i++)
{
    System.out.print(i + " ");
}
```

This will produce the following console output:

```
46 47 48 49 50 51 52 53 54 55
```

Depending on what you are trying to do, the loop control variable's starting and ending values may not matter as much as **how many loops you intend to occur** because of them. Consider the following, where the first ten numbers from one to ten are added (here, the iterative values of `i` **do** matter, since they are used in the calculation):

Code Snippet 5.4

```
int sum = 0;
for (int i=1; i<=10; i++)
{
    sum += i;
}
System.out.println("The Sum is: " + sum);
```

In this example, the code loops while `i` is less than or equal to the value of `10` and starts the loop at `i = 1`. All the values of `i` during looping will be `1` through `10`, whereas with the earlier example, the values were `0-9`, since code execution looped while less than `10`, starting at `0`. Careful attention to the starting and loop-until conditions will yield the number of loops you need in a `for` statement.

Using a `for` loop for `String` and text manipulation: Loop structures like the `for` loop are very helpful for string and character manipulation. Consider the following example, where the words in a phrase are counted by cleverly counting the spaces (blank space characters) in the `String` variable:

Code Snippet 5.5

```
String phrase = "I cannot wait to bring my Java book with me on my date this weekend!";

int wordCount = 0;

for (int i=0; i<phrase.length(); i++)
{
    if (phrase.charAt(i) == ' ')
        wordCount++;
}
System.out.println("There are "
        + wordCount
        + " words in the phrase!");
```

This will produce the following output (which is **not** the correct count—you will see why shortly):

```
There are 14 words in the phrase!
```

Notice first the way the `for` loop header has been set up. The loop control variable starts at zero and loops while `i` is less than the length of the phrase. Remember how index notation works: the last value in a sequence is always at `length - 1`. If a `String` value is ten characters long, the index positions of the characters are zero through nine (`length - 1`). The `String` method `.length()` reports the length of the phrase, and then the logic loops to the last character (at the index position one less than the length). The loop increments `i` by one using the post-increment operator so that each and every character is processed.

Now manually count the words in the phrase. Yes, by hand. Uh-oh. If you did, you hopefully noticed that **the count is not correct**! You have a logic error (the program executed successfully, but the desired outcome was not achieved). Examine the logic here carefully, and you should see the issue: each blank space (assuming there is no errant one at the start/end of the phrase) has a word on its left and right. The last blank space has a word on its right, but only the blank spaces themselves are being counted and are used as a proxy for the number of words. The count is low by one because the code misses the count of the last word. This is corrected by adding one to the `wordCount` value **after the loop has ended**:

Code Snippet 5.6

```
String phrase = "I cannot wait to bring my Java book with me on my date this weekend!";
int wordCount = 0;
for (int i=0; i<phrase.length(); i++)
{
    if (phrase.charAt(i) == ' ')
        wordCount++;
}

wordCount++;

System.out.println("There are "
        + wordCount
        + " words in the phrase!");
```

This fixes the issue for **this phrase**, but consider the following situation:

```
String phrase = "";
```

If this empty String variable is processed with the above code, it would produce the following output:

```
There are 1 words in the phrase!
```

Oops! Another logic error. In this case, for whatever reason, the `String` was blank (perhaps it was blank in the field that was read in from a database table, or blank in a data file, or typed in empty). This is fixed with a bit of boolean logic:

Code Snippet 5.7

```
String phrase = "";
boolean blankFlag = false;
int wordCount = 0;

for (int i=0; i<phrase.length(); i++)
{
    if (phrase.charAt(i) == ' ')
    {
        blankFlag = true; // Set to true if any blank encountered
        wordCount++;
    }
}

if (blankFlag)   // if blankFlag == true
    wordCount++; // increase wordCount by 1

System.out.println("There are "
        + wordCount
        + " words in the phrase!");
```

And for this `String` variable, this will produce the following console output:

```
There are 0 words in the phrase!
```

Much better. But as happens in many information systems data-processing scenarios, the data may be "dirty," and you may encounter a string value that looks like this:

Code Snippet 5.8

```
String phrase = "EastonFenix";
```

Someone forgot to type in the blank space during data entry, or a logic error in code that processed this data neglected to include the blank space character between the two names. If you processed this String using the above code, it would report the following:

```
There are 0 words in the phrase!
```

This is not correct either! You can fix this by setting a boolean flag to true if the length is greater than zero. Meaning that if there are any characters in the String, there is at least one word. And if any blank space characters are encountered, then there is **more** than one word:

Code Snippet 5.9

```
String phrase = "EastonFenix";
boolean blankFlag = false;
boolean anyWords = false;
int wordCount = 0;

for (int i=0; i<phrase.length(); i++)
{
    anyWords = true;  // Will set to true if loop runs, length > 0

    if (phrase.charAt(i) == ' ')
    {
        blankFlag = true; // if you encounter blank, set to true
        wordCount++;
    }
}

if (blankFlag || anyWords) // if blankFlag OR anyWords is true
    wordCount++;           // Increase wordCount by 1

System.out.println("There are "
        + wordCount
        + " words in the phrase!");
```

This logic now tackles several of the potential major scenarios that might be encountered in a single `String` value. Of course, the code here cannot fix the name that is missing a blank space in between the first and second names, but you can at least count that there is one word in this `String` and none in a blank one.

Break and continue statements: Loops like the `for` loop are not fixed in their quantity of loops, and Java (like many languages) provides a way to alter the behavior of loop statements from **within**. You have seen the `break` statement used in both types of `switch` structures. Placing a `break` within a loop will cause the loop to end immediately, and code execution will leave the loop and move to the next line of code following the loop. Consider the following example:

Code Snippet 5.10

```
for (int i=0; i<10; i++)
{
    System.out.print(i + " ");
    break;
}
System.out.println("END");
```

This code will produce the following output to the console when run:

```
0 END
```

Notice that even though the `for` loop header is set to run ten times, it only performs part of the first iteration (prints the current value of `i`) and then encounters the break statement, which completely ends the loop and moves execution out to the next line of code after the `for` loop, which is the printing of the word "`end`." Typically, you would consider using `break` if there is a condition or scenario that you want to monitor in your loop, and if that condition occurs, it would be dangerous (a logic error or even a runtime error) to continue the loop, so it is best to end and move on. Consider the following example, where the results of division are performed:

Code Snippet 5.11

```
int numerator = 9;          // Hard-coded example value
int denominator = 5;        // Hard-coded example value

for (int i=10; i>0; i--)
{
    System.out.println(numerator + "/"
            + denominator
            + " = "
            + ((double)numerator/denominator));

    numerator--;
    denominator--;

    if (denominator == 0)
        break;
}
```

This will produce the following output:

```
9/5 = 1.8
8/4 = 2.0
7/3 = 2.3333333333333335
6/2 = 3.0
5/1 = 5.0
```

Notice that the `break` statement helps us avoid a division by zero error. Also, notice that within the `for` loop header, the count can run backward with the loop control variable needed. Simply use the post-decrement operator to decrease `i`'s value by one in each iteration. Additionally, the `numerator` and `denominator` are both decremented by one after using a cast operator to divide the two `int` values and up-convert the result to a `double` in order to preserve decimal data. It is safer to check for a denominator value of `0` at the start of each iteration. The logic can be altered as follows (in **bold**):

Code Snippet 5.12

```
// These could be captured via Scanner and console input also
int numerator = 9;
int denominator = 5;

for (int i=10; i>0; i--)
{
    if (denominator == 0) // Check at start of iteration
        break;

    System.out.println(numerator + "/"
            + denominator
            + " = "
            + ((double)numerator/denominator));

    numerator--;
    denominator--;
}
```

Realistically, the numerator and denominator would be not hard-coded but captured from user input or other sources. A second real-world example could look like the following. In it, a `String` variable is used as a password, and the logic ensures it contains one of three special characters specified by gathered business requirements:

Code Snippet 5.13

```
String password = "java!rocks#";
boolean passwordNotSecure = true;

for (int i=0; i<password.length(); i++)
{
    if (password.charAt(i) == '!'
            || password.charAt(i) == '#'
            || password.charAt(i) == '$' )
    {
        passwordNotSecure = false;
        break;
    }
}
```

This logic starts with the assumption that the password does not comply with the business's security rules for a password, and the characters it contains set the security audit flag to true. The code loops a number of times equivalent to the character length of the `String` variable and checks each character. As soon as a character that exactly matches one of the three required is encountered, the security audit "flag" is set to `false`, and the `break` statement is executed, leaving the loop and ending all iterations. The `String` class method `.contains()` could be used here to eliminate the need for a loop if you were pushing for efficiency. In situations where some business rules require more than one of a special character, `.contains()` would fall short, returning your logic to the need to write your own loop code to check all characters.

To understand the `continue` statement, consider the following example, where you want to count the characters in a `String` but omit the counting of blank spaces:

Code Snippet 5.14

```
String phrase = "Every book is an adventure and a journey not through distant places but through
yourself";
int characterCount = 0;

for (int i=0;i<phrase.length();i++)
{
    if (phrase.charAt(i) == ' ')
        continue;

    characterCount++;
}
System.out.println("Blanks in String: "
        + (phrase.length() - characterCount));
System.out.println("Alphabetic Characters: "
        + (characterCount));
System.out.println("String Length: "
        + phrase.length());
```

This particular phrase will produce the following output:

```
Blanks in String: 14
Alphabetic Characters: 74
String Length: 88
```

Notice how the value for `characterCount` is lower than the value for the length of the `String` itself. The continue statement causes the **current** loop iteration to end immediately and tells the `for` loop to move on to the postiteration action and on to the **next** loop iteration. Use the `continue` statement whenever the rest of the code or logic in your loop has been determined to not apply to a current case or scenario—for example, if you are altering `String` fields in a database table and find that the current value you are examining does not qualify for the complicated logic, performing an extensive financial calculation based on income values and find the current one you are examining in a loop does not need those performed, skipping the invocation of other code if login credentials are incorrect, and so on. There are many reasons why you might want to skip the rest of the logic in a current loop and move on to the next loop (and next value in a sequence). The added benefit here is that your application processes data in a smarter fashion and could see a speed benefit from "skipping" some processing that does not need it.

Control variable scope and alterations and optional `for` loop header expressions: A few last things to point out regarding `for` loops that are less commonly used but are valid in the Java syntax. First, you are not required to declare your loop control variable inside the `for` loop header. You can declare and initialize your control variable outside the `for` loop, and this will move its scope (i.e., life-span) outside the `for` loop itself. Consider the following valid example:

Code Snippet 5.15

```
int counter = 10;

for ( ; counter >= 0; counter--)
{
    System.out.print(counter + "...,");
}

System.out.println("\nBlast Off!");
```

Here the variable `counter` is used as the loop control variable, and it is created outside / prior to the `for` loop itself, meaning that its "life" does not begin and end with the beginning and end of the `for` loop. Notice as well that the first expression in the `for` loop header is **blank**! All the expressions within a `for` loop header are **optional**; you can leave them out, but you will still need to include the semicolons. What happens when you do that? Consider the following:

Code Snippet 5.16

```
for ( ; ; )
    System.out.print("Loop... ");
```

No loop control variable, no loop-until condition, no postiteration action. What has been done here is to create an **infinite loop**. This will run, but you will have to manually stop the application (i.e., "hard stop") because its logic never allows it to naturally end! Infinite loops are logic errors. You usually do not want a loop to go on forever but want some way for either the values or the usage of the application to cause the loop to end (eventually). Again, it is important to carefully consider your logic in the `for` loop header and the data you are processing or interacting with to ensure that your application steers clear of infinite loops. Carefully setting up your decision structures within your loop's code to handle cases where the loop should end will help prevent these infinite loops.

When would declaring the loop control variable outside of the `for` loop come in handy in a realistic scenario? Consider this example, where the password characters example is revisited and the counter used to determine at which specific index position a security character was **first** encountered:

Code Snippet 5.17

```
int position = 0;
String password = "eyeLove#Java!";

for ( ; position < password.length(); position++)
{
    if (password.charAt(position) == '#' ||
            password.charAt(position) == '!' ||
            password.charAt(position) == '$')
        break;
}

if (position != password.length())
    System.out.println("Required Character at position: "
            + position);
else
    System.out.println("Password NOT in compliance!");
```

As soon as one of the special characters is encountered, the `break` statement ends the loop entirely, and execution moves on to the code following the loop. Since the variable position was declared outside the loop, its life extends past that of the `for` loop, and you can use it after the loop has ended! Notice as well the logic check of `position`'s value versus the length of the `String` variable. Remember that if the `for` loop does not end early, its counter's value will be increased **one last time**, which will then cause the loop-until condition to evaluate to `false`, ending the loop naturally. If the characters are not found in the `String`, then the position will be incremented to exactly the value of the `String`'s length, causing the strict less-than loop-until condition to fail, ending the loop. These are the kinds of nuanced behavior in loops that you the developer should keep particularly in mind!

SUMMARY POINTS

- The `for` loop is a test-before-looping loop structure in Java. If the loop-until condition evaluates to false from the very beginning, the first loop will never occur.
- The `for` loop is useful in situations where you know before looping how many repetitions you will approximately need.
- The `for` loop header contains three expressions that help control the behavior of the `for` loop: the loop control variable initial condition, the loop-until condition, and the postiteration action or alteration to the control variable.
- All loops in Java, including the `for` loop, can have either one line of code without curly braces or multiple lines of code in a code block defined by curly braces associated with it.
- A loop control variable declared in the header of the `for` loop has a life-span that equals the duration of the `for` loop's life. When the loop ends, so does the variable. A loop control variable declared outside the `for` loop will have a "larger" scope and lives past the life of the `for` loop.
- Traditionally, loop control variables have single-letter names, but this is not a syntax requirement in Java. You can choose any name you wish as long as it is not a reserved keyword or command in Java.
- The `break` statement ends the current iteration of a loop and instructs the loop to end immediately.
- The `continue` statement ends the current iteration of a loop and instructs the loop to immediately move on to the next loop in the sequence.
- The three expressions in a `for` loop header are optional and, if omitted, will change the behavior of the `for` loop, possibly creating an infinite loop scenario.

QUICK PROBLEMS

1. **Coding:** Use a `for` loop to print the numbers one hundred through to zero backward to the console, starting with one hundred and counting down all the way to zero.
2. **Think:** What will happen if you manually change the value of a loop's control variable from inside the associated code of the loop itself? How might this alter the loop's behavior?
3. **Coding:** Store a first name and second name in a `String` variable. Use the appropriate `String` class method to find the location of the blank space character in the `String`. After this, use two successive `for` loops to print the characters one by one that are to the left of the blank space and to print the characters one by one that are to the right of the blank space in the `String`, respectively. *Hint:* Find the length of the `String` to help control the number of loops in the second `for` loop.

5.3 Nesting `for` Loops

At some point, every information systems professional interacts with tabular-style data. These are most commonly seen in the form of spreadsheets and/or database tables. They are prolific throughout the business world. Rows and columns of data are useful because of their predictable structure, their compact and concise nature, and their ability to represent and store multiple characteristic values about entities and their associations (most notably in relational databases). Programmers who build software to interact with tabular data will use a technique that involves **nested `for` loops** in order to **traverse** or "walk" along both the rows and the columns of tabularly structured data. Like `if` statements, you can nest `for` loops as deeply as you wish (three, four, five levels, etc.), but from three on, things get very complex and confusing. Normally, a single nested `for` loop is used, consisting of an **outer** and **inner `for` loop**. Figure 5.4 shows the nested nature of this typical usage.

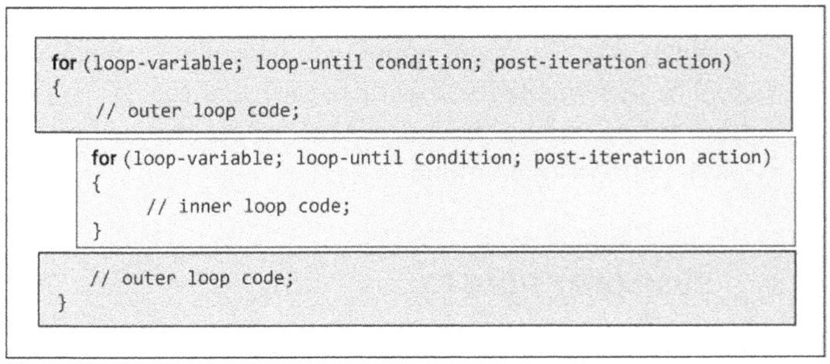

Figure 5.4. Structure of a Singly Nested `for` Loop with Outer and Inner `for` Loops

With tabular data that consists of rows and columns, normally the outer `for` loop is used to determine which row is currently being processed. The inner `for` loop then traverses each column **within the row indicated by the outer.** This is **not** a definite and concrete rule, just a rule of thumb and a usual way of processing rows and columns. Looking at figure 5.3, the way to understand the execution of a nested `for` loop structure is as follows: **for every single loop of the outer `for` loop, the inner `for` loop will iterate all of its defined number of times.** It is a loop within a loop! Consider the following example that will have an outer `for` loop defined to iterate three times and an inner `for` loop that will iterate three times **for each and every loop of the outer**:

Code Snippet 5.18

```
int printVar = 1;
for (int i=0;i<3;i++)
{
    for (int j=0;j<3;j++)
    {
        System.out.print(printVar + " ");
        printVar++;
    }
}
```

If you execute this code, it will print the following to the console:

```
1 2 3 4 5 6 7 8 9
```

Notice that the outer `for` loop is set up to loop three times (`i`'s values will be `0`, `1`, and `2`). The inner `for` loop will loop three times for each and every loop of the outer. The variable `j` is used as the control name for the inner loop, since `i` is already declared and used in the header of the outer loop. The inner `for` loop is defined to loop three times as well (`j`'s values will be `0`, `1`, and `2`), but this loop will run all three of its iterations each and every time the outer `for` loop runs. To visualize this better, change the code just a bit to look like this:

Code Snippet 5.19

```
int printVar = 1;

for (int i=0;i<3;i++)
{
    for (int j=0;j<3;j++)
    {
        System.out.print(printVar + " ");
```

```
        printVar++;
    }
    System.out.println("");
}
```

This prints the following:

```
1 2 3
4 5 6
7 8 9
```

Now you should be able to visualize the nature of the nested loop! The code associated with the outer `for` loop consists of an inner `for` loop (this is executed first and loops all three of its times) and then a second line of code, the call to `.println()`, which prints a new-line character to the console, moving output to the next line below. And the outer loop will execute both of these in each and every one of its three iterations. Just like with a singular `for` loop, you can use the values of the control variables while the nested `for` loop is executing:

Code Snippet 5.20

```
for (int i=0;i<3;i++)
{
    for (int j=0;j<3;j++)
    {
        System.out.print(j + " "); // printing value of j
    }
    System.out.println("");
}
```

The output to the console will look like the following:

```
0 1 2
0 1 2
0 1 2
```

This helps visualize the nature of the nested `for` loop, printing the value of `j` while the inner `for` loop runs. Notice how there are three rows (this is the outer `for` loop working), and within each row, the inner `for` loop runs all three of its loops, printing the value of `j` on each loop. Each time printing moves to a new row (which is moving to the next iteration of the outer `for` loop), the inner `for` loop restarts from its beginning, and `j` starts back at zero (because the variable `j` is redeclared each time). To help visualize this even more, consider the following code and output:

Code Snippet 5.21

```
for (int i=0;i<4;i++)
{
    System.out.print("Row " + i + ": "); // print value of i

    for (int j=0;j<5;j++) // Loops 5 times for each outer loop
    {
        System.out.print(j + " "); // printing value of j
    }

    System.out.println(""); // new line at end of this "row"
}
```

Console output:

```
Row 0: 0 1 2 3 4
Row 1: 0 1 2 3 4
Row 2: 0 1 2 3 4
Row 3: 0 1 2 3 4
```

Both the outer and the inner loops have been changed somewhat. The outer will loop four times, and the inner will loop five times for each loop of the outer. In this example, note that the values of both `i` and `j` are printing, which helps you visualize how these variables' values change as the loops run. Keep in mind that the outer `for` loop will not finish its **first** iteration until **all the code** associated with that inner loop has **finished**.

For the software within an information system, using a nested `for` loop to print a tabular report is highly common in many business contexts. Just because data is stored in a spreadsheet or in a database table (or in a tabular style in a query result), that does not mean the data will print or be processed that way. Consider the following example, where five rows of randomly generated data are printed:

Code Snippet 5.22

```
System.out.println("Row:\tNum1:\tNum2:\tNum3:");

for (int i=1;i<=5;i++)
{
    System.out.print(i + "\t");
    for (int j=0;j<3;j++)
    {
        System.out.print(Math.round(Math.random() * 50) + "\t");
    }
    System.out.println("");
}
```

Console output:

```
Row:    Num1:   Num2:   Num3:
1       1       16      43
2       16      21      50
3       36      31      25
4       25      19      11
5       15      33      1
```

Notice that escaped tab space characters are concatenated into the printed `String` values. The `.random()` and `.round()` methods of the Math class are used to generate random whole numbers for each column, all printed in a professional-looking columnar report. Notice as well that the column headers are printed prior to both loops. A common **mistake** is to place the print for the headers inside the outer `for` loop as its first line of code. Consider the following, where this mistake is made for you already:

Code Snippet 5.23

```
for (int i=1; i<=5; i++)
{
    System.out.println("Row:\t\tNum1:\t\tNum2:\t\tNum3:");
    System.out.print(i + "\t\t");
    for (int j=0;j<3;j++)
    {
        System.out.print(Math.round(Math.random() * 50) + "\t\t");
    }
    System.out.println("");
}
```

Console output:

```
Row:    Num1:   Num2:   Num3:
1       22      43      50
Row:    Num1:   Num2:   Num3:
2       21      31      28
Row:    Num1:   Num2:   Num3:
3       36      7       30
Row:    Num1:   Num2:   Num3:
4       47      16      0
Row:    Num1:   Num2:   Num3:
5       1       25      31
```

Oops! Remember that your computer really, really likes loops. And it will process them in a truly mechanical manner. Any code you place inside a loop's associated code block will execute with each and every iteration of the loop. Placing the column header print inside the outer loop will cause it to print each time the outer loop iterates and executes. There may be occasions where you want this to occur. It all depends on the client's reporting and business needs. Consider the following, which uses format specifiers to display the report in a more sophisticated manner:

Code Snippet 5.24

```
for (int i=1;i<=5;i++)
{
    System.out.println("Employee " + i + ":");
    System.out.print(String.format("%-12s", "Division:"));
    System.out.print(String.format("%-12s", "Sector:"));
    System.out.print(String.format("%s", "Rank:\n"));
    for (int j=0;j<3;j++)
    {
        System.out.print(
                String.format("%-12d",
                        Math.round(Math.random() * 50)
                )
        );
    }
    System.out.println("\n");
}
```

Console output:

```
Employee 1:
Division:   Sector:     Rank:
49          16          17

Employee 2:
Division:   Sector:     Rank:
48          11          1

Employee 3:
Division:   Sector:     Rank:
12          42          23

Employee 4:
Division:   Sector:     Rank:
19          35          20

Employee 5:
Division:   Sector:     Rank:
22          4           37
```

The values for each column are still randomly generated (here for simplicity and ease of demonstration), and using format specifiers, left-justification flags, and column widths keeps everything cleanly lined up and predictable.

The `break` and `continue` statements still work the same way, even with `for` loops that are nested. Consider the following example, where each word of a `String` is printed on its own line (with brackets added for visual clarity):

Code Snippet 5.25

```
String text = "Java is a powerful language useful for development on many different platforms";
int position = 0;

for ( ; ; ) // OUTER for loop
{
    if (text.length() == 0) // Is text empty?
```

```
        break; // if so, break the outer loop

    System.out.print("["); // Print the word's opening bracket

    for ( ; ; ) // INNER for loop
    {
        if (position < text.length()) // if you are not to end of text
        {
            if (text.charAt(position) != ' ') // if it is not a blank
                System.out.print(text.charAt(position++)); // Print
            else // If the character is a blank space
                break; // Break the inner loop and end it
        }
        else
            break; // if at end of text, break the inner loop.
    }

    System.out.print("]\n"); // print the ending bracket

    if (position == text.length()) // if you are at the end
        break; // break the outer loop
    else
        position++; // increase the position again to the next word
}
```

Console output:

```
[Java]
[is]
[a]
[powerful]
[language]
[useful]
[for]
[development]
[on]
[many]
[different]
[platforms]
```

Notice that both the outer and the inner loops are **infinite loops**. Be careful to use **break** statements to end infinite loops when appropriate! The outer loop "walks" along each successive word, and the inner `for` loop processes and prints each character of that word, checking for both the end of the string value (`position == text.length()`) and a blank space. The post-increment operator is used to increment `position`, moving along to the next character in the `String` value. Notice that the **break** statement is used within the `for` loop it applies to, and this rule applies to **continue** as well. It is typically not a great idea to use infinite loops for any logic, as this can introduce frustrating logic errors. In the next section, a better way will be introduced via the `while` loop.

SUMMARY POINTS

- Nested loop structures, especially `for` loops, can be very useful in situations where there is a tabular-style structure to the data consisting of "rows" and "columns," though nesting is not limited to only these scenarios.
- When one `for` loop is nested within another, the inner `for` loop (the one nested) will loop all of its number of times for each and every single loop of the outer (the containing) `for` loop.
- The inner `for` loop will have access to the control variable of the outer `for` loop, but the outer `for` loop code cannot see the inner loop control variable.

- The number of repetitions an inner `for` loop will carry out when nested can be determined by multiplying the number of loops of the outer by the number of loops of the inner, since the inner loop runs X times for each outer loop.
- Nesting of loop structures can be useful not only for incoming data but for output and console/ report printing.

QUICK PROBLEMS

1. **Coding:** Use a nested `for` loop to print out the numbers ten through twenty, twenty through thirty, and thirty through forty, each on its own row of console output.
2. **Think:** Suppose you have a triple-nested `for` loop (an outer `for` loop with an inner loop that itself has one more `for` loop nested within). If all three loops are implemented to run five loops each, how many times will the innermost `for` loop run in total?
3. **Coding:** Create a `String` variable with your name stored as its value. Using a nested `for` loop, print the characters of your name from the `String` variable, printing only three characters per row. Print characters until there are no more in the `String` to print, then ensure both loops end.

5.4 `while` Loops

The `while` loop differs from the `for` in ways that are useful for situations where the number of loops you will need is **not exactly known** before processing occurs. It is additionally useful in situations where you know looping needs to end when a certain condition is encountered but you do not know exactly when this will occur. Where the `for` loop gives you a predictable, structured method of looping, the `while` loop provides flexibility for certain situations. Figure 5.5 shows the simpler header for the `while` loop, just containing a boolean expression that will be evaluated to `true` or `false`. The `while` loop is a **test-before-looping** loop structure (see table 5.1), meaning that it will evaluate the boolean expression first before performing **any** loops at all. If the evaluation fails prior to the first loop, no loops are performed, and execution moves completely past the `while`. If the expression evaluates to `true`, then the first loop is performed, the code is executed, and then the expression is evaluated again, repeating.

```
while (boolean expression)
   // Single line of associated code;
```

```
while (boolean_expression)
{
  // Multiple Lines;
  // Associated Code;
}
```

Figure 5.5. Basic Structure of Single-Line and Multiline `while` Loops

Consider the following very simple example of the while loop in action:

Code Snippet 5.26

```
int aNum = 0;

while (aNum < 10)
{
    System.out.print(aNum + " ");
}
```

This code intends to print the numbers zero through nine similar to the first `for` loop example earlier. When this code executes, the following prints to the console:

```
0 0 0 0 0 0 0 0 0 0 0 0 0 0 . . .
```

An infinite loop occurs! The `while` loop truly gives you more flexibility, but you have to do a bit more work. Notice that unlike the `for` loop, the `while` will not increment a loop control variable, and you cannot create one in the `while` loop header. The main mistake here is a logic error: we neglected to ensure the `while` loop will fail by incrementing `aNum` at the end of each loop. You can fix this as follows (by being a little nerdy, which is OK):

Code Snippet 5.27

```
int aNum = 0;

while (aNum < 10)
{
    System.out.print(aNum++ + " "); //post-increment operator
}
```

You can efficiently use the post-increment operator in-line within the `.print()` parameter, as it will only increase the variable's value by one after the print occurs. The console shows the results of this change:

```
0 1 2 3 4 5 6 7 8 9
```

The `while` loop gives you more flexibility, but you must carefully consider the logic used and the boolean expression you have it evaluate to make sure that at some point, the loop will end. Within information systems development scenarios, very common occurrences for the use of a `while` loop include but are not limited to the following:

- Reading in records from a data file where you do not know how many records there will be.
- Capturing the results of a query whose record count could change on each run.
- Receiving a stream of data from an internet/web source where the quantity of data may not be known ahead of time.

Consider this simpler example, which creates a small application that adds two numbers and prompts the user if they wish to continue and sum another pair of numbers (or not):

Code Snippet 5.28

```
String choice = "y";
int numOne = 0, numTwo = 0;
Scanner in = new Scanner(System.in);

while (choice.equalsIgnoreCase("y"))
{
    System.out.println("================");
    System.out.println("Enter two numbers to add, separated by a space: ");

    numOne = in.nextInt();
    numTwo = in.nextInt();

    System.out.println("\nThe sum of "
            + numOne + " and "
            + numTwo + " is: "
            + (numOne + numTwo));

    System.out.println("Continue? y or n: ");

    choice = in.next(); // Capture single character input
}

System.out.println("Finished!");
```

Looping this a few rounds gives the following console output:

```
================
Enter two numbers to add, separated by a space:
10 16

The sum of 10 and 16 is: 26
Continue? y or n:
y
================
Enter two numbers to add, separated by a space:
```

```
56 98

The sum of 56 and 98 is: 154
Continue? y or n:
n
Finished!
```

Note how useful the `while` loop is in this situation: the user may choose to add two numbers any quantity of times. There is no way to predict this beforehand. A `for` loop would force a certain quantity of usages of the application on the user—not a good thing. The user is allowed to decide when the loop should end, and the `while` loop will continue looping until that occurs.

Consider an additional example, a program that will calculate the average of an unknown quantity of positive numbers for a client building a statistical application:

Code Snippet 5.29

```
Scanner in = new Scanner(System.in);
double sum = 0.0;
double average = 0.0;
int numQuantity = 0;
int enteredNumber = 0;

System.out.println("Enter numbers to average with spaces (-1 to quit:)");

while (enteredNumber != -1)
{
    enteredNumber = in.nextInt();

    if (enteredNumber == -1)
        continue; // Skip the rest of this iteration

    else
    {
        numQuantity++; // Valid number entered, increase count
        sum += (double)enteredNumber; // Increase the sum
    }
}

average = (sum / numQuantity); // Calculate average AFTER loop ends
System.out.println("Calculated Average: " + average);
```

An example run of this program would look like the following:

```
Enter numbers to average with spaces (-1 to quit:)
5 16 56 42 1 48 74 65 -1
Calculated Average: 38.375
```

Notice that `break` and `continue` can be used in a `while` loop just like in the `for` loop. Here, the `continue` causes the rest of the code in the current iteration of the loop to be skipped if the entered number is equal to `-1`. At the end of the current iteration, the boolean expression is evaluated again and this time found to be `false`, ending the loop entirely and allowing the average calculation and print to occur. The call to `.nextInt()` only occurs once each loop, so each loop reads in a number, evaluates it against the "quitting" number, and if it is valid, adds it to the sum. Notice that the average calculation does not occur **until after the loop has finished and all numbers have been read in.** The `while` loop is useful here, since you cannot know ahead of time how many numbers the user may enter. You certainly would not want to restrict them from entering any quantity they wanted in this particular situation.

Nested `while` loops: Finally, consider the example from earlier in the chapter where two `for` loops were used to infinitely loop and parse a `String` variable and print each word in decorative brackets. Since infinite loops are not a great idea in any application, consider this use of the `while` loop to accomplish the same task:

Code Snippet 5.30

```
String text = "Java is a powerful language useful for development on many different platforms";
char currentChar = '-'; // Initialize with nonalphabet character
String currentWord = "";
int position = 0;

if (text.length() > 0)
    while (position < text.length()) // OUTER while loop
    {
        currentWord += "["; // Decorative bracket

        while (position < text.length() && currentChar != ' ')
        { // INNER while loop
            currentChar = text.charAt(position++);
            if (currentChar == ' ')
                continue;
            else
                currentWord += currentChar; // up-convert char
        } // End of INNER while

        currentWord += "]"; // Decorative Bracket

        System.out.println(currentWord); // Print current word

        currentWord = ""; // Reset currentWord to blank
        currentChar = '-'; // reset currentChar;
    } // End of OUTER while
```

The console output from running this code is the same as the earlier version:

```
[Java]
[is]
[a]
[powerful]
[language]
[useful]
[for]
[development]
[on]
[many]
[different]
[platforms]
```

Remember that like nested `for` loops, a nested `while` loop (the **inner** while loop) will loop however long it is able to for each loop of the **outer** while. In this case, the outer while loop moves to the next word in the `String` variable, while the inner `while` loop processes each character in that word until a blank space is reached. Notice how useful it is to reset several of the variables back to their starting values after the inner while loop is finished but **before** the outer while loop begins its next loop. The variable `position` is the only one that is not reset, as it helps control both loops and prevents us from encountering an `IndexOutOfBounds` error.

The `while` loop can be much more useful than the `for` loop in many different application and data-processing situations. But with this increased flexibility comes more responsibility on your part to prevent logic errors and infinite loops. Remember that it is important **to not assume** that the computer or Java will **know what you want it to do**. Remember that computers are **very** mechanical in their processing of your code. Computing devices will do exactly what you tell them to do, exactly as you told them to do it. You must be precise and careful in setting up your logic. Be careful of uncommon scenarios and out-of-the-norm occurrences that can occur during data processing. For example, in the word-processing example earlier, the possibility that someone typed in two spaces in between two words was not accounted for, nor was the possibility of a space at the beginning or the end of the String's value. Real-world data is messy, and you will encounter issues like these and more from time to time. Of course, this means that the data-cleaning routines you will be involved with are just as important as—if not more than—the data-processing/analytics logic you may write.

SUMMARY POINTS

- The while loop can be more flexible than for loops, since they are useful in situations where you do not know exactly how many repetitions you will need prior to data processing.
- The header of a while loop is simpler than that of the for loop headers: they only evaluate a boolean expression to true or false and continue looping while the expression evaluates to true.
- A developer using a while loop must ensure that they set up the logic properly so that the loop will eventually end. Though infinite loops are occasionally used in programming, they are often frowned upon as bad program design.
- If needed, a while loop can be set up to logically execute in a similar, fixed fashion to a for loop.
- Keep in mind that similar to an if statement, a while loop's evaluation expression expects a true or false value to eventually resolve, no matter how complicated the boolean expression. Assignment operations are **not** permitted in the parentheses of a while loop.
- Computers are "dumb": they will do exactly what you tell them to do, exactly as you tell them to do it. Double-check your logic and assumptions, always!

QUICK PROBLEMS

1. **Coding:** Write a small program that will use a while to loop, and accept one character typed into the console at a time until a blank space is entered, ending the loop. Print the entered characters back to the console.
2. **Think:** What are several ways that an infinite loop could occur with a while loop? How would you prevent each case?
3. **Coding:** Create a String variable, and store your name within as its value. Using a while loop, append one character at a time from the String to another new String variable. Continue to append until thirty characters have been appended. If you reach the last character in the String that contains your name, restart the copying of characters from the start of the name String.

5.5 do…while Loops

The do…while loop (structured in figure 5.6) and the while loop are similar in most aspects except for one key difference: the do…while loop evaluates its boolean expression **after** the first loop. The do…while loop's test after the loop type of structure is handy in certain situations. To understand how this type of loop is beneficial, consider the following example, where a while loop is used to process a password:

```
do
    // Single line of code;
while (boolean_expression);

do
{
    // Multiple Lines;
    // Associated Code;
}
while (boolean_expression);
```

Figure 5.6. Basic Structure of a Single-Line and Multiline do…while Loop

Code Snippet 5.31

```
Scanner in = new Scanner(System.in);
String password = "";
String correctPass = "eyeLove#Java";

while (correctPass.equals(password) == false)
{
    System.out.println("Enter Password: ");
    password = in.next();
}
System.out.print("Login Successful!");
```

How many times will the `.equals()` method be called if the user gets the password right on the first try? After careful examination of the code, you will see that the password comparison is performed twice: once when starting when you know they will not match and then again after the user has attempted a login. It is slightly inefficient to perform the comparison twice. In other situations, this first comparison could involve invoking a method that is time or resource consuming, which could make it an efficiency issue. Since you know that the passwords will always mismatch on the first comparison, you can skip this first comparison. Allow the user to enter the password, **then** compare them, then continue to loop if they get it wrong. Here, the `do...while` loop will make this code a bit more efficient:

Code Snippet 5.32

```
Scanner in = new Scanner(System.in);
String password = "";
String correctPass = "eyeLove#Java";

do
{
    System.out.println("Enter Password: ");
    password = in.next();
}
while (!correctPass.equals(password));

System.out.print("Login Successful!");
```

Figure 5.4 and the example here show the unique structure of the `do...while` loop. The do statement is followed by either one line of code or a code block like other decision structures, and the code associated with the do statement will always execute at least one time. The `while` follows this code block, and this is the only time you will purposefully see a semicolon at the end of a `while` statement (note that in a normal `while`, there is no semicolon at the end, similar to `for` and `if` statements). Note as well that the not (`!`) operator is used, causing the code to loop while the result of `.equals()` is not `true`. The comparison is performed only one time, after the first attempted password entry. Be careful of assumptions and logic errors with the `do...while` loop. Consider the following example, where the business rules need the first three characters of names entered for part of an email address and where you can process more than just one name entered:

Code Snippet 5.33

```
String firstName = "";
String emailPart = "";
Scanner in = new Scanner(System.in);

do
{
    System.out.println("Enter Name: ");
    firstName = in.nextLine();
    for (int i=0;i<3;i++)
    {
```

```
        emailPart += firstName.charAt(i);
    }
}
while (!firstName.equals("quit"));
```

With this code, what if the user hits enter without typing anything in? What if a name is entered that is two or fewer characters? Think of using an external data source; what if the `firstName` is blank or outside the rules in the source for the current record you might be reading in? In that case, the do…`while` loop may not be optimal, since it assumes the first loop will run correctly, which, in the example here, it will not (you will receive a `String Index out of Range` error since the `firstName` came in blank from console entry). A simple bit of decision structure logic can mitigate this in the case of manual user input.

Code Snippet 5.34

```
String firstName = "";
String emailPart = "";
Scanner in = new Scanner(System.in);

do
{
    System.out.println("Enter Name: ");
    firstName = in.nextLine();

    if (firstName.length() < 3)
        System.out.println("First Name Must Be 3 or More Characters");
    else
        for (int i=0;i<3;i++)
        {
            emailPart += firstName.charAt(i);
        }
}
while (!firstName.equals("quit"));
```

How would you change this code to handle a name that is only one or two characters long?

Processing user choices for application functionality is another great example of where a do…`while` loop can come in handy. Consider this example, where a user can choose to print the first name or second name of an entered full name, or they can choose to quit the application immediately without using any feature:

Code Snippet 5.35

```
int menuChoice = 0;
String fullName = "";
String partialName = "";
Scanner in = new Scanner(System.in);
System.out.println("Enter a full name: ");
fullName = in.nextLine();
String menu = """
              ===================
              Enter your Choice:
              1: Print first name
              2: Print second name
              3: Quit the application
              """;
do
{
    System.out.println(menu);
    menuChoice = in.nextInt();
    switch (menuChoice)
```

```
    {
        case 1: partialName =
                fullName.substring(0, fullName.indexOf(" "));
        System.out.println("First Name is: " + partialName);
        break;
        case 2: partialName =
                fullName.substring(fullName.indexOf(" ") + 1);
        System.out.println("Second name is: " + partialName);
    }
}
while (menuChoice != 3);
System.out.println("Exited!");
```

An example run of this application with user inputs would look like the following:

```
Enter a full name:
Textbook Author
===================
Enter your Choice:
1: Print first name
2: Print second name
3: Quit the application

1
First Name is: Textbook
===================
Enter your Choice:
1: Print first name
2: Print second name
3: Quit the application

2
Second name is: Author
===================
Enter your Choice:
1: Print first name
2: Print second name
3: Quit the application

3
Exited!
```

The `do...while` loop is useful in this context, since it allows us to capture the user's first menu choice after entering a name. They can choose option 3 right from the start if they wish to quit the application or another option to process the name in different ways. In all of these cases, barring any data issues, the `do...while` loop has been useful in situations where you know the first loop that contains some sort of processing is needed and possible (first user choice, first login attempt, first data entry) and in cases where you do not want to unnecessarily evaluate a boolean expression when you know it will always fail on the first check. There are lots of occasions where the `do...while` loop can help keep code clean, simple, and much easier to read, to understand, and to maintain. As with the while loop, you must be careful to ensure that the `do...while` loop will eventually evaluate its boolean expression to `false` and end, preventing an infinite loop. The `break` and `continue` statements can be used within a `do...while` also, same as you have seen in previous examples. Consider your logic carefully, and leverage the power of these loops to do a lot of the repetitive and tedious processing work for you!

SUMMARY POINTS

- The `do...while` loop is a loop-after-testing type of loop structure in Java, where at least the first loop is executed before evaluating any boolean expression to determine if the loop should continue.
- Because of their unique syntax structure, a `do...while` loop is the only loop structure with a semicolon at the end of the entire statement.
- Similar to `while` loops, the developer using the `do...while` types of loop structures should take care to set up their evaluation logic so that the loop will eventually end.
- Similar to `for` and `while` loops, the code associated with the "do" part of a `do...while` loop can consist of one line of code without curly braces or curly braces forming a code block with multiple lines of code.

QUICK PROBLEMS

1. **Coding:** Using a `do...while` loop, generate a random `int` value between one and one hundred. Continue to loop and generate random integers between one and one hundred until the number eighty-seven is generated. Exit the loop once this occurs.
2. **Think:** Think about the applications, websites, and systems that you use on a daily basis (mobile sites, desktop apps, tablet apps). What are some actions/activities you engage with in those software products where a `do...while` loop could be in use?
3. **Coding:** Write a small program that will ask the user for two pieces of information: an amount of money to deposit into a savings account (as a double) and the monthly interest rate earned on the savings (as #.#, but convert into the appropriate mathematical form). Use a `do...while` loop to calculate how long until the money in the account has grown to one million US dollars ($1,000,000.00). Print the number of months until this is reached as well as the final balance when reached. Test with several different inputs in varying ranges.

Summary

In this chapter, you have learned about three of the four types of looping structures present in both the Java language and most any and all contemporary programming languages. You have examined how structured and rigid `for` loops can be in their behavior and how useful they are when you know approximately how many loops you might need your code to execute. The nesting of one `for` loop within another for the processing of structured, often tabular data has shown a great deal of promise for many of the scenarios that information systems professionals encounter during system development and implementation. The flexibility of `while` loops has become apparent, useful in situations where the number of loops may change from one run of the application to the next. And the benefits of the unique nature of `do...while` loops show their applicability to many additional data-processing and code-looping scenarios that you might encounter. Combined with your knowledge of decision structures and code branching, loops can help take software to a level of clever automation and hands-off decision-making for many situations. In the next chapter, you will examine how to make these powerful processing and logic combinations available for use throughout your application with the creation and usage of your own custom Java methods.

Practice Problems

Terminology

Match the following terms from the chapter with their most appropriate definition:

1. Looping behavior	a. The range of code that delimits the life-span of a variable, from point of creation to point of garbage collection.
2. Test before looping	b. Statement in Java that will cause the loop iteration it is executed within to stop and additionally causes the loop to skip all remaining loops, ending the loop structure's processing.
3. Test after looping	c. Scenario where a loop structure's logic never causes the loop to cease its repeated actions, continuing on without stopping.
4. Loop header	d. Within nested loop logic, this loop structure is contained within another loop structure and is part of the code associated with it.
5. Loop control variable	e. A particular execution of the code associated with a loop structure. One of potentially many repeated executions of this code.
6. Variable scope	f. Statement in Java that will cause the loop iteration it is executed within to stop and cause the loop to move on to its next repeat iteration.
7. Loop-until condition	g. Leveraging code repetition in an application to process data and simplify the repeat of code activities.
8. After-iteration action	h. Within nested loop logic, this loop structure contains one or more loop structures within its associated code.
9. Iteration	i. Test-before-looping type of loop structure useful in situations where the quantity of loops is approximately known before processing occurs.
10. Infinite loop	j. Logic in a `for` loop header that contains the boolean expression(s) used to determine when a `for` loop should cease its repetitions.
11. Break	k. The object-oriented version of the primitive data types.
12. Continue	l. Test-after-looping type of loop structure that allows the first execution of associated loop code before evaluating a boolean expression.
13. Nested loops	m. Type of loop in programming that evaluates a boolean statement prior to executing a loop's associated code.
14. Outer loop	n. Test-before-looping type of loop structure that simply evaluates a boolean expression and is useful when the number of loops is not well known prior to processing.
15. Inner loop	o. The line of code in a loop structure where logic to control the extent of looping behavior lies. Often the first line of code in the structure but can be the last in a test-after-looping loop.
16. Wrapper class	p. Code in a `for` loop header that determines how a loop control variable will be altered after each iteration of the `for` loop.
17. `for` loop	q. Type of loop in programming that evaluates a boolean statement after at least one iteration of a loop has executed.
18. `while` loop	r. Logic where a loop structure is part of the associated and repeated code of another loop structure. Typically, this consists of one loop within another but can be more complex.
19. do...`while` loop	s. Variable whose value is compared to a threshold value and can be part of the logic used to control a loop's behavior.

Find the Error

In each of the following problems, carefully examine the code given, and determine the error(s)/issue(s) with each. Keep in mind, the error(s) could be syntax (code) or logic (intended outcome) based or both!

1.

```
// Print each value of i squared
for (int i=0;i<10;i++;)
{
    System.out.println(i + "*"
            + i + "="
            + (i*i));
    i=0;
}
```

2.

```
// Generate Random Numbers
// Print only when "10" occurs
// Stop after the 15th print.
int number = 0;
while (count < 15)
{
    int count;
    number = (int)Math.random() * 15;
    if (number = 10)
        System.out.println("10 Found! Found "
                + count + " times!");
        count++;
}
```

3.

```
// Produce a sum of random numbers
// Stop addition when sum exceeds 100
int sum = 0;
do while (sum < 100)
{
   sum += (int)Math.random() + (int)10.9;
};
```

4.

```
int n1 = 5;
int n2 = 5;
double quotient = 0.0;
while (n1 <= 10)
{
    quotient = n1 / n2;
    System.out.println(n1 + "/" + n2 + "=" + quotient);
    n1++;
    n2--;
}
```

5.

```
// Print all the numbers 0–100
// in a table
for (int i=0; i<10; i++)
{
    for (int j=i; j<10; j++)
    {
        System.out.print(j + " ");
```

```
    }
    System.out.println("");
}
```

6.

```
// Copy the characters of a String
// one at a time to another String
String firstString = "These are tricky problems!";
String secondString = "";

while (!firstString.equals(secondString))
{
    secondString += firstString.charAt(i++);
}
```

7.

```
// Process a String's characters
// and stop if an '!' is encountered
String phrase = "Hello!there!fellow!developer!";
for (int i=0;i<phrase;i++)
{
    if (phrase.charAt(i++) == '!')
        System.out.println("! encountered!");
        break;
}
```

8.

```
// Process a String's characters
// and replace if an '!' is encountered
String phrase = "Hello!there!fellow!developer!";
String cleanedPhrase = "";
int position = 0;
while (position < 29)
{
    if (phrase.charAt(position++) != '!')
        cleanedPhrase += phrase.charAt(position);

    if (phrase.charAt(position) == '!')
        continue;
}
```

9.

```
// Have a user type in numbers and report
// the largest value entered.
Scanner in = new Scanner(System.in);

System.out.println("Enter numbers (-1 to end): ");
for (int i=0; i<8; i++)
{
    int largest = 0;
    int current = 0;

    current = keyboardIn.nextInt();
    if (current > largest)
        current = largest;

    if (current == "-1")
        continue;
}
System.out.println("Largest Number: " + largest);
```

10.

```
// Concatenate three String variables
// by processing their lengths and
// characters.
String s1 = 'Computer';
String s2 = 'Information';
String s3 = 'Systems';
String full = '';

while (full < 3)
{
    if (s1.length() == 0)
        break;

    for (int i=0;i<s1.length();i++)
        full += s1.charAt(i);

    for (int j=0;i<s2.length();j++)
        full += s2.charAt(j);

    for (int k=0;k<s2.length();k++)
        full += s2.charAt(j);
}
```

Think about It

1. Why are machines, like computers, really good at looping behavior? Why are people often really bad or suboptimal at it?
2. What are the big similarities between `for` loops, `while` loops, and do…`while` loops? How are they different?
3. In what types of scenarios is a `for` loop most useful? What would be a situation where you may not want to use a `for` loop?
4. Describe the purpose of the `for` loop header. What are some things that a developer must keep in mind when writing the statement for a `for` loop header?
5. Describe when you would want to use curly braces after a `for` loop header and when you might not want to. Do these same guidelines apply to the other loop types described in this chapter?
6. Describe occasions where parts of the `for` loop header may be left blank and the advantages of this.
7. Where are semicolons needed when implementing a `for` loop? Where are they not needed? What can happen if semicolons are used incorrectly in a `for` loop?
8. Describe the life cycle of the loop control variable. Where is it declared? When can you use it? Where can you not use it?
9. Describe the use of the break statement within a `for` loop. What effect will its usage have on the behavior of the `for` loop?
10. Describe the use of the continue statement within a `for` loop. What effect will its usage have on the behavior of the `for` loop?
11. Describe the behavior of a nested `for` loop structure. How can you count the number of times in total a nested loop (as opposed to an outer loop) will repeat?
12. What are some common scenarios in information systems contexts where a nested `for` loop may be useful?
13. How does the nesting of one `for` loop within another impact your ability to use the loop control variables of the `for` loops within their code? What impact does `for` loop nesting have on the inner `for` loop's control variable life cycle?
14. Describe the general behavior of the `while` loop. What are some common scenarios where the use of a `while` loop may be appropriate?
15. What is the main way that a `while` loop differs from a `for` loop?
16. Describe how logic that uses a `while` loop can be written that will exactly match the behavior of a `for` loop.
17. How is a loop control variable optional for a `while` loop?
18. Describe the main way in which a do…`while` loop differs from a `while` loop.

19. What is unique about the syntax/structure of a do...while loop that differs from other loops in Java? How does a semicolon impact this structure?

20. Describe some common scenarios in which the use of a do...while loop might be appropriate.

Short Syntax Problems

1. Using your research from chapter 2 about a particular national lottery, rewrite your problem from that chapter, and use a for loop to generate the play and special numbers for a random drawing. Print these to the console as you generate them in a clean, well-formatted manner.
2. Use any loop structure you like to print a more realistic progress bar. Given a value between zero and one hundred, print a progress bar to the console that fills in from the left to right, similar to a download status bar when downloading a large file from the web. Use whatever character you would like to represent the "filling" of the bar. For example, 76% might look like this:

   ```
   [========  ]
   ```

   Or 44% could look like this with another character used:

   ```
   [****      ]
   ```

3. Write a small program that will prompt the user to enter a string value on the console. Store that in a String variable. Then use a for loop to print all the characters from that String in reverse order. Omit any blank space characters from the print.
4. Write a small program that will prompt a user to enter a String value on the console. Store that in a String variable. Then use a while loop to count the quantity of each vowel (a, e, i, o, u, and y) in that String's value. Print the results to the console in a professional-looking and report-ready fashion.
5. Write a small program that stores a long paragraph or block of text in a String variable (seven or more sentences). Prompt the user to enter a single character they would like the application to report a quantity count of within that text. Using any loop structure you like, count the number of times that character occurs in the text (either upper- or lowercase). Report that count to the user on the console in a professional-looking and report-ready fashion.
6. Write a small program that will use a single nested for loop (one outer and one inner) to print the multiplication table for numbers zero through nine using rows and columns of output.
   a. **Added challenge:** In the first column and first row, print the numbers zero through nine. Then show their multiplication in the matrix itself.
   b. **Added challenge:** Format the table print so that all numbers take up the same amount of space, keeping all rows and columns perfectly aligned.
7. Write a small program that will calculate the average exam grades for students in a class. Use a loop structure to keep accepting inputs until the value -1 (negative one) is entered. Do not include -1 in your calculations. Use an appropriate variable to sum the grades as they are entered and a separate variable to keep track of the count of variables entered. Your program should allow the user to enter as many grades as they wish, and it should report the average.
8. Write a small program that will prompt a user for a String value that is a phrase or sentence and for a number that will represent the number of both rows and columns. Print the characters of the phrase to the console in an n-rows and n-columns fashion (where n is the value the user first entered). If you reach the end of the String value while printing, restart at the first character in the String. Omit the blank space characters from the print, but do not allow this omission to reduce the number of characters printed per row! The user can enter any phrase and row/column size they wish. See an example run below:

   ```
   Please enter a phrase:
   Java is a GREAT programming language!

   Square Matrix Size (as n)?:
   12

   J a v a i s a G R E A T
   p r o g r a m m i n g l
   a n g u a g e ! J a v a
   i s a G R E A T p r o g
   r a m m i n g l a n g u
   a g e ! J a v a i s a G
   R E A T p r o g r a m m
   i n g l a n g u a g e !
   J a v a i s a G R E A T
   p r o g r a m m i n g l
   a n g u a g e ! J a v a
   i s a G R E A T p r o g
   ```

Full Problems

1. Write a game that will be used in an educational setting that will allow the user to practice their knowledge of the multiplication table. Implement the game as follows:
   a. Prompt the user for their first name at the beginning of the game, and store it.
   b. The game will have five rounds per play. In each round, the user will be presented with a multiplication of two numbers chosen randomly. Once presented with the two numbers, the user will have three tries in order to guess the correct answer.
      i. If the user guesses the answer correctly, they are able to move on to the next round.
      ii. If the user guesses incorrectly, they have two more tries. Once they have guessed incorrectly three times, they have "lost" the round.
   c. In the first two rounds, multiplication problems involving numbers zero through four will be presented. In the next two rounds, five through seven. In the final round, numbers seven through nine will be presented in multiplication problems.
   d. Once a user has played five rounds (win or lose), they will be prompted and asked if they would like to play again. The user can only play a total of three sets of five rounds.
   e. Each time a user wins a round, they will earn five hundred points. If they lose a round, they will lose two hundred points. Allow for the possibility that their score could go into negative values!
   f. After the game is completely over (after three plays of five rounds each, or once the user chooses to not play anymore), print the user's name and their total score before exiting the program.
2. Write an application that will print an amortization table for an automobile loan. Prompt the user for their name, initial loan amount for a new vehicle, interest rate (as #.#), duration of loan (number of months), and amount the customer anticipates paying monthly (how much they can afford). Research what a typical amortization table looks like and what they do on the web if you are unfamiliar with them.
   a. Print on the first row the column headers for the remaining loan balance, monthly interest, payment amount, and balance after that month's payment. Keep in mind that the amount remaining will use the following formula:

      (remaining balance + monthly interest amount) – monthly payment
   b. On every row, print the values for each month of the duration of the loan under the column headers.
   c. If the amount remaining of the loan for a month drops below the amount of the monthly payment, then the monthly payment for that month should just be the remaining balance, not the borrower's monthly payment.
   d. If the borrower's monthly payment is insufficient to cause the remaining balance to decrease, do not print a table; instead, print a message to this effect to the user, and ask them to enter a new monthly payment. Continue prompting for a monthly payment if the payments are insufficient to cause the remaining loan balance to decrease.
   e. Once the table has fully printed, print the **total amount** of interest that was paid by the borrower over the life of the loan.
3. Write an application that will mimic a bank account for a banking customer with a starting balance of $1,000.00. The application will function in the following ways:
   a. The user will be prompted with two options: "`1: Deposit`" or "`2: Withdrawal`."
   b. Based on the user's choice, an amount and a description of the transaction will be entered. Deposits will increase the amount, and withdrawals will decrease the amount.
   c. A third option, "`3: Print History`," will print the record of all the transactions (amount and description, along with whether it was a deposit or withdrawal) performed so far. *Hint:* Use a `String` variable and concatenate a text description of the event along with a new-line character escaped into the `String`.
   d. The user can choose any of the menu options they wish. If they make a series of transactions, first print the history, then make a few more transactions—for example, printing history should show the new, longer list of events.
   e. Present the user with a "`4:` Exit" menu option to end the application. *Hint:* Do **not** use `System.exit()` to end the application; have the logic of your loop structure end based on the menu choice itself.

4. Write an application that will display a calendar in the console. The application should behave in the following manner:
   a. Prompt the user for the month (1–12) and the day of the week the month starts on (1–7, where 1 is "Sunday" and 7 is "Saturday").
   b. Assume the year is not a leap year. Research how many days are in each month (some are thirty, some are thirty-one, and one is twenty-eight).
   c. Print the calendar for that month based on the user's inputs and the number of days in the entered month. Print the names of the days of the week along the top. Use loop structures to print each row ("week") on a separate line of output in the console.
5. Write an application that will fully process a paragraph in the following ways:
   a. Prompt the user to enter a single paragraph of text, hitting the Enter key at the end to end the input. Be sure the paragraph includes appropriate punctuation.
   b. Process the block of text and, using only the methods and code you have learned through this chapter, print to the console the following information:
      i. The number of words in the paragraph
      ii. The number of characters (omitting blank spaces and punctuation) in the paragraph
      iii. The longest word
      iv. The shortest word (omitting any that are two characters or less)
      v. The number of words in the longest sentence
      vi. The number of words in the shortest sentence
      vii. The vowel that occurred with the highest quantity

Chapter 6

Methods

What You Will Learn in This Chapter

Writing well-organized, readable, maintainable, and highly effective code is a goal that all programmers should strive for. In this chapter, you will learn about an additional foundational topic in programming: the creation and usage of methods. Methods bring many benefits to application development efforts: they can help keep code organized and well written, decrease repetition of logic, and increase the effectiveness of development efforts by making complex code easy to use anywhere in the application. Prior to this chapter, you have invoked methods that are included with the Java language in its various classes. In this chapter, you will learn how to create and invoke your own.

Specifically, this chapter will help you do the following:

1. Understand some of the major benefits of methods and why they are found in most programming languages
2. Understand the differences between a method's definition and its usage and the major parts of the method definition
3. Understand how to specify the level of security on a method and determine what code can use your method, how your method relates to the class it is defined in, and how this also impacts its future usage
4. Understand how to implement the parameter list for a method so that it can accept data and how to determine what data the method should return to the invoking code
5. Understand how method invocation differs from the method's definition and how the return type impacts invocation
6. Understand what happens when various data types are used as arguments and their values are passed to a method and how this impacts both the method's code and the arguments themselves
7. Understand what impact scope has on variables found both inside and outside of methods and where these can be accessed
8. Understand what method overloading is, how to overload your custom methods, and what its benefits are

Opening Scenario

After several days of work, you have made some significant and partial progress with your data-cleaning logic. Taking a fresh look at your code listing one morning, you notice that it is a very long, complex arrangement. Lots of times, you are processing similar data in similar ways in different locations throughout your code. You have tried to "copy and paste" code and adapt it into various locations as best you can, but this was an error-riddled process that took at least two days to clean up. Looking ahead at your data quality to-do list, you know that lots of the logic you have already duplicated will need to be copied again into other similar efforts later on. You have also noticed that some of the code you already have working (some loops and decision structures, copied and adapted into various places) will all need to be changed slightly as the client updates your team with new data definitions and quality rules. A few of your fellow colleagues have taken a look at your code listing, and the words "confusing," "hard to follow," "repetitive," and "hard to maintain" have been mentioned. Looking things over, you realize now that you need to bring a bit more sophistication into your coding efforts and reduce the duplication and difficulty in reading the code and ease the maintenance across the board. A colleague with programming experience has recommended using methods to move some of the complicated logic "off to the side" so you can "call it wherever you need—it will clean things up!" Looking over some examples on the web, you realize this is a bit different than the line-to-line coding style you have gotten used to. But the examples using methods seem clear, concise, and easy to use. Methods seem to almost be tools or "appliances," as one article described: you create them and then can take them off the "shelf" to use their abilities wherever you need them in your code. This seems like a really good way to go! Zip code checks, address cleanups, name stylings, and so on—all these data quality issues can have a method built, and maybe you can do it in a flexible way to handle each one, whenever you need it, without overcomplicating your main logic. Methods seem like the answer! As you have done before, you set your work aside to learn more about methods in Java and how you can use them in the most effective way possible . . .

6.1 Why Are Methods Useful?

The creation and usage of methods are critical concepts that programmers who wish to be proficient in any programming language must learn. Up until this point in your Java studies, you have gotten lots of practice at the latter, the usage of methods. You have invoked (i.e., used) methods to print to the console (`.println()`), to read in user input (`.nextInt()`) from the console, to compare two numbers (`.max()`), to compare string values (`.equals()`), and to create professional-looking output (`.format()`). In all these cases, you have used methods that were created by someone else and used them to your advantage to do something, well, useful!

Figure 6.1. Methods and Blenders Have a Lot in Common
Source: "Blender Blender Blender Blender" by miss karen is licensed under CC BY 2.0, https://www.flickr.com/photos/47489771@N00/2947260485.

Keep in mind that for each of these methods and the others that you have seen, you did not have knowledge of or understand anything about the code listed inside these methods that makes them "run." Think about what you **have** known: the methods' **names** and descriptions, what types of **parameter inputs** they require, and what type of data they **return**. For each of these and other methods that you have used so far, the programmers who wrote those methods thought about a problem (i.e., comparing two strings, finding out which of two numbers is larger, etc.), considered the logic involved in solving that problem, and then wrote Java code that implements that logic. They have already done all the hard work. When you encounter the same problem that these programmers faced, instead of having to figure out the logic and implement the code yourself, you can simply invoke a method that tackles that problem already. This is a critical point in understanding why methods are so useful: the code in a method often performs a task and was placed inside a method because the programmer believed that the logic the code implements is useful both to them and perhaps to **other programmers** who might face the same problem at some point in the future.

What does this imply about the characteristics of methods? There are three main ideas that methods, by their nature, implement:

Blended java to enjoy while studying Java!
Source: "Caramel Frappuccino" by mastermaq is licensed under CC BY-SA 2.0, https://www.flickr.com/photos/24311648@N00/485577211.

- **Reusability/generalizability:** Notice that with the methods you have studied so far, you can use them (i.e., invoke them) from anywhere in your code, anytime you wish, as many times as you wish (as long as you have performed any proper imports, etc.). This makes methods **reusable**, meaning that you do not have to rewrite the code for a small part of logic that solves some specific problem over and over every time you need to use it. You can write the code once, store it in a method, and then invoke that method whenever and wherever you need that code's help in tackling some problem. This further implies that methods are **generalizable**, meaning that they can be used in various situations and programs as long as certain criteria are met (inputs are appropriate, permissions allow invocation, return types if any are used, etc.). Think of it this way: imagine that you want to make a coffee drink to enjoy while you are studying Java in this textbook. You typically use a blender appliance to make the treat. You would not go out and buy a new blender each time you want to make a new coffee. You reuse the same blender each time: you give it inputs and allow it to process them, and its "returned data" is the blended drink you want to enjoy. Also, a blender is generalizable in the fact that you can place almost anything (even cell phones!) in, and it will process them in the same way. Methods, like blenders, are reusable.

- **Modularity:** Earlier you learned how classes implement object-oriented programming ideals in Java by separating the implementation of code and the data it manages from the places it's used. Methods work in the same way. Since methods are bundles of code that implement logic, there is only one copy of that code and only in one place. But you can use it anywhere and anytime you wish and as many times as you wish. This makes a method somewhat **modular** in that you just plug it in and invoke it wherever needed in your code.
- **Maintainability:** Methods help keep code neat and tidy. Instead of having ten copies of some logic that you need to solve a problem repeatedly throughout your code listing, place one copy of the code in a method. Then simply invoke that ten times wherever you need it throughout your code. What if you need to make a change to the way the method works or correct some issue with your logic? Since you have bundled the code in a method, code is edited in **one place**, and that change "trickles out" to all places where you have **invoked** the method! This makes your code much more maintainable and easier to update when needed.

Understanding how to both use and create your own methods will greatly increase your skills as a programmer in Java, and these same skills transfer to other languages that also use methods. Methods enable you to move repetitive code off into its own bundle, decreasing the confusion and mess that may occur otherwise in your code listing. Using methods also increases the sophistication of your code in that you can perform increasingly complex actions with simpler and simpler code (invoking a method takes a lot less code and effort than rewriting the code within). Most modern programming languages use methods (sometimes called procedures, routines, or subroutines in those other languages), and Java is no exception.

SUMMARY POINTS

- Methods simplify the task of calling "chunks" of code logic repeatedly and without unnecessarily lengthening your code or increasing its complexity / decreasing its readability.
- Programmers can take advantage of the logic and problem-solving that other programmers have already engaged in by invoking their methods.
- Methods have three main benefits: they make often complex code reusable without unnecessary duplication; they increase the generalizability and flexibility of logic in terms of the data it can handle; and they adapt ideals of modularity, containing code in plug-and-use "bundles" as well as increasing maintainability by storing only one copy in one place.
- Methods are ideal when you have similar logic duplicated in several places in your application or when you want to reduce complex logic to more sequential method invocations (which take far less code) on the front end.

QUICK PROBLEMS

1. **Think:** Consider an application where a new password entered by a user is checked against a set of business rules for password composition (needs numbers, caps, special characters, etc.). How would moving this logic into a method and having one copy of it simplify maintenance of the application if the rules change? How would this enable more flexible application implementation?

2. **Think:** Consider a few of the program examples in chapter 5 that used a menu to prompt the user for functionality choices. How could method help clean up the `main()` method of these applications, increasing code readability and maintenance?
3. **Think:** What are some of the characteristics of the class methods you have invoked so far from the Java library that have made them useful? How have you provided data to these methods so they can do their "job"?

6.2 Method Definition: The Structure of Methods

Recall that Java is a class-based language. So far, you have created new **Java main classes**, which are classes that have a `main()` method defined within. To simplify your understanding of methods in Java from the start, keep two overall syntax rules in mind:

- A method must always be within a class in Java.
- A method cannot be defined within another method (no method nesting).

Notice that you cannot create a Java file with just a method in it and no class structure. Since everything is class based, you must have at least the basic structure of a class that a method is within. Figure 6.3 shows the relationship between methods, classes, and the **packages** that classes are contained within and will be referred to often throughout the chapter.

General method concepts: Methods are **defined**, whereas variables are declared. The method **definition** refers to the code you wrote that defines the structure of the method itself and the code that you bundled inside that method. Keep in mind that the method definition is different from the method **invocation**. You define a method by creating it and writing the code that makes it "run." You invoke a method when you call it and have it execute the code you wrote. These will happen in different places in your code! Remember too that a method will not run until you invoke it.

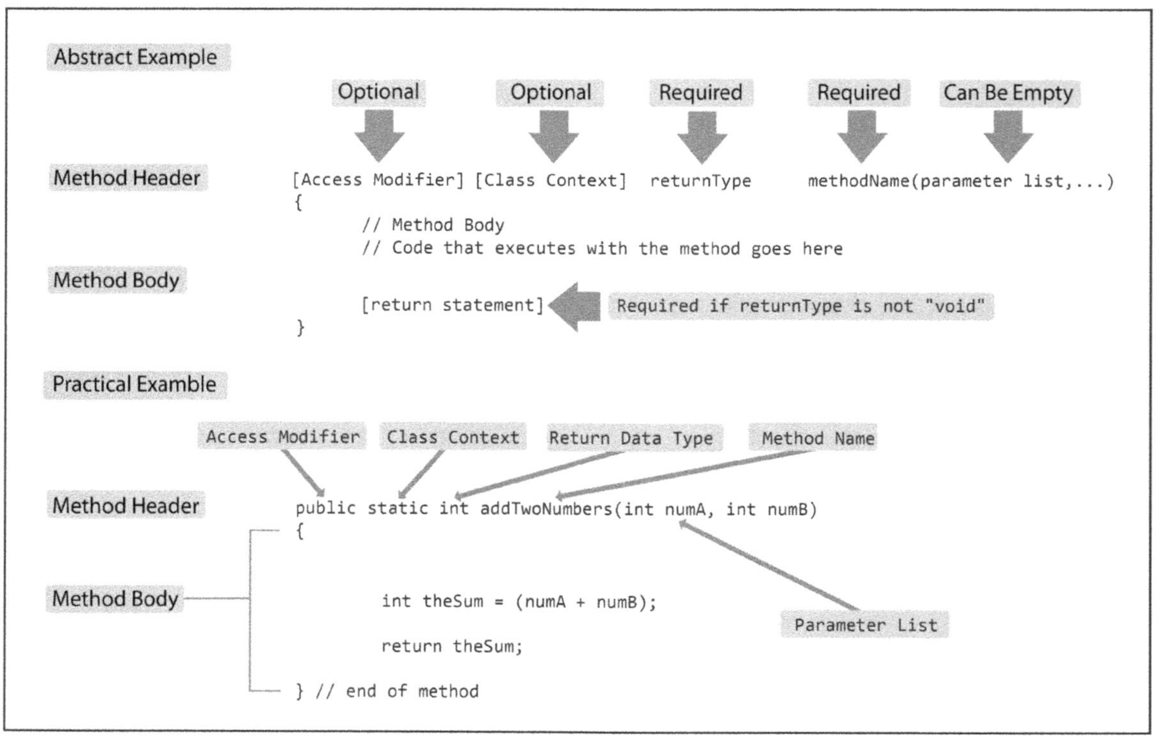

Figure 6.2. Diagram of the Basic Method Header and Body

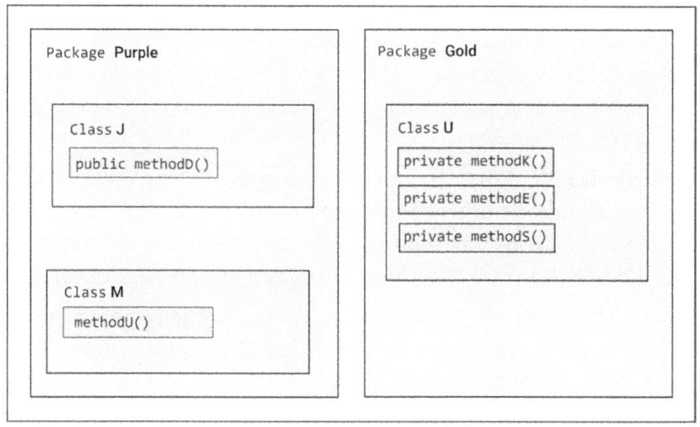

Figure 6.3. Relationship among Java Methods, Classes, and Packages

Note in figure 6.2 that a method definition has two parts, the method **header** and the method **body**, each with its own options and settings. Though a method can have a single line of code following its header (like with decision structures), this is not recommended. Good practice always encloses the method body in curly braces, even if there is only one line of code. Remember too that methods are never defined within other methods, but methods are always defined inside of a class.

Another key point to keep in mind when defining methods is that you have a great deal of **flexibility** in how you set up the method header and how it is defined. Methods in general are flexible, and this makes them much more useful to Java programmers who need them to help solve complex problems. So though the flexibility can be a tiny bit frustrating at the beginning, you will come to find the benefits are outstanding as you conquer these concepts. Again referring to figure 6.2, consider each part of the method header and the flexible options you have with each.

Access modifier concepts: Think of this setting as the "security" for the method, determining what other code is allowed to invoke it. To understand this, again remember that a method is **always** inside a class, and the class it is in is **always** inside a **Java package** (a way of keeping classes that are similar to one another grouped easily—think "folder"). So a Java package can contain many classes, and each of those classes can contain many methods. You can think of a class that a method is within as the **containing class** to simplify things. For the access modifier, you have several options that you can use when defining your method's header:

- `public`: The `public` access modifier opens the security door wide: any code anywhere can invoke your method without restrictions. Code inside or outside the method's containing class can invoke your method. Code in a class in another package can too.
- `private`: The `private` access modifier is the opposite: only code that is inside the containing class can invoke a method given this as its access modifier. The door is "closed" to all other code anywhere outside the containing class that might want to invoke this method.
- `protected`: The `protected` access modifier is not useful to us just yet. Chapter 9 will discuss **class inheritance**, where another class can be specified as the "child" of a preexisting class (which enables benefits of its own). The `protected` modifier means that a method can be invoked by any code in its containing class **and** by any code in the containing class's subclass (inherited class).
- **Just leaving this option blank:** If you choose to put nothing at all for this method header option (which is OK!), then Java gives your method default access security. This means that code in the containing class can invoke your method, **and** code in any other class **that is in the same package** as the containing class can invoke it as well. Code in classes outside the containing class's package is just out of luck!

To understand access modifier options better, refer to figure 6.3. Notice that each of the methods in the classes listed in figure 6.3 has either `public`, `private`, or omitted access modifiers. Let's see how this impacts these:

- `.methodD()`: Notice that `.methodD()` in Class `J` has a public access modifier. This means that any code, anywhere in either Class `J` or any of the other classes, can invoke this method and use it. Classes in package `purple` or in any other package can also access this method.
- `.methodK()`, `.methodE()`, and `.methodS()`: Notice that all three methods in Class `U` have the private access modifier. This means that only the code that is inside of Class `U` can invoke and use these methods. The code in any other classes that are also in package `gold` will not be able to invoke these methods here or in any other packages. The door is shut tight!

- `.methodU()`: Notice in figure 6.3 that this method has **no** access modifier associated with it. The programmer purposefully (or maybe accidentally?) omitted an access modifier with this method. That means that Java will give it a default level of access security: code in Class `M` will be able to invoke the method, and code in any other classes in package `purple` will be able to as well, including Class `J`. But classes in other packages outside of `purple` will not be able to use `.methodU()`.

Static versus nonstatic option concepts: As the creator of a new method, you can choose whether your method should be an **instance** method (callable upon instance objects of your class, as you will see in later chapters) or a **static** method that can only be invoked via the class itself. The following clarifies what options you can use in the method header when defining your method:

- `static`: You will actually write `static` as the option following the access modifier if you wish the method to be static. For now, `static` will be the option used most often.
  For example, the `Math.max()` method is a `static` method that you have used before.
- **Just leaving the option blank:** As with the access modifier option, if you leave this option blank and **do not specify** `static`, then Java will assume that your method should be an **instance** method.

For example, the `String` class method `.length()` is an instance method. You must use it on an instance object of the `String` class like so:

```
String myName = "Author"; // String instance object myName
System.out.println(myName.length()); // Invoke upon instance
```

Return type concepts: Just as with the other options, you have some flexibility here as well. A method is **not required** to actually return any data back to its invoking code. This is an option that is **completely up to the programmer!** Notice that when you invoke `System.out.println()`, for example, you never write any code that looks like this:

```
someVariable = System.out.println();
```

For other methods that return data, like `Math`'s `.max()` or `String`'s `.length()`, their results are assigned to some variable or as another method's argument. It is left up to the programmer to decide what data, if any, their method needs to return back to the invoking code.

Two quick return type syntax rules:

- You cannot leave the return type blank for a method definition. Java requires you to indicate the return type behavior of your method.
- Methods can only return one "chunk" of data: either a copy of a primitive data type or a reference to an instance object. Java methods cannot return back two or more separate variable values at the same time.

So what are your return type options?

- `void`: If you want the method to not return back any data, use the void return type option here instead of a blank (you cannot use a blank!). With this option, the method will execute its code and then just finish, with no data returning back to the invoking code.
- **Primitive data type or complex class type:** If you do want the method to return back data of a certain type, then you simply list the data type you expect to be returned as this option. **You would not list a variable name or any expression here,** just the data type's name. If you want the method to return an int, you would list `int` as the return type. Same for `String`, `Scanner`, and so on.

Naming your method: A method name is required, and its name follows the same rules as those for naming a variable (cannot start with a number; cannot contain a special character such as # or !; cannot use a Java-reserved word). Camel-case notation is recommended for your method names: `thisIsAMethod()`. Choose a simple yet descriptive name for your method. The method name will be a big hint to other developers who use your code as to its purpose and usage.

Parameter list concepts: You may have noticed that throughout this text, parentheses have always been included at the end of any method name. This is a key to determining if some named entity is a method or a variable. Two quick syntax rules here:

- When **defining** a method, you must include parentheses, even if you do not need input parameters for your method.
- When you **invoke** (i.e., call) a method, you must include parameter parentheses along with whatever arguments are required for the method (if any).

Consider the following definition for a small method that returns the sum of two numbers:

Code Snippet 6.1

```
// Example method
public static int addTwoNumbers(int numA, int numB)
{
    return (numA + numB);
}
```

Here are some general rules and concepts to remember about parameters in a method header:

- **Methods can be defined with any quantity of parameters:** A method can have zero parameters, one parameter, two, three, and so on—as many as you need. For `addTwoNumbers()`, you need the method to receive two int values, so define two `int` parameters.
- **Any defined data type can be used as a parameter:** Both primitive and class data types can be defined as a method parameter. For `addTwoNumbers()`, use `int` data types, as they are primitives and defined in Java. You easily could change the method definition to use other defined data types (primitive or user-created class types) as well.
- **You cannot use an expression as a method parameter:** Java requires that a method's defined parameter(s) be **variable declarations**. You **cannot** initialize a method's parameter in the parameter list! You will see later how the method's parameters gain their value.
- **Each declared method parameter is separated by a comma:** This helps Java differentiate between them. There is no comma needed after the last one.
- **Each declared method parameter has its method's execution life as its scope:** This means that a method parameter is "born" when the method is first invoked, and it "dies" when the method has finished and execution has returned to the calling code. The life-span of a variable and code areas where it can be accessed from are known as its **scope**. A method parameter declared in a method header **cannot be accessed by code outside the method**! For `addTwoNumbers()`, the two parameter variables `numA` and `numB` begin existence when the method is invoked, and they are destroyed sometime after the method finishes execution.
- **The variable length argument list `varargs` can be used as a method parameter:** You can keep the number of parameters defined in the parameter list flexible and tell Java to place the values into an array structure to be used inside the method. This will be explored later in the textbook.

Though there may be a lot of rules to the parameter list of a method header, once you get the "hang" of them, they will come naturally.

End of the method header: Just like with control statements and loop structures, there is no semicolon needed at the end of any method header. Also, you will **not** place a semicolon at the end of the last curly brace that makes up the **method body** either. Just like with an if statement, Java can see that this is a special structure to your logic and that no line termination is needed. For example, the following method definition would include two semicolons by mistake:

Code Snippet 6.2

```
public static int addTwoNumbers(int numA, int numB);  // NO!
{

    return (numA + numB);

};  // NO!
```

Method body concepts: This last part of the method definition is the "easiest" to understand in terms of its structure. The method body is enclosed by opening and closing curly braces and contains the code that you want to execute every time its method is invoked. The method body defines the scope and life-span of the method's parameter variables. Also, if there are any other variables in your class that have a high enough scope (i.e., class-level variables), they can be accessed from within the method body.

Return statement concepts: The last bit of flexibility here involves the `return` statement. The following are some syntax rules regarding the return statement:

- If your method's return type is `void`, you will **not** need a `return` statement in your method body. Otherwise, you will.
- Typically, a `return` statement is the last line of code in a method body. You can have other `return` statements in decision structures in your code, but the execution of your method's code must **not prevent** any `return` statement from being reached.
- Any code written **after** a return statement in a method body will **not** be executed (unreachable code statement error).
- The type of data you return in a `return` statement must match the data type you defined as the return in the method's header.

Consider the following example return statement:

```
return someVal;
```

In this example, "`someVal`" could be an actual literal value (like `2` or "`false`"), or it could be the name of a variable, or it could be the returned data from another method invocation (like `Math.max(2,7)`). Notice that in the `addTwoNumbers()` example, the result of an expression can also be returned. Since two `int` values are added, and `int` is defined as the method's return type, the `int` sum can be returned.

Table 6.1 summarizes the parts of the method definition that are optional versus not and the options that you can set for each. Table 6.1 is **not** all-inclusive, as there are additional modifiers that assist with multithreaded code execution and exception-throwing modifiers that will help prevent application-ending errors. For now, what has been covered will suffice as you start to explore methods.

Table 6.1. Summary of Structural Parts of the Java Method Definition

Method definition			
Method header	Access modifier	Optional	`public`, `private`, `protected`, or blank
	Class context	Optional	`static` or blank
	Return type	Required	`void` or data type
	Method name	Required	Follows variable naming rules
	Parameter list	Required	Zero, one, or many parameters
Method body	Method body	Required	Between curly braces, follows method header
	Return statement	Depends	Required if return type is not `void`

Method definition examples: A few examples that explore the flexibility of your options will help clarify how to use these and what "works" in Java. Consider again the quite simple `addTwoNumbers()` example with a change from its earlier definition (omitting "`static`"):

Code Snippet 6.3

```
public int addTwoNumbers(int
numA, int numB)
{
    int sum = numA + numB;
    return sum;
}
```

First, the access modifier used is "`public`," which means that any code, inside the containing class or outside of it, can invoke this method. Next, the class "context" modifier has been omitted. Java will interpret this method as nonstatic (meaning you would have to invoke it upon an instance object of the containing class). The return type is `int`, which defines this method as returning an `int` value (does not matter what the value is as long as it is an `int`). The method name is `addTwoNumbers`, which is pretty descriptive: this method adds two numbers together. The parentheses for the parameter list are **not optional**, but how many and what types of parameters included are. Two are used, both `int` variables with the names `numA` and `numB`. These variables are only usable **inside the method body**. If you try to use `numA` in code that is outside the method, Java will throw an error.

Now take a look at an example with no return type:

Code Snippet 6.4

```
private static void printAWord(String theWord)
{
    System.out.println("The word is: " + theWord);
}
```

This is a simple example. The access modifier `private` is used, meaning this method can only be invoked by code from inside its containing class. The use of `static` means this is a class-invokable method and cannot be called upon for specific instance objects of this class (remember this is similar to `Math.max()`, where `.max()` is a `static` method, and you invoke it by using the name of the class `Math`). By using `void` as the return type, you instruct the method to not return any data at all. The method name `printAWord()` is fairly self-explanatory, with the one single parameter being a `String` called "`theWord`," obviously the `String` value to be printed. You pass that value into the method from the outside (from the invoking code).

Notice that these methods are the following:

- **Modular:** The code is bundled in these methods, and the method can be invoked repeatedly from anywhere in your code.
- **Generalizable:** The first can add any two numbers within language limits, and the second can print any String, giving us great flexibility.
- **Maintainable:** You have only one place to change the adding or printing behavior in all the places in the code where these methods are invoked.

As you define methods, keep these benefits in mind. Any repeated code in an application could be a good candidate for being moved into a method. Then invoking the method where you previously had the code repeated would clean and simplify your logic. There are many ways in which creating a method can benefit and simplify your development efforts.

SUMMARY POINTS

- Methods in Java are always found or "defined" within a Java class, never outside.
- Methods in Java are always defined outside of other methods. All methods in a class are at the same "level" of definition within the class's structure.
- Methods are first defined and then invoked in your code.
- A method definition contains two major parts: the method header and the method body. The method header has several parts, some of which are optional and others that are not.
- The access modifier of a method defines its "security," meaning what access and permissions code in other areas of your application have in calling or invoking your method.
- The "class context" modifier defines how your method will be interacted with in the context of its usage with a class. The static modifier forces invocation on the class name (when code outside of the class is invoking the method). Omitting this modifier defaults your method to a nonstatic context (invokable only upon an instance object of the class).
- The return type of a method is not optional. It must be either "void" or the data type of whatever value you intend for the method to return to the calling code.
- The name of the method is required and follows the same rules as those for naming a Java variable.
- The parameter list always includes at least the parentheses. The parameter list for a method definition can contain zero, one, or many parameters, as many as you need.
- The method code body follows the method header and is always enclosed in curly braces.

The code that executes when the method is invoked is placed between the curly braces.

- If your method has a return type of anything other than "void," you are required to place a `return` statement as the last line of code in your method code body and `return` a value that matches the defined return data type.
- If you have any decision structures in your method, you must make sure a `return` happens with all possible execution paths (decision paths) as well. Typically, a `return` statement as the very last line of the method outside of any decision structures will do the trick.

QUICK PROBLEMS

1. **Coding:** Define a method that can be called by any code, and give it a static modifier. The method will accept three String values and concatenate them together with a blank space in between each. Return the concatenated String back as the return type. Give the method a descriptive and useful name.
2. **Think:** Can you think of several reasons why a class may want to have all its methods with a private access modifier? If the class stores sensitive data in its objects, would this align with a private access modifier?
3. **Coding:** Write a static method that can be called by any code. The method will accept three int parameters. The method will return back the largest number of these three parameters. Give the method a descriptive and useful name.

6.3 Method Invocation: How to Use Methods

You have likely noticed by now that the code used to **invoke** (i.e., use) a method looks very different from the code used to **define** that method. The invocation code is usually a lot simpler, as it should be. In most contemporary programming languages, methods are defined only once but can be used multiple times afterward. In figure 6.4, you can see the overarching relationship among the definition of a method and its usage, the parts of the method definition that relate to specific parts of the method usage, and the flow of data between the invocation and method definition.

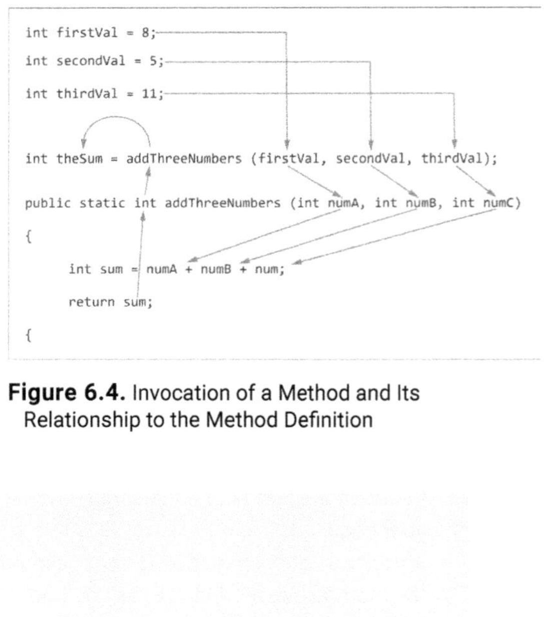

Figure 6.4. Invocation of a Method and Its Relationship to the Method Definition

The diagram shown in figure 6.4 highlights parts of the following full code listing (method definition in **bold**):

Full Program 6.1

```
package com.javaforis.chapter6;

public class ToolBox {

    public static void main(String[] args) {

        int firstVal = 8;
        int secondVal = 5;
        int thirdVal = 11;

      // Invocation of method:
        int theSum = addThreeNumbers(firstVal, secondVal, thirdVal);
        System.out.println("The sum of "+ firstVal
                + ", " + secondVal
```

```
                + ", and " + thirdVal + " is: "
                + theSum);

    } // end of main()

    // Static method's definition (header and body)
    public static int addThreeNumbers(int numA, int numB, int numC)
    {
        int sum = numA + numB + numC;
        return sum;
    }
}
```

Reexamining the `main()` method: Take a second look at the method header for `main()`. The parts should seem much less mysterious now:

- The `main()` method for a Java main class that an IDE will create for you will have the `static` modifier, meaning it is invoked upon the class name itself. Who invokes the `main()` method? The JVM looks for a `main()` method in your class when the IDE compiles and runs your program. Remember that `main()` is the starting point for the application. Additionally, it has the `public` access modifier for this reason: so that it can be invoked by external code.
- The return type for `main()` is `void`. Recall that you have not had to use a return statement in any `main()` method application so far (and will not!). Any method with a `void` return type will not have a `return` statement.
- The lone parameter for the `main()` method definition is an array of `String` values called `args`. Since you do not invoke this application from the command line, this parameter variable is not used at all.

Understanding the `addThreeNumbers()` definition: This is a much more practical usage of `addThreeNumbers()`. Note how the purpose and intended usage of the method impact your choices of how to structure its header:

- The method definition for `addThreeNumbers()` is **outside the code body of main**. Since `main()` and the method are both methods contained in this class `ToolBox`, they are at the same "level" in the class's code listing.
- Since instance objects of class `ToolBox` will not be needed and because the method `addThreeNumbers()` is to be invoked from within the static `main()` method, the "`static`" modifier is used on `addThreeNumbers()` as well.
- The method `addThreeNumbers()` is given a `public` access modifier, which allows any code to invoke it.
- It will return an `int` value, so notice that in the `main()` method, you can account for that behavior by storing the `int` value it returns in a variable. You could also have placed the invocation to `addThreeNumbers()` in the concatenated parameter for the `.println()` call as well (as you have done with several other methods in the past).
- There are three `int` variables created and passed to the method through its parameter list during invocation.

Before parameter passing is discussed in detail, carefully note the differences between the code that defines the method and the code that invokes it. Notice that in the definition, three parameters are declared: `int numA`, `int numB`, and `int numC`. When the method is invoked, **you do not have to declare them in the argument list of the invocation**. Since the values are passed from the `main()` method to the `addThreeNumbers()` method, you can use them in the positions of the parameter list: one in the first position, one in the second, and one in the third. Here are some rules to remember when using parameters in a method invocation:

- When you **define** a method, the values it accepts through its parentheses are called **parameters**. When you are **invoking** the method and placing variables or values in those parameter positions, you call them **arguments**. Arguments are the values **passed to the method**, and parameters **receive the values that were passed to them**. Think baseball: arguments are the pitchers, and they throw the ball to the catchers (the parameters).

- If a method is defined with X number of parameters, then when you invoke it, you must use the same number of arguments in the invocation line of code. In the example above, the method `addThreeNumbers()` is defined with three parameters, so with this method, you must use three arguments to invoke it.
- You must provide arguments in the same **arrangement (order), quantity (number), and data types** as called for in the method definition. Say, for example, a method is defined with two parameters, a `String` (as the first parameter) and a `double` (as the second parameter). When you invoke that method, you **must** provide a `String` as the first argument and a `double` as the second. If you try to provide more than two arguments, Java will throw an error. If you try to provide two `String` arguments, Java will also throw an error.
- Like with any other method you have used, you can use a literal value, a variable, or the return of a method invocation as an argument when you invoke a method, as long as whichever you use matches the data type specified for the parameter at that position in the parameter list of that method.
- Parameters receive their values and data from whatever code invokes them. In your method, there is usually no need to assign values to your parameters, as the **method starts with values already placed in your parameter variables!** The call to your method cannot occur unless the calling code passes values to your required parameters, so you can always be 100% confident that **some data** is stored within them. But you **cannot** always be sure that the data is of a high quality or accurate—additional logic on the part of the developer might be needed to ensure this.
- **The names of the variables used as arguments do not have to match the names of the expected parameters.** The only concern is with the data types of the values in those variables, not with their names.

Java considers **both** the **name of the method** and the **order, quantity, and data types** of the method's parameters as the "signature" of the method. Think of the last time you signed your name. You used your signature as a unique identifier of you, specifically you and no one else. The method name and its parameter list definition are its unique signature, and Java will use that to **identify which method in particular you are trying to invoke**.

Understanding pass(ing) by value: Now that you understand how to use arguments to pass data to a method's parameters, it is critical to understand just exactly how that data is being "sent" to the method. Where does the data go? Does the data type of the argument impact how the data is sent? These are questions that need answering before moving on, as they will impact how you understand the execution of methods from here on out. This is a critical language concept in Java! Refresh your blended coffee or other delicious drink, as this is an especially important section.

Unlike other programming languages, Java always handles parameter passing in what is known as a "pass-by-value" manner. Other languages will handle parameter passing either in a pass-by-value manner for primitive data types or in a "pass-by-reference" manner for reference types (we would know them as class/complex types or reference variables). What does this mean exactly? A simple breakdown is needed:

- **Pass by value** means that when an argument is used in a method invocation, a **copy** of its value is passed to the method. If the method makes a change to that copy, **nothing changes in the original variable or value that was passed.**
- **Pass by reference** means that when an argument is used in a method invocation, if that method makes a change to the **corresponding parameter**, those changes "trickle up" back to the argument that was originally passed.

I hope this paper was passed by value!

Source: "Overcoming Writer's Block—Crumpled Paper on Wooden Floor—Crushed Paper" by photosteve101 is licensed under CC BY 2.0, https://www.flickr.com/photos/42931449@N07/5263540555.

Think of it this way: pass by value is like making a copy of a sheet of paper and then handing it to your best friend. You tell your friend, "Write all over it, finger paint, crumple it up, and throw it away!" Once they are done, your original is still pristine and untouched! Pass by reference would be handing your friend your **only copy** of your sheet of paper and letting them make changes, and then they hand it back to you. Your original was changed, and now you have the ruined piece of paper. **Java always handles argument passing in a pass-by-value manner.** How do the data types of the arguments passed to a method impact this rule? They do not, but the rules for this will become particularly important later on.

- **Primitive data types:** For variable types like int, double, boolean, and so on, a **copy** of their value is passed to the method via the argument. If the method makes a change to the copy, nothing happens to the original variable in the invoking code ("calling" code). For primitive data types, this is like the copy of a sheet of paper being used: nothing happens to the original.
- **Class ("complex") data types / reference data types:** Java also follows pass by value for these, but there is a bit more thought that goes into understanding how these behave. Remember that a reference type is a variable that stores an address of an object somewhere in memory. It is a variable that is basically a "bucket" that stores an address of an object. The real data is in the object somewhere in memory. When a reference data-type variable is used as an argument, **a copy of its reference address is passed to the corresponding parameter**. If you make a change to the parameter's reference value itself, the original argument **does not change**. But if you make a change to the **object itself that is referenced by the variable**, then you **will see the change to the object back up in the invoking code!** Think of this example: You write the address of your house down on a sheet of paper. You then copy that address to a second sheet of paper. You hand that copy to your friend and tell them, "Please go paint my house in lots of bright colors." Your friend paints your house using lots of colors and then throws away their copy of the address paper. Both you and your friend had **references** to your house (the "object"). Your house is now colorful. So your friend (the method) changed the object, and now you see the change to the object through your reference. But when they destroyed their sheet of paper, it did not change **your** address paper. This is analogous to what happens when you pass a reference variable to a method.

You painted my object!
Source: "Painted House in Basel" by mabi2000 is licensed under CC BY-SA 2.0, https://www.flickr.com/photos/43846837@N00/43214814.

To help you better understand pass by value in Java when reference types are used, it's best to walk through an example. Imagine that the application has access to a class called `SomeObject`. Instance objects of this class (chapter 2) store two pieces of data: an `int` and a `String` value. Now imagine that you have a class method named `changesSomeObject()` that will make a change to the instance objects of this class that are passed to it. Consider the following code:

Code Snippet 6.5

```
// in main():
// Create the new SomeObject instance
SomeObject myObj = new SomeObject(12, "Java");

// invoke the method and pass the object to it.
changesSomeObject(myObj);

// . . . later on, outside of main()

// The method definition for changesSomeObject()
public static void changesSomeObject(SomeObject anObj)
{
    anObj.changeMyValues(5, "hello");

    anObj = new SomeObject(10, "words");
}
```

We do not know what code runs when a `SomeObject` object is created. But that is OK: you know that each of these objects stores an `int` and `String`. You can see that in `main()`, the `SomeObject` instance object `myObj`

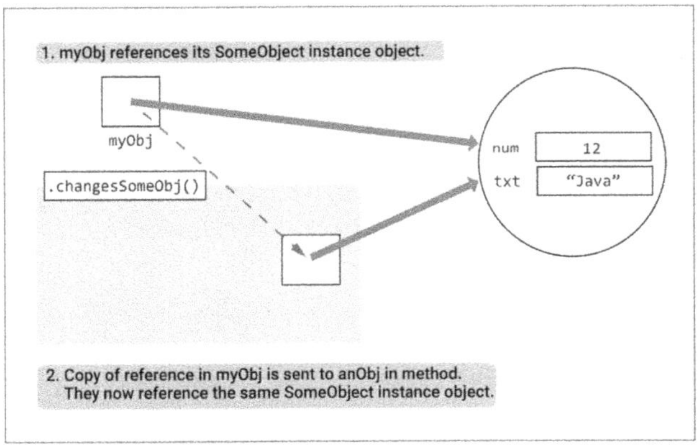

Figure 6.5a. Reference Variable Is Passed by Value to the Method `.changesSomeObj()`

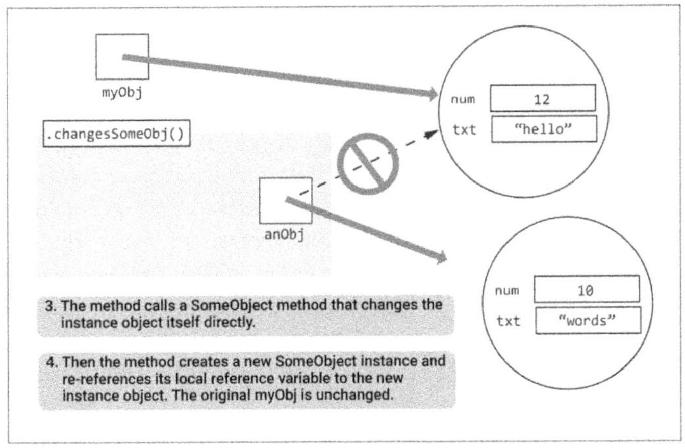

Figure 6.5b. Variable `anObj` Is Rereferenced to a New Object

is created with a `12` and the word "`Java`" is stored within via the constructor call (chapter 2). Then **a copy of the reference stored within `myObj` is passed via the one argument is passed to the method.** When the method `changesSomeObject()` begins execution, its parameter `anObj` has a **copy** of the reference that points to the location of the object in memory that `myObj` pointed to. Both reference variables now point to the same single `SomeObject` instance object in memory.

The method first calls a `SomeObject` class method that changes the values inside the object referenced by `anObj`. You make a change to the object itself, not the reference (we paint the house, but the copy of the address remains the same). The second line of code changes **the value of the reference variable itself.** When the method finishes and execution returns back up to `main()`, the original reference variable `myObj` **has not changed.** Why? Because pass by value only passes a copy. But the object that `myObj` references **has changed.** The house has been painted, and now you can see the new colors. The `SomeObject` instance object had new values placed within, and now those values are accessible. Figure 6.5 shows you the sequence of these events visually.

The way to keep this easily in mind is to ask yourself, Is the object referenced being changed, or is the reference to the object what is changed? **If you understand this key point, then the rest of the topics in this textbook will not be difficult at all!**

Handling returned data: Recall that when you create a method whose return type is not set to "`void`," then you must include a `return` statement as the last line of code in the method's code body. If you try to place any code after the `return` statement in a method, the Java compiler will most likely give you an `Unreachable Statement` error or something similar. Statements such as `return` work the same way as parameter passing but in the other direction: a copy of the value is returned to the calling code. Using the fictitious `SomeObject` class, consider the following `main()` method code and two methods that are invoked (we make a change to the method from earlier here as well):

Code Snippet 6.6

```
// in main():

int aValue = 20;
int secondValue = changeInt(aValue);

SomeObject anObj = new SomeObject(314, "Number");
SomeObject secondObject = changesSomeObject(anObj);

//. . . outside of main();

// Method Definition - returns a primitive
public static int changeInt(int value)
```

```
{
    return (value * 15);
}

// Method Definition - returns a class object reference
public static SomeObject changesSomeObject(SomeObject theObj)
{
    int newValue = theObj.getNumberValue();
    String newString = theObj.getStringValue();


    SomeObject newObject = new SomeObject(newValue, newString);
    return newObject;
}
```

Our first method `changeInt()` accepts an `int` as its single parameter. It receives a **copy** of the `int` argument passed to it, makes a change to that copy, and then returns back a **copy** of that value to the invoking code. The value eventually stored in the variable `secondValue` in `main()` when that segment of code is completed is a copy of the `int` value that was in the method `changeInt()`. Copies everywhere!

In the second method, the now adapted `changesSomeObject()` method, which returns a reference to a `SomeObject` instance object, receives a **copy** of the **reference** to the object that `anObj` references in `main()`. As with the previous example, now `anObj` in `main()` and `theObj` in `changesSomeObject()` **both reference the exact same single object in memory**. Some class instance methods are invoked to extract the `int` and `String` from within the object, and those values are used as parameters in the `SomeObject` constructor to create a new `SomeObject` instance object. Finally, the method returns a **copy of the reference to that new object** back to the calling code. (Take note here, it does **not** return a copy of the object itself, only a copy of the **reference** to the new object!) When execution returns to the `main()` method, the new reference variable `secondObject` receives a copy of that reference returned by the method, and it now "points" or references at the newly created `SomeObject` instance object in memory. Keep in mind that the `SomeObject` class does not exist; it is made up for this example.

Variable scope in the context of methods: Recall that scope means the "life-span" as well as the "accessibility" of a variable. Where it comes into memory, where it leaves memory, and what code can use the variable (as well as what code **cannot**) are all wrapped up in the idea of variable scope. When a variable is declared inside of a method, either in the parameter list of the method header or in the code body, that variable is said to be "local" to that method. This means its scope is limited to the start and end of that method. Consider the following two methods where the first method invokes the second:

Code Snippet 6.7

```
public static void firstMethod(int a, double b)
{
    a = a * 2;
    b = b * 2.0;

    double product = secondMethod(a, b);
}

public static double secondMethod(int wNumber, double dNumber)
{
    return (wNumber * dNumber);
}
```

Notice that both of these methods have parameter variables declared in their method headers. In method `firstMethod()`, variables `a` and `b` are **local** to `firstMethod()`. Their "life-spans" begin whenever the method is called, and the variables are removed from memory (they go to the "great compiler in the sky") when the method has finished execution. The same goes for the two parameter variables in `secondMethod()`; they are local in scope to that method.

What does this mean for being able to use these variables? Consider what would happen if you attempted to add these lines of code to the method `secondMethod()`:

Code Snippet 6.8

```
int copyOfA = a;
int copyOfB = b;
```

If you tried adding these lines of code to `secondMethod()`, you would receive a `Cannot Find Symbol` error from the Java compiler. Why? Remember that `a` and `b` are local to `firstMethod()` only and can only be "seen" in that method. This is scope! **Code in `secondMethod()` cannot see the variables used in the code of `firstMethod()`.** But you **can** invoke one method from within the other (since they are defined at the same "level" in the class). In essence, you do not need to be able to see variables `a` and `b` from `secondMethod()` because their data values are passed in and stored in the method's parameters `wNumber` and `dNumber`. Remember the following:

- The code in any method cannot see any variables declared in the other(s). The majority of the time, you must pass data to a method via input parameters.

For an exception to this, consider the following code example, where a "class-level" data field has been added to the `ToolBox main()` method application class (in bold):

Full Program 6.2

```
package com.javaforis.chapter6;

public class ToolBox {

    public static int recentProduct = 0; // Static Data Field

    public static void main(String[] args) {

        System.out.println(multiplyTwoNumbers(5, 8));
        System.out.println(multiplyTwoNumbers(10, 14));

        System.out.println(recentProduct);
    }

    public static int multiplyTwoNumbers(int a, int b)
    {
        recentProduct = (a * b);
        return a * b;
    }

}
```

The variable `recentProduct` has been added as a static data field to the class `ToolBox`, meaning it is declared and initialized outside of either method. So it is considered to be at a "higher" level of scope. In this case, you do not need to pass the variable `recentProduct` as a parameter, since the code in **both methods** can directly see it and access it. Keep in mind that the code in `main()` **cannot** see variables `a` or `b` in `multiplyTwoNumbers()` because they are local only to the `main`'s code body and not accessible outside of it.

SUMMARY POINTS

- The method invocation is much simpler to write than the method definition. Once you have defined the method, you are ready to use it.
- In the method invocation, you place the arguments or values that you want to pass to the method's parameters. The method header defines the parameters, which receive the data

passed to them by the method invocation. The arguments are copied into the parameters in the order in which the arguments are placed (first into first, second into second, etc.). The order/quantity/data types of your arguments must exactly match the order/quantity/data types as defined in the method header.

- Parameter variables are only declared in the parameter list. You will not initialize them in the parameter list. Likewise, when you invoke a method, you do not need to declare variables in the invocation; simply use values or variables as arguments, and Java will pass their values to the parameters for you.
- You cannot place an expression or formula in the parameter list of the method header or method calls. Only variable declarations. Variable initializations are not needed, since the values passed to the parameters will initialize them.
- The names of any variables used as arguments in the method invocation do not have to match the variable names defined in the method header. Only the order/quantity/data type arrangement matter.
- Java uses pass by value for all parameter passing, even for reference data-type variables.
- A method that receives an object reference as a parameter can make a change to the object referenced by the parameter, but a change to the parameter reference itself will not change the reference argument in the calling code that was passed to it.
- If you have a return type other than "void" in your method header, you must return a data value that matches that type. The return statement must be the last line of code in your method code body.
- Methods return copies of the returned values similar to how they receive only copies. You can think of this as "return-by-value," though this is not official Java language terminology.
- Defined parameter variables and any variables declared inside a method are considered "local" in their scope to that method's life-span and cannot be accessed directly by code outside the method. If there are variables that are at a higher level of scope in the method's containing class, then code inside a method can see and use these higher-scoped variables, but it cannot see variables defined/declared in other methods.

QUICK PROBLEMS

1. **Coding:** In your `main()` method, create a Scanner object used for reading in console input. Then in your class, define a static method with no return type. The method will accept one parameter, a reference to a `Scanner` object. In the method, have it prompt for a user to enter a phrase, capture the phrase, and print it right back out to the console. Finally, in `main()`, invoke the method, and pass as the argument the reference to your `Scanner` object.
2. **Think:** What will happen if when invoking a method that accepts two double values as each argument, you instead pass two int values in each argument position?
3. **Coding:** Write the `addThreeNumbers()` method from the examples in 6.3. Then create a new method called `.subtractThreeNumbers()` that will subtract the second parameter from the first and then the third from their difference, and have this method return back that difference. For each argument position in the invocation of `.subtractThreeNumbers()`, invoke `addThreeNumbers()`, and use `Math.random()` to generate a number between zero and ten for each parameter in `addThreeNumbers()`.

6.4 Method Overloading: Increasing Method Flexibility

For many of the methods exampled so far, you may have noticed multiple versions of each. Recall the `Math` class and its various methods, like, for example, the `.max()` method. Table 6.2 summarizes the different versions of the `.max()` method that can be found in the Oracle documentation for class `Math`:*

Table 6.2. Overloading of the `Math` Class Method `.max()`

Method signature	Description
`static double max(double a, double b)`	Returns a copy of the largest of the two `double` values a and b
`static float max(float a, float b)`	Returns a copy of the largest of the two `float` values a and b
`static int max(int a, int b)`	Returns a copy of the largest of the two `int` values a and b
`static long max(long a, long b)`	Returns a copy of the largest of the two `long` values a and b

Why are there four different versions? Shouldn't Java be able to tell the larger of any two numbers? Remember that Java is a type-strict (i.e., "strongly typed") language. If there were only one version of `.max()` that took two parameters, both `int` values, then using two `double` values would not work. Recall that the **signature** of a method is both its name **and** the order, quantity, and data types of its parameters. If you attempted to invoke this imaginary version of `.max()` as follows, the Java compiler would throw a type mismatch error:

Code Snippet 6.9

```
double larger = Math.max(5.6, 7.8); // int only .max() method
```

Because it is a type-strict language, a two `int` parameter version of the method would **not** accept two `double` values (or even one `double`!). Java developers branched off the method into separate versions to **increase its flexibility and convenience**. These are **overloaded** versions of the method. The `.max()` method has several other overloaded versions available to programmers.

You can take advantage of overloading with your methods also. Consider the following example, where a method prints out all the numbers between those passed to it as parameters, numbers inclusive:

Code Snippet 6.10

```
public static void printNumbers(int firstNum, int secondNum)
{
    for (int i=firstNum; i<=secondNum; i++)
    {
        System.out.print(i + " ");
    }
}
```

The application that will use this method might benefit from a second defined version, where `firstNum` and `secondNum` could be multiplied each by a third number and "scaled" to increase the print range. The method should still be named `printNumbers()` so it is obvious to other developers what both of these methods do. The second version of the method should behave a little differently than the first. How will Java differentiate between the two when they are called? Here are the rules for method overloading:

- The overloaded version of the method must have the same name as the old version.
- The overloaded version of the method must differ in **one or more** of the following aspects: the ordering of the parameters, the number of parameters, or the data types of the parameters. The overloaded version can differ in one, two, or all three aspects (mix and match).

* https://docs.oracle.com/en/java/javase/15/docs/api/java.base/java/lang/Math.html.

- The overloaded version **can also** differ in the return type and the access modifiers from what the original version has.
- The overloaded version does **not** have to have the same parameter names as the older version.
- The overloaded version's code **does not** have to exactly match the older version's code.

Using the rules, you might create a second version, an overloaded version, of the method like so:

Code Snippet 6.11

```
public static void printNumbers(int firstNum, int secondNum, int scale)
{
    for (int i=(firstNum*scale); i<=(secondNum*scale); i++)
    {
        System.out.print(i + " ");
    }
}
```

Notice in this version, both `firstNum` and `secondNum` are multiplied by the scale. What if you wanted a version of the method that accepts double values and prints every `.1` between the two numbers? You could create another overloaded version like so:

Code Snippet 6.12

```
public static void printNumbers(double firstNum, double secondNum)
{
    double printNum = firstNum;

    while (printNum <= secondNum)
    {
        System.out.printf("%.2f ", printNum);
        printNum += .1d;
    }
}
```

Now consider the **invocation** of these method versions. What if you invoke the method in the following way:

Code Snippet 6.13

```
printNumbers(1.5, 2.5);
```

Remember that the signature of a method is both its name and the order/quantity/data types of its defined parameter list. How does Java know which method you want to invoke? It simply checks all accessible versions of this method and finds the following:

- It finds a method that matches the name `printNumbers()`.
  - Then of those that match that name, it finds which method has a double as the first defined parameter and a double as the second defined parameter.
    - If it finds a method that matches both, it will execute that method and pass the arguments to its parameters.
    - If it does not find a matching method, the compiler will throw a "No Suitable Method Found" error on your invocation.

Method overloading when creating methods is useful in cases where you may want the method to execute one way with a certain set of inputs and differently with another. This is not to say that decision statements are not needed in a method: you can still branch the execution of your logic within a method based on the values that are passed. But if you think both yourself and other developers who might use your code will benefit from having differing versions of your method with various configurations of parameter inputs, then you might consider method overloading. You will see many overloaded methods throughout your Java studies.

SUMMARY POINTS

- Creating different versions of the same method, where differences are found in the defined order/quantity/data types of its parameters, is known as method overloading.
- Overloaded methods can also differ in the return type and/or access modifiers.
- Method overloading is useful in increasing the flexibility by which your method can be used by yourself and other programmers.
- Overloaded methods must have the same name as the earlier version but differ in some aspect in the defined parameter list.
- The overloaded method version's parameter names and code body can differ without impacting the overloading behavior.

QUICK PROBLEMS

1. **Coding:** Consider the versions of the `printNumbers()` method discussed in this section. Create another overloaded version of the method that accepts three parameters: the first two with data type `int` and a third `int` called `widen`. This version of the method will print all the numbers from the first `int` minus the value of `widen` to the second `int` plus the value of `widen` (the range of numbers printed is "widened" by the third parameter).
2. **Think:** Consider a chunk of logic that you have moved into a method. This logic's behavior is based on user input. For example, if the user enters a "1," it will perform one task, and if they enter a "2," it performs another (using chapter 4 concepts). If you are moving this logic to a method, would you need overloaded versions for each of these options? Why or why not?
3. **Coding:** Consider the method you created for quick problem #3 in section 6.2. Create an overloaded version of this method that accepts three double parameters and again returns back a copy of the largest value of the three.

Summary

The creation and usage of methods are foundational skills for any developer using a modern programming language. Sometimes called routines or functions in other languages, their creation and usage improve applications in many ways. Complex logic that is repeated (not in a loop context) can be moved into a method to "clean up" your code listing, replaced with much simpler single-line invocations of the method where you "bundled" your logic. Since your logic is now in one single place, the maintainability of your code has improved. A change made to your method-bundled logic will now "trickle out" to all the locations in your code listing where you invoked the method and its logic. And since your logic is now bundled within a method, you can plug and play this logic wherever you need in your code and even chain the usage of several methods together, invoking complex processing with very simple method calls. Methods are truly a valuable concept that, once you have practiced well, will take your programming skills well into the intermediate level of ability. Paring the creation and use of methods with loops (chapter 5) and decision statements (chapter 4) opens your development efforts up to very sophisticated processing capabilities. And understanding how to create methods will only increase your ability to understand how to use those methods created by other developers in the Java libraries. In the next chapter, you will begin to create custom "complex" variables by examining how arrays work in Java.

Practice Problems

Terminology

Match the following terms from the chapter with their most appropriate definition:

1. Method	a. A technique of creating successive versions of a method that have the same name as the original but differ in the order, the quantity, or the data types of parameters in the new version's parameter lists.
2. Parameter	b. A Java modifier that binds the invocation of a method or the usage of a class resource to the entire class itself, not any particular instance object of the class.
3. Invocation	c. A value placed in a parameter location when a method is invoked. This is a value that will be passed to the method.
4. Method definition	d. An access modifier used to provide complete access to code both inside and outside a class to either its methods or other resources.
5. Method header	e. A behavior where a copy of a variable's value is passed to a method. Changes to that value in the method do not propagate back to the passed variable.
6. Method body	f. The complete identification of a method by the Java compiler that includes both the name of the method and the specific order, quantity, and data types of its defined parameters.
7. Access modifier	g. The declared data type of the data, if any, that a method will pass back to the code that invoked it.
8. `Static`	h. An access modifier used to allow access to a class's methods or other resources to only code either inside the class or in one of its subclasses.
9. Return type	i. Last line of a method's body where the value, variable, or other data is specified to be passed back to the code that invoked the method.
10. Parameter list	j. The "calling" of a method from a location in your application. This call allows for the passing of any data to the method and executes the code defined in the method's body.
11. `return` statement	k. An access modifier used to prevent access to a class's methods or resources to any code not inside the class.
12. `public`	l. The second part of a method definition. This defines the code that will execute each and every time a method is invoked.
13. `private`	m. Part of the method header that defines the quantity, data types, and ordering of local method variables that will receive data when their method is invoked. Methods can have zero or as many of these variables as needed.
14. `protected`	n. A "bundle" of code with a surrounding structure including a name for invocation, parameters for data passing, and the potential to return data back to the invoking code.
15. Pass by value	o. A Java command that declares the ability of code both inside and outside of a method's containing class to invoke the method.
16. Pass by reference	p. The first part of a method definition. This part defines the accessibility for the method, its relationship to its containing class, its return type (if any), its name, and what (if any) data will be passed to it via parameters.
17. Argument	q. A variable declared in the method header. Code that calls a method can pass data to this variable when the method is invoked.
18. Method overloading	r. A behavior where a variable is passed to a method and changes to its value in the method propagate back to the originally passed variable.
19. Method signature	s. The declaration of a method, its structure, and the code that will execute when this method is invoked.

Find the Error

In each of the following problems, carefully examine the code given, and determine the error(s)/issue(s) with each. Keep in mind, the error(s) could be syntax (code) or logic (intended outcome) based or both!

1.

```
public static int addTwoNumbers{int a, int b}
(
   return a + b;
   System.out.println("Sum: " + (a + b));

);
```

2.

```
public String getEmployeeStatus(int employeeCode,)
{
    String status = "";
    employeeCode = 0;

    if (employeeCode == 1)
        status = "Active";
    else if (employeeCode == 2)
        status = "Inactive";

    return status;
}
```

3.

```
private boolean checkZipLength()
{
    boolean check = false;

    if (zipCode.length() >= 5)
        check = true;

    return true;
}
```

4.

```
public String concatText(String a, String b)
{
    if (findLonger(a))
        return (a + " " + a);
    else
        return (b + " " + b);

    public int findLonger(String a, String b)
    {
        if (a.length() >= b.length())
            return a;
        else
            return b;
    }
}
```

5.

```
public int numCheck(int a, int b)
{
```

```
    if (a >= b)
        return "a is larger!";
    else
        return "b is larger!";
}
```

6.

```
// In executing code:
int a=5, b=7, c=9;
addSomeNumbers(a; b; c;); // Method invocation
System.out.println("The sum is:  + theSum");

// Method Definition
private static void addSomeNumbers(int a, int b, int c)
{
    int theSum = a + b + c;
}
```

7.

```
// In executing code:
String st = "VT";
int lvl = 8;
double payCode = 5.5;
hiringCheck(paycode, st, lvl); // Method invocation

// Method Definition
protected boolean hiringCheck(String state; int refLevel;)
{
    . . . . // Code omitted
}
```

8.

```
private nonstatic convertName(String name)
{
    name = name.toUpperCase();
    return convertName(name);
}
```

9.

```
// Elsewhere in executing code:
int randomNumber = methodA() = methodB() = lower;

. . .

// Method Definition
public int methodA()
{
    // Generate a random number between 0 and 100;
    return (methodB(Math.random()*100));
}

// Method Definition
public int methodB(int lower)
{
    // Generate a random number between lower and (100 + lower)
    return ((Math.random() * 100) + lower)
}
```

10.

```
public static void (String studentName, double GPA)
     String print = "Student Name:  " + studentName;
     print += ", GPA:  " + GPA;
     if (GPA > 3.5)
          print += ": Honor Roll";
     else
          print += ": n/a";

     return print;
     System.out.println(studentName + "  processed!");
}
}
```

Think about It

1. What are some of the benefits of using methods in your application? What are the potential benefits to other developers when you add methods to your application?
2. When does duplicated logic belong in a method, and when might it belong in a loop structure instead?
3. How is the method definition different from the method invocation?
4. What are the two main parts of the method definition?
5. What parts of the method header are optional? Which are not optional? Why are these nonoptional parts required?
6. What does the access modifier do? How does it impact the usage of your method?
7. How does the inclusion of the static modifier in your method header change the way your method will be used?
8. How many parameters are required in a method header? How are method parameters different from method arguments?
9. What are the options for the return type part of the method header? How many possible options are in there total?
10. Describe how the concept of variable scope operates both inside and outside a method. Where can the variables that are declared inside a method be accessed? What variables can the code inside your method access?
11. How is the method body similar to the code body of a loop or control statement?
12. What is the rule on including a return statement in your method's body? Where should it be placed?
13. How is the code you write for the method header's parameter list different than the code you would write for the arguments in the invocation?
14. Describe what happens when you pass a variable whose data type is primitive as a method argument.
15. Describe what happens when you pass a variable whose data type is a class/complex type as a method argument.
16. In your own words, describe the parameter-passing behavior that Java uses.
17. What are some of the most important rules for method overloading in a Java program?
18. What are some benefits of method overloading?
19. How does the Java compiler know which overloaded version of a method should be called?

Short Syntax Problems

For all of these problems, implement the methods in a Java `main()` application. Write any appropriate `main()` method application code necessary to invoke, test, and run your implemented methods.

1. Create a method called `.vowelCount()`. The method will have one parameter, a `String` called `phrase`. It will return an `int`. The method will take any `String` input and count the number of English-language vowels found within the phrase (include *y* in this count). It will return this count as the `int` return. Account for differences in case (*a* vs. *A*). Test your method out on several phrases.
2. Create a method called `.averageGenerator()`. The method will have one parameter, an `int` called `quantity`. The method will return back a `double`. The method will generate a quantity of randomly generated numbers (between one and one thousand) and will sum them up. The parameter that is passed in will determine how many random numbers to generate and sum. Then it will calculate the

average by dividing that sum by the quantity. Return the average as the return value. If the quantity is equal to one, simply return the single number that is generated. Test your method out several times.

3. Create an overloaded version of method `.averageGenerator()`. The method will accept two parameters: an `int` called `quantity` and a `boolean` called `print`. The method will return a `double`. The method will work the same way as in #2, except that if the parameter `print` contains `true`, the method will print each randomly generated number as it is printed (with a blank space in between each). Otherwise, if `print` is `false`, it will not print anything as it generates the numbers and calculates the average to return.
4. Create a method called `.zipCodeCheck()`. It will accept one parameter: a `String` called `zipCode`. It will return back a `boolean`. The method will examine the passed in `String` and check for either a five-digit US zip code (i.e., `#####`) or a nine-digit one with a dash (`#####-####`). If a dash is found in the `String`, it will verify that five numbers precede it and four numbers follow it. If a dash is not found, it will check for five digits. Also in either case, letters are not allowed in any part of the `String`. If any of these checks fail, return `false`; otherwise, return `true`.
5. Write a method called `.totalVowelCount()`. This method will accept one input parameter, a String called phrase. It will return back a `String`. This method will count the quantity of all English-alphabet vowels in phrase. It will return back a professionally formatted String that displays all the vowels and their counts. Include *y* in your count. Be sure to handle letters with different cases (i.e., `a` vs. `A`).
6. Write a method called `.createMatrix()`. The method will accept two input parameters: an `int` called `rows` and an `int` called `cols`. The method will return back a `String`. The method will create a text matrix consisting of rows number of rows and cols number of columns. Each row-by-column cell will be either a `1` or a `0`, randomly chosen. Concatenate the text into a `String`, and **maintain the rows and columns/matrix nature in the String**. Return this back as the return value. In your application, test this method out to ensure that a true and well-aligned matrix of rows and columns is returned by printing the return to the console.

Full Problems

For all of these problems, implement the methods in a Java `main()` application. Write any appropriate `main()` method application code necessary to invoke, test, and run your implemented methods.

1. Create/expand from earlier your method called `zipCodeCheck()`. It will accept one parameter: a `String` called `zipCode`. It will return back a `boolean`. The method will examine the passed in `String` and check for either a five-digit US zip code (i.e., `#####`) or a nine-digit one with a dash (`#####-####`). If a dash is found in the `String`, it will verify that five numbers precede it and four numbers follow it. If a dash is not found, it will check for five digits.
   i. In either case, letters are not allowed in any part of the String. (*Hint:* Try to do this using what you have learned up until this point using either character codes [appendix C] or another String to cleverly compare characters against.) If any of these checks fail, return `false`; otherwise, return `true`.
2. Create a method called `passwordCheck()`. The method will accept one parameter, a `String` variable called `userPassword`. The method verifies new passwords entered by a user on the console by assessing the passed `String` against these business rules, returning `true` if it adheres to them all (`false` otherwise):
   i. The password must contain a `!`, `#`, or `$` symbol.
   ii. It must contain at least one capital letter and one number.
   iii. It must not begin with a number.
   iv. It must be at least ten characters long.
   v. No character can be duplicated sequentially. For example, "`aa`" would not be permitted within the password `String`, but "`. . . afa . . .`" would, and so on.
3. Create a method called `amortAutoLoan()`. The method returns back a `String`. The method will accept several parameters:
   i. The principal balance on an automobile loan (as a `double`)
   ii. The yearly interest rate for the loan (as a `double` in #.# format, which your method will convert to its appropriate math form)
   iii. The amount the customer would like to pay on the loan each month (as a `double`)

   The method will behave in the following way:

   i. If the customer's desired monthly payment is insufficient to cover the interest on the loan, the method will return back a `String` phrase "`Insufficient Monthly Payment`" to the calling code.
   ii. Otherwise, the method will concatenate (in the returned `String` using appropriate column headers and professional String formatting and columns) the listing of the monthly principle, interest amount, payment, and remaining amount, month after month, for the entire life of the loan. Be sure to include a row header indicating the month number.

4. As you have learned, the `String` class (chapter 3) has a method defined called `.contains()`. This method will return `true` if the parameter `String` is found within the `String` variable/value you invoke the method upon. **Without using the `.contains()` or the `.matches()` methods of the String class**, write your own method that **duplicates** the functionality of the `String` class `.contains()` method. Give it a different name, one unique to your application. For this method, it will accept two `String` parameters: the first String will be the `phraseToSearch`; the second parameter `String` will be the smaller `phraseToFind` to search for in the first. Your method will return a `boolean` if `phraseToFind` is found within `phraseToSearch`. *Hint #1:* You can use `.equals()`, `.equalsIgnoresCase()`, and `.substring()` for this task. *Hint #2:* Using a piece of paper, write out a sentence, then write out a small word in the sentence or part of that sentence. Compare the two visually. How could you compare the smaller phrase to "chunks" of the larger, chunk by chunk, character by character, to see if the smaller phrase is present? How would you know when the phrase is found? What would have to be true?

5. A client has need for a small Java statistical application that will calculate three separate values on demand: the average of a set of numbers, the largest and smallest values in a set of numbers, and the standard deviation of that set of numbers. The client does not want all these to print at once but rather wants to be able to choose from one of three menu options; each option will calculate one of these values. After a menu item is selected, the user is prompted for numbers to enter and can enter any quantity (this application will work with only positive numbers). After entry, the desired value for that menu option is entered. They have asked you to write this application. Tackle this using methods in the following way:
   i. First, write a method called `findAverage()`. This method will have no input parameters and will return a `double`. When the method runs, it will first prompt the user to enter numbers and will sum them up as the user enters them. The method will keep track of the quantity entered as they are entered as well. The user can enter -1 in order to stop entry, and the -1 will not be part of the average. After entry, the sum will be divided by the quantity and this average returned.
   ii. Next, write a method called `findMinAndMax()`. This method will have no input parameters and will return a `String`. The method will prompt the user to enter numbers, one after the other, entering -1 to stop the entry (and omitting -1 from the work). As the numbers are entered, the method should keep track of the lowest and highest number entered and compare each newly entered number to them. If one is lower or higher, that number is remembered as the newest "champion." The method will return a `String` when processing is complete that states the min and max numbers in professionally formatted output.
   iii. Third, write a method called `standardDeviation()`. This method will have no input parameters and will return a `double`. You will need to perform external research and look up the formula for standard deviation for this problem. The method will prompt the user to enter numbers one after the other, entering -1 to stop entry. Use the entered numbers and call any Math class methods needed to calculate the standard deviation of the numbers entered. Return this calculated value as the method's return value.
   iv. Finally, in the `main()` method of your application, prompt the user for a menu option, capture it, and within a `switch`, handle the processing of the option. For each option, invoke the associated method above.
   v. Place all of this in a loop so that the user can calculate several successive values. Include a menu option in your `switch` that will end the loop and the application.

Chapter 7

Working with Data in Arrays

What You Will Learn in This Chapter

Working with data is a core task that developers face in any programming language, not just in Java. Developers take advantage of data structures like **arrays** to help efficiently store and provide easy access to data. Programming languages use array-based concepts, logic, and syntax to help developers create and manage sequences of data effectively. Many Java language features you will learn in the future are based on basic array concepts. As a developer implementing information systems to solve business problems, arrays are a critical concept inseparable from the work you will do and the data you will manage. The concepts and use of arrays are worth spending time on as an information systems developer.

Specifically, this chapter will help you do the following:

1. Learn what common array-based structures of data are in IS and how they compare with "regular" variables in Java, along with some of their benefits in programming
2. Learn how arrays are treated as complex objects and how to use their reference variables
3. Learn how arrays can be multidimensional and how arrays of increasing dimensionality are handled by Java and managed in memory
4. Learn how loops can be effectively used along with arrays to perform several common data-processing tasks
5. Learn how to avoid common mistakes and errors that can occur in the use of arrays and how to avoid them
6. Learn how the rereferencing of array variables affects their use and common issues to watch out for when working with array variables
7. Learn how useful the static methods of the Java class arrays can be in common data sequence processing tasks

Opening Scenario

Your efforts at creating effective data-cleaning and data-processing logic in Java have been successful! After some initial verification of your logic, your colleagues on the prototype team have given the green light to your efforts. The team is pretty confident the data will be well structured, well modeled, and clean for the prototype information system being built for the client. Now your project manager has moved you to the core implementation team as the project moves into its main phase. Recall that your team is tasked with developing a prototype desktop IS in Java as a "proof of concept" to see if a larger system is feasible for the company.

After extensive requirement-elicitation efforts by the project manager and other team members, a to-do list has been generated, and the team has asked you to coordinate the development of the core feature: inventory management. The client has a limited number of stores in one area and has used spreadsheets and other highly manual efforts to manage their inventory, their customer information, their employees and time sheets, and more. At this early stage, you decide that arrays would be a great way to store inventory information in memory (for now). "Go for it," your project manager states. "Your code will be relatively easy to convert over to database access when we are ready." You have not worked with arrays much, though you have a general idea of what they do and the benefits they yield. Additional web searching has yielded many array examples that seem complicated and difficult, though you respect the sophistication of the logic. Single-row and multiple-row arrays; arrays with varying numbers of columns to save space in memory; arrays that duplicate spreadsheet workbooks (multiple tables each with rows and columns)—lots of array concepts to think about. You decide to start with the basics so that you can gain a solid understanding of array structures before tackling the store's inventory management needs . . .

7.1 Arrays versus Primitive Data-Type Variables

Arrays are a great next step in learning how to do more with less code. Additionally, they serve as an effective transition between the usage of primitive data types and more object-oriented "enabled" Java syntax. The `String` and `Scanner` classes have given you some practice in object-oriented concepts. While the basic arrays in Java are not instance objects of a class per se, Java manages them in a similar manner. This will help you gain more confidence in object-oriented concepts before diving deeper into class creation and usage in later chapters.

Figure 7.1. Solar Panel Array Providing Power to a Home in the Western United States

Source: "Utah House Solar Panels" by ricketyus is licensed under CC BY 2.0, https://www.flickr.com/photos/7261722@N08/5052486185.

What is an array? In most programming languages, an **array** is a sequence of data stored in a memory-efficient (i.e., compact) manner within one "data structure," a variable with a complex internal structure. This makes arrays a "complex" data-type variable that Java handles similarly to a class object, but they are not instance objects of classes. Typically, all the data in the sequence are of the same data type. Consider figure 7.1, a solar panel array. Each panel consists of rows and columns of solar "cells" collecting light and generating energy for a home. These panels are compact and efficient: all the cells are clustered together in an efficient and space-saving way that is easily usable. You can quickly point out a particular cell by identifying its row and column on that row. Arrays in Java are the same: they allow you to store multiple data values in a single object in a compact, memory-efficient, and easily accessible manner.

Consider all the students in one of your classes. What is an easy way to gather and print all their names? How could you do this in a Java application? An easy way would be to conduct a count of how many students are in the class and then create a similar quantity of String variables to store each of their names. For example, say there are ninety-seven students in a classroom:

```
String name1 = "Blair";        // 1st String Variable
String name2 = "Cameron";
String name3 = "Easton";
.
.
.
String name97 = "Makoto";      // 97th String Variable
```

This works, but look at all the manual effort you expended! What if you then want to print a list of the names in a roster style? You would have to write ninety-seven `.println()` statements. You might cleverly think that you can just concatenate them all into one long `String`:

```
String nameList = "Blair" + "Cameron" + "Easton" + . . . + "Makoto";
```

OK, this might work at a basic level as well. But how would you separate the names for printing? What if you need to change someone's name due to a misspelling? What if a student drops the class, and you need to remove the student's name entirely? Concatenation into one long `String` would not work too well either and is still a lot of effort. An array that contains a sequence of `String` variables would make easy work of this task. Here is how a `String` array would be created in Java:

Code Snippet 7.1

```
String[] nameArray = new String[97];      // Size 97 Array
nameArray[0] = "Blair";                   // First Element
nameArray[1] = "Cameron";                 // Second Element
nameArray[2] = "Easton";                  // Third Element
.
.
.
nameArray[96] = "Makoto";                 // Last Element
```

We will explore later in this chapter how the above code works. Essentially, this is one single variable that can store many different `String` values. And each `String` value is separate and distinct from the others. You can make a change to one without impacting others. You have ninety-seven different names stored in one variable, and Java does all the hard work of keeping them stored, separated, and easily accessible.

An array can be used to store multiple values of any data type. Because of this, an array is **complex** and has internal structure different from the normal primitive data-type variables that you are familiar with. Java manages arrays the same as it would an instance object of a class, but arrays are **not** instance objects. In the prior example of student names, the variable `nameArray` is **not** the array itself! It is a **reference variable** to the array of `String` values. Java keeps the array itself in the heap area of memory. The reference variable `nameArray` is kept in the method's memory frame on the frame stack where it was declared (in the example, you can imagine it is stored in `main()`'s frame). In this case, the reference variable `nameArray` references the location in the computer's memory where the array (the actual data) is located at. Though an array is not an instance object of any class, it is treated like one. Figure 7.2 shows this object-oriented nature with accompanying reference variable.

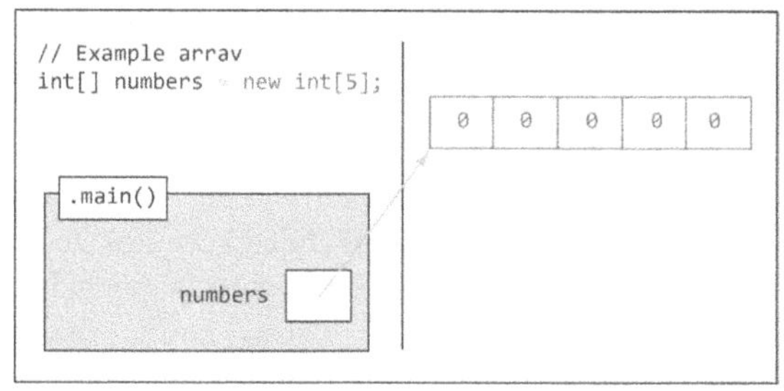

Figure 7.2. An Example Array on the Heap and Its Reference Variable in `main()`

There are some overall concepts that you should remember that will help you use arrays in Java more effectively. These concepts deal with the nature of Java arrays and how they manage the data stored within them:

- **The array itself and its reference variable are two different objects:** The actual data of an array is not stored in its reference variable. Rather, its reference variable stores the location of the actual array in memory. If needed, multiple reference variables can store the address of a single array. This happens particularly when a reference to an array is passed to a method.
- **Arrays are a sequence of the same type of data:** An array in Java can only store the type of data it was declared with. You cannot mix and match data types in a single standard Java array. For class data types, both the class and its subclass types can be referenced from the array's elements—as will be discussed later in the textbook.
- **Array "chunks" are known as elements:** Each value or "chunk" of data stored in an array is known as an element of the array. Arrays are a sequence of elements.
- **Standard Java arrays cannot be resized (made larger or smaller) once created:** Once you create an array in Java with a certain size, that array will stay that size forever until it is destroyed (out of scope or when the application ends). An array reference variable can be rereferenced to a larger, newly created array if needed.
- **Elements of Java arrays are mapped using index notation:** Recall that a String can be thought of as a sequence of character (`char`) values and that index notation is used to map the characters in that string. The first character is at index position 0, and the last character is at index position length minus one. Java arrays are mapped in a similar manner, with the first element of the array at index position `0` and the last at `length - 1`. An array consisting of 10 `int` elements will be mapped at index positions 0 through 9.

- **Data is not inserted into a Java array but is copied into an array element:** Because Java arrays cannot be resized, you cannot "insert" a new value into the array, which implies a change to the array's size. Elements of arrays are overwritten when new data is copied in.
- **Java does not manage the data you place into an array in any way:** Data are not automatically placed into a standard Java array in any sorted manner. An array does not care where you place the data or in what order in the array. An index position must be specified when copying data into an array.
- **Using the assignment operator (=) does not copy an array:** Remember that arrays use reference variables. If you set two reference variables equal to each other, you are **not** copying the data they refer to; rather, you are copying the value of one reference variable into another. The data in the arrays they referred to remain untouched (unless garbage collection occurs due to an array being orphaned). Copying array data takes a little more work.
- **Any valid/defined data type can be used to create an array in Java:** Standard Java arrays can be declared as any valid or defined data type, including class data types.
- **Arrays can be multidimensional:** You will be the most popular person at the party this weekend when you demonstrate a three-dimensional array to your friends and/or family! Arrays in Java can be created with structures of increasing dimensionality. The most common are one-, two-, and three-dimensional arrays. Figure 7.3 gives examples of various dimensional arrays. A one-dimensional array would be a single row of data (e.g., a row of a database table). Two-dimensional arrays are like spreadsheets or an entire database table. A three-dimensional array would be **like an entire database** (an array of tables). A four-dimensional array (not shown) would be an **array of databases**, and so on.

The usage of arrays is fairly common across most programming languages and is considered a basic skill that developers have to conquer to be considered proficient in most modern contexts. For information systems professionals, the use of arrays and processing highly structured data are critical concepts. When working with loops, you learned how their structure can assist with either read/write operations with database tables or any structured data-processing task. These same loops will work with two-dimensional arrays. Database integration and read/write operations to a database table often come with a lot of processing overhead, meaning it can slow an application down (ever so slightly). Often, it will be more efficient to store data in an array in memory for further processing or even cleaning rather than constantly pushing and pulling data to your database, writing the data out at the end of the task. Additionally, becoming effective at the use and processing of arrays will help with your learning later on with more advanced data structures that perform more automatic data-handling tasks (such as stacks and queues). There are many, many benefits for the IS professional to become proficient at the creation and use of arrays in Java, as have been discussed.

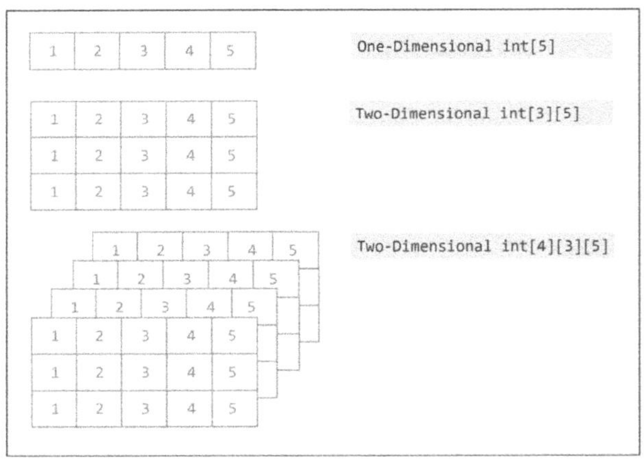

Figure 7.3. Examples of `int` Arrays with Increasing Dimensionality (Basic Visualization)

SUMMARY POINTS

- Arrays make storing multiple, related values in memory easy as compared to having many different variables for each value.
- Arrays in Java are complex data-type objects. Though arrays are complex, they can store both primitive and class data-type values.
- Arrays consist of an object in memory that is "pointed to" or addressed by its reference variable, similar to other class data-type variables.
- Arrays store values in elements, and values are copied into each element of an array.

- Standard arrays in Java are a fixed size after creation. Once created, they cannot be lengthened or shortened.
- Like with String values, index notation is used to map each individual element of an array in Java.
- Arrays can consist of one, two, or multiple dimensions in their structure. One- to three-dimensional arrays are most common in Java and other languages.

QUICK PROBLEMS

1. **Think:** Thinking about your daily life, what would be an example of information that you might store in a **one-dimensional array** (one row, several columns)?
2. **Think:** Thinking about your daily life, what would be an example of information that you might store in a **two-dimensional array** (several rows, each with several columns)?
3. **Think:** Thinking about your daily life, what would be an example of information that you might store in a **three-dimensional array** (several tables, each with several rows and several columns)?

7.2 One-Dimensional Arrays

Declaring and initializing one-dimensional arrays: Figure 7.5 covers the basics of the creation of a dimensional array in Java. Notice the ellipses after the brackets in figure 7.5, indicating you can add as many pairs of brackets as you need to increase the dimensionality of the array. For a one-dimension array, there will only be one pair of brackets on both the reference variable and the array creation. Recall that

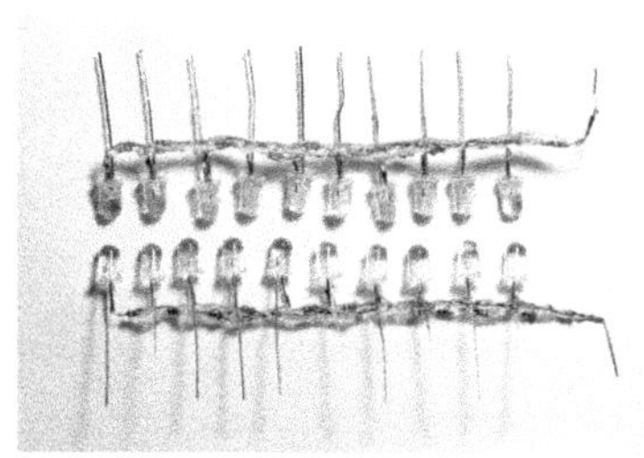

Figure 7.4. Two Separate One-Dimensional Arrays of LEDs
Source: "LED Arrays" by steve_lodefink is licensed under CC BY 2.0, https://www.flickr.com/photos/32547150@N00/2183899433.

- an array can be declared using any valid/defined data type in Java, and
- the reference variable is **not** the array itself but refers to the actual array in a different location of memory.

The data type of your array's reference variable should match the data type you want each element of the array to store. For example, a simple array of ten integers would look like this:

Code Snippet 7.2

```
int[] numberArray = new int[10]; // Array of 10 integers
```

Notice that like any variable, the name of the reference variable is totally up to you. The square brackets are the **bracket operator** and are associated with array creation and use in Java. There are two different objects in memory after this line of code executes. Since arrays in Java are handled as if they were instance objects, the `new` operator is used to create the array in the heap area of memory.

An array of ten elements is created, where each element is an `int` data-type variable. When you first create the array, the number you use in the brackets **always indicates the size** of the new array being created. On the left of the assignment operator, a **reference variable** is created that will provide access to the array in memory. Notice the brackets are blank/empty. The **data type** of this reference variable is `int[]`. You include the brackets with the `int` data type to indicate that this is a **reference variable that stores the location in memory of an array of integers.** The assignment operator itself copies the address of where the array is located in memory into the reference variable, completing the execution of the line of code.

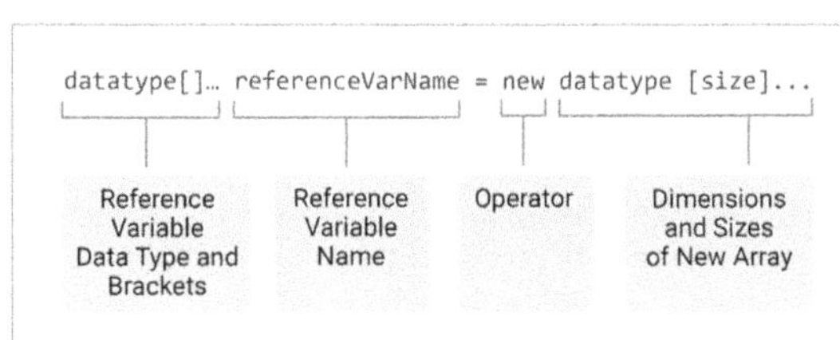

Figure 7.5. Array Declaration Template in Java

Alternatively, Java also allows you to create an array by placing the empty brackets next to the reference variable instead of beside the data type of the array it refers to:

Code Snippet 7.3

```
int numberArray[] = new int[10];  // Alternative declaration.
```

When discussing this array's data type, you would still refer to it as an `int[]`. You can use any data type to create an array in Java and arrays of any size you wish:

Code Snippet 7.4

```
String[] listOfNames = new String[50]; // Array of names
double[] examScores = new double[37]; // Array of double values
boolean[] binaryValuesList = new boolean[15]; // Array of booleans
```

Like other variables in Java, you can split up these tasks of array creation and reference variable declaration into two separated steps:

```
int[] listOfHeights; // reference variable contains NULL
.
.
.
listOfHeights = new int[45]; // Reference to array object copied
```

This should further demonstrate how the reference variable is **not** the array but references/points to the array in memory. The size 45 `int` array is not created until sometime after the reference variable is declared.

You can also use both a variable and an expression to indicate the size of the array at the time of creation:

Code Snippet 7.5

```
int arraySize = 20;
int[] mySequence = new int[arraySize];
int[] anotherSequence = new int[arraySize * 20];
```

Java allows you to create an array using what is known as an **array initializer** (sometimes called a "shortcut array"):

Code Snippet 7.6

```
int[] smallArray = {56, 93, 54};
// Small array created via array initializer
```

This syntax is different from the normal array creation examples seen earlier. Notice that the reference variable part stays the same. The array creation step on the right of the assignment operator is different. Here, curly braces are used instead of using the new operator. Also, the values here are **the actual data values you want to store in the array, not the size**. Notice that each value is separated by a comma. How does this work?

1. Java counts the number of elements you place in the curly braces with commas separating them. It recognizes this syntax as a command to create a new array with a size equal to the number of elements you typed in.
2. Java then infers the data type as best it can based on the actual elements you typed in.
3. It creates the array with size and element data types based on your shortcut list. The values in your shortcut list are copied in each element of the array (first into the first, second into the second, etc.).
4. Finally the reference to the array is copied into the reference variable you declared.

Arrays created like this are ideal for situations where you only need a small number of elements in an array and where you already know ahead of time the values that you will need. Additionally, you can use variable values in place of literals in the curly braces if needed:

Code Snippet 7.7

```
    int first = 5;
    int second = 10;
    int third = 15;

    int[] smallList2 = {first, second, third};
```

The following are some common **mistakes** with general array creation that you should avoid:

1. **The reference variable's data type and the array's data type do not match:** In this case, you will get an incompatible types error if you fail to match up the data types of the reference variable and the array. Remember, the reference variable's data type defines what **type** of array it will reference, and Java is fairly strict about this. Consider this mistake:

```
int[] grades = new double[34];  // Nope!
```

Your IDE will most likely give you an **incompatible types** error here, as Java sees the `int[]` as one data type and `double[]` as strictly another. Normally, an `int` can be stored (or up-converted) into a double, but here the array versions of these will not work the same way. You have defined the reference variable `grades` as referencing an array of `int`, but you tried to point it at an array of `double` values! Java will not compile this code.

2. **You forgot to indicate the size of your newly created array:** Another common mistake is neglecting to indicate how large your newly created array will be. The shortcut method takes care of this because Java can guess how large it should be by the number of elements you typed between the curly braces. But if you use the normal array creation style, Java cannot guess how large the array needs to be. Consider the following errant code:

```
double[] studentScores = new double[]; // Nope! Size required
```

The array needs an indicated size at creation. Multidimensional arrays (later in this chapter) will alter this rule a bit.

How to read and write from/to a one-dimensional array: After an array has been created, any number placed in the brackets beside the reference variable refers to the **index location of a specific element in the array**. Consider the arrays created earlier in this section: they already exist in memory and are ready to be worked with:

Code Snippet 7.8

```
numberArray[0] = 316;
listOfNames[3] = "Dr. Java";
```

Notice the operator `new` is missing from these lines of code. Once the arrays exist and have a reference to them, you can simply use the arrays and start writing data in and reading data out. The numbers here refer to the index positions of particular elements you want to work with. When copying the value `316` into `numberArray`, it can be read as "Copy the value 316 into the element at index position 0 (the 0th element) in the array referenced by the reference variable `numberArray`." Arrays typically start out "empty," filled with default values based on their data types (0 for `int`, 0.0 for `double`, `null` for `String` and other reference types, etc.).

Consider the shortcut array from earlier, `smallList2`. You can change its values too, even though you created and initialized it all in one step:

Code Snippet 7.9

```
smallList2[1] = 44;
```

Reading from the array uses the same syntax: refer to a specific element in the array, and Java will give you a **copy** of that element to work with. For example, if you wanted to print all the elements of the shortcut array `smallList2`, it is relatively simple, since it is a, well, small list:

Code Snippet 7.10

```
System.out.println(smallList2[0]);
System.out.println(smallList2[1]);
System.out.println(smallList2[2]);
```

As always, the code in the method parameter executes first, so on each line of code, you retrieve a copy of the zeroth, first, and second elements in the array referenced by smallList2 (respectively), and then that copy is printed to the console. Keep in mind that every element will be printed here, **even elements that you may not have placed data into**. For an `int` array, elements with their "default" values will be `0`, so you will have a `0` print to the console for these specific elements.

What if you want to print the contents of `numberArray` or `listOfNames`? These arrays are a lot longer than `smallList2`, and it would be awkward to copy and paste `System.out.println()` over and over for each element. Let Java do all the hard work and use a loop for these. Specifically, a `for` loop. The creation of the array and the placing in of data for convenience are both shown in this example:

Code Snippet 7.11

```
int[] numberArray = new int[10];
numberArray[0] = 316;
numberArray[8] = 47;

for (int i=0; i<10; i++)
{
    System.out.println(numberArray[i]);
}
```

The console output for this code after execution would look something like this, and notice that unchanged elements are also printed (with values of `0`):

```
316
0
0
0
0
0
0
0
47
0
```

Notice in the `for` loop, the loop is "hard coded" to only run ten times. Each array in Java "knows" its own length via a `length` property that you can use to make the `for` loop more generalizable to any array size:

Code Snippet 7.12

```
for (int i=0; i<numberArray.length; i++)
{
    System.out.println(numberArray[i]);
}
```

The same console output will print as you saw earlier, but now the `for` loop can determine the length of the array on its own. This will be useful in situations where you may not know the size of an array ahead of time.

You can change this example again to print the index positions of each printed array element:

Code Snippet 7.13

```
int[] numberArray = new int[10];
numberArray[0] = 316;
numberArray[8] = 45;

for (int i=0; i<numberArray.length; i++)
{
    System.out.println("Index Position " + i
            + ": " + numberArray[i]);
}
```

The console output for this would be the following:

```
Index Position 0: 316
Index Position 1: 0
Index Position 2: 0
Index Position 3: 0
Index Position 4: 0
Index Position 5: 0
```

```
Index Position 6: 0
Index Position 7: 0
Index Position 8: 47
Index Position 9: 0
```

The following are some common mistakes with array usage that you should avoid:

1. **Trying to use an array without first creating it:** It is critical that your reference variable must reference an actual array; otherwise, you will not be able to use it. Consider the following code example:

Code Snippet 7.14

```
String[] wordList;
wordList[5] = "Sixth Word"; // null Reference Exception
```

Notice that creating the reference variable does **not** automatically create the array you want it to reference! In the second line of code, it is assumed that an array exists, that the reference variable points to it, and that it is large enough to have a sixth element that can be written to (at index position `5`). Many assumptions here! Trying to write to an element will not automatically create the array either. This code can be corrected as follows:

Code Snippet 7.15

```
String[] wordlist = new String[10];
wordList[5] = "Sixth Word";
```

Now the array actually exists and is large enough to have an index position of `5`.

2. **Trying to copy data into an array element that does not exist:** In this error, the array exists, but you are trying to access an element that does not. The assumption is that the array is longer than it really is. Consider the following:

Code Snippet 7.16

```
String[] wordList = new String[3]; // Size 3: 0, 1, 2
wordList[5] = "Sixth Word"; // Index 5 does not exist!
```

If you run this code, you would receive an error from the Java compiler similar to this:

```
java.lang.ArrayIndexOutOfBoundsException: Index 5 out of bounds for length 3
```

The `ArrayIndexOutOfBoundsException` occurs when an array element does not exist. Usage of the `length` property of an array will help minimize this error.

3. **Assuming there is something at an array index position when there is not:** For this example, consider an array of `String` values. Recall that the `String` class has many instance methods that can be invoked on `String` variables to help with their processing. Consider the following example:

Code Snippet 7.17

```
String[] phrases = new String[3];
phrases[0] = "Arrays in Java can be very helpful!";

for (int i=0; i<phrases.length; i++)
{
    System.out.println("Phrase " + i
            + " Contains \"Java\"?: "
            + phrases[i].contains("Java"));
}
```

For the first String in the array phrases, your console output would look like this:

```
Phrase 0 Contains "Java"?: true
```

But immediately after this, you would receive an error similar to this:

```
java.lang.NullPointerException: Cannot invoke "String.contains(java.lang.CharSequence)" because
"phrases[i]" is null
```

In this example, it is assumed that there was a `String` value at index positions `1` and `2` (second and third positions, respectively), but there was not. So when the `String` method `.contains()` is invoked upon the assumed `String` elements at those positions, Java found `null` at those two positions instead, generating the `NullPointerException`. There were no `String` elements to invoke the method upon!

4. **Invoking the `String` class method `.length()` instead of accessing the array property length:** This can be a common mistake, since `Strings` and arrays are both used so commonly in Java. The `String` class has an instance method called `.length()` that will report the number of characters in a `String` variable. Java arrays all have a `length` property (*think:* instance data field) that will report the number of elements in the array (empty or not). It is easy to confuse the two, but keep in mind that one is a method, and one is a property:

Code Snippet 7.18

```
String[] phrases = new String[3];
System.out.println(phrases.length()); // no method exists!
```

This will not compile, as the compiler will not be able to find a length method that corresponds to an array.

5. **Forgetting that the array property length reports only the length of the array, not how many elements have values in the array:** Consider the following example:

Code Snippet 7.19

```
int[] numberArray = new int[10];
System.out.println(numberArray.length);
```

The console output for this would be the following:

```
10
```

Notice that the array is brand new and empty, and the length property's value is printed to the console, telling you the size of the newly created array. In this specific array example, all the elements are "empty" (they all contain the value `0`), and length will still report `10`. In order to determine the number of nonzero elements in this integer array, you will have to do a little more work:

Code Snippet 7.20

```
int[] numberArray = new int[10];

numberArray[0] = 316;
numberArray[8] = 47;

int counter = 0;
for (int i=0; i<numberArray.length;i++)
{
    if (numberArray[i] != 0)
        counter++;
}
System.out.println("Nonzero elements in array: " + counter);
```

This will effectively identify how many elements have been changed. Keep in mind that based on the business rules and context of the application, a value of `0` in your array may be valid! Be careful of the context and what constitutes an "empty" array element.

For an array that contains a `String`, you will have to use the `null` value in Java to see which elements have or have not had a string value copied in:

Code Snippet 7.21

```
String[] phrases = new String[3];
int phraseCounter = 0;

phrases[0] = "Arrays in Java can be very helpful!";
```

```
for (int i=0; i<phrases.length; i++)
{
    if (phrases[i] != null)
        phraseCounter++;
}
```

Using the `for-each` loop: Like many other modern programming languages, Java provides a convenient variant of the `for` loop that makes traversing or walking along each element of an array easier. The `for-each` loop works just like a regular `for` loop, though it does more of the "work" of looping for you. Often you will see this looping structure called the "enhanced" for loop. The `for-each` loop finds the array length, starting at the beginning of the array, and traverses each element to the last. Additionally, the `for-each` loop will obtain a **copy** of each array element as it walks along and makes that copy available to you for use in the loop's code body. Figure 7.6 shows the general structure of the `for-each` loop and examples its behavior over the **first two** of its loops for an example array of `int` data.

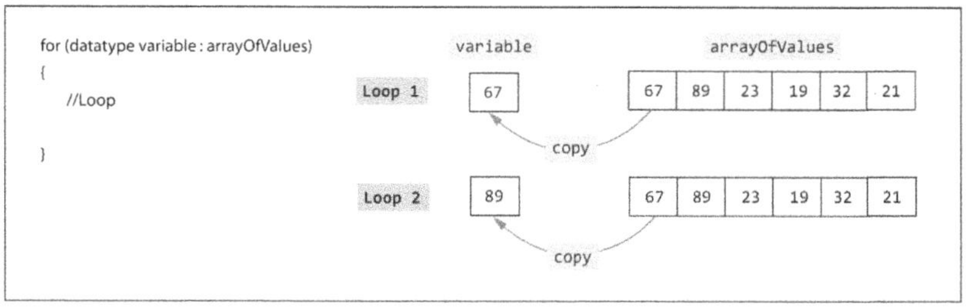

Figure 7.6. General Template and Example Behavior for the `for-each` Loop

Consider the following `int` array with both a normal `for` loop and the enhanced `for` loop for comparison (they both do the same thing in this case: print the values of the array):

Code Snippet 7.22

```
int[] ageList = {67,89,23,19,32,21};          // "Shortcut" array

for (int i=0;i<ageList.length;i++)            // "Regular" for loop
{
    System.out.print(ageList[i] + " ");       // .print()
}

System.out.println();                         // Separates console lines
for (int element : ageList)                   // for-each loop header
{
    System.out.print(element + " ");          // .print()
}
```

Console output:

```
67 89 23 19 32 21
67 89 23 19 32 21
```

For the element copy variable, you can choose any name you want (as you would in any variable declaration). The name `element` is used here for clarity. The `for-each` loop copies the value of each element in the array sequence into the loop variable `element`, and the array it is copying values from is `ageList`. Notice that the `for-each` loop does not need you to specify the length or where to start looping (a loop control variable). It handles all this for you. Additionally, on each loop, the value within the variable `element` is replaced with a copy of the next element in the array sequence, meaning you never need to specify an index location in the array during looping. The `for-each` loop can be a quick and easy way to carry out **read-only** processing with an array. This leads to two cautions to keep in mind with these loops:

1. The `for-each` loop makes a copy of each element in the array on each loop (one element copied per loop). This means that if you change the value of the element copy variable before a loop has ended, you are **not** changing the value of the original array element! You are only working with a copy of the value in the `for-each` loop.

2. If you need to refer to an index position in the array within a `for-each` loop, this can be difficult and tricky to do, since the `for-each` loop has no loop control variable that it increments! The variable used in the `for-each` loop is a copy of an array element, **not** the index position (I have stated this a couple of times now; must be important!).

A good rule of thumb and recommendation is as follows:

- If you need to **change** values of array elements or access their index positions in reverse or in a nonsequential way, or possibly only accessing a limited number of index positions, use a regular `for` loop.
- If you simply need to **read** or **make copies** of **all** the array elements (for printing, statistics, additional processing, etc.), the use of a `for-each` loop can be effective and valuable.

SUMMARY POINTS

- Arrays in Java consist of two parts: a reference variable and the array in a separate location in memory. The reference variable stores the address of the array, whereas the array itself stores the actual data you will work with.
- The data type of the reference variable should match the data type of the object it is referencing. This is true for arrays and other objects you will work with later.
- When creating an array, brackets are used with a number between them to indicate the size of the one-dimensional array. The new operator creates the array with each element structured with the appropriate data type and creates an element sequence length (the size of the array) as indicated by the bracketed number.
- The array initializer is a "shortcut" syntax that allows you to create, size, data type, and fill an array with data all in one line of code. An array of any size can be created with the array initializer but shorter arrays are more common.
- After an array is created, the use of brackets and a number with its reference variable indicates a specific index position of an element in the array, where data can be copied into (write) or copied from (read).
- Arrays and `for` loops often work well together: arrays have an unchanging size, and `for` loops work well when you know ahead of time the number of loops you need (i.e., size of array is the number of loops, one loop per element).
- Always ensure that an array's reference variable actually references an array before use and that an index position in an array exists before trying to use it. Both scenarios can cause runtime exceptions.
- The length property of an array reports only its size and nothing about its contents.
- The `for-each` loop handles the logic behind the size of the array and copying elements from each successive index position for you. They are most easily used when you only need to passively read from an array and not make changes.

QUICK PROBLEMS

1. **Coding:** Write some code that will prompt a user to enter the size of an array of names. Capture that size, and create a `String` array to that size. Then loop and have the user enter names one at a time, copying them into the array. Loop once more at the end, and print the list of names entered.
2. **Think:** Why might it be better (programmingwise) to create an array of `Strings` instead of simply concatenating one long list of `String` values?
3. **Coding:** Create a `double` array, and fill about one-third of the elements in the array with values randomly (just pick one-third). Then loop through the array, count the nonzero values, and calculate the average of only the elements with values greater than zero. Report the array's length, quantity of contents, and average of nonzero contents.

7.3 Two-Dimensional Arrays

Figure 7.7. The Two-Dimensional Array Game of *X*s and *O*s

Source: "Tic-Tac-Toe, Noughts and Crosses" by Matthew Paul Argall is licensed under CC BY 2.0, https://www.flickr.com/photos/79157069@N03/14080255255.

If you think about it, you use arrays every day without even thinking about it: What is my to-do list for the day? What groceries should I pick up this afternoon? What are the next eight errands that I need to run? These would be examples of one-dimensional arrays: simple lists, each item separate and distinct from one another. Two-dimensional (two-dim) arrays are just as common: the last time you used a spreadsheet application, looked at an address book, or considered the structure of a solar panel, you were working with a two-dimensional data structure. Rigidly structured data is present in many aspects of our daily lives.

With two-dimensional data, information systems professionals are often dealing with spreadsheets, work breakdown structures (WBS) in a project, or more commonly, database tables (including the metadata tables that often accompany them). The concept of the relational database depends on well-structured, two-dimensional data interacting with one another, although the efforts of "big data" experts have moved some databases away from this traditional structure. Two-dimensional arrays are often used to store structured data that will eventually be written out to a database table, data that was just read in from a table, or complex user-entered data, among others. Usually this consists of records or rows, and each row contains multiple attributes or columns of additional information that belong to that record. Two-dimensional arrays in Java have added flexibility in that each row can be a different length than others, or rows can be entirely swapped.

Declaring and initializing two-dimensional arrays: In Java, declaring and creating a two-dimensional array simply involves adding an additional bracket to both the reference variable declaration and the creation of the array, as can be seen in the following example:

Code Snippet 7.23

```
int[][] numberGrid = new int[3][3];
```

The data type of the reference variable would be `int[][]`, or a two-dimensional `int` array reference. When the array is created using the new operator, notice that two dimension sizes are required. The brackets are arranged in order, left to right, of higher to lower dimensions:

- The first bracket refers to the number of **rows** in this two-dim array.
- The second bracket refers to the **number of columns on each row** of the array.

Note that each lower dimension is dependent on the higher one above it. With two-dimensional arrays, you should get into the habit of not considering the number of columns **without also making sure to which row you are referring**. The number of columns can be different from row to row, so you have to think about the number of columns on a particular row you are working with. For the array `numberGrid`, there are three rows (the first bracket/dimension) and then three columns on each of those rows (the second bracket/dimension).

How two-dimensional arrays are stored in memory: As figure 7.8 shows, there are two primary ways of visualizing a two-dim array as it is stored in the computer's memory. The simplest-but-not-quite-accurate way for this particular array is displayed first on the left of the figure as a three-by-three grid of `int` values. You still have a reference variable declared in `main()` or elsewhere, and it references the two-dim array on the heap. In the second representation (in the right half of figure 7.8), you have the more accurate representation of the two-dim array. In reality, a two-dim array is really an **array of one-dimensional arrays**. An array of arrays! The reference variable first references the one-dim

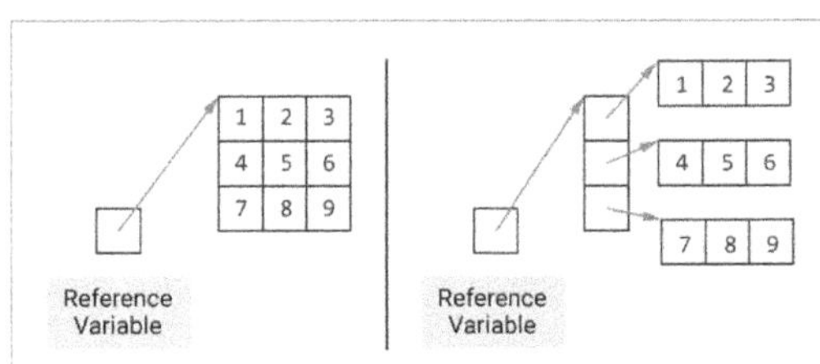

Figure 7.8. Alternate Visualizations of a Two-Dimensional Array in Java

array that keeps track of the number of rows. Each element in this internal array contains a reference (i.e., address) to other one-dim arrays that make up the particular rows. Each row is itself a one-dim array of the data type specified after the `new` operator. So the reference variable references a one-dim array of reference variables, each of which references a one-dim `int` (in this example) array.

Read and write to a two-dimensional array: To work with the rows as well as the columns on particular rows (note the precise wording there), nested `for` loops work well. In order to set the loops up properly, you need to understand how to access the number of rows and number of columns on each row using the `length` array property from earlier. Consider the following:

Code Snippet 7.24

```
String[][] fullNameGrid = new String[5][3];
System.out.println("Number of Rows: " + fullNameGrid.length);
System.out.println("Number of Cols per Row: "
        + fullNameGrid[0].length);
```

Console output:

```
Number of Rows: 5
Number of Cols per Row: 3
```

Keep in mind that the two-dim array is an **array of arrays**. So using the `length` property on only the name of the array tells you the length of the one-dim reference array that keeps track of the number of rows in the array. But if you use `length` on a **particular row of the array**, in this case the row at index position `0`, you will find the length of one particular row. Consider the following:

```
fullNameGrid[0].length
```

A full description of this line of code would be along the lines of the following: "In the reference array, which is itself referenced by the variable `fullNameGrid`, report the length of the one-dim array referenced at index position `0`." In simpler terms, the code requests the number of columns on row `0` in the array. Now a nested `for` loop can be used to place values in the three-by-three `numberGrid` array from earlier:

Code Snippet 7.25

```
int[][] numberGrid = new int[3][3];
int value = 1;
for (int i=0; i<numberGrid.length; i++)
    for (int j=0; j<numberGrid[i].length; j++)
        numberGrid[i][j] = value++;
```

Core Concept

Notice that for each loop of the **outer** `for` loop, you are working with a **row** in the two-dim array. For each loop of the **inner** `for` loop, you are working with a particular column **on the current row iterated on by the current outer loop**. On the first loop of the outer `for` loop, row `0` is the "current" row due to the value of `i`. The inner loop works with values of `j`, so that you are iterating on column `j` **of row** `i`—in other words, the columns for the row at `i` = 0. When the inner `for` loop is done, it exits back out to the outer loop, finishes, and moves on to the next iteration of the outer loop, iterating `i` to a value of `1` (now the second row of the array), and the inner starts over again, traversing columns 0, 1, and 2 **on the row at index position 1**. Notice as well that no matter what row or column currently iterated upon, the value of the variable increments as the inner `for` loop completes each loop. The second dimension depends on the first.

To print the contents of this array after filling it with values, consider the following pseudocode:

- For each row in the array
    - For each column on the current row
        - Print the value of the element at the row/col with a space
    - Print a new-line character to the console after the inner `for` loop has finished

The code for this might look like the following (after the earlier code has executed and with `i` and `j` in **bold** to help you note the row and column indications):

Code Snippet 7.26

```
for (int i=0; i<numberGrid.length; i++)
{
    for (int j=0; j<numberGrid[i].length; j++)
        System.out.print(numberGrid[i][j] + " ");

    System.out.println();
}
```

The output to the console for this code would be the following:

```
1 2 3
4 5 6
7 8 9
```

Notice that two events occur in each and every loop of the outer `for` loop: an inner `for` loop runs, and when it is finished, an invocation to `.println()` occurs that inserts a nice carriage return on the end of the output, printing the numbers in a grid-like fashion similar to the array's internal structure.

If you neglect to include the outer loop's `.println()` invocation, then all the elements of the two-dimensional array will print on the same line, like so:

Code Snippet 7.27

```
for (int i=0; i<numberGrid.length; i++)
{
    for (int j=0; j<numberGrid[i].length; j++)
        System.out.print(numberGrid[i][j] + " ");

    // no outer loop .println()
}
```

Output:

```
1 2 3 4 5 6 7 8 9
```

Notice that many of the same interaction concepts that are true for one-dim arrays are also true for two-dim:

- You can copy data in and read data out from any index position in any order you wish.
- The array does not manage the data (sorting, arranging, etc.) at all. That is up to you (the developer).
- You cannot change the sizes of any of the particular one-dim row arrays in the two-dim array, nor can you change the number of rows in total of the array.
- You have to be careful with both `nullPointerErrors` (assuming something is at an array element when it is not) and the lengths of the number of rows and columns on a row (to avoid an `arrayIndexOutOfBounds` error).
- The `length` property will only tell you sizes of rows/columns, not quantities of contents or quantities of nonempty elements.
- An array initializer ("shortcut" array) can be used to create a two-dimensional array as well. In this case, an outer set of curly braces defines the overall two-dim array; internal sets of curly braces and comma-separated values, the brace sets themselves also divided by commas, define the rows and columns. Re-creating the above `numberGrid` using an array initializer looks like the following:

Code Snippet 7.28

```
int[][] shortcutGrid = { {1,2,3}, {4,5,6}, {7,8,9} };
```

Java performs the same actions of inferring the quantity and data types of values on each row (determining the number of columns) and, additionally here, the number of rows and then creating the array for you under these assumptions. This works well with smaller sets of values and usually with sets that will not change often (though they can be changed).

Two-dimensional array example: To demonstrate an information systems-related usage of a two-dim array, consider a small application that will allow a user to enter a short list of contact information for individuals.

In this case, you might want to store a name, email address, and phone number for a list of individuals. The structure of the data would look something like this with additional rows similarly structured:

McKensie Lyndon	mlyndon@javacorp.net	123-555-2232
Pemberly Remy	pemremy@javacorp.net	123-555-8897

For this application, you can have the user type in just five records of this type. Notice that the full name (first and second name) as a whole, then the email, then the phone number will all be captured. No user input checking is needed (but you are free to do so afterward as an additional challenge). Have the user enter all the rows and columns in this example, and each column is prompted within the loop. A pseudocode plan for this problem might look like the following:

- Create a 5 × 3 String array
- In an outer loop that loops five times (five rows in the array)
    - In a nested inner loop that loops three times for each loop of the outer (three columns per row)
        - Switch on column number (`0`, `1`, `2`)
            - Case 0: prompt for name
            - Case 1: prompt for email
            - Case 2: prompt for phone

This is not a bad plan! Use a `switch` statement to do all the hard work of handling the appropriate prompt. Since all elements in the array are `String` values, this will make the use of `Scanner` much easier:

Code Snippet 7.29

```
// Assume proper imports are included
Scanner in = new Scanner(System.in);
String[][] contactList = new String[5][3];

for (int i=0; i<5; i++)
{
    System.out.print("Contact #" + (i+1) + "\n");
    for (int j=0; j<3; j++)
    {
        switch (j)
        {
            case 0: System.out.print("Enter Name: ");
            contactList[i][j] = in.nextLine();
            break;
            case 1: System.out.print("Enter Email: ");
            contactList[i][j] = in.nextLine();
            break;
            case 2: System.out.print("Enter Phone: ");
            contactList[i][j] = in.nextLine();
            break;
        }
    }
    System.out.println("Contact #" + (i+1) + " entered!");
}
```

The interaction on the console as the application looks like the following (only the first two record inputs are shown):

```
Contact #1
Enter Name: Test Person A
Enter Email: testpersona@javacorp.net
Enter Phone: 123-555-3423
Contact #1 entered!

Contact #2
```

```
Enter Name: Test Person B
Enter Email: testpersonb@javacorp.net
Enter Phone: 123-555-3322
Contact #2 entered!
. . . // rest of application interaction not shown
```

To print the contents of the array after the user has filled it with data, you can use another nested `for` loop structure. An enhanced, nested `for-each` loop structure would look like this (you can place this code after the input `for` loop structure from earlier):

Code Snippet 7.30

```
System.out.println("Printing Contact List");
int recordNumber = 1;
for (String[] record : contactList) // Outer Loop
{
    System.out.print("Record Number: " + recordNumber++ + ": ");

    for (String element : record) // Inner Loop
    {
        System.out.print(element + " ");
    }
    System.out.println();
}
```

Remember that a two-dim array is an **array of arrays**. So in the outer `for-each` loop, you are copying the **reference** to the one-dim array that represents each row in the two-dim array. Then using that reference to a row, the inner `for-each` loop walks through each **column on that row** and simply prints the contents. Notice as well that because `for-each` loops are used, index position number information is not used or available. An `int counter` variable is used instead and incremented as the loop moves from one row to the next to print a professional-looking record number.

Using ragged/"uneven" arrays: Remember that a two-dimensional array is simply an **array of arrays**. The first dimension in the array is a one-dim array of references to other one-dim arrays given the data type of the array specified at its creation (see figure 7.8). When you execute a line of code like the following, Java creates both the "rows" array and each individual three-element one-dim int array that will represent each row:

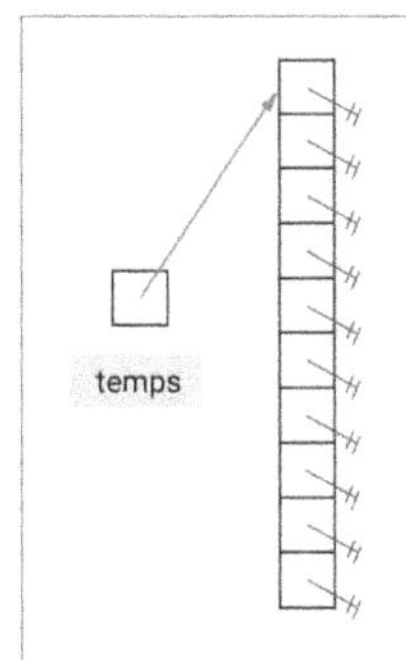

Figure 7.9. Two-Dim Array in Memory with No Rows Created Yet

Code Snippet 7.31

```
int[][] squareNums = new int[3][3];
```

These are known as **symmetrical** arrays, since they are an even square (three rows and three columns on each row). But since this is an array of arrays, you have the alternative choice of creating each row **one at a time** and later after the two-dim array is declared. How does this help? Imagine you are collecting temperature readings from volunteers in your area every day. Each day, they email you their temperature readings, but since these are volunteers, they may not all report in every single day. One day you might have five volunteers report in, the next you might have eleven, and so on. You also perform some processing on these reported temperatures (possibly the average, the max and min, etc.), so you need to keep the values distinct. A two-dim array where the number of columns **differs** from row to row would work well here. Consider the following array declaration along the lines of this example:

Code Snippet 7.32

```
double[][] temps = new double[10][];
```

Notice that a row count is specified (this first dimensional value can never be blank), but the columns-per-row value is blank. Figure 7.9 shows what this array would look like in memory at this point, before you create the rows.

The two-dim array's internal reference array has `null` for all its elements (shown with a double-slashed ending line, a reference to nothing), since you have not yet created any actual rows for the array. These must be created one by one. For example,

Code Snippet 7.33

```
double[][] temps = new double[10][];
temps[0] = new double[5];
temps[1] = new double[9];
temps[2] = new double[17];
temps[3] = new double[3];
. . .// rest of row creations omitted
```

At each row, create a new one-dimensional `double` array with the size needed, and store a reference to that new one-dim array at the index position of the "row array" in the two-dim array. Creating each row separately allows you to create **ragged** arrays. Because ragged arrays are allowed in Java, this makes using the length property even more important:

Code Snippet 7.34

```
// To print the array's contents simply
for (int i=0; i<temps.length; i++)
{
    for (int j=0; j<temps[i].length; j++)
    {
        System.out.print(temps[i][j] + " ");
    }
    System.out.println();
}
```

This is a great way to handle varying row lengths: each time your loop moves to a new row, you programmatically determine the number of columns on that row and limit the inner loop to that quantity. The risk of `arrayIndexOutOfBounds` errors is dramatically reduced. You may not know ahead of time how many columns there are per row, if the array is symmetrical, or even how many rows there are in total.

To finish the weather example, calculate the average of each row of temperatures, and report that average. The average can be stored in a one-dimensional `averageTemp` array. The pseudocode for this would look something like the following:

- Create a two-dim `temps` array
- Create a one-dim `averageTemp` array
- Create a `double average`
  - Create each temps array row and populate it with values
- In an outer `for` loop that loops over each row
  - In an inner `for` loop that loops over each column of each row
    - Sum each temperature value from this row into `average`
  - Divide the sum stored in `average` by the length of this particular row
  - Store the value in `average` in the `averageTemp` array at index position row
  - Reset the average variable back to 0.0 prior to the next row

Notice that you can use the variable `average` to store both the sum and then the average of the temperatures on each row. The variable `average` is reset back to 0.0 before moving to the next row so that the values on one row do not "contaminate" the average temperature calculation on the next row. Also, if there are ten days of temperature data, then there will be ten separate averages. The `averageTemp` array (one-dim) is given the same length as the number of rows in the `temps` array (two-dim). These sync up well. The code for the above might look like this (we will use an array initializer here, whereas in an actual application, you might have more logic to gather the temperatures, create each row separately one at a time, etc.):

Code Snippet 7.35

```
double average = 0.0;

double[][] temps = {
    {92.0, 87.9, 91.2},
    {78.2, 89.2},
    {99.5, 100.2, 98.9, 90.1, 44.5}};

double[] averageTemp = new double[temps.length];

for (int i=0; i<temps.length; i++)
{
    for (int j=0; j<temps[i].length; j++)
    {
        average += temps[i][j];
    }
    average /= temps[i].length;
    averageTemp[i] = average;
    average = 0.0;
}

for (int i=0; i<averageTemp.length; i++)
{
    System.out.println("Day " + (i+1) + " Temperature Average: "
            + String.format("%.1f F", averageTemp[i]));
}
```

A regular `for` loop is used to print the average temperatures along with the day number. This formats the daily average temperature print professionally.

The console output for this code after execution looks like the following:

```
Day 1 Temperature Average: 90.4 F
Day 2 Temperature Average: 83.7 F
Day 3 Temperature Average: 86.6 F
```

Note that the extra "F" in the format specifier used in the `.format()` method reports to the user the temperature units for this data (Fahrenheit). Notice also that the average is not calculated until **after all** the temperatures on a row have been summed up. You have to capture all values and sum them first, and then the division by the quantity can occur.

Modifying the contact list example: Recall that the `Scanner` class method `.nextLine()` returns a `String`. The `String` also implements method `.split()`, which will conveniently break a `String` apart into a one-dimensional `String` array for you. For the inner `for` loop, you could cleverly modify it by chaining an invocation to `.split()` to act on the `String` returned by `.nextLine()` and let Java do some of the hard work of splitting up the data (changes in **bold**):

Code Snippet 7.36

```
// Assume proper imports are included
Scanner in = new Scanner(System.in);
String[][] contactList = new String[5][]; // Ragged Array

for (int i=0; i<5; i++)
{
    System.out.println("Enter name, email, and phone (with spaces):");

    contactList[i] = in.nextLine().split(" "); // Add whole array

    System.out.println("Contact #" + (i+1) + " entered!");
}
```

```
System.out.println("\nPrinting Contact List");
int recordNumber = 1;
for (String[] record : contactList)
{
    System.out.print("Record Number: " + recordNumber++ + ": ");

    for (String element : record)
    {
        System.out.print(element + " ");
    }
    System.out.println();
}
```

The inner `for` loop is removed from the first loop entirely. The `.nextLine()` method returns the entire `String`, and chain invoking `.split()` upon it creates a one-dim `String` array with each separate "chunk" of data split across elements. The `.split()` method requires a parameter that is the `String` "expression" that identifies how the text will be divided (where the substring chunks stop and start). The generated one-dim array is then stored as the row at row `i` in the outer loop. Very convenient! Executing this code with some test data would look like this:

```
Enter name, email, and phone (with spaces):
First LastA firstlastA@javacorp.net 123-555-8993
Contact #1 entered!
Enter name, email, and phone (with spaces):
First Middle LastB firstmlastB@javacorp.net 123-555-3342
Contact #2 entered!
Enter name, email, and phone (with spaces):
First LastC firstlastC@javacorp.net 123-555-3423
Contact #3 entered!
Enter name, email, and phone (with spaces):
First LastD firstlastD@javacorp.net 123-555-2223
Contact #4 entered!
Enter name, email, and phone (with spaces):
First LastE firstlastE@javacorp.net 123-555-9991
Contact #5 entered!

Printing Contact List
Record Number: 1: First LastA firstlastA@javacorp.net 123-555-8993
Record Number: 2: First Middle LastB firstmlastB@javacorp.net 123-555-3342
Record Number: 3: First LastC firstlastC@javacorp.net 123-555-3423
Record Number: 4: First LastD firstlastD@javacorp.net 123-555-2223
Record Number: 5: First LastE firstlastE@javacorp.net 123-555-9991
```

Notice that without any additional effort, the code can handle first and second names easily. One record could even have a three-part name (as found in the second input), and the ragged/uneven array column size on that row will accommodate it. Now that the records are in a two-dim array, you could easily print just a list of the email addresses (even accommodating for the possibility of a middle name) to be used in a mailing list:

Code Snippet 7.37

```
for (int i=0; i<contactList.length; i++)
{
    if (contactList[i][2].contains("@"))
        System.out.println(contactList[i][2]);
    else
        System.out.println(contactList[i][3]); // next col to right
}
```

Notice that the column being printed on each row is always the one at index 2 or 3. The column at index 3 is printed in case the name is a three-part one, and you can test this by seeing if the `String` value at the column contains an `@` sign. If the data quality is high and accurate, then the email addresses in the data should contain one. This code would yield the following console output:

```
firstlastA@javacorp.net
firstmlastB@javacorp.net
firstlastC@javacorp.net
firstlastD@javacorp.net
firstlastE@javacorp.net
```

Understanding the concepts of multidimensional arrays in Java and practicing their use effectively will open up a great deal of possible uses for them across your applications. In information systems, you will encounter dimensionally structured data constantly. Many different operations will be needed on all or parts of that data (as you have seen so far). Becoming proficient in the use of multidimensional arrays in Java will help you with these tasks not only in Java but in other programming languages and platforms as well.

SUMMARY POINTS

- Two-dimensional arrays are commonly encountered in our daily, digitally ubiquitous lives—spreadsheets, grocery store aisles, database tables, and so on.
- It is easy to think of a two-dimensional array in Java as rows and columns, but it is actually an array of arrays. The first array contains reference variables, each referencing a one-dimensional array of the specified data type at declaration time.
- With two and higher dimensional arrays in Java, the first bracket used to create the array always indicates the size of the highest dimension, with each successive bracket indicating a lower dimension that is dependent on the higher. You have to think of columns as on a particular row and tied to that row, not as independent columns.
- Nested `for` loops help work with two-dimensional array structures, though any nested loop structure will work well, perhaps with some additional effort.
- Two-dimensional arrays that have the same number of columns per row as there are rows are known as symmetrical arrays. Asymmetrical arrays can have varying numbers of columns on each row, with each row different from the others. These are often called "ragged" or uneven arrays as well.
- When creating an asymmetrical array, you will leave the "columns" dimension blank at the time of creation. Each row must be created using the new operator later by creating one-dimensional arrays whose references are stored at the row positions in the two-dim array.

QUICK PROBLEMS

1. **Coding:** Use a nested loop to calculate the multiplication table from zero to nine. Store the results of each multiplication in a `10 × 10` two-dimensional `int[][] array`. Use another nested `for` loop to print the contents of the array when finished.
2. **Think:** What are some real-world scenarios where an asymmetrical/"ragged" two-dimensional array would come in handy (where each row or "record" might need to be of differing lengths)?
3. **Coding:** Use `Math.random()` to generate five numbers between one and ten (inclusive). Store these numbers in a one-dimensional array. Then using a nested loop structure, create a two-dim array where each row will have a size that consists of that number plus a quantity of zeros after it, where the quantity is the number. For example, if the number seven was generated for the first number, then the first row of the two-dimensional array would look like this:

   ```
   7 0 0 0 0 0 0 0
   ```

   with seven zeros following the seven. Copy the randomly generated number into the first element, then follow with seven zeros, and so on for the other numbers.

7.4 Advanced Array Concepts

Because of the way that Java handles arrays as complex objects in memory, working with arrays can be a bit trickier than using normal "primitive" data-type variables. You have seen some of these concepts already in this chapter, especially with the basics of two-dimensional arrays. It will be useful to cover some more advanced concepts and features of arrays in Java to ensure that you can tackle any development challenge you might encounter in various information systems contexts. Understanding how these advanced concepts work will help your learning in subsequent chapters and the topics covered in them as well.

Figure 7.10. Two Parallel Sets of Train Cars—Similar to Two Parallel One-Dimensional Arrays
Source: "Long Train" by bradleygee is licensed under CC BY 2.0, https://www.flickr.com/photos/13951072@N00/3687736192.

Rereferencing array reference variables and copying arrays: Recall from earlier that arrays in Java consist of two parts: a reference variable that references the actual array (that contains the data) in a different area of memory. Consider the following line of code, and recall the warning that using the assignment operator does not work in copying arrays:

Code Snippet 7.38

```
int[] listOne = {5,10,15,20};
int[] listTwo = new int[listOne.length];

listTwo[0] = 100;
listTwo[1] = 200;

listTwo = listOne; // does not copy the array listOne!

for (int num : listTwo)
    System.out.print(num + " ");
```

The console output when this code executes is the following:

```
5 10 15 20
```

What happened to values `100` and `200`? It certainly looks like a copy of the array `listOne` was made and its values were copied into `listTwo`. But this is not the case. Keep in mind that `listOne` and `listTwo` are reference variables, so the address reference from `listOne` is copied and overwrites the address that was stored in `listTwo`. Recall that this is known as **rereferencing** a reference variable. Figure 7.11 shows what memory looks like after this code executes.

Notice in figure 7.11 that both `listOne` and `listTwo` now reference the same array, the one originally created along with `listOne`. When this happens, there are no longer any references to the array originally created with `listTwo` (in which values `100` and `200` are stored), and it will eventually be garbage collected and destroyed. This means the values stored in that array will be lost as well. In the attempt to copy, an entire array is destroyed! It is important to always be aware of when you are working with a **reference** to an array as opposed to when you are working with an **element** of an array. Usually, the presence of brackets and an index location tell you that a specific element (in one-dim arrays) is being worked with (remember that in a two-dim array, the first dimension is a reference, so this would be an exception).

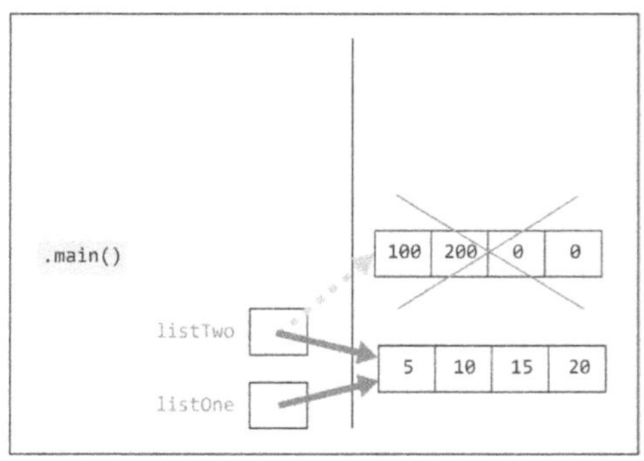

Figure 7.11. Contents of Memory after `listTwo` Has Been Rereferenced

Code Snippet 7.39

```
someArray = someOtherArrayReference;  // Working with references
twoDimArray[1] = someArrayReference;  // Working with references
someArray[8] = 89;                    // Working with a specific element
twoDimArray[2][9] = "PersonName";     // Working with a specific element
```

If you need to copy one array's contents into another, the use of a loop is usually effective. There are a couple of things to remember when you need to copy arrays (even though there are methods available to do this for you, a proficient developer should know how to do this "manually"):

- The two arrays must be declared with the same data type, or one array's data type must be up-convertible into the other (copying int values into double elements in the second array, for example).
- The array you are copying **into** should be **as long or longer** in length than the array you are copying **from**. If the reverse is true, you will encounter an `arrayIndexOutOfBounds` exception error when you try to copy into an element in the **to** array that does not exist.
- Normally, copying happens by aligning the index positions in both arrays, meaning that a regular `for` loop will probably work better. The `for-each` loop has no index value available, so you can copy out of the **from** array, but there is no easy way to indicate where in the **to** array the value should go.

An example of copying to `int` arrays would look like this:

Code Snippet 7.40

```
int[] fromArray = {65,23,12,43,23,11,98,49,32};
int[] toArray = new int[100];

for (int i=0; i<fromArray.length; i++)
{
    toArray[i] = fromArray[i];
}

for (int num : toArray)
    System.out.print(num + " ");
```

The console output of the contents of `toArray` looks like this:

```
65 23 12 43 23 11 98 49 32 0 0 0 0 0 0 0 . . . // remaining omitted
```

Notice this works, since the target array has a length as large or larger than the array being copied from. The data types of the two arrays match as well, yielding no compatibility errors from the compiler. Lastly, the data in the original array is still there, since there is a reference to the original array from its original reference variable. What if you wanted an exact copy of your array but in reverse? In this case, create an additional array of the exact same size and data type, and copy the elements over in reverse:

Code Snippet 7.41

```
int[] fromArray = {65,23,12,43,23,11,98,49,32};
int[] reverseArray = new int[fromArray.length];
int location = 0;

for (int i=fromArray.length - 1; i>=0; i--)
    reverseArray[location++] = fromArray[i];

for (int value : reverseArray)
    System.out.print(value + " ");
```

Console output:

```
32 49 98 11 23 43 12 23 65
```

Notice the values. Here an `int` called location is used to determine where in `reverseArray` the value should be copied to. If you wanted to use a little bit of clever math, the following code could be used (changes in **bold**):

Code Snippet 7.42

```
int[] fromArray = {65,23,12,43,23,11,98,49,32};
int[] reverseArray = new int[fromArray.length];

for (int i=fromArray.length - 1; i>=0; i--)
    reverseArray[(fromArray.length - 1) - i] = fromArray[i];

for (int value : reverseArray)
    System.out.print(value + " ");
```

You should be able to see from this that Java allows expressions to be evaluated within the square index position brackets of an array: subtract the current value of `i` (on each loop) from the length of the array minus 1 (which refers to the position of the last value in `fromArray`). On the first loop, the value is 9 – 9, which is 0, the index position in `reverseArray` where the first value should be copied to.

Using arrays with methods: Arrays are commonly used with methods and make transporting these complex sequences of data to and from method logic easy when needed. Now that you have a clearer understanding of how reference variables work with methods, the same concepts apply to methods. Consider the following simple example, a static method that will print the contents of a one-dim array:

Code Snippet 7.43

```
// In main()
int[] applicationArray = {1,2,3,4,5};
printArray(applicationArray); // pass a copy of the array's reference

// . . .

// Application Method Definition
public static void printArray(int[] anArray)
{
    for (int num : anArray)
        System.out.print(num + " ");
}
```

Console output:

```
1 2 3 4 5
```

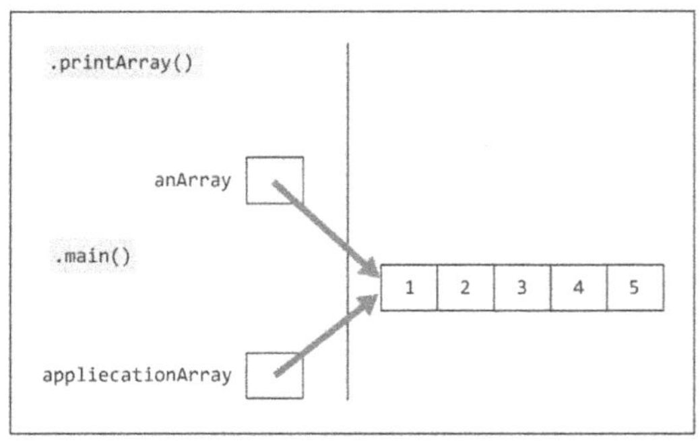

Figure 7.12. Reference for One-Dimensional Array Passed to Method `printArray()`

Figure 7.12 visually shows how the reference to this array is being passed to the method `printArray()`—one array but two references to it.

Recall two primary benefits of methods: abstraction and modularity. With the example method `printArray()`, you have a method that will print the contents of **any** one-dim int array whose reference is passed via the parameter. Notice that in the line of code where the method is invoked, you **do not** need to indicate any index position: it is the job of the method to handle that. You simply pass a **copy of the reference to the <u>entire</u> array** to the method.

In the parameter of the method definition, notice that an `int` array reference variable is declared. The method expects to receive a copy of a reference to an `int` array via the parameter. The process here is similar to the array rereferencing example earlier: you are simply copying an array reference from one reference variable to another. In this case, the reference is the parameter for a method. For a two-dim array, the process is very similar:

Code Snippet 7.44

```
// In main()
int[][] twoDim = {
    {1,2,3},
```

```
    {4,5,6,7,8,9}};

printTwoDimArray(twoDim); // Pass copy of array reference to method

// . . .

// Application Method Definition
public static void printTwoDimArray(int[][] twoDimArray)
{
    for (int[] row : twoDimArray)
    {
        for (int element : row)
            System.out.print(element + " ");

        System.out.println();
    }
}
```

Console output:

```
1 2 3
4 5 6 7 8 9
```

The key here is to define the method's parameter with the appropriate data type. Recall that the names of the arrays do not have to match, since a copy of the reference variable's value is passed to the parameter. Figure 7.9 shows this process visually.

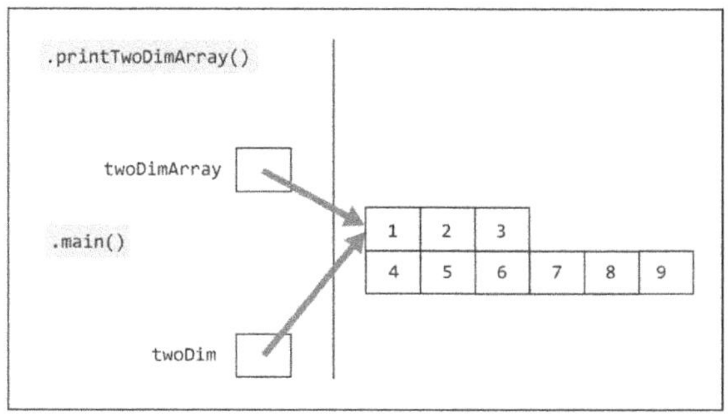

Figure 7.13. Passing a Copy of a Reference to a Method Parameter

Methods can return back references to arrays as well. Keep in mind that the actual array is always created in the heap area of the memory allocated by the JVM. So a method can pass a copy of a reference to the array back to the calling code (e.g., to a reference variable in `main()`) easily. Consider the following example, where a method generates a randomly sized and filled one-dim int array:

Code Snippet 7.45

```
// In main()
int[] randomArray = createRandomIntArray();

// . . .

// Application Method Definition
public static int[] createRandomIntArray()
{

        // Random size between 1 and 100
    int value = (int)((Math.random() * 100)+1);

    // Create the array with the randomly generated size
    int[] returnArray = new int[value];

    for (int i=0; i<returnArray.length; i++)
    {
        // Each element given a random value
        //  between 1 and 100
        returnArray[i] = (int)((Math.random() * 100)+1);
    }
```

```
    // Return copy of reference to this array
    //  back to the calling code.
    return returnArray;
}
```

The array reference variable is declared locally in the method code and given a reference to the array created in the method (but stored on the heap). Once the array is sized and filled with random values (adding `1` to the value to ensure an index size larger than `0`—just to be sure), a **copy** of the array's reference is returned back to the line of code that called it in `main()`. This reference copy is stored in the `randomArray` reference variable declared locally in `main()`. For a brief moment, there are two references to the same array, before the method `createRandomIntArray()` leaves memory.

Earlier, the average value of temperature data stored on rows of a two-dim array is calculated. Using a method, you can perform a similar task. By setting the method up to accept a one-dim int array, you can loop through the two-dim array in `main()` and let the method do all the hard work of averaging the values:

Code Snippet 7.46

```
// In main()
int[][] temps = {
    {99,45,23,12,100,12},
    {45,64,78},
    {89,78,45,34,65,87,33,23,12,90}};

for (int[] row : temps)
    System.out.println(
            String.format(
                    "Average Temp: %.1ff",
                    arrayAverage(row)));
.
.
.
// Application Method Definition
public static double arrayAverage(int[] array)
{
    double average = 0.0;
    for (int num : array)
        average += num;
    average /= array.length;

    return average;
}
```

The console output here would be the following:

```
Average Temp: 48.5f
Average Temp: 62.3f
Average Temp: 55.6f
```

Notice that the method has no idea that every single array it receives is a row from a two-dim array, nor does it care as long as it receives the proper data-type reference. In `main()`, the `for-each` loop is used advantageously, as it makes a convenient copy of each row reference from the two-dim array and passes it cleanly to the method.

Altering an array via passed parameter reference: Changes to an array made in a method's code are seen back in the invoking code. Keep in mind that since copies of array reference variables are passed to methods via their parameters, there is only a **single** array. If the code in the method makes a change to the array, then later, when the method has left memory and execution has returned to the calling code, those changes **can be seen** in the calling code! Think of this example: You know the location of your home or apartment and write down the address on a piece of paper (you have a reference to an object: your house). You copy the address to another piece of paper and give it to a friend (now there are two references to one object: you and your friend both know where your house is at). Now you ask your friend to paint your house neon green. They do so and then throw the paper away and leave. They changed your house, and you can see the change.

Consider the following code to see this in action (we again use the custom `printArray()` method here):

Code Snippet 7.47

```
// Application code
int[] myArray = {1,2,3,4,5,6,7,8,9};
changeArray(myArray);
printArray(myArray);

// . . .

// Application Method Definition
public static void changeArray(int[] array)
{
    for (int i=0;i<array.length;i++)
        array[i] = 0;
}
```

The console output for this would look like the following:

```
0 0 0 0 0 0 0 0 0
```

Notice that when the array reference is passed to the method, the array contained values other than zero. The array uses the reference to access and change the array. When the method is done, the original reference is still valid. The array referenced was changed by **some other code**, and **those changes can now be seen by the invoking code.**

Usage of the `Arrays` class: Developers working on information systems problems and in business contexts will often encounter the need to manipulate, compare, sort, and search sequences of data such as those stored in arrays. Searching for a value in an array is a common task, as is sorting a list of numbers, names, and so on in various orders. Other problems like determining the equality of two arrays, or if one array contains another (subsets) do frequently occur in the course of development work in various contexts. Contained within the Java library is the `Arrays` class, which contains several static methods ("utility" methods) that can perform these tasks for us.* Consider the following four arrays that will be used to examine and gain practice with these methods. (*Note:* For all the methods covered, the `int[]` overloaded version of the method will be shown and discussed, and many of the methods in the `Arrays` class have **several** overloaded versions to cover arrays of many different data types.)

Code Snippet 7.48

```
int[] randomNumbers = {
    61,72,18,39,92,
    48,65,75,28,81,
    76,63,45,95,92,
    8,60,98,14,24,
    22,82,85,5,41,
    25,43,66,75,44};

int[] smallArray = {1,2,3,4,5};
int[] anotherArray = {1,2,4,3,5};
int[] largeArray = {1,2,3,4,5,6,7,8,9,10};
```

Note: You will need to import `java.util.Arrays` or use `java.util.*` as the import statement as used before to define the `Arrays` class for your application.

---

* https://docs.oracle.com/en/java/javase/15/docs/api/java.base/java/util/Arrays.html.

- **Sorting an array in numeric order from smallest to largest:** Often values in a sequence of data will first need to be sorted before they can be worked with. The `.sort()` method of the `Arrays` class can do this easily for arrays of many different data types:

```
public static void sort (int[] arrayToBeSorted)
```

The static method has no return type and will alter the array whose reference you pass to it. For example, using a large, random value array with the method results in the following (we will call the `.printArray()` method from earlier also):

Code Snippet 7.49

```
Arrays.sort(randomNumbers);
printArray(randomNumbers);
```

Console output:

```
5 8 14 18 22 24 25 28 39 41 43 44 45 48 60 61 63 65 66 72 75 75 76 81 82 85 92 92 95 98
```

- **Searching an array for a value quickly:** Computer scientists have developed useful algorithms for searching sequences of data, all with varying speeds and efficiency (a discussion of which is beyond the scope of this textbook). One powerful search method is binary search, which requires an array to already be sorted. This approach chooses the midpoint of a sorted list of data, compares the value you are looking for to that midpoint value, chooses the half of the values lower or higher than your value, and repeats this process on just that half. An efficient technique that can quickly find a value, even in a very long sequence of data.

```
public static int binarySearch(int[] array, int valueToLookFor)
```

Notice the `int` return type on the method. It will return back the index position of where in the array the searched value is found. If the value is **not** found, it will return a negative number:

Code Snippet 7.50

```
Arrays.sort(randomNumbers); // Array MUST be sorted first!
System.out.println(Arrays.binarySearch(randomNumbers, 45));
System.out.println(Arrays.binarySearch(randomNumbers, 9000));
```

Console output:

```
12
-31
```

In the sorted version of the long array, the number `45` is indeed in index position `12` (the thirteenth position) in that sorted list (see the printed sort earlier). When you search for the value `9000`, that number is not found in the array, so a negative number is returned (this will change based on various characteristics of the list, but a "not found" will always be indicated by a negative position). Binary search is highly efficient, even with very large arrays—as long as the array is sorted first.

- **Determining if two arrays are the same:** The `Arrays` method `.equals()` can report whether or not two arrays have the same values **and** if the values in both arrays are in the same order:

```
public static boolean equals(int[] firstArray, int[] secondArray)
```

Interestingly, sorting these arrays before this comparison is not a hard-and-fast requirement. For example, if you sort `smallArray` and `anotherArray` above, they will be compared as equal to each other. Sometimes you may want to make an equality comparison on unsorted arrays as follows:

Code Snippet 7.51

```
System.out.println(Arrays.equals(smallArray, anotherArray));
```

This comparison returns `false`.

- **Finding the index position at which two arrays differ from each other:** Pairing nicely with the earlier example demonstrating `.equals()`, the `.mismatch()` method can identify at what index position in the arrays the values start to differ:

```
public static int mismatch(int[] firstArray, int[] secondArray)
```

Expanding on the previous example, you get the following:

Code Snippet 7.52

```
boolean equalResult = Arrays.equals(smallArray, anotherArray);
if (!equalResult)
    System.out.println("Arrays differ at index position: "
            + Arrays.mismatch(smallArray, anotherArray));
else
    System.out.println("Arrays are equal (length, content, order)!");
```

This code will result in a mismatch found at index position 2 (which is the value 3 in one array and the value 4 in the other), describing where the two arrays diverge in values.

- **Making a copy of an array into one with equal or greater length:** Earlier, you wrote the code for this very action. The `Arrays` class provides a convenient method that will perform this action:

```
public static int[] copyOf(int[] copyFromArray, int newArraySize)
```

You can copy `smallArray` into a new array using this method (again the custom `.printArray()` method is used here):

Code Snippet 7.53

```
int[] newArray = Arrays.copyOf(smallArray, 100);
printArray(newArray);
```

Console output:

```
1 2 3 4 5 0 0 0 0 0 0 0 0 0 0 0 0 0 0 . . .// rest of array omitted
```

If the `newArraySize` you specify is smaller than the array you are copying from, this method will not copy any more values from the original array past that size/location in the original. It will "cut off" the rest of the values from entering into the new array. If the new array is longer, as in the example, it will pad the rest of the values with zeros or other default values when needed.

- **Easily printing the contents of an array:** A method that will perform this very task was exampled earlier in the chapter. Yet it is worth looking at the `Arrays` class's implementation just the same:

```
public static String toString(int[] arrayToPrint)
```

If you use this method on `smallArray`:

Code Snippet 7.54

```
System.out.println(Arrays.toString(smallArray));
```

Console output:

```
[1, 2, 3, 4, 5]
```

The main difference between this method and the custom version from earlier is that the custom printing method prints directly to the console, whereas the `Arrays` version returns a `String` representation of the array. The method prints the decorative brackets and the commas.

These are just a few of the many static methods available in the `Arrays` class.

Using parallel arrays to manage mixed data types: As previously noted, a standard array in Java can only store one type of data—the type it is declared with (with exceptions for subclasses of class data types). One common technique in business programming to store mixed data types in arrays is to use a technique called **parallel arrays**. For example, consider the need to store an array of employee names along with their salaries. You would like to use arrays due to the simplicity of index notation and the efficiency of storing data. But when declaring an array, you have to make a choice: `String` or `double`. But using two arrays in **parallel** can get around this restriction. Your code is written in such a way as to "synchronize" the two arrays. For example, consider the following full code listing that will add employees and salaries to two arrays (size `100`). Take note of the variable `keeper` that place-keeps the next available location to write data to in **both** arrays:

Full Program 7.1

```
import java.util.*;

public class EmployeeSalary {

    public static void main(String[] args) {

        // Arrays kept in parallel with one another
        String[] employeeNameArray = new String[100];
        double[] employeeSalaryArray = new double[100];
        int keeper = 0; // notes the next free array index

        String tempName = "";
        double tempSalary = 0.0;

        Scanner keyIn = new Scanner (System.in);

        while (true)
        {
            System.out.print("Enter Employee Name (\"na\" to finish): ");
            tempName = keyIn.nextLine();

            if (tempName.equals("na")) // Compare tempName to "na"
                break; // Exit the loop.

            System.out.print("Enter Employee Salary: ");
            tempSalary = keyIn.nextDouble();
            keyIn.nextLine(); // Clear out remaining return character

            employeeNameArray[keeper] = tempName;
            employeeSalaryArray[keeper] = tempSalary;

            keeper++; // Increment keeper
        }

        // Print the contents of the two arrays:
        for (int i = 0; i < keeper; i++) {
            System.out.println("Employee: " + employeeNameArray[i]
                    + ", \tSalary: $"
                    + String.format("%,.2f", employeeSalaryArray[i]));
        }

    } // end of main()

} // end of class
```

The user can enter data, and the resulting application output will be the following:

```
Enter Employee Name ("na" to finish): Sarah
Enter Employee Salary: 100000
Enter Employee Name ("na" to finish): Marizah
Enter Employee Salary: 104000
Enter Employee Name ("na" to finish): Jameia
Enter Employee Salary: 110000
Enter Employee Name ("na" to finish): na
Employee: Sarah,     Salary: $100,000.00
Employee: Marizah,     Salary: $104,000.00
Employee: Jameia,     Salary: $110,000.00
```

Notice the use of an infinite loop here (there are better ways to write this). The two arrays work in parallel, and one single `int` variable acts as the placeholder for the next available free element in both arrays. If one array is changed, another is at the same time and in the same index position. This allows the first salary amount to correspond to the first employee named and so on.

Resizable arrays using the `ArrayList<E>` class: Java provides another useful class that allows you to create an array that will dynamically grow and shrink as you add and remove items from it. The `ArrayList<E>` class is a generic type class, meaning it can flexibly store any data type within its structure. Generic classes will be covered later in the textbook.* For now, understanding the basic usage of `ArrayList<E>` will suffice:

Full Program 7.2

```
import java.util.*;

public class ArrayListUsage {
    public static void main(String[] args) {

        ArrayList<String> employeeList = new ArrayList<>();

        employeeList.add("Meridith");
        employeeList.add("Jameiah");
        employeeList.add("Guo");

        // Print size of ArrayList:
        System.out.println("Employees: " + employeeList.size());

        // Print the second element:
        System.out.println("Second Employee: " + employeeList.get(1));

        // Remove the first element:
        employeeList.remove(0); // Resizes list to 2 employees

        // Print remaining list:
        for (String s : employeeList) {
            System.out.println("Employee: " + s);
        }

    } // end of main()
} // end of class
```

When you run this code, the following output will occur:

```
Employees: 3
Second Employee: Jameiah
Employee: Jameiah
Employee: Guo
```

Notice that an `ArrayList` object uses methods to add, remove, and access elements in its structure. Index notation is still used but as a parameter to methods with no brackets involved. Notice that a size was not indicated in the declaration or initialization of the `employeeList` object. `ArrayList` handles all this for us, growing and shrinking as elements are added and removed, respectively. Notice as well that when declaring an `ArrayList<E>` object, the `E` is replaced with the data type you want to store in the object. One rule here: you cannot use primitive data types in an `ArrayList`—you are required to use their "wrapper" class equivalents, like so (notice the capital letter on the primitive data types—the class equivalents are named the same):

Code Snippet 7.55

```
ArrayList<Integer> intList = new ArrayList<>();
ArrayList<Double> doubleList = new ArrayList<>();
ArrayList<Boolean> boolList = new ArrayList<>();
// . . . and so on
```

---

* https://docs.oracle.com/en/java/javase/18/docs/api/java.base/java/util/ArrayList.html.

Explore the official Oracle documentation for more information on the methods available when you use an `ArrayList` object.

SUMMARY POINTS

- Rereferencing can occur with reference variables of any type, not just those for arrays. Since nonnull reference variables contain addresses of the objects they reference, copying one reference variable into another simply copies an address. Where a reference variable may have previously referenced one object, it now may reference another, leaving its original one possibly orphaned.
- Copies of references to arrays are passed to methods. If the method code uses that reference to make a change to the array that is being referenced, viewing the array through the original reference when execution returns will show those changes. Two references are "pointing" to the same object. Any changes to that object will be "seen" by both references.
- Methods can return back a reference to an array as their return type. If the invoking code receiving that reference stores it in a reference variable, the array being referenced will not be orphaned and lost. This makes for a useful technique for the creation and modification of arrays occurring in methods and away from the main application code.
- Java makes the `Arrays` class available along with numerous useful static methods that can perform valuable processing tasks with arrays. Sorting, searching, comparing, copying, and printing methods are available, just to name a few.
- Using arrays in parallel is an often useful application technique for keeping elements of data "synchronized" with one another.
- Java provides the `ArrayList<E>` class, making a dynamically resizable array available to developers when needed.

QUICK PROBLEMS

1. **Coding:** Write the definition for a method that will accept a reference to an int[] array. In the method, take each element's value, and multiply it by three, storing the product back into the same element. Have the method return void. In your calling code, print the contents of the array both before and after the invocation of the method.
2. **Think:** Consider an int[] array where every element contains the number two. What happens if this array is sorted? What happens if you search this array for the number two?
3. **Coding:** Write your own incomplete search algorithm that finds the smallest **and** the next smallest number (just those two) in an array of `int[]` values. Print those numbers to the console. Then use the `Arrays.sort()` method to sort your array, and print the first two elements in that sorted array to see if they match your algorithm's results.

Summary

In this chapter, you have taken your ability to capture, store, and process data one step further through the use of arrays in Java. Arrays are ubiquitous with contemporary programming languages and platforms, and their ability to store data in a structured manner is highly useful, as you have seen. The fact that arrays in Java store a sequence of the same data type leads the language to handle them as complex objects, further introducing you to the use of practical object-oriented concepts. Further, becoming proficient with arrays will help with your learning later when integrating databases with Java applications. Data structures like the `ArrayList<>`, `List`, `Stack`, `Queue`, `PriorityQueue`, and `LinkedList` (see companion chapter 5) have their nature and functionality based on the concepts you learn with standard arrays. And arrays are found across most all programming languages. As a contemporary developer, especially as an information systems professional, understanding how to leverage the power of arrays in Java is incredibly beneficial to your programming skills. The effective processing of the data you encounter in information systems often requires the use of arrays or array-based syntax and/or logic in order to be successful. The time you spend in this chapter becoming skilled with Java arrays will pay off dividends far into the future.

Practice Problems

Terminology

Match the following terms from the chapter with their most appropriate definition:

1. Array	a. An error encountered when a reference variable is used to attempt an operation on its assumed referenced object but the reference variable contains `null`.
2. Index notation	b. An array that contains a single sequence of data.
3. Reference variable	c. A two-dimensional array where the sizes of both dimensions are the same.
4. Element	d. Instance method of the String class that reports the number of characters stored in a String variable.
5. Array dimensionality	e. Error where access to a nonexistent index position in a data sequence was attempted.
6. Bracket operator	f. A Java class included in the Java library that contains many useful methods that assist in array and data sequence processing.
7. `null` value	g. A two-dimensional array where the sizes of the multiple individual sequences of data could be different from one another. Often called a "ragged" array.
8. Array initializer	h. Arrays class method that can efficiently search a large sequence of data to find a value.
9. `length`	i. Replacing the address stored in a reference variable with another address.
10. `.length()`	j. Arrays class method that identifies the index position of the first element that differs between two array sequences.
11. Index out of bounds exception	k. One "chunk" of data in a sequence of data.
12. Null pointer exception	l. Arrays class method that will return a reference to a copy of a method. Can be used to create a new array that is larger than the old one but contains the old array's data.
13. `for-each` loop	m. An array that contains multiple individual sequences of data.
14. One-dimensional array	n. Arrays class method that will sort a sequence of data in ascending order.
15. Two-dimensional array	o. Java data structure that stores a sequence of data of all of the same data type.
16. Asymmetrical arrays	p. Often called an "enhanced" `for` loop; can iterate over a sequence of data, handling the start, end, and copying of data sequence values automatically.
17. Symmetrical arrays	q. The default value of a reference variable where it does not reference anything in memory.
18. Rereferencing	r. Arrays class method that can compare the order, size, and values of two arrays and determine if they are identical.
19. `Arrays` class	s. Variable that stores an address of a complex object in the JVM's memory.
20. `Arrays.sort()`	t. Array property that reports the total size of the array but does not report on the values stored within.
21. `Arrays.binarySearch()`	u. The internal structure of a variable that stores a sequence of data that allows increasingly higher data structuring and design.
22. `Arrays.equals()`	v. A "shortcut" method of creating, sizing, data-typing, and filling values into an array, all in one step.
23. `Arrays.mismatch()`	w. Operator that helps assign a size to an array at time of creation or index location of data in an array.
24. `Arrays.copyOf()`	x. Numerical mapping of locations of data in a sequence.

Find the Error

In each of the following problems, carefully examine the code given, and determine the error(s)/issue(s) with each. Keep in mind, the error(s) could be syntax (code) or logic (intended outcome) based or both!

1.

```
int[] numArray == {1 2 3 4 5}:
```

2.

```
int[4][5] table[][] = new int[][];
```

3.

```
String[] words;
    String phrase;
    for (String word: words)
    {
        phrase = word;
    }
    System.out.println("Concatenated: " + phrase);
```

4.

```
int[] values = int[10];
    int sum = 0;
    for (int i=0;i<10;i++);
    {
        values[i] = i;
    }
    for (int num ; values)
        sum = num;
    System.out.println("Sum of Values: " + sum);
```

5.

```
// Each row is filled and longer
//  than the prior row
int[][] numberSteps = new int[10][];
    for (int i=1; i<=10; i++)
        for (int j=0; j<i; j++)
        {
            numberSteps[i] = new int[j];
            numberSteps[i][j] = i;
        }
```

6.

```
// Merging two arrays into one
    // Duplicates Allowed
    int[] fArr = {3,9,2,1,5,3,2,4};
    int[] sArr = {9,2,5,3,2,5,7,8,2};
    for (int i=0; i<(fArr.length + sArr.length); i++)
    {
        if (i < fArr.length)
            fArr[i] = fArr[i];
        else
            fArr[i] = sArr[i];
    }
```

7.

```
// Printing all the characters
    // of the string values in a
```

```
    // String array.
    String[] sArr = {"Java","is","Great!"};
    for (String s : sArr)
    {
        System.out.print(sArr.charAt(s));
    }
    System.out.println(); // next word on new line
```

8.

```
// Method to reverse the values in an array
public static int[] reverseArray(int[] array)
    {
        int[] returnArray = new int[array.length];
        return returnArray;

        for (int i=array.length - 1;i>=0;i++)
        {
            returnArray[0] = array[i];
        }

        return array;
    }
```

9.

```
boolean[] boolVals = new boolean[10];
    for (boolean val: boolVals)
    {
        switch(boolVals)
        {
            case true: System.out.println("True!");
            break;
            case false: System.out.println("False!");
            break;

            boolVals++;
        }
    }
```

10.

```
// Method to sum the values in an array
public static int[] sumArray(int[] array)
    {
        array = new int[array.length];


        for (int[] num : new int[array.length])
        {
            array += num;
        }

        return array[i];
    }
```

Think about It

1. Why is the usage of an array better than creating X number of single variables to store values in?
2. What are two primary characteristics of arrays in Java?
3. What makes an array in Java a "complex" data type?
4. Where is an array kept in the computer's memory? Where is its declared reference variable kept?

5. How are the various elements stored in an array mapped and accessed?
6. How is creating an array using an array initializer different from the "normal" way?
7. What happens if you try to read from or write to an element in an array that does not exist?
8. Why is an unused element of an array never truly empty?
9. What does the `length` property of basic Java arrays report? What does it not describe regarding arrays contents?
10. How is the process of finding the length of a String different from that of finding the number of elements in an array?
11. What are two ways a `NullPointerException` can be generated when working with arrays?
12. How does a `for-each` differ from a `for` loop? What are the advantages of using a `for-each` loop?
13. What is a common scenario where the use of a regular `for` loop might work better when interacting with an array? When would the use of a `for-each` loop possibly work better?
14. Describe how two-dimensional arrays are encountered in your everyday computing and data-processing lives.
15. Describe how a two-dimensional array is really an "array of arrays."
16. How are array initializers used differently when creating two-dimensional arrays?
17. How can a ragged/uneven/asymmetrical array be useful?
18. How is the creation of asymmetrical arrays different from that of symmetrical two-dimensional arrays?
19. Describe what occurs when rereferencing occurs. How does this affect arrays and changes made to them?
20. Why is the assignment operator ineffective in copying the values of one array into another?
21. When passing an array to a method, why is the index notation **not** used in the method invocation argument?
22. Why is sorting an array necessary before using some of the Arrays class methods? Describe a particular example of where it is needed.

Short Syntax Problems

1. Write code that will count the occurrence of English vowels (`a`, `e`, `i`, `o`, `u`, and `y`) in a `String` phrase. Use an array to store the counts of each vowel. Print these to the screen with appropriate labels and descriptions.
2. Write code that will loop through an `int[]` array of values and determine the largest (`max`) and smallest (`min`) values in the array. Report these values to the console in a descriptive and appropriate manner.
3. Write code that will take a String phrase and create a `char[]` array from the characters in the String, one character per array element.
4. Create a method using the logic in problem #1 but have the method parameter accept a `char[]` array, as you developed in problem #3. Count the vowels and store them in an array, and return that count array back to the calling code.
5. Create a method called `.wordsToLetters()`. The method will accept one parameter, a `String[]` array called `words`. The method will return back to the calling code a `char[][]` two-dim array called `letters`. The method will extract the letters from each `String` in the `words` array and add those one at a time to the corresponding row in the `char[][]` array (first word is the first `char[][]` row, second is the second, and so on).
6. Create a method called `.lettersToWords()`. The method will accept a two-dim `char[][]` array called `letters`. The method will return back a `String[]` array. For each row of the two-dim `char[][]` array, the method will concatenate the characters on that row into a `String` and store that `String` as one element of the `String[]` array to be returned back.
7. Create a method called `.diagonalWord()`. The method will accept a String called phrase. First, the method will start at the beginning of the phrase and search until the first vowel is encountered. Make a copy of that character. Second, create a symmetrical two-dimensional `char[][]` array with a row and column count both equal to the length of the String phrase parameter. Along the diagonal, copy the letters from phrase in order. If an array element is not along the diagonal, copy the vowel that was determined earlier. Return back this array. See below for an example. Your method should be able to handle **any** String of **any length and content!** Be sure to account for upper- or lowercase letters in any way you see fit.

   Example invocation:

```
diagonalWord("programming");
```

Console output from the method call (the diagonal is shown in **bold** to clarify requirement—your program **does not** need to print it in bold!):

```
p o o o o o o o o o o
o r o o o o o o o o o
o o o o o o o o o o o
o o o g o o o o o o o
o o o o r o o o o o o
o o o o o a o o o o o
o o o o o o m o o o o
o o o o o o o m o o o
o o o o o o o o i o o
o o o o o o o o o n o
o o o o o o o o o o g
```

Full Problems

1. Write a Java program that will conduct a national lottery. First, have the user enter six numbers between one and seventy-five, followed by a "supernumber" that is between one and one hundred. The application will store these in an array. After this, present the user with three menu options:
   a. **Play:** This will randomly generate six numbers and one random supernumber using the ranges described earlier. The numbers will be displayed. You will also store the numbers in a two-dimensional `int` array of size one hundred rows and seven columns.
      i. For each drawing, indicate which numbers from the random drawing also matched the player's numbers they played. Also highlight if the "supernumber" matched.
   b. **History:** Display all the past random lottery drawings. Be sure to highlight the "supernumber" separately for each drawing.
   c. **Exit:** Exit the program by naturally having the loop end.
2. Create an inventory management program for the mom-and-pop grocery store. First, use a one-dimensional String array (with sufficient size) to store the names of products in the store ("eggs," "milk," etc.). Then use a two-dimensional double array (same number of rows as the number of elements from the product name array) to store numeric information on the products: item number (five digits), quantity ordered; quantity remaining, and price. Using a looping menu system, give the user the following options:
   a. **Enter a new item:** Prompt for the item name, item number, quantity ordered, quantity remaining (assume some have been sold already), and price of each. The user should be able to enter as many new items as they wish (exit back out to main menu, then into this one, back out, etc.).
   b. **Display inventory:** This will display all inventory with all information for each in a professionally formatted, business-appropriate report.
   c. **Display revenue:** For each item in inventory, subtract the quantity remaining from the quantity sold. Multiply this difference by the price for each item. In a business-appropriate report, display the revenue generated for each item. At the bottom of the report, display the total revenue generated across all items.
   d. **Exit:** Give the user an option to exit the application.
3. Create a program that will manage a dynamically resizing `int[]` array, starting with an array of size one element. Use only a basic Java array for this program. Use array rereferencing to accomplish the heart of this program's functionality. The program will, in a menu loop, offer the following options and functionality and continue to prompt for a user choice until they choose an option to exit the application:
   a. Add a value to the array:
      i. First, check to see if the value is already in the array. If it is, **do not** allow the addition, and prompt the user to this effect.
      ii. Second, if the value is not present in the array, expand the array by creating a second array of `oldArray + 1` and add the new value to it.
      iii. Third, sort the array.
      iv. Finally, print the array so that the user can see the effect of their change.
   b. Remove a value from the array:
      i. First, create a second array with size `oldArray - 1`.
      ii. Second, copy all the elements from the `oldArray` to the `newArray` except for the value to be removed.
      iii. Finally, print the array so the user can see the effect of their change.

c. Report the current average of the values in the array.
d. Report the current max and min values in the array.
e. Include an option to exit the program.

4. Expand the contact record example given earlier in this chapter, and create a program that will fully manage a list of contacts (name, email, and phone number). Create a two-dim `String[][]` array of sufficient size to test out your logic (one hundred or larger). The program should continue to prompt for task choices until the user chooses an option to quit the program. Include the following menu options:
   a. **Add a contact:** your application should be aware of the **next free** location in the `String[][]` array where a new record can be added without destroying any prior records.
   b. **Edit a contact:** Your application will print a list of all the contacts along with an index location and prompt the user for the location of the record to be changed. Then prompt them for all the information for the record. Overwrite the row in the array with the new, updated information.
   c. **Remove a contact:** Your application will "delete" a row's information, and it should keep track of the next free location. *Note:* You will need to determine how to manage rows that become empty due to a record deletion, think of a simple way to keep records, and empty rows shuffled together/consolidated. Any counter you keep for the next free row will need to be updated as well.
   d. **Search for a contact:** You can prompt the user for a name (full name or first and/or last) and perform a search of all records. Print only those rows that match the search. Be sure to handle upper-/lowercase letters appropriately in your search logic.

5. You have been tasked to write a small test Java program to manage undergraduate student data at a small college. The college keeps track of six pieces of student data: their name (`String`), their GPA (`double`), their completed semester hours (`int`), their advisor (`String`), their student level (i.e., freshman, sophomore, etc.), and their eligibility for graduation (`true` or `false`). Create six arrays of sufficient size for testing (i.e., size ten), one array for each of these pieces of data. You will keep these arrays synced. For example, the student in index position 0 of the name array will correspond to all the data also in index position 0 in the other five arrays (they are "aligned"). In a program with a menu that allows the user an option to exit when they are ready (menu in a loop), implement the following options:
   a. **Add a student to the registry:** You will prompt for all six pieces of information. You will add them all to the next available index position across the six arrays that do not already have data in that position. Update the next available position after a student is added.
   b. **Print all students according to their student level:** This menu option will prompt the user for which category level to print. For example, if the user chooses "junior," then only the student records that correspond to that level will print (with all six pieces of information that correspond to that student).
   c. **Print all students according to GPA:** The user can print all students whose GPAs fall above a value **or** below a desired value.
   d. **Print all students according to semester hours:** The user can print all students whose completed hours fall above **or** below a desired value.
   e. **Exit the application:** This menu option will cause the program to quit.

PART 2

Intermediate Java Concepts

Chapter 8

Object-Oriented Programming with Java Classes

What You Will Learn in This Chapter

Most contemporary programming languages implement the concepts and syntax of object-oriented programming to some degree. Java is no different. It intermingles programming paradigms in order to increase the language's usefulness to a wide variety of developers with varying skill sets. Object-oriented programming languages dominate the professional landscape as well, benefiting developers who need to architect ever larger and more complicated software. The object-oriented development paradigm, though not without its critics, has increased developer productivity, increased the ease of maintenance for software, and increased the reusability, flexibility, redundancy, and in some cases, data integrity of code. For information systems professionals, the object-oriented paradigm aligns well with the concept of digitizing real-world entities and representing them within easily scaled and architected information systems. In this chapter, you will learn how to think about, create, and leverage user-defined classes beneficially in your Java programs.

Specifically, this chapter will help you do the following:

1. Explore the basic concepts and benefits of object-oriented programming and allow you to be able to discuss how it is both similar and different from traditional programming
2. Investigate a real-world example of how creating your own class in Java can yield benefits for the design and benefits of an application
3. Learn the syntax, structure, and contents of a basic user-defined class in Java
4. Understand the purpose of and learn the syntax for defining the data fields of the class, their level of access, and their relationship to class objects
5. Understand the purpose of and learn the syntax for a class constructor, its parameters, and the nature of its return type
6. Understand the purpose of member methods of a class, learn how to think about and define them, and understand their relationship to class objects
7. Learn how to manage class objects in memory and understand their nature and life-span

Opening Scenario

After learning the ins and outs of arrays in Java, you have successfully implemented "Version A" of the client's prototype grocery inventory management system. You decided to use parallel arrays to keep track of the different data types of information associated with each item "record": name, price, and quantity. Your implementation works, though a little awkwardly. Keeping the arrays in sync has become frustrating, logic-wise. You can already foresee frustrations this design will cause with future functionality, not to mention the limitations the design places on future scalability of the application. Even so, the prototype works well and gives your implementation colleagues a good idea of how some of the core functionality will work. The client was also pleased with the initial system and gave some valuable feedback to your project manager (PM).

Now the team would like you to leverage the benefits that a fully object-oriented version of the application can bring. Primarily, the system should scale easily and not make later database integration difficult. A colleague, busy with her own implementation of client functionality, has suggested that class objects would work well for the inventory items. You quickly find out how right she is: class objects can bundle their own actions and data; they are easily managed in memory, and classes would bring the benefits of modularity, maintainability, readability, and scalability to the application. As the system grows, moving some logic and data into classes would allow the team to work on the system in a distributed fashion, each completing their own parts of the code.

Once again, you know there is a lot to learn. Several other colleagues have lamented that they "never learned that object stuff all that well" and that they "wish they had." Your prior exposures to programming did not dive too deeply into the object-oriented paradigm either. An initial skim shows lots of new terminology and behaviors of code that seem complex. Even so, the benefits object-oriented development can bring to the system are worth it. Classes seem to bring sophistication and modernity to the development efforts, not to mention imbuing the philosophy of letting the code do more work with less effort. Once again you decide to dive in . . .

8.1 Classes and Object-Oriented Programming

Figure 8.1. Instance "Objects" of `People` Enjoying the Outdoors
Source: "People" by ThisParticularGreg is licensed under CC BY-SA 2.0, https://www.flickr.com/photos/41084935@N00/362937046.

Up until this point, you have been writing Java code and developing programs in a more straightforward style of programming. Beginners in a language often start learning syntax in this manner. You start with the first line of code, move on to the next, then the next. Maybe you invoke a method here and there, but a major intent of the program is to move from the first to the last line of code and then finish. From A to B.

Experienced programmers view this straightforward manner as a process-focused approach, where the design of the application depends on what has to be done or what the programmer is trying to accomplish. With this style of programming, the program's planned structure sees data as a secondary, though important, focus of the overall design. Data processing might be one goal among many. Several modern programming languages in use today leverage a more procedural approach to development, the C language a prominent example.

As systems grew more complex, developers found that programs became unwieldy. It became increasingly difficult to manage these large and often necessarily dynamic systems. A more modular style of programming was developed to alleviate difficulties in building large systems. This style involved breaking an application up into multiple source code files that can call upon one another. This decomposing of work into smaller chunks helps teams tackle large programming tasks by dividing and conquering. Maintenance and improvements to a modular-style software system are much easier: make a change to one small chunk of the source code instead of the entire system at once.

Object-oriented (OO) programming leverages the benefits of modular development. OO programming was developed as an approach that allows the data, in addition to the processing of it, to guide development efforts. As information systems professionals, a focus on data is highly important! Remember that with the "linear," procedural approach, the software is built around the process and the steps to be completed. With an OO approach, the data and any logic that directly manages it are bundled together! This bundle is called an object. This approach provides several benefits:

- OO programming moves your application into more of a nonlinear style, leveraging modularity and easing the task of building complex systems.
- Objects, which bundle data and logic inside of them, can present to the "outside world" an interface through which code external to the object can interact with the data and logic inside. This allows each object to control access to its own data.
- Because objects contain their own data and logic, developers can make a change to the internal code for both with no need to change the code of an application that interfaces with these objects. Changes can occur internally, with external code having no knowledge of what is going on inside.

- In order for application developers to use and interact with these objects, they are not required to have any knowledge whatsoever of the code inside!

Blueprints detail the look, characteristics, and behavior of future buildings.

Source: National Park Service, US Department of the Interior. (1950, September 8). *White House north elevation*. National Archives Catalog. https://catalog.archives.gov/id/17370293?objectPage=2.

OO programming allows us to develop complex applications quickly and easily (once you learn all the basics) by building the application up part by part. This is typically thought of as a bottom-up approach. Think of how a house is typically built: an area is prepared for construction, a foundation or floor is laid down, walls are built up, a roof is installed on top, and then the internal work is refined and completed. It is a big job, but it is accomplished piece by piece and usually by multiple people on a team.

Java is primarily an object-oriented language. Classes are the primary way of creating objects. The code for a class is typically placed in its own Java file called a class definition file (CDF). Why? Remember that objects in OO programming contain both data and the logic that manages the data. Remember too how the OO approach provides modularity to development efforts. If the class is written in a separate file, another developer can work while you or another team member works on the application. Application code and class code are separated and distinguished. Figure 8.2 shows this relationship between the `main()` and instantiable classes.

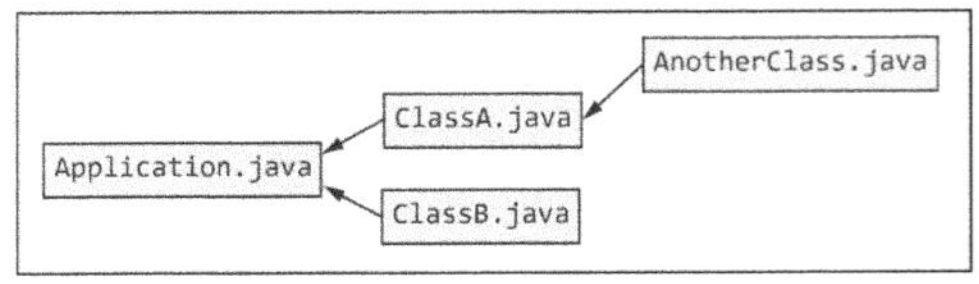

Figure 8.2. An Application and the Classes It Uses in Multiple Java Files

With OO programming, the approach to the development of a system is influenced strongly by the data that system will work with. The data will determine the structure of classes, how they behave, how the application will create them, and the way in which other code will interact with class-based objects.

Transitioning to classes with an example: As a thought experiment, imagine you have been tasked with writing an application that will represent and store information about people. This could be employees at the mom-and-pop grocery store, or students enrolled at a university, or actors at a casting agency hiring for movie roles. For now, the example can be just for a general person in no specific context. Your application will need the ability to create and process these entities of real-world people in its digital context.

From a Java programming standpoint, you have two approaches: a more all-in-one approach, which has been used so far in this textbook, or an object-oriented approach. What requirements have been elicited? In this case, you need the application to handle general people objects, so simple characteristics like eye color, height, age, and name will suffice. A pay rate variable will need to be kept as well, as people generally like to get paid! Finally, keeping track of one person will not be enough, so the application will need to be able to store information on many people, say thirty or more. The ability to sort on characteristics like pay rate and age might be useful in most contexts as well.

So far in the textbook, you have studied basic Java syntax, formulas and text formatting/output, conditional statements, loops, methods, and arrays. Thinking about how to create digital "people" in your application, you may have already imagined various ways to implement the general requirements. You will examine these and see how they may be insufficient for the client's needs.

First try: How about an entire Java application for a single person?

It should be a simple matter to create variables for all the needed attributes of a person, prompt for their entry, and read them in (as you have learned in previous chapters). Your first try might look like this:

Full Program 8.1

```
import java.util.*; // Scanner and others

public class PersonApp {
    public static void main(String[] args) {

        String eyeColor = "";    // "green"
```

```
        int height = 0;         // In inches
        int age = 0;            // In years
        String name = "";       // "Suzie"
        double payRate = 0.0;   // In US Dollars

        String prompt = """
                        Please enter their:
                        Name (First and Last)
                        Eye Color (single word)
                        Height (in inches)
                        Age (in years)
                        Pay Rate (as 0.0)
                        """;

        Scanner typeIn = new Scanner(System.in);

        System.out.println(prompt);

        name = typeIn.nextLine();
        eyeColor = typeIn.next();
        height = typeIn.nextInt();
        age = typeIn.nextInt();
        payRate = typeIn.nextDouble();
    }
}
```

This works somewhat, but the major problem is that it only works to keep track of one single person. This will not work for more than one person, not to mention thirty or more. Also, you probably will not want to create thirty separate Java source code files and name each one of them uniquely. There has to be a better solution.

Second try: What if you use arrays in parallel?

At this point, you might remember how useful arrays can be and that they can store a sequence of data of the same data type. Some related pseudocode that leverages arrays might look like this:

```
Start an array counter at 0
In a loop that loops 30 times
   Prompt for attribute variables
   Read them in
   Copy them into their respective arrays at index location counter
   increment counter by 1
End loop
```

Now you might think, "Aha, I've got it! I'll use arrays in parallel to sync information on each person." The code for this logic could look like the following:

Full Program 8.2

```
import java.util.*; // Scanner and others

public class PersonApp {
    public static void main(String[] args) {
        String[] eyeColor = new String[30];
        int[] height = new int[30];
        int[] age = new int[30];
        String[] name = new String[30];
        double[] payRate = new double[30];
        int counter = 0;

        for (int i=0; i<30; i++)
        {
            String prompt = """
                            Please enter their:
```

```
                        Name (First and Last)
                        Eye Color (single word)
                        Height (in inches)
                        Age (in years)
                        Pay Rate (as 0.0)
                        """;
            Scanner typeIn = new Scanner(System.in);

            System.out.println(prompt);
            name[counter] = typeIn.nextLine();
            eyeColor[counter] = typeIn.next();
            height[counter] = typeIn.nextInt();
            age[counter] = typeIn.nextInt();
            payRate[counter] = typeIn.nextDouble();
            ++counter;

        } // End of the for loop
    } // End of main()
} // End of the Class
```

OK, this might work, but the approach is not entirely ideal. Why not? First, the above approach is not very flexible. These standard Java arrays are statically sized. If the application needs to process more people, you will have to change the application code to increase the array sizes. This approach is not easily scalable and will not be able to handle more people in a flexible way. If the application itself needs to grow in functionality and usage, you will most likely need to use methods to modularize any repetitive code. What if the application needs to store more characteristics of people or the business context of their usage requires additional data captured? This would mean adding more arrays and more maintenance headaches. What about sorting? If you wanted to sort the "people" represented by these parallel arrays, say by age, you would have to perform the same sorting logic in five separate arrays. Any index location change happens in five arrays instead of one. No, this approach is increasingly messy and will not work very well as the application's needs grow.

Smarter approach: Use a Java class to define and create `Person` objects.

Thinking about the characteristics of object-oriented programming discussed earlier hints that this design philosophy might be a better route. Instead of trying to match five different arrays on an index, it would be handy to have all five variables bundled together in a single object. If another part of the application needs to use the data in any particular object, you can just pass the reference to that object over. You can also use an array to keep track of all the `Person` objects created. A resizable array like `ArrayList<E>` can grow as you add more people without complication. Any sorting logic could be stored in the class as well, saving further implementation work on the part of the application developer. There are many benefits to using an OO design paradigm. Notice the focus here on the data, not necessarily on the process that surrounds the data. This focus guides the development of the system.

Now that you have learned **why** object-oriented programming is useful, you can begin learning **how** to program in an object-oriented manner!

SUMMARY POINTS

- Object-oriented programming moves us from a more traditional/listing style of development to a more nonlinear, modular style.
- Object-oriented programming heavily leverages concepts of modularity in order to break down large system implementations into smaller, delegable tasks, often allowing for a bottom-up approach to software development.
- The traditional, simple listing style of programming is thought of as having more of a process/task focus, whereas object-oriented programming has more of a data focus.
- Objects bundle both data and actions together (encapsulation) and provide to code outside these objects a simple interface with which to interact (abstraction).

QUICK PROBLEMS

1. **Think:** Consider how difficult it was to create a "person" in a Java application using a traditional programming style. What additional difficulties are encountered if you wanted to also have "students" in your application (a type of person)?
2. **Think:** If you implemented a "person" as demonstrated in this section (by declaring lots of variables and methods in your application), how would another developer use your "person" code in their application? Who controls what a "person" does in a Java application if this happens? How easily can changes be made?
3. **Think:** If you create class data-type objects in your application like `Person`, how will this impact the way you use them with methods and arrays?

8.2 Classes and Instance Objects

Proper class design and implementation are important to the success of the system under development. There are several questions that information systems professionals involved in this process should answer:

- What will be the purpose of the objects (their overall usage)?
- What data will they store?
- How should they be created?
- What actions/behaviors should they be capable of?
- How does the business's logic, elicited requirements, or data needs impact the data managed by the class and the actions it is capable of?

The answers to these questions will guide development of every part of a Java class. A class is typically placed in a separate Java source code file (.java file). You will occasionally see a separate class defined in the same file as a Java `main()` class, but this is not as common. The basic template for a Java CDF looks like this:

```
[access modifier] class ClassName [inheritance and interface usages]
{
   // Data Field(s) (instance and static)

   // Constructor(s)

   // Methods (instance and static)

} // end of the class
```

The parts enclosed by brackets ("[]") are optional and have various values the developer can use. Generally, a Java class consists of a class header first with the word `class` preceding the class name. The header is where you detail any inheritance and interface interactions for the class. The access modifier is similar to that for methods. Since you typically want to be able to use your class in application code, `public` is the typical access modifier. Later in the textbook, the uses of `private` and `protected` will be covered for classes.

Curly braces are used to denote the class's code body. Typically, three sections of code are written for a class within the body:

- **Data fields:** The variables that each instance object will contain within or variables that store data for the entire class.
- **Constructors:** Methods invoked one time upon newly created instance objects of the class that perform initialization tasks.
- **Member methods:** Methods that can be invoked at any time after instance object creation, either on objects of the class or via the class itself.

At a minimum, you should have some data fields. But the presence of constructors and methods in your CDF is not a requirement. Good class design suggests always including all three sections in your classes, but this is not a requirement.

How does a Java class work at a high conceptual level?

- You can think of your CDF as a blueprint or template. Figure 8.3 shows this concept. Remember the house example above: a team of construction professionals may have assembled the house, but they did not start until they had a blueprint to follow while building. **Your CDF is your class's blueprint.**
- What is the blueprint used for? Developers (you, your colleagues, or others) can use the CDF blueprint to create objects that will ultimately represent entities in the system. The terminology here is "The CDF is used to create instance objects of your class." Why is it called an instance object? Oracle officially calls an object created using a CDF an "instance of the class," but you will colloquially hear them called instance objects. These are objects that have been **created with an internal structure that is defined in your CDF blueprint** and that are **capable of actions** (i.e., code logic) that are also defined in the CDF. Each class object is a created "instance" of the objects intended/purposed by the CDF, the same as an actual, physical house is an "instance" of the house intended to be built by a construction blueprint.
- Once an application (or code in other classes) has used your class's CDF to create instance objects, they can store data, process data, interact with objects from the same class (and possibly others), and perform other actions. Remember that **data and logic are bundled together** in these class instance objects.

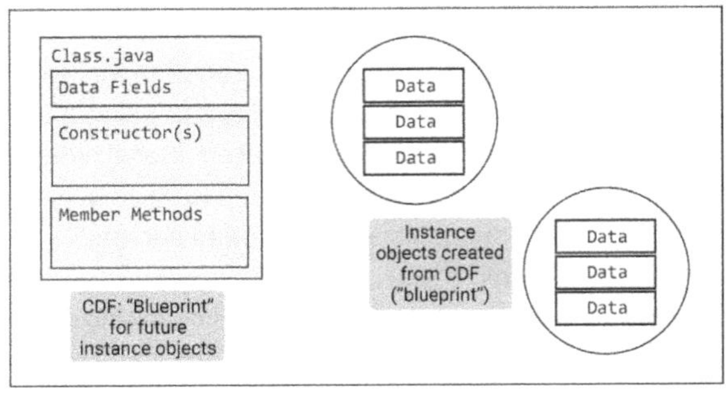

Figure 8.3. The CDF as a Blueprint for Future Class Instance Objects

Getting Started with the Class Definition File

This chapter allows you to follow along with the coding of the `Person` class, learning about various aspects of Java classes as you go. It is recommended you create a new Java project in your IDE of choice. If the IDE does not create an initial package for you, do so first. Within the package folder for your new project, create a new Java class file (**not** a `main()` method file), and name it "`Person.java`." Notice in this case, you are **not** creating a Java `main()` class file. You will code the instantiable class first, then the application is created later.

The autogenerated code in class `Person` should look close to this:

Code Snippet 8.1

```
public class Person
{


}
```

The file you just created, `Person.java`, is a CDF. This is the blueprint where your class defines what future instance objects of the `Person` class will look like (structurewise) and how they will behave (what actions they will be capable of).

If your IDE autogenerates any code for you, it will be sparse (as the listing above shows). If your IDE creates an empty file, just copy/type the `Person` class code listed here into your file and save it.

Notice the difference between this class file and the usual Java `main()` class files: there is no `main()` method! An instantiable Java class file, by itself and by design, is **not executable**. A CDF alone does not constitute a complete, executable Java application. That is why this file is only a blueprint and the class objects are created later in an executable application (or in another class). The general parts of the `Person` class CDF code are indicated in figure 8.4.

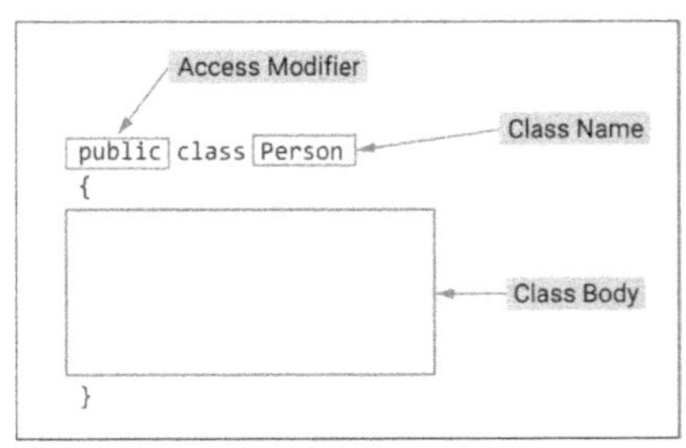

Figure 8.4. Diagramming the Initial Structure for Class `Person`

Declaring data field(s): A class is not required to have data fields. Class `Person` is intended to represent real-world people and store data on each person's characteristics. With this requirement, class `Person` will have data fields defined. A **data field** is a variable, defined by your CDF, which will (either) be stored inside of instance objects (or) be associated with the class itself. Simply declare however many variables in the CDF are needed to satisfy whatever data requirements are present for instance objects of the class. The object-oriented concept of **encapsulation**, the storage and sometimes hiding of data inside an object, is accomplished with data fields. Encapsulation allows the developer to enact security and control access for the data within class instance objects. Typically, developers following good practices will "lock down" all the data inside an object by using access modifiers to restrict direct access and relax that security for a small subset of the data where the system logic calls for it.

Instance objects of class `Person` will store information on the age, name, height, eye color, and pay rate of individuals. Each individual will have different values for these characteristics. This idea is key: nonstatic (instance) data fields are present in each and every instance object that is created using a class's CDF. Every `Person` instance object needs to store data on these characteristics, and each instance object will represent a different, distinct real-world person. You can enable instance objects of `Person` to store this information by adding five data fields to the CDF's code body:

Code Snippet 8.2

```
public class Person {
    public String eyeColor;
    public int height;
    public int age;
    public String name;
    public double payRate;
}
```

Note that these variables are declared as you have done previously, except for the addition of the access modifier. But now they are declared within a CDF instead of a `main()` method. **Any** valid data type can be used as a data field in a class. All future instance objects of class `Person` will be created with these variables inside each object. For example, if you have one hundred `Person` objects, each object will have a **distinct and separate** `eyeColor`, `height`, `age`, and so on. All variable naming conventions and syntax rules still apply, even to data fields.

Figure 8.5. A Real-Life Access Modifier
Source: "British Guard" by Starshyne09 is licensed under CC0 1.0, https://www.flickr.com/photos/10202505@N05/4704581569.

Understanding access modifiers: Think about a guard who restricts the ability to access a location (like the Buckingham Palace guard in figure 8.5). An access modifier acts in a similar way: changing its value allows or restricts external access to any one part of a class (data field[s], constructor[s], or method[s]). In other words, you open up or close off the ability of other code outside your class to access something inside your class. The full rules on this can get pretty complex (class vs. package vs. inheritance). The following are simple descriptions of access modifier values:

- `public`: The door is wide open! Code both inside and outside the class can freely access (or invoke) class resources given this access modifier.
- `private`: The door is shut tight! Only code within the class can freely access (or invoke) class resources given this access modifier.
- `protected`: Code inside the class can access class resources given this access modifier, and code within classes that are subclasses (or child classes) of this class can access these resources (we will talk about subclasses in the next chapter).

Good design practices recommend that developers "lock down" parts of their class, especially data fields, and only open up access as needed. Why would you want to prevent parts of your class from being accessed or used? The idea here is that class objects might contain sensitive information or that there is functionality that should be carefully controlled and secured—for example, if a class object stores sensitive medical information or identity data. Auditing, financial, medical, privacy, or other business rules may govern how certain data or processes are used or how they should run. There can be many reasons why parts of your class should be freely accessible and others strictly controlled. Data fields for class `Person` will have a `public` access modifier for now, as the concepts of a class are explored. This will allow code in the application to directly access and change `public` data fields within any particular instance object.

Instance versus static: Recall that nonstatic data fields declared in a CDF are present in each and every instance object of a class created using the CDF blueprint. What is meant by nonstatic? Static? Think of it in a real-world sense: every living, breathing person has an age (hopefully not `-21` years old; that would be awkward), a name, a height, and an eye color. These will also be present in each and every person instance object that you will create. Sometimes these are called **instance variables** because they are data fields present in each and every instance.

What would be a real-world example of a variable that is not present in each and every instance object but is associated with the class overall? For a count of all the people in a room, a person count data field can be used that describes some overall characteristic and is not tied directly to any one person in particular. In Java, this would be known as a **static data field** (or **static member variable**). Its "static" because as instance objects are created and destroyed, static data fields are not affected at all. Instance objects can come and go, and your static data fields will stay around in memory, available for use. Static data fields are found outside instance objects and are related to the overall class itself.

A static data field should be added to class `Person` so that it can keep track of how many of its instance objects have been created:

Code Snippet 8.3

```
public class Person {
    public String eyeColor;
    public int height;
    public int age;
    public String name;
    public double payRate;

    public static int personCount;

} // end of class Person
```

The creation of a static data field is very easy: simply add the `static` reserved keyword prior to the data type. Figure 8.6 diagrams the parts of a static data field declaration.

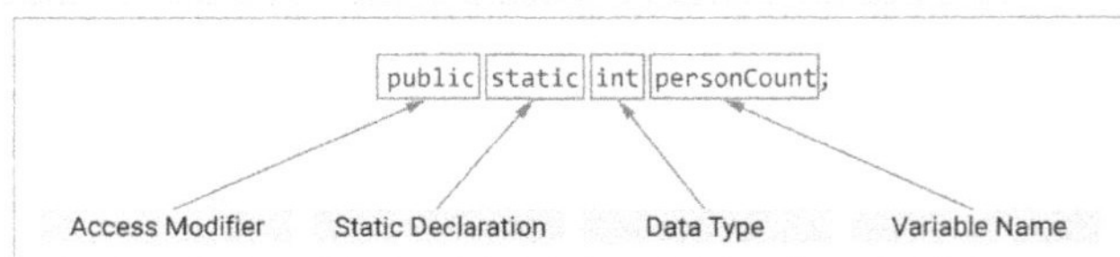

Figure 8.6. Diagram of Code Declaring a Static Data Field in `Person` Class

If you do not include the keyword `static` in your data field declaration, the Java compiler will assume it is an instance variable.

Initializing data field variables: In the past, you have typically initialized variables at the same time as they are declared. In the case of class data fields, a different approach is taken. In a Java class, initialization for data fields follows these generally accepted guidelines:

- **For nonstatic (instance) data fields of a class:** Initialization occurs in the class constructor(s), not along with declaration.
- **For static data fields:** Initialization typically happens at declaration.

Though constructors will be covered later, you can apply these guidelines to the static data field `personCount`, which has been added to `Person`:

Code Snippet 8.4

```
public class Person {

    // Instance Data Fields Initialized Later in Constructor(s)
    public String eyeColor;
    public int height;
    public int age;
```

```
    public String name;
    public double payRate;

    public static int personCount = 0; // Initialized here

} // end of class Person
```

SUMMARY POINTS

- A Java class is typically placed in a separate `.java` file but can be implemented as an inner class, one in the same class file as your application.
- A Java class is implemented as a class definition file (CDF), which can be thought of as a blueprint for how future instance objects of the class will be internally structured and what actions they can perform.
- The data fields of a class determine what variables will be found in each and every instance object (nonstatic data fields) and which variables will be overall in the class itself (static data fields). Any valid data type can be used as a declared data type for a class data field.

QUICK PROBLEMS

1. **Coding:** Create a Java class for your favorite fruit (your choice). Make sure to capitalize the name of the class. Add at least three data fields of various data types to your class to describe the fruit (e.g., size, weight, color, nutrition info, etc.).
2. **Think:** Why does it make sense for each class object to contain its related data fields? How does this simplify the organization of your class objects?
3. **Coding:** Create a Java class called "`Car`." Add data fields for the make, model, and year using appropriate data types. Add an array data field called "owners," size 10, that will keep a list of names of prior owners of the vehicle.

8.3 "Test Driving" the User-Defined Class `Person`

Testing your class out at this point would be a good idea, as it will allow you to practice accessing the data fields stored in the `Person` instance objects you create. Create a new Java `main()` class file called "`PersonApp.java`" in the same package where `Person.java` is located. From here on out, you will begin working with multiple `.java` files. The term "application" will refer to the Java `main()` class file that is the starting point for your overall project/program. In your application, declare a new instance object of class `Person` in `main()`:

Full Program 8.3

```
public class PersonApp {

    public static void main(String[] args) {

        Person suzy = new Person(); // Instance Object

    }
}
```

Figure 8.7 diagrams the sequence of events that occurs with this line of code.

This line of code executes in a certain sequence that highlights how an instance object is created differently from a regular variable:

1. The `new` operator is executed first. This operator instructs Java to create a new instance object of whatever class you have referred to on this line (in this case, `Person`). Remember that the CDF is a blueprint, so Java creates and structures the instance object following the instructions in the `Person` CDF blueprint. So after step 1 is finished, an instance object of class `Person` exists in memory, and inside this object are five data fields: `eyeColor`, `height`, `age`, `name`, and `payRate`.

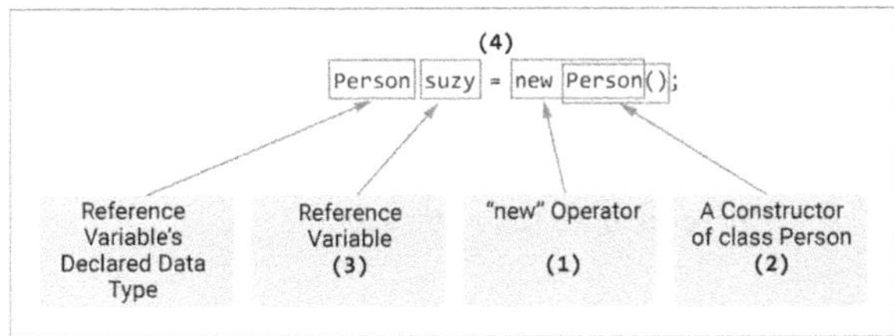

Figure 8.7. Creation of a `Person` Class Instance Object with Sequence of Events

2. The specific constructor method you specify is invoked. Recall that each method has a signature: the name of the method and the order/number/types of its parameters. Constructors are just a special type of method. There might be more than one constructor in a class. Java uses the name and the order/number/type of the parameters, if any are present, of the constructor to know which particular one you want to invoke. Any code in the constructor method runs and executes.
3. A reference variable is created in the application. This variable will store the address of where your class instance object is located in memory. Initially, this reference variable is created empty (in step 3). Notice as well that the data type that is declared for "`suzy`" is `Person`. User-defined classes like `Person` are also considered a data type and can be used as such.
4. The assignment operator copies the object's location reference into the reference variable. Unlike a normal method, constructors have no defined return type. This is because all constructors return back the address of the instance object they initialize.

Looking at the line of code above, you probably have a feeling of déjà vu. Recall the creation of a `Scanner` variable for reading in console input (with the `Person` instantiation line above it for comparison):

Code Snippet 8.5

```
Person suzy = new Person();
Scanner in = new Scanner(System.in);
```

These lines of code have the same general structure. Declaring variables with complex data types creates an instance object and a reference variable that refers to that instance object. The creation process can be split across separate lines of code, as you have seen before:

Code Snippet 8.6

```
Person bob;          // Declaration, reference contains null
bob = new Person(); // Initialization
```

How do you place data into an instance object? This can be done in three ways:

- Passing in data through the constructor method's parameters
- Directly accessing the instance object's data fields
- Invoking class methods that act upon particular instance objects of the class

The second method will work well at this point. Data can be placed within instance objects directly using the dot notation (.). Consider the following code:

Full Program 8.4

```
public class PersonApp {
    public static void main(String[] args) {

        Person  suzy = new Person();
        Person bob;
        bob = new Person();
```

```
        suzy.name = "Suzy";
        suzy.age = 21;
        suzy.payRate = 85.0;

        bob.age = 45;
        bob.payRate = 80.0;
        bob.height = 70;
    }
}
```

Since data fields are stored within instance objects, you have to reference the instance object first and then specify which variable stored inside will be worked with. You want to change `suzy`'s `name` only. We want to assign a `height` to only `bob`. Keep the following critical idea in mind:

- **If a data field in one instance object is changed, it has no impact on the other data fields stored in other instance objects.**

You are creating separate, distinct instance objects that do not directly impact one another. Even though every `Person` may contain a variable `age`, the `age` variable in the `suzy` instance object is completely different from the `age` variable in `bob`.

In addition to changing an instance object's data fields, you can use their values in your logic. Consider the following code:

Full Program 8.5

```
public class PersonApp {
    public static void main(String[] args) {

        Person  suzy = new Person();
        Person bob;
        bob = new Person();

        suzy.name = "Suzy";
        suzy.age = 21;
        suzy.payRate = 85.0;

        bob.age = 45;
        bob.payRate = 80.0;
        bob.height = 70;

        System.out.println(suzy.name + " is " + suzy.age + " years old!");
        System.out.println("Bob is: " + (bob.height / 12.0)
+ " feet tall");
    }
}
```

The output from this will be the following:

```
Suzy is 21 years old!
Bob is: 5.833333333333333 feet tall
```

The dot notation can be used to access resources inside the instance object as well as the actions available to the objects (like class methods).

SUMMARY POINTS

- A user-defined Java class that contains only data fields yields a class with a minimum amount of usefulness for data bundling (encapsulation).
- The `new` keyword in Java creates a new instance object of a class or complex-type variable in memory. New class objects are created following the "blueprint" as represented by the class definition file.
- Where the new object is located in memory is stored in a reference variable. These variables have one purpose: to store the address (a "reference") to objects in memory.
- The members of a class (data fields and member methods) can be accessed by using the dot notation (`.`) on a class object.

QUICK PROBLEMS

1. **Coding:** Using your fruit class from quick problem #1 (if you created it) in section 8.2, instantiate three objects. Copy values into a few of the data fields of the newly created instance objects.
2. **Think:** Where have you seen the new operator used before? How did it serve a similar purpose then?
3. **Coding:** Using your `Car` class from quick problem #3 (if you created it) in section 8.2, create an instance object of `Car`. Set its make, model, and year. Add two names of owners to the first two elements of the data field array for your `Car` object. (*Hint:* Use the dot notation to access the array inside the referenced object, then proceed with normal array code.)

8.4 Class Constructor Methods

Recall the following line of code, where an instance object of class `Person` was created:

Code Snippet 8.7

```
Person suzy = new Person();
```

Note that anytime you see parentheses, a method is being invoked. With this line of code, a **constructor method** of class `Person` is being invoked. What does a constructor do? An analogy will help: Think about the last time you used a printer (ink-jet, laser, thermal, etc.), maybe one you own. You purchased the printer, but you didn't construct it—someone else built the printer, probably according to a blueprint. What did **you** do? You **initialized** the new printer object: unboxed it, unwrapped it, installed ink cartridges, put some paper in, powered it on, and connected your devices to it. Maybe you and several friends use the printer. After it was initialized, you didn't have to purchase another printer: you and your friends can just use it over and over when needed.

The constructor method acts the same as you: it does not build the object, but it initializes the newly created object. The constructor's job is to assign values to some or all of the data fields of a newly instantiated class object. As the designer of a Java class, you get to decide how many constructors your class will have and how they will initialize your class's instance objects. The following are some rules for constructors to keep in mind:

- A class can have one or more (i.e., overloaded) constructors, but only one constructor can be invoked per each instance object. Once an instance object has been initialized with a constructor, it is ready for use.
- A constructor must have the same name as the class it is in. For the `Person` class, any and all constructors that are defined will have the name `Person()`. The parentheses will differ based on each constructor's definition in the CDF.
- A constructor will differ from a regular method in that you will not specify any return type for it, not even `void`. All constructors return the address of the class instance object that they just finished initializing by default.
- A constructor method **acts upon** the newly created instance object of the class, the one created by the `new` operator. The constructor (typically) changes the data fields inside that brand-new instance object.

- There are two scenarios for how Java will interact with your class based on the number of constructors that you have defined in your CDF:
  - **If you define no constructors at all in your CDF:** Look at the `Person.java` listing. No constructor has been defined in the class so far. In this case, when you attempt to create an instance object and you call the zero-argument version of your class's constructor (`Person()`), Java creates a temporary version of this constructor for you and invokes it.
  - **If you define one or more constructors in your CDF** (recommended): Java will invoke the specific constructor you call based on its method signature. Keep in mind that if you define any constructors at all in your CDF, Java **will not** create one for you. If you have defined only one constructor, for example, in your CDF, then that is the only one that will be valid to invoke upon new instance objects.

As the class developer, you can decide how many constructors to define in your class. Each constructor can be defined to accept parameter inputs for none, some, or all of your data fields as well. It is up to you. Adding a zero-argument constructor to class `Person` looks like this:

Code Snippet 8.8

```
public class Person {

    public String eyeColor;
    public int height;
    public int age;
    public String name;
    public double payRate;

    // Zero-parameter constructor
    public Person()
    {
        eyeColor = "";
        height = 0;
        age = 0;
        name = "";
        payRate = 0.0;
    }

} // end of class Person
```

In this case, the constructor accepts no initial incoming data when a `Person` object is created. The developer of class `Person` decides, then, how to initialize each data field. Business rules for an organization may define, for example, that a blank name in their system should contain "n/a" or "empty" so that these fields are highlighted as needing future entry. Including a defined zero-parameter constructor gives those developers who use your class a quick and easy way to create instance objects without writing further logic to collect initial data values that they may not have until later.

At this point, with only one constructor defined in the class, the following line of code is valid:

Code Snippet 8.9

```
Person joaquim = new Person();
```

Now instead of calling a "temporary" constructor provided by Java, this will invoke the zero-argument constructor you have defined in the CDF. Note that the following line of code would **not** work:

Code Snippet 8.10

```
Person spencer = new Person("blue",70,32,"Spencer",12.00);
```

Since you have only defined one single constructor in your class, this attempt to invoke a five-argument version will throw an error when this application executes (if the IDE does not flag it first). This version of the constructor does not exist and is not defined in the CDF.

You have to add this new version of the constructor to the CDF. You can define the new constructor after the first one in the CDF, and this will be considered to be an **overloaded** version of the first constructor:

Code Snippet 8.11

```
public Person(String incomingEyeColor,
        int incomingHeight,
        int incomingAge,
        String incomingName,
        double incomingPayRate)
{
    eyeColor = incomingEyeColor;
    height = incomingHeight;
    age = incomingAge;
    name = incomingName;
    payRate = incomingPayRate;
}
```

The parameters have been prefixed with the word "incoming" and the data field names with matching data types. This highlights which ones represent incoming parameter data and which are the data fields in the instance object that will be initialized in the future. These parameter names will be changed later on in this chapter.

Notice how the incoming parameters have their data copied into the data fields. The user of the class provides the data they want placed in the new instance object. And that is a key point: the new constructor is ready for use in `PersonApp` application:

Code Snippet 8.12

```
// In PersonApp.java:
Person sam = new Person("Blue", 57, 35, "Sam", 90.0);
```

A third instance object of class `Person` is now present in memory. The reference variable is `sam` with a declared data type of `Person`. Values are provided as invocation arguments that match the defined parameters. You are required to provide arguments in the same order/number/types as you have defined this arrangement as parameters in your CDF. Figure 8.8 shows this alignment between invocation arguments and defined parameters visually.

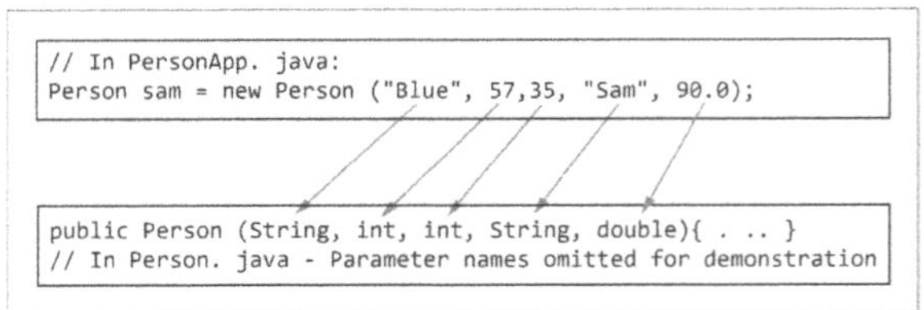

Figure 8.8. Argument and Parameter Alignment during Constructor Invocation

This alignment is a requirement. Why? Again, remember that the signature of any method consists of both its name and the order/number/type of its parameters. If you call it by the wrong "signature," then Java may call the incorrect constructor method (if one exists that matches your invocation attempt) or may throw an error (if no constructor exists that matches the invocation).

You can test that the values were indeed copied into the instance object after the use of this constructor:

Code Snippet 8.13

```
// In PersonApp.java:
Person sam = new Person("Blue",57,35,"Sam",90.0);
System.out.println("Name: " + sam.name);
System.out.println("Age: " + sam.age);
System.out.println("Pay Rate: $" + sam.payRate);
```

The following is the console output after this code is executed:

```
Name: Sam
Age: 35
Pay Rate: $90.0
```

SUMMARY POINTS

- The constructors of a class are special methods that execute only one time ever per instance object, and their job is to initialize the newly created instance objects.
- The primary job of the class constructor is to initialize newly instantiated class objects. You should always plan to place code for initializing a newly created instance object inside the constructor. This could include setting values for data fields or calling any other necessary methods.
- A class can have zero, one, or many constructors. The developer should choose to add constructors to a class definition based on a determination of how flexible they believe future users of this class may need object initialization to be.
- When creating an instance object of a class, the application developer has the choice of invoking whichever constructor they wish, but they can only invoke one of them, and only once per newly created instance object.

QUICK PROBLEMS

1. **Coding:** Using your `Fruit` class from quick problem #1 (if you created it) in section 8.2, create two constructors: a default and a fully implemented constructor that takes values for all the data fields in each object. Test this out in your application.
2. **Think:** Consider a class called `Employee`. Think about what common data fields might apply to any employee of a business. In the default (zero-arg) constructor for this class, what are some starting values you might implement?
3. **Coding:** Using your `Car` class from quick problem #3 (if you created it) in section 8.6, create one constructor that accepts values for all data fields except for the owner array. Test this constructor out in your application, adding two owners after the object instantiation.

8.5 Defining Class Member Methods

So far, the `Person` class has data fields that will be present in each and every future instance object and two constructors that give developers a choice as to how to initialize newly instantiated objects. A big benefit of classes is that their objects bundle data and **behaviors** together. The **member methods** of a class represent the actions that can be performed on and by its objects (and the class itself). As with data fields, member methods can have their access restricted or opened through the use of access modifiers. Any member methods defined with the public access modifier are considered part of the **interface** of the class—the way by which external code can interact with the class and its objects.

Some of the key differences between constructors and class member methods are as follows:

- **Constructors are invoked only one time per newly created instance object.** The constructor method's job is to initialize the newly instantiated class objects. Instance objects will only have a constructor invoked upon them one time ever: right after instantiation. After this there is no need—the object is already initialized.
- **Member methods are available on demand after the instance object of a class has been initialized.** Member methods can be called as many times as needed upon as many class instance objects as you wish. These are the behaviors that the objects are capable of, and they can be invoked on the objects as long as those objects are still in memory.

Member methods, like data fields, can be present in a class as both nonstatic and static methods. There can also be two categories of method in a class that are distinguished by their intended purpose as well. These can be briefly summarized as follows:

- **Nonstatic methods are common.** These are methods of a class, defined in your CDF, that can be invoked directly upon future instance objects of the class. These make up the common "behaviors" of these objects that can be used by application developers.
- **Static methods, like static data fields, are not tied to any particular instance object but instead are invoked upon the class itself.** Earlier you defined `personCount` as a static data field of class `Person`. There is only one copy, as it keeps track of how many `Person` instance objects have been created. It is not tied to any particular instance object. Static methods are invoked on the overall class itself. Building on this, a static member method could be defined in the class that returns a copy of the value stored within `personCount`. This method would be invoked via the class, not upon any instance object.
- **"Getter" and "setter" methods are focused on data field access.** Generally in OO programming, a method that retrieves a value from a data field in an object is called an "accessor," and a method that changes a value of a data field in an object is called a mutator. Conversationally, you can think of these as "getter" and "setter" methods.
    - Getters "get" or retrieve data **from** a data field **inside the instance object**.
    - Setters "set" or copy new data **into** a data field **inside the instance object**.

Typically, getters and setters focus on one thing, interacting with a single data field, and do little else. Getter and setter methods can exist for both nonstatic and static data fields. Also, you can have getter and setter methods for both public and private data fields. **Data fields with the private or protected access modifier most typically have a getter and often (but not always) a setter method.**

Adding "getter" and "setter" methods: There is no fixed rule as to how many you should have, but naming them does follow certain conventions. Some things to consider regarding getter and setter methods:

- **Does the class have any private data fields?** If yes, then these are good candidates for defining getter/setter methods for the CDF. Private data fields are not directly accessible from outside the instance object/class. Normally, secure programming insists upon making **all** data fields private initially and opening up only the ones needed as public by other code.
- **What is the data type of each data field?** For example, if a data field is a reference to an array, should the getter/setter work with the reference itself or an index position within the array? Each data field will require a different nature of interaction with it.
- **How complex are the business rules regarding a data field?** A value for a data field may be complex to calculate or set, requiring a great deal of logic and value checks. In cases like these, you might decide to make the data field `private` and define a getter (and/or setter) method to carefully control the accepted values of the field in any particular instance object.

All the data fields of the `Person` class have `public` access modifiers. But for practice, you can add a getter and setter method for a few data fields: `eyeColor`, `age`, and `payRate`. The template for a getter/setter method is the same as you have seen before with most methods:

```
[access modifier] [return type] get[DataFieldName] ( [parameters] )
{
     // method body
     [return statement]
}

[access modifier] [return type] set[DataFieldName] ( [parameters] )
{
     // method body
     [return statement]
}
```

A method's name communicates its intent like with variable names. Typically, developers have the words "`get`" and "`set`" precede the names of the data fields these methods target. The data field name is commonly capitalized after "get" or "set" in the method name. Some external code in the Java library expects this naming convention to be followed. After the constructors in the Person class, add one getter and setter method for each of the three data fields mentioned earlier:

Code Snippet 8.14

```
// in Person.java
// . . .earlier code omitted for brevity

public String getEyeColor()
{
    return eyeColor;
}

public void setEyeColor(String newEyeColor)
{
    eyeColor = newEyeColor;
}

public int getAge()
{
    return age;
}

public void setAge(int newAge)
{
    age = newAge;
}

public double getPayRate()
{
    return payRate;
}

public void setPayRate(double newPayRate)
{
    payRate = newPayRate;
}
```

Taking a closer look at one getter/setter set will help the rest make sense:

- `.getEyeColor()`: The access modifier is `public` (and will be for most getters and setters, typically). The return type is `String`. This makes sense: if retrieving the `eyeColor` (a `String` data-type data field) from inside a future instance object, then the method needs to return back the same data type that the data field is defined as. There is no parameter needed: the data needed is already inside the instance object this method will be invoked upon in the future. There is no need to send data in because the data is already inside the object. A copy of the needed data is being retrieved from within the object. In the method's body, return a copy of the `String` value in `eyeColor`. Getter methods should typically **never** change the value of the data field they are getting from!
- `.setEyeColor(String newEyeColor)`: The access modifier is `public`. The return type for this setter is `void`. Why? Well if you are sending new data into the object to replace a value, there is usually no need to return any data back. Occasionally, a return type for a setter may be `boolean` so that the method can report back to the calling code if the change was successful or not. The method defines one incoming parameter: `newEyeColor`. If you are changing the value of `eyeColor` that is already inside the object, then the parameter is needed in the new value. In the method body, the value of `newEyeColor` is copied into the instance object's data field `eyeColor`.

The detailed breakdown for the `get/setEyeColor` methods applies to all the other method pairs as well. You can test these out in the application by adding the following code to the listing:

Code Snippet 8.15

```
// in PersonApp.java

suzy.setEyeColor("Green");
bob.setEyeColor("Polka-Dot");
sam.setAge(50);
bob.setPayRate(60.0);

System.out.println("Suzy's Eye Color: " + suzy.getEyeColor());
System.out.println("Bob's Eye Color: " + bob.getEyeColor());
System.out.println("Sam's Age: " + sam.getAge());
```

This will generate the following output:

```
Suzy's Eye Color: Green
Bob's Eye Color: Polka-Dot
Sam's Age: 50
```

Notice that since the setter methods have `void` return types, there is no data returned from these invocations. The getter methods return back data from within the instance objects they are invoked upon. These values are concatenated `String` literals in the `.println()` invocations.

Adding member methods: Adding a member method to the `Person` CDF is similar syntaxwise. The purpose of member methods is typically broader in scope than getters and setters. Member methods embody the behavior/actions of the objects of the class: they can perform a calculation, compare one object with another, provide access to more complex resources in the class, handle an array, and so on. They enable the actions that are available to instance objects of the class (and to the class itself).

An important point to keep in mind: Member methods **abstract** otherwise complex code behind a simple interface (a method invocation). Think about what logic or processing might be useful to a developer who is using your class in their application. Your member methods can implement this logic, saving them the trouble of writing it. A developer using your class does not need to know details of the code written in member methods. All they have to know is how to invoke the method and what data it needs/returns.

You have a choice in your class's design of defining either nonstatic or static member methods. Consider first a nonstatic member method. Looking at the `Person` class, notice that each individual's `height` is stored as inches. Add a method that will convert this to feet and return back that as a `double`:

Code Snippet 8.16

```
// in Person.java
public double heightInFeet()
{
    return (height / 12.0);
}
```

Notice also that no input parameter is needed here because the needed data (the `Person` instance object's `height` data field) is already stored **inside** the instance object. The value of the `height` data field is divided by `12.0` (to ensure the result does not drop the decimal data), and this calculated value is returned back. This method can be tested in the application after implementation:

Code Snippet 8.17

```
System.out.println("Bob is " + bob.heightInFeet() + " feet tall!");
System.out.printf("Bob is %.2f feet tall!\n", bob.heightInFeet());
```

And the console output for this code is the following:

```
Bob is 5.833333333333333 feet tall!
Bob is 5.83 feet tall!
```

If you remember, you implemented this calculation earlier in the application's code for `bob`. This code has now been moved into a nonstatic class member method. Because it is nonstatic, you must invoke the method upon instance objects of the class. The instance objects store the `height` data field, so they must be the target of the method's action.

Adding static member methods: The static keyword can be added to resources of a class that you want to be part of the overall class itself and not tied directly to any particular instance object. In fact, any data fields or methods that are declared static can be accessed before even the first instance object of your class is created. The static data field personCount was added to the Person class earlier. It should be incremented each time a new instance object is initialized by any constructor. Why? Because you do not know ahead of time which particular constructor a developer will invoke and you need to make sure that the incrementation occurs in all existing constructors. Modify both Person constructors with the following (changes in **bold**):

Code Snippet 8.18

```
public Person()
{
     eyeColor = "";
     height = 0;
     age = 0;
     name = "";
     payRate = 0.0;

     personCount++; // Increment static data field
}

public Person(String incomingEyeColor,
        int incomingHeight,
        int incomingAge,
        String incomingName,
        double incomingPayRate)
{
     eyeColor = incomingEyeColor;
     height = incomingHeight;
     age = incomingAge;
     name = incomingName;
     payRate = incomingPayRate;

     personCount++; // Increment static data field
}
```

Now anytime that either of the constructors is invoked, each invocation will increment personCount by one. Let the class itself handle the Person instance object count.

How do you print the value of personCount in the application? Remember that static data fields differ from "nonstatic" ones (instance data fields) in that there is only one copy of the data field for the class overall. Instance data fields are found in each and every instance object. Every Person has an eyeColor; every Person has an age. **But there is only one variable that stores the count of how many Person objects there are.** Since personCount also has a public access modifier, you can print it directly by using the class name itself. Think of it this way: static data fields are a data field of the overall class, so it makes sense to use the class's name:

Code Snippet 8.19

```
// In PersonApp.java

System.out.println("Person Count: " + Person.personCount);
```

This code will print the following to the console:

```
Person Count: 3
```

This makes sense: the new keyword has been used three times in the application to create Person instance objects and invoked one or the other of the constructors of this class each of these three times. Each time a constructor was invoked, personCount was incremented by one.

Notice that the variable personCount cannot be accessed via any particular instance object; it is a static data field. You must use the class's name as a qualifier in order to access any static resource of a class. Typically, static member methods will be responsible for allowing the application to interact with static data fields (and other static methods) of a class, forming part of the class's interface. Now add into the Person class a static member method that will return back the count value stored in the static data field:

Code Snippet 8.20

```
public static int countOfPersons()
{
   return personCount;
}
```

Adding the static keyword makes this a static member method. Right from the start, notice the big difference in this class member method's code versus the application code written earlier. The class name must be used as a qualifier to access this data field (i.e., Person.personCount). Why? Well, the static data field is inside the class, and the application contains code external to that class. When you add a static member method, by the very word "member," it means that the method is part of the class / inside the class, and its code can already see (i.e., has a symbolic definition for) personCount. Now invoke the method by revising the prior line of code:

Code Snippet 8.21

```
// Revised line of code in PersonApp.java
System.out.println("Person Count: " + Person.countOfPersons());
```

This generates the same output as earlier:

```
Person Count: 3
```

As you can see, it is a static method. This code is added to the main() method in the application and is external to the class. This means you must use the class's name in order to qualify where the method that you want to invoke is defined.

Class design tip: Normally, most data fields in a class are private, and the developer carefully chooses which ones to make public. Normally, personCount would also be private (or protected) so that the class has total control over altering the data field's value. You would not want a rogue developer setting personCount to one thousand when there are only three data fields!

SUMMARY POINTS

- Member methods of the class, including getters and setters, constitute the actions that a class and its objects are capable of. This completes the "bundle" of data with actions.
- Getter (accessor) and setter (mutator) methods typically focus on just one data field and govern external access to it.
- In an application, the dot notation is used to access the member resources (data fields and methods) of a class and/or its objects.
- Nonstatic resources of a class are accessed via dot notation on an instance object of a class.
- Static resources of a class are accessed via dot notation on the class name itself (not one of its objects).

QUICK PROBLEMS

1. **Coding:** Using your fruit class from quick problem #1 (if you created it) in section 8.4, add a static data field for the count of the fruit created, incrementing it in your constructor. Add a static method that will return this count.
2. **Think:** When might the use of a class instance method be preferable to just directly accessing an instance object's data field? When might the reverse be true (just accessing the data field)?
3. **Coding:** Using your Car class from quick problem #3 (if you created it) in section 8.2, add a nonstatic method called .describeCar(). The method will return back a String that concatenates all the data field values for any specific car in a professional, descriptive statement of the vehicle.

8.6 Using References to Instance Objects

Understanding how references to objects work is a key concept in object-oriented programming. Earlier, you learned that the `Person` variables `bob`, `suzy`, and `sam` are reference variables. These are not the `Person` class instance objects themselves but references to where the objects are in memory. A reference variable simply stores an address and is given class data types ("complex"). It is a bucket of **address** data. Understanding this yields a strong understanding of how objects can be "passed" and referenced: you are passing around **references** to objects and not the objects themselves.

Copying reference variables: Consider the following two examples of making a variable copy:

Code Snippet 8.22

```
int a = 5;
int b;
b = a;

Person personA = new Person();
Person personB;
personB = personA;
```

Both examples may appear to be doing the same thing: one variable being copied into the other. This is true for the `int` variables: the value of `a` is being copied into the `int` variable `b`. But in the case of the `Person` variables, this is not the case. The `personA` object is not being copied into the `personB` object. Instead, the **reference address** that is stored in the reference variable `personA` is being copied into the reference variable `personB`. In other words, the address in one "bucket" is copied into the other "bucket." Additionally, there is only one instance object of `Person` in memory, as the `new` operator was only used once. One object, two references to it. Figure 8.9 shows this visually.

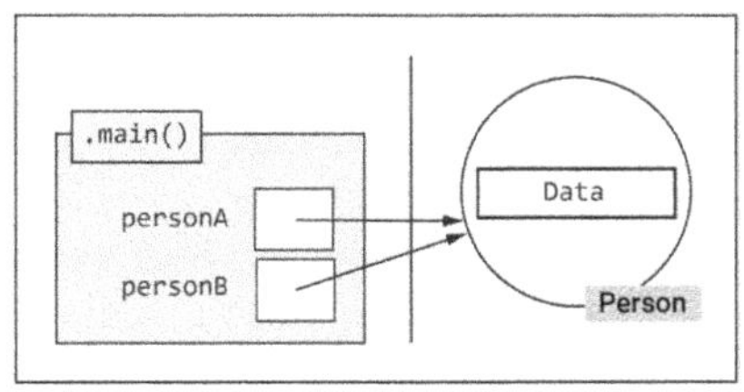

Figure 8.9. Referencing Two Reference Variables at the Same `Person` Instance Object

A real-world analogy to rereferencing is again helpful here: You know the address of your favorite grocery store (they have that brand of java you like to brew so much!). Your friend laments to you that their grocery store is subpar and disappoints them greatly. So you write down the address of your favorite store and give it to them. In doing so, you did **not** make a copy of the entire store. Instead, **you made a copy of the address to the store.** You and your friend now both have a reference to the one single grocery store! The same situation occurs with the example code earlier: both `personA` and `personB` have stored within them references to the location in memory where one single `Person` instance object is located.

Using class data types in arrays: How else can you use references to instance objects? Remember that a class is a type (the classes you create are brand-new data types that are valid in your project). Remember also that an array can use any valid data type for its elements. Putting these concepts together, consider the following application code:

Code Snippet 8.23

```
Person[] personArray = new Person[3];
personArray[0] = new Person();
personArray[1] = new Person();
personArray[2] = new Person();

personArray[1].name = "Michelle";
personArray[1].setEyeColor("Blue");
System.out.println(personArray[1].name
        + "'s eye color: "
        + personArray[1].getEyeColor());
```

This creates an array of reference variable elements instead of an array of `int`, `double`, and so on. So each `personArray` element has a class data type, making it a reference variable, and each element can reference a `Person` instance object. Remember that when you create a standard Java array, it is initially created empty unless an array initializer is used. The same is true with `personArray`. Notice that at each array element location, a reference to a `Person` instance object is stored. Each object is created using `new` and initialized with the zero-argument `Person` constructor. An element at a specific index position in the array is identified to store the reference to a newly created `Person` instance object. Figure 8.10 shows what this looks like in memory.

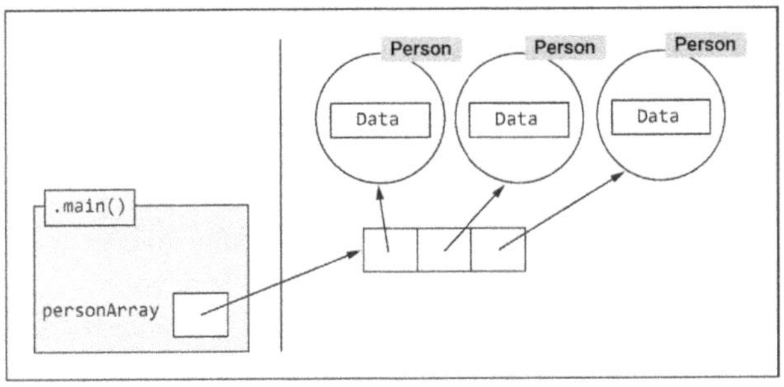

Figure 8.10. An Array of `Person` Instance Object References in Memory

To fully grasp the use of references to objects, consider this example, which makes changes to the `personArray` after you have added the three objects to it:

Code Snippet 8.24

```
personArray[1] = personArray[0];
personArray[2] = personArray[0];
```

Recall that this code copies references to instance objects (right to left). After this new additional code runs, the reference to a `Person` instance object that is stored at element `[0]` in `personArray` is now copied into and overwrites the reference address that was stored in `personArray` at elements `[1]` and `[2]`. The result of this code will ultimately be that all three `personArray` elements will now store the same reference to the same, single instance object. The references to the other two instance objects that were stored in the second and third array elements have been lost. When an instance object has no more references to it from anywhere, the Java garbage collector takes it to that "great compiler in the sky." Figure 8.11 shows how the two `Person` objects are "orphaned" when their only references are overwritten in the array.

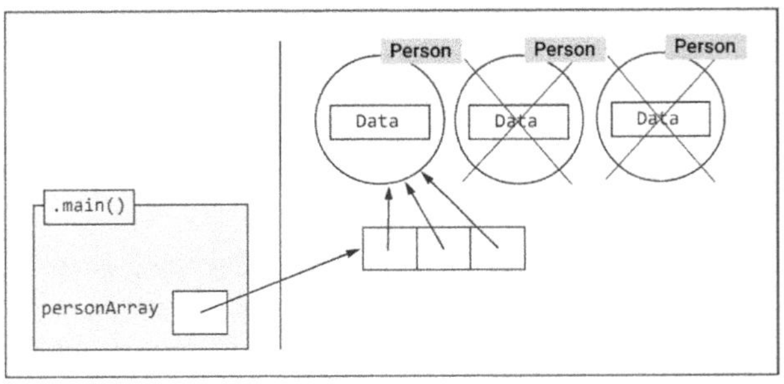

Figure 8.11. Contents of the `personArray` after Two References Are Overwritten

Passing a reference to an instance object: Now you know how to manipulate and copy references to instance objects. A reference to an instance object can also be passed as a method parameter. To demonstrate this, a `static` method can be added to `PersonApp.java` that will create a `String` concatenated with the information for any `Person` instance object that the method receives a reference to. The method will return a reference to the created `String` back to the calling code:

Code Snippet 8.25

```
public static String personDetails(Person aPerson)
{
    String returnValue = "Name: " + aPerson.name + "\n"
            + "Age: " + aPerson.getAge() + "\n"
            + "Eye Color: " + aPerson.getEyeColor() + "\n"
            + "Height: " + aPerson.height + "\n"
            + "Pay Rate: " + aPerson.getPayRate() + "\n";

    return returnValue;
}
```

Use this in the `main()` method of `PersonApp`:

Code Snippet 8.26

```
// In PersonApp.java
System.out.println(personDetails(sam));
```

This line of code will cause the following to print to the console:

```
Name: Sam
Age: 50
Eye Color: Blue
Height: 57
Pay Rate: 90.0
```

The method `personDetails()` defines a parameter called `aPerson`, and the data type for this parameter is `Person`. This means that this method accepts one parameter, a reference to any `Person` instance object. The method does not know where the reference comes from, and it does not care, as long as it receives one. In the application, the reference stored within the reference variable "`sam`" is copied down to the method parameter "`aPerson`." In this case, the code **does not** make a second copy of the instance object that "`sam`" references, just the reference itself is copied. That is why "pass by reference" doesn't exist as a parameter-passing behavior in Java: even with objects, you are still passing a **copy** of a variable. Since the parameter references a `Person` instance object, you can use the dot notation to access resources in the instance object the references refer to. Figure 8.12 visually shows the two references to the `Person` instance object.

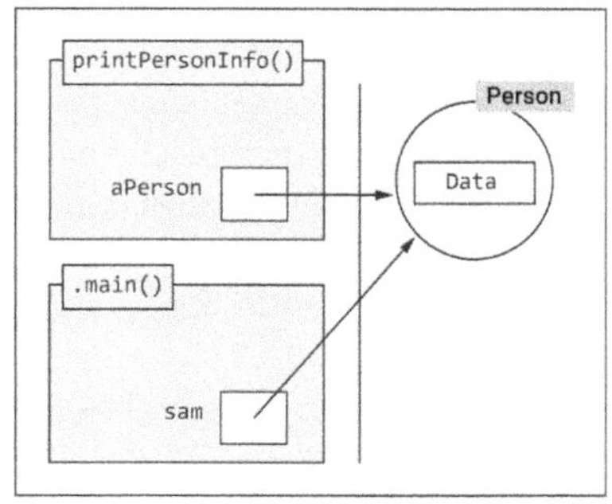

Figure 8.12. Passing a Reference to a `Person` Instance Object to a Method

Using the `this` keyword: You have seen now how to use references to your class instance objects from within an application. How can you refer to an instance object from **within the code of the class itself**? For example, recall that when the code of a constructor is executing, it is acting upon a new instance object of its class. How can you refer to the instance object that a constructor or regular member method is acting upon at that moment? The `this` keyword allows you to do this.* A couple of things to keep in mind with `this`:

- The `this` keyword is Java's **built-in reference variable** that references the instance object that is currently being acted upon / targeted within a class method.
- You will only ever see `this` used in a class method, and it only ever appears in **nonstatic methods of that class**. Why? Because `this` refers to an instance object, which static methods do not act upon.
- The `this` keyword can help clarify variable name conflicts or vague variable name usage when a **data field and a method parameter have the same name**.

That last point is important. Typically, constructor parameters and getter/setter parameters that are passing in values for data fields will **have the same name** as the data field they are targeting. For example, consider this fictional setter method:

Code Snippet 8.27

```
public void setSomeDataField(int dataField)
{
    dataField = dataField;
}
```

The incoming parameter is named the same as the data field of the class this setter is defined in. What impact does this have? Notice the line of code in the method body. Unless you clarify which variable is the data field and which is the parameter, Java will assume the line of code refers to the incoming parameter on both sides and will copy it over top of itself. The data field's value will not change! How do you tell Java to copy the incoming parameter into the target data field? By using the `this` keyword. The alteration is in **bold**:

* https://docs.oracle.com/javase/tutorial/java/javaOO/thiskey.html.

Code Snippet 8.28

```
public void setDataField(int dataField)
{
    this.dataField = dataField;
}
```

Conversationally, this is translated as "The `dataField` of the instance object that this **method is currently acting upon** will have its value replaced by that of the incoming parameter dataField." So this allows you to reference whatever instance object this class member method happens to be acting upon. In a fictional application, you might have something like this:

```
SomeClass objA = new SomeClass();
objA.setDataField(100);
```

So when the code of `setDataField()` executes, the `this` keyword will reference the instance object that `objA` references. Why? Because that is the object that `setDataField()` was invoked upon using the dot notation. You invoke the nonstatic instance method `setDataField()` upon the instance object referenced by `objA`, so that's the "target" object that `this` references.

Developers typically name incoming constructor parameters the same as the data fields they target. Make the following changes (in **bold**) to the `Person` class to adhere to this industry standard:

Code Snippet 8.29

```
public Person()
{
    this.eyeColor = "";
    this.height = 0;
    this.age = 0;
    this.name = "";
    this.payRate = 0.0;

    personCount++;
}

public Person(String eyeColor,
        int height,
        int age,
        String name,
        double payRate)
{
    this.eyeColor = eyeColor;
    this.height = height;
    this.age = age;
    this.name = name;
    this.payRate = payRate;

    personCount++;
}
```

With the constructors, you can conversationally say that "`this` references the instance object that the constructor is currently initializing." Again, how do you know which particular "current" instance object is being initialized and referenced by `this`? By examining your application code and looking at which constructor is being invoked. Change your setters in the same way (changes in **bold**):

Code Snippet 8.30

```
public void setEyeColor(String eyeColor)
{
    this.eyeColor = eyeColor;
}

// some code omitted. . .
```

```
public void setAge(int age)
{
    this.age = age;
}

// some code omitted. . .

public void setPayRate(double payRate)
{
    this.payRate = payRate;
}
```

The `this` keyword tells Java where the new, incoming value is being copied. To visualize this, consider the following example code that invokes `.setAge()` on the `Person` instance object. Figure 8.13 shows how the `this` keyword references the `Person` instance object the instance method was invoked upon.

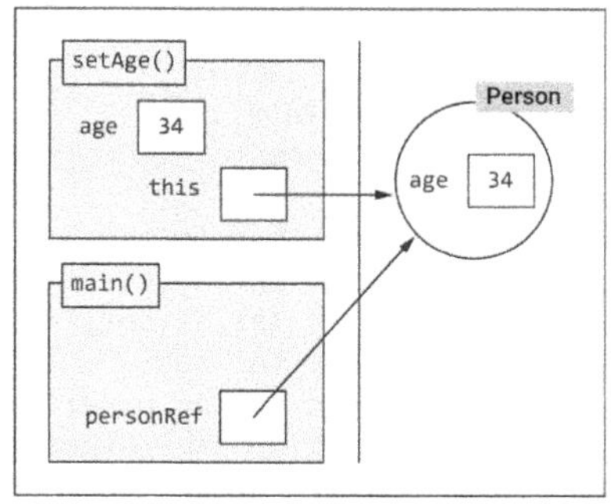

Figure 8.13. Role of the `this` Reference Variable in Data Field Alteration

Code Snippet 8.31

```
// In Application
Person personRef = new Person();
personRef.setAge(34);
```

SUMMARY POINTS

- Reference variables store to a class instance object that is found in memory. These types of variables can be used in an application, as a method parameter, or as a data field of a class, among other uses.
- The "this" keyword's usage is primarily within the code of a class and always in a nonstatic method of a class.
- The "this" keyword is a built-in reference variable that Java creates, and it always refers to the particular instance object being acted upon by the method the keyword is found within.

QUICK PROBLEMS

1. **Coding:** Using your fruit class from quick problem #1 (if you created it) in section 8.6, create a static application method that accepts a reference to an instance object of your class. Have the method print to the console the values of the data fields stored within the object whose reference was passed to it.
2. **Think:** Reference variables have a default value of `null` in Java. What happens if you set a reference variable for an instance object to `null` and there are no other references to the object?
3. **Coding:** Using your `Car` class from quick problem #3 (if you created it) in section 8.5, add an instance method to the class that accepts a reference to another `Car` instance object as a parameter. Call this method `.compareCars()`. The method will return back `true` if "this" instance object's model year is older than the parameter `Car`'s model year.

8.7 Using Complex-Type Data Fields in Your Class

A data field of a Java class can be declared with any valid data type. Remember that classes, even those you develop, are newly created data types as well and are valid to use in your code wherever you declare a data type. Combining these two concepts together, you can use a class (i.e., complex) data type for a data field in your class. You can also use complex data types like arrays as data fields in your class. This further extends the ability of your objects: you can give instance objects the ability to refer to other instance objects in memory!

To demonstrate this, you can give `Person` instance object the ability to refer to another `Person` instance object. For example, what if each new employee in the mom-and-pop grocery store initially trains with a coworker upon hire? The `Person` CDF will need a nonstatic data field or data typed as `Person` to mimic this real-world entity relationship:

Code Snippet 8.32

```
// some code omitted. . .

public class Person {
    public String eyeColor;
    public int height;
    public int age;
    public String name;
    public double payRate;
    public Person trainer;

// some code omitted. . .
```

Keep in mind, since this is a nonstatic data field, it is the **constructor's job to initialize this data field**. Here, since it is a reference variable to a `Person` object, the reference is `null` or empty:

Code Snippet 8.33

```
public Person()
{
    this.eyeColor = "";
    this.height = 0;
    this.age = 0;
    this.name = "";
    this.payRate = 0.0;
    this.trainer = null;

    personCount++;
}

public Person(String eyeColor,
        int height,
        int age,
        String name,
        double payRate)
{
    this.eyeColor = eyeColor;
    this.height = height;
    this.age = age;
    this.name = name;
    this.payRate = payRate;
    this.trainer = null;

   personCount++;
}
```

Now your constructor, which is placed into this data field, depends on the business's logic, rules, and so on. Can a `trainer` be determined when a `Person` object is first created, or is this not decided until much later? You should go with the second scenario and additionally add a getter and a setter for this new data field:

Code Snippet 8.34

```
public Person getTrainer()
{
    return this.trainer;
}
```

Class design tip: Adding a data field to an existing class is like throwing a stone in a pond: it causes ripples. Doing so should trigger a series of questions about what changes are needed in all of the constructors and what changes are needed, if any, in the member methods (including existing or needed new getter and setter methods).

The constructors set `trainer` to `null`, since you do not know which particular `Person` object `trainer` will reference ahead of time. Add a setter method so that `trainer` can have a `Person` reference copied into it from the application at a later time:

Code Snippet 8.35

```
public void setTrainer(Person trainer)
{
    this.trainer = trainer; // Usage of this
}
```

What is going on with `.setTrainer()` is simple: some code somewhere, typically an application, will invoke the method and pass via its parameter a reference to some other `Person` object. (*Note:* The reference could also contain a `null` value.) The reference flows into the parameter and then is copied into the `trainer` data field of the instance object that this method is acting upon. For example,

Code Snippet 8.36

```
sam.setTrainer(suzy);
```

The reference to the `Person` instance object stored inside the "`suzy`" reference variable is sent to the `.setTrainer()` method's parameter, and then the method copies it into the `trainer` data field of the instance object that "`sam`" refers to. Figure 8.14 shows the changes to all the reference variables before `.setTrainer()` finishes its invocation.

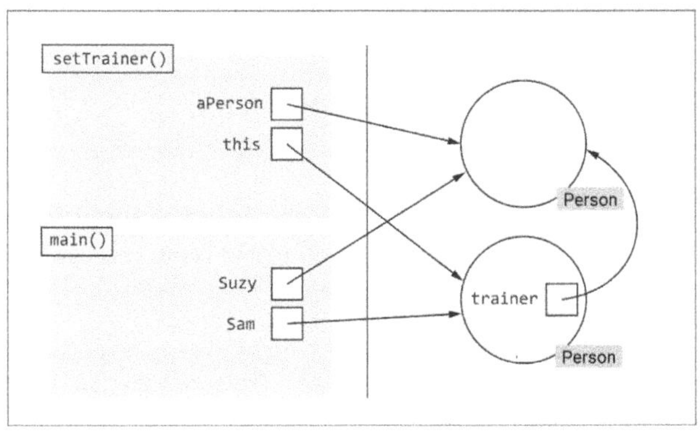

Figure 8.14. Referencing One `Person` Instance Object from Another

Using arrays as a data field: You can combine the idea of object references and complex data fields in another way. It might be nice for the class itself to keep a record of all the instance objects created. What if you added a static array, data typed as `Person`, that would store a reference to each new `Person` instance object? The class will statically store a copy of these references, similar to a roster of individuals. Add a new array to `Person` like so (in **bold**):

Code Snippet 8.37

```
// In Person.java
// . . .
public static int personCount = 0;
public static Person[] roster = new Person[30];
// . . .
```

Notice that since this is a static data field, it is initialized right at declaration. This creates a new size-`30` element array in memory, and each element is able to store a `Person` reference value.

Class design note: Ideally, in a production-ready IS, you would want to use a Java data structure that can dynamically resize, like the `ArrayList<E>` class, so that you are not limiting your array to an unchanging size.

Where can you get a copy of the reference to each and every instance object initialized by the class constructors? With each constructor invocation! The constructor has access to the `this` keyword, and it is by default a reference to the instance object currently being acted upon by the constructor. A copy of its value can be copied into the array at the next available location, which happens to synchronize with `personCount` (which starts its count at 0, the first element of the array). Make the following changes to your constructors (in **bold**):

Code Snippet 8.38

```
public Person()
{
    this.eyeColor = "";
    this.height = 0;
    this.age = 0;
    this.name = "";
    this.payRate = 0.0;
    this.trainer = null;

    roster[personCount] = this;
    personCount++;
}

public Person(String eyeColor,
        int height,
        int age,
        String name,
        double payRate)
{
    this.eyeColor = eyeColor;
    this.height = height;
    this.age = age;
    this.name = name;
    this.payRate = payRate;
    this.trainer = null;

    roster[personCount] = this;
    personCount++;
}
```

How would you put this to use in the application? Remember the method `personDetails()` that is implemented in the application class? Now you can use both it and the `roster` in `Person` to your advantage:

Code Snippet 8.39

```
// In PersonApp.java
// Print details for all Person objects in memory
for (int i=0; i<Person.roster.length; i++)
{
  if (Person.roster[i] != null)
  {
      System.out.println(
              personDetails(Person.roster[i])
              );
  }
  else
      System.out.println("Null Reference at index " + i);
}
```

Since each element of `roster` is a reference variable, you must check to see if the value of that reference value is not equal to `null` (i.e., no reference at all). If it is not, then pass the reference at that array element to

`.personDetails()` as an argument. Otherwise, signal that there was no reference at that index location. The loop will print the following when executed:

```
Name: Suzy
Age: 21
Eye Color: Green
Height: 0
Pay Rate: 85.0

Name:
Age: 45
Eye Color: Polka-Dot
Height: 70
Pay Rate: 60.0

Name: Sam
Age: 50
Eye Color: Blue
Height: 57
Pay Rate: 90.0

Null Reference at index 3
Null Reference at index 4
Null Reference at index 5
. . . [omitted for space] . . .
Null Reference at index 28
Null Reference at index 29
```

It is interesting to note here that if you did not check for a `null` reference, then as soon as you attempted to use a `roster` index location that has a `null` reference stored in it and use that in `personDetails()`, Java would throw a `java.lang.NullPointerException`. A `NullPointerException` is thrown when your code attempts to access the resources of an instance object at a reference, **when in actuality there is no object address in that reference at all**! In other words, the line of code as written assumes that an object exists at that reference, but in reality, there is no object at the referenced memory location, so you cannot do anything via that reference.

SUMMARY POINTS

- Any valid data type can be used as the type for a class's data fields.
- Adding data fields to existing classes will necessitate the developer to consider changes to all preexisting constructors and their code and the possibility of adding new constructors based on the purpose of the class being written.
- A reference variable is a single reference to the instance object of a complex data type and is given this data type in its declaration. When an array is created and declared with a complex data type, it becomes a sequence of reference variables whose values are all `null`.
- If a reference variable is empty (i.e., contains `null` as a value), then attempts to access resources of the class through that variable will result in a `NullPointerException` being thrown by the compiler.

QUICK PROBLEMS

1. **Coding:** Using your fruit class from quick problem #1 (if you created it) in section 8.5, add a `Person` data field to the class definition. Change whatever constructors exist or add additional ones to accommodate this change. This data field will store a reference to the `Person` who "owns" the fruit. Test this relationship out in your application.
2. **Think:** Consider an application that has `Teacher`, `Student`, and `Class` objects. How would you add these classes as data field references to one

another to mimic a real-world relationship between a class, its students, and the teacher of the class?

3. **Coding:** Using your `Car` class from quick problem #3 (if you created it) in section 8.4, convert the `String` array previously added into a `Person` array. Make any appropriate changes to your constructors and methods. Test things out in your application to ensure the conversion works without error.

Summary

In this chapter, you learned about the basic concepts, benefits, and ways in which Java implements object-oriented programming. Classes allow us to increase the modularity, reusability, and ease of maintenance and update applications. Developing object-oriented programs can help increase programmer productivity and collaborative efforts. You learned how to create a basic class definition file; explored its basic structure; and learned about data fields, constructors, and member methods. You learned how to manage instance objects in memory through reference variables and how static members of a class differ from nonstatic members in terms of their locations in memory. Additionally, you learned how other complex data types, including other classes, can be used within class instance objects to make them far more useful. Where previously, variables were limited to only one data type or a sequence of the same data type, now variables declared as instance objects of classes can bundle both various data types and various member methods as actions to make developing software of increasing complexity and sophistication easier.

Practice Problems

Terminology

Match the following terms from the chapter with their most appropriate definition:

1. Reference variable	a. An object created in memory according to a class blueprint.
2. Class	b. Sets security for a class resource so that only code in the class and its subclasses can access the resource.
3. Constructor	c. Declares a class resource to be overall to a class and not in any particular instance object.
4. Member method	d. A special type of class method that only executes one time per instance object. Its job is to initialize newly created instance objects.
5. Reference	e. Declares a class resource to be repeated and found in each and every instance object built using the class.
6. Data field	f. Sets security for a class resource so that only code within that resource's class can access it directly.
7. Static	g. A built-in reference variable that always refers to a class instance object being acted upon by the nonstatic method that the reference is found within.
8. Public	h. A member method whose focus is to retrieve the value (or a particular value) from a single data field.
9. Accessor (getter)	i. A variable that stores within it the address of an instance object in memory.
10. Instance object	j. Sets security for a class resource so that it is directly accessible by code both within and outside a class.
11. Nonstatic	k. A variable defined to be found either within a class's instance object or in the class itself.
12. Private	l. An address to an object in memory.
13. Protected	m. A member method whose focus is to change the value (or a particular value) of a single data field.
14. Mutator (setter)	n. Can be used to build a digital entity represented by objects that bundle data and actions, leveraging modularity and increasing development efficiency.
15. this	o. A method that is particularly part of a class and that constitutes the actions/behaviors of that class and/or its objects.

Find the Error

In each of the following problems, carefully examine the code given, and determine the error(s)/issue(s) with each. Keep in mind, the error(s) could be syntax (code) or logic (intended outcome) based or both!

1.

```
// Application - Assume any classes used are defined
FineClass classVariable;
classVariable.someValue = 5;
classVariable.someOtherValue = 10;
```

2.

```
// Application - Assume any classes used are defined
FineClass someClassVariable = new FineClass();
someClassVariable.FineClass();
someClassVariable = 60;
```

3.

```
// Constructor
public PaintedSprocket(String typeOfSprocket, int sprocketWeight)
{
    this.typeOfSprocket = sprocketWeight;
    this.sprocketWeight = sprocketWeight;
}

// Application
PaintedSprocket sprocket = new PaintedSprocket("heavy", 2.5, 5);
```

4.

```
// Constructor
public PaintedSprocket(String typeOfSprocket, int sprocketWeight)
{
    this.typeOfSprocket = "NoName";
    this.sprocketWeight = 0;
}

// Application
PaintedSprocket sprocket = new PaintedSprocket("heavy", 5);
```

5.

```
public class DataBit
{
    public int firstData;
    public static int secondData;

    // Rest of class omitted, assume constructors are defined. . .
}

// Application
DataBit bitOne = new DataBit();
DataBit bitTwo = new DataBit();
bitOne.firstData = 5;
bitOne.secondData = 10;
bitTwo = bitOne;
```

6.

```
public class DataBit
{
   public int firstData;
```

```
    public static int secondData;

    // Rest of class omitted, assume constructors are defined. . .
}

// Application
DataBit bitOne = new DataBit();
DataBit bitTwo = new DataBit();
bitOne.firstData = 10;
bitTwo.firstData = 20;

// Swap the references.
bitOne = bitTwo;
bitTwo = bitOne;

// Print the 10 and the 20
System.out.println(bitOne.firstData + " " + bitTwo.firstData);
```

7.

```
// Application - Assume any classes used are defined
FineClass[] fineArray = new FineClass[5];
fineArray[0].someData = 50;
fineArray[2].someData = 100;
fineArray[1] = fineArray[2];
```

8.

```
public class DataBit
{
    public int firstData;
    public static int secondData;
    public static int [] dataArray = new int[5];

    // Rest of class omitted.
}

// Application
DataBit firstBit = new DataBit();
firstBit.dataArray[0] = firstBit;
firstBit.dataArray[10] = new DataBit();
```

9.

```
public class DataBit
{
    public int firstData;
    public static int secondData;
    public DataBit coData;

    // Rest of class omitted.
}
// Application
DataBit one = new DataBit();
one.coData = new DataBit();
one.coData.coData = new DataBit();
one.coData.coData.secondData = 10;
```

10.

```
public class DataBit
{
    public int firstData;
```

```
    public static int secondData;
    public DataBit coData;

    // Rest of class omitted.
}

// Application
DataBit one = new DataBit();
one = null;
one.firstData = 10;
one.coData = new DataBit();
```

Think about It

1. What are several differences between a simple listing style of programs and more object-oriented programs? What are the pros and cons of each?
2. What are the three typical sections that are added to a Java class?
3. What is the difference between static and nonstatic data fields?
4. What are the main points to keep in mind when defining and writing the code for a constructor?
5. What are the data types that are valid for usage as the declared type of a data field?
6. How can you determine which constructor was called based on code in an application that creates a class instance object?
7. What are the similarities between a single reference variable and an array whose data type is a class (i.e., complex)?
8. Describe what happens when the assignment operator (=) is used between two class reference variables.
9. Assume you have two instance objects of a class, objA and objB. The variable objA has data within it, and objB does not. How would you copy all the data from objA to objB? Describe this process conversationally.

Short Syntax Problems

1. Declare three nonstatic data fields for a class: an `int` for the day of the week, a `String` that holds the name of a weather observer, and an array of one hundred temperature observations as `double` values. Increase the security on the array so that it cannot be directly accessed outside of the class.
2. Write a constructor for a class called `Animal`. The constructor will accept two parameters: `animalName`, a `String`, and `animalWeight`, a `double`. Have the constructor initialize data fields by the same names.
3. Write both a getter and a setter for the `String` that holds the name of a weather observer from problem #1 (short syntax) above.
4. Write both a getter and a setter for the int that holds the day of the week for problem #1 (short syntax) above. Add logic to both that restricts the values interacted with to actual days of the week (1 through 7). Print an error message to the console if the application sends a day outside this range.
5. Write a getter and setter method for the weather observation array in problem #1 above (short syntax). Write logic for these that ensures the targeted index is within the array's range. **Extra:** Decide whether the getter will return a reference to the entire array or if it will return a specific index from the array (business logic).
6. Write a method for class `Animal` from problem #2 (short syntax) above. The method will be called `.compareAnimal()`. It will be a nonstatic method that accepts one parameter: a reference to an `Animal` instance object. The method will compare the `animalWeight` data fields of the parameter and the object it is invoked upon. It will return a boolean: true if the invoked animal has a heavier weight, false if the parameter animal's weight is larger.

Full Problems

1. Implement a full class called `BankAccount`. Instance objects of this class will represent bank accounts for customers. Structure your CDF so that you store a customer name, create an ID number that is unique for each customer (*Hint:* you might need a static variable to keep the next ID available), a bank

account balance, a customer address, and a customer email. Determine the business-appropriate level of access modifier security for each data field. Add a zero-parameter and "full" parameter constructor, each. Implement any needed getters and setters. Finally, implement two methods: one method for making deposits and one method for returning a String that contains a report-ready description of the account's balance and status. **Extra:** If the account is overdrawn (negative balance), include a message to this effect in the reporting method.

2. Create a Java class called Sprocket. Include one static data field, `sprocketCount`; one instance data field, `sprocketWeight` (a `double`); and finally a data field for the name of the Sprocket (which will be the word "sprocket" concatenated with the total number created at that time—e.g., "sprocket1," "sprocket2," etc.). In a loop, create one hundred `Sprocket` instance objects, and give each a randomly generated weight. Add a reference to each `Sprocket` object into an array. Then pass the array to an application method that will loop through the array and find the Sprocket with the **largest** weight. Return a reference to that largest `Sprocket` object and print its name to the console.
3. Implement two classes as follows:
   a. First, implement a Book class. Store information on the book's title, subtitle, ISBN number, price, year published, publisher, and page count. Determine appropriate access modifier security levels for each. Add only one constructor that accepts all the above information through parameters. Add appropriate getters/setters. Finally, add a method that returns a String that contains the book's description.
   b. Second, implement a second class called Author. This class will store an author's name, their email address, and their age. Implement a constructor to initialize each object. Add any needed getters and setters. Finally, add a method that returns back a String that contains the Author's description.
   c. Lastly, add a nonstatic data field to Book that will contain a reference to an Author instance object. Make any necessary changes to the classes existing constructors. Change the code in the reporting method for Book so that it calls the reporting method of the Author class and incorporates the Author instance object's returned description in the Book's description. Account for the possibility of a `null` reference in this process.
4. Create a class called `Friend`. Each instance object will have a data field for the name of a person ("me") and a data field that references another `Friend` instance object. When one `Friend` references another Friend object, they are "friends."
   a. Create seven or more Friend instance objects. Pair four of them off as friends (A with B, B with C, and C with D; D will have a `null` for their "friend" data field).
   b. Write an application method that accepts a reference to a Friend instance object. It will print the Friend pairs until it encounters a Friend whose "friend" data field is `null`.
5. Create a full Java application for a small school system that will use classes for `Teacher`, `Student`, and `Course`. The application should be capable of the following functionalities:
   a. The `Teacher` class will store a name, years of service, and rank ("Instructor," "Assistant," and "Full"). Choose appropriate data types for each.
   b. The `Student` will store a name, year in school (1–12), and GPA. Choose appropriate data types for each.
   c. The `Course` will store a subject ("Chemistry," "Math," . . . etc.), a title ("1," "2," . . . etc.), an array that stores students enrolled in the class (use references to `Student` objects), and a data field that stores who the instructor is (use a reference to a `Teacher` object).
   d. The application will use a menu system to allow the user to create `Teachers`, `Students`, and `Courses`. Additional menu options will allow for the association of a `Teacher` with a `Course` and enroll a `Student` in a `Course`. Keep in mind that your application should allow a `Student` to be enrolled in multiple courses.
   e. A final menu option will allow a full information roster to be printed for any course. The course information, the teacher, and the students enrolled in the course with their professionally displayed information will be printed to the console.
   f. Include a menu option to exit the application.

Chapter 9

Class Inheritance and Polymorphism

What You Will Learn in This Chapter

Developing software using modern object-oriented techniques such as creating your own data types through classes can greatly benefit your coding efforts. One major benefit to contemporary object-oriented development is in its ability to let developers easily and quickly build off the work of others. Classes can be extended and adapted through the concept of class inheritance. Instead of reimplementing what could be a large amount of work, developers can simply extend a class, add custom functionality for some specific scenario or context they are developing in, and continue their work without too much effort. Their new classes carry with them all the abilities and data modeling of those that came before but with useful and contextually relevant class characteristics now added. In this chapter, you will learn about class inheritance and how to extend classes and understand the behavior of inherited classes and their interaction with data.

Specifically, this chapter will help you do the following:

1. Help you explore the details of how class inheritance works in Java and the benefits it brings to development efforts
2. Guide you in thinking about what classes could be extended, their usefulness in specific application or data-modeling contexts, and how to create the subclass file
3. Teach you how inheritance impacts the data fields of classes, which are accessible, and what additional ones are needed in the subclass
4. Guide you through the sequence of constructor invocations that occurs when instantiating an object of a subclass, what additional initialization efforts are needed in the subclass, and what instance objects are impacted in this process
5. Show you how subclass methods are defined, how methods from parent classes can be redefined, and how method overloading operates in an inheritance context
6. Help you better understand the concept of polymorphic behavior and how Java guides the behaviors of objects, and the invocation of their methods, in an inheritance context

Opening Scenario

After extensive study in modern object-oriented concepts and after a great deal of work, the mom-and-pop inventory system prototype has been completed and implemented in Java. After all the data cleaning, data modeling, and object-oriented planning and implementation efforts, you are fairly satisfied with the system as it stands. Your team has examined the prototype you have built, and they are happy at this point. Your colleague, still working through part of the client's requirements for this project, noted that in your inventory system, there is no way to indicate what type of inventory item is being stored in the system. "You have a details field, but this is not nearly enough to help this client," she notes, and you have to agree. The client would eventually like to see reports detailing the inventory by product type and store area. They've noted that some of their broader product categories (produce, deli meats, boxed dry goods, and dairy) all have unique characteristics, some of which help determine the prices, time on shelf, and reorder dates from suppliers. The prototype as it stands is nice but is not very useful to the client.

Thinking about how your data objects would behave in a reporting environment, you can already see tedious work ahead in trying, for example, to retrieve a full description for each category of object, each with its unique set of characteristics. Feeling frustrated, you dive back into your studies of modern object-oriented concepts to see if there is a smart way to tackle this problem. The topic of class inheritance is a popular one—how classes can be extended and structured to behave differently in various contexts and based on how they are used. This could be a solution! You decide to dive back into your studies to see how the mom-and-pop inventory prototype can be modified to handle the store's inventory categories and items in a more sophisticated manner . . .

9.1 Class Inheritance: Basics and Benefits

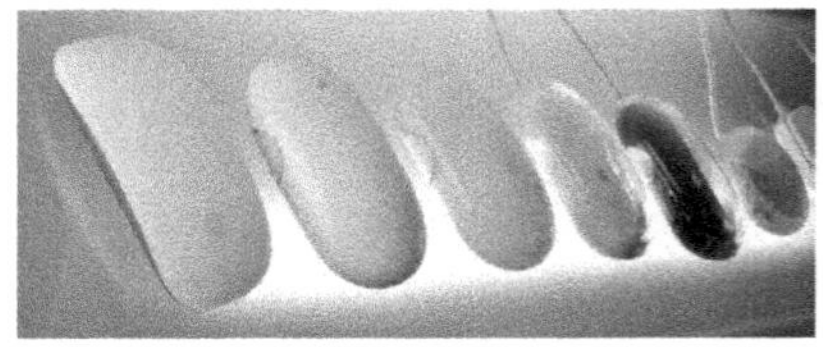

Figure 9.1. Evolution of Computer Mice: Each Inheriting Features from the Last
Source: "25 Years of Apple Mouse Evolution" by raneko is licensed under CC BY 2.0, https://www.flickr.com/photos/24926669@N07/4204026760.

Concept of inheritance: Object-oriented programming provides the information systems developer with numerous conceptual tools like modularity, abstraction, encapsulation, state, actions, and the building of our own custom types using classes, just to name a few. These enable the IS professional to model real-world entities or concepts in a programmatic way and build ever more sophisticated systems, enabling more functionality with less coding work. OO development also enables other developers to easily build on work that has come before, using the classes and codes shared by programmers in new ways or in new application contexts. All of this works wonderfully toward enhancing the productivity of developers and the quality of the systems that they build.

OO development also enables programmers to not only use classes created by others but also expand their features, functionality, and characteristics, building on the work that has come before. Remember that syntax that will allow us to do more (functionality) with less code (time spent developing it) is the ideal goal. The idea of **class inheritance** is the next big benefit of OO programming that we will discuss in this chapter, and it enables this concept of building or expanding on the work that other programmers have done. Java, like most other modern OO programming languages, allows the developer to create a new class (i.e., type) that is related to some preexisting class by specifying a direct, purposeful expansion of the features and functionality of the old class into the new. When this happens, the new class can perform all the actions of the old class, and its objects can store the same data that the old class can. Not only can the new class inherit all these actions and data-storage capabilities, but it also can add new and unique actions and data.

The shoebill stork: Definitely a bird. Probably a dinosaur. Definitely a dinosaur. Is it looking at me?
Source: "Shoebill {balaeniceps rex)" by Drew Avery is licensed under CC BY 2.0, https://www.flickr.com/photos/33590535@N06/3712942432.

Examples of inheritance in the real world: It will help to think of some examples. First, think about a bird. You probably are thinking about not a bird **in general** but a **very specific bird**: maybe a cardinal you saw this morning, a parrot you keep as a pet, or a shoebill stork. The specific bird that came to mind can be thought of as a subtype of the more general category of bird ("A chicken is a specific type of bird"). You could break this down even more: a peregrine hawk is a subtype of "hawk," and "hawk" is a subtype of "bird." Professionals in the field of biology would wince at these descriptions, but they will suffice for our discussion. Notice that a **hierarchy** between these entities forms quickly when you relate them together in this manner. Another example would be for students: A student is a specific type of person. A graduate student is a specific type of student (i.e., a student who is enrolled in graduate school past undergraduate studies). So you already see a hierarchy here: person ← student ← graduate student. Think about some actions and characteristics ascribable to most people:

Person	
Actions:	Walk, talk, sleep, eat
Characteristics:	Height, age, eye color, name

A student can be described in the same way, with some additional actions and characteristics unique to them:

Student	
Actions:	Walk, talk, sleep, eat, **study, attend class**
Characteristics:	Height, age, eye color, name, **GPA, class year, major**

Importantly, understand that a student can do **everything** a typical person can do, but because they are a **person in a specific context** of being a student, they can do more and have more characteristics ascribed to them. In other words, the student **inherits** actions they can perform and characteristics from being a person, but because they are a student, they extend what a typical person can do into a new context. Finally, consider a graduate student:

Graduate Student	
Actions:	Walk, talk, sleep, eat, study, attend class, **write thesis**
Characteristics:	Height, age, eye color, name, GPA, class year, major, **thesis advisor**

The grad student can still do everything a student can do (who can do everything a person can do), but they have an additional action they perform and have an extra characteristic that is unique to just them. In this you can see the chain of inheritance from person to grad student.

Inheritance in the opening scenario: Thinking about these examples and about the mom-and-pop grocery store opening scenario that runs through the textbook, you might already have some ideas about how inheritance can apply. For inventory items, they are not capable of many actions intrinsically. Actions could be defined **for** them as part of a larger information system (reporting needs, data management needs, etc.).

Consider the more abstract concept of an `InventoryItem` as a Java class (with methods and data fields):

`InventoryItem`	
Actions (methods):	`setPurchasePrice; getPurchasePrice; itemProfit(); getDescription(); setDescription();`
Characteristics (data fields):	`purchasePrice; sellPrice; description;`

An item in a grocery store by itself is not capable of any actions, but you can define actions that can be performed by/upon the item in an abstract, digital way as an entity in an information system. Consider the following two entity classes that could inherit all these actions and characteristics and add some (in **bold**) of their own:

`Dairy (inherits from InventoryItem)`	
Actions (methods):	`setPurchasePrice; getPurchasePrice; itemProfit(); getDescription(); setDescription();` **`getExpirationDate(); getProductSize();`**
Characteristics (data fields):	`purchasePrice; sellPrice; description;` **`expirationDate; productSize();`**

`Produce (inherits from InventoryItem)`	
Actions (methods):	`setPurchasePrice; getPurchasePrice; itemProfit(); getDescription(); setDescription();` **`getWeight(); getQuantityPerBundle();`**
Characteristics (data fields):	`purchasePrice; sellPrice; description;` **`weight; quantityPerBundle;`**

Finally, to complete the hierarchy, consider these two classes: one that inherits from class `Dairy` and one that inherits from class `Produce` (each with its added actions and characteristics in **bold**):

`Yogurt (inherits from Dairy)`	
Actions (methods):	`setPurchasePrice; getPurchasePrice; itemProfit(); getDescription(); setDescription(); getExpirationDate(); getProductSize();` **`getFlavor();`**
Characteristics (data fields):	`purchasePrice; sellPrice; description; expirationDate; productSize;` **`flavor;`**
`Grapes (inherits from Produce)`	
Actions (methods):	`setPurchasePrice; getPurchasePrice; itemProfit(); getDescription(); setDescription(); getWeight(); getQuantityPerBundle();` **`getType();`**
Characteristics (data fields):	`purchasePrice; sellPrice; description; weight; quantityPerBundle;` **`type;`**

Note that for some of these classes, you have a "get" and "set" method that correspond to data fields that can change. For other data fields, you have only "get" methods for data fields that will not change (the weight of a product, its quantity in a sold bundle, etc.). Figure 9.2 shows how these mom-and-pop grocery store Java classes are hierarchically related to one another.

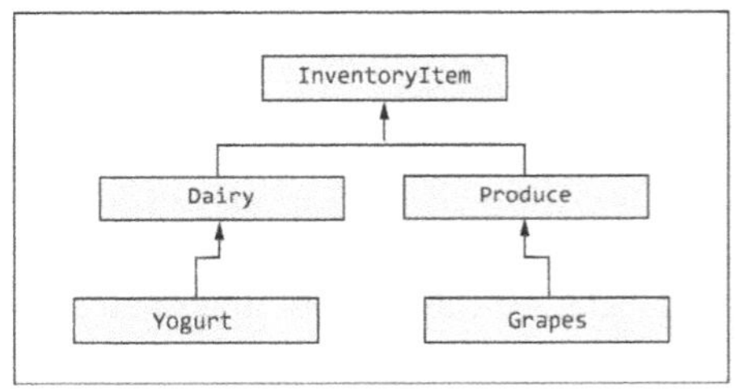

Figure 9.2. Inheritance Relationship between Mom-and-Pop Grocery Store Classes

Each class inherits characteristics from the one above it. This means that objects created from the `Grapes` and `Yogurt` classes will still share some characteristics and actions, but they will possess unique aspects of both, useful in their contexts within an information system. Objects of each class will contain information useful to them within the system and be capable of actions that are relevant to their object types. Notice as well that the "top-level" class, `InventoryItem`, contains both purchase price and sell price information as well as a method that allows for the profit for each item sold to be reported. Since all our inventory classes inherit from this top-level class, every item in our system can report its own potential profit after a sale. As a developer in an information system, you only have to define that behavior once, and it "trickles down" to all the objects in the inheritance hierarchy.

Later in the chapter, the code for all these inventory classes will be defined and used in an example. There is a lot to talk about before getting to that point! For now, it will benefit your studies of inheritance in Java to first focus on a simpler, more relatable example: persons, students, and graduate students.

Benefits of class inheritance: Class inheritance works pretty much the same in most object-oriented languages. A developer can define a new class in a way that tells Java that it inherits from, or **extends**, an older preexisting class. The new class (known as the **subclass**) will inherit the data fields and methods of the old class (known as the **superclass**).

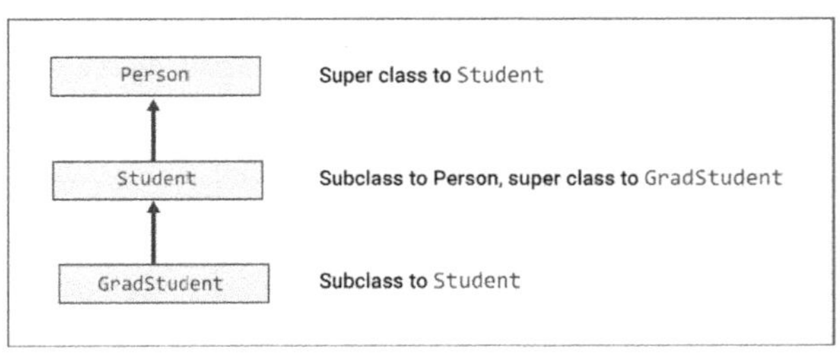

Figure 9.3. Relationship among `Person`, `Student`, and `GradStudent` Classes

Figure 9.3 shows this relationship with these terms using our person / student / graduate student example from earlier. Class inheritance provides a big benefit to developers in several ways. First, the developer writing the new class does not have to spend a great deal of time and effort rewriting all the code and functionality of the old class when defining the new one. The new subclass will inherit all that work, allowing the developer to get started on system building fast. Additionally, the developer may not even be able to view the source code of the preexisting subclass (if it is compiled already or proprietary)! Classes can (typically though with some exceptions) still be inherited from allowing the developer to build on their functionality. Since the developer does not have to duplicate the code and reimplement the old class's functionality, they can focus their time on the new actions and data the subclass will be capable of. Since some previous developer has already spent the time to figure out the implementation of the superclass's logic, the developer expanding this class with a new one can bring their expertise (in the subclass's specific context) to bear. Finally, class inheritance enables objects of **future** classes that do not exist yet to work with applications and systems that **currently exist** without having to change any of the current system's code. Because those future classes inherit from existing ones, they will have similar characteristics and behave in similar ways as current classes, making them predictable and possessing features similar to currently existing code.

Major concepts of class inheritance in Java: Before you dive in with a specific example of class inheritance, there are some important concepts to keep in mind about how this works in the Java programming language and some terms to be aware of:

- A **subclass** is the new class you (the developer) are creating and extends a preexisting class. A **superclass** is that preexisting (old) class that has actions and data you want to extend/expand upon. Since classes in Java are synonymously known as types, these are sometimes called **subtype** and **supertype**, respectively. You will also occasionally hear these called **child** and **parent** classes, and these terms will also be used occasionally in the textbook to help clarify relationships between classes. Table 9.1 helps summarize and assign these terms.
- The modifiers `public`, `private`, and `protected` will impact how certain superclass members (data fields and methods) can be accessed by the subclass. These will be defined and explored later in this chapter.

Table 9.1. Commonly Used Class Inheritance Terms

Old class you are expanding	New class that inherits from old
Superclass	Subclass
Supertype	Subtype
Parent class	Child class
Base class	Derived class

- In Java, **all** classes are in an inheritance relationship. Every class has a superclass, whether one is **explicitly** (purposefully) defined or not (**implicitly** defined by the compiler). Any particular class could be a subclass, inheriting from a parent class, and simultaneously be a superclass itself to another (child) class that inherits from it. Think of a family tree in the real world: a person could be a child to their parent and also have children of their own.
- In Java, a class can only inherit from **one parent class**, but a parent class can have **many child classes** inheriting from it.
- Powerful behaviors can be enabled via instance objects of classes in an inheritance relationship, behaviors that can happen automatically without additional code on the part of the developer.
- A method inherited from a superclass can be redefined in the child class to behave differently if the method is invoked upon a child class instance object.
- The constructor methods for our classes become **very important**, and you have to carefully consider which constructors exist in the superclass, what they do, and what additional functionality our subclass constructors might need.

All of these points will become clearer as you work through the examples and concepts in this chapter. Similar to the way that object-oriented programming makes you think a little differently and out of the box about development, class inheritance requires a similar shift in thinking. Remember that if development efforts are conducted wisely, then more work can be done with less code. Class inheritance benefits the IS developer: a great deal of time in IS is spent defining and representing real-world entities in systems through data models, business logic, and database design. The use of classes can be expanded to match any sophisticated subtyping efforts in our systems analysis and design and align both our development and data efforts.

SUMMARY POINTS

- Class inheritance allows a developer to build upon the work found in a preexisting class and extend that class's abilities into a new class that is more suited for a specific context.
- Class inheritance also prevents a developer from needing to duplicate what could be a great deal of work involved in implementing the logic found in a previous class. The developer can inherit that work and build upon it to speed along system development.
- A superclass is the preexisting class that is being inherited from, and the subclass is the new class that extends the abilities of that preexisting class.
- If a developer does not explicitly define a class as having a parent, Java will implicitly assume that the class's direct parent is the top-level `Object` class.
- A class can only define one parent class but can have many children classes.

QUICK PROBLEMS

1. **Think:** Consider an airplane as a general superentity / parent entity. What are some of the general characteristics of an airplane? Now think about a specific example of a plane (fighter jet, commercial airliner, etc.). What characteristics does the specific example inherit? What are new characteristics specific to that subentity / child entity?
2. **Think:** How can the developer save time by taking advantage of class inheritance? What is a major future benefit of existing object-oriented code that is provided by class inheritance?
3. **Coding:** Define a small Java class called `Event`. Objects of this class will store a `String` of the event's description and a `String` containing the date of the `Event`. What are some possible subclasses of `Event` that you could create? What new data fields and methods might they implement?

9.2 Defining the Subclass

In chapter 8, class `Person` was defined and explored in order to understand the basics of class definitions and usage in Java. In this chapter, class `Person` will be slightly modified, removing some of the previous methods and data fields. The access modifier for the `age` data field will be changed to `private`, and the modifier for the static data field `personCount` has been changed to `protected`. The shortened, full code listing for class `Person` is as follows:

Code Snippet 9.1

```
public class Person {
    public String eyeColor;
    public int height;
    private int age;                          // Changed to private
    public String name;
    protected static int personCount = 0;     // Changed to protected

    public Person()
    {
        this.eyeColor = "";
        this.height = 0;
        this.age = 0;
```

```
        this.name = "";
        personCount++;
    }

    public Person(String eyeColor,
            int height,
            int age,
            String name)
    {
        this.eyeColor = eyeColor;
        this.height = height;
        this.age = age;
        this.name = name;
        personCount++;
    }

    public String getEyeColor()
    {
        return eyeColor;
    }

    public void setEyeColor(String eyeColor)
    {
        this.eyeColor = eyeColor;
    }

    public int getAge()
    {
        return age;
    }


    public void setAge(int age)
    {
        this.age = age;
    }

    public double heightInFeet()
    {
        return (height / 12.0);
    }

    public static String countOfPersons()
    {
        return "Person Count: " + personCount;
    }

} // end of class Person
```

Access modifiers, class inheritance, and industry best practice: Information systems professionals should keep in mind that industry-experienced developers almost **never** assign data fields in a class a `public` access modifier. Data fields are typically given a `private` or `protected` access modifier to follow best practices for encapsulation. Doing so helps increase the security on your instance objects and protects their state from accidental, misguided, or malicious modification. For the `Person` and later `Student` classes exampled in the chapter, keep in mind that while some data fields are `public`, this is merely for learning purposes as you explore class inheritance in the Java language. The later full mom-and-pop grocery store example will use industry best practices for access modifiers.

Remember that access modifiers change permissions for class data fields and methods in the following ways:

- The modifier `public` opens access to the class member for code both inside and outside the class.
- The modifier `private` restricts access to the class member to **only** the code inside the class.
- The modifier `protected` restricts access to the class member to both code inside the class and code residing in children/subclasses of this parent class, with some exceptions for package location and subclass/non-subclass relationships that other classes may have with our class.

The `age` data field now has its access modifier set to private, severely restricting the ability of external code to change it or retrieve its current value. Only the code inside the class definition file (CDF) of `Person` can directly access `age`. The private access modifier will also prevent child class (subclass) code from directly accessing `age`, even though they inherit the data field. This will mean that our child classes will need to invoke methods of the parent class that **can** access it. A developer can make this data field access decision when, for example, they only want access to a data field to come through the getter and setter (accessor and mutator) methods, where things can be tightly controlled.

With the static data field `personCount` given a `protected` access modifier, code in the child classes of `Person` **can** directly access it and change it, but outside code (i.e., application code) cannot. This "keeps things in the family," as it were. In our case, though, both classes and our application all reside in the same package, meaning that this `protected` data field is "effectively" `public`. Developers coding the subclass will have to be aware of the access modifiers of the members of the parent class and adjust their class implementation accordingly.

Inheriting from class `Person`: The ins and outs of class inheritance in Java can be explored by continuing implementation of the person/student/graduate student example from earlier. The data fields and methods of class `Person` are already defined and will be inherited. For a subclass called `Student`, which inherits from `Person`, new data fields will be defined, such as GPA (as a `double`), class year (as an `int`), and their major (as a `String`), as additional data fields. Implementing the constructors for this new class as well as the accessors and mutators will help clarify how to think about class design and implementation in the context of class inheritance well.

Step 1: Create the `Student.java` Subclass File

Start with a new Java class file called `Student.java` (remember that it is a good habit to place each class within its own Java file). Create the new `Student` class file in the same package folder where the `Person` class sits. The new class will have the following listing when it is first created (`package` line of code not shown):

Code Snippet 9.2

```
public class Student {



}
```

Step 2: Indicate That Class `Student` Inherits from Class `Person`

So far, this is only a stand-alone class. Remember that all classes inherit from some other class, even if no inheritance is explicitly specified. Since a parent class is not explicitly defined here, Java will **implicitly** (i.e., indirectly or without you doing anything) set this class's parent class to the `Object` class. Class `Object` is the top-level class in Java: it has no parent, and **all** other classes in the Java package library eventually inherit from `Object`. The `Person` class also implicitly inherits from `Object`, since no parent is explicitly specified. While inheriting from `Object` is not a bad thing necessarily, you want `Student` to extend class `Person`'s functionality. You need to explicitly specify the inheritance relationship as follows (edit in **bold**):

Code Snippet 9.3

```
public class Student extends Person {



}
```

The `extends` keyword tells Java that this class directly and intentionally inherits from another class (whose name follows the `extends` command). `Student` explicitly inherits from class `Person`. Figure 9.4 now shows the "family tree" of these classes. Notice that the arrow of indication points up to the parent that a class inherits from.

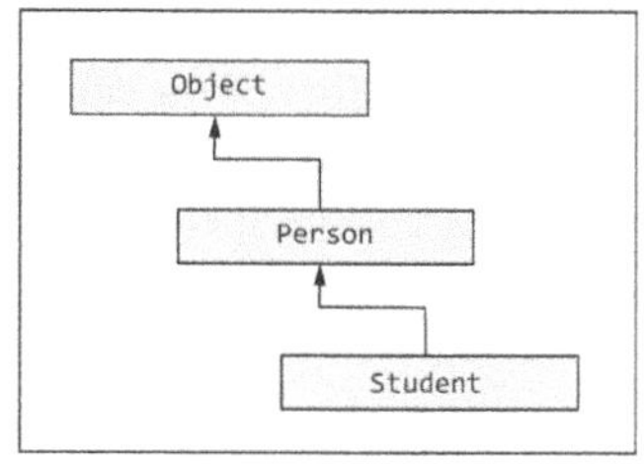

Figure 9.4. Classes `Object`, `Person`, and `Student` and Their Inheritance Relationship

Step 3: Testing Out Your New Subclass and Its Inherited Members

Due to class inheritance and the access modifiers set in class `Person`, instance objects of class `Student` will have access to all the methods that objects of class `Person` can access. Instance objects of `Student` will also contain all data fields inherited from class `Person`. For example, age was inherited from `Person` and has a public access modifier allowing direct access within a `Student` instance object:

Code Snippet 9.4

```
Student infoSysA = new Student();
infoSysA.name = "Sarah";
```

Since `Student` inherits from `Person`, each `Student` instance object has all the same data fields contained within that `Person` instance objects also have. `Student` objects have a `name` data field, and so do `Person` instance objects.

A few things to remember:

- In this example, an instance object of class `Student`, **not** an instance object of class `Person`, has been created. Inheritance relationships between classes do not mean that the parent class automatically has an object created at the same time that a child class object is instantiated. This is a common misunderstanding. **Creating an instance object of a child class only creates one object—the one for that class. In this example, only a `Student` instance object is created.**
- Remember that when you do not explicitly specify a constructor for your class, Java will implicitly create a "default"/zero-argument constructor for you temporarily each time you create an instance object of that class. Since you do not have any constructors for class `Student`, Java is "creating" one for you. This will stop as soon as you define **any** constructors for class `Student`. Java is also invoking the `Person` class's default constructor, and we will discuss how/why this happens later.
- Notice that the above code works just fine, and in the CDF for class `Student`, you did **not** have to redeclare any of the data fields from class `Person`, nor did you have to re-create any of the methods of class `Person`: class inheritance allows us to inherit these for all of the `Student` class instance objects!

Consider the following line of code for our application:

```
studentSarah.age = 25;
```

If you write this line of code, the compiler will flag it with the error "`age has private access in Person`." Remember that the access modifier for `age` in `Person` was changed to `private`, severely restricting access. In this case (as you will have to do for the `Student` class constructors shortly), invoke one of the inherited parent class's methods that do have access:

```
studentSarah.setAge(25);
```

Understand the sequence here:

- The `.setAge()` setter method is defined in class `Person`. Since it is defined in that class, it has access to all the `private` data fields of class `Person` and can change them.
- Class `Student` inherits all the public member methods and data fields of class `Person`. Since `.setAge()` is a `public` method in class `Person`, `Student` can inherit it, and instance objects of class `Person` can have this method invoked upon them, as you have done here.

You do not have to redefine a `.setAge()` method for `Student`, since one is already inherited from `Person`. The developer of the `Person` class has already solved this problem, and there is no need to "reinvent the wheel."

Step 4: Adding Data Fields That Are Unique to Subclass `Student`

The ability of the subclass to inherit data fields and inherit access to the member methods of the parent class is extremely helpful. Even so, child classes should expand on the abilities of a parent class by defining functionality for a more specific context. Remember that you do not have to spend (i.e., waste) time redefining everything inherited from the parent class. The **new** data fields, methods, and functionality of the subclass will be the focus. A good place to start is with the data fields of the child class (a good place to start for any Java class):

Code Snippet 9.5

```
public class Student extends Person {

    private double GPA;              // Subclass Data Field
    public int classYear;            // Subclass Data Field
    public String majorSubject;      // Subclass Data Field

}
```

Careful consideration of the data fields and their access modifiers is important, especially for IS professionals who are trying to align the object code with the data model / business logic elicited for the IS implementation. In this case, it is probably a good idea to control access to the `Student` object's `GPA` so that external code cannot change it directly. You can use a mutator method to protect the values that can be set for this data field. Assigning it a `private` modifier ensures that any future child classes will need to use our mutator logic as well, since their code will not have direct access. For `classYear` and `majorSubject`, giving these `public` access modifiers will allow full and direct access to these from both the subclass and the application as well.

Are these all that are needed? More data fields could be added if the elicited requirements and business logic require it (planning you should have done prior to writing any code, by the way!). Keep in mind that since this class inherits from class `Person`, instance objects of class `Student` will contain the same data fields as are found in all `Person` instance objects. You can change those that are given `public` or `protected` access modifiers directly, while you will need to use the parent class's methods to change or access those marked `private`.

You can test out access to both the parent and child class data fields like so:

Code Snippet 9.6

```
Student studentDakota = new Student();

studentDakota.GPA = 4.0; // Error: Private Access only
studentDakota.majorSubject = "CIS";
studentDakota.classYear = 3;
studentDakota.name = "Dakota";
studentDakota.setAge(21);
```

The student's `GPA` is not directly accessible, since it has `private` access. A mutator (i.e., "setter") method will be defined later for class `Student` to provide a means to access `GPA`. `Student` inherits `age`, but it is `private` as well, so the inherited method `.setAge()` should be used to change it. The others are `public` and can be changed directly.

Step 5: Defining Constructor(s) for Your Subclass

When a constructor is not defined in your subclass, Java creates a zero-argument constructor for you (like it does for all classes in this situation). Good development practice is to specifically define all constructors and not let Java create any transitory ones during execution. Keep in mind these constructor behaviors:

- Since all classes inherit from other classes (or from class `Object` if there is no explicit inheritance defined by the developer), every constructor of a class automatically invokes the zero-arg ("default") constructor of its parent class. Our classes have been doing this the whole time without us knowing! For example, when an instance object of `Person` is created like the following, the `Person()` constructor invokes, behind the scenes and automatically, the default constructor of the `Object` class (which would be `Object()`):

```
Person someone = new Person();
```

This does not have a major impact on development efforts, but you should be aware it's happening. If you define a parent class that does not have a default constructor and then define a child class and Java attempts to invoke your parent's default constructor (and does not find it), an error will occur. That's why it is always **good habit** (and often a **requirement** of many frameworks) to create a zero-arg constructor for all classes!

- The exception to that prior point (automatic constructor calling) is if you specify in your child class's constructors exactly which parent class constructor you want to invoke. The rule here is that this call to the parent class constructor **must** be the **first line of code in the constructor!** If you tell Java which constructor to invoke, you control more of the process.
- Having a child class constructor invoke a constructor from its parent continues the idea of **not repeating a lot of code and effort**. Remember that the parent class constructor has access to any private data fields, has logic in it that some other developer already took the time and effort to perfect, and might do 80% of the initialization work you need. Take advantage of that (the "Do not reinvent the wheel" rule)!
- From **within the code of the child class**, you can access members (constructors, methods, and data fields, if you need to) of the parent class using the keyword `super`.

To start simple, let's define a zero-arg constructor for our `Student` class, and you can see all the points discussed here in action:

Code Snippet 9.7

```
public Student()
{
    super(); // Invokes superclass's zero-arg constructor
    // Has to ALWAYS be the first line of code in constructor!
    this.GPA = 0.0;
    this.classYear = 0;
    this.majorSubject = "n/a";
}
```

Notice the first line in the body of this constructor. Normally, a constructor is invoked from the application side like so: `Person()`. The keyword `super` allows access to something in the parent class. The `super` keyword is a placeholder for the parent class's name. This first line of code instructs Java to invoke the default constructor of the class (`Person`) that is the parent of this class (`Student`). That constructor in `Person` has access to all the inherited data fields, including the private ones, so it can do a lot of the work that you would have to do (and some of the work that you may not have permission to do!). The parent class constructor in `Person` will also perform the work of incrementing the static data field `personCount` so you do not have to keep up with it—a `Student` is a person after all! After it has performed its work, it ends, and execution returns to our (`Student`) constructor, then you can initialize all of the rest of the data fields that are "new" to our local class. Figure 9.5 shows this sequence.

A **very** important point to keep in mind here: remember that in all of this, you are initializing a newly instantiated object of

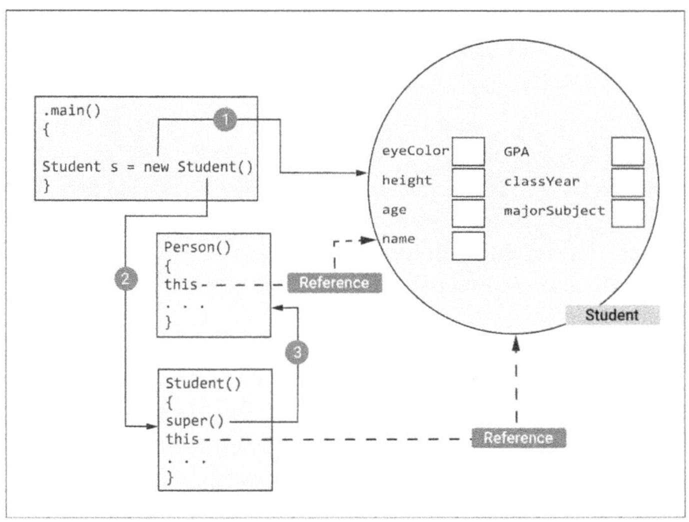

Figure 9.5. `Student` Instance Object Creation and Constructor Invocation Sequence

the Student class only. Even though the Person zero-arg constructor is being invoked from the Student zero-arg constructor, remember that **constructors do not create objects—they merely help initialize them**! The new operator creates the object. Have you ever had a parent or friend help you build or construct something (a building-block version of a shoebill stork maybe)? Calling the parent class constructor is like asking someone for help: "I am building this one thing, and I need you to walk in the room and help me. When you are done, you can leave, and I'll finish the job." This is a great way to think about parent class constructor invocation from the child's constructor: **there is one instance object, and both the child class's constructor and the parent class's constructor are helping initialize it**!

A second, multiparameter constructor is needed for the Student class:

Code Snippet 9.8

```
public Student(String eyeColor,
            int height,
            int age,
            String name,
            double GPA,
            int classYear,
            String majorSubject)
{
    super(eyeColor, height,
            age, name);
    this.GPA = GPA;
    this.classYear = classYear;
    this.majorSubject = majorSubject;
}
```

Remember that either of the Student class constructors can be invoked from an application or code written somewhere else. In either case, it will be that invoking code's responsibility to pass the correct argument data into the Student constructor invoked. For this new student constructor, all the data for both the inherited Person data fields and the data for the Student class data fields is required. Notice that in the first line of this constructor's body, the four-argument Person constructor is invoked first and passes the data it requires. The Student constructor then performs the work of using that data to initialize the Student object's data fields. Control then passes back to the child class constructor so it can finish initialization of the Student object (with GPA, majorSubject, and classYear).

Another very important point: since you are invoking the parent class constructor from the child class's constructor, the reference variable this that you have seen previously always refers to the instance object of the invoking class. Remember that all this was kicked off with a line of application code similar to this:

```
Student someStudent = new Student("Blue",70,21,"Julie", 4.0, 4,"CIS");
```

This line of code in an application starts the chain of constructor invocations. Notice that before the constructor is ever called, the new operator creates the Student instance object **first**. After this, the Student constructor is invoked, and it acts upon the newly created instance object. When the Student constructor "calls for help" from its parent class's constructor, the parent constructor helps initialize **the Student instance object**. In both invocations, the reference variable this **always refers to the instance object you are initializing, the one created using the new operator**.

Step 6: Defining Methods for the Subclass

Methods can be added to the subclass to enable actions that are specific to both it and its objects. The easiest would be to add accessors ("getters") and mutators ("setters") for all data fields. For those data fields with a private access modifier, this is especially important. Any logic that targets data field values, ranges, masking, and so on should be placed in the accessors/mutators as well. Implementing these for the GPA data field would look similar to this:

Code Snippet 9.9

```
public double getGPA()
{
    return this.GPA;
}

public boolean setGPA(double GPA)
{
    if ((GPA >= 0.0) && (GPA <= 5.0))
    {
        this.GPA = GPA;
        return true;
    }
    else
    {
        return false;
    }
}
```

Notice that `.setGPA()` returns a `boolean` value instead of simply having `void` as its return type. This is one strategy (of many) to prevent bad-quality data or ranges of the `GPA` that might fall outside of the business rules of the client. In this case, GPA for students should be between 0 and 5.0, inclusive. If the range of the received parameter value is OK, the `Student` instance object's `GPA` data field is set to the value and returns `true` (to indicate success). Else a value of `false` is returned and does nothing. In some cases, it might be a good idea to let the application determine the upper range, which would change the setter like so:

Code Snippet 9.10

```
public boolean setGPA(double GPA)
{
    if (GPA >= 0.0)
    {
        this.GPA = GPA;
        return true;
    }
    else
    {
        return false;
    }
}
```

Here, no upper limit is checked, as other usage contexts in the future may allow GPA values higher than 5.0. Since other `Student` class data fields are `public`, getters and setters are not specifically needed, but you should implement them for good practice. Since industry best practice states "No public data fields at all!" in your class, changing them to `protected` and creating getters/setters for them would be a great next step in your learning.

Summarizing the Steps to Define and Implement a Subclass

1. Create your subclass Java file **without** a `main()` method.
2. Add the `extends` keyword followed by the name of the superclass you are extending.
3. Test your subclass out by creating an instance object of it (optional). Note how you can access any public members inherited from the superclass via the instance object's reference variable.
4. Define any data fields that are unique and new to the subclass. Any inherited data fields do **not** have to be redefined.
5. Define any and all constructors you feel your subclass should have. A zero-argument constructor should at least be added (as good industry practice recommends).
6. Define any and all methods of your subclass. Any methods that are inherited from the superclass do **not** have to be defined, though they might be overloaded in the subclass (see later in this chapter).

SUMMARY POINTS

- The access modifiers assigned to the class members of a superclass can impact the code and implementation approach of the subclass, potentially restricting direct access to some class members.
- The extends keyword is used to define a direct, explicit inheritance relationship between a class and another class intended as its superclass.
- Though Java will "create" a temporary zero-arg constructor for your classes (including subclasses) if you do not define one, it is recommended to explicitly define a zero-arg constructor for every class you create, even subclasses.
- Since a subclass inherits all the data fields from the parent, redeclaring these data fields in the subclass is not necessary, though some data fields may not be directly accessible due to access modifier settings.
- Invocation of a superclass's constructor from a subclass constructor must occur on the first line of the constructor body; otherwise, the compiler will throw an error.
- Invocation of a superclass's constructor suspends the need for the developer to rewrite all the potentially complex initialization code that has already been implemented in the superclass's constructors.
- When a subclass constructor invokes a superclass constructor, both constructors work to initialize the subclass instance object. The `this` reference variable refers to this instance object.
- The developer of a subclass can define and add as many methods to the subclass as they need. These new methods will then be available to the application developer using the subclass along with any methods inherited by the subclass.

QUICK PROBLEMS

1. **Coding:** Add a partial constructor to the `Student` class. This constructor will only require some of the data fields as input parameters from the application. You can choose which ones to require. Initialize your data fields with these parameter values.
2. **Think:** What would happen if every constructor in the subclass simply called the zero-arg constructor of the superclass for each and every subclass constructor?
3. **Coding:** Think of an appropriate data field to add for a `Student` class. Add this data field to the CDF. Modify all your constructors to account for this new data field.

9.3 Method Overriding

The ability of developers to extend a class's functionality and data model into another class can save time and bolster development efforts within an information system. Any number of child classes can be extended, each with its own adapted data model and functionality, each useful in specific contexts. Inheritance enables the developer to quickly adapt to many processing possibilities, keeping their applications and system flexible to real-world data and logic needs. Inheritance also enables future code to be compatible with code that is written today.

Changing inherited method behavior: When engaging in class inheritance, developers may want to not only inherit functionality from a parent class but also **redefine** that functionality and have it behave differently when child class objects are in use. Methods inherited from the parent class may change or use the values of only the inherited data fields (which is always the case by the way: the developer who wrote the parent class could not predict the future data fields you would put in your class!). You may have cases where many other developers are accustomed to calling a specific method from the parent class in their applications, and when using your class, you would want them to invoke the same method (many times; doing otherwise would "break" existing code!). So in these cases, it is helpful to **override** the method inherited from the parent class to define different functionality for it to carry out when invoked in the context of your child class. The method will work one way on objects of the parent and a different way when working with objects from your child class. Figure 9.6 gives you a general idea of what method overriding will look like in the context of class inheritance.

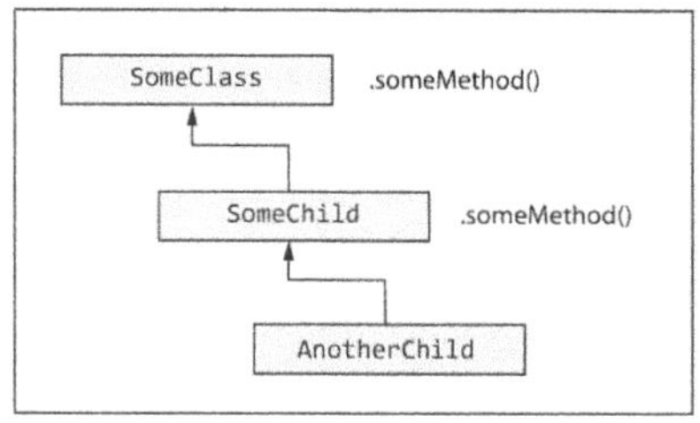

Figure 9.6. Some Example Classes with an Overridden Method in the Child Class

There are a few rules to keep in mind when overriding a method:

- For the method you wish to override, the **signature** of the method in the **child** class **must exactly match** the signature of the method in the **parent** class: same name, same order/number/data types of the parameters.
- The access modifier for the method must be the same (it is part of the signature, after all).
- The return type must be the same.
- The body (code of the method) **can** be different—of course, this is the whole point of method overriding! The code is the behavior, and you want behavior for the child class version that differs from the parent class version.

Overriding the `.toString()` method of the `Object` class: To demonstrate methods overriding simply, consider the "family tree" of classes that you saw in figure 9.5: `Object`, `Person`, and `Student`. Recall that the `Object` class is the top-level class for **all** classes in Java.* Since our `Person` class does not explicitly extend another class, Java implicitly extends the `Object` class in class `Person` (as it does for all classes with no explicit parent specified). The `Object` class has several methods that are common to all classes and their objects in Java (since all classes inherit from it eventually). One of these methods is the `.toString()` method. Here is a summary of the official Oracle documentation for this method:

Return type	Name	Description
`String`	`.toString()`	Returns a `String` value that describes the object the method is invoked upon

Notice that this method is not `static`, meaning it is intended to be invoked upon instance objects of classes that inherit this method from class `Object`. The `.toString()` method is one that is often overridden by Java developers who want to give their class's instance objects a way to describe themselves. This description could simply be "I am a `Person` object!" or a concatenation of data field values yielding a useful description of a particular object. Additionally, since the `.toString()` method is inherited by all Java classes from the `Object` class, there are many other classes and their code in the Java library that expect that your class has overridden `.toString()`, and those classes will often invoke this method upon your object automatically. As a OO Java developer, it is a good habit to override `.toString()` in all your classes and think carefully about the description it will return.

For example, consider the invocation of `.toString()` upon some already instantiated `Student` objects:

Code Snippet 9.11

```
System.out.println(studentSarah.toString());
System.out.println(studentDakota.toString());
```

This code produces the following output when the application runs:

```
com.javaforis.chapter9.Student@28a418fc
com.javaforis.chapter9.Student@5305068a
```

Notice that no error occurs. `Person` inherits the `.toString()` method from `Object`, and since `Student` inherits from `Person`, `Student` objects can have `.toString()` invoked upon them also. In all these cases, **the version of the `.toString()` method as defined in class `Object` is the one invoked**! Notice the output is not

* https://docs.oracle.com/en/java/javase/14/docs/api/java.base/java/lang/Object.html.

very descriptive (unless you really like hexadecimal representations of memory objects . . .). But you can see that the default behavior of the `.toString()` method is to literally describe the objects in memory.

Many of the classes in Java will often assume you have `.toString()` implemented and automatically invoke the `.toString()` method upon your objects. It can do this because all classes inherit from Object. For example,

Code Snippet 9.12

```
System.out.println(studentSarah);
System.out.println(studentDakota);
```

Running these will print the same object descriptions. Java knows that since all classes inherit from Object, any attempt to print a complex data-type object will automatically invoke `.toString()` upon it. Since a hexadecimal description of `Person` and `Student` objects is not very helpful, it would be helpful to override `.toString()` to behave differently in these classes.

First, start the overriding process in the parent class `Person`. Recall the `.toString()` method signature from the Oracle documentation displayed earlier:

```
public String toString()
```

Per method overriding rules, the signature is re-created exactly in the parent class `Person` (child to class `Object`) in order to signal to Java that overriding is occurring:

Code Snippet 9.13

```
// Added to class Person:
public String toString()
{
    return "Name: " + this.name
           + ", age: " + this.age;
}
```

The method's signature is exactly the same as is found in the parent class `Object`. The code of the method differs, and this is appropriate: you want this method to behave differently when invoked upon `Person` instance objects. You can test this out in your application by instantiating some `Person` objects and invoking `.toString()` upon them:

Code Snippet 9.14

```
Person somePerson = new Person();

somePerson.name = "Skyler";
somePerson.setAge(30);

System.out.println(somePerson.toString());
```

When you run this, it will produce the following code:

```
Name: Skyler, age: 30
```

Notice that now you have redefined how the `.toString()` method will work when `Person` class objects are the target. Because the `Person` class has its own **locally defined version** (local to the `Person` class), Java will invoke the `Person` version instead. And since the `Student` class inherits methods from `Person`, consider the following code and its output using both our `Person` object and our earlier `Student` objects (here, the explicit and implicit invocations of `.toString()` are mixed):

Code Snippet 9.15

```
System.out.println(studentSarah);
System.out.println(studentDakota);
System.out.println(somePerson.toString());
```

The output for this code when it is executed is the following:

```
Name: Sarah, age: 25
Name: Dakota, age: 21
Name: Skyler, age: 30
```

The Student class inherits the specific version from Person (its immediate parent). Since Student has not overridden .toString() itself, that Person class version is invoked when used upon Student instance objects. You can now override .toString() within the Student class and in doing so see a second use for the super keyword (in **bold**):

Code Snippet 9.16

```
// Added to class Student
public String toString()
{
    String returnString = super.toString();
    returnString += ", Major: " + this.majorSubject
            + ", Year: " + this.classYear
            + ", GPA: " + this.getGPA();

    return returnString;
}
```

Here is a summary of the major activities happening in this overridden method version:

- The Person class version of .toString() was overloaded by re-creating the signature for the method exactly in the Student class. Now the Student class has its own specific version.
- The method starts by invoking the .toString() version of the Person class. Think about this: somewhere, someone will invoke the Student class's .toString() method on a Student object (we want the Student object to describe itself). That means through all of this, the this reference variable references a Student instance object. If you invoke the Person class's version of .toString(), it will describe the Student class instance object you are working upon. Since both a Person object and a Student object have a name and age data field, the parent class's .toString() will be able to describe them both. You retrieve this description and store it in a local variable.
- Once the parent class's .toString() has performed its work, it extracts the major, year, and GPA of the Student object it is acting upon and adds it to the description.
- This description is returned as the method's String return type.
- The invocation of the parent class's .toString() method was completely optional. The compiler does not require this. In this case, it was convenient to do, since we wanted to include the age value in the description, and the child class does not have direct access to that data field.

Now that you have a version of .toString() in **both** the parent and the child class, an interesting behavior can be observed. Consider our three print statements from earlier. **Without changing anything about them**, you will now see a different output:

Code Snippet 9.17

```
System.out.println(studentSarah);
System.out.println(studentDakota);
System.out.println(somePerson.toString());
```

Console output:

```
Name: Sarah, age: 25, Major: n/a, Year: 0, GPA: 0.0
Name: Dakota, age: 21, Major: CIS, Year: 3, GPA: 0.0
Name: Skyler, age: 30
```

Java invoked the version of the .toString() method found in the Person class for Person instance objects, and it invoked the version found in the Student class for Student instance objects. All we, the developer, had to do was to simply call the method and let Java figure out which version to call. This is often called "method versioning," and its part of the dynamic abilities that class inheritance allows us to leverage. Figure 9.7 walks you through two different method-versioning scenarios and how Java searches the "family tree" for the most-locally-declared version of an inherited method. Notice that in "scenario A" of figure 9.7, the .toString() method is only overridden in the Person class, so when invoked upon a Student instance object, it is the Person class's version that is called.

Overriding versus overloading: Chapter 6 discusses the topic of method overloading (where a second version of a method is created in the same class). In this section, you have now learned about overriding. When defining a child class, both of these concepts can coexist. Consider the `.getAge()` method defined in the `Person` class. For demonstration's sake, you can both override the version inherited from the `Person` class and overload it. This will create a second version locally in the `Student` class:

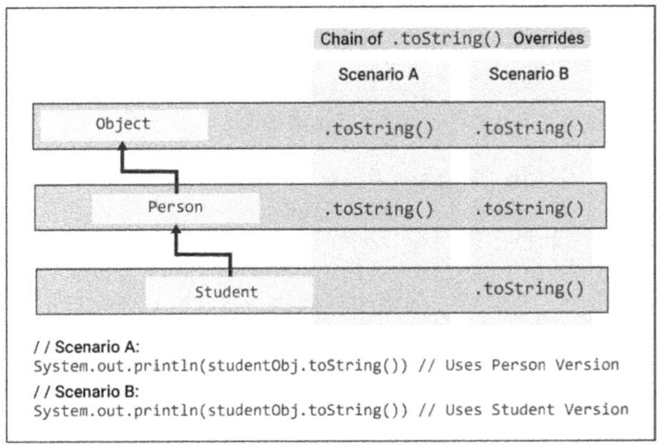

Figure 9.7. Method Versioning and Depth of Method Overriding

Code Snippet 9.18

```
// Both of these are added to class Student

// This is the overriding version:
public int getAge()
{
    System.out.print("Student Age Requested!");
    return super.getAge();
}

// Here is the overloaded version in the same Student class:
public int getAge(int ageThreshold)
{
    if (super.getAge() < ageThreshold)
    {
        System.out.println("Student Age Under Threshold");
        return ageThreshold;
    }
    else
        return super.getAge();
}
```

Here are the invocations:

```
System.out.println(studentDakota.getAge());
System.out.println(studentDakota.getAge(30));
```

The console output is the following:

```
Student Age Requested!
21
Student Age Under Threshold
30
```

There are some important points to notice in these two methods:

- This code overrides the `.getAge()` from the parent class in the `Student` (child) class.
- This code then overloads `.getAge()` in the `Student` class, defining a second version.
- To prevent an infinite recursive loop, be careful to use `super` to call the parent class version from the child class code. If the code `this.getAge()` was used by mistake, the method would just call itself locally in the `Student` class forever (infinitely looping).

Notice that with both invocation lines of code, first Java figures out which version of `.getAge()` to invoke. Since the `Student` class has versions defined locally, it finds these versions. Then based on the method signature,

Java determines which version within `Student` to call. Java does all the hard work of determining which class and which method version within that class to invoke.

Overriding a parent class's method is an optional choice for the developer. In many cases, the inherited method will work just fine. Often, the developer will want to change or extend the functionality (as you have seen in this chapter's examples) of inherited methods to ensure they enhance the value of the abilities of the child class better. In our examples earlier, you very well could have simply overridden `.toString()` in the `Person` class and left it at that; the descriptions would have been fine. But for our purposes, giving more descriptive info for `Student` objects could help the class add value to whatever application or system you are building. Overriding decisions will be up to you as you build classes that extend previous ones. You will need to consider questions like "Will this enhance the functionality of the system?" or "Will other developers who might use this child class find it useful?" to determine how much and to what extent you implement method overriding in your child classes.

SUMMARY POINTS

- Developers implementing a subclass often want an inherited method to behave differently when invoked upon/by that subclass's objects. This is known as method overriding.
- Successfully overriding an inherited method depends on re-creating the method's signature exactly (access modifier, return type, name, and parameter list configuration).
- The body of an overridden method can differ and in fact should: this is where the locally different behavior emerges.
- Methods of the Object class, like the `.toString()` method, are commonly overridden by Java developers, since all classes inherit from this top-level class and these methods are common to all classes. This helps increase compatibility of unrelated classes in some application context.
- Method versioning occurs when Java tries to determine which inherited or overridden method to invoke based on how "locally" defined the method is in comparison to where the invoked-upon instance object's class sits in the "family tree" of class inheritance the class belongs to.
- You can invoke an overridden (parent class) method from the code body of the overriding (child class) method when the previous version performs logic that might come in handy.

QUICK PROBLEMS

1. **Coding:** Override the `.heightInFeet()` method so that the height value it returns is rounded up to the nearest foot for `Student` objects.
2. **Think:** What happens if you invoke a child class method whose parent also inherited the method? Where does Java go to attempt to find a definition for the method?
3. **Think:** What happens if you change the parameter list for an overridden method in a child class to differ from the one defined for the parent class version?

9.4 Understanding Polymorphism

For any given class, you cannot fully predict what future classes will be created that inherit from either your class or any one of the subclasses that you or other developers have created. But because of how class inheritance works in Java, you can know that future classes will inherit the methods and data fields of your parent class. We have discussed how class inheritance enables current code to be compatible with future classes that do not exist yet. Class inheritance enables you to predict both the future behavior of classes and the future behavior of code that **uses those classes.** Through a concept known as **polymorphic behavior,** future instance objects of child classes can work wherever code has been written that expects instance objects of a parent or ancestor class. Commonly, you hear polymorphism described as the ability of objects to take on "many forms" (which is what polymorphism literally means: many forms!). In this case, the "many" part of "many forms" would refer to the data types of the object's ancestor classes. We can demonstrate this with a few examples.

Dynamic binding during method invocation: Class inheritance in Java can impact the way you use reference variables and the behavior that is expected when methods are invoked upon their referenced objects. Recall that objects are created and stored on the heap (i.e., "free store") and that you work with variables whose value is an address where that object can be found (i.e., reference variables). These variables reference the object on the heap, and so far both the reference variable and the object have the same data type. To understand how class inheritance impacts our usage of reference variables, consider the following three scenarios:

Code Snippet 9.19

```
// Scenario A:
Person aPerson = new Person("green",72,21,"Braden");
System.out.println(aPerson.toString());

//Scenario B:
Person bPerson = new Student("blue",70,20,"Julie",4.0,4,"CIS");
System.out.println(bPerson.toString());

//Scenario C:
Student cPerson = new Person(); // Type Conversion Error
cPerson.toString(); // Will not execute due to error on prior line
```

What will be the output when these run? For the first two scenarios, the output will look like this:

```
Name: Braden, age: 21
Name: Julie, age: 20, Major: CIS, Year: 0, GPA: 4.0
```

The creation and usage of a `Person` object in scenario A look very normal. In scenario B, look carefully at the instantiation line. On the left of the assignment operator, the reference variable is given a data type of `Person` but copied into it the reference for a newly created `Student` object. A `Person` reference variable references a `Student` object. This is allowed by the compiler and demonstrates polymorphic behavior. To understand polymorphism, consider what actually printed and what occurred when scenarios A and B executed (scenario C will be discussed soon):

- In scenario A, the reference variable with data-type `Person` references an actual instance object of the `Person` class. Java invokes the `Person` version of the `.toString()` method that was implemented earlier.
- In scenario B, the reference variable with data-type `Person` references an instance object of the `Student` class. **Java allows a parent class–type reference variable to reference an object instantiated from a child class type.** When the `.toString()` method is invoked upon this `Person` reference variable, Java invokes the `Student` version of the `.toString()` method.
- Notice that with scenario C, the reverse is not true: **a subclass-type reference variable cannot reference an instance object of one of its parent class objects.**

Although the reference variable itself has a `Person` data type, notice that Java is deciding which version of the `.toString()` method to invoke (either the `Person` or `Student` class version) according to **the data type of the actual object referenced!** Java's ability to do this is a critical component of polymorphic behavior in modern object-oriented code. Keep in mind as well that these instance objects do not exist until the application is actively running. So this choice of which class's method version to invoke when the line of code in scenario B is executed is what is known as a **runtime decision**, and this decision overall is known as **dynamic binding.** Java dynamically binds, or associates, a method version as the one that will be executed when that method is invoked upon a particular reference variable. To understand the "dynamic" part of this process, think about the following example:

Code Snippet 9.20

```
Person dPerson = new Student(); // References Student Object
System.out.println(dPerson.toString());

dPerson = new Person(); // References a Person Object
System.out.println(dPerson.toString());
```

Console output:

```
Name: , age: 0, Major: n/a, Year: 0, GPA: 0.0
Name: , age: 0
```

Notice that the reference variable `dPerson` retains its data type of `Person` throughout after declaration. Initially, it is given the address of a `Student` instance object, then rereferenced after the first call to `.toString()` with the address of a `Person` instance object, then the method is called again. These objects are not created until the application is running ("runtime"), and so Java has to dynamically, on the fly, decide which version of `.toString()` to call, since the method invocation is, both times, on the same reference variable `dPerson`. Since, in the first invocation of `.toString()`, the reference variable references a `Student` instance object, Java binds the calls to `.toString()` on the reference variable `dPerson` to the `Student` class version of the method. After this, the reference variable is reassigned, and then Java binds the `Person` class version to the invocations on that variable. So the rule of thumb here is to always observe which class the object referred to has been instantiated from, and you will always know which method version will be invoked!

Polymorphic code—two examples: To understand how useful polymorphic behavior in object-oriented code can be, consider two more examples. Consider the following application code that uses both the `Person` and the `Student` classes (this could be another Java main class in the same package if you wanted to create a second file to try this code out):

Code Snippet 9.21

```
public static void main(String[] args) {
        Person a = new Person();
        a.name = "Jamie";
        Person b = new Student();
        b.name = "Kris";
        Student c = new Student();
        c.name = "Merrill";

        printPersonDescription(a);
        printPersonDescription(b);
        printPersonDescription(c);

    }

    public static void printPersonDescription(Person p)
    {
        System.out.println(p.toString());
    }
}
```

So we have added a static method `printPersonDescription()` to this new application, and the method accepts a reference to a `Person` instance object. It might be better to say it **expects** a reference to a `Person` instance object. Polymorphic behavior allows us to use a reference to an object of the `Person` class **or any of its child classes** in the place of the expected referenced defined in the method's header. Notice now the application code. Three objects are created, one `Person` and two `Students`, and these are referenced by two `Person` instance objects and one `Student` instance object, respectively. And that's OK: when we are invoking the static method `printPersonCount()`, we pass to it all three references. Because of polymorphic behavior, all three invocations will work: in each case, Java will examine the data type of the actual object passed and dynamically bind the appropriate version of the `.toString()` method from the class the object is instantiated from to that method call for that reference variable. This binding will stay with that reference variable until it references another instance object data type, then the binding will be dynamically reset again, and so on at runtime.

With this example, you can clearly see how code that is written today can be compatible with future classes that may not even exist yet. For example, if you define a `GradStudent` class, you can then use its objects in the application the same as you would any of the two ancestor classes (`main()` and other class header information omitted here). First, the `GradStudent` class definition:

Code Snippet 9.22

```
public class GradStudent extends Student {
    public Person thesisAdvisor;

    public GradStudent()
    {
        super();
        this.thesisAdvisor = null;
    }

    public Person getThesisAdvisor()
    {
        return this.thesisAdvisor;
    }

    public void setThesisAdvisor(Person thesisAdvisor)
    {
        if (thesisAdvisor != null)
            this.thesisAdvisor = thesisAdvisor;
    }

    public String toString()
    {
        String resultString = super.toString();
        if (this.thesisAdvisor != null)
            resultString += "\n\tAdvisor: "
+ this.thesisAdvisor.toString();
        else
            resultString += "\n\tAdvisor: N/A";

        return resultString;
    }

} // End of GradStudent
```

With the GradStudent class defined, it can now be used in the application:

Code Snippet 9.23

```
public static void main(String[] args) {

    // In the Application
    Person a = new Person();
    a.name = "Jamie";
    Person b = new Student();
    b.name = "Kris";
    Student c = new Student();
    c.name = "Merrill";

    // GradStudent object
    GradStudent d = new GradStudent();
    d.setThesisAdvisor(a);
    d.name = "Noel";

    System.out.println((new Person()).toString());

    printPersonDescription(a);
    printPersonDescription(b);
    printPersonDescription(c);

    // Send GradStudent reference to
    //  app method.
```

```
    printPersonDescription(d);

}

public static void printPersonDescription(Object p)
{
    System.out.println(p.toString());
}
```

The output for this is similar to earlier but now with the output for the `GradStudent`:

```
Name: Jamie, age: 0
Name: Kris, age: 0, Major: n/a, Year: 0, GPA: 0.0
Name: Merrill, age: 0, Major: n/a, Year: 0, GPA: 0.0
Name: Noel, age: 0, Major: n/a, Year: 0, GPA: 0.0
   Advisor: Name: Jamie, age: 0
```

Developers who extend your classes one, two, or ten years from now can use your application (and particularly the application's method) to print the description for their classes. If their future classes have a `.toString()` method implemented, then that version will invoke when they pass their objects to your method. If not, then the most recently defined `.toString()` method closest to the classes they have created will invoke (this could be the one in `GradStudent` or the one in `Person` if they started their descendent classes from that point in the "family tree"). Polymorphic behavior allows objects of one descendent data type to "take the form" of the data type of one of its ancestors and work just fine. Finally, you could adjust the application method like this and make it even more broadly compatible (changes in **bold**):

Code Snippet 9.24

```
    public static void printPersonDescription(Object p)
    {
        System.out.println(p.toString());
    }
```

Notice now that the method expects a reference to an `Object` class instance object instead of `Person`. Since **all classes** in Java **eventually** inherit from the `Object` class, now every possible object of every class, present and future, is compatible with your method.

Classes, subclasses, and `ArrayList<E>`: Consider a third example where polymorphic behavior of class objects can come in handy: when they are used with the `Collections` framework as well as with simple Java arrays. Consider this full program listing, which uses the `Student` and `GradStudent` classes from this chapter:

Full Program 9.1

```
import java.util.*;

public class PersonCollectionApplication {

    public static void main(String[] args) {

        // For simplicity, only using
        // the zero-arg constructor and setting
        // a name for each.

        Person advisorSarah = new Person();
        advisorSarah.name = "Dr. Sarah R.";

        Student studentMikah = new Student();
        studentMikah.name = "Mikah L.";

        Student studentTyrie = new Student();
        studentTyrie.name = "Tyrie S.";

        GradStudent gradBillie = new GradStudent();
```

```
        gradBillie.name = "Billie H.";
        gradBillie.setThesisAdvisor(advisorSarah);

        // Using a simple array:
        Person[] studentArray = new Person[3];
        studentArray[0] = studentMikah;
        studentArray[1] = studentTyrie;
        studentArray[2] = gradBillie;

        // Using ArrayList (chapter 7)
        ArrayList<Person> studentList = new ArrayList<>();
        studentList.add(studentMikah);
        studentList.add(studentTyrie);
        studentList.add(gradBillie);

        for (var per : studentArray)
            System.out.println(per.toString());

        System.out.println("");

        for (var per : studentList)
            System.out.println(per.toString());

     // Figure 9.8 depicts memory contents at this point

    } // end of main()
} // end of class PersonCollection
```

The output when this program is run will be as follows:

```
Name: Mikah L., age: 0, Major: n/a, Year: 0, GPA: 0.0
Name: Tyrie S., age: 0, Major: n/a, Year: 0, GPA: 0.0
Name: Billie H., age: 0, Major: n/a, Year: 0, GPA: 0.0
   Advisor: Name: Dr. Sarah R., age: 0

Name: Mikah L., age: 0, Major: n/a, Year: 0, GPA: 0.0
Name: Tyrie S., age: 0, Major: n/a, Year: 0, GPA: 0.0
Name: Billie H., age: 0, Major: n/a, Year: 0, GPA: 0.0
   Advisor: Name: Dr. Sarah R., age: 0
```

For simplicity sake, only the name data field was changed for each class object created, with the exception of setting the advisor for the graduate student "Billie." The class objects engage in polymorphic behavior here, since the array and the `ArrayList<E>` are both data types with `Person`. Wherever a reference to a `Person` object is expected, a reference to an object of one of its subclasses can be provided instead. Again, this provides "future compatibility": you can use subclasses of class `Person` that do not even exist yet in code where references to `Person` objects are expected, like with the array and `ArrayList<E>` in this example. Figure 9.8 shows the (partial) contents of memory and the relationship between all these objects just before the `main()` method completes.

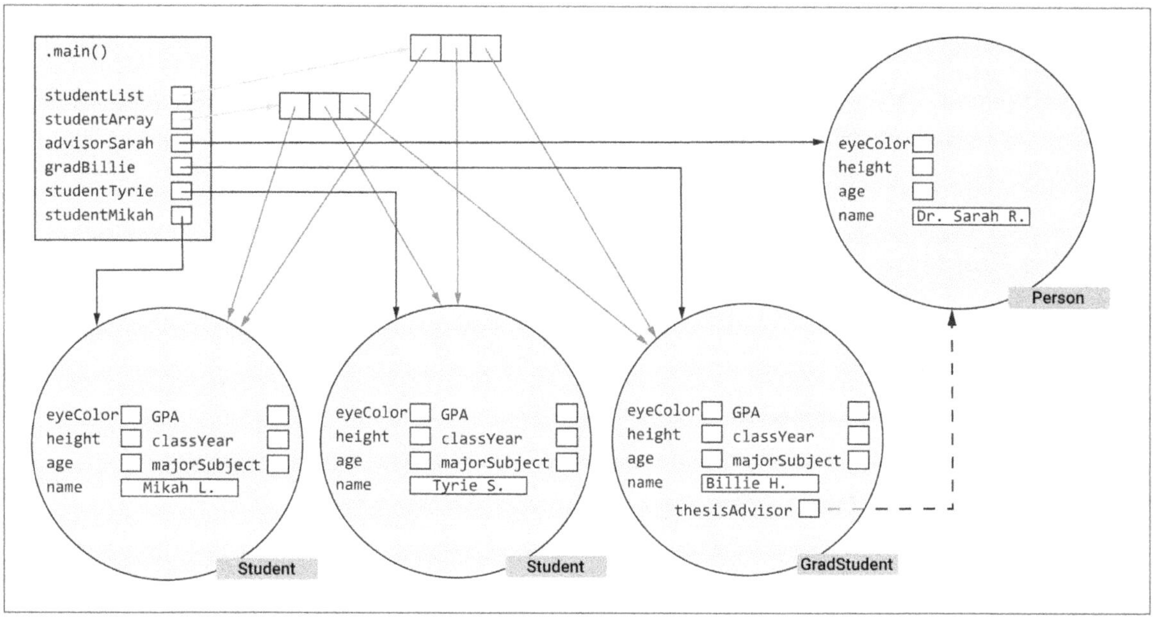

Figure 9.8. `Person`, `Student`, `GradStudent`, `Array`, and `ArrayList<E>` Objects in Memory

SUMMARY POINTS

- Dynamic binding is a runtime decision by Java as to which method version to invoke based on the class data type of the actual instance object addressed by a reference variable that the method was invoked upon.
- "Future compatibility" is enabled by the combination of dynamic binding and class inheritance, where objects of future child classes can be used in any place that objects of the ancestor, parent class are expected by Java code/applications.

QUICK PROBLEMS

1. **Coding:** Create an array with a data type of `Person`. Create a few `Person`, `Student`, and `GradStudent` instance objects, and store references to these objects in the array. Using a loop, invoke the `.toString()` method on each object referenced, and print their descriptions to the console. Account for any null/empty locations in the array.
2. **Think:** What happens if a subclass does not have a method defined but the superclass does and a reference variable references a subclass object when the superclass's method is invoked upon it? How do dynamic binding and method versioning work in this situation?

Summary

In this chapter, you have learned about the major benefits that class inheritance can yield for contemporary development efforts. You have learned how to define and adjust the subclass to indicate an extension of a previously existing class. You have seen how data fields can be inherited from the parent class and added to with your subclass's new fields. You have learned how constructors are invoked when instance objects of a subclass are created and how subclass constructors can invoke those in the parent class to assist with object initialization. You have additionally seen the benefits of both overriding the method of a parent class in the child's definition file and overloading an inherited method in the child. How polymorphic behavior relates to class inheritance and method overriding has been explored, and you've learned how code can be made "future compatible" if inheritance and the right planning are done. These are all very powerful features of OO languages like Java and will make your development efforts more productive and effective. In the next chapter, you will explore the Java exception class system and learn how to increase the stability and reliable nature of your applications in the prevention and handling of program exceptions.

Practice Problems

Terminology

Match the following terms from the chapter with their most appropriate definition:

1. Class inheritance	a. The redefining of one class's method in one of its child classes, re-creating the signature of the method exactly.
2. Class member	b. A class that extends the capabilities and characteristics of a previously existing class.
3. Data field	c. The period of time when a Java application is executing in memory.
4. Class method	d. A keyword that allows convenient access to members of a superclass from within the code of a child class.
5. Constructor	e. The ability of Java to determine the appropriate version of a method to invoke when called on a reference variable based on the data type of the object referenced by that variable.
6. new	f. Access modifier that allows unrestricted access to the member of a class.
7. Superclass	g. Access modifier that, depending on the location of accessing code and the target class code, can either restrict or allow access to a class member assigned this modifier.
8. Subclass	h. The redefining of a method with a slightly different signature either in the same class or in a child class that inherits the original version.
9. public	i. A resource of a class, usually a data field or a class method.
10. private	j. The period of time when a Java application is first compiled, the data types are symbolically checked, and initial syntax errors are detected.
11. protected	k. A behavior of object-oriented code where objects can take on the identity of their ancestor classes and be used in locations where the ancestor class data type is expected.
12. extends	l. Operator that instructs Java to create an object of the requested data type on the heap (i.e., "free store").
13. super	m. Represents the action possible either by the class or upon objects instantiated from the class.
14. Method overriding	n. The parts of a method's header that help Java identify the version of a method to invoke, especially if there are multiple versions. Primarily, the method name + the order/quantity/data types of defined parameters.
15. Method overloading	o. Keyword that explicitly defines an inheritance extension between one class and another.
16. Method signature	p. The ability for a class to build on the actions and state of a previously existing class by extending that class with additional or redefined actions and state.
17. Method versioning	q. Access modifier that severely restricts access to the member of a class to only the code within that class.
18. Polymorphism	r. Represents the supertype or parent class that future classes can extend.
19. Dynamic binding	s. A class method that performs the initialization steps for a newly created class instance object. Only invokable one time per new object.
20. Runtime	t. Helps represent the state of objects of a class, the values stored (or encapsulated) within the object.
21. Compile time	u. The ability of Java to examine a class inheritance hierarchy and decide which method version to invoke: usually the most recently/locally defined version.

Find the Error

In each of the following problems, carefully examine the code given, and determine the error(s)/issue(s) with each. Keep in mind, the error(s) could be syntax (code) or logic (intended outcome) based or both!

Use the following `SuperClass` code listing (assume no errors in this listing) to examine the errors found in the problems:

```
public class SuperClass {

    public int dataA;
    private String dataB;

    public SuperClass ()
    {
        this.dataA = 0;
        this.dataB = "";
    }

    public SuperClass (int dataA, String dataB)
    {
        this.dataA = dataA;
        this.dataB = dataB;
    }

    public String describeObj()
    {
        return this.dataA + " " + this.dataB;
    }

}
```

1. For a class `SubClass` intended to be a child class of `SuperClass` above:

```
class SubClass
{
    int dataC = 7;
    public SubClass ()
    {
        super();
        dataC = 7;
    };
}
```

2. For an application that resides in the same package as `SuperClass` (above) and `SubClass` (from #1):

```
SubClass cB = new SubClass ();
cB.dataA = 10;
cB.dataB = 7;
cb.dataC = "Object";
System.out.println(cb.toString());
```

3. For an application that resides in the same package as `SuperClass` (above) and `SubClass` (from #1):

```
SuperClass cA = new SubClass ();
System.out.println(cA.toString());
```

4. For a class `SubClass` intended to be a child class of `SuperClass` above:

```
class SubClass extends SuperClass
{
    int dataC = 7;
    public SubClass ()
    {
        dataC = dataA;
```

```
        dataB = "object";
        dataA = new ClassA(17);
        super.constructor();
        super.describeObject = "new object";
    }
}
```

5. For an application found in the same package as `SuperClass`:

```
SuperClass cA = new SuperClass();
cA.dataC = 40;
```

Think about It

1. What are some of the benefits of having one class inherit from another?
2. How many parent classes can a child class have? How many child classes can a parent class have? How does this impact your ability to model real-world entities in an information system?
3. Why is a child class considered better suited to a more specific context? How is a parent class "more general" in its usage?
4. Why is a parent class called a "supertype" and a child class called a "subtype"?
5. What happens if you do not purposefully specify a parent class for a class you have just created?
6. What parts of a parent class are inherited by a child class? What parts of a parent class are accessible by a child class?
7. Why does the child class not need to redeclare all the data fields of the parent class?
8. How does invoking the constructor of a parent class from the constructor code of a child class benefit the developer of the child class? What rules are there for doing so?
9. When a child class object is instantiated, how many instance objects are created?
10. Why is it a "good habit" to always create a zero-arg default constructor in all of your classes?
11. How does method overriding differ from method overloading? How can both of these occur in a child class?
12. Describe what happens during dynamic binding. How can this impact the behavior of our applications?
13. How can polymorphism benefit the developer and the flexibility of the applications that they write?

Short Syntax Problems

For these short syntax problems, create a new Java class file called "`Faculty.java`," and specify that this class inherits from the `Person` class used in this chapter.

1. Implement the following data fields for the `Faculty` class: office number, building name, email address, department abbreviation, and hourly pay rate (as a private data field).
2. Define the zero-arg constructor for the `Faculty` class. Invoke the zero-arg constructor from the `Person` class in your new constructor.
3. Define a partial constructor for the `Faculty` class. Invoke the zero-arg constructor in this new constructor. Define the constructor parameters to accept a `name`, email address, and department abbreviation.
4. Define both a mutator ("setter") and an accessor ("getter") for the hourly pay rate data field.
5. Override the inherited `.toString()` method for the `Faculty` class. Have it print only the information you accepted in the second constructor in short syntax problem #3.
6. Add two new data fields to the `Faculty` class: a `Student` array called `advising` and an `int` called `arrayKeeper`. Have your constructors initialize this array to size ten and the `arrayKeeper` variable to a value of `0`.
7. Add a method called `.addAdvisee()` to the `Faculty` class. The method will accept one parameter, a `Student` reference called `advisee`. Copy the reference from the `Student` parameter into the advising data field array at the next free location as indicated by `arrayKeeper`.
8. Add a method called `.printAdviseeList()` to the `Faculty` class. The method will print to the console a well-formatted list of the `Students` being advised by this `Faculty` member (as found in the `advising` array). Invoke the `.toString()` on each `Student` reference in the array to accomplish this. Account for any null/empty locations in the data field array.

Full Problems

1. Create an application called `CourseScheduler` that resides in the same package as the `Person`, `Student`, `GradStudent`, and `Faculty` (short syntax problems) classes. This application will have the following functionality:
   a. The application will enable the user to create a college course, represented by an instance object of class `Course`. The `Course` will have the characteristics of a start date, end date, day of the week it meets, and time of day. Each course object will store an array of references to the `Student` objects that represent students enrolled in the course. It will also contain a reference for the faculty member who teaches the course.
   b. The application will allow the user to select from existing courses and add a student from an existing list to that course. You will need to enable the application to have an option for creating `Students` before they can be added to the course.
   c. The application will allow the user to assign a faculty member to a specific course. You will need to enable the application to have an option for creating `Faculty` members before they can be assigned to teach a course.
   d. The application should have a way of printing the details of the course (date range, day and time, faculty assigned to the course, and the listing of students enrolled).
   e. The application should have a way of removing a particular student from a particular course.
2. Create a Java application called `AirTrafficControl`. This application will allow various types of aircraft to "take off" from an airport, report estimated flight times to a destination, report on what aircraft are in the air, and detail which flights have completed.
   a. Create a superclass called `Airplane`. Objects of the class will store a **public** `String` of `callSign` (consisting of the company that owns the plane and a three-digit number), a **private** int of `maxPassengers`, and a **private** `double` of `maxSpeed` (in knots/hr.).
      i. Add an instance method called `travelTime()`. For any particular `Airplane` or its subclasses, the method will accept a double of distance (in miles) and will report the time (in hours) that it will take the aircraft to fly that distance, using each aircraft's `maxSpeed` data field. *Hint:* You will need to do the conversion from knots/hr. to miles/hr.
   b. Create a subclass called `Jet`.
      i. When `Jet` objects are created, set the `maxPassengers` to 20 and the `maxSpeed` to 500 knots/hr.
      ii. Add a private `String` data field called `ownerName`, since jets at this airport are usually owned by private individuals.
      iii. Override the `.toString()` method so that the information about the `Jet` is printed, including the ownership.
   c. Create a subclass called `Commercial`.
      i. When `Commercial` objects are created, set the `maxPassengers` to 240 and the `maxSpeed` to 700 knots/hr.
      ii. Add a private int called `crewCount`. This will be the count of how many crew members are working the craft during its upcoming flight.
      iii. Override the `.toString()` method to print the `Commercial` aircraft's information, including crew count.
   d. Create a class called `Flight`.
      i. Each `Flight` object will contain an `Airplane` data field that references the subclass craft involved in a flight plan.
      ii. Each `Flight` should contain a data field (you choose data type) that will indicate whether the `Flight` is in progress or completed.
      iii. Each `Flight` object will also store a `String destination` for a destination label and a double `flightDistance` that contains the length of the flight in miles.
   e. The `AirTrafficControl` application should have the following abilities:
      i. Initiate takeoff: This allows the user to create a `Flight` with its details, select the type of aircraft, instantiate its class object, and specify details of that aircraft.
      ii. Initiate landing: The user can indicate that any `Flight` has landed.
      iii. Print details on a particular `Flight`: the user should be able to print the details of any particular flight to the console.
      iv. Print details on all flights: The user can print details for all flights. These should be divided into "in-progress" flights printing first, with "complete" flights printing second.
3. Create an application for the mom-and-pop grocery store called `SimpleInventory`. This application will allow for the creation of four types of inventory

items for a grocery store: produce, product, dairy, or meat.

a. Create a superclass / parent class called `Inventory`. Objects of `Inventory` will have the following data fields: `quantityInStock`, `purchasePrice`, `sellPrice`, `category`, `description`, and `dateStocked` (this is the date the item was put out on the grocery store floor).
b. Create a subclass for each of the four types of inventory items that the store will sell. For each, inherit from the parent class `Inventory`. Each class's constructor will initialize the inherited category data field according to its type ("Produce" for produce instance objects, etc.). Each class will have additional data fields as follows:
   i. `Produce`: `weight`, `daysFresh` (this is how many days we can sell before needing to discard the item)
   ii. `Product`: `packaging` (canned or boxed), `brand`
   iii. `Dairy`: `dairyType` (milk, cheese, cream, dessert), `brand`
   iv. `Meat`: `weight`, `type` (type of protein)
c. Enable the user of the application the ability to choose a category to add an item to and then to enter the specific information for that item in all four categories (users will not add an inventory instance object to the system).
d. Enable the user to print a report that shows the following:
   i. All the items in stock in a certain category
   ii. All the items in stock in the entire store
   iii. The potential profit for all the items in a certain category (total sale price of all + total price paid for all)
   iv. The potential profit for all the items in the store (same approach as in **d.iii**)

Chapter 10

Exceptions, Good Practice, and Professional Java

What You Will Learn in This Chapter

Learning the syntax of the Java programming language is just one step toward becoming a well-rounded Java developer. Now that the basics of object-oriented programming in Java have been covered, it will be beneficial to review topics such as handling code exceptions, professional approaches to common business-related programming issues, and general good practices in the language. In this chapter, you will build upon the good practices that have already been discussed or implied throughout prior chapters in this textbook and explore how to increase the reliability and stability of your applications, considering how your applications are interconnected within a software system.

Specifically, this chapter will help you do the following:

1. Learn about the Java exception class system, explore its object-oriented nature, and learn when exceptions occur in Java applications
2. Learn how to handle the occurrence of exceptions in Java programs using try...catch statements, how to catch issues more broadly or zero in on a specific type of exception, and how exception handling can impact the execution of your application
3. Learn how to purposefully cause exceptions to occur in your code based on logic spurred by suboptimal or undesired conditions
4. Learn how to increase the level of security on class objects to adhere to business, regulatory, or data privacy needs
5. Learn how to create methods that communicate better with their invoking code, how to mask sensitive data effectively, how to minimize repetitive class qualifications in syntax, and how to thoroughly and effectively document your code to help others understand its purpose and nature

Opening Scenario

After additional development efforts, you have implemented a sophisticated class structure for the mom-and-pop grocery store inventory system. Poring over the client's requirements with your colleague yielded quite a few more product categories that you felt needed subclasses. After further prototype testing, everything seems to work well. In a large system such as this, with many information systems professionals working on parts of the system, you've noticed some strange issues. For example, you have often noticed that errors related to missing objects, or parameters passed `null` references, have been popping up. User input from the console when typing in inventory product details is not checked, and you have mistyped several times, crashing the entire application. Some developers on the project are struggling with array structures, with many index errors occurring in some of the busier code sections. Things seem disjointed, with expectations for various parts of the code base not "lining up" with other parts of the system. At this point in the systems development effort, you and the team have not had a chance to go back through the code to try to rewrite certain areas where these errors are popping up, improving the logic or writing more sophisticated code. Indeed, if the application would just stop crashing, much of the testing could be completed without having to type in inventory test data all over again, among other things. Frustration abounds.

Your project manager has asked you to switch over and coordinate error-handling efforts to stabilize the prototype until several of the application's issues can be revisited later on. "At this point," she states, "there is no way we can demo this to the clients again. I think we got lucky there were no errors last week!" You have to agree: right now this system is not client-ready. Once again, you dive back into your study efforts to discover all the ins and outs of the exception-handling capabilities of the Java programming language . . .

10.1 Understanding Exception Handling in Java

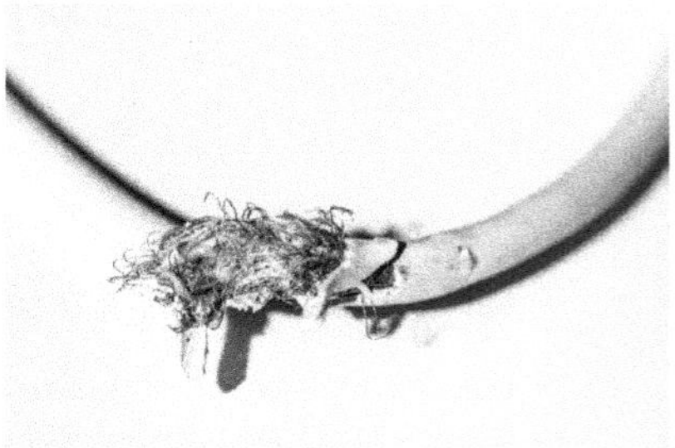

Figure 10.1. Things Sometimes Go Wrong: Your Software Should Be Ready
Source: "Puppy Problems" by spurekar is licensed under CC BY 2.0, https://www.flickr.com/photos/63324741@N04/48898338131.

Maybe you have heard the saying "The best defense is a good offense." Another saying, often used in many of the business classes you may have taken, is "Better to be proactive than reactive." Anticipating problems before they happen, trying to prevent them, and mitigating their negative impact are all activities that the modern information systems professional engages in on a daily basis. For large system planning and implementation projects, IS professionals try to ensure the success of these projects (which can take many years and cost hundreds of millions of dollars) by preventing project failures and mitigating them when they do happen. IS developers engaged in the programming and coding efforts of a project try to do the same with their systems development: prevent errors when possible and give their software the ability to handle any when they arise.

Throughout this textbook, you have seen several instances where an error in syntax or in logic can cause an error to occur in your program, making it "crash" and display a message. For example, in a new Java `main()` class file (create one if you wish, named `Chapter10Examples.java`), recall the following when you try to access a location in an array that does not exist:

Full Program 10.1

```
// Package line omitted

import java.util.*;
public class Chapter10Examples {
    public static void main(String[] args) {

        int[] anArray = new int[5];
        anArray[10] = 100;          // ArrayIndexOutOfBoundsException

    }
}
```

When you attempt to run this code, you get the following error:

```
Exception in thread "main" java.lang.ArrayIndexOutOfBoundsException: Index 10 out of bounds for
length 5
  at com.javaforis.chapter10.Chapter10Examples.main(Chapter10Examples.java:8)
```

You have seen this error message before: `ArrayIndexOutOfBoundsException`. Notice that most of these messages try to tell us the error type and some details about where the compiler thinks the error occurred (the line number on the end of the file name `Chapter10Examples.java`). There is more to this error as well that you can now better understand:

- Notice the name of the error: `ArrayIndexOutOfBoundsException`. The first word is capitalized, and as you have seen, classes also have their first word capitalized. This error appears to be referring to some Java class.
- The fully qualified name of the error is `java.lang.ArrayIndexOutOfBoundsException`. This is detailing a package location for this error class: `java`, the top-level package, and the `lang` subpackage that is imported by default in all Java classes.

In Java, these errors are known as **exceptions**, and exceptions in Java are defined by **exception classes**. Since everything in Java is class/object based, so are its errors! When an error like this occurs in your program, the compiler is creating an instance object of the class `ArrayIndexOutOfBoundsException` and is "throwing" (*think:* flag is thrown on a play in a US football game) this exception. Because the application stopped execution (i.e., "blew up"), this error was an **unhandled exception**, meaning that the application did not **catch the exception**, and this caused the program to stop. Developers in any programming language, including Java, should be as proactive in catching and actively handling exceptions in their code as possible so that their application can process the error and continue executing without a hiccup. This involves a bit of proactive coding of smartly reactive exception handling.

To understand when exceptions are thrown in Java, consider the following small class and `main()` method code in an application that uses it:

Code Snippet 10.1

```
class LittleClass {
    int num;
    public LittleClass(){
        this.num = 0;
    }
    public LittleClass(int num){
        this.num = num;
    }
}

. . .

// Following Code can be added to the Chapter10Examples.java
//     application

// Will be flagged as an error before the program can compile/run!
LittleClass lilC = new LittleClass(316);
System.out.println((String)lilC);
```

It would be great to print the value of `num` stored in the `LittleClass` instance object `lilC` in the application (you might be thinking, "Well, you should have overridden the `.toString()` method!" and you would be right). Here, the object referenced by the reference variable `lilC` is cast as a `String` object to print it. A good try, but this will not work in this situation. Before this program runs, the compiler notices that the data type `LittleClass` is not a subclass of class `String`, so this cast is not allowed. A compilation error occurs. Remember that these compiler errors occur for things like syntax issues (forgetting a semicolon, ending a code block, misspelled variable name causing a symbol not found error, etc.). But what if you change our application code to look like this:

```
// Code in an application main() method
// Reference variable rereferenced to Object
Object lilC = new LittleClass(316);
System.out.println((String)lilC);
```

This code is allowed to be compiled and executed. Think about why both `String` and `LittleClass` are subclasses of class `Object` (the top-level parent class of all classes in Java, as you saw in chapter 9). So initially, there's nothing wrong with casting the object referenced as a `String`, since `String` is a subclass of `Object`. Remember as well that the instance object will not be created until runtime (when the program is executing). When you run your application with this code, the following **exception** occurs at runtime:

```
Exception in thread "main" java.lang.ClassCastException: class
com.javaforis.chapter10.LittleClass cannot be cast to class java.lang.String
   at com.javaforis.chapter10.Chapter10Examples.main(Chapter10Examples.java:12)
```

When the program runs, the object is created and its data type known, and then the `ClassCastException` is thrown. Since `LittleClass` and `String` are **unrelated classes** (not a parent/child of each other), they are unable to be cast as each other. This exception can also be thrown if you try to cast a parent class object as one of its children:

Code Snippet 10.2

```
// Parent and Child Classes
class LittleClass {
    int num;
    public LittleClass(){
        this.num = 0;
    }
    public LittleClass(int num){
        this.num = num;
    }

    public String toString()
    {
        return "LittleClass!";
    }
}

// Newly added child class
class BiggerClass extends LittleClass{
    int secondNum;

    public BiggerClass(int num, int secondNum)
    {
       super(num);
       this.secondNum = secondNum;
    }

    public String toString()
    {
        return "BiggerClass!";
    }
}

. . .

// Application Code

// Casting a parent reference as a child
LittleClass lilC = new LittleClass(5);
System.out.println(((BiggerClass)lilC).toString());
```

Notice the use of parentheses here: first the cast operator is applied to the reference variable, then that is isolated within parentheses and the dot operator used on that cast reference to attempt to call the `BiggerClass.toString()` method.

Java exception classes' family tree: Then handling of exceptions in Java as class objects is a sensible step for a modern OO language. The exception classes are related to one another in an inheritance relationship, which give developers a lot of flexibility in how they watch for and handle these exceptions (not to mention the ability to create their own exception classes through extending the ones already present!). Figure 10.2 shows the hierarchy of exception class inheritance and some of the more common exceptions that you will explore in this section.

Figure 10.2 details two terms you should be aware of as you move forward in our discussion of exception classes:

- **Checked exceptions:** Java forces developers to actively watch for and handle some exceptions if you write code that might throw (i.e., cause) them. For example, if your application is attempting to open and read

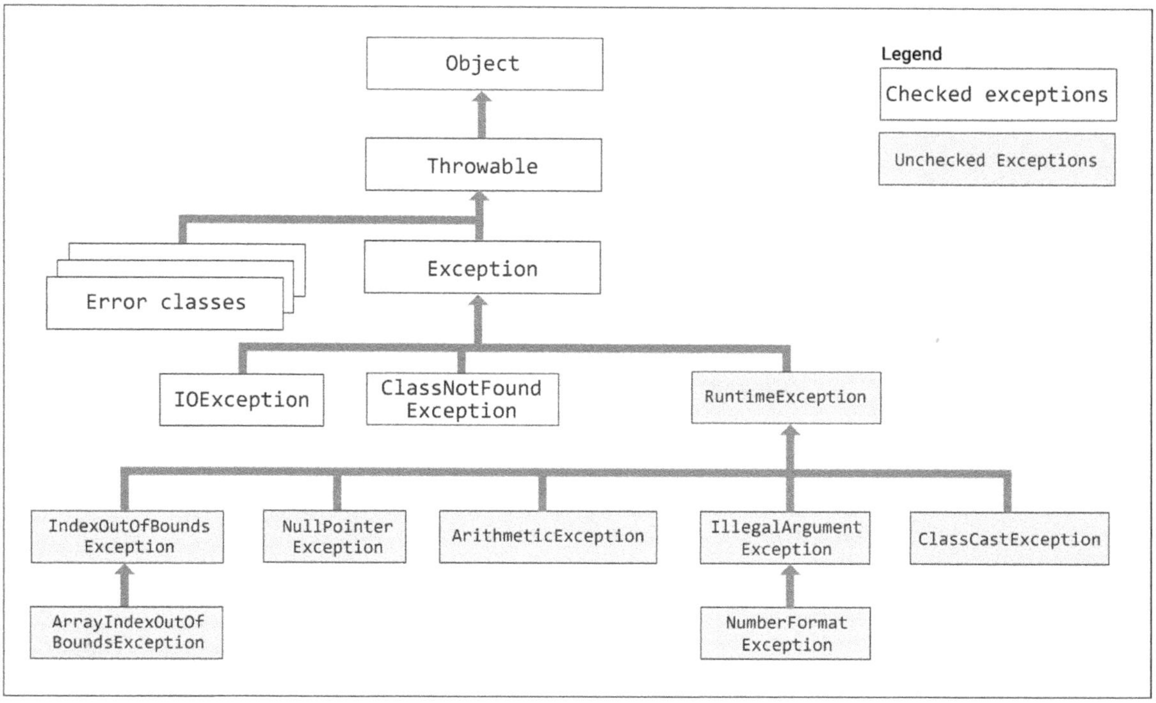

Figure 10.2. A Partial View of the Java Exception Class Inheritance Hierarchy

from a text file, what happens if the file is not present? What happens if a network connection drops while your program is communicating across that connection? These are pretty severe, and Java requires you to write code that proactively watches for these. Java requires you to implement **checked exceptions** for any code that could possibly generate these types of issues. Java will examine your code at compile time to see if there is even the possibility that a checked exception might be thrown and will alert you that you need to alter your code to handle these (most IDEs will flag this code as well).

- **Unchecked exceptions:** These are exception types that the compiler does not look for when first examining your code at compile time. These types of exceptions occur at runtime, and the developer has the option of watching for and handling them . . . or not. Of course, **not** handling these exception types can cause your program to halt/crash. Typically, these are considered logic exceptions, since they (often but not always) reflect some issue with the logic in your application—for example, our out-of-bounds array error or trying to use a reference when its actually `null`/empty. Unchecked exceptions allow us to catch those "oops!" moments, which can still occur despite our best efforts.

Notice that in figure 10.2, the hierarchy of these classes starts with the `Throwable` class (itself a subclass of Object).* All the exception classes in this hierarchy inherit from `Throwable`. The following is a summary of some of the Oracle documentation details of `Throwable` objects and all instance objects of its subclasses:

- Instance objects of subclasses of `Throwable` are created and thrown either by the Java Virtual Machine (JVM) or by code that explicitly throws (i.e., instantiates) an exception.
- Each exception class (any subclass of `Throwable`) object contains, among other data, the message of the exception and the stack trace (*think:* chain of methods) of code execution that led to the code that caused the exception to be thrown. This can be helpful in tracing how your application's execution got to the point where an issue occurred.

* https://docs.oracle.com/en/java/javase/17/docs/api/java.base/java/lang/Throwable.html.

- The exception subclasses inherit from `Throwable` many instance methods for accessing that helpful information like the exception message or stack trace print.
- All the exception subclasses of the Throwable class are checked exceptions, **except** for the `RuntimeException` class and all its subclasses. This branch of the "family tree" contains **unchecked exceptions** that you can choose to watch for and handle . . . or not.

Table 10.1 provides a quick listing of the exception classes shown in figure 10.2 along with short descriptions of when you might encounter an exception of this type (these are not all the Java exception classes by any means—see the earlier footnote for the Oracle documentation for class `Throwable` for a full listing).

Table 10.1. Listing of Some Commonly Used Java Exception Classes

Exception class name	Checked?	Description
`Throwable`	Yes	Parent class of all exception and error (different from syntax error) classes in Java. Defines many methods inherited by the exception classes that provide information on the exception thrown.
`Exception`	Yes	Direct superclass of all exception classes.
`IOException`	Yes	Generally means that an exception has occurred with an input/output (I/O) activity. Typically associated with reading and writing from/to external files.
`ClassNotFoundException`	Yes	When a developer tries to programmatically load or use a class (outside of normal reference variable declaration) and no definition for a class by the name used can be found.
`RuntimeException`	No	The direct superclass of all exception classes that are unchecked and whose objects can be thrown during execution of a program.
`ArrayIndexOutOfBoundsException`	No	Thrown when an index location in an array does not exist but is attempted to be used by your code.
`NullPointerException`	No	Thrown when you attempt to call an instance method or use a data field of an instance object referenced by a reference variable, but the variable contains `null` instead and no object is referenced by it.
`ArithmeticException`	No	Thrown typically when you have a division by zero but can occur with other formula/mathematical exceptions.
`IllegalFormatException`	No	Thrown when a formatted string has been composed incorrectly (wrong use of a format specifier, etc.).
`NumberFormatException`	No	Thrown when trying to convert a `String` to an `int`, and the `String` does not contain characters appropriate for the conversion.
`IllegalArgumentException`	No	Can be thrown when a value passed to a parameter is determined to not be in the right format, value, range, etc.
`ClassCastException`	No	Thrown when one class is typecast as another, unrelated class or when a parent is cast as one of its subclass data types.
`InputMismatchException`	No	Type of exception thrown by the `Scanner` class to indicate that the data type of the value typed or read in does not match what was expected. *Note:* This exception is located in the `java.util` package along with the `Scanner` class. You must import it separately or import everything in `java.util` to catch it.

Try...catch statements: As has been mentioned, your first option for handling exceptions in your application is to do nothing at all. This is not good since some exceptions are required to be handled (the checked exceptions), and others will cause your program to halt when they are thrown. An overall great practice (and your second option) for Java developers is to proactively handle exceptions by identifying code that may throw an exception during runtime (for unchecked exceptions) and placing that code within a **try...catch statement**. For both checked and unchecked exceptions, the try...catch statement will allow you to intercept or "catch" the generated instance object of the exception class, execute any code that you feel needs to run if the exception occurs, and allow your program to continue executing. This is big: now your program will not crash but continue on, having smartly handled the exception.

The try...catch statement looks like this in general:

Code Snippet 10.3

```
try
{
   // Your code that might throw an exception
}
catch (Exception exc)
{
    // Code here will execute if the exception is thrown.
    // The "catching" occurs by a reference variable
    //  to the exception being stored in the parameter of
    //  the catch statement.
}
finally
{
    // The finally block is optional. Here you will
    // place code that will execute regardless of
    // whether an exception was thrown or not.
}
```

For checked exception classes, you are forced by the compiler to surround code that can throw them with a try...catch statement. For example, any code that might want to read from or write to a file will be required to be placed in a `try` block, with the catch block handling any exceptions. Typically, checked exceptions are thrown when interacting with some resource that is **outside** of your application or outside the control of Java: the operating system or some other software deleting a file or locking access to it, a network connection going down, and so on. These are severe enough that the good practice of handling them is required of the developer. For unchecked exceptions, other parts of your application or user interaction with your program may cause an error that, while not severe, is bad enough that unhandled, it would crash the application. To try to mitigate this as much as possible, it is recommended to use try...catch in these locations.

Notice that the catch statement has a parameter declaration (similar to what you would see in a method header). You can choose any name for the parameter name that you want. Notice as well that this is a reference variable, and you are using any exception class that you intend to "catch" objects of when exceptions are thrown. Finally, remember that all the exception classes are in an inheritance hierarchy. This means that you can catch a reference to a specific exception class **or** you can catch a reference for any of its subclasses instead. For example, consider the following application code (assume all needed imports have been added):

Full Program 10.2

```
import java.util.*;

public class Chapter10Examples {

    public static void main(String[] args) {

        Scanner in = new Scanner(System.in);
        int[] anArray = new int[5];
        int index = 0;

        System.out.println("Enter numbers: ");

        while (in.hasNext())
```

```
        {
            anArray[index++] = in.nextInt();
        }
    }
}
```

Console interaction and output:

```
Enter numbers:
1 2 3 4 5 6 7 8 9 10 11
Exception in thread "main" java.lang.ArrayIndexOutOfBoundsException: Index 5 out of bounds for
length 5
   at com.javaforis.chapter10.Chapter10Examples.main(Chapter10Examples.java:14)
```

Notice that in this code, it was assumed that the user would only enter five numbers, but the application really didn't specify to them how many numbers to actually type in. The user typed in eleven numbers, and the program threw an `ArrayIndexOutOfBoundsException` object when they attempted to write to a nonexistent array location. This exception can be caught by modifying this code like so:

Code Snippet 10.4

```
try
{
    while (in.hasNext())
    {
        anArray[index++] = in.nextInt();
    }
}
catch (ArrayIndexOutOfBoundsException indexException)
{
    System.out.println("Array filled!");
}

for (int element : anArray)
    System.out.print("[" + element + "]");
```

Notice again that you can name the parameter reference variable anything you want, but typically it should be named with some sort of abbreviation that describes the type of exception it references. Now when the exception is thrown, our program catches it, prints a message, and continues program execution, printing the array contents with new code after the try...catch block:

```
Enter numbers:
1 2 3 4 5 6 7 8
Array filled!
[1][2][3][4][5]
```

The program no longer crashes! Since exception classes are in an inheritance hierarchy, you can "cast a wider net" by defining a catch parameter for one of the parent class exception types (modified code in **bold**):

```
catch (Exception ex)
{
    System.out.println("Array filled!");
}
```

For this, the console interaction and output will be the same. Here again is the polymorphic behavior of our objects in action. Generally, deciding to catch an exception class data type that is higher in the exception family tree is useful when one or more exceptions might be thrown by the code you are referencing and you are not sure beforehand which might occur. Consider the following input with our above code:

```
Enter numbers:
1 2 3 a 5 6 7 8
Array filled!
[1][2][3][0][0]
```

Notice that the user accidentally typed in a letter instead of a number. Here an `InputMismatchException` was thrown by the `Scanner` class, but our catch statement handled it. The first three letters were filled, but the loop was stopped by the exception being thrown. This code has a logic issue; we have not accounted for the possibility of a user entering a letter, and our exception-handling code has alerted us to it. A smarter way to handle this might look like the following:

Full Program 10.3

```
import java.util.*;

public class Chapter10Examples {

    public static void main(String[] args) {

        Scanner in = new Scanner(System.in);
        int[] anArray = new int[5]; // ArrayList<E> works better...
        int index = 0;

        System.out.println("Enter numbers: ");

        while (true)
        {
            if (index == anArray.length)
                break;
            else if (in.hasNextInt())
                anArray[index++] = in.nextInt();
            else
            {
                in.next();
            }
        }


        for (int num : anArray)
            System.out.print("[" + num + "]");

    }

}
```

Console interaction and output:

```
Enter numbers:
1 2 3 a 5 6 7 8 9
[1][2][3][5][6]
```

An infinite loop is used **carefully** here to keep processing numbers until the array is filled, skipping the errant letter. Typically, exception handling is not used for debugging, but messages thrown like this in a process of system prototyping or testing can help developers identify logic issues in the code that they may have otherwise missed. Careful adaptation of our logic can take out the possibility that certain exceptions happen at all, though you will not be able to prevent them all. This makes the exception-handling features of Java very useful.

Printing exception information: The `Throwable` exception class passes to all its inherited children various instance methods that allow the developer to print information about the exception thrown. As a simple example, you can modify the catch from the earlier array example as follows:

Code Snippet 10.5

```
. . .
catch (ArrayIndexOutOfBoundsException indexException)
{
    System.out.println("Array filled!");
    System.out.println(indexException.getMessage());
    indexException.printStackTrace();
}
. . .
```

Console output:

```
Enter numbers:
1 2 3 4 5 6 7 8
Array filled!
Index 5 out of bounds for length 5
java.lang.ArrayIndexOutOfBoundsException: Index 5 out of bounds for length 5
   at com.javaforis.chapter10.Chapter10Examples.main(Chapter10Examples.java:19)
[1][2][3][4][5]
```

The ability to print exception messages is especially helpful when you are catching a parent exception class and want to debug what particular type of exception occurred. For example, with our prior number entry code, printing the exception message will show both `ArrayIndexOutOfBounds` and `InputMismatchExceptions` as well as any others, if they occur.

Exception chaining and multicatch: Java allows you to chain together a string of catch statements where the developer may want to perform different logic when different exceptions are caught. For example, consider this version of the number entry code from earlier:

Full Program 10.4

```
import java.util.*;

public class Chapter10Examples {

    public static void main(String[] args) {

        Scanner in = new Scanner(System.in);
        int[] anArray = new int[5];
        int index = 0;

        System.out.println("Enter numbers: ");

        try
        {
            while (true)
            {
                anArray[index++] = in.nextInt();
            }
        }
        catch (ArrayIndexOutOfBoundsException indexEx) // Child Class
        {
            System.out.println("Array Filled!");
        }
        catch (InputMismatchException inputEx) // Parent Class
        {
            for (int i=0;i<anArray.length;i++)
                anArray[i] = 0; // Clear the array to try again later

            System.out.println("Only Letters Can Be Entered for Input!");
        }
    }
}
```

Notice that one catch block can follow another. To do this in Java, there are two primary rules:

- If the exceptions you want to chain are a parent class instead of a child class, then the child class must be used in the first catch block. Subsequent catch blocks must move **up** the family tree, casting a wider exception-handling "net" each time.
- If the exceptions are **siblings** (same level of the family tree) or if they are in **unrelated packages** (i.e., `java.lang` for most exceptions and `java.util` for `InputMismatchException`), then the catch order does not matter.

For example, note that the `ArrayIndexOutOfBoundsException` class is a subclass (after `IndexOutOfBoundsException`) of the `Exception` class. Consider the following code:

Code Snippet 10.6

```
catch (Exception inputEx)
{
    for (int i=0;i<anArray.length;i++)
        anArray[i] = 0;
    System.out.println("Only Letters Can Be Entered for Input!");
}
catch (ArrayIndexOutOfBoundsException indexEx)
{
    System.out.println("Array Filled!");
}
```

Note that the superclass `Exception` has been coded first, prior to its subclass. The Java compiler (and most IDEs) will flag this as a syntax error and state that "`ArrayIndexOutOfBoundsException has already been caught`." This is because the higher-level exception class already catches all of the exception class instance objects in the family tree below it. Reverse these so that the subclass is chained first, and the problem will resolve.

In the case of the second rule, and especially where you are working with exception classes that are not directly related to one another, a **multicatch** block can be used. Here you only use one reference variable name and list all the exception class data types you want to look for, separated by an OR operator:

```
catch (ArrayIndexOutOfBoundsException | IllegalArgumentException exc)
{
    // do something. . .
}
```

Notice that there is only one reference variable. Whichever exception thrown that is caught by this block (if its data type matches one of these two) will be used as the data type for the variable. This can be useful in fostering a succinct and more easily readable code listing (as well as saving you some typing).

Explicitly throwing exceptions: An additional option you have to handle errors and issues in your code is to purposefully throw an exception instead of allowing the JVM to do it. Using the keywords **throws** and **throw** allows a developer to trigger the instantiation and throwing of an exception class object whenever a condition or issue has occurred that is not wanted for their application. For example, consider the following `static` application method:

Code Snippet 10.7

```
public static LittleClass assignObject(LittleClass objRef)
        throws IllegalArgumentException
{
    if (objRef == null)
        throw new IllegalArgumentException(); // instance object
    else
        return objRef;
}
```

The **throws** keyword is always used in a method header or class header: it signals to the compiler that the following code is capable of throwing exception class objects of the specified type and that this code should be "listened" to for those throws. Then within the code itself, the **throw** keyword does the actual creation of the exception class instance object. In the example here, the `throws` keyword indicates that this method can throw an `IllegalArgumentException`. This means that if the code that invokes this method passes parameter data (from their side, an argument) that is in error or is `null`, an exception can be thrown. Notice that because you are dealing with exception classes and creating an instance object of the desired class, the **new** keyword and the default constructor must be used with the throw keyword. The code that invokes this method must be ready to handle this unchecked exception with a try...catch statement or the exception throw can cause the application to halt:

Code Snippet 10.8

```
// in main()
LittleClass cls = null;
try
{
    LittleClass cls2 = assignObject(cls);
}
catch (Exception ex)
{
    System.out.println(ex.getMessage());
    ex.printStackTrace();
}
```

If your code throws an unchecked exception, the invoking code's exception handling will be optional. On the other hand, if you design your code so that it throws one of the checked exceptions, this will **force** the invoking code to handle your exception. Consider the following unrealistic example, which modifies the `assignObject()` method from earlier:

Code Snippet 10.9

```
public static LittleClass assignObject(LittleClass objRef)
        throws IllegalArgumentException, ClassNotFoundException
{
    if (true) // Always evaluates to true
        throw new ClassNotFoundException(); // instance object

    return null;
}
```

Notice that you can indicate the possibility of throwing more than one exception class type by using a comma after the first exception type. Here this code always returns a `ClassNotFoundException` (purely for demonstration purposes). Back in the invoking code, if this throw is unhandled, the compiler (and most IDEs) will show an error of

```
"unreported exception ClassNotFoundException; must be caught or declared to be thrown"
```

You will most likely see this code when working with advanced Java (file I/O, database integration, multithreading, etc.) whose code will often throw checked exceptions.

As stated at the start of this section, the best defense is a good offense. Proactively handling exceptions and suboptimal conditions in your code through Java's exception-handling functionality will help increase the reliability and usability of your code. At the very least, it will help you in debugging logic errors and to write better code that minimizes even the possibility of throwing any of these exceptions. For the other cases where exceptions cannot be helped, handle them, and allow your application to smartly respond and continue running.

SUMMARY POINTS

- Anticipating errors and exceptions in your code through good logic design is a great overall best practice. Handling any exceptions that you might not be able to anticipate beforehand is the next best practice afterward.
- Java uses exception classes as the framework for interacting with and handling exceptions that occur.
- An unhandled exception will cause your application to halt and end.
- Exceptions that are handled are "caught," and catching exceptions allows your application to continue running, increasing its reliability and robustness against errant conditions.
- The exception classes in Java are part of an inheritance hierarchy that starts with the parent class Throwable.
- Exceptions that fall in the checked category are required by the developer to have code written that handles them before the application will even compile. Other unchecked exceptions can occur at runtime. Handling them is considered a best practice but is optional.
- A try...catch statement can be used to attempt potentially exception-generating code and "catch" the exception instance object thrown by that code when the exception occurs.
- Code that should execute whether there was an exception thrown or not should be placed in an optional "finally" block at the end of the try...catch statement.
- Multiple exceptions can be handled through chained catch statements. Exception chains should be ordered from more specific subclass to more general superclasses.
- Exceptions from nondirectly inherited classes can be watched for together in a multicatch statement.
- `Exception` class's instance objects inherit methods from the `Throwable` class, enabling the extraction of information about the exception that occurred.
- Developers can purposefully cause exceptions to be thrown, applying their usage to logic not normally considered errant by the JVM.

QUICK PROBLEMS

1. **Think:** How do exception classes in Java demonstrate the primary benefits of class inheritance in an object-oriented language?
2. **Coding:** Write some code that will attempt to divide an integer by zero. Enclose that code in a try...catch block, and set up your catch block to watch for `RuntimeException` objects to be thrown. Print the available information from the exception object to the console.
3. **Think:** How can loop structures be used effectively with exception handling in a Java program? (*Hint:* How do you give your user another "chance" after the error is caught?)

10.2 Java Development Good Practices

Good practice in Java development encompasses much more than event handling and carefully planned and implemented logic in our applications (though these are two very important starts). There are many entire books dedicated to the subject, with extensive discussion of good practice in specific Java language contexts such as security, program reliability, defensive programming, program readability, developer assumptions and bad habits, general programming, and application performance/speed/efficiency. Many of the language areas of Java that have been covered so far cross-reference with these broad topics for good practice with the language syntax. Java developers who spend decades in their career field often only encounter a small percentage of the good practice topics that have been written about. An extensive and in-depth discussion of this broad topic is beyond the scope of this textbook. But many good practices can be examined in the context of what you have learned so far and apply to your development efforts, particularly in information systems development contexts. You will find a use for all the following at some point in your careers!

Good practices (thus far) summarized: Good practices and key ideas for Java development have been sprinkled and implied throughout the chapters covered in this textbook so far. Table 10.2 provides a quick summary and convenient reference of **some** of these in the order that they have been discussed, along with a short description of each.

Table 10.2. Summary of This Textbook's Good Practices So Far

Chapter 0: Basics of Java Programming

Subject	Best practice
Commenting	Include sufficient but not excessive commenting with your code.
Formatting	Keep your code well tabbed, spaced, and cleanly aligned to improve readability.
Variables	Give your variables short, descriptive names, and use `camelCaseNotation` to name them.
Variables	It is a good idea to declare one variable per line of code.

Chapter 1: Putting Data to Work with Operators

Subject	Best practice
Operators	Remember that the assignment and equality operators behave differently!
Data types	A lower-precision numeric data type will be up-converted the higher one in a formula.
Operators	Using short circuit boolean operators can increase evaluation efficiency in some cases.
Data ranges	Be careful of inclusivity/exclusivity in checking for ranges of values.
Operators	Good use of parentheses can bring predictability to the processing of operators in a formula.

Chapter 2: Using Object-Oriented Java

Subject	Best practice
Classes	Think of a class as a blueprint that guides the building, state, and actions of future objects.
Classes	Constructors do not construct; they initialize newly constructed objects.
Classes	There is only ever one copy of a static data field of a class created upon class usage.

Chapter 3: Strings and Text Formatting

Subject	Best practice
String	A `String` can be thought of as an array of char values.
String	The equality operator will not reliably compare two `String` variables. Use a comparison method.
Index notation	The first index position is always at 0; the last index position is always at length – 0.

Chapter 4: Decision Logic and Code Flow

Subject	Best practice
Logic flow	The `if` statement causes mutually exclusive logic branching: one route or another at a time but not both.
Code blocks	With some, but not all, Java syntax, curly braces are optional in a one-line-of-code body.
Switch statement	A `switch` cannot compare all data types, only a small set of them.

Chapter 5: Loops, Loops, Loops, Loops . . .

Subject	Best practice
Looping behavior	Java will execute your loops exactly the way you set them up. Consider loops carefully!
Loop variables	Altering a loop control variable's value inside a loop body can change the loop's behavior!
Nested loops	The inner loops will run their number of times for each and every outer loop iteration.
Loop types	Some loops test prior to looping; one tests after the first loop iteration has occurred.

Chapter 6: Methods

Subject	Best practice
Methods	Methods allow for reusable, modular, and more maintainable code.
Defining methods	Method headers have required and optional parts and values for each that change usage.
Defining methods	Methods are always defined within a Java class, even static application methods.
Return types	Any return type other than "`void`" requires a returned value by the method code body.
Naming methods	Method names should use `camelCaseNotation`, consist of a verb, and describe its purpose.
Method signature	The signature of a method consists of its name and parameter configuration.
Parameter data	Method parameters are completely pass by value in Java, even for complex data types.

Chapter 7: Working with Data in Arrays	
Subject	**Best practice**
Arrays	Arrays use index notation for element mapping.
Array data types	Primitive data-type arrays contain values; complex-type arrays contain reference elements.
Arrays	Normal arrays in Java are nonresizable once they are first created.
Copying arrays	The equality operator copies only array references and not array contents.
Multidim arrays	Two-dimensional arrays are an array of arrays in memory.

Chapter 8: Object-Oriented Programming with Java Classes	
Subject	**Best practice**
Classes	Classes easily bundle actions and data together in objects and increase system scalability.
Member access	Access modifiers change the ability for code outside the class to access it.
Member access	Industry best practice recommends private/protected access modifier for class data fields.
Class names	Class names should be capitalized and should typically contain nouns.
Constructors	It is a good idea to always define a zero-arg, "default" constructor with your classes.
Methods	Accessor and mutator methods should be carefully considered for all data fields.

Chapter 9: Class Inheritance and Polymorphism	
Subject	**Best practice**
Inheritance	Try to limit class inheritance to your own classes / same package classes for code stability.
Inheritance	Carefully consider the more specific context that your inherited class may operate in.
Inheritance	Try to avoid wasteful overloading/overriding of methods. Ensure value is added each time.
Polymorphism	Consider allowing polymorphic abilities to prepare your application code for the future.

Minimal privilege approach: Taking a development approach of providing minimal and strict access to the members of a class object is a popular technique for increasing the security of the data processed by an information system. In addition to proper restrictions to data residing in databases, external files, and networked resources, the information systems professional should be mindful that information systems often keep a great deal of data in memory—for example, during transaction processing and data analytics activities. Contemporary systems often use class objects to keep that data in memory and to make it easily accessible and manipulatable.

For example, JSON (JavaScript Object Notation) data is often the transmitted data of choice in web application environments, and often where REST (representational state transfer) services are consumed/processed. Developers in these environments (which include many Java developers) often follow contemporary practices in deserializing JSON data into class objects to make it easier to work with and change (if needed). Then the class objects (and their data fields) can be serialized back into JSON data easily, without the need for messy string manipulation of the JSON text itself. While those objects are in memory, they could contain highly sensitive data regulated by strict business rules and/or governmental regulatory practices (student data, health information, etc.). Implementing a strict data policy for the structure and nature of the class definition files themselves is often a must. An example of a retail order in JSON format might look like this:

```
{
  "custId": 123,
  "ordId": 4567,
  "orderItems": [
    {
      "prodId": 1,
      "price": 9.99,
      "title": "Orange Juice"
    },
    {
      "prodId": 78,
      "price": 95.98,
```

```
      "title": "Blender"
    },
    {
      "prodId": 1985,
      "price": 3.00,
      "title": "Dr. E's Candy Bar"
    }
  ]
}
```

A poorly designed class whose instance object contains this data, added to what could be security exploits in the information system where the data is in memory, could pose a risk to this customer's data (not to mention the reputation and legal standing of the organization). Businesses will often adopt the philosophy of network professionals in "locking it all down and opening up only what you need opened." This approach is a **minimal privilege** approach to class design and is considered to be a good practice for the contemporary Java developer.

Often this approach is taken to an extreme where, once created, class instance objects cannot be altered. These are known as **immutable class objects**. String instance objects actually fall in this class. Think about the following code:

```
String myName = "Dr. E";
myName = "Dr. Ezell";
```

Now that you know more about String object construction (chapter 3) and rereferencing of reference variables (chapters 2 and 8), look at what is happening here: you do not change the original `String`; you merely replace the reference to the old `String` instance object with a new reference to a new `String` instance object. The `String` class has been given the `final` modifier, meaning it cannot be extended into any custom subclasses. A quick look at the `String` class's official Oracle documentation shows that no data fields are public or exposed, none of the methods alter the `String` stored in the instance object, and the one overloaded version of the `String` constructor that actually takes another `String` as a parameter makes a copy of that parameter.[*] This helps prevent a malicious or careless programmer from building a direct reference to any internal data fields of the object. The following formally states some of these common rules for immutable class objects:

- The class and many/all of its methods are given the `final` modifier so that extending the class through class inheritance is prohibited.
- A constructor that copies any objects passed to it instead of passing through a reference variable's value is preferred so that no direct links to internal data fields can be surreptitiously achieved.
- None of the instance methods of the class return back a reference variable directly to any data fields. For example, if a data field is an array, there may be a method that returns a copy of an element at an index position of the array. The method will never expose a reference to the array data field directly, keeping strict control of internal object resources in the hands of the class's internal code only.
- All data fields are given the `private` access modifier, locking down external access to them.
- Sometimes, even the constructor is given the `private` modifier, controlling even the creation of instance objects of the class more tightly.

As an information systems developer, you will need to carefully consider business rules and logic, regulatory requirements, and security approaches in the system overall, as you are involved with the planning and implementation of classes. A class could fall on the extremes of immutable, as described here, to completely `public` in every defined member.

More informative methods: Consider the following example of a method of a class that has access to a data field consisting of an array of `LittleClass` instance objects called `lcArray`. This array receives two parameters, an int `oldValue` and an int `newValue`, and will change the num data field of the `LittleClass` instance object that contains `oldValue` to `newValue`:

---

[*] https://docs.oracle.com/en/java/javase/17/docs/api/java.base/java/lang/String.html.

Code Snippet 10.10

```
public void replaceValue(int oldValue, int newValue)
{
    for (int i=0; i<lcArray.length; i++)
    {
        if (lcArray[i].num == oldValue)
        {
            lcArray[i].num = newValue;
        }
    }
}
```

What has to happen for this method to function correctly? First, all the elements in the array have to be non-null reference variables that actually reference `LittleClass` instance objects. If the first requirement is met, then secondly, one of the objects referenced by the array will need to have a num data field that actually contains `oldValue`. What happens if the first requirement fails? As you saw earlier, a `NullPointerException` will be thrown. What happens if the second requirement fails? This isn't an exception, but if the `oldValue` is not found within the num data field of any of the referenced objects, then nothing happens. Lastly, a more important question: How will the invoking code know if the value of `oldValue` was found and replaced or not in the array? A good practice in Java is to make your methods **more informative**, signaling to invoking code the status or the results of some operation or indicating that an error or suboptimal condition has occurred. The following might be a better version of this method:

Code Snippet 10.11

```
public boolean replaceValue(int oldValue, int newValue)
        throws NullPointerException
{
    // Assume at first the value will not be found.
    boolean searchResult = false;

    for (int i=0; i<lcArray.length; i++)
    {
        if (lcArray[i] == null)
            throw new NullPointerException();
        else if (lcArray[i].num == oldValue)
        {
            // Replace the value
            lcArray[i].num = oldValue;
            // Change the boolean "flag"
            searchResult = true;
        }
    }

    // Communicate the success or failure back to the
    // invoking code
    return searchResult;
}
```

Our method can communicate back to the invoking code in two main ways: First, if a `null` reference is found, a new `NullPointerException` instance object is thrown back to the calling code instead of letting the JVM discover this during runtime. Second, a `boolean` value is returned so that the invoking code can place the call to this method within an if statement or some other decision structure, allowing their code execution to flow appropriately based on the results of this search and replace operation. Developing methods that communicate results and/or state is good practice for Java developers.

Sanitizing sensitive output: You have most likely seen sanitized output in software systems and applications so much now that you have become desensitized to their presence. A basic, sensible step that developers should implement in business and regulatory rules in an information system is to mask sensitive, private data whenever possible. The idea here is that when information like passwords, identification numbers, personal contact numbers (phone, cell, etc.), sensitive salary amounts, and the like have to be shown in certain unsecure contexts (reports, selection screens, etc.), every effort to make them useless to malicious individuals should be taken. Here are a few common examples:

- Many contexts call for the printing of part of a password to remind the user which they should use during authentication. Some example code can be easily written to enable the masked reveal of a password:

Code Snippet 10.12

```
String password = "12345SecurePassword"; // Bad idea!
System.out.print("Password: ");
for (int i=0; i<password.length() - 2; i++)
{
    System.out.print("*");
}
System.out.print(password.substring(password.length()-2));
```

Console output:

```
Password: *****************rd
```

- Identification numbers, such as US Social Security numbers, can often be masked in the same way:

Code Snippet 10.13

```
String ssn = "000-00-1234"; // Never store this in a variable!
String ssnMasked = "####-##-" + ssn.substring(ssn.length() - 4);
System.out.println("ID: " + ssnMasked);
```

Console output:

```
ID: ####-##-1234
```

- Monetary amounts are often hidden by rounding up or down or providing a range of values that the actual value falls in between. For example, in the US, the stock transactions of the members of Congress are often shown as ranges to protect financial privacy:

Code Snippet 10.14

```
double trade = 758443.32;
String senatorPrintRange = "";

if ((trade <= 500000) && (trade > 0))
    senatorPrintRange = "$0 - $500K";
else if ((trade > 5000) && (trade <= 1000000))
    senatorPrintRange = "$500K - $1M";
else
    senatorPrintRange = "> $1M";

System.out.println(
        "Senator Codebase's 2024 Stock Trades: "
                + senatorPrintRange);
```

Console output:

```
Senator Codebase's 2024 Stock Trades: $500K-$1M
```

During the systems analysis and design process and particularly during requirement elicitation, the IS professional should thoroughly investigate the level and extent of potentially private/sensitive information revealed in reports, visualizations, and areas of the UI: which employees can see them, which employees **should** see them, and how much of that data should be shown and/or masked.

Cleaner Java syntax with static imports: An infrequently discussed but often useful feature of the Java programming language is the ability to perform static imports of specific members of a class or all members of a class (the data fields and the methods). This can be useful when you are using a method, usually a static method, of a class over and over and have to write repetitive, qualifying syntax to ensure the method definition is found. A common exemplar of the usefulness of a static import involves the member methods of the Math class:

Code Snippet 10.15

```
// Somewhat inefficient code. . .
// Generating Lottery Numbers
for (int i=0; i<7; i++)
{
    if (i % 2 == 0)
        System.out.print(
                Math.max(
                        Math.round(Math.random()*100),
                        Math.round(Math.random()*100)));
    else
        System.out.print(
                Math.min(
                        Math.round(Math.random() * 100),
                        Math.round(Math.random()*100)));

    if (i < 6)
        System.out.print(", ");
}
```

That's a lot of "`Math.`" and "`System.`" used throughout the code. By adding the following import statements to the top of our code, you can static import the methods of these two classes and eliminate much of the repetitive syntax:

```
import static java.lang.Math.*;
import static java.lang.System.*;
```

Notice the use of the dot operator after the class name followed by the asterisk. This indicates that you want to import all methods and data fields from the class into your application. If you wanted only a specific member, you would replace the asterisk with the member's name. Now the code can be simplified like so:

Full Program 10.5

```
import java.util.*;
import static java.lang.Math.*;
import static java.lang.System.*;

public class Chapter10Examples {

    public static void main(String[] args) {

// Somewhat inefficient code. . .
// Generating Lottery Numbers
for (int i=0;i<7;i++)
{
    if (i % 2 == 0)
        out.print(
                max(
                    round(random()*100),
                    round(random()*100)));
    else
        out.print(
                min(
                    round(random() * 100),
                    round(random()*100)));

    if (i < 6)
        out.print(", ");
}
   }
}
```

This feature "inherits" the methods and data fields of the classes you static import from into your application and allows your application to consider them to be "locally defined" in your application, as if you wrote the methods yourself in your Java `main()` class file. This can be convenient in specialized situations where repetitive syntax occurs. **But be warned:** it is considered **good practice to only use this sparingly!** Undesired issues can arise with the use of static imports as well. For example, if there are data fields with the same name in two or more of the classes you static import from, then the compiler will not be able to determine which you wish to use and will raise an error. **This is not a technique to apply in every application you develop!**

Documenting your code: Early in the textbook we discussed—and you have now seen throughout the book—examples of leaving code comments in your Java files. The ideal best practice here is to comment your code sufficiently but not excessively. Also, comments that repeat what can be obviously ascertained from a cursory glance at the code being commented are to be avoided as well. The logic of a program can often become complex and difficult to understand without some notes or guidance. Code comments help communicate to the next developer (or to you, after a year or so of not looking at the code) what is going on in this one particular section of code, how to use it, when not to use it, who wrote it and when, and why it was needed.

In addition to code comments, documenting your code is equally important. If the code you will use is proprietary, then other developers may not be able to see your source listing at all. They may only gain access to the documentation (*think:* metadata) about the code itself. Java provides an easy syntax for generating very descriptive syntax of your code. The Oracle `javadoc` tool can parse the documentation syntax of your code, generating an HTML document containing your comments.[*]

Each `javadoc` comment block begins with `/**`, and most IDEs will autocomplete the rest of the block and expand it as you add `javadoc` parameters (and many IDEs will add those as well based on the structure of the code itself).

Here is an example small class appropriately commented in the syntax that the `javadoc` tool can understand:

Code Snippet 10.16

```
/**
 * Creates Class Objects whose data fields
 * can be stored or swapped.
 *
 * @author Dr. E
 *
 */
public class NumberSwap {

    /**The First Number Stored */
    public int firstNum;
    /**The Second Number Stored */
    public int secondNum;

    /**
     * Default Constructor
     */
    public NumberSwap()
    {
        this.firstNum = 0;
        this.secondNum = 0;
    }

    /**
     * Two-Parameter Constructor
     *
     * @param firstNum
     * @param secondNum
```

* https://www.oracle.com/technical-resources/articles/java/javadoc-tool.html.

```
     */
    public NumberSwap(int firstNum, int secondNum)
    {
        this.firstNum = firstNum;
        this.secondNum = secondNum;
    }

    /**
     * Swaps firstNum into secondNum
     * and secondNum into firstNum
     * without data loss.
     */
    public void swapForward()
    {
        int tempNum;
        tempNum = this.firstNum;
        this.firstNum = this.secondNum;
        this.secondNum = tempNum;
    }

    /**
     * Swaps secondNum into firstNum
     * and firstNum into secondNum
     * without data loss.
     */
    public void swapBackward()
    {
        int tempNum;
        tempNum = this.secondNum;
        this.secondNum = this.firstNum;
        this.firstNum = tempNum;

    }
}
```

Most IDEs will provide a one-click method for generating the `javadoc` HTML page and giving you the link to where that HTML page is located in your local project folder. Viewing that generated HTML, you will notice its style is almost identical to the official Oracle documentation for most Java classes and features. Figure 10.3 gives you a partial view of the generated doc. Since it is a locally created HTML file, this makes it very easy to share across a corporate network or on the web. Finally, the `javadoc` tool will dynamically describe the methods that are part of your class through inheritance and list those in the generated documentation as well. It is very useful and a good practice to generate descriptive documentation in and about your code.

Table 10.3 summarizes a few of the more commonly used parameters in a `javadoc` comment block in your application (often the IDE will generate these for you when you begin that specific comment block and allow the IDE to autocomplete the rest). The parameters shown in the table must be used in that order when used, and the official Oracle documentation goes into detail for the rest.

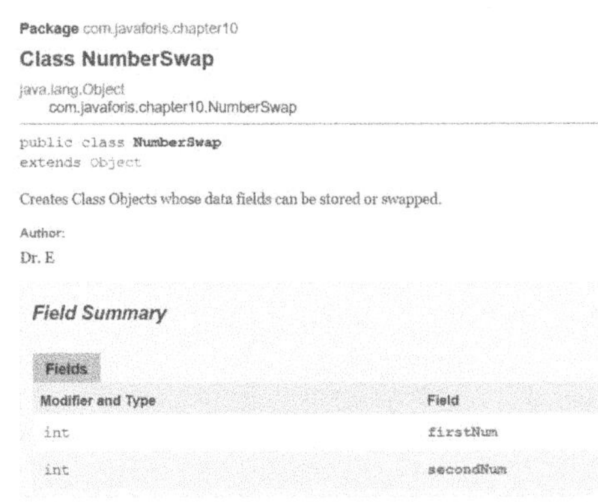

Figure 10.3. Partial View of `javadoc` Tool–Generated HTML for the `NumberSwap` Class

Table 10.3. Common `javadoc` Tool Parameters Used in Documentation Comments

`javadoc` parameter	Description
`@author`	Used typically for a class. Lists the author(s).
`@param`	Used typically for a method. Lists the input parameters defined for the method. Repeat for as many parameters as are present.
`@return`	Used typically for a method. Describes the data type returned.
`@throws`	Used typically for a method. Describes the exception class data type that could be thrown by this method's code.

SUMMARY POINTS

- The concept of minimal privilege in a Java class involves restricting as much of the class as possible from outside access. At the extreme, immutable classes most effectively demonstrate this security principle.
- When possible, it is good practice to enable your method to communicate back with its invoking code so that that code's logic can adapt to the success or failure of the method to perform its task(s) accordingly or handle any exceptions thrown by the method's actions.
- Both business and personal data are often sanitized/masked/obscured in areas where nonauthorized individuals may see it or where malicious individuals may be able to use it to their advantage.
- Static importing in Java can be useful, though it is good practice to use it sparingly to clean up the syntax in your code.
- Using both normal code documentation and `javadoc`-generated documentation, syntax can improve the ability of others to understand and use your code and is an excellent professional practice for developers working in the language.

QUICK PROBLEMS

1. **Coding:** Take the example `LittleClass` class used in this chapter and implement the principles of class immutability within. How does this impact the functionality of `BiggerClass`?
2. **Think:** Why might it be preferable to purposefully throw an exception instead of waiting for the JVM to encounter a situation where it generates one?
3. **Think:** Describe the benefits of creating thorough documentation for the Java classes you define. What are the ways you can "document" the class from within the class itself (variable names, method names, etc.)?

Summary

As mentioned in the chapter, there are many more commonly discussed and accepted best practices for Java developers to consider while building their applications and systems. Many of these are applicable to the usage of higher-level syntax and language concepts that are beyond the scope of this book. Where applicable, in the remaining chapters and supplemental contents, good practices with topics newly discussed from here on out will be highlighted. Now that you have completed your exploration of the major object-oriented development topics in Java, this chapter presents a good opportunity to pause and reflect on both practices discussed before and new ones like exception handling and other practices applicable at this point. Well-thought-out and designed logic, purposeful and thorough exception handling and mitigation, and succinct, efficient code are great first steps in good practice in using the Java language for your information systems development efforts at all levels. Now that the majority of the basics of contemporary OO are behind us, in the next chapter, you will explore the class-based JavaFX library, used to create modern look-and-feel desktop application user interfaces.

Practice Problems

Terminology

Match the following terms from the chapter with their most appropriate definition:

1. `Exception`	a. The last block of a try...catch statement. Code placed here will execute regardless of the occurrence of a thrown exception or not.
2. Error	b. The top-level class in the exception class inheritance hierarchy. All other exception classes inherit from it.
3. Unhandled exception	c. Allows for the importation of class members into your application in such a way as your application considers them to be local. Best used sparingly!
4. Exception catching	d. Syntax structure in a Java application that allows potential exception throwing code to be examined and any exceptions generated by the code to be caught.
5. Checked exceptions	e. The use of exception syntax in a Java program to process exceptions and allow an application to continue running.
6. Unchecked exceptions	f. The usage of multiple catch blocks in a try...catch statement in order to broaden your application's ability to catch a wider array of exception data-type objects thrown. Typically used for directly inherited exception classes.
7. `Throwable`	g. An exception thrown in a Java application when a reference to a parent class object is attempted to be cast as one of its children.
8. `ClassNotFoundException`	h. A security approach that secures all unnecessary access to a resource or data, opening up access only in a strict, as-needed basis.
9. `NullPointerException`	i. Java keyword that actively throws an exception class instance object. Followed by the exception class object's instantiation using `new` and constructor call.
10. `ClassCastException`	j. Either a problem with the syntax of a Java program or a severe issue that occurs during program execution.
11. Try...catch statement	k. Keyword used in a method header to indicate that its code intends to throw an exception class type when needed.
12. `finally`	l. Oracle tool used to easily generate professional-looking HTML documentation for your code.
13. Exception chaining	m. Exception types that are not required to be examined by exception-handling syntax.
14. Multicatch	n. An exception thrown in a Java application when a class name is attempted to be used programmatically but the class source file cannot be found or the class name resolved.
15. Throwing exceptions	o. An occurrence in Java that represents abnormal or undesired program behavior.
16. `throw`	p. A class developed under a strict security approach. For example, it may prevent unmanaged access to its internal data, use a copy-style constructor, and prevent extension by other classes.
17. `throws`	q. Writing code to purposefully throw an exception to indicate to invoking code that an undesirable or suboptimal outcome has occurred during program execution.
18. Minimal privilege	r. An exception thrown in a Java application that represents an attempt to use an object referenced by a variable when no object exists at that reference.
19. Immutable class	s. An exception in a Java program that is not caught or processed. Will cause a program to halt and display an error.
20. `import static`	t. Succinct syntax catching multiple, directly unrelated, exception class objects thrown in a single catch block statement.
21. `javadoc`	u. Exceptions in Java that, when caused by certain syntax, are required by the compiler to be caught/handled before the program can be compiled/run.

Find the Error

In each of the following problems, carefully examine the code given, and determine the error(s)/issue(s) with each. Keep in mind, the error(s) could be syntax (code) or logic (intended outcome) based or both!

1.

```
public static int sumNums(LittleClass objA, LittleClass objB)
        throw NullPointerException
{
    int theSum = 0;
    objA = null;
    objB = null;
    objA = LittleClass(5);
    objA = LittleClass(7);

    if (theSum = 0)
        throws NullPointerException();
    else
        theSum = objA.num + objB+num;

    return NullPointerException(theSum);
}
```

2.

```
Scanner in = new Scanner(System.in);
System.out.print("Enter first name:");
try
{
    in = in.nextLine();
    catch (IOException ioex)
    {
         in = in.next();
    }
}
```

3.

```
Scanner in = new Scanner(System.in);
string name = "";
System.out.print("Enter first name:");
try
{
    name = in.nextDouble();

}
catch (
        Exception(InputMismatchException) exA
                | Exception(RuntimeException) exB)
{
     in = in.nextLine();
}
finally
{
    throws Exception();
}
```

4.

```
Scanner in = new Scanner(System.in);
String name = "";
System.out.print("Enter first name:");

try
```

```
{
    name = in.nextLine();
}
catch (Exception | InputMismatchException ex)
{
    System.out.println(ex.getMessage());
}
catch (NullPointerException npex | InputMismatchException ex)
{
    System.out.println(ex.getMessage());
}
```

5.

```
public static String inputName()
{
    Scanner in = new Scanner(System.in);
    String name = "";
    System.out.print("Enter first name:");

    try
    {
        name = in.nextLine();
        return name;
    }
    catch (InputMismatchException ex)
    {
        System.out.println(ex.getMessage());
        return "NONAME";
    }
    finally
    {
        System.out.println("Method Done!");
    }
    catch (Exception ex)
    {
        System.out.println(ex.getMessage());
        return "NONAME";
    }
    finally
    {
        System.out.println("Method Done!");
    }
}
```

Think about It

1. How does Java handle exceptions that occur in its applications? How does this align with the overall nature of the Java programming language?
2. What are the two types of exceptions in Java? When are they watched for or thrown?
3. How does the developer of a Java program using exceptions code their applications differently in regard to the two main types of Java exceptions?
4. How does class inheritance impact the way a developer uses the try...catch statement?
5. What should a developer keep in mind when chaining catch blocks in a try...catch statement?
6. What is the main difference between the chaining of catch blocks and a multicatch statement?
7. What are some of the benefits of code that purposefully throws an exception?
8. What are several ways that the security of your code can be tightened?
9. What is a benefit of generating official documentation for your code?
10. How does making methods more “communicative” benefit the logic of the invoking code?

Short Syntax Problems

1. Write a small program that prompts a user to enter two numbers, and display the result of dividing the first by the second. Convert the inputs to doubles for the division. Handle any possible exception that might arise. Use a boolean variable to prompt the user to "Try Again," and allow them to reenter the second number on the same, current loop if they enter a `0` for the second number.
2. Using the `LittleClass` definition from this chapter, write a method that will accept a reference to a `LittleClass` instance object, an int location, and a reference to a `LittleClass` array. The method will attempt to copy the reference to the parameter `LittleClass` object, into the referenced array, at the particular location. Set up the method so that it uses a multicatch statement that will catch either a `null` reference or an out-of-bounds index position in the array. Return a boolean to indicate if either of these causes the operation to fail or if it succeeded.
3. Modify your method from short syntax problem #2 so that the method throws both of your exceptions instead, and remove the boolean return type. Write invoking code that handles either of the exceptions if it is thrown and displays an appropriate message.
4. Modify the method `.addAdvisee()` from short syntax problem #7 in chapter 9 to throw a `IllegalArgumentException` if the student reference passed to it is null.
5. Modify your student class from full problem #1 in chapter 9 to add a method called `.printStudentDetails()`. This will print a list of all students in a report-like format with column headers and the data for each student below. When printing the GPA, mask this sensitive data by printing the range for each student's GPA (0 to 1, 1 to 2, 2 to 3, 3 to 4, and 4+).
6. Modify your application from full problem #4 in chapter 7 to add a menu option for "Print All Contacts." This option will print a professional report of all the contacts stored in the system, along with column headers. For each contact, mask all but the last four numbers of the phone number and all but the first and last two characters and the @ symbol of the email address when printing each contact's details.
7. Modify the `.createMatrix()` method from short syntax problem #6 in chapter 6. Throw an `IllegalArgumentException` if either of the input parameters is negative. Write invoking code, and test out your exception handling.

Full Problems

1. Write a full program that will be used by a small catering company to help them plan out the seating arrangement for small gatherings of VIP guests. The program will have the following abilities implemented in a menu system (which will include a "Quit Application" option as well):
   a. The program will use two arrays to represent the two rows of seats on each side of a long table. One array is one side of the table, and the other is the opposite side. The application will ask how many seats are needed for a row, and the opposite side will match that quantity.
   b. The arrays will store references to `Guest` instance objects. The `Guest` class should store the guest's name, organization, and a list of food allergies (you can store this in one String). Make sure the `Guest` class has many of our security concepts discussed in this chapter implemented.
   c. The program will allow you to first create `Guest` objects. The user will have the option of choosing a table side and then a seat number. The Guest object will be created and referenced by that element in the appropriate array. Be sure to translate seat 1 to array index 0, and so on.
   d. The program will have the option of moving a `Guest` one seat to the left or right, with the following checks:
      i. An exception will be thrown if a `Guest` is assumed to be at a seat location and that seat is empty.
      ii. If the `Guest` is at the end of a row, they cannot move left (at the start) or to the right (if they are at the end).
      iii. If a `Guest` is seated next to someone, swap that `Guest` and the person next to them in whichever direction they move. If no one is seated next to a `Guest` in the direction you want to move them, make sure to empty the seat the `Guest` was previously in.
      iv. The user can choose to move the `Guest` a far distance to another seat in the same row or a seat in the opposite row. The application

should handle and prompt for any exceptions dealing with a seat being filled, no Guest at a seat to be moved, or an invalid target seat index location.

e. The application provides an option to print the seating chart at any point in its usage.

2. Write a full Java application that will keep track of a cohort of students and generate a report on their academic characteristics.
   a. Create a `CohortStudent` class. Each `CohortStudent` object will keep track of a student's name, major, and GPA. Use some of the best practices regarding access modifiers and exception handling for the data fields and methods in this class.
   b. Each `CohortStudent` object should have the ability to compare their GPA with that of another `CohortStudent` object. A returned value of "true" indicates that the student's GPA is higher or equal to the one compared to. Use exception handling to ensure that no `null` references are attempted to be used.
   c. Your application should allow the user to create `CohortStudent`s. Any `CohortStudent` can be selected to have their characteristics printed to the console. Mask their GPA by reporting its assignment to a GPA range (0 to 1.0, 1.0 to 2.0, etc.).
   d. Use a normal array of size ten to test things out. Use exception handling to prevent an issue if the user tries to enter more than ten `CohortStudent` details into the system.
   e. Allow the user to print a report showing all `CohortStudent` objects. Print them in groupings by their GPA range, highest to lowest. Use grouping titles to separate out each listing per group.

Chapter 11

Creating Java User Interfaces with JavaFX

What You Will Learn in This Chapter

Information systems professionals who are well rounded in their design and development skills should have some experience in the planning, implementation, and refinement of a user interface (UI) for their applications. The majority of contemporary information systems use a graphical user interface (GUI), though console-based text interface systems are still in use. The JavaFX GUI framework provides an easy-to-learn, object-oriented class library that can help Java developers quickly build professional, business-ready Java GUI applications. Intended as the successor to the Java Swing library, JavaFX is growing in popularity and is well worth the information systems professional's time and effort to learn.

Specifically, this chapter will help you to do the following:

1. Understand the similarities and differences between the Abstract Window Toolkit (AWT), Swing, and JavaFX graphical libraries
2. Understand the nature of the JavaFX library and its approach to designing a GUI-based Java application
3. Understand how to use layout panes and JavaFX controls, specify a visual relationship between these, and display them as a GUI-based application
4. Understand how to handle user-generated events in a JavaFX application, the event delegation model, and the three techniques for event handling
5. Understand the approach to multiform GUI development in JavaFX in both a compact and secondary window approach
6. Understand the manner in which many JavaFX controls store data and how to interact with that data
7. Understand the nature of and examples of the built-in JavaFX charting and visual displays to develop clean- and professional-looking visualizations

Opening Scenario

After extensive work, you and your team have developed an object-oriented, class-based data model for the mom-and-pop grocery inventory system. Using Java's exception-handling classes and studying best practices in Java development efforts, your team has prepared error-checking and error-mitigation logic to be integrated into the client's system. After a thorough review, your project manager believes both you and the team are ready for the final stage in the prototype development, prior to a "so-far" demo to the client: "We need to bring this application into the twenty-first century." The next step is to develop a GUI front end for the application, as the console-based menu system is a little awkward. Your project manager continues, "Since they use GUI-based applications on their personal computers, the owners are not going to want to see a console-based, 'type -a-number-1-here-type-a-number-2-there' system. For this client, it just won't be a good fit. People want to point and click."

Sitting down at your development machine, you realize that you have never thought a lot about how the software that you use every day looks and feels. Immediately all the occasions where applications have frustrated you come to mind—like those times you have spent many minutes trying to find this or that menu option or this and that feature of the application and so on. You recall how some software has been easy to learn and how some applications needed a very thick manual that you now set your coffee cup on. "We have to be mindful of ease of use as well," you think, knowing that time spent carefully designing the look and feel of the client's system will be just as important as time spent writing its code and implementing the client's business rules. You've heard about a few Java GUI libraries but have never needed to take a closer look until now. One more time, refill your coffee mug and dive into the research. You think, "If we can get this right, the clients will be very happy with our abilities and will want to continue this project far into the future . . ."

11.1 Overview of GUI Frameworks in Java

Figure 11.1. Wireframe Diagrams Are Often Used during User Interface Design
Source: "Wireframes" by Christian_Campos is licensed under CC BY 2.0, https://www.flickr.com/photos/23438340@N02/3883508604.

The development and refinement of the graphical user interface (GUI) truly helped bring computing to the masses. Forms, folders, icons, images, "physical" controls—all these real-world things were digitally analogized in the form of the GUI interface, eliminating the need for people to learn terse, and often confusing, command-line syntax. This opened personal computing up to broader usage and laid the groundwork for the web, mobile, artificial intelligence (AI), and "metaverse" platforms so popular today. Companies like Microsoft in the 1980s and later Apple, among others, pioneered early work in adding a GUI layer over top of their operating systems for personal computing systems. This is not to say that earlier computing platforms (both consumer and business focused) did not have a visual user interface. Companies like Xerox and Amiga had earlier (than Apple and Microsoft) introduced point-and-click quasi-graphical systems, but their use was limited and often found only in experimental and lab usages.* Personal computer operating systems interfaces ranged from simple console-like command interfaces (like MS-DOS) to text-/menu-based systems that allowed free movement between commands. The move to GUI systems was often rapid and (again, in the case of Microsoft and Apple) contentious, but innovation along with the more natural and effective use of computing that comes with a GUI drove this computing interface approach to dominance.

Today, computer users leverage the user interface that works best for them and the tasks they want to accomplish. In business, you will find a mix of both console-based applications and GUI-driven software. Often, console applications are running in a GUI-based operating system (i.e., Windows PowerShell for issuing advanced OS commands within Windows). But the GUI design philosophy reigns supreme, both in desktop applications and in web, mobile, and tablet software implementations. In information systems (IS) scenarios, software interactions occur through form-based data entry, tabular reporting, tabbed organization of information, visual display of analyzed data through charting and other visualization types, and so on. As IS professionals, you will encounter these and other GUI scenarios in your daily planning and implementation work.

Directly related to the consideration of a GUI implemented for a system are questions such as the following: Is this data entry method effective? Should this screen be redesigned? How can we reduce the amount of time it takes to accomplish a task? Is the UI intuitive, easy, and efficient? Researchers in IS tell us that the two primary reasons (among many) why users choose to either adopt and use or reject an IS are due to their perception of self-benefit ("Will using this system help me in my job?") and ease of use ("Is this system easy to use, easy to learn, and better than the 'old' way?"). For the IS professional engaged in systems analysis and design, potentially working on the future "to-be" system, these are big hurdles to overcome. Part of your planning and design work should be laser-focused on these two questions when considering a redesign of an existing system or the planning for a new.

Many contemporary, popular programming languages include a framework for developing a GUI application. This includes Java, which has two built into the language and a third that was recently moved out of the official JDK by Oracle to an open-source community. Now that prior chapters have prepared you with a solid basis of

* Eric Raymond tours much of this earlier work at http://www.catb.org/~esr/writings/taouu/html/ch02s05.html.

understanding Java's object-oriented (OO) nature, learning how to use the two most recent GUI frameworks in the language will not take long. They, like the base Java language itself, are class based and help developers quickly build a UI for their applications.

This chapter covers the usage of JavaFX, the most recent Java GUI framework and the one moved out to the open-source community (though still a project Oracle cheers on, even though it does not directly control the development of the framework anymore). First, it will help your learning to briefly discuss the predecessors to JavaFX: AWT and Swing. Companion chapter 1 will walk you through the Swing framework if you are interested (or if your instructor covers that framework instead).

Abstract Window Toolkit (AWT): This was the earliest official framework for creating a graphical, windowed user interface for a Java program. AWT was innovative and made GUI development easily available to Java developers. Originally developed by Sun Microsystems (the originators of the Java language), it was popular in its time, but it had several drawbacks:

- AWT Java applications were not easily portable: AWT GUI elements (buttons, scroll bars, check boxes, etc.) were not part of AWT themselves. Rather, the framework required the use of whatever native controls were available through the operating system. If you wanted to move your AWT Java application to another OS, some rewriting of code was required to use that OS's controls. This made regular Java programs much more portable than AWT-based Java programs. This tie to the underlying OS limited the controls that could be used. If you wanted a new control, you had to code it from scratch.
- There was no "separation of concerns": In contemporary application development, separation of concerns is an approach where the logic of an application and its user interface functionalities are developed separately. With AWT, you were limited in writing logic and UI together with no alternative, decreasing modularity and hindering ease of maintenance by multiple developers.
- AWT was considered a resource-inefficient GUI library: The objects created by using the AWT framework were bulky (back when computing resources were more limited), and the behavior of AWT programs could be buggy/inconsistent.

Swing: Developed by Sun Microsystems through a partnership with Netscape in the 1990s, the Swing framework resolved many of the AWT drawbacks and became a popular successor. Swing was built upon the AWT framework and shares some compatibility with it. Swing is still in broad use today. Many of its benefits include the following:

- Platform independence: Swing controls are part of framework itself, so the developer is not forced to use those built into the OS. Swing applications use AWT to create a window, and then Swing handles the creating/display of controls and interactions with the OS generated by user clicks and activity. This allows for easy portability of a Swing Java application from one OS to another, as Swing interprets the activity generated and decides how to send that to the OS instead of having the developer make those OS calls directly. Think of it like a minigraphical virtual machine (VM) for GUI-based Java applications!
- Since Swing controls were part of the framework itself, this gave developers a much higher variety of controls to work with other than just those natively included on the OS within which the application was running (see figure 11.3 for an example of this variety).
- Since Swing handles its own controls, it has a much richer set of them than any one OS. Due to Swing's portability, the user experience is consistent across operating systems: a button in a Swing app running on Windows will look and act (mostly) the same as one on Mac OS X, Linux, and so on.
- Swing allows for a "model-view-controller" approach to GUI app development, which adheres to the "separation of concerns" design paradigm. The user interface code can be separate from the logic that executes when the UI is used. This allows easier maintenance: one or more developers can work on the UI separately and in parallel with

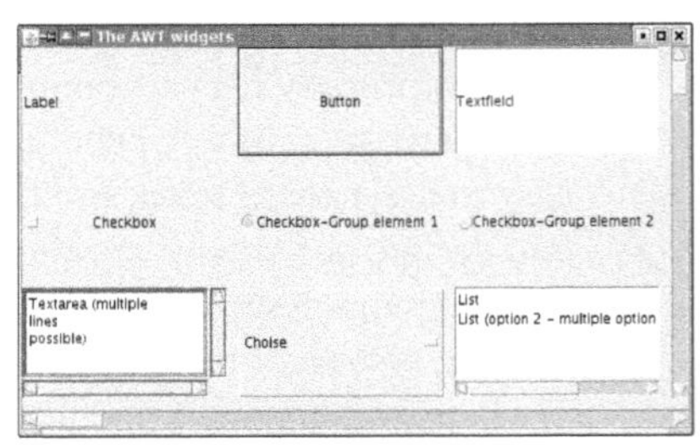

Figure 11.2. Example of an AWT Java Application in Linux
Source: "AWT_at_Linux.jpg" by Sven is public domain, https://commons.wikimedia.org/wiki/File:AWT_at_Linux.png.

other developers who might be working on the application's logic.

- Swing is still relatively popular today. Developers like its reliability (far less buggy!), consistency, and ease with which development can occur.

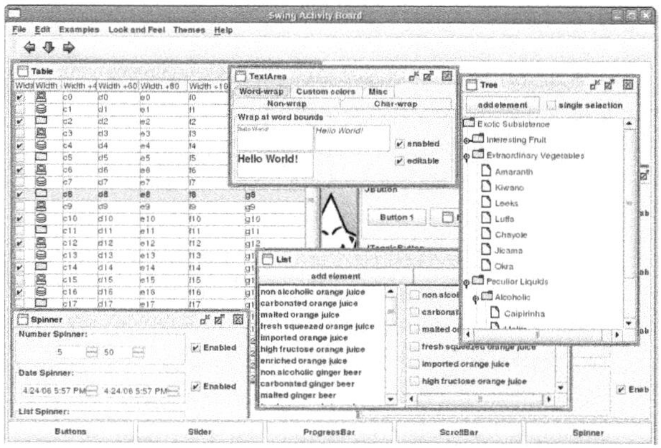

Figure 11.3. Example of a Java Swing GUI Application
Source: "The Swing (Graphics User Interface) Demo of the GNU Classpath Project" by Audrius Meskauskas is licensed as free software under the GNU General Public License, https://commons.wikimedia.org/wiki/File:GC_SwingDemo.PNG.

JavaFX: Developed originally by Sun Microsystems and expanded upon by Oracle, JavaFX was intended as the natural successor to Swing (and still is to some extent). In 2018, Oracle moved JavaFX from "in-house" development and out under the umbrella of OpenJDK (open-source version of Java), into the OpenJFX project.[*],[†] JavaFX is no longer included as a native part of the newest Java JDK releases, though it is still included in JDK 8. This adds some extra steps needed to run a JavaFX project in your IDE of choice (see appendix A for JavaFX installation instructions), but this allows the framework to thrive under speedy community development. Some of the advantages that the JavaFX framework adds above and beyond Swing are the following:

- **Web-ready GUI framework:** JavaFX was intended to be compatible with the web. Web content can be embedded within a JavaFX program, and a JavaFX program can be deployed as a website itself.
- **JavaFX supports multitouch scenarios:** Multitouch, along with a web-compatible nature, makes JavaFX a great development choice for desktop-, web-, mobile-, or tablet-based use cases. Like Swing, JavaFX applications are portable across operating systems, enabling a consistent user experience across both platforms and devices.
- **2D and 3D graphics and animations, rich text, advanced charting, and multimedia support:** JavaFX allows for a much richer user experience than Swing. Visual effects such as rotation, opacity, blurring, shadows, and more can be defined for almost any control on a JavaFX form. Paired with animations, developers can create fairly rich UI "front ends" for their information systems. JavaFX has visually appealing charting ability built in, giving developers quick access to business-ready visualizations.
- **High-degree of customizability and continued MVC support:** Almost every aspect of a JavaFX program can be altered aesthetically through Cascading Style Sheet (CSS) styling. Similar to Swing, JavaFX continues support for the MVC design paradigm, allowing the UI and the logic to be built separately.

Oracle and the development community have for some time intended for JavaFX to be the natural successor to Swing, though there is room for both frameworks in your toolbox. You will find both in use across the Java development world, and you will examine JavaFX in detail in this chapter. The basics, nature, and customizability of JavaFX (as well as Swing) are quickly learned, enhancing your skills as a developer working in the Java language. Figure 11.4 shows an example of a Java application that uses the JavaFX library.

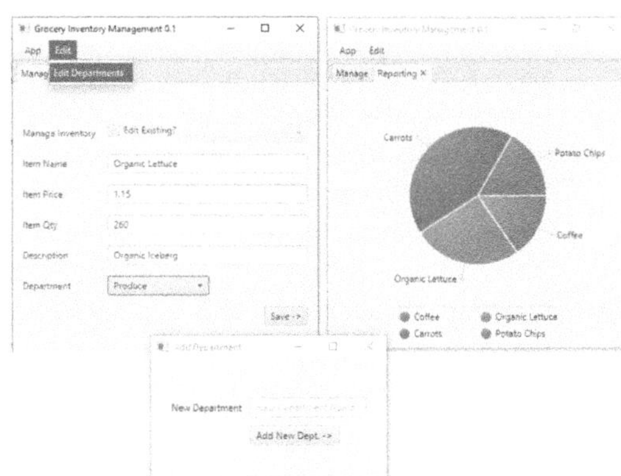

Figure 11.4. Example of a JavaFX Form with Charting and Other Controls

* https://wiki.openjdk.java.net/display/OpenJFX/Main.
† https://openjfx.io/.

SUMMARY POINTS

- The graphical user interface is the dominant method by which users interact with software and computing-based systems.
- Information systems professionals consider several factors when designing software and the interface through which users will interact with it, focusing on issues like self-efficacy and ease of use.
- The Abstract Window Toolkit (AWT) was the earliest GUI framework used in the Java language for creating a visual user interface for Java applications. The framework was heavily dependent on the UI resources of the operating system the Java application was targeted for.
- The Swing framework, next offered as a GUI library for Java, improved upon AWT's weaknesses—namely, through operating system independence and internally implemented UI controls.
- The JavaFX framework, now outsourced to the OpenJFX group with Oracle consultation, modernizes both the GUI controls available for Java applications and their functionality in web/internet contexts.

QUICK PROBLEMS

1. **Think:** Think about the various computing-based devices you interact with on a daily basis. What are some of the things that are common across all of them in terms of the GUI / user interface? Can all tasks (i.e., spreadsheet editing) work effectively on device screens of all sizes (i.e., your smartphone)?
2. **Think:** What is a benefit to having a GUI framework in Java be "operating system independent," and how does this mirror the benefits of the Java language itself?
3. **Think:** Can you perform wireframing and user interface planning for non-GUI applications, like a console/terminal application?

11.2 Building a Basic JavaFX Application

Sun Microsystems, Oracle, and now the OpenJFX project have continued to develop JavaFX as a Java API, which gives it access to the base Java language and allows developers to build a GUI overlay to their Java applications.* Like the Java language itself, the JavaFX libraries are object-oriented (OO). The OO programming approach you have learned in Java in prior chapters will pay off here. Creating the parts of a JavaFX program are relatively easy once you know how constructors and instantiation work (which you do!). Using data fields and invoking member methods of the classes (and their instantiated objects) that make up JavaFX are both done just as you have learned previously.

Understanding the JavaFX framework: You learned in chapter 9 about the hierarchical nature of the Java API. Classes have sibling classes as well as subclasses, and each class only has one parent. JavaFX uses this same hierarchical arrangement in its class libraries. Additionally, since JavaFX is concerned with displaying things **visually**, it approaches the display and drawing of GUI elements on the screen in a hierarchical manner as well. Oracle calls this arrangement approach the **scene graph**, and this arrangement in memory is used to enable efficient renderings (i.e., drawings) of visual elements on screen that represent the underlying class instance objects the developer creates.† Since everything in JavaFX is object oriented (classes), the developer may create an instance object of, say, the `Button` class, which would place the instance object somewhere on the heap. When the JavaFX application runs, instance objects are created on the heap, and the JavaFX scene graph defines a visual relationship among screen-displayed elements that represent those objects. Figure 11.5 shows examples of how JavaFX classes translate to instance objects in a running JavaFX application.

* https://docs.oracle.com/javase/8/javafx/JFXST.pdf.

† https://docs.oracle.com/javafx/2/scenegraph/jfxpub-scenegraph.htm.

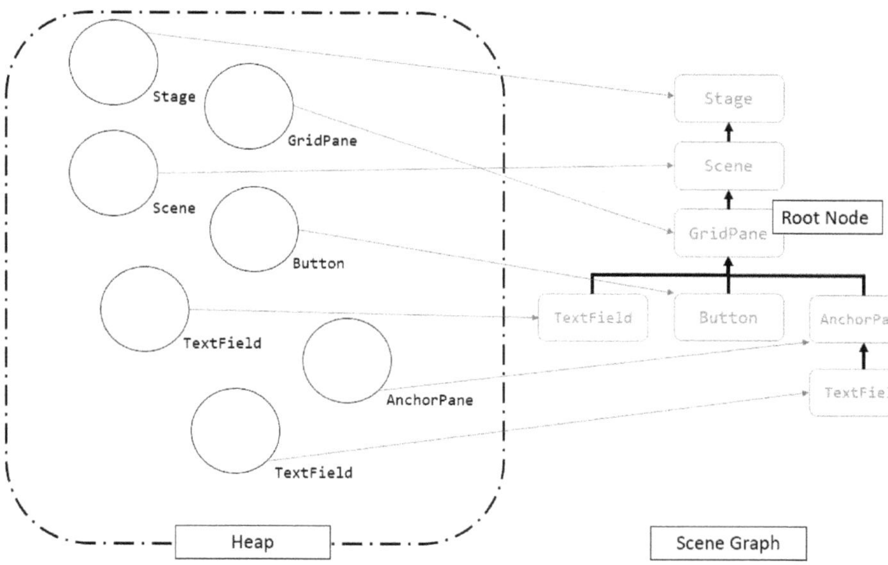

Figure 11.5. Instance Objects and the Scene Graph

The lowest (visual) level of a JavaFX application is the `Stage` (notice the capital letter, it is a class). The `Stage` will contain a `Scene` (another class). The `Scene` will then contain a root-level object of the `Node` class. This root `Node` will then contain all the other `Node` objects and subobjects **nested** within. Visually, the `Stage` is the lowest-level object displayed by JavaFX, but in the visual rendering hierarchy, the `Stage` is the topmost object. Notice in figure 11.5 that the `Stage` is higher in organization than the `Scene`, and the `Scene` is higher in the hierarchy than the layout objects and controls that can be placed in a scene. Think of a plate of pancakes: the `Stage` would be the "lowest" pancake, the `Scene` the next one up, and so on. Keep in mind that the scene graph is merely an arrangement that JavaFX uses to efficiently determine object rendering order.

Anatomy of a JavaFX program: The ideas of "nesting" and "stacking" are key to understand a JavaFX program's structure: a `Scene` is nested within a `Stage`, and a (root) `Node` is nested within a `Scene`. Usually this root `Node` instance object is a layout of some kind: an instance of the `Pane` class or one of its subclasses. You can also make a regular JavaFX control the root `Node` (all controls and layouts of JavaFX are subclasses of class `Node`). So when you are looking at a JavaFX GUI application, consider a plate of pancakes and how you look down on them from above. This gives you an idea of the nested nature of a JavaFX program: controls and layout panes are at the topmost level visually, underneath these might be a root `Node` (usually a single layout pane), then the `Scene` underneath this, and finally the `Stage` at the very bottom.

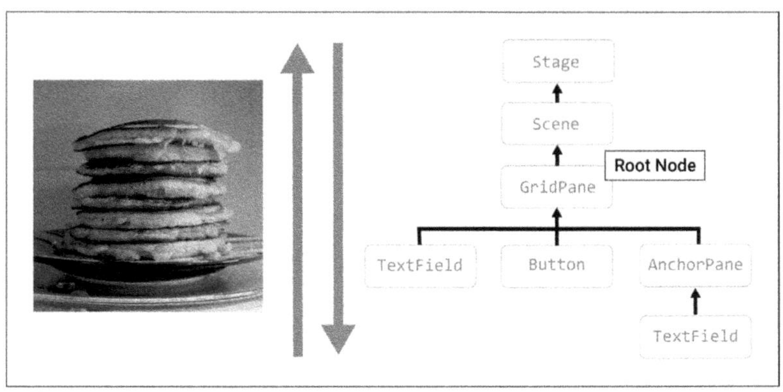

Figure 11.6. Stack of Pancakes and a Scene Graph Compared
Source: "A Full Stack (IMG_5126)" by trekkyandy is licensed under CC BY-SA 2.0, https://www.flickr.com/photos/87054972@N00/6727786205.

Figure 11.7 shows a very simple application that has two `Label` controls, two `TextField` controls, a `Button`, and a `TextArea` control below the button. These controls are placed within a `GridPane` (a subclass of class `Pane`, itself a subclass of `Node`), which is placed within a `Scene`, which itself, finally, is placed within a `Stage`. Keep this simple JavaFX development approach in mind:

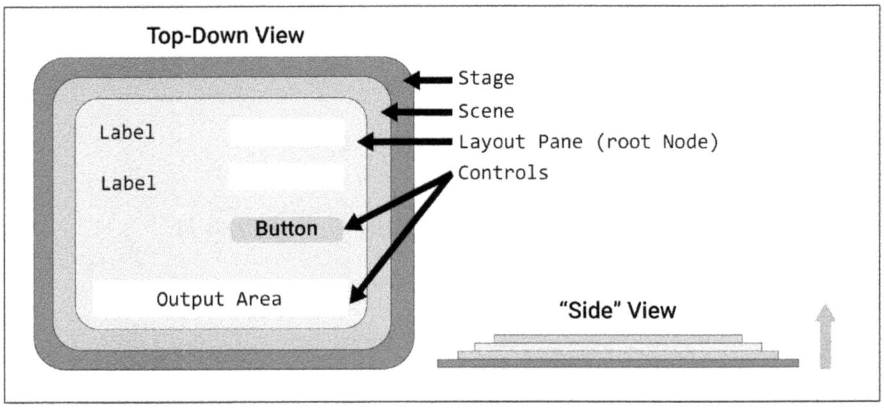

Figure 11.7. Sample JavaFX Application with Indicated Nested Layers

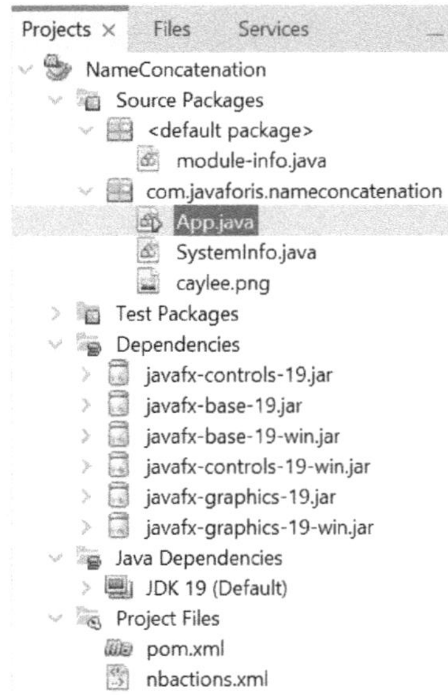

Figure 11.8. The Basic Project Structure for a New JavaFX Project (Maven) in NetBeans

Controls in a Pane → Pane in a Scene → Scene in a Stage

Understanding the basic JavaFX program: Appendix A gives you instructions for installing JavaFX, getting it set up within some of the more common IDEs, and creating a basic JavaFX project. Create a new JavaFX project called `NameConcatenation` on your computer. Once your project is created, find your Java main class file (in NetBeans, the default JavaFX project will call its main class file "`App.java`"). Figure 11.8 shows the structure of a new JavaFX project in NetBeans, which **may differ** slightly in Eclipse and other IDEs. No matter which IDE you are using, the key is to find the main JavaFX application file in your project, which is where the JavaFX code will be added and edited.

In this project, `App.java` will be where all code for this first example will be placed. For most new JavaFX projects in most IDEs, the `main()` class file might contain the following example code by default:

Full Program 11.1

```
package com.javaforis.nameconcatenation;

import javafx.application.Application;
import javafx.scene.Scene;
import javafx.scene.control.Label;
import javafx.scene.layout.StackPane;
import javafx.stage.Stage;

/**
 * JavaFX App
 */
public class App extends Application {

    @Override
    public void start(Stage stage) {
        var javaVersion = SystemInfo.javaVersion();
        var javafxVersion = SystemInfo.javafxVersion();

        var label = new Label("Hello, JavaFX " + javafxVersion
                + ", running on Java " + javaVersion
                + ".");
        var scene = new Scene(new StackPane(label), 640, 480);
        stage.setScene(scene);
```

```
        stage.show();
    }

    public static void main(String[] args) {
        launch();
    }
}
```

Notice that the structure and contents of this new JavaFX app are different from what you are used to with a new Java main class or a new Java class file. New JavaFX main class files come with expanded example code to help developers gain an understanding of how these applications work. In brief, here are some things to be aware of with this code:

- The application class, here called `App` (in our `NameConcatenation` project), itself extends the JavaFX class `Application`.*,† The power of inheritance helps here, as you do not have to rewrite all the complicated code to get visual elements rendered, manage the scene graph, and so on. JavaFX does all this for you.
- Note that there are two methods within the class: the normal `main()` method you have seen before and the method `start()`. Notice as well that the `start()` method is preceded by an optional `@Override` tag, meaning that you are overriding a method from the superclass (`Application`) in this subclass `App`.
- The method `main()` is **not where you will write your code in a JavaFX application!** The `start()` method is the natural starting point for code execution in a JavaFX application. Notice that all the code is in `start()`, whereas `main()` only calls another method, `launch()`.
- Notice the `import` statements that are provided by default. Again, because JavaFX is not part of the base `java.lang` package, the definitions for the JavaFX classes that are needed are imported. Notice as well that the imports are very specific, defining specific, single classes. You will change these soon.

Compile and run your project without making any changes. If everything works correctly (i.e., if the author consumed a sufficient amount of a caffeinated beverage while writing appendix A), your application should launch and look like the following (your output may differ on your machine than in my screenshot):

A quick examination of the code will show why the app looks the way it does:

- The example JavaFX app comes with a class called `SystemInfo` that merely provides some static class methods for retrieving the system info. This information is concatenated into a `String` used as a constructor parameter for the `Label` class. You will not need work with this file for now.
- A new `Scene` instance object is created, and an in-line constructor call for a new `StackPane` instance object (`StackPane` is a subclass of `Pane`; these are layout objects allowing us to arrange our controls the way you want) is used in the `Scene` constructor. A window width and height are provided for the `Scene` as well. This nests the `StackPane` (with its nested `Label`) in the `Scene`.
- Notice that the `start()` method is passed a reference to an already created `Stage` instance object via reference variable stage. Somewhere in the process of launching the JavaFX application, a `Stage` object is instantiated. The instance method `.setScene()` is called, and a reference to the `Scene` is passed to it. This nests the `Scene` in the `Stage`.

Figure 11.9. Beginning JavaFX Application Provided by NetBeans

* https://docs.oracle.com/javase/8/javafx/api/javafx/application/Application.html.

† https://docs.oracle.com/javase/8/javafx/JFXST.pdf.

- Finally, the instance method `.show()` is called on the `Stage` reference variable, and this causes the JavaFX GUI window to appear (become visible). This triggers the traversal of the scene graph, rendering the `Stage`, `Scene`, and `Node` objects nested within.

Though this works, this example is difficult to understand. Perform the following steps in your code:

- Replace the `import` statements with the ones shown in the code below.
- Remove (carefully!) all the code **inside** the method body of `start()`.

When you are done, your code in `App.java` will look like the following (changes in **bold**):

Full Program 11.2

```
package com.javaforis.nameconcatenation;

import javafx.application.Application;
import javafx.scene.*;                          // Import all classes
import javafx.scene.layout.*;                   // Import all classes
import javafx.scene.control.*;                  // Import all classes
import javafx.event.*;                          // Import all classes
import javafx.stage.Stage;

public class App extends Application {

    @Override
    public void start(Stage stage) {

        // All the example code deleted - starting from scratch!
        // All code will be added inside start()

    }

    public static void main(String[] args) {
        launch();
    }
}
```

Working with controls: The controls in a JavaFX application are what the user will interact with. Start by creating these and adjusting their properties in whatever way you need. The real first step for IS professionals, prior to diving in and hammering out code, will be to plan out and design what the UI will look like and think about its effectiveness, efficiency, and ease of use.

Our example application `NameConcatenation` will have a few requirements:

- The user can enter their first and last names.
- The user can click a button that will cause the two names to be concatenated and displayed in another location in the app.

Pretty simple! During the requirement-elicitation process, IS analysts may often use visualizations and UI prototype sketches (or cleaner wireframes as you see in figure 11.1) to help spur discussion over how the user should interact with the software to create a refined user experience. A possible sketch for our concatenation application may look like figure 11.10.

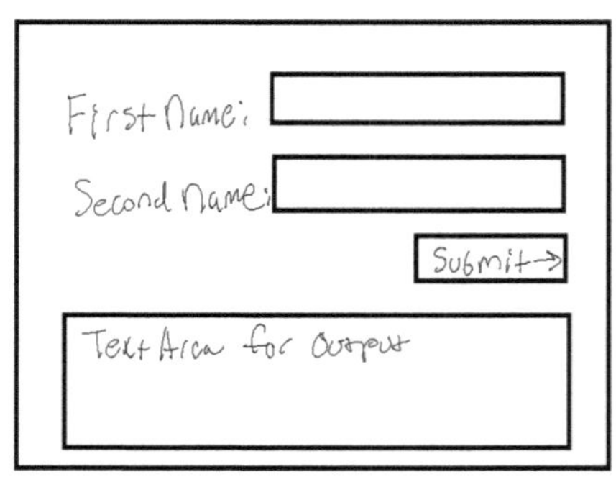

Figure 11.10. A Rough Wireframe Sketch of the Name Concatenation Application

It looks like a rough sketch, and it is supposed to be. Often you might sketch these out on the fly while discussing the to-be system with a client. Or it may be a quick design idea for your own application. It always pays to plan before you code. Notice that in our sketch, you have two label prompts for the names to the left of two text entry boxes. A "`Submit ->`" button below these indicates to the user that they should type something in first, then next click the button to kick off the concatenation action. Finally, the output will appear on the form itself (we are not displaying any user-needed output in the console anymore; they cannot see it!). By using a top-down design, you communicate an intuitive and easy-to-understand UI to the user: they know where to start, what to do next, and where to look for results. As your applications grow more complex, planning and UI sketching will become a critical phase of the systems analysis and design process, particularly to ensure client requirements are understood and included in the design.

There are four different types of JavaFX controls that will be needed: `Label`, `TextField`, `TextArea` (the larger text box), and a `Button`.[*,†,‡,§] Remember the development approach/sequence:

Controls in a Pane → Pane in a Scene → Scene in a Stage

A clear first step is to instantiate the controls you need. With the import statement

```
import javafx.scene.control.*;
```

all the classes from the control subpackage are imported without having to add a statement for each and every JavaFX class that might be needed. As with all other classes, use the new operator and the class's constructor to instantiate an object of the class. Add the following code to the now empty `start()` method:

Code Snippet 11.1

```
// Create two labels for data entry prompts
Label lblFirstName = new Label("Enter First Name:");
Label lblSecondName = new Label("Enter Second Name:");

// Create two TextFields for the data entry
TextField txtFirstName = new TextField();
TextField txtSecondName = new TextField();

// Create a button that will conduct the
//  concatenation action
Button btnSubmit = new Button("Submit ->");

// In this app you will use a TextArea for output.
TextArea txtaOutput = new TextArea();
```

Notice that most of these controls' constructors are overloaded and have multiple versions. This will usually be the case for controls that can display visual text. (You can use the zero-argument constructor or a constructor version that takes a String as an argument. Explore the Oracle documentation for each to see what constructors are available.) Notice also that the names for the reference variables for each control start with an abbreviation of the control's class name. This is a **recommended** good practice but not required, and this naming style (along with camel case for each) will be used throughout this chapter. Finally, note that instantiating controls will not automatically cause them to be displayed in your application. You have to add them to a `Pane` (or one of its subclasses) and continue through the sequence of controls → layout pane → scene → stage before you can display a form. Table 11.1 lists many of the common controls in a JavaFX application and what they look like.

Oracle has a handy tutorial showing how to use all of these and more, and there are many additional examples online.[¶,**] Many of those in table 11.1 will be demonstrated in this chapter. For many controls (like `Label` and `Button`), images can be added, and many can be styled in custom ways (i.e., font styling) that are beyond the scope of this chapter (but for you to explore later in your studies).

---

[*] https://docs.oracle.com/javase/8/javafx/api/javafx/scene/control/Label.html.
[†] https://docs.oracle.com/javase/8/javafx/api/javafx/scene/control/TextField.html.
[‡] https://docs.oracle.com/javase/8/javafx/api/javafx/scene/control/TextArea.html.
[§] https://docs.oracle.com/javase/8/javafx/api/javafx/scene/control/Button.html.
[¶] https://docs.oracle.com/javafx/2/ui_controls/jfxpub-ui_controls.htm.
[**] Jakob Jenkov has many fantastic tutorials on every JavaFX aspect at http://tutorials.jenkov.com/javafx/overview.html.

Table 11.1. Some Common JavaFX Controls and Example Displays of Each

Control class name	Visual example of control
`Label`	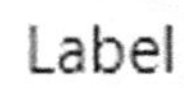
`TextField`	
`TextArea`	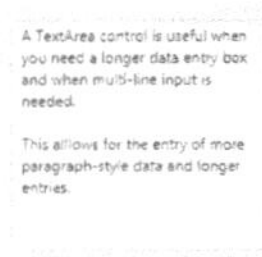
`Button`	
`RadioButton` (used with a `ToggleGroup` object to make the controls aware of one another and only one selectable at a time)	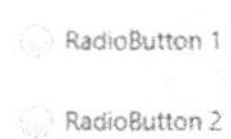
`CheckBox`	
`ChoiceBox`	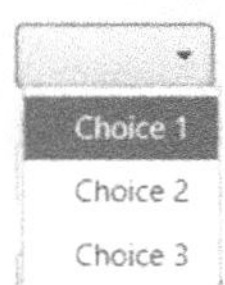
`ComboBox`	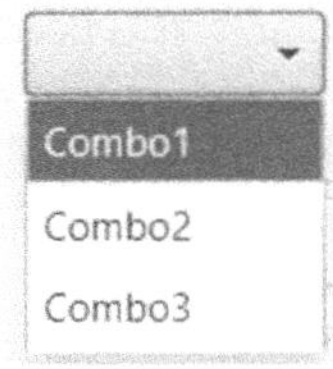
`Slider`	
`ProgressBar`	
`ListView`	
`MenuBar, Menu, MenuItem`	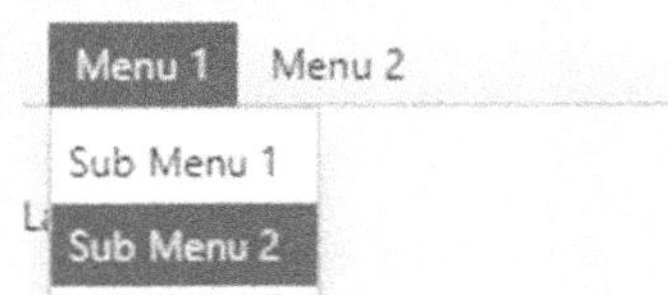
`ImageView`	

Since each control is a class instance object, each has many instance and class member methods that can be invoked as needed. In our example application, you have instantiated `TextField`, `Label`, `Button`, and `TextArea` controls. A brief look at some of the common methods available with each of these controls is helpful. There are **many** more than just those listed here:

- `TextField`: Inherits methods from the `TextInputControl`, `Control`, `Region`, `Parent`, and `Node` classes.
  - `.getText()` **and** `.setText(String s)`: The reference to a `TextField` instance object does not contain its text; this is stored in the actual instance object. As you saw in chapter 8, getters (accessors) and setters (mutators) are available for many of the data fields in these controls. `TextField` objects have a "text" data field, and you can `.get`_____ and `.set`_____ on text to retrieve/change the displayed text value.
  - `.setPrefColumnCount(int i)`: Easily set the character column width of the `TextField`.
  - `.setEditable(boolean b)`: Toggle the editability of a `TextField` using a boolean. Useful when you need to display a value but do not want a user to be able to change it.
  - `.setPromptText(String S)`: Displays a prompt inside the `TextField` that disappears when the user begins typing. Alternatively, you can display a `Label` next to the `TextField`, but using this method saves UI space.
- `Label`: Inherits methods from the `Labeled`, `Control`, `Region`, `Parent`, and `Node` classes.
  - `.getText()` **and** `.setText(String s)`: Same behavior as with the `TextField` control.

- `.setWrapText(boolean b)`: You can toggle on and off the ability of the `Label` to wrap the text it displays in its width and height.
- `.setFont(Font f)`: Change the font face and/or size of text in the `Label` by passing to it a reference to a new `Font` instance object.
- `.setTextFill(Paint p)`: An easy way to change the color of the font displayed in a `Label`. The `Paint` class has a subclass, `Color`, an instance object of which is normally used as the argument (polymorphism!).
- `.setGraphic(Node n)`: A `Label` can display a graphic within it! Again, polymorphism allows the developer to use any subclass of `Node` in place of the argument. In a `Label` you can display an `ImageView`, `Shape`, and more!

- `Button`: The `Button` class shares many of the same methods listed above with `Label` and `TextField`. The following are some notable differences:
  - The `Button` constructor has an overloaded version that accepts the display text and a second parameter for a graphic (defined as `Node`, but the `ImageView` control can be polymorphically substituted).
  - `.setStyle(String css)`: The `.setStyle()` method accepts a `String` that can be a full JavaFX CSS style definition that has a slightly different syntax than the normal website CSS you might be used to.*

Working with `Pane` and its subclasses: It is not enough to simply create controls. You next have to "nest" them within a layout pane and define how they will be arranged. Looking at the wireframe UI plan, our application will need a `Label` and `TextField` in the first "row" of the UI, another pair beneath these, a button beneath this, and finally a `TextArea` at the bottom of the UI. JavaFX provides several layout classes, or "panes" (*think:* windowpane) to give you flexibility on how to arrange the controls on your form. The `Pane` class is the top-level layout class and has several subclasses with specific layout behaviors. All layout panes can allow other panes to nest within them. It will be helpful to briefly describe these layout pane classes:

- `Pane`: The `Pane` class is the top-level class (superclass) for all the other pane-based classes. Recall that the higher in a class inheritance tree you go, the more general or generic the class's behavior. This is true for `Pane`, which only has one defined method, `.getChildren()` ("children" is the term for the `Node` objects associated with or "nested within" a layout pane object). The `Pane` class does not try to arrange controls for you. For each control, you must call the `.setLayoutX(double n)` and `.setLayoutY(double n)` methods to tell each control precisely (to the pixel!) where to go. Subclasses of `Pane`, with more specific implementations, will arrange your controls according to certain rules based on the nature of the layout class itself. This can save you time.
- **`BorderPane`, `hBox`, and `vBox`:** These three layout panes are commonly used together. The `hBox` and `vBox` `Pane` instance objects are typically nested within the regions of a `BorderPane`. A `BorderPane` layout will simply divide up the areas of the form (see figure 11.11) so that you can nest various other panes within those areas. An `hBox` pane adds controls to itself to form an easy horizontal row of controls. The `vBox` does the same but adds them in a vertical column. For example, you might create two `vBox` panes, add controls to them, place them in "left" and "right" areas of an overall `BorderPane`, and then do the same for two `hBox` panes in the "top" and "bottom." Each `hBox` and `vBox` pane would individually manage the controls placed within them, and by placing these panes in the overall `BorderPane`, they themselves are arranged to the "border" areas, keeping things tidy overall. Typically, controls like `MenuBar` are used in the "top" area, and any status output is in the "bottom" area, similar to other web and desktop applications.
- `FlowPane`: Another very useful `Pane` subclass that allows you to specify its width, and then it will add controls, wrapping them to a new row when the width is exceeded.
- `AnchorPane`: Layout class that allows you to "anchor" controls (or nested pane objects) to various regions within it: top, bottom right, bottom left, top left, and

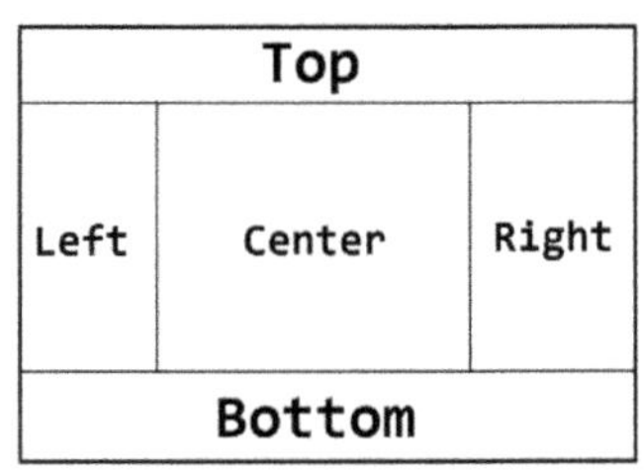

Figure 11.11. Areas of a `BorderPane` Used for Nesting Other Layout Pane Objects

* The Oracle JavaFX CSS Reference Guide can be found at https://docs.oracle.com/javafx/2/api/javafx/scene/doc-files/cssref.html.

so on. If the `AnchorPane` takes up the full form, the controls will stay in their locations, even if the form is resized manually by the user.

- **`GridPane`:** Very useful layout class that allows the developer to add controls (or other panes) in a column and row fashion. The number of columns and rows does not have to be specified beforehand and will grow dynamically as you add controls. Also, you do not have to add controls to columns or rows sequentially. A control could be added to column `4` and then next added to column `10` if you wished.

In the `NameConcatenation` application, there are several choices for layout classes to use to arrange the application's controls. `GridPane` is a fairly straightforward and easy layout class to learn. The `GridPane` class has the `.add(Node n, int column, int row)` method, which accepts a reference to the control or pane you are adding, then the int column and int row to add it to. `GridPane` asks for the column number first to match the nature of computer graphics (`x` and `y` coordinates). Figure 11.12 details what the wireframe drawing may look like with `GridPane`'s columns and rows applied.

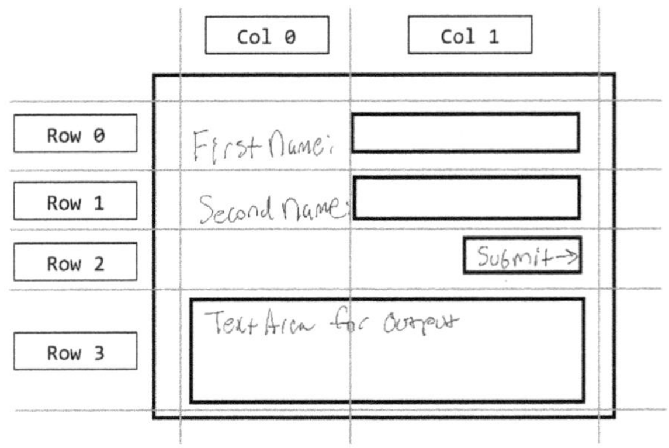

Figure 11.12. `NameConcatenation` Wireframe Overlayed with `GridPane` Columns and Rows

Take note here that similar to arrays, index notation is used, and counting starts at `0`. Unlike arrays, you must specify the **column location first** and then the row when using the `.add()` method. Add the two `Label` and two `TextField` controls to a `GridPane` object like so (add this code after the instantiations from earlier):

Code Snippet 11.2

```
GridPane gPane = new GridPane();
gPane.add(lblFirstName, 0, 0);
gPane.add(txtFirstName, 1, 0);
gPane.add(lblSecondName, 0, 1);
gPane.add(txtSecondName, 1, 1);
```

Notice that the first `Label`, `lblFirstName`, is added at column `0`, row `0`. The `TextField txtSecondName` is added at column `1` (the **second** column) and row `1` (the **second** row).

The `.add()` method also has one overloaded version:

```
.add(Node n, int col, int row, int colspan, int rowspan)
```

In cases where you have a wide or tall control and you need it to span across columns or span across rows, this second version of the method comes in handy. Notice again our wireframe: the `TextArea` is pretty big and will span across two columns. You can use the second version of `.add()` for this. Add the rest of the controls like so:

Code Snippet 11.3

```
gPane.add(btnSubmit, 1, 2);
gPane.add(txtaOutput, 0, 3, 2, 1); // column span and row span in bold
```

Finishing the `Scene` and `Stage` and displaying the UI form: Even though you have arranged controls within a layout pane object, there are a few more steps to go: placing the `Pane` within a `Scene` as the root `Node` and nesting the `Scene` within the `Stage`. Creation of a `Scene` object and specification of a root `Node` (here a root `Pane`) both occur with the instantiation of the `Scene` object:

Code Snippet 11.4

```
// Specify root node, window width, window height
Scene mainScene = new Scene(gPane, 300, 300); // gPane used
```

A reference to the `GridPane` object `gPane` is passed as a constructor argument along with a chosen window width and height. Finally, you tell the `Stage` to use this scene and to display itself. Luckily, as noted earlier, when the `start()` method begins, a reference to an **already** created `Stage` object called `stage` is passed into `start()`, eliminating the need to create one ourselves. The final steps will look like this:

Code Snippet 11.5

```
// Specify the Stage's Scene:
stage.setScene(mainScene);

// Set the Window's title:
stage.setTitle("Name Concatenation FX");

// Instruct the Stage to become visible:
stage.show();
```

At this point, you can now run the FX project, which should produce a window similar to that shown in figure 11.13.

Figure 11.13. Name Concatenation Form Built in JavaFX

You have a form! But things seem a little cramped: looks like the form is taller than is needed but not nearly wide enough. Also, while the `Button` is in the correct column, it would be nice to move it to the far right as in the wireframe plan. Here is a summary of the changes needed to neaten things up:

- Increase the width and decrease the height slightly.
- Add some space between the controls by adjusting the `GridPane` object's `Hgap` and `Vgap` properties (using the included setters for these).
- Center our controls in the `Scene` by adjusting `GridPane`'s alignment property. (Depending on your IDE, an import for `javafx.geometry.Pos` might be added automatically, or you might need to manually add this import if an error is indicated.)
- Move the `Button` to the right of the second column using an `AnchorPane` and placing that in the `GridPane` instead.

Adjust your code in the `start()` method to look like the following (changes in **bold**):

Code Snippet 11.6

```
@Override
public void start(Stage stage) {

     // Create two labels for data entry prompts
     Label lblFirstName = new Label("Enter First Name:");
     Label lblSecondName = new Label("Enter Second Name:");

     // Create two TextFields for the data entry
     TextField txtFirstName = new TextField();
     TextField txtSecondName = new TextField();

     // Create a button that will conduct the
     // concatenation action
     Button btnSubmit = new Button("Submit ->");

     // In this app you will use a TextArea for output.
     TextArea txtaOutput = new TextArea();

     GridPane gPane = new GridPane();
     gPane.add(lblFirstName, 0, 0);
     gPane.add(txtFirstName, 1, 0);
```

```
    gPane.add(lblSecondName, 0, 1);
    gPane.add(txtSecondName, 1, 1);

    AnchorPane aPane = new AnchorPane();
    aPane.getChildren().add(btnSubmit);

    // Anchor the Button to the right
    //  0 pixels from the right edge of the Anchor Pane in the Column
    AnchorPane.setRightAnchor(btnSubmit, 0.0);

    gPane.add(aPane, 1, 2); // AnchorPane, which contains the Button
    gPane.add(txtaOutput, 0, 3, 2, 1);

    // Alignment is set using an enumerated type of the Pos class
    gPane.setAlignment(Pos.CENTER);

    gPane.setHgap(15); // 15 pixel horizontal gap between columns
    gPane.setVgap(15); // 15 pixel vertical gap between rows

    // Specify root node, window width, window height
    Scene mainScene = new Scene(gPane, 500, 350);

    // Specify the Stage's Scene:
    stage.setScene(mainScene);
    // Set the Window's title:
    stage.setTitle("Name Concatenation FX");

    // Instruct the Stage to become visible:
    stage.show();

} // End of the start() method
```

Now your form should look like that shown in figure 11.14 when you rerun the project *Note:* Do not forget to first close your FX form before making code changes—closing the form shuts down the Java application displaying it.

This is closer to the initial wireframe design. At this point, the form performs no actions. You can type in the `TextFields` and click the `Button`. Notice that the controls have a modern styling and match your computer operating system's visual style. The next step will be to enable name concatenation to occur when the user clicks the `Button` and to produce output in the `TextArea` when this finishes by handling JavaFX events.

Figure 11.14. Revamped Name Concatenation Form

SUMMARY POINTS

- JavaFX is an object-oriented GUI library for use in Java applications, using concepts such as object references, constructors, and invocation of member methods similar to other Java classes, among others.
- JavaFX uses a scene graph to relate objects that are to be rendered and displayed visually to one another in a hierarchical manner, making both development and graphical rendering efficient.
- Elements in a JavaFX program nest within one another, forming the "leaves" and "branches" of the scene graph hierarchy.
- The root `Node` is the highest-level JavaFX element nested within a `Scene` object. Other layout panes and controls are nested within and branch out from the root `Node`.
- Unlike regular Java programs, the `.start()` method is the beginning of code execution in a JavaFX application.

- Controls and other layout pane objects can nest within a layout pane, which then nests within a `Scene` object, which must then nest within a `Stage` object.
- Some JavaFX controls may depend on other controls being present. For example, a `TabPane` must have other Tab objects, a `MenuBar` must have `Menu` and `MenuItem` objects, and `RadioButton` controls must be assigned to a `ToggleGroup` object so that only one `RadioButton` at a time can be clicked by the user.
- The `Pane` class is the parent of the other layout pane classes. The subclasses of `Pane` provide automatic control arrangement and styling based on their specific nature.

QUICK PROBLEMS

1. **Coding:** Use a `vBox` pane, and in a small JavaFX application, add three `RadioButton` controls and two `CheckBox` controls. Add a `Button` at the bottom. *Hint:* See the example earlier adding controls to an `AnchorPane` pane for the method to use with the `vBox`.
2. **Think:** Why is it important to think about and plan the design of your GUI application before you begin coding? What are the positive and negative impacts the design will have on the application's usage?
3. **Coding:** In the example in this section, change the alignment of the `GridPane gPane` to other settings (TOP_RIGHT, BOTTOM_LEFT). What happens to the controls?

11.3 Understanding Event Handling in JavaFX

Learning about the nature of JavaFX, how controls work, the layout panes that FX provides for styling your GUI forms, and the customizations to all of these that can be made are merely half the battle. In order to be useful, the JavaFX GUI forms must be capable of user-initiated actions. GUI actions can include (but are not limited to) executing code logic, processing information a user enters in an JavaFX form, and visually updating part of the GUI. **Event handling** is the ability of a GUI framework to execute intended code when the user interacts with the visual elements of the application. In JavaFX, classes and objects are involved in the event-handling process. Oracle's official event-handling documentation goes into considerable additional detail, much of which is beyond the scope of this chapter's focus on the basics but would be worth further study later.*

Event delegation model: In chapter 10 you learned how runtime errors can be mitigated through error handling, where `Exception` class (and its subclasses) objects are "thrown" when a specific issue arises. This same concept of "throwing" and "catching" objects generated by some occurrence is the same for event handling. JavaFX's event handling follows the **event delegation model.** In a GUI form, when a `Button` is clicked, a letter is typed in a `TextField`, a mouse cursor hovers over a control (or hovers out / leaves a control), and so on, all these actions will generate an event. In JavaFX, the `Event` class and its subclasses have instance objects created and thrown for these actions. With an event delegation approach, the **control that generates the event is not the control that handles the event.** The control delegates the responsibility of handing the event off to other code (*think:* hot potato!). The developer can specify that some other **target** object will handle the event by executing code, and the **source** object's job (the control that generated the event) is simply to pass the `Event` instance object. This increases flexibility because in JavaFX, you could conceivably change how an event for a control is handled on the fly (during runtime) if you wanted. Figure 11.15 presents an example of event delegation in action.

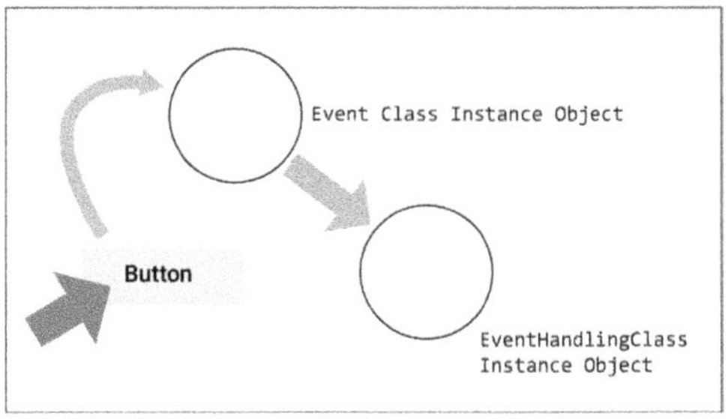

Figure 11.15. Event Delegation When a Button Is Clicked

* https://docs.oracle.com/javase/8/javafx/JFXED.pdf.

In JavaFX `Node` objects and their subclasses can generate `Event` objects through user activity. On a JavaFX form, controls such as `Button`, `TextField`, `Slider`, and the `Scene` itself are common, where user interaction causes event actions to be fired off. Many of these control classes have methods implemented that allow for the **registration of an event handler**, which is how event delegation occurs in JavaFX. For example, when a user clicks a `Button` on a form, it will create and throw (or "fire off") an `ActionEvent` instance object. The developer will delegate what object will catch and handle the `Event` object thrown, and this is done by invoking the appropriate event registration method on the `Button` instance object and passing to it a reference to an event-handling object.

Three ways of handling events in JavaFX: A simple example using a `Button` will help. You can "wire up" the "`Submit ->`" button on the `NameConcatenation` form so that when a user clicks it, test output is printed to the `TextArea` on the form. To handle events, you need several things to be in place:

1. A **Source** object is needed: In this case, the `Button` instance object that is clicked is our source.
2. A **Target** object is needed: This will be the instance object of a class that can handle Events. You will need to create this class and instantiate an object from it. There are three ways to do this:
   a. A full inner (i.e., nested) event-handling class
   b. An anonymous inner event-handling class
   c. The use of a lambda expression (*think:* shortcut syntax)
   A class can handle events when the class implements the `EventHandler<>` interface (see companion chapter 4 for more detail on interfaces in Java).
3. An **event registration method** must be invoked: Based on the desired event to be handled, you will need to select and invoke an event registration method upon the **source** object and pass a reference to the **target** object as a parameter to that method invocation.
4. The appropriate **scope** must be chosen for JavaFX controls: Any GUI controls that the event-handling object may change (like changing text, color, etc.) should be defined at the data field level due to scope.

We already have a `Button` object on the form. It has an event registration method defined for `Button` clicks, called `.setOnAction()`, that you can invoke when needed. So all that you need is the event-handling class and an instance object of that class. As noted earlier, there are three ways to create this class, and these can be demonstrated easily. The third technique is **the easiest to use**, though covering the first two will help you understand the third.

Event-handling technique #1—inner event-handling class: Java classes allow for another class to be defined within their class body (but outside of any method body). These are considered nested or inner classes. Since an object must handle events and classes are the definitions for objects, you must define an event-handling method. In our code listing, after the end of the `start()` method, code the following class (you will want to make sure this code is outside of the `start()` method but inside the `App` class—see figure 11.16 for proper placement):

Code Snippet 11.7

```
class ButtonClickHandler implements EventHandler<ActionEvent>
{
    public void handle(ActionEvent event)
    {
        txtaOutput.setText("Event Handled!");
    }
}
```

There are a few things to note here:

- The `EventHandler<ActionEvent>` part of the class header tells Java that this class implements an interface known as `EventHandler`. This is required by classes whose objects you want to handle events. An **interface** is simply a way of relating classes together that are not normally related to one another at all (not in an inheritance relationship). The < and > brackets indicates a **generic data type** for the interface, meaning that the `EventHandler` interface can use any valid data type for its internal data fields.

- If a class implements an interface, it is usually **required** to include a definition for a method that is part of the interface class's definition. Notice you have a `handle()` method. This is defined in the `EventHandler` interface. Since our class implements this interface, you are forced (i.e., Java law!) to implement a **local, concrete definition of this method**.
- Notice that after all this, the code you want to have execute (placing some text in the `TextArea`) is the code within the `handle()` method. The method literally handles the event! When an `Event` object is passed to the instance object of this class, the `handle()` method will **automatically** be called to handle the event.

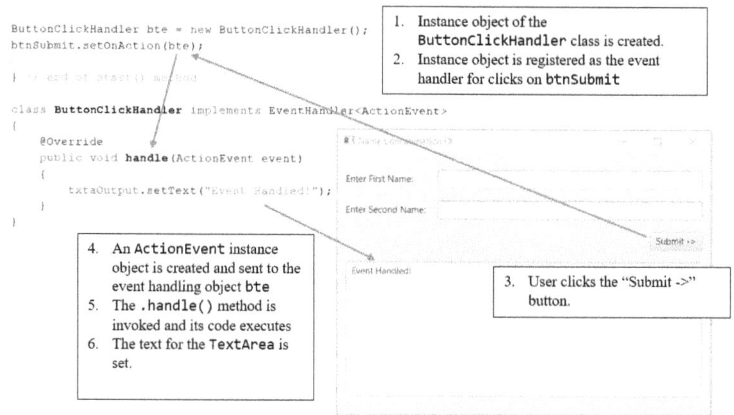

Figure 11.16. Event-Handling Sequence When Inner Class Is Used

Now back in the `start()` method, you can create an instance object and register that object as the handler for any click events from the button:

Code Snippet 11.8

```
ButtonClickHandler bte = new ButtonClickHandler();
btnSubmit.setOnAction(bte);
```

Figure 11.16 details the sequence of events that happens when the user clicks the button.

For this to work, the method of the event-handling object must be able to see (i.e., scope) the `TextArea`. To accomplish this, **the definition for the `TextArea` has been moved to the data field level of the App class.** Here is our full code listing for reference (with new changes in bold):

Full Program 11.3

```
package com.javaforis.nameconcatenation;

import javafx.application.Application;
import javafx.scene.*;
import javafx.scene.layout.*;
import javafx.scene.control.*;
import javafx.event.*;
import javafx.geometry.Pos;
import javafx.stage.Stage;

public class App extends Application {

// Data Field Level of App class

// In this app you will use a TextArea for output.
// Instantiation moved to data field level to ensure
//  proper event-handling scope.
TextArea txtaOutput = new TextArea();

    @Override
    public void start(Stage stage) {
    // Create two labels for data entry prompts
    Label lblFirstName = new Label("Enter First Name:");
    Label lblSecondName = new Label("Enter Second Name:");

    // Create two TextFields for the data entry
```

```
    TextField txtFirstName = new TextField();
    TextField txtSecondName = new TextField();

    // Create a button that will conduct the
    // concatenation action
    Button btnSubmit = new Button("Submit ->");

    GridPane gPane = new GridPane();
    gPane.add(lblFirstName, 0, 0);
    gPane.add(txtFirstName, 1, 0);
    gPane.add(lblSecondName, 0, 1);
    gPane.add(txtSecondName, 1, 1);

    AnchorPane aPane = new AnchorPane();
    aPane.getChildren().add(btnSubmit);
    AnchorPane.setRightAnchor(btnSubmit, 0.0);

    gPane.add(aPane, 1, 2);
    gPane.add(txtaOutput, 0, 3, 2, 1);

    gPane.setAlignment(Pos.CENTER);
    gPane.setHgap(15);
    gPane.setVgap(15);


    // Specify root node, window width, window height
    Scene mainScene = new Scene(gPane, 500, 350);

    // Specify the Stage's Scene:
    stage.setScene(mainScene);
    // Set the Window's title:
    stage.setTitle("Name Concatenation FX");
    // Instruct the Stage to become visible:
    stage.show();

    ButtonClickHandler bte = new ButtonClickHandler();
    btnSubmit.setOnAction(bte);

    } // end of start() method

    class ButtonClickHandler implements EventHandler<ActionEvent>
    {
        @Override
        public void handle(ActionEvent event)
        {
            txtaOutput.setText("Event Handled!");
        }
    }

    public static void main(String[] args) {
        launch();
    }
}
```

Event-handling technique #2—anonymous inner event-handling class: JavaFX's event-handling syntax allows us to simplify technique #1 a bit by combining both the class definition and event-handling instantiation into one step and placing this in-line within the event registration method of the `Button` object. In this example, you do not need an inner class placed outside the `start()` method: you will define and use the class all in one step and do this within the parameters of the `.setOnAction()` method like so:

Code Snippet 11.9

```
btnSubmit.setOnAction(new EventHandler<ActionEvent>()
{
    public void handle(ActionEvent event)
    {
        txtaOutput.setText("Event Handled!");
    }
}
); // end of the setOnAction() parentheses
```

JavaFX knows what you are attempting to do here and allows this shortcut syntax. Notice that you use the interface `EventHandler<>` but the class is not given a name, as was done in technique #1. This is known as an **anonymous inner class**, anonymous because it is nameless. Notice as well that all this is done within the parameter parentheses of the `.setOnAction()` method. A new, nameless class is being defined, one that implements the `EventHandler<>` interface, and a new instance object of that class is being instantiated and registered as the event handler for `Button` clicks, all in one step! The full class defined outside the `start()` method earlier has been removed, as it is no longer needed.

Event-handling technique #3—event handling using a lambda expression: This technique is even easier and is the recommended way to handle events for the time being. In Java (and in most modern OO languages), **lambda expressions** have become very popular because of their very short syntax and ease of use. The easiest way to understand them is to think about the input, processing, and output/return nature of a method. A lambda expression simplifies this with a very simple syntax:

```
( input parameter(s) ) -> { expression }
```

Notice here that the arrow is actually part of the syntax; it is the **lambda operator**. Lambda expressions in Java are normally passed to another method as a parameter. Instead of needing an entire method (or class containing that method), a lambda expression simplifies the gathering of one or multiple parameters and their use in an expression. Typically you see lambda expressions used where a reference to an instance object is expected, and that instance object is one of a class that implements an interface. Sound familiar? You can use a lambda expression to replace the anonymous inner event-handling class with a **much** simpler syntax:

Code Snippet 11.10

```
btnSubmit.setOnAction((e) -> {
    txtaOutput.setText("Event Handled!");
});
```

That's it! JavaFX knows that you are accepting a single parameter and code that are executing. You are using this lambda expression where a reference to an event-handling class instance object (that implements the `EventHandler<>` interface) is expected and where that class implements the `handle()` method. JavaFX figures out the rest and executes the code in the lambda expression when events are generated by `Button` clicks. This is the easiest way to handle events.

Now you can replace the test print to the `TextArea` with the actual purpose of the application. Notice that you will need to move the instantiations of the `TextField` controls to the data field (i.e., class) level of the application so that the event-handling lambda expression can "see" them. The full code listing here would be the following (again with changes in **bold**):

Full Program 11.4

```
package com.javaforis.nameconcatenation;

import javafx.application.Application;
import javafx.scene.*;
import javafx.scene.layout.*;
import javafx.scene.control.*;
import javafx.event.*;
```

```
import javafx.geometry.Pos;
import javafx.stage.Stage;

public class App extends Application {

// Data field level of the App class

// In this app you will use a TextArea for output.
TextArea txtaOutput = new TextArea();

// Create two TextFields for the data entry
TextField txtFirstName = new TextField();     // Moved to Class Level
TextField txtSecondName = new TextField();     // Moved to Class Level

    @Override
    public void start(Stage stage) {

    // Create two labels for data entry prompts
    Label lblFirstName = new Label("Enter First Name:");
    Label lblSecondName = new Label("Enter Second Name:");

    // Create a button that will conduct the
    // concatenation action
    Button btnSubmit = new Button("Submit ->");

    GridPane gPane = new GridPane();
    gPane.add(lblFirstName, 0, 0);
    gPane.add(txtFirstName, 1, 0);
    gPane.add(lblSecondName, 0, 1);
    gPane.add(txtSecondName, 1, 1);

    AnchorPane aPane = new AnchorPane();
    aPane.getChildren().add(btnSubmit);
    AnchorPane.setRightAnchor(btnSubmit, 0.0);

    gPane.add(aPane, 1, 2);
    gPane.add(txtaOutput, 0, 3, 2, 1);

    gPane.setAlignment(Pos.CENTER);
    gPane.setHgap(15);
    gPane.setVgap(15);

    // Specify root node, window width, window height
    Scene mainScene = new Scene(gPane, 500, 350);

    // Specify the Stage's Scene:
    stage.setScene(mainScene);
    // Set the Window's title:
    stage.setTitle("Name Concatenation FX");
    // Instruct the Stage to become visible:
    stage.show();

    btnSubmit.setOnAction((e) -> {
        String fullName = "Your full name is: "
                + txtFirstName.getText()
                + " " + txtSecondName.getText();
        txtaOutput.clear();
        txtaOutput.setText(fullName);
```

```
    });

    } // end of start() method

    public static void main(String[] args) {
        launch();
    }
}
```

Handling events generated by various controls: An extensive discussion of how to handle all the types of events from all the types of controls would be beyond the scope of this chapter. The official Oracle documentation and many tutorials online dive into these extensively.[*,†,‡] Now that you have the basics handled (I figured you needed a pun after all that!), a few of the more commonly encountered events and how these are registered and handled can be examined. Table 11.2 examines a sampling of these that you might commonly find useful in your applications. Keep in mind that since our controls all share class `Node` as a parent, many of the controls will inherit/implement the same registration methods (e.g., a mouse hover can occur with a `Button`, `Scene`, `TextField`, etc.; a click can occur with a `Button`, `Scene`, etc.).

Table 11.2. Some Common UI Events and How to Handle Them

Source control	Events	Event type thrown	Registration method
`Button`	Button click	`ActionEvent`	`.setOnAction(EventHandler<ActionEvent>)`
	Mouse enters above it	`MouseEvent`	`.setOnMouseEntered(EventHandler<? super MouseEvent>)`
	Mouse exits from above it	`MouseEvent`	`.setOnMouseExited(EventHandler<? super MouseEvent>)`
`TextField`	Keyboard key pressed	`KeyEvent`	`.setOnKeyPressed(EventHandler<? super KeyEvent>)`
`ListView`	List item clicked/selected	`MouseEvent`	`.onMouseClicked(EventHandler<? super MouseEvent>)`

You can put table 11.2 to use. With a little clever coding, the `Button` on our form can be removed altogether, and the concatenation action can occur when the user hits the Enter key in the second `TextField`. The modified code for this would look like this (with changes in bold):

Full Program 11.5

```
package com.javaforis.nameconcatenation;

import javafx.application.Application;
import javafx.scene.*;
import javafx.scene.layout.*;
import javafx.scene.control.*;
import javafx.event.*;
import javafx.geometry.Pos;
import javafx.stage.Stage;

public class App extends Application {
```

* https://docs.oracle.com/javase/8/javafx/JFXED.pdf.

† https://docs.oracle.com/javase/8/javafx/api/javafx/event/Event.html.

‡ Again, Jakob Jenkov, along with others, does a great job of extensively covering events for controls: http://tutorials.jenkov.com/javafx/index.html.

```
// Data field level of the App class

// In this app you will use a TextArea for output.
TextArea txtaOutput = new TextArea();

// Create two TextFields for the data entry
TextField txtFirstName = new TextField();
TextField txtSecondName = new TextField();

    @Override
    public void start(Stage stage) {
    // Create two labels for data entry prompts
    Label lblFirstName = new Label("Enter First Name:");
    Label lblSecondName = new Label("Enter Second Name:");

    // Create a button that will conduct the
    // concatenation action
//  Button btnSubmit = new Button("Submit ->"); // Commented Out

    GridPane gPane = new GridPane();
    gPane.add(lblFirstName, 0, 0);
    gPane.add(txtFirstName, 1, 0);
    gPane.add(lblSecondName, 0, 1);
    gPane.add(txtSecondName, 1, 1);

//    AnchorPane aPane = new AnchorPane();           // Commented Out
//    aPane.getChildren().add(btnSubmit);            // Commented Out
//    AnchorPane.setRightAnchor(btnSubmit, 0.0);     // Commented Out

    //gPane.add(aPane, 1, 2);
    gPane.add(txtaOutput, 0, 3, 2, 1);

    gPane.setAlignment(Pos.CENTER);
    gPane.setHgap(15);
    gPane.setVgap(15);

    // Specify root node, window width, window height
    Scene mainScene = new Scene(gPane, 500, 350);

    // Specify the Stage's Scene:
    stage.setScene(mainScene);
    // Set the Window's title:
    stage.setTitle("Name Concatenation FX");
    // Instruct the Stage to become visible:
    stage.show();

    // Register a key press event instead of a Button click
    txtSecondName.setOnKeyPressed(e -> {

        if (e.getCode().getName().equals("Enter"))
        {
            String fullName = "Your full name is: "
                + txtFirstName.getText()
                + " " + txtSecondName.getText();
            txtaOutput.clear();
            txtaOutput.setText(fullName);
        }

    });
```

```
    } // end of start() method

    public static void main(String[] args) {
        launch();
    }
}
```

Notice that the click event registration method call for the `Button` is commented out, and so is the `Button`! The application now handles a `KeyPress` event for `txtSecondName`. In the event-handling logic, `e` is the parameter passed to the lambda expression, and this is also the reference to the `KeyPress` instance object thrown by the press of a key in the `TextField`. For each key press, check to see if the specific key pressed is the `Enter` key. If so, concatenate the names, and print the output. Simple! Figure 11.17 shows the modified form both before and after user interaction. Though this is a clever way to kick off the concatenation action, you probably should have a `Button` on most forms—most users expect one, and it sends them a clear "What do I do next?" signal. Using a `Button` and kicking off the event with an Enter key press are common.

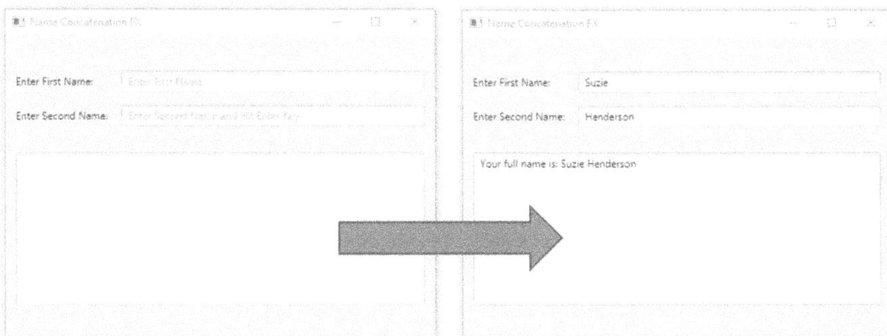

Figure 11.17. State of Modified Form before and after User Interaction

SUMMARY POINTS

- JavaFX uses the event delegation model, which allows controls being interacted with by the user in the GUI to pass the event-handling responsibility to code located elsewhere in the application, in other objects' class implementations.
- `Event` is the top-level class for all events generated in a JavaFX application. Events are thrown by the controls that experienced an event-generating action. Subclasses of `Event` relate to specific types of events generated in a JavaFX application.
- Events can be handled by instance objects of classes that implement the generic-type `EventHandler<>` interface. These classes can be defined and used in a traditional, stand-alone object sense; as an anonymous inner class; or as a lambda expression within the parameter of a control's event registration method.
- A big benefit of using an event-handling class (technique #1) is that an instance object of this class can be registered to handle events from several different objects at the same time. Though using a lambda expression ties the event handling to only one control (technique #3), it saves the developer time and provides a much simpler syntax.
- To properly handle an event, the developer must be aware of what type of control threw the event object, the specific event data type of the object, and the appropriate event registration method to use on the source control.

QUICK PROBLEMS

1. **Coding:** Write a small JavaFX application that will include two `TextField` controls: the first will accept a phrase and the second a search term. Include a `Button` that when clicked will display the message "Found!" on the form if the search term is found within the phrase and "Not Present!" otherwise.
2. **Think:** Using event-handling technique #1, why would it be useful to have one event-handling object process events from more than one control?
3. **Coding:** Write a small JavaFX application that accepts a phrase in a `TextField`. When a `Button` is clicked, report on the form in a Label control the number of characters in the phrase along with the number of words.

Summary

In this chapter, the basics and some advanced techniques for using the JavaFX GUI library to build a modern, functional GUI-based Java application have been covered. The skills used in this chapter were highly integrative, using concepts from all the chapters you have studied throughout this text. The popularity of using JavaFX is still growing, and Oracle and the OpenJFX group intend for this library to serve as the eventual full successor to the Swing libraries still used today. Your studies and practice in this area of Java will put you ahead of your peers in the market who may not be familiar with the many features of JavaFX. Additionally, as information systems professionals, experience gained in concepts involving the "front-end" design of your IS is invaluable toward your becoming a well-rounded expert in your field. How easy users find your system to learn and use, how the system fulfills business requirements, and how helpful users perceive the system to be will all be heavily influenced by the design of the form, handling of events, and variety of controls plus the manner in which information is displayed in the application. Spending time in this area will help your future IS projects to succeed! In the next and last chapter of this textbook, you will explore how to integrate database technology into your Java application to fully finish out the functionality of a contemporary, business-ready system.

Practice Problems

Terminology

Match the following terms from the chapter with their most appropriate definition:

1. Graphical user interface	a. Approach to event handling in JavaFX that allows a control object to pass the processing and effect of an action event in the UI to code associated with another object.
2. Swing	b. A JavaFX layout class from which all other layout classes inherit. Allows to-the-pixel arrangement of controls on a form.
3. Abstract Window Toolkit	c. A subclass of `Pane` that allows for quick arrangement of controls on a form via control wrapping to the next row on overflow.
4. JavaFX	d. Top-level class for all `Event` objects that can be thrown and handled in the JavaFX event delegation model.
5. Scene graph	e. JavaFX control that can contain a layout pane or control that allows for a compact, multiwindow design to an application.
6. `Node`	f. Java graphical library that introduced platform independence, a variety of UI controls, and enhanced stability.
7. Root `Node`	g. The approach of arranging JavaFX elements in the scene graph relationship.
8. JavaFX controls	h. A shortcut type of expression that is similar to the structure of a method, accepting parameter inputs and returning a value, though with more limitations than a method.

9. `start()` method	i. An approach of relating visual elements in a hierarchical manner, enabling nesting associations of visual elements, and increasing rendering efficiency.
10. `Pane`	j. A subclass of `Pane` that allows for the directional arrangement and alignment of JavaFX panes and controls on a form. Is window-resize aware.
11. Wireframe model	k. The top-level `Node` object in a JavaFX scene graph. Anchors all other visual elements to the JavaFX Scene object.
12. Nesting	l. Methods defined for most JavaFX controls that allow the developer to associate an event-handling object with a specific type of events thrown from a control.
13. `GridPane`	m. Visual display that allows interaction with software with more than just keyboard/console commands, such as with mouse and touch input.
14. `AnchorPane`	n. A subclass of `Pane` that allows for the quick arrangement of subpanes on a JavaFX form to the edges and center of an application window.
15. `BorderPane`	o. The top-level class of most JavaFX classes.
16. `FlowPane`	p. Java graphical library that introduces web integration, web-like styling, 2D/3D graphical rendering, and multitouch usage scenarios.
17. Event delegation model	q. Part of the systems analysis and design process where users who might be typical for the system under development attempt to complete general user tasks with software to help identify usage and design issues and refine the system design.
18. Event handler	r. Subclasses of `Node` that represent the visual UI elements users can interact with during usage of a JavaFX application.
19. Event registration method	s. A subclass of `Pane` that allows the arrangement of JavaFX layout panes and controls in a two-dimensional grid.
20. `Event` class	t. Earliest Java graphical library that allowed developers to develop GUI for Java applications. Was platform dependent and resource inefficient.
21. Lambda expression	u. Class in JavaFX that implements the `EventHandler<>` interface and overrides the `handle()` method, providing code that executes when the event is detected.
22. User testing	v. The starting point for code execution in a JavaFX application.
23. `Tab`	w. A software design tool used, often in meetings with clients, to confirm and clarify requirements of a system and refine UI design.

Find the Error

In each of the following problems, carefully examine the code given, and determine the error(s)/issue(s) with each. Keep in mind, the error(s) could be syntax (code) or logic (intended outcome) based or both! Assume any JavaFX code is listed within an appropriate `start()` method unless stated otherwise. Where ellipses (. . .) are indicated, assume that necessary but unrelated code has been omitted for clarity.

1.

```
TextField tOne = new TextField();
TextField tTwo = new TextField();
GridPane gP = new GridPane();
gP.add(tOne, 0, 0);
gP.add(tOne, 0, 1);
Scene pS = new Scene(tTwo, 100, 100);
stage.show();
```

2.

```
TextField firstNum = new TextField();
TextField secondNum = new TextArea();
. . .
btnAdd(e -> (
int numA = firstNum;
int numB = secondNum;
System.out.println(numA * numB);

));
```

3.

```
TextField tOne = new TextField();
TextField tTwo = new TextField();
Button btnAdd = new Button();
GridPane gP = new GridPane();
gP.add(tOne, 1, 0);
gP.add(tOne, 0, 1);
gp.add(btnAdd,1,1,2);
```

4.

```
ComboBox cmboNames = new ComboBox();
TextArea txtNames = new TextField();
cmboNames.add("Suzie");
cmboNames.add("Breyea");
. . .
for (int i=0;i<10;i++)
{
    txtNames.setText(name.toString());
}
```

5.

```
Button btnFinish = new Button();
Label lblStatus = new Label("");
. . .
btnFinish.setOnKeyTyped(new interface handle(
   lblStatus.getText("Button Finished Clicked!");
 ));
```

6.

```
AnchorPane aPane = new AnchorPane(Pos.Center);
aPane.add(btnSubmit, 0, 0);
AnchorPane.setAlignment(btnSubmit, 0.0);
gPane.add(aPane, anchorRight);
```

7. (Use Chapter 11 Opening Scenario Application Supplemental for this problem)

```
Button btnUpdateList = new Button();
ComboBox cmboList = new cmboBox();
ArrayList<Integer> numberList = new ArrayList<>();
. . .
// code that gathers numbers from the UI and
// adds them to numberList
. . .
btnUpdateList.setOnAction(e -> {
    for (Integer int : numberList)
    {
        cmboList.add(int);
    }
});
```

8. (Use Chapter 11 Opening Scenario Application Supplemental for this problem)

```
Tab tbStudentList = new Tab("Students");
Tab tbFacultyList = new Tab("Faculty");
tbStudentList.setContent(new TabPane());
GridPane gP = new GridPane(TabPane(), 0, 0);
gP.setAlignment(pos.CENTER);
```

9. (Use Chapter 11 Opening Scenario Application Supplemental for this problem)

```
// Assume the Person class is included and
// any methods invoked upon its objects are
// defined.
Person personOne = new Person();
Person personTwo = new Person();
Label lblStatusArea = new Label("");
ComboBox personList = new ComboBox();
personList.add(personOne);
personList.add(personTwo);
. . .
lblStatusArea.setText(personList
        .getSelectionModel()
        .getSelectedIndex()
        .getPersonName());
```

10. (Use Chapter 11 Opening Scenario Application Supplemental for this problem)

```
GridPane gP = new GridPane();
Button addTextFields = new Button("Add New Field");
int col = 0, row = 0;
// . . .
addTextFields.setOnAction(e -> {
    gP.add(new TextField(), col, row);

    TextField().setText("TextField #" + row);
});
```

Think about It

1. What advantages does a GUI application have over a console-based application? What advantages does a console-based application have over a GUI one?
2. Why was AWT's lack of portability between platforms a hindrance for developers?
3. What characteristics does the Swing Java GUI library share with JavaFX? What differentiates JavaFX from Swing?
4. How is JavaFX an object-oriented GUI library?
5. How are objects related to one another in the JavaFX scene graph? How does this help make development of JavaFX applications easier to understand?
6. What is the root `Node` in a JavaFX application, and why is it important? What relationship does it have to the rest of the Nodes/controls in the application?
7. Where does code execution start in a JavaFX application?
8. What is the top-level object in a JavaFX application?
9. What is the suggested order of object creation in a JavaFX application? Why is this efficient for the developer?
10. What is the difference between a `TextField` and a `TextArea` in a JavaFX application?
11. What is the difference between the `Pane` and `GridPane` classes?
12. What is the data type returned by the `.getItems()` method on a `ComboBox`? What is the relationship between the referenced object and the `ComboBox`?
13. What is the general approach that JavaFX uses to handle GUI events?
14. How is event handling in JavaFX similar to error handling in the main Java language?
15. Why is it beneficial to have subclasses for the `Event` class?
16. What type of parameter do event-handling registration methods for controls accept? Where does the parameter come from?

17. What are the benefits to using a lambda expression in an event-handling method?
18. How is creating a second form in your JavaFX application related to the object-oriented nature of JavaFX?
19. What is important to keep in mind when pulling data from and putting values into JavaFX `TextField` controls?
20. What is the difference between a `ComboBox` and a `ListView` control?

Short Syntax Problems

1. Develop a JavaFX application that will accept the entry of a user's name. Include a `Button` that when clicked, the user's name will be displayed in a `Label` on the form, but with the letters printed in reverse.
2. Develop a JavaFX application that will allow a user to type in a long paragraph in a `TextArea`. Ensure that the text wraps within the `TextArea`. Include a `Button` that when clicked will pop up a secondary form that will report the number of each of the English vowels (`a`, `e`, `i`, `o`, `u`, and `y`) found in the paragraph entered.
3. Develop a JavaFX application that will ask the user to enter two numbers to generate a quantity of random numbers between those two numbers. Include the quantities five through ten in a `ComboBox` on the form. Include a button that when clicked will read the quantity selected in the `ComboBox` and generate that quantity of random numbers between the first and second entered somewhere on the form. Include a small bit of logic making sure the second number is larger than the first. Include a warning on the form if this is **not** the case, and do not let number generation occur if so.
4. Develop a JavaFX application that allows the user to enter a paragraph in a `TextArea`. In a `ComboBox`, include three text editing options: "Remove all blank spaces," "Convert to lowercase," "Remove all vowels." Include a `Button` that when clicked will carry out the currently selected command and edit the contents of the `TextArea` accordingly.
5. Develop a JavaFX application that includes a single `Button` control in the center. When the `Button` is clicked, it will move to a random x and y location on the form. *Hint:* Use a Pane, get the current width and height of the Scene, and use the `.setLayoutX()` and `.setLayoutY()` methods appropriately.

Full Problems

1. Complete the functionality for the "`Grocery Inventory Management 0.1`" JavaFX application by implementing the following:
   a. Research how to programmatically exit the application, and enable the App -> Quit App `MenuItem` to close the application out.
   b. Rename the "Reporting" tab to "Charting," and add a new tab labeled "Reporting." Add a `TextArea` to this new tab. Fill the `TextArea` with a listing of all the items in inventory in a report style (similar to your work in chapter 9). Be sure to use `String.format()` to format the `TextArea` information appropriately. Cause the `TextArea` to update anytime a new `InventoryItem` is saved on the form.
   c. Add a new menu called "Summary" with a `MenuItem` called "Generate Summary." When the user clicks this `MenuItem`, another secondary form will pop up and list the total revenue that would occur if every item in the grocery store was sold. Make sure to format the information appropriately as a monetary amount.
2. Researchers in the information systems discipline generally include references to their research that follow the style detailed in the *Publication Manual of the American Psychological Association*. A template for the reference style for a regular academic journal article looks like the following (minus any alignment requirements):

   Author, A. A., Author, B. B., & Author, C. C. (Year). Title of article. *Title of Periodical, volume number*(issue number), pages.

   Develop a JavaFX application that prompts for the following information:
   - Year of article
   - Title of article
   - Title of the periodical
   - Volume number
   - Issue number
   - Pages (in style ##–##)
   - First author's name

   Include a button that allows the user to dynamically add another `TextField` if there is a second author, another if there is a third, up to six authors.

When the "Add Author" button is clicked, a new `TextField` should be dynamically instantiated and displayed. A final button, "Generate Reference," should display all the entered information according to the reference style above in a `TextArea` so that the user can copy and paste it elsewhere. *Hint:* You'll need to keep references to all the new `TextField` objects generated so that you can gather author names from them.

3. Make changes to short syntax problem #3 from earlier. Replace the `ComboBox` with a `TextField` that will allow the user to type in any quantity of random numbers to be generated. Ensure that the number is one or greater (and not zero). Include a JavaFX `PieChart` on the form that will display the quantity of each whole number between the first and second numbers as a visual chart. For example, if the two numbers are 2 and 4, and the user wants to generate six random numbers, the numbers may be 2, 3, 3, 4, 4, 2; the quantities generated would all be two of each and the `PieChart` would have three equal slices.

Chapter 12

Java Applications and Database Integration

What You Will Learn in This Chapter

In contemporary business environments, a modern information system will connect to and use a relational database (among other data sources). As an information systems professional engaged in development efforts, it is important that you gain experience not only in interacting with a database but in integrating database access into the applications you help plan and develop. This chapter covers connecting to and interacting with an Oracle database from within a Java application. Oracle has implemented many Java classes that serve as the interface through which database interaction in a Java application can occur. Along the way, many of the challenges and choices that an IS developer faces when integrating database access within their application will be discussed.

Specifically, this chapter will help you do the following:

1. Learn how the modeling of a business's data needs can impact the development of a system and its implementation of a client's requirements
2. Briefly refresh your database and Structured Query Language (SQL) skills and understand the common database-related tasks that an information systems professional faces when working with relational databases
3. Understand the nature of the Oracle Java database connectivity (OJDBC) classes and practice their usage
4. Understand some of the project settings needed for a Java (with Maven) project to allow connections to a database using OJDBC
5. Understand how `String` manipulation helps format query results into business-ready, well-formatted reports
6. Understand the nature and usage of major OJDBC class objects and how they help with database integration
7. Explore the challenges of connecting both a console-based Java application and a GUI (JavaFX)–based Java application to a database

Opening Scenario

Both your project manager (PM) and the rest of your implementation team were very happy with the GUI developed for the mom-and-pop grocery inventory application. The clients were also happy to see an interactive, easy-to-use version of the application. "This finally feels like it is really happening!" one of the clients exclaimed. The GUI itself served as a visualization tool that spurred several hours of both clarification of understood requirements and brainstorming for what would be "nice-to-have" future features. Your PM, careful to prevent scope creep, took their suggestions and carefully steered expectations for the first completed version soon to come. Overall, the GUI integration moved the needle strongly toward project success.

"Now the last step—developing a database for this application," one of your colleagues says while walking out of the meeting. The whole team knew this would be the next big step. As part of the initial requirements gathering phase, both yourself and colleagues have already gathered information on the client's data needs for the application. Additionally, you have begun producing definitions for their data and some rough entity relationship diagram (ERD) sketches. Much of the application's planned design has been guided by the team's understanding and common vision of the client's data needs. This is one prepared team! You feel that your prior experience developing and directly managing databases has paid off and helped the planning process. What you lack is experience in actually integrating databases into application development. You have mentioned to your colleagues that you can write "solid SQL queries in an editor all day long," but getting an application to talk to a database is something you're "still a little rusty at."

As has been your approach to the whole project, you decide it is time to shake the rust off in this area. Encouraged by the positive client prototype feedback, you decide to get this done. You dive into the basics of connecting a Java application to an Oracle database. Major changes to the UI are not needed, so you aim to make the integration as seamless as possible. You have heard of the OJDBC but are unsure how to use it in a Java application. One more time, you dive into your research, determined to help finish this last piece of the prototype system . . .

12.1 Database Basics: ERDs, Database Tables, and SQL

A computer-based information system "collects, processes, stores, analyzes, and disseminates information for a specific purpose . . . getting the right information to the right people at the right time, in the right amount, and in the right format."* All the programming logic, the business rules implemented using that logic, and the greatest of UI designs would all mean nothing if not for the information that information systems contain and process. The modern IS can store data (raw facts), information (data with context), and knowledge (information with actionable steps). Data is the most important of these three. Why? Everything an IS does, how users interact with it and find it useful in solving their problems, and its overall quality start with the data placed within. You may have heard the old saying "Garbage in, garbage out." This is particularly impactful for an IS. If the data is bad, if it is structured in its relationships incorrectly, or if the data itself is low quality (inaccurate, incomplete, inconsistent, old or untimely), then all the processing and dissemination of that information by the IS and possibly the decisions made in the organization based on that dissemination could be bad. While issues of data quality are beyond the scope of this text, the model and structure for your data and how your Java-based IS interacts with that data are not. To wrap up your studies of how to use Java to develop an IS, it is critical to understand how to integrate databases with Java applications.

Figure 12.1. An Array of Hard Disk Drives Storing Data in a Central Location
Source: "Research on Massive Amount of Climate Data Requires Fast Access" by j_cadmus is licensed under CC BY 2.0, https://www.flickr.com/photos/97810305@N08/17203388288.

Modeling the data relationships: As discussed in chapter 11, the system planning process is highly important. Requirement-elicitation meetings with the client and GUI design planning are both highly critical parts of the IS development and implementation process. Included in this planning process is the modeling of the system's data needs and modeling of the relationship between the data processed by the system.

An **entity relationship diagram** (ERD) is often used to show the representation of data entities (*think:* people, places, things, events, etc.) in a system as well as any cardinality relationships between them (one-to-one, one-to-many, many-to-many). For example, a `Person` may work at several `Employer` locations, but any one `Employer` only has one of that particular `Person` (one-to-many relationship). The ERD helps an IS implementation team to clarify the data needed in the system, the most efficient way to represent it, and the modeling of its real-world relationships in the system. ERDs are a great communication tool, as they present a common **vision** for the data needs of the system to the entire team. They can also help the client to understand the design of the system and clarify any mistakes or omissions the team might have missed. The ERD is a critical part of a successful IS implementation. Concepts behind ERD design are beyond the scope of this textbook, but they serve as an important planning and communication tool for information systems professionals such as yourself.

* Rainer, R. K., Prince, B., & Cegielski, C. (2014). *Introduction to information systems* (5th ed.). John Wiley & Sons, p. 14.

Figure 12.2 shows the ERD for a database that you will build and use in the first half of this chapter. As you can see, there are four tables: Customer, Item, CustOrder, and CustOrderItems. Each of these will be explained as this section of the chapter progresses.

This chapter will use the Oracle Express 21c database installed locally on your Windows PC operating system. A couple of things to note before moving on:

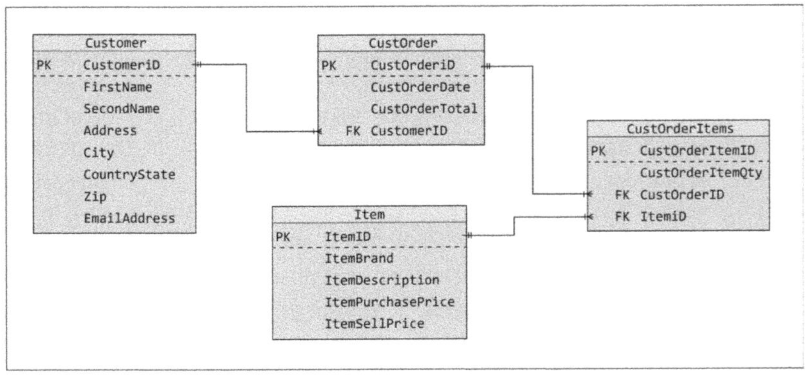

Figure 12.2. Entity Relationship Diagram for a Simple Customer Order Database

- **Appendix A** demonstrates how to install **Oracle Express 21c DB** for local use on your computer. If you do not have it installed on your Windows PC, follow the instructions in appendix A to install, configure, and test out a connection to it (through the NetBeans IDE).
- This chapter also assumes you have *some* experience with SQL, so examples will serve as a refresher. If you **do not** have prior experience with database concepts, that is **OK** too. You can still follow along with the examples.
- If you have an Oracle DB set up in a networked location in your school or work environment, you can change the URL connection string in the later code to point there instead. Check with your campus's lab services or IT help desk or speak with your instructor for more help.

For this database example, you will build a very simple customer order database. This database (DB) will then be integrated with a Java console-based application and allow data to be written and read directly from the DB through the application. The biggest benefit here is that the data will still exist even if you stop and restart the application.

Notice that in this simple DB, there are two **entities**, `Customer` and `Item`, which here could be considered **strong entities**, since they are "stand-alone" and do not depend on any other entities for their existence. The other two tables are considered **weak entities**, since they require both a `Customer` and an `Item` to exist for their records to be complete. Each table has its own **primary key**, or a column filled with unique identifiers, for each record. The weak entity tables have a column that refers to the primary key in another table, something called a **foreign key**. The foreign key in a record in one table links that record to a record in another table where the foreign key matches the primary key.

The `CustOrder` table represents information overall for a single order. In that single order, there could be multiple items purchased, or `CustOrderItems` (a quantity of an item purchased within a particular order). Imagine a trip to the grocery store: you purchase five things on this trip, and the next day, you stop by and buy eight things. Each trip overall is a `CustOrder`, and each item you purchase on a particular trip might be a `CustOrderItem` record.

The design for an ERD is somewhat flexible, and you may see a lot of variety in the layout, symbols, and cardinality used. Figure 12.2 uses the **crow's-foot** notation for showing the relationship between entities. A primary key attribute is marked with a "PK" symbol and foreign key attribute with a "FK." Notice what the ERD communicates about the relationships between the indicated entities:

- A `Customer` may have many `CustOrder` records (may have many orders), but each `CustOrder` only has one `Customer` associated with it.
- An `Item` may be purchased as a part of many `CustOrderItem` records, but each `CustOrderItem` record will only associate with one particular `Item`.
- Each `CustOrder` may be associated with many `CustOrderItems`, but each single `CustOrderItem` record will only be associated with one particular `CustOrder`.

Notice as well that the `CustOrderItems` table has two one-to-many relationships associated with it. What this really represents is a many-to-many relationship between `CustOrder` and `Item`. The best way to show these is to use what is commonly called a **bridge** or **associative** table (often called "association" or "intersection" tables as well). A `CustOrder` can have many `Items`, but each `Item` can be a part of many `CustOrders` (lots of people may purchase an item). So it is best to represent this many-to-many relationship in a bridge table.

Creating the database tables: Creating the tables for our simple customer order DB will provide a refresher in SQL. **Appendix A** demonstrates how to run queries through the SQL command editor built into NetBeans after you have Oracle DB installed. Keep in mind that the SQL you will use here has some **Oracle database–specific syntax**. If you want to execute these queries in MySQL or Microsoft's SQL Server, the syntax may differ.[*,†,‡]

The `CREATE TABLE` command facilitates the creation of DB tables and the setting of primary and foreign keys and specifies a convenient autoincrement for the primary key's value. The SQL query to create the `Customer` table looks like this in Oracle DB:

SQL Snippet 12.1

```
CREATE TABLE Customer (
    CustomerID INTEGER GENERATED BY DEFAULT ON NULL AS IDENTITY,
    FirstName VARCHAR2(100),
    SecondName VARCHAR2(100),
    Address VARCHAR2(255),
    City VARCHAR2(255),
    CountryState VARCHAR2(2),
    Zip VARCHAR2(10),
    EmailAddress VARCHAR2(255),
    CONSTRAINT customer_pk PRIMARY KEY (CustomerID)
);
```

You can execute this command in either the Oracle SQLPlus command-line window or the NetBeans DB UI (**appendix A demonstrates how to do both**).

Consider this part of the command:

```
    FirstName VARCHAR2(100),
```

Here, `FirstName` is the name of an attribute (i.e., column) for the `Customer` table. `VARCHAR2` is an Oracle database data type, "variable character length field type 2."[§] In the parentheses that follow is the width of the attribute's column. Each `FirstName` will have a maximum of one hundred characters in length (for really long first names). There are some reserved words that you will not be allowed to use as attribute names, but the ones chosen here should work well.[¶]

Notice as well the settings for the primary key in the `Customer` table:

```
    CustomerID INTEGER GENERATED BY DEFAULT ON NULL AS IDENTITY,
    . . .
    CONSTRAINT customer_pk PRIMARY KEY (CustomerID)
```

In Oracle Database versions 12c and forward, you can indicate that a primary key should autoincrement as records are inserted using the `GENERATED BY DEFAULT ON NULL AS IDENTITY` command. This is specific to Oracle's syntax, as is the addition of the constraint for indicating that this attribute is a primary key (the last line in the command). The constraint is given a name of its own and stored as a separate object in the table, and the intended primary key attribute is named in the parentheses at the end of the line. Since this is a strong entity table, no foreign key is indicated. The SQL for creating the `Item` table is similar:

---

* https://www.mysql.com/.

† https://www.microsoft.com/en-us/sql-server/.

‡ W3Schools.com has an excellent, quick run-through of how the syntax for some things differs among three common platforms: Oracle, MySQL, and Microsoft T-SQL: https://www.w3schools.com/sql/default.asp.

§ https://docs.oracle.com/en/database/oracle/oracle-database/21/sqlrf/Data-Types.html.

¶ https://docs.oracle.com/en/database/oracle/oracle-database/21/sqlrf/Oracle-SQL-Reserved-Words.html.

SQL Snippet 12.2

```
CREATE TABLE Item (
    ItemID INTEGER GENERATED BY DEFAULT ON NULL AS IDENTITY,
    ItemBrand VARCHAR2(255),
    ItemDescription VARCHAR2(255),
    ItemPurchasePrice NUMBER,
    ItemSellPrice NUMBER,
    CONSTRAINT item_pk PRIMARY KEY (ItemID)
);
```

For the weak entity and bridge tables, foreign keys are needed. This implements the planned relationship with cardinality indicators in the ERD (figure 12.2).

For `CustOrder`:

SQL Snippet 12.3

```
CREATE TABLE CustOrder(
    CustOrderID INTEGER GENERATED BY DEFAULT ON NULL AS IDENTITY,
    CustOrderDate TIMESTAMP,
    CustOrderTotal NUMBER,
    CustomerID INTEGER,
    CONSTRAINT order_pk PRIMARY KEY (CustOrderID),
CONSTRAINT cust_fk FOREIGN KEY (CustomerID) REFERENCES Customer(CustomerID)
);
```

Notice in the Oracle SQL syntax that for the foreign key constraint, you have to indicate both the local attribute (`CustomerID`) that will serve as a foreign key and the attribute in the **other** table that it references (`CustomerID` in `Customer`). Matching the names in both tables is not required but is good design, though be careful that the data type and sizes of the `PRIMARY KEY` / `FOREIGN KEY` columns in each **should** match. Notice as well the `TIMESTAMP` data type used for storing date and time information for each order's occurrence.

Finally, you can create the bridge table like so:

SQL Snippet 12.4

```
CREATE TABLE CustOrderItems(
    CustOrderItemsID INTEGER GENERATED BY DEFAULT ON NULL AS IDENTITY,
    CustOrderItemQty INTEGER,
    CustOrderID INTEGER,
    ItemID INTEGER,
    CONSTRAINT custorderitem_pk PRIMARY KEY (CustOrderItemsID),
    CONSTRAINT custorderid_fk FOREIGN KEY (CustOrderID) REFERENCES CustOrder(CustOrderID),
    CONSTRAINT itemid_fk FOREIGN KEY (ItemID) REFERENCES Item(ItemID)
);
```

The `CustOrderItems` table has two foreign keys, as it represents the many-to-many relationship between the `Item` and `CustOrder` tables. Again, you have to include two attributes in this table and then specify which foreign table attributes they relate/map to.

Inserting test data: Now that the tables are created with constraint relationships defined between them, test data can be inserted into each to test the DB design. Prepopulating your DB with test data helps later test IS functionality requirements and business logic. This also grounds the overall design in reality: Does the data match the client's needs? The client's business requirements? Does the data design make the development effort overly difficult or simplify the process?

The `INSERT` command allows you to populate records into DB tables. Since each table's primary keys are set up to autoincrement, the DB will create a unique identifier for each new record inserted automatically. Though you can handle creating these through logic, it is much easier to have the DB do this for you. Creating test data for the `Customer` table would look like this:

SQL Snippet 12.5

```
INSERT INTO Customer (FirstName,SecondName,Address,City,CountryState,Zip,EmailAddress) VALUES
('Casey','Darra','443 Garland St.','Nashville', 'TN','37201','cdarra@javais.org');

INSERT INTO Customer (FirstName,SecondName,Address,City,CountryState,Zip,EmailAddress) VALUES
('Fernley','Finnegan','120 N. Main','Martin', 'TN','38238','ffinne@javais.org');

INSERT INTO Customer (FirstName,SecondName,Address,City,CountryState,Zip,EmailAddress) VALUES
('Jesse','James','43 South Ave.','Rahway', 'NJ','07065','jjames@javais.org');

INSERT INTO Customer (FirstName,SecondName,Address,City,CountryState,Zip,EmailAddress) VALUES
('Mani','Makoto','43089 Hwy 12','Buxton', 'NC','27920','mmakoto@javais.org');

INSERT INTO Customer (FirstName,SecondName,Address,City,CountryState,Zip,EmailAddress) VALUES
('Pemberley','Quinby','71 Bluestone Dr.','Harrisonburg', 'VA','28301','pquinby@javais.org');
```

For most `INSERT` commands on most SQL platforms, the listing of the columns at the start of the command is optional **only** if you are inserting data for each and every column. In this case, since the tables are handling the autoincrement of our primary keys, you need to list all the columns, since only a subset of the columns are altered through the SQL command.

Our other tables can be **populated** with test data similar to the following:

SQL Snippet 12.6

```
INSERT INTO Item (ItemBrand,ItemDescription,ItemPurchasePrice,ItemSellPrice) VALUES
('ViewGood','80-inch OLED TV',450.50,899.99);

INSERT INTO Item (ItemBrand,ItemDescription,ItemPurchasePrice,ItemSellPrice) VALUES
('Choppie','Super Blender 2000',49.99,129.99);

INSERT INTO Item (ItemBrand,ItemDescription,ItemPurchasePrice,ItemSellPrice) VALUES
('CodeIT','Dark Roast Java Beans',1.99,6.99);

INSERT INTO Item (ItemBrand,ItemDescription,ItemPurchasePrice,ItemSellPrice) VALUES
('Applesoftcle','15.9 iThinkBookPad',999.99,1299.99);

INSERT INTO Item (ItemBrand,ItemDescription,ItemPurchasePrice,ItemSellPrice) VALUES
('Prospect Press','How to IS: A Comprehensive Guide',39.99,40.02);

INSERT INTO CUSTORDER (CUSTORDERDATE,CUSTORDERTOTAL,CUSTOMERID)
VALUES (TO_TIMESTAMP('2023-03-16 15:16:00', 'YYYY-MM-DD HH24:MI:SS'),136.98,1);

INSERT INTO CUSTORDER (CUSTORDERDATE,CUSTORDERTOTAL,CUSTOMERID)
VALUES (TO_TIMESTAMP('2023-04-16 16:45:00', 'YYYY-MM-DD HH24:MI:SS'),1340.01,2);

INSERT INTO CUSTORDER (CUSTORDERDATE,CUSTORDERTOTAL,CUSTOMERID)
VALUES (TO_TIMESTAMP('2023-05-16 11:24:00', 'YYYY-MM-DD HH24:MI:SS'),899.99,3);

INSERT INTO CUSTORDERITEMS (CUSTORDERITEMQTY,CUSTORDERID,ITEMID)
VALUES (1,16,2);

INSERT INTO CUSTORDERITEMS (CUSTORDERITEMQTY,CUSTORDERID,ITEMID)
VALUES (1,16,3);

INSERT INTO CUSTORDERITEMS (CUSTORDERITEMQTY,CUSTORDERID,ITEMID)
VALUES (1,17,4);

INSERT INTO CUSTORDERITEMS (CUSTORDERITEMQTY,CUSTORDERID,ITEMID)
VALUES (1,17,5);

INSERT INTO CUSTORDERITEMS (CUSTORDERITEMQTY,CUSTORDERID,ITEMID)
VALUES (1,18,1);
```

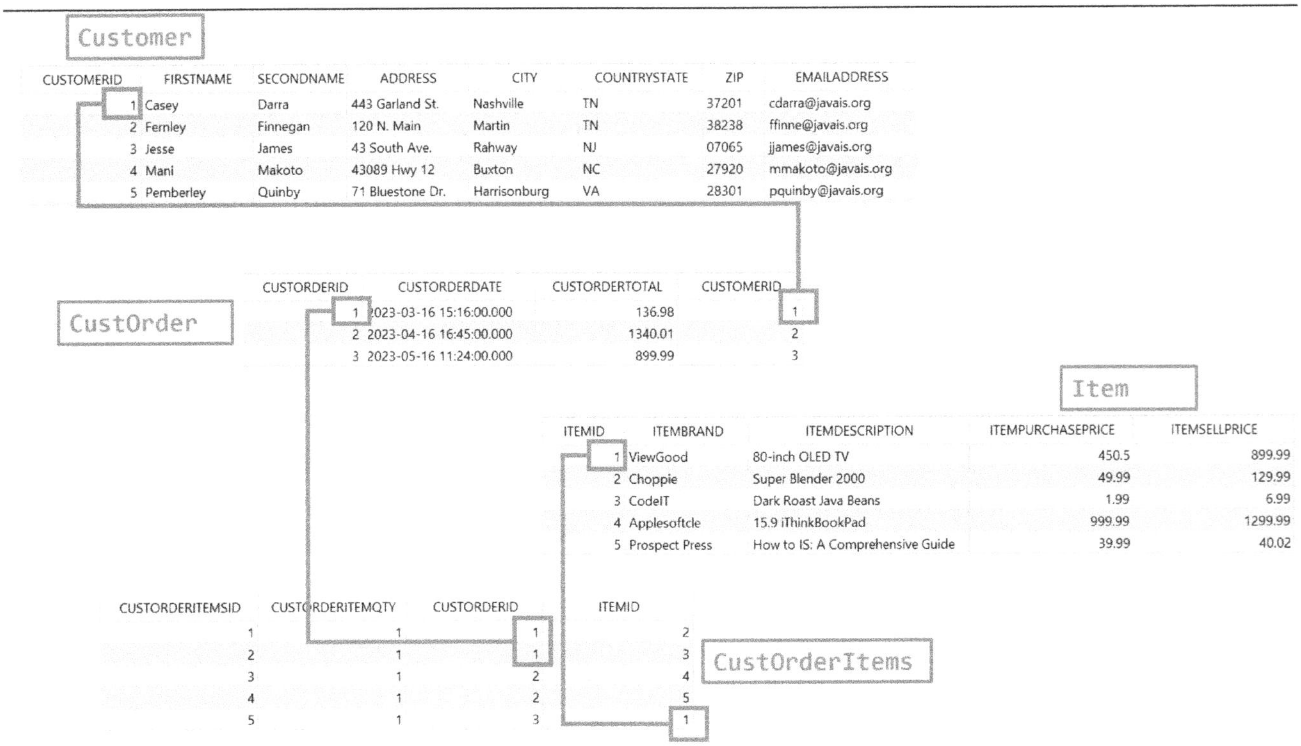

CUSTOMERID	FIRSTNAME	SECONDNAME	ADDRESS	CITY	COUNTRYSTATE	ZIP	EMAILADDRESS
1	Casey	Darra	443 Garland St.	Nashville	TN	37201	cdarra@javais.org
2	Fernley	Finnegan	120 N. Main	Martin	TN	38238	ffinne@javais.org
3	Jesse	James	43 South Ave.	Rahway	NJ	07065	jjames@javais.org
4	Mani	Makoto	43089 Hwy 12	Buxton	NC	27920	mmakoto@javais.org
5	Pemberley	Quinby	71 Bluestone Dr.	Harrisonburg	VA	28301	pquinby@javais.org

CUSTORDERID	CUSTORDERDATE	CUSTORDERTOTAL	CUSTOMERID
1	2023-03-16 15:16:00.000	136.98	1
2	2023-04-16 16:45:00.000	1340.01	2
3	2023-05-16 11:24:00.000	899.99	3

ITEMID	ITEMBRAND	ITEMDESCRIPTION	ITEMPURCHASEPRICE	ITEMSELLPRICE
1	ViewGood	80-inch OLED TV	450.5	899.99
2	Choppie	Super Blender 2000	49.99	129.99
3	CodeIT	Dark Roast Java Beans	1.99	6.99
4	Applesoftcle	15.9 iThinkBookPad	999.99	1299.99
5	Prospect Press	How to IS: A Comprehensive Guide	39.99	40.02

CUSTORDERITEMSID	CUSTORDERITEMQTY	CUSTORDERID	ITEMID
1	1	1	2
2	1	1	3
3	1	2	4
4	1	2	5
5	1	3	1

Figure 12.3. Database Test Data and Primary Key / Foreign Key Relationships

Notice that for the `CustOrder` and `CustOrderItems` tables, some of the values inserted are the numeric primary keys from the `Customer` and `Item` tables. Text in SQL is indicated by single quotes. For the `TIMESTAMP` data field, the `TO_TIMESTAMP()` Oracle SQL function converts the timestamp text into the appropriate `TIMESTAMP` data-type value according to the formatting mask (the second parameter). Figure 12.3 shows the data in the tables after insertion with notation showing the `PRIMARY KEY` / `FOREIGN KEY` relationships.

Note that in these `INSERT` statements, the `CustOrderTotal` for each `CustOrder` record is manually inserted. In a typical business scenario, this would be programmatically calculated and not stored in the table itself. It is included here with the `INSERT` commands for the sake of simplicity and demonstration.

Working with SQL queries—oh CRUD! The real power in SQL lies in its ability not only to manipulate and create data but to read from and combine the results of multiple tables in informative and decision-making-supportive ways. Seeing as the data tables have several defined relationships, some clever use of the SQL syntax can produce information very helpful in generating insights into data patterns and customer activity. You can also duplicate these SQL commands programmatically in Java and generate the same "views" upon the data within Java applications also.

Keep in mind that the task of most SQL commands can be summed up in the acronym CRUD: create, read, update, delete. Table 12.1 summarizes these actions.

As you interact with your database, either manually or through a Java application, most of what you will do will fall under CRUD. A brief review of some of the more common SQL commands will be helpful here. Take note of the semicolon at the end of each SQL statement: when using an SQL editor or command line, a semicolon is needed to define the end of the statement, separating it from the one after it. Also, SQL queries can be split across multiple lines when needed to make them easier to read without impacting results at all:

Table 12.1. CRUD Actions, Descriptions, and Associated Example SQL Commands

Action	Description	Example SQL command
Create	The creation or addition of data to your database or its tables	INSERT… CREATE TABLE…
Read	The passive reading of data from your database tables	SELECT…
Update	The editing of data already stored within your database tables or changing of table characteristics	UPDATE… UPDATE TABLE…
Delete	The removing of data or entire tables from your database	DELETE FROM… DROP TABLE…

- `SELECT`: Used to select rows of data from one or more tables. The asterisk (*) is used as the "all," as in "Select all rows from table Item." Some examples:

```
SELECT * FROM ITEM;
```

ITEMID	ITEMBRAND	ITEMDESCRIPTION	ITEMPURCHASEPRICE	ITEMSELLPRICE
1	ViewGood	80-inch OLED TV	450.5	899.99
2	Choppie	Super Blender 2000	49.99	129.99
3	CodeIT	Dark Roast Java Beans	1.99	6.99
4	Applesoftcle	15.9 iThinkBookPad	999.99	1299.99
5	Prospect Press	How to IS: A Comprehensive Guide	39.99	40.02

```
SELECT ItemBrand, ItemDescription from Item;
```

ITEMBRAND	ITEMDESCRIPTION
ViewGood	80-inch OLED TV
Choppie	Super Blender 2000
CodeIT	Dark Roast Java Beans
Applesoftcle	15.9 iThinkBookPad
Prospect Press	How to IS: A Comprehensive Guide

The `SELECT` command has several clauses that can help filter the results or perform actions upon the data returned:

- `WHERE`: This command filters the query results to include only those rows whose column matches the value indicated:

```
SELECT * FROM Item WHERE ItemSellPrice > 100;
```

ITEMID	ITEMBRAND	ITEMDESCRIPTION	ITEMPURCHASEPRICE	ITEMSELLPRICE
1	ViewGood	80-inch OLED TV	450.5	899.99
2	Choppie	Super Blender 2000	49.99	129.99
4	Applesoftcle	15.9 iThinkBookPad	999.99	1299.99

- `AND/OR`: You can include boolean clauses to further filter the data:

```
SELECT *
FROM Item
WHERE ItemSellPrice > 100
AND ItemPurchasePrice > 500;
```

ITEMID	ITEMBRAND	ITEMDESCRIPTION	ITEMPURCHASEPRICE	ITEMSELLPRICE
4	Applesoftcle	15.9 iThinkBookPad	999.99	1299.99

- `IN`: Provides a concise way of searching for multiple values for a specific column at once:

```
SELECT *
FROM ITEM
WHERE ITEMBRAND IN ('ViewGood','CodeIT');
```

ITEMID	ITEMBRAND	ITEMDESCRIPTION	ITEMPURCHASEPRICE	ITEMSELLPRICE
1	ViewGood	80-inch OLED TV	450.5	899.99
3	CodeIT	Dark Roast Java Beans	1.99	6.99

- ORDER BY...ASC/DESC: Sorts the rows returned by the statement based on the values in the specified column in either ascending (ASC) or descending (DESC) order:

```
SELECT *
FROM Item
WHERE ItemSellPrice > 100
ORDER BY ITEMSELLPRICE DESC;
```

ITEMID	ITEMBRAND	ITEMDESCRIPTION	ITEMPURCHASEPRICE	ITEMSELLPRICE
4	Applesoftcle	15.9 iThinkBookPad	999.99	1299.99
1	ViewGood	80-inch OLED TV	450.5	899.99
2	Choppie	Super Blender 2000	49.99	129.99

- COUNT: Some analytical clauses are available like Count, which will give you a count of the results in terms of quantity of rows returned:

```
SELECT COUNT(*)
FROM ITEM
WHERE ItemSellPrice > 100;
```

COUNT(ITEMSELLPRICE)
3

The COUNT clause can be especially useful in scenarios where a login occurs to determine if the username and/or password given by the user is in the database. Notice that COUNT simply returns a number, keeping the actual data itself in the database table. If you used a normal SELECT * to check the login, the actual username and password data would be returned, and their interception would pose a possible security risk.

- GROUP BY: Allows you to "collapse" results into categories defined on a field—for example, to view the average of some value by country, school, or grade:

```
SELECT COUNT(CustomerID), CountryState
FROM CUSTOMER
GROUP BY COUNTRYSTATE;
```

COUNT(CUSTOMERID)	COUNTRYSTATE
1	NJ
1	NC
1	VA
2	TN

- AVG: You can have the database calculate the average of a field:

```
SELECT AVG(ITEMSELLPRICE)
FROM ITEM;
```

AVG(ITEMSELLPRICE)
475.396

This will work for multiple columns at the same time as well:

```
SELECT AVG(ITEMPURCHASEPRICE),
AVG(ITEMSELLPRICE)
FROM ITEM;
```

AVG(ITEMPURCHASEPRICE)	AVG(ITEMSELLPRICE)
308.492	475.396

- SUM: Allows you to add up all the values returned for a field.

```
SELECT SUM(ItemSellPrice)
FROM Item;
```

SUM(ITEMSELLPRICE)
2376.98

- `LIKE`: Allows you to return results based on similarity to part of all of a specific column. Paired with the `WHERE` clause:

```
SELECT *
FROM Item
WHERE ItemDescription LIKE '%TV%';
```

ITEMID	ITEMBRAND	ITEMDESCRIPTION	ITEMPURCHASEPRICE	ITEMSELLPRICE
1	ViewGood	80-inch OLED TV	450.5	899.99

  - `'%TERM'`: Searches for a match where any number of characters can precede the search term.
  - `'TERM%'`: Searches for a match with any number of characters following the term.
  - `'%TERM%'`: Allows for any number of characters to either side of the search term.
  - `'a%z'`: Searches for a term that begins with `a` and ends with `z`. Can be any number of characters, like `'sa%ha'` (which would find "`samantha`").
  - `'_a'`: Finds rows where the field contains `a` as the second character from the left. This works for `'a__'` as well, with the quantity of underscores representing the spacing pattern to look for.
- Select queries with `Join`:
  - `Inner Join`: Returns rows for which there is a match between two tables on a specific column. This allows you to pull columns from two different tables, defining columns that correspond to a foreign key instead of simply displaying the foreign key. This works well with bridge/associative tables:

SQL Snippet 12.7

```
SELECT Customer.FIRSTNAME,
Customer.SECONDNAME,
CustOrder.CUSTORDERDATE,
CustOrder.CUSTORDERTOTAL
FROM Customer
INNER JOIN CustOrder
ON Customer.CUSTOMERID = CustOrder.CUSTOMERID;
```

FIRSTNAME	SECONDNAME	CUSTORDERDATE	CUSTORDERTOTAL
Casey	Darra	16:00.0	136.98
Fernley	Finnegan	45:00.0	1340.01
Jesse	James	24:00.0	899.99

You can combine the `INNER JOIN` with a `WHERE` clause also. For example, you can display all the items that were part of `CustOrder` #16:

SQL Snippet 12.8

```
SELECT CustOrderItems.CUSTORDERITEMQTY,
CustOrderItems.CUSTORDERID,
Item.ITEMBRAND,
Item.ITEMDESCRIPTION,
Item.ITEMSELLPRICE
From CustOrderItems
INNER JOIN Item
ON CustOrderItems.ITEMID=Item.ITEMID
WHERE CustOrderItems.CUSTORDERID = 16;
```

CUSTORDERITEMQTY	CUSTORDERID	ITEMBRAND	ITEMDESCRIPTION	ITEMSELLPRICE
1	1	Choppie	Super Blender 2000	129.99
1	1	CodeIT	Dark Roast Java Beans	6.99

Especially handy is the ability to join multiple tables at the same time by using successive `INNER JOIN` statements in a row. When you do this, you **must** remove the table name qualifiers from each column you want to include. Also, the `USING()` clause is used in place of the `ON` clause in a single `INNER JOIN`:

SQL Snippet 12.9

```
SELECT
FIRSTNAME || ' ' || SECONDNAME as CustName,
CUSTORDERDATE,
CUSTORDERITEMQTY,
ITEMDESCRIPTION,
ITEMSELLPRICE
FROM Customer
INNER JOIN CustOrder USING(CustomerID)
INNER JOIN CustOrderItems USING(CustOrderID)
INNER JOIN Item USING(ItemID)
ORDER BY CUSTOMERID ASC;
```

CUSTNAME	CUSTORDERDATE	CUSTORDERITEMQTY	ITEMDESCRIPTION	ITEMSELLPRICE
Casey Darra	16:00.0	1	Dark Roast Java Beans	6.99
Casey Darra	16:00.0	1	Super Blender 2000	129.99
Fernley Finnegan	45:00.0	1	How to IS: A Comprehensive Guide	40.02
Fernley Finnegan	45:00.0	1	15.9 iThinkBookPad	1299.99
Jesse James	24:00.0	1	80-inch OLED TV	899.99

Keep in mind that this syntax is Oracle database specific. In MySQL, for example, the multiple table join syntax will differ.

- `UPDATE`: Allows you to change the data in one or more columns across one or more rows using a `WHERE` condition that can be as simple or complex as you would like. Notice the use of the `NOT` clause here to exclude changing the price of the coffee:

SQL Snippet 12.10

```
UPDATE Item
SET ItemPurchasePrice = 59.99
WHERE ItemPurchasePrice < 50.00
AND
NOT ItemID = 3;
```

ITEMID	ITEMBRAND	ITEMDESCRIPTION	ITEMPURCHASEPRICE	ITEMSELLPRICE
1	ViewGood	80-inch OLED TV	450.50	899.99
2	Choppie	Super Blender 2000	59.99	129.99
3	CodeIT	Dark Roast Java Beans	1.99	6.99
4	Applesoftcle	15.9 iThinkBookPad	999.99	1299.99
5	Prospect Press	How to IS: A Comprehensive Guide	59.99	40.02

- `DELETE`: Allows you to remove rows from a database table where one or more columns match on `WHERE` search criteria. First, a bad row of data is inserted for demonstration:

SQL Snippet 12.11

```
INSERT INTO Item (ItemBrand, ItemDescription, ItemPurchasePrice, ItemSellPrice)
VALUES
('Mistaken','Product',-5.00,-10.00);
```

ITEMID	ITEMBRAND	ITEMDESCRIPTION	ITEMPURCHASEPRICE	ITEMSELLPRICE
1	ViewGood	80-inch OLED TV	450.50	899.99
2	Choppie	Super Blender 2000	59.99	129.99
3	CodeIT	Dark Roast Java Beans	1.99	6.99
4	Applesoftcle	15.9 iThinkBookPad	999.99	1299.99
5	Prospect Press	How to IS: A Comprehensive Guide	59.99	40.02
21	Mistaken	Product	-5.00	-10.00

Oops! You can use `DELETE` to remove this bad row of data:

```
DELETE FROM Item
WHERE ItemPurchasePrice < 0.00
```

ITEMID	ITEMBRAND	ITEMDESCRIPTION	ITEMPURCHASEPRICE	ITEMSELLPRICE
1	ViewGood	80-inch OLED TV	450.50	899.99
2	Choppie	Super Blender 2000	59.99	129.99
3	CodeIT	Dark Roast Java Beans	1.99	6.99
4	Applesoftcle	15.9 iThinkBookPad	999.99	1299.99
5	Prospect Press	How to IS: A Comprehensive Guide	59.99	40.02

Better! Notice that if you attempt to `DELETE` any of the other items, you will get an SQL integrity constraint error, since the primary key of these items has been used as foreign keys in other database table records (in `CustOrderItems`).

There is a lot more to the SQL syntax than what is just shown here. This was, hopefully, a shake-off-the-rust refresher in the syntax if it has been a while since you last worked with SQL. You will find many of these more common commands and clauses in the next section as you develop a console-based Java application that will use this simple customer order database.

SUMMARY POINTS

- An entity relationship diagram is an important part of the data-modeling, requirement-elicitation, and planning processes for new information systems.
- A strong entity table is one where records in the table do not depend on any other table's records for completeness.
- A weak entity table contains records whose fields are often primary key values from other table records, creating a dependency for completeness.
- A primary key is a unique identifier for each database table record, and this identifier should not change.
- A foreign key is the inclusion of a table's primary key values in a column in a separate table's column, allowing the association of one record in one table to a record in another.
- Inserting test data into your database tables during the information systems development process is a great way to both confirm your implementation of the client's requirements and aid in testing out system functionality.
- The CRUD acronym summarizes the majority of database-related tasks an information systems professional will face: creating tables and records, reading records, updating information in records, and deleting records when needed and where appropriate.
- The SQL syntax for common database tasks may differ slightly from one database platform to another.

QUICK PROBLEMS

1. **Modeling:** Draw out an ERD for the process of paying your bills every month. Include entities PERSON and BILLTYPE along with a bridge table for the actual payment activity.
2. **Think:** What are the benefits of using an ERD during the systems development process? How can it impact all the members of an IS planning and development team? How can it benefit a single developer?
3. **Modeling:** Draw out an ERD for the process of going to see a movie. Include entities for GUEST, MOVIE, and THEATER and any needed bridge tables for the actual showings, along with dates and times.

12.2 Database Integration with Console-Based Java Applications

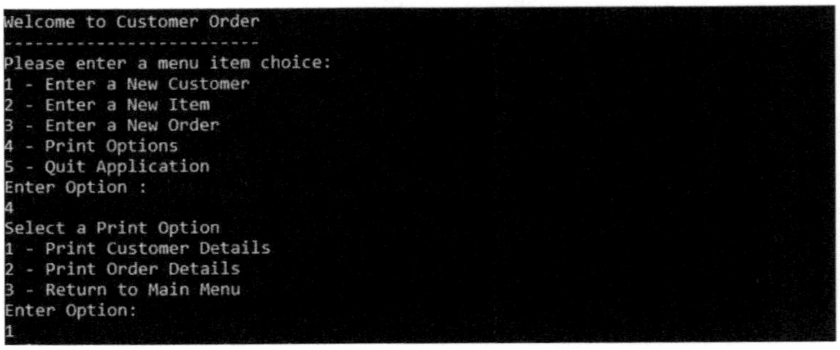

The Java database connectivity (JDBC) language API is defined within the `java.sql` package within the Java API.* Oracle provides the `java.sql` package (the module is named the same) to serve as the base API for connecting to a DB as well as tabular-formatted data from a Java application. Object-oriented development is leveraged heavily here, as the `java.sql` package itself facilitates the abstract classes (see companion chapter 4 for more details on abstract classes) and the interfaces that are used by other code to make a connection to a database. Oracle, IBM, Sybase, PostgreSQL, Microsoft SQL, and other third-party database vendors all have created driver `.jar` JDBC driver files that provide concrete implementations of the classes and interface methods provided in the JDBC. This allows each third-party driver to "roll its own" version of the JDBC that matches the nature and functionality of its underlying database technology. Figure 12.4 shows this relationship in a very abstract form.

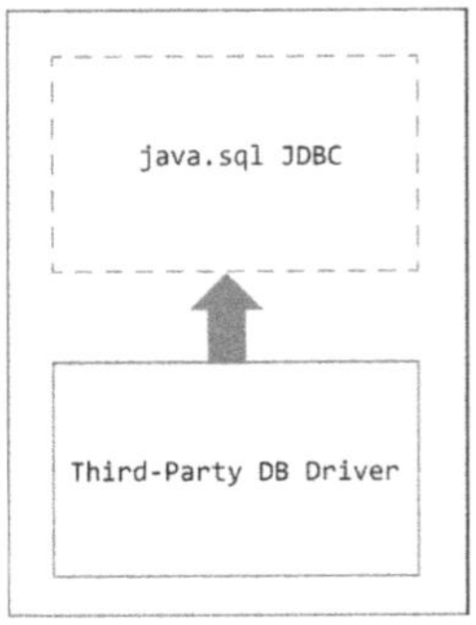

Figure 12.4. Implementation Relationship between JDBC and a Third-Party Driver

For the examples in this chapter, you will continue to use Oracle Express Database 21c as our locally installed database as well as the Oracle JDBC (OJDBC) thin client driver file to enable Java applications to connect to the local database. **Appendix A** has the **full instructions** for installing Oracle DB 21c Express Edition and setting up both NetBeans and your Java project to connect to and use the DB.

The OJDBC `.jar` file discussed in appendix A contains Java classes that provide concrete implementations to the classes and interface methods in `java.sql` JDBC (interfaces such as `Driver`, `Connection`, `PreparedStatement`, etc.).

Create a new Java (non-JavaFX, for now) project called "`CustOrder`" along with a Java `main()` class file by the same name ("`CustOrder.java`"). For this Java application, you will need to include the database driver in our project as a dependency. **See appendix A for full instructions.** For each and every Java project where you want your Java code to interact with the Oracle DB, you will need to do the following:

- Include the dependency XML tags and their content in `pom.xml`
- Click the "Build Project" button to have your project download the related `.jar` files

Figure 12.5 visually summarizes the changes that are detailed fully in appendix A. **Perform the steps listed there first!**

After this, you are ready to use the OJDBC Java DB classes in your application. Add the following import statement to your Java `main()` class:

```
import java.sql.*;
```

Since you will be using the Oracle JDBC driver to enable our application to connect to the Oracle Express 21c DB, include the following imports as well:

Code Snippet 12.1

```
import oracle.jdbc.pool.*;      // DB-related Java classes in .jar file
import oracle.jdbc.*;           // DB-related Java classes in .jar file
import java.util.*;             // For Scanner and other classes
```

Testing the database connection: Now that the proper driver has been included in the project, you can test the connection to the database from Java code itself. As you saw in appendix A, NetBeans can connect to and interact with the database separately from your Java code. **Your Java code does not require a connection from**

* https://docs.oracle.com/en/java/javase/17/docs/api/java.sql/java/sql/package-summary.html.

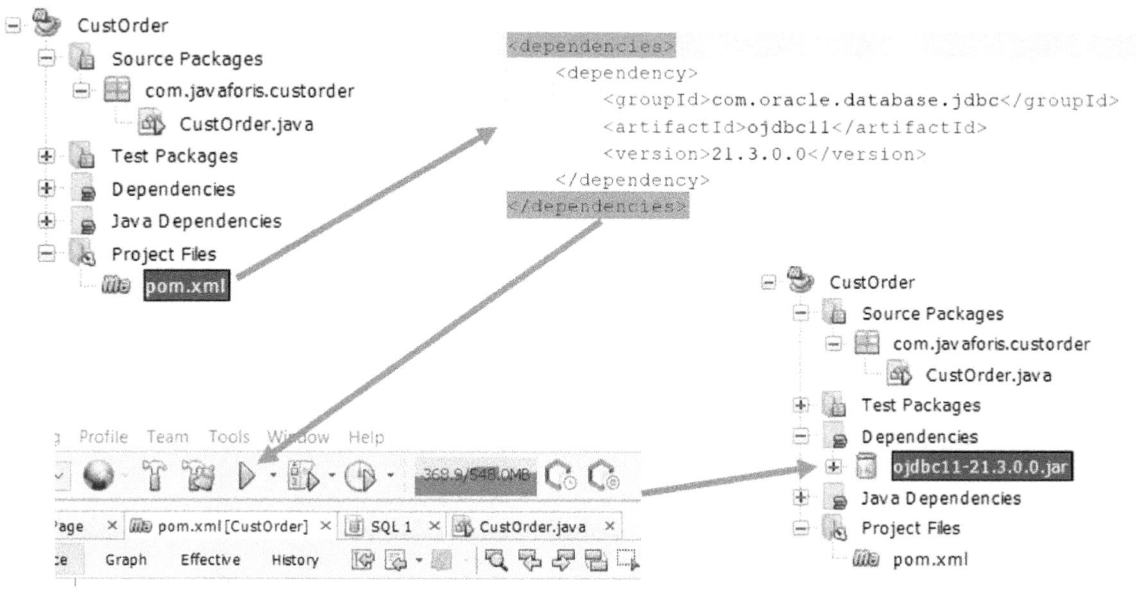

Figure 12.5. Editing the `pom.xml` Project File to Include the OJDBC Driver in NetBeans

NetBeans to the DB in order to connect itself! The IDE connection and the connection from your code are two separate avenues of interacting with the DB. The ultimate goal is to interact with the DB from Java code. IDE connection to the DB can be very helpful for debugging and fine-tuning our Java code and its DB interactions. In your `main()` method, include the following test code. Take note that for this code to work, you will need the simple customer order tables created and filled earlier in this chapter:

Code Snippet 12.2

```
// In main()
try
{
   // java.sql Interface Classes
   Connection jsqlConn;
   PreparedStatement jsqlStmt;
   ResultSet jsqlResults;

   // Oracle jdbc driver Class in oracle.jdbc.pool
   OracleDataSource oDS;

   // Change the URL, user, and pass according to the
   // Database you have access to. If you use
   // appendix A's steps, these will work. Otherwise
   // use the settings for your corporate/educational
   // database (user, pass, network address, and name)

   // Connecting to the XEPDB1 Database Container
   // on a local machine using the Oracle thin client
   // driver
   String URL = "jdbc:oracle:thin:@localhost:1521/XEPDB1";
   String user = "javauser";
   String pass = "javapass";

   // Query you want to test out.
```

```
    String sqlQuery = "SELECT * FROM Item";

    // The only code that uses an oracle.jdbc.pool class
    // The OracleDataSource Class implements the javax.sql.DataSource
    // Class, which the Java Documentation recommends as a better
    //  connection approach (resource efficient).
    // Part of the oracle.jdbc.pool package, the class keeps a pool
    // of connections to make connecting to the DB more
    //  resource efficient.
    oDS = new OracleDataSource();
    oDS.setURL(URL);

    // Makes the connection to the database.
    jsqlConn = oDS.getConnection(user, pass);

    // Sets up the PreparedStatement object with the query.
    jsqlStmt = jsqlConn.prepareStatement(
            sqlQuery,
            ResultSet.TYPE_SCROLL_INSENSITIVE,
            ResultSet.CONCUR_READ_ONLY);

    // Executes the Select Query and retrieves a ResultSet
    jsqlResults = jsqlStmt.executeQuery();

    // .next() must be called to move the ResultSet
    //  pointer to the first row of results. Otherwise
    //  an error will occur. The while() loop invokes it to
    //  move to the next row of results each time.

    while (jsqlResults.next())
    {
        System.out.print(jsqlResults.getInt(1)
                + "\t" + jsqlResults.getString(2)
                + "\t\t" + jsqlResults.getString(3)
                + "\t" + jsqlResults.getDouble(4)
                + "\t" + jsqlResults.getDouble(5) + "\n");
    }

}
catch (SQLException sqle)
{
    // Something went wrong - Print the Exception Message
    System.out.println(sqle.toString());
}
```

If everything is set up correctly (DB installation and settings, `pom.xml` changes, import statements—appendix A), this code should produce the following output when the project is run:

```
1     ViewGood            80-inch OLED TV                       450.5      899.99
2     Choppie             Super Blender 2000                    59.99      129.99
3     CodeIT              Dark Roast Java Beans                  1.99        6.99
4     Applesoftcle        15.9 iThinkBookPad                   999.99     1299.99
5     Prospect Press      How to IS: A Comprehensive Guide      59.99       40.02
```

Success! The Java application's **code itself** is communicating with the database and retrieving data from it. That is really the hardest part. First, clean up the formatting of the output using some `String` formatting approaches from chapter 3:

Code Snippet 12.3

```
// Chapter 3 String formatting
System.out.printf(
        "%-5s%-15s%-33s%-7s%-7s\n",
        "ID",
        "Brand",
        "Description",
        "Price",
        "Sell");

String border = "";
for (int i=0; i<70; i++)
    border += "-";
System.out.println(border);

while (jsqlResults.next())
{
    // Chapter 3 String formatting
    System.out.printf(
            "%-5d%-15s%-33s$%-,7.2f$%-,7.2f\n",
            jsqlResults.getInt(1),
            jsqlResults.getString(2),
            jsqlResults.getString(3),
            jsqlResults.getDouble(4),
            jsqlResults.getDouble(5));
}
```

This will produce output that looks like the following:

```
ID   Brand          Description                      Price  Sell
----------------------------------------------------------------------
1    ViewGood       80-inch OLED TV                  $450.50 $899.99
2    Choppie        Super Blender 2000               $59.99  $129.99
3    CodeIT         Dark Roast Java Beans            $1.99   $6.99
4    Applesoftcle   15.9 iThinkBookPad               $999.99 $1,299.99
5    Prospect Press How to IS: A Comprehensive Guide $59.99  $40.02
```

Some adjustments to the widths of each "column" might be necessary to get it looking just right (business ready).

An examination of a few of these lines of code separately will help in understanding them better, along with the methods being invoked upon the objects in use:

- **Usage of the `ResultSet` object `jsqlResults` and its methods:** Especially when a `SELECT` query is processed, a `ResultSet` object will store the results, in a row and column format, of the query. If you explore the documentation for the `ResultSet` class, you will see many "getter" methods that are named with the data type they retrieve from the object.[*] Keep in mind that invoking `.next()` prior to the first call to a `ResultSet` getter method moves an internal pointer to the first row of data (if there is data). A couple of handy things to remember about a `ResultSet` object:
  - Most of the "getter" methods will accept either a column label parameter as a String (i.e., the actual name of the column from the query results you want to retrieve) or an index number for the column you want to retrieve data from. `ResultSet` columns **start at** `1`, not `0` like with arrays!

    For example, with our `Item` table results, you can use

    `jsqlResults.getInt("ItemID")`

    or

    `jsqlResults.getInt(1)`

    to get the data for the first column in the query results, the ItemID column.

[*] https://docs.oracle.com/en/java/javase/17/docs/api/java.sql/java/sql/ResultSet.html.

  - Keep in mind also the data type of the column you are trying to retrieve, and use the appropriate getter (i.e., `.getString()` for String data, `.getDouble()` for double precision numbers, etc.).
  - If there are rows of data in the returned `ResultSet` object as a result of the query processed, you must call `.next()` at least once to move the internal pointer to the first row of data. Notice the invocation in the example code within a `while` statement. The method `.next()` returns a `boolean true` if there is another row and `false` if not.
- **Creating a data source for the connection:** After defining the URL, username, password, and query as String variables, an `OracleDataSource` object is instantiated, and the `.setURL()` method is invoked upon it.
- **Creating a connection to the database:** Next, you use this `OracleDataSource` object to `.getConnection()` and store this in a `java.sql` Connection object reference. The JDBC documentation recommends using a class that implements the `DataSource` interface over the `DriverManager` class to establish a connection to your database due to resource efficiency. In the Oracle DB driver, the `OracleDataSource` class implements this JDBC `DataSource` interface and you use it to get a connection from a connection pool.
- **Understanding the `PreparedStatement` object:** For the other objects, like `ResultSet`, `PreparedStatement`, and `Connection`, the interfaces are imported from `java.sql` but the Oracle driver implements classes that use these interfaces behind the scenes. For example, the `PreparedStatement` reference variable does not actually reference an instance object of `PreparedStatement` (you cannot instantiate interfaces!) but is instead a polymorphic reference to an instance object of an ODJBC class that implements the `PreparedStatement` interface.
- **Creating a `PreparedStatement` object:** You then use the `jsqlConn Connection` object to create a `PreparedStatement`. The Oracle documentation recommends these over `Statements`, and they are highly useful (they can be used for precompiled, parameterized queries!). You will notice that the `.prepareStatement()` method of `Connection` takes three parameters: the query you want to execute, the selection of traversal behavior in the eventual `ResultSet` object you want returned back, and the read/write behavior of the eventual `ResultSet` object you want returned.* The Oracle documentation for `ResultSet` breaks these down, but here is a summary:†
  - `ResultSet` "type":
    - `TYPE_FORWARD_ONLY`: When reading the results of the `ResultSet`, only allow the internal "pointer" to move forward from start to end.
    - `TYPE_SCROLL_INSENSITIVE`: Allows the internal pointer (which row you are on in the `ResultSet`) to move forward or backward. The "insensitive" part means that if the table or underlying results of the query processed changed, the data in the `ResultSet` will **not** update dynamically.

      The following are some of the methods of `ResultSet` that allow this movement:

      `.next()`: Moves the cursor forward one row in the `ResultSet`
      `.previous()`: Moves it back one row
      `.first()`: Moves the cursor to the first row of data
      `.last()`: Moves the cursor to the last row of data
      `.absolute(int r)`: Moves the cursor to the rth row
      `.relative(int re)`: Moves the cursor re number of rows forward or backward from the row its currently on

      For example, you might invoke these in this way:

```
// After a ResultSet object has been populated by
//   a query execution and assuming there are a
//   sufficient number of rows in the results
jsqlResults.first();
jsqlResults.next();
```

* https://docs.oracle.com/en/java/javase/17/docs/api/java.sql/java/sql/Connection.html#prepareStatement(java.lang.String,int,int).

† https://docs.oracle.com/en/java/javase/17/docs/api/java.sql/java/sql/ResultSet.html.

```
jsqlResults.next();
jsqlResults.last();
jsqlResults.previous()
```

    - `TYPE_SCROLL_SENSITIVE`: Same as for the "insensitive" type, but here the `ResultSet`'s data will change dynamically to match the underlying data or results.
  - `ResultSet` read/write behavior:
    - `CONCUR_READ_ONLY`: The `ResultSet` is read-only in terms of its connection to the underlying table or data. Changes made to the `ResultSet`'s data will not change the source data.
    - `CONDUR_UPDATABLE`: Changes to the `ResultSet`'s data will change the source data the query pulled the results from.
- **Methods used with a `PreparedStatement` object:** The `PreparedStatement` method has three main methods invoked to process an SQL command or query:
  - `.executeQuery()`: This method is mainly used with SELECT queries and its return type is `ResultSet`.
  - `.executeUpdate()`: This method is handy for other types of CRUD queries, such as `UPDATE`, `INSERT`, or `DELETE`. The method's return type is an int that indicates how many rows in the target table were affected by the command.
  - `.execute()`: This method is a catchall for any other types of SQL commands you may want to issue. It will return a boolean to indicate if a `ResultSet` was generated at all by your command (true if so, false if the return is a count of rows affected or no results).
    - If true is returned, use the inherited `.getResultSet()` method on the `PreparedStatement` object to retrieve a reference to the `ResultSet` returned.
- **Specifying the connection String:** String URL contains the connection string needed to connect to an Oracle DB installed on a local machine. If you have another DB installed or a different type installed on a networked location, the connection string will look different. There are several great guides online to show how to format a connection string for various third-party DB systems.* A brief look at the one used in this chapter:

  `"jdbc:oracle:thin:@localhost:1521/XEPDB1"`

  `jdbc:oracle:thin`: This instructs the `OracleDataSource` object that uses the URL to use the Oracle thin client driver.

  `:@localhost:1521`: This is the network location of the database install and the port that it listens on (at that location) for communication.

  `/XEPDB1`: Oracle Express DB (since version 12c) follows a cloud-inspired and cloud-compatible multitenant architecture. The Oracle DB architecture can host many separate "pluggable," isolated database environments. PDB1 is "Pluggable Database 1" and is set up by default when you install Oracle DB 21c (see appendix A). So in addition to the port (1521), you have to specify which particular PDB to connect to.
- **Sending the username and password in plain text:** Obviously, this is a big security issue. For the purposes of learning how to integrate a database with a Java application, you are OK to use a test username and password like "javauser" and "javapass," but it would not be a good idea to include the credentials for a production-ready database in plain text in your Java code. There is a possibility of reverse-engineering and extracting these and allowing a malicious party to gain access. Two things to keep in mind that can help you sleep easier at night:
  - The Oracle thin client driver does encrypt the credentials as it connects to the Oracle database and verifies the information. This helps with an intercept of the data between the client and the server. Oracle's documentation discusses many of the security features of the current OJDBC driver above and beyond this.† In a corporate setting, many applications would sit on-network or even on-server with the database, eliminating the need for a login altogether.

---

* Codejava.net has a very helpful write-up: https://www.codejava.net/java-se/jdbc/jdbc-database-connection-url-for-common-databases.

† https://docs.oracle.com/en/database/oracle/oracle-database/21/jjdbc/client-side-security.html.

- One technique to consider is to hash the credentials using a modern algorithm like PBKDF2 and store these values in a `nameoffile.properties` file in your project.[*,†] Then when you need the credentials to connect to the database, you can read in the individual properties in the file into a Properties instance object, decrypt the password, and then use it with the OracleDataSource object.[‡] This will add another layer of frustration to any malicious actors!

Implementing the customer order application: Now that the Java application's database connection has tested OK, you can quickly build the customer order application. A console-based application will be built first before creating a database-connected JavaFX GUI application (later in this chapter).

First things first: you can make the sending and processing of queries a lot easier in the application. Alter your Java main class `CustOrder.java` to look like the following, and note the addition of the static method (in **bold**):

Full Program 12.1

```
import java.sql.*;
import oracle.jdbc.pool.*;
import oracle.jdbc.*;
import java.util.*;
import java.time.*; // For order timestamps

public class CustOrder {

    // Class Data Field Level Variables
    public static OracleDataSource oDS;
    public static Connection jsqlConn;
    public static PreparedStatement jsqlStmt;
    public static ResultSet jsqlResults;
    public static Scanner keyboardIn = new Scanner(System.in);

    public static void main(String[] args) throws SQLException {

   // Application and method calls here
    }

    public static void runDBQuery(String query, char queryType)
    {
        // queryType - Using the CRUD acronym
        // 'r' - SELECT
        // 'c', 'u', or 'd' - UPDATE, INSERT, DELETE


        try
        {
            String URL = "jdbc:oracle:thin:@localhost:1521/XEPDB1";
            String user = "javauser";
            String pass = "javapass";

            oDS = new OracleDataSource();
            oDS.setURL(URL);


            jsqlConn = oDS.getConnection(user, pass);
            jsqlStmt = jsqlConn.prepareStatement(
                    query,
```

* https://howtodoinjava.com/java/java-security/how-to-generate-secure-password-hash-md5-sha-pbkdf2-bcrypt-examples/.

† Dev2qa.com has a great write-up on this, and you can find mentions of it in other security circles: https://www.dev2qa.com/how-to-load-jdbc-configuration-from-properties-file-example/.

‡ https://docs.oracle.com/en/java/javase/17/docs/api/java.base/java/util/Properties.html.

```
                    ResultSet.TYPE_FORWARD_ONLY,
                    ResultSet.CONCUR_READ_ONLY);

            if (queryType == 'r')
                jsqlResults = jsqlStmt.executeQuery();
            else
                jsqlStmt.executeUpdate();
        }
        catch (SQLException sqlex)
        {
            System.out.println(sqlex.toString());
        }

    } // End of runDBQuery() method
}
```

Moving the instantiation of the database-related objects to the class level and the actual connection and execution of the query into a method will make our coding efforts easy. As discussed in chapter 6, this will ease maintenance (if any is needed) and remove duplication from our code. Also, since the two query execution methods of the `PreparedStatement` class you want to use return different data types (`ResultSet` or `int`), a small bit of selection logic and a second parameter to the `runDBQuery()` method will help keep things clean. The beauty of this approach is that you can run a query from anywhere in the code and see any results in the `jsqlResults` object from anywhere in the code (since it is a static data field of this application class). Lastly, notice that a `throws` statement has been added to the `main()` method header to handle any `SQLException` objects that may be thrown due to any issues. This is needed, since you access the `ResultSet` object from within the `main()` method, and any database-related code generates checked exceptions (chapter 10) that must be handled.

The customer order application will need to have several functional requirements:

- The ability to enter a new customer into the system
- The ability to enter a new item into the system
- The ability to start a new `CustOrder`, add items and their quantities in a loop, and then close the order
- The ability to print all this information, including an overview of all orders for a particular customer and the details on a particular `CustOrder`

A looping menu system with methods can tackle this effectively. You can easily set up the menu system first in `main()`:

Code Snippet 12.4

```
// in main()
int menuChoice = 0;
String menuPrint = """
                    Please enter a menu item choice:
                    1 - Enter a New Customer
                    2 - Enter a New Item
                    3 - Enter a New Order
                    4 - Print Options
                    5 - Quit Application
                    Enter Option :
                    """;
System.out.println("Welcome to Customer Order");
System.out.println("------------------------");
do
{
    System.out.print(menuPrint);
    menuChoice = keyboardIn.nextInt();
    switch (menuChoice)
```

```
        {
        case 1: addCustomer();
            break;
        case 2: addItem();
            break;
        case 3: addOrder();
            break;
        case 4: printOptions();
            break;
        case 5: // Do nothing let the do…while catch it
            break;
        default: System.out.println("Invalid Menu Choice");
        }
    } while (menuChoice != 5);
    System.out.println("Application Exiting. . . ");
```

Several methods are invoked from the menu switch that will keep the code clean and "modular" and allow for easy future changes. There are several tasks to complete to get this database-connected application working, and these follow one by one:

Adding Customers and Items

Using knowledge of how to connect to a database, you can implement the `addCustomer()` and `addItem()` methods as follows (these would be static class methods added to this `CustOrder` class outside of `main()`, as in previous chapters):

Code Snippet 12.5

```
public static void addCustomer()
{
    keyboardIn.nextLine(); // consume newline from menu entry

    String firstName, secondName, address,
            city, countryState, zip, email;
    String insertQuery = "";

    System.out.println("Enter new customer information: ");
    System.out.println("First Name: ");
    firstName = keyboardIn.nextLine();

    System.out.println("Second Name: ");
    secondName = keyboardIn.nextLine();

    System.out.println("Address: ");
    address = keyboardIn.nextLine();

    System.out.println("City: ");
    city = keyboardIn.nextLine();

    System.out.println("Country/State: ");
    countryState = keyboardIn.nextLine();

    System.out.println("Zip Code: ");
    zip = keyboardIn.nextLine();

    System.out.println("email Address:  ");
    email = keyboardIn.nextLine();

    insertQuery =
        "INSERT INTO CUSTOMER (FirstName, SecondName, "
```

```
        + "Address, City, CountryState, Zip, EmailAddress) VALUES (";

    // Build the rest of the query using the inputs
    insertQuery += "\'" + firstName + "\',\'"
            + secondName + "\',\'"
            + address + "\',\'"
            + city + "\',\'"
            + countryState + "\',\'"
            + zip + "\',\'"
            + email + "\')";

    // Invoke our DB method, send create code
    runDBQuery(insertQuery, 'c');
}

public static void addItem()
{
    keyboardIn.nextLine(); // Consume newline from Menu entry

    String itemBrand, itemDescription;
    String insertQuery = "";
    double itemPurchasePrice, itemSellPrice;

    System.out.println("Enter new item information: ");
    System.out.println("Brand Name: ");
    itemBrand = keyboardIn.nextLine();

    System.out.println("Item Description: ");
    itemDescription = keyboardIn.nextLine();

    System.out.println("Item Purchase Price ");
    itemPurchasePrice = keyboardIn.nextDouble();

    System.out.println("Item Sell Price ");
    itemSellPrice = keyboardIn.nextDouble();

    insertQuery = "INSERT INTO ITEM (ItemBrand, ItemDescription, "
            + "ItemPurchasePrice, ItemSellPrice) VALUES (";

    insertQuery += "\'" + itemBrand + "\',\'" + itemDescription
            + "\'," + itemPurchasePrice + "," + itemSellPrice + ")";
    // Invoke our DB method, send create code
    runDBQuery(insertQuery, 'c');
}
```

Of the methods that make changes to the database, these are the simplest. Because these two methods add records to the strong entity database tables of customer and item, the code is relatively simple. The overall idea here is to do the following:

- Gather each piece of the new record from the user on the console
- Use concatenation to build a String that contains the `INSERT INTO` query
- Send the query to the `runDBQuery()` method with appropriate action code

The part of each method where the query `String` is concatenated is the most important. Keep in mind that in an SQL query, string/text values must be surrounded by single quotes. Notice in these methods, an escaped single quote `"\'"` is used to ensure that it is properly concatenated within the `String` variable. It is **critical** as a developer that you check the "final product" of the query string before sending it to the database. This can be accomplished by printing it to the console first, commenting out the call to `runDBQuery()`, and then copying/pasting the dynamically generated query and trying it out in your query editor or command line.

For example, if you want to add a customer and print the dynamically generated query using this code, it would look like this:

Code Snippet 12.6

```
System.out.println(insertQuery); // Remove when done testing
//runDBQuery(insertQuery, 'c'); // Uncomment when done testing
```

This print would be the following:

```
INSERT INTO CUSTOMER (FirstName, SecondName, Address, City, CountryState, Zip, EmailAddress)
VALUES ('Test','Customer','123 Java Lane','Bytecode','OR','12345','Test@javaforis.com')
```

This is an important step, as it is **very easy** to miss a single quote, a comma separating data values, and so on. Notice that the first half of the query is always the same. It is the input received from the console that must be "glued" together carefully. This query can now be copied/pasted into an SQL command window in NetBeans and executed, allowing you to tackle any SQL syntax issues and/or resulting code adjustments (do not forget to take out the query print and uncomment the call to `runDBQuery()` after you are done).

Adding a Customer Order

This will be the most complicated part of the implementation (grab the caffeinated beverage of your choice at this point). Notice that an order in the planned database consists of two parts: a customer record for the order in `CustOrder` and individual item records in `CustOrderItems` that correspond to a `CustOrder` record. The general sequence of events in our `addOrder()` method will go something like this:

- Get the current timestamp, and save it for `CustOrder` use later.
- Print a list of the current customers, and allow the user to select one to add an order for.
- Insert a `CustOrder` record using the timestamp and the selected customer. Leave the `CustOrderTotal` as 0.00 for now.
- Use the timestamp from insertion to retrieve the dynamically created primary key value for the `CustOrder` record. You will need this for the records in `CustOrderItems`.
- In a loop, allow the user to select an item and quantity to add to the order. For each completed selection, insert a `CustOrderItems` record using the `CustOrder` record you are associating these new records with along with the `ItemID` and `Quantity`.
- Finally, after all items have been added, loop through `CustOrderItems` on the `CustOrderID` you have been working with, and sum up the price paid multiplied by the quantity. Calculate the total of the order and `UPDATE` the `CustOrder` record you have been working with to reflect the accurate total.

The code for `addOrder()` will look like this. Notice the throwing of the `SQLException` in the method header, since you are working with a `ResultSet` object:

Code Snippet 12.7

```
public static void addOrder() throws SQLException
{
    String selectQuery = "";
    String insertQuery = "";
    String updateQuery = "";
    int customerSelection = -1;
    int itemSelection = -10;
    int custOrderID = -1;
    int itemQuantity = 0;
    double custOrderTotal = 0.0;

    // Use current time for the order timestamp
    // Chapter 3
    String custOrderDate =
        String.format(
                "%tF %tT",
                LocalDateTime.now(),
```

```
            LocalDateTime.now());

// Make the selection of the customer ID
System.out.println("Select a Customer for the Order: ");
System.out.println("---------------------------------");
selectQuery = "SELECT CustomerID, "
    + "FirstName || \' \' || SecondName as CustName, "
    + "EmailAddress from Customer ORDER BY CustomerID ASC";

runDBQuery(selectQuery, 'r');

// Print the list of Customers
while (jsqlResults.next())
{
    System.out.println(jsqlResults.getInt(1) + " "
            + jsqlResults.getString(2) + " "
            + jsqlResults.getString(3));
}

// Capture User Selection:
System.out.println("---------------------------------");
System.out.println("Enter Customer: ");
customerSelection = keyboardIn.nextInt();

// Create the CustOrder Entry with No Total
insertQuery = "INSERT INTO CustOrder "
        + "(CustOrderDate,CustOrderTotal,CustomerID) VALUES";

insertQuery += "(TO_TIMESTAMP(\'" + custOrderDate + "\',\'"
        + "YYYY-MM-DD HH24:MI:SS\')," + 0.0 + ","
        + customerSelection + ")";

// Insert the CustOrder entry.
runDBQuery(insertQuery,'c');

// Retrieve the CustOrderID that was autogenerated
// for the just inserted CustOrder record
// using the same timestamp you just used.
selectQuery = "SELECT * FROM CustOrder " +
    "WHERE CustOrderDate = TO_TIMESTAMP(\'"
        + custOrderDate
        + "\',\'YYYY-MM-DD HH24:MI:SS\')";

runDBQuery(selectQuery,'r');

while (jsqlResults.next())
    custOrderID = jsqlResults.getInt("CustOrderID");

// Build the Order
selectQuery = "SELECT * from ITEM";
runDBQuery(selectQuery, 'r');

do
{
    System.out.println("Select Item Number (or -1 to finish) "
            + "followed by Quantity");
    while (jsqlResults.next())
    {
        System.out.println(jsqlResults.getInt(1) + "\t"
                + "$" + jsqlResults.getDouble(4) + "\t"
```

```
                    + jsqlResults.getString(2));
        }
        System.out.println("Item Selection: ");
        itemSelection = keyboardIn.nextInt();

        if (itemSelection != -1)
        {
            System.out.println("Quantity: ");
            itemQuantity = keyboardIn.nextInt();

            // Move cursor in ResultSet back to before
            // the first row. No need to re-query the DB.
            jsqlResults.beforeFirst();

            // Build the order query:
            insertQuery = "INSERT INTO CustOrderItems "
                    + "(CustOrderItemQty,CustOrderID,ItemID) "
                    + "VALUES (";

            insertQuery += itemQuantity + ","
                    + custOrderID + "," + itemSelection + ")";

            // Insert the CustOrderItemRecord
            runDBQuery(insertQuery, 'c');
        }

    } while (itemSelection != -1);

    // Now that the CustOrder record is added
    // and the CustOrderItem records have been
    // added, calculate the order total and
    // update the CustOrder record

    // Using a Join
    selectQuery = "SELECT CustOrderItems.CustOrderItemQty,"
        + " Item.ItemSellPrice "
        + "FROM CustOrderItems "
        + "INNER JOIN Item ON CustOrderItems.ItemID = Item.ItemID "
        + "WHERE CustOrderID = " + custOrderID;

    runDBQuery(selectQuery, 'r');

    // Loop through all items and quantities associated
    // with the order and sum up the total
    while (jsqlResults.next())
    {
        custOrderTotal +=
                (jsqlResults.getInt(1)
                * jsqlResults.getDouble(2))
    }

    // Finally, update the CustOrder record with the order total
    updateQuery = "UPDATE CustOrder SET CustOrderTotal = "
            + custOrderTotal + " WHERE CustOrderID = " + custOrderID;

    // Use the update code character
    runDBQuery(updateQuery, 'u');

} // end of addOrder() method.
```

Since the `ResultSet` in `runDBQuery()` has the property SCROLLABLE_INSENSITIVE set, you can use `jsqlResults.beforeFirst()` within the method in several places to move the `ResultSet`'s cursor back to the beginning without requerying the DB, eliminating a resource-expensive operation.

Printing Order Lists and Order Details

Compared to the `addOrder()` method, the printing tasks are a piece of cake! First, since `printOptions()` is invoked from the main menu, you can add that submenu method first:

Code Snippet 12.8

```
public static void printOptions() throws SQLException
{
    int printChoice = 0;
    String printOptions = """
                  Select a Print Option
                  1 - Print Customer Details
                  2 - Print Order Details
                  3 - Return to Main Menu
                  Enter Option:
                  """;
    do
    {
        System.out.print(printOptions);
        printChoice = keyboardIn.nextInt();
        switch (printChoice)
        {
            case 1: printCustomer();
                break;
            case 2: printOrder();
                break;
            case 3: // Do nothing.
                break;
            default: System.out.println("Invalid Menu Choice - Try Again!");
        }
    } while (printChoice != 3);
}
```

In this method, you invoke two more methods that will each work with the application's `ResultSet`, so the `throws SQLException` statement has been added to this method's header, as it will be to the others. The code for `printCustomer()` and `printOrder()` look like the following and are relatively straightforward:

Code Snippet 12.9

```
public static void printCustomer() throws SQLException
{
    int customerSelection = -1;
    String selectQuery = "";

    System.out.println(
            "Select Customer to Print Order Summary For: ");

    selectQuery = "SELECT CustomerID, "
            + "FirstName || \' \' || SecondName as CustName, "
            + "EmailAddress from Customer ORDER BY CustomerID ASC";

    runDBQuery(selectQuery, 'r');

    // Print the list of Customers
    while (jsqlResults.next())
    {
        System.out.println(jsqlResults.getInt(1) + " "
```

```
                + jsqlResults.getString(2) + " "
                + jsqlResults.getString(3));
    }
    System.out.println("Select Customer: ");
    customerSelection = keyboardIn.nextInt();

    // Print all CustOrder records for this customer number

    selectQuery = "SELECT * from CustOrder WHERE CustomerID = "
            + customerSelection;

    runDBQuery(selectQuery, 'r');

    if (jsqlResults.next() == false)
    {
        System.out.println("===== No Orders Found! =====");
    }
    else
    {
        System.out.println("\nOrders for Customer: ");
        System.out.println("--------------------------------");
        System.out.printf("%-25s$%-10s\n","Order Date","Order Total");
        System.out.println("--------------------------------");

        jsqlResults.beforeFirst();

        while (jsqlResults.next())
        {
            // Print out the order date and the total
            // Chapter 3 String Formatting
            System.out.printf(
                    "%-25s$%-10.2f\n",
                    jsqlResults.getString(2),
                    jsqlResults.getDouble(3));
        }
        System.out.println("--------------------------------");
    }

} // End of printCustomer()

public static void printOrder() throws SQLException
{
    String selectQuery = "";
    int orderSelection = -1;
    String rowBorder = "";

    System.out.println(
            "Select a Customer Order to Print Details For: ");

    selectQuery = "SELECT CustOrder.CUSTORDERID, "
    + "Customer.FIRSTNAME || ' ' || Customer.SECONDNAME as CustName, "
    + "CustOrder.CUSTORDERDATE, "
    + "CustOrder.CustOrderTotal "
    + "From Customer "
    + "INNER JOIN CustOrder "
    + "ON Customer.CUSTOMERID = CustOrder.CUSTOMERID "
    + "ORDER BY Customer.CUSTOMERID ASC";

    runDBQuery(selectQuery, 'r');
```

```
    System.out.println("---------------------------");
    while (jsqlResults.next())
    {
        // Chapter 3 String Formatting
        System.out.println(
                String.format(
                        "%-5d%-25s%-25s$%-10.2f",
                        jsqlResults.getInt(1),
                        jsqlResults.getString(2),
                        jsqlResults.getString(3),
                        jsqlResults.getDouble(4)));
    }
    System.out.println("---------------------------");
    System.out.println("Select Order #: ");
    orderSelection = keyboardIn.nextInt();

    selectQuery = "SELECT Item.ItemBrand, "
            + "Item.ItemDescription, "
            + "CustOrderItems.CUSTORDERITEMQTY, "
            + "Item.ItemSellPrice "
            + "FROM CustOrderItems "
            + "INNER JOIN Item "
            + "ON CustOrderItems.ITEMID = Item.ITEMID "
            + "WHERE CustOrderItems.CustOrderID = " + orderSelection;

    runDBQuery(selectQuery, 'r');

    System.out.println("Printing Order Details: ");
    System.out.println("----------------------------------");
    System.out.println(String.format(
        "%-18s%-40s%-10s%-10s",
        "Brand:",
        "Description:",
        "Qty:",
        "Price:"));

    for (int i=0;i<78;i++)
        rowBorder += "-";

    System.out.println(rowBorder);

    while (jsqlResults.next())
    {
        System.out.println(String.format(
                "%-18s%-40s%-10d$%-10.2f",
                jsqlResults.getString(1),
                jsqlResults.getString(2),
                jsqlResults.getInt(3),
                jsqlResults.getDouble(4)));
    }

    System.out.println(rowBorder);
}
```

Notice the use of `String` formatting in several places (chapter 3) and the use of `INNER JOIN` queries to make the data selection and display tasks much easier. The power of SQL really helps the developer to get business-ready applications up and working quickly.

Sample Run of the Application

Time to take the application for a test-drive. A `Customer`, `Item`, and `Order` will be added, and the results printed using our print system. (*Note:* Some spacing has been manually added to this output for ease of reading—feel free to edit the code later to match the spacing you see printed here.)

```
Welcome to Customer Order
-------------------------
Please enter a menu item choice:
1 - Enter a New Customer
2 - Enter a New Item
3 - Enter a New Order
4 - Print Options
5 - Quit Application
Enter Option :
1

Enter new customer information:
First Name:
Sarah

Second Name:
Surenson

Address:
123 Java Way

City:
Elizabeth

Country/State:
NJ

Zip Code:
07201

emailaforis.com

Please enter a menu item choice:
1 - Enter a New Customer
2 - Enter a New Item
3 - Enter a New Order
4 - Print Options
5 - Quit Application
Enter Option :
2

Enter new item information:
Brand Name:
JView

Item Description:
WiFi Extender

Item Purchase Price
99.99

Item Sell Price
129.99

Please enter a menu item choice:
```

```
1 - Enter a New Customer
2 - Enter a New Item
3 - Enter a New Order
4 - Print Options
5 - Quit Application
Enter Option :
3

Select a Customer for the Order:
-----------------------------------
7 Cajavais.org
8 Fernleyjavais.org
9 Jejavais.org
10 Majavais.org
11 Pemberljavais.org
24 Sarahaforis.com
-----------------------------------
Enter Customer:
24

Select Item Number (or -1 to finish) followed by Quantity
1     $450.5      ViewGood
2      $59.99     Choppie
3       $1.99     CodeIT
4     $999.99     Applesoftcle
5      $59.99     Prospect Press
22     $99.99     JView
Item Selection:
22

Quantity:
1

Select Item Number (or -1 to finish) followed by Quantity
1     $450.5      ViewGood
2      $59.99     Choppie
3       $1.99     CodeIT
4     $999.99     Applesoftcle
5      $59.99     Prospect Press
22     $99.99     JView
Item Selection:
5

Quantity:
1

Select Item Number (or -1 to finish) followed by Quantity
1     $450.5      ViewGood
2      $59.99     Choppie
3       $1.99     CodeIT
4     $999.99     Applesoftcle
5      $59.99     Prospect Press
22     $99.99     JView
Item Selection:
-1

Please enter a menu item choice:
1 - Enter a New Customer
2 - Enter a New Item
3 - Enter a New Order
```

```
4 - Print Options
5 - Quit Application
Enter Option :
4

Select a Print Option
1 - Print Customer Details
2 - Print Order Details
3 - Return to Main Menu
Enter Option:
1

Select Customer to Print Order Summary For:
7 Cajavais.org
8 Fernleyjavais.org
9 Jejavais.org
10 Majavais.org
11 Pemberljavais.org
24 Sarahaforis.com
Select Customer:
24

Orders for Customer:
----------------------------------
Order Date              Order Total
----------------------------------
2021-12-22 20:10:34     $170.01
----------------------------------
Select a Print Option
1 - Print Customer Details
2 - Print Order Details
3 - Return to Main Menu
Enter Option:
2

Select a Customer Order to Print Details For:
----------------------------
16   Fernley Finnegan        2023-03-16 15:16:00      $136.98
17   Mani Makoto             2023-04-16 16:45:00      $1340.01
18   Pemberley Quinby        2023-05-16 11:24:00      $899.99
29   Sarah Surenson          2021-12-22 20:10:34      $170.01
----------------------------
Select Order #:
29

Printing Order Details:
-----------------------------------
Brand:           Description:                       Qty:      Price:
-------------------------------------------------------------------------------
JView            WiFi Extender                      1         $129.99
Prospect Press   How to IS: A Comprehensive Guide   1         $40.02
-------------------------------------------------------------------------------
Select a Print Option
1 - Print Customer Details
2 - Print Order Details
3 - Return to Main Menu
Enter Option:
3

Please enter a menu item choice:
```

```
1 - Enter a New Customer
2 - Enter a New Item
3 - Enter a New Order
4 - Print Options
5 - Quit Application
Enter Option :
5

Application Exiting. . .
```

Eureka! It looks like everything works really well. You can add a `Customer` and an `Item`, build a `CustOrder` for that new `Customer` using both old and new `Items`, and then print various reports for that `Customer` and their `CustOrder`, with all details accurate. Oracle's JDBC makes it quick and simple to connect to any third-party database platform from your Java application. The added benefit here is that since you are not storing anything in memory (in arrays or `ArrayList<E>`), you can shut down the application and run it again tomorrow and the same data will show, since the data is stored external to the application. Additionally, the data is being written in real time. Of course, various databases may be configured to commit actions differently, which may force you to call `.commit()` on the `Connection` object in use (check with your database administrator).

SUMMARY POINTS

- Java's JDBC provides an incomplete API for connecting a Java application to a database and allows third-party database makers to implement complete versions of the JDBC as their database drivers, specific to their technology.
- Your Java application can establish its own connection to an underlying database separate from the connection used by your IDE, which is provided as a convenience.
- `ResultSet` objects store the results of the execution of a query in a tabular (row and column) format. Column counting in a `ResultSet` object starts at `1`, unlike arrays that start at `0`.
- A `Connection` object is used to generate a `PreparedStatement`, and the `Connection` object can be instructed to specify a type and behavior of the eventual `ResultSet` object that the `PreparedStatement` will return later.
- Printing the contents of a query string dynamically generated through concatenation can allow the developer to inspect the results quickly and visually prior to query execution, to check SQL syntax and concatenation accuracy, and so on.

QUICK PROBLEMS

1. **Coding:** Add another print option that will print the sum total for each item sold in aggregate across all customers.
2. **Think:** Why was it useful to keep many database-related sections of logic associated with various application tasks separated into their own methods?
3. **Coding:** Add another print option that will print the summed quantity of items sold grouped by each item.

Summary

In this highly integrative final chapter, you have learned about Java's database connectivity and integration abilities. You have explored the nature of the JDBC and how third-party database drivers leverage and implement its classes. You have gained a brief refresher in SQL syntax and interacting with data in database tables. You have also walked through thorough examples of both console-based and UI-based Java applications that use a database for data storage and retrieval. All these examples help broadly cover all the skills, challenges, syntax, and (much of the) planning that an information systems professional working on a systems development and implementation project will face in contemporary business environments. The challenges of integrating a database with any system are highly similar no matter the platform, be it a Java environment or another technology stack. Gaining end-to-end experience in this as you have with this chapter is an incredibly valuable stepping-stone to not only a rewarding career working with Java in systems development but working with any platform. Gaining a strong understanding of these skills in Java sets you apart as a highly valuable information systems professional ready to tackle challenging contemporary business problems right from the start. Additionally, you have gained these development and integration skills in one of the most popular and enduring development languages, Java, in the world. Such a widely used language and development library such as Java will not diminish from use for many, many years, if ever. Java is here to stay, and your work in the language throughout this book has given you an enormous head start in your career and personal skills. Though you've done a lot of work, the learning journey is just beginning!

Practice Problems

Terminology

Match the following terms from the chapter with their most appropriate definition:

1. Entity relationship diagram	a. A database table that represents a many-to-many relationship between entities in other tables. Often called an associative table.
2. Record	b. SQL command used to retrieve copies of records from one or more database tables, often with logic to filter the number of results.
3. Field	c. Oracle's concrete implementation of the interface classes found within the JDBC. Used for connections to Oracle database systems.
4. Primary key	d. SQL command used to edit existing data within a database table.
5. Foreign key	e. SQL command used to "collapse" records returned in a SELECT command into convenient categories for aggregation and analysis.
6. Strong entity	f. JDBC interface class, implemented by third-party database drivers, that represents a precompiled SQL statement. Useful when a parameterized query is needed and generally a more resource-efficient way of querying the database.
7. Weak entity	g. JDBC interface class that must be implemented by all third-party database driver APIs.
8. Cardinality	h. A single column in a database table used for storing a single piece of data on an entity. Sometimes called an attribute.
9. Bridge table	i. Method of the JDBC interface class `ResultSet` that moves an internal `ResultSet` object cursor forward over rows of query-returned data.
10. `CREATE TABLE`	j. A representation in a database that depends on the existence of other entities or records.
11. `INSERT`	k. A single field or multiple fields in a database table used to store a unique identifier for a record stored within another table. Implements a relationship between entities.
12. `UPDATE`	l. SQL command used to return a set of database records from two or more tables where fields in all tables match.
13. `DELETE`	m. JDBC interface class, implemented by third-party database drivers, that represents a connection to a database.
14. `SELECT`	n. Planning tool useful during system design to visualize the relationships between data entities, communicating a shared vision for the system's data model.
15. JDBC	o. A symbolic way of describing the nature of the relationships between entity tables in a database, often numerically.

16. OJDBC	p. A representation in a database that depends on no other entities or records in the database in order to be properly represented.
17. `INNER JOIN`	q. JDBC interface class implemented by a third-party database driver that stores an object representing the records and fields returned from SQL query execution.
18. `GROUP BY`	r. SQL command used to place data into a database table.
19. `Driver`	s. A single row in a database table, usually to represent one entity or a relationship between entities.
20. `Connection`	t. SQL command used to remove one or more records from a database table.
21. `PreparedStatement`	u. Java API that implements the Java database connectivity language. Third-party database drivers implement concrete versions of the interface classes found within the JDBC.
22. `ResultSet`	v. Single or multiple fields used in a database table to represent a unique identifier for entity records.
23. `.next()`	w. SQL command used to define and implement an entity table within a database, including unique identifiers and relationships with other tables.

Find the Error

In each of the following problems, carefully examine the code given, and determine the error(s)/issue(s) with each. Keep in mind, the error(s) could be syntax (code) or logic (intended outcome) based or both!

For these code segments, assume the following exists and has been properly declared/initialized/created:

- A `ResultSet` object called `results`.
- A method that will properly execute an SQL query and populate the results object, called `runDBQuery()`. The method takes a `String` parameter, the SQL query.
- Various variables used in the questions that match the field names, which have been properly populated with data from application activity. These will be used for concatenation.
- A `Student` class with data fields `studentName`, `year`, `major`, and `email`.
- A database with tables:
  - STUDENT with fields `StudentID`, `Name`, `ClassYear`, `Major`, `Email`.
  - FACULTY with fields `FacultyID`, `Name`, `Department`, `Email`, `Phone`.
  - COURSE with fields `CourseID`, `Major`, `Number`, `MaxEnrollment`.
  - A bridge table called SEMESTERCOURSE with fields `SemesterID`, `CourseID`, `FacultyID`, `SemesterYear`, `SemesterPeriod` ("Fall," "Spring," "Summer").
  - A bridge table called ENROLLMENT with fields `EnrollmentID`, `SemesterID`, and `StudentID`.

1.

```
String students = "SELECT ALL FROM STUDENT";
runDBQuery(student);
while (next())
{
    system.out.println(results.next(0)) + results.next(1));
} do (results.getString(i));
```

2.

```
String insertS = "INSERT INTO STUDENTS ("
        + "Julie Studious"
        + "Senior"
        + "," + "CIS" + "'" + "jstudious@javaforis.com";
runDBQuery(inserts);
```

3.

```
String insertQ = "INSERT INTO "
        + "STUDENT (NAME,CLASSYEAR,COURSEID,"
        + "SEMESTERID,FACULTYID) "
```

```
        + "VALUES (" + studentName + "'," + classYear ","
        + courseID + "," + facultyYear + ") "
        + "INNER JOIN COURSE ON STUDENTID = COURSEID "
        + "INNER JOIN FACULTYID=FACULTYID "
        + "ORDER BY STUDENTID ASC";
```

4.

```
String printEnrollment =
        "SELECT * FROM SEMESTERCOURSE "
        + "ORDER BY SEMESTERID DESC";

runDBQuery(printEnrollment)

while (results.next(true));
{
    System.out.println(
            results.getInt(
                    CourseID,
                    FacultyID,
                    SemesterYear,
                    SemesterPeriod,
                    StudentID));
    results.beforeFirst();
}
```

5.

```
Student[] studentList = new Student[100];
// . . .array is partially populated
// . . . . through application usage
String insertStudents = "";
for (int i=0;i<studentList.size();i++)
{
    for (int j=0;j<studentList.size();j++)
    {
        insertStudents = "INSERT INTO STUDENT ("
                + studentList[i].studentName
                + "," + studentList[j].year
                + ",""" + "studentList[i].major"
                + ",""" + studentList[j].email + "',)";
        runDBQuery(insertStudents);
    }
    results.next();
}
```

Think about It

1. Why is it important for an information systems professional to learn about database technologies and how to integrate them into applications they develop?
2. Why is an entity relationship diagram a useful tool in information systems planning and development?
3. How can a properly modeled and well-structured database help system development efforts? How can a poorly modeled and structured database hinder system development efforts?
4. What are some of the "real-world" things that an entity can model in an ERD? Can events be modeled?
5. Describe what a bridge/associative table does within a database.
6. What benefit is there to allowing a database to autoincrement your table's primary key field? What are some of the difficulties this might cause during development?
7. What are some of the benefits of creating test data in a database used by a system in development?

8. What does the CRUD acronym mean? How does this relate to system development activities?
9. Describe the primary benefit of a JOIN-type query in SQL. Why would it be difficult to reproduce a JOIN query's results programmatically if these types of queries did not exist?
10. What benefits could there be to allowing third-party database drivers to provide their own implementations to the interface classes in the JDBC?
11. What benefit could there be to the ability to reset a `ResultSet` object's internal data cursor back to the "beginning" of the `ResultSet`?
12. What are some of the pros and cons of storing all application data "in memory" (i.e., variables in the stack and heap) versus storing everything in database tables?
13. What are some things the developer should keep in mind when building a query dynamically using input data from an application's console or user interface?
14. Deleting records in a database used by an information system is typically a bad idea. What is the alternative to deleting a record? How does this impact the information system development efforts?

Full Problems (Console-Based Java Applications with Database Integration)

1. Develop a console-based application that will manage a user's to-do list. The application should be able to accept a new to-do item, assign a category to it, and assign a numeric rank to the item (1, 2, 3, etc.). The application can print out the list either by category or by numeric rank, and to-do items should be able to be marked as complete and "drop off" the list. Store your data in properly structured and related database tables.
2. Develop a console-based application that will allow a user to enter information on people and assign familial relationships between them ("Father," "Mother," "Children"). Store all information in database tables, with one entity table called PERSON and a bridge table for each of the three familial relationships. The application will then allow a user to print information out on one person, which will print out all relationships for that person.
3. Develop a console-based application that will keep track of information for an animal shelter. Create entity tables for SHELTER, VOLUNTEER, and ANIMAL. Create any needed bridge tables. The application will allow the creation of new animal or volunteer records and associate them with a specific shelter. The application will also allow the user to record a transfer of an animal from one shelter to another. The application can print all this information in business-ready format.
4. Develop a console-based application that will manage course enrollment for students at a university. Create entity tables for STUDENT, COURSE, FACULTY, and SEMESTER. The SEMESTER table will store which semester a course is offered in (fall, spring, or summer) and the year. The application will allow the user to create students, faculty, courses, and semester records in the database. Choose reasonable attributes to store for each. The application will also allow the user to enroll a student in a course, assign a faculty member to that course, and assign the course to a semester. (*Hint:* Use a bridge/associative table for these associations.) Finally, using the database and its bridge/associative tables, the application will have options for printing:
   a. All the students in a course
   b. All the courses a student takes
   c. All the courses a faculty member teaches
   d. All the courses offered in a particular semester
5. Develop a queuing system for customers who have called the support center of a business. You will need entity tables for CUSTOMER, SUPPORTSPECIALIST, and CALLCENTER. The business has three different call centers (for now), each staffing support specialists who answer the phone and help address customer complaints. Create each entity table with reasonable attributes to store on each. The application will allow for the creation of entity records for all three tables. The application will also be capable of the following:
   a. The application should assign a customer to a specific support specialist. As multiple customers are added to a support specialist's queue (i.e., line), keep track of the customer's place in the queue (1, 2, 3, etc.).
   b. Support specialists can drive into any of the three call centers to work that day. The application should allow for the assignment of a support specialist to a call center.
   c. The application should allow a customer's place in the queue to be changed to "bump them up" in line to be handled next. For example, a customer who was fifth in line for a specific customer support specialist can now be first in line.

d. The application should generate a general report that will print summary information for each support specialist, including how many customers are in line for each.
e. The application should generate a detailed report showing the customers in line for a specific customer support specialist.
f. The application should generate a general report showing how many customers are queued up for **all** customer support specialists at each of the three call centers the company operates.

Full Problems (GUI-Based Java Applications with Database Integration)

1. Develop a UI-based, database-integrated application (JavaFX or Swing) for short syntax problem #1. Use an appropriate control to display the to-do list and to change the ranking/ordering of its items. Add the ability to select one item and to click a button that will open a second window, where additional details can be entered in paragraph form and then saved.
2. Develop a UI-based, database-integrated application (JavaFX or Swing) for short syntax problem #3. Add the ability to add vaccination and health events for any animal in the shelter and for those records to stay associated with the animal if they move to another shelter location. Store and capture appropriate information on volunteers. Add the ability to print all activity for a specific animal, and have that information appear in a second reporting window.
3. Develop a UI-based (JavaFX or Swing), database-integrated `Student` management application. The application will allow the user to do the following:
   a. Create students, faculty, and classes. Classes should have a maximum enrollment of fifteen students. Student information should include their class year (1, 2, 3, or 4) and their current GPA.
   b. Assign a faculty member to teach a class in a specific year and semester.
   c. Enroll a student in a class in a specific year and semester.
   d. Print a report for the past enrollment of a specific student in all classes.
   e. Print the full information for an upcoming class, including the assigned faculty member, the year and semester, and all currently enrolled students.
   f. Prevent a student from enrolling in a course twice.
   g. Prevent more than fifteen students from enrolling in a course.
   h. Show a summary of information for a course by student enrolled year—for example, how many first-year students, second-year students, and so on are enrolled in a course.

Appendix A

Java Development Kit, Java IDEs, Oracle DB Setup, Debugging, and jShell

How to Use This Appendix

Appendix A gives you a brief tour of a few of the more popular free-to-download IDEs where Java development can occur, describes how to set up Oracle Express DB in Microsoft Windows, and gives a brief tutorial on the usage of the Oracle Java tool `jShell`. These topics can serve as a supplement to your in-classroom activities (depending on the IDE used in your curriculum) or as further exploration of functionality apart from your directed learning. The tour of IDEs is meant to complement chapter 0. The instructions for setting up Oracle Express DB can help you get started with chapter 12. `jShell` can serve as a handy, quick way to test out small snippets of Java code as you study topics throughout all chapters in this textbook.

Installing the Java Development Kit

Before installing and using any of the IDEs discussed in this appendix, you **must** first install the Java Development Kit (JDK). This installs both the Java Virtual Machine and the development-related files that let you compile and document your Java applications.

1. The Official Oracle Java Development Kit can be downloaded from here: https://www.oracle.com/java/technologies/downloads/.

   Select your version of Java (latest is 19 as of this writing) and your operating system (recommended: Windows). Download the "x64 Installer" for compatibility with 64-bit modern CPUs.
2. Oracle also works with the OpenJDK project to provide an open-source version of Java and the JDK at https://jdk.java.net/. The latest release candidate for the Java JDK (version 19) can be downloaded here: https://jdk.java.net/19/.
3. Once you have downloaded the installer, double-click to run it. Installation should be straightforward. **It is recommended to reboot your computer after the installation.**

A.1 Java-Integrated Development Environments

Since about the 1990s, demand for individuals skilled in software development has exploded. Languages like COBOL, FORTRAN, and RPG (among others) have been popular for a long time and are still used in many business and governmental areas. The rise of modern, object-oriented languages in popularity has brought with it a similar rise in demand for individuals skilled in development in these languages. Part of this rise comes about due to what many have deemed a shift toward "information economies" rather than production economies in much of the developed world. From this comes a mainstreaming of software development, spurring the development of software tools that help more individuals develop applications and systems easily. Traditionally, software development involved some sort of text editor and issuing compilation and execution commands on a command terminal or window. Many developers today still prefer this simple way of application building, and indeed, Java programs can be created in this way (command-line compilation of text edited code—see figure A.1 for an example in Java).

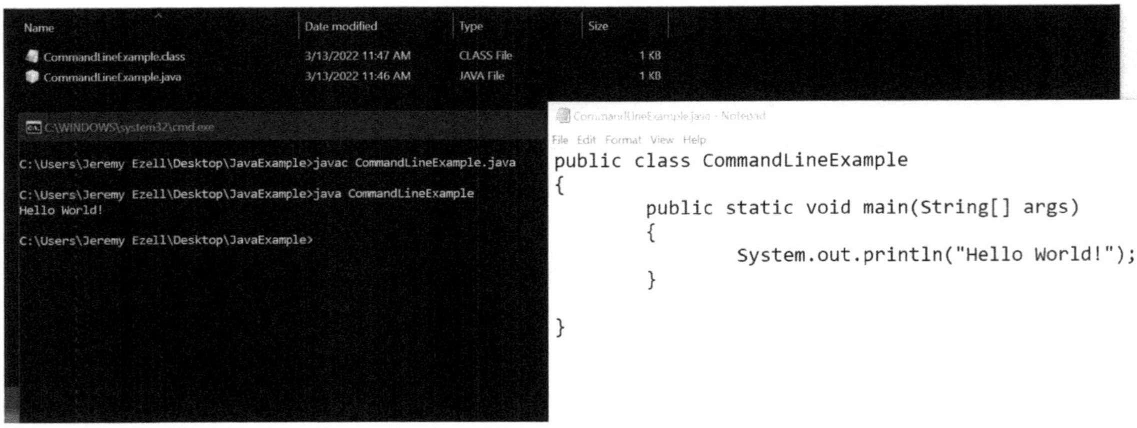

Figure A.1. Text-Editor-Written and Command-Line-Compiled Java Program (Windows)

Integrated development environments (IDEs) were created by both language authors and third-party groups to ease the development process. Most IDEs offer built-in, feature-rich text editors for composing code; the ability to call the language's native compiler; and the ability to both run and "debug" a program all as major features. Most IDEs offer the ability to create projects in multiple languages to attract developers from various backgrounds. This is often the case, since many languages and development technologies complement one another when building a larger system (e.g., ASP.net, C#, and SQL, or Java, HTML5, and CSS).

Some Popular Java-Focused IDEs

Prior to 2016, NetBeans was owned and developed by Oracle. Since 2016, Oracle has handed NetBeans over to the open-source community of the Apache Software Foundation, who has coordinated development and new releases of the IDE through the Apache NetBeans community.* As of this writing, the latest version is NetBeans 18, which is the IDE used in the authoring of code and examples throughout this textbook. NetBeans makes it easy to create Java projects. The Apache NetBeans community provides several tutorials on using NetBeans to create Java applications, debugging, using JavaFX and Swing, and more.†

The Eclipse Foundation emerged from the Eclipse Project started by IBM but has grown to coordinate numerous open-source projects, the Eclipse IDE being one of them. They target the adoption of their software and projects for both commercial and open-source environments. The Eclipse IDE is a popular IDE for Java development, among other languages. If you install Eclipse, you will be asked which development environment you prefer: Java, Enterprise Java/Web, C/C++, PHP, and others. Based on your choice, the IDE will arrange its UI and menu functions to align with these development preferences. Eclipse is fully featured: editing, compiling, autocompleting code while writing, debugging, and much more. The Eclipse community has published an extensive set of documentation for the IDE, including a step-by-step tutorial guide for creating a Java application in Eclipse.‡,§

The jGRASP IDE is a lightweight IDE that can be used with many languages besides just Java, though the IDE itself was written in Java and is focused on this language. Developed by faculty in the Department of Computer Science and Software Engineering in the Samuel Ginn College of Engineering at Auburn University, jGRASP appears "bare-bones" at first but contains many helpful features: control structure diagramming, debugging, automatic UML diagram building, among many others. jGRASP does not feature the autocompletion of code when editing like NetBeans and Eclipse do. Many developers who are more comfortable with the language

* https://netbeans.apache.org/community/index.html.
† https://netbeans.apache.org/kb/docs/java/index.html.
‡ https://help.eclipse.org/latest/index.jsp.
§ At the documentation, click Java Development User Guide > Getting Started > Basic Tutorial.

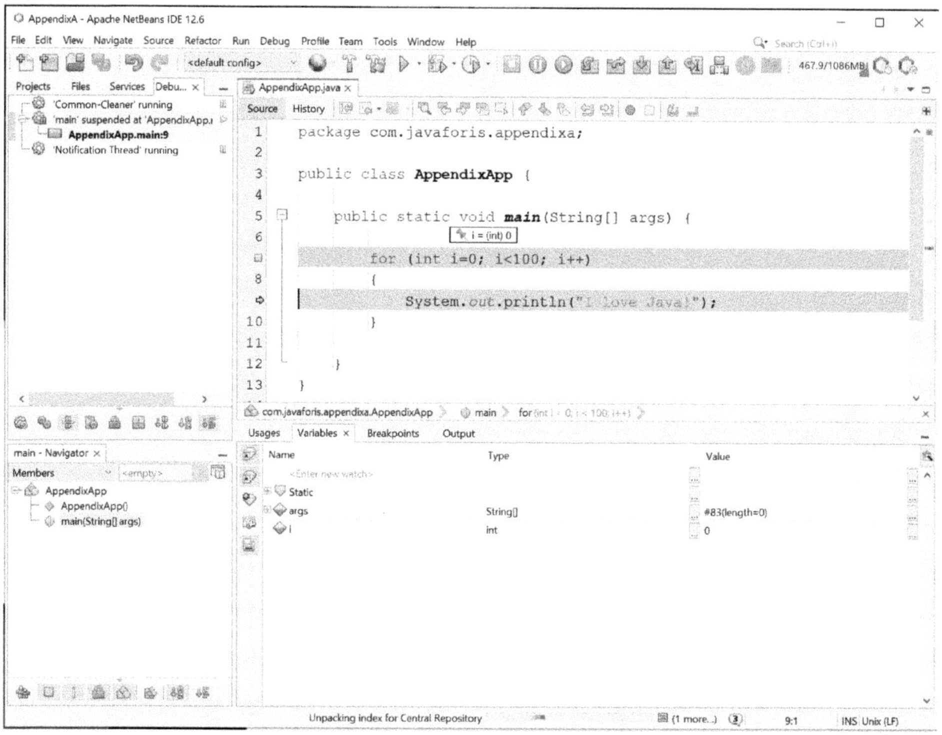

Figure A.2. Apache NetBeans IDE: Editing and Debugging a Java Application
Source: Apache NetBeans IDE, https://netbeans.apache.org/. Copyright © 2017–2024 The Apache Software Foundation.

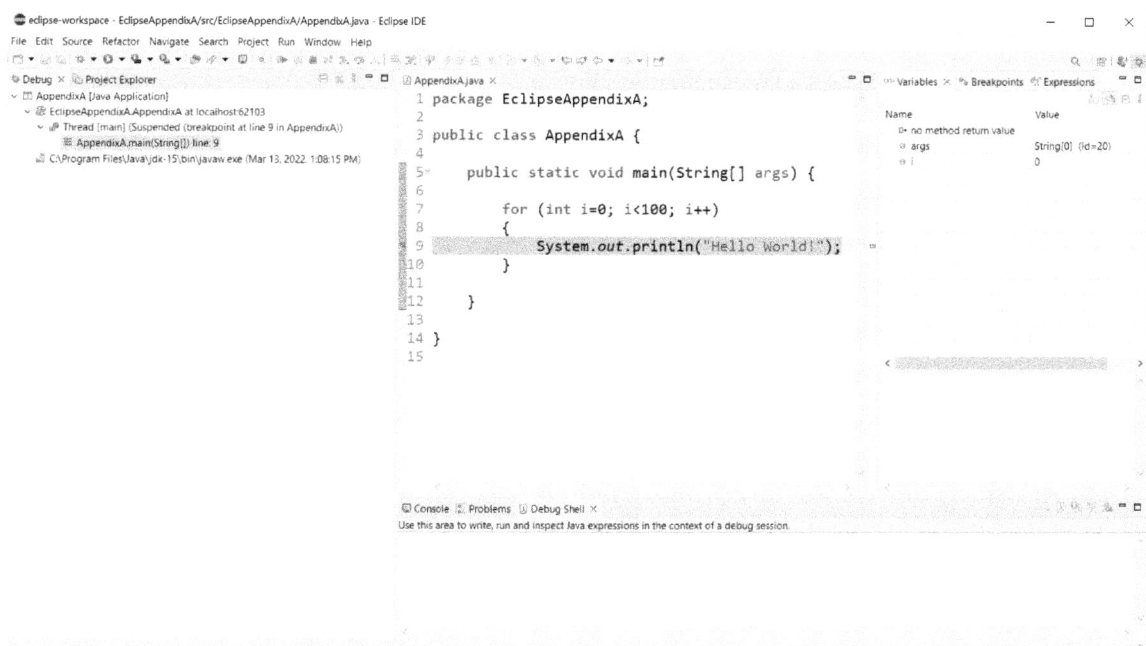

Figure A.3. Eclipse IDE: Editing and Debugging a Java Application
Source: Eclipse IDE, https://www.eclipse.org/eclipseide/. Copyright © 2022 Eclipse Foundation. All Rights Reserved.

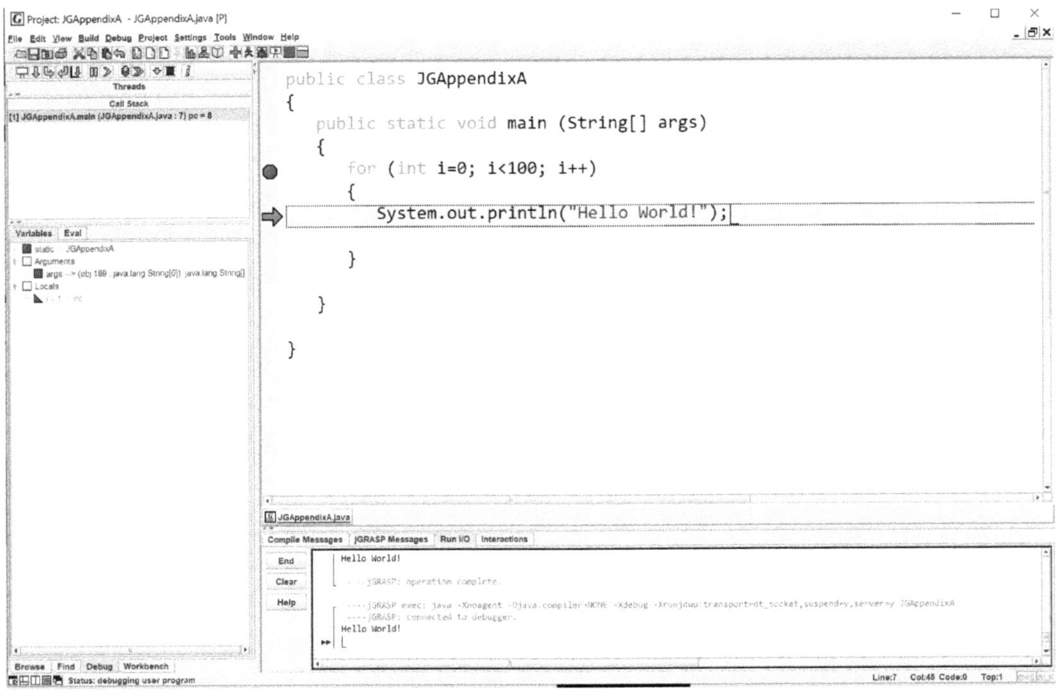

Figure A.4. jGRASP IDE: Editing and Debugging a Java Application
Source: jGRASP IDE, https://spider.eng.auburn.edu/user-cgi/grasp/grasp.pl?;dl=download_jgrasp.html. Copyright © 1999–2022 Auburn University.

will use jGRASP to quickly create Java applications in this lightweight IDE. The developers provide both an overview of the IDE and an extensive "Getting Started" tutorial on their website.*,† A notable feature of jGRASP is its ability to handle and visualize‡ class definition files (CDFs) and object hierarchies within a Java project.

Java Code Errors, Warnings, and Logic Issues

A big benefit of most IDEs is that they help the developer easily spot most issues and errors present in code. For errors that are not so easy, IDEs provide several tools, primarily debugging tools, to help the developer walk through their code's execution and track down issues. We will discuss a few of these scenarios here.

Compiler errors: These are usually the most obvious errors and issues to spot in your code. Most IDEs will attempt to flag code you've written that will cause a compiler error before compilation happens. Figure A.5 highlights a common error: misspelling of an object or class name. In this case the IDE, Apache NetBeans, has highlighted the error with a red underline showing that this is a severe problem. Often you can hover your mouse cursor over the line to see a tool tip containing the specific error message causing this flag. This is similar to how misspellings may be flagged in many popular text-editing software packages in use today.

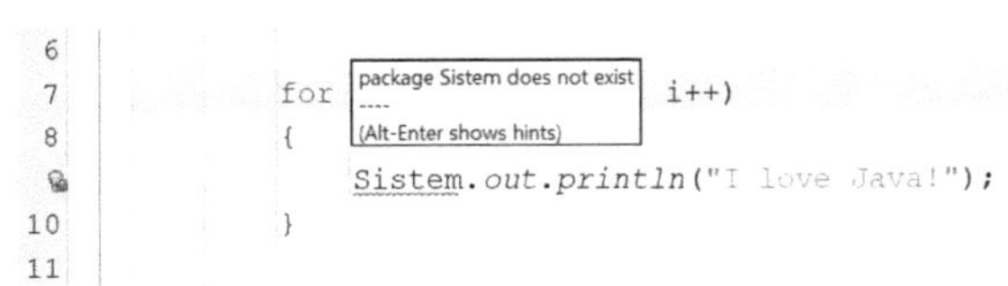

Figure A.5. Misspelling in Java Syntax Flagged by the Apache NetBeans IDE

If you were to compile this program with the error in place, most IDEs will return the message generated by the Java compiler itself, like so:

* https://www.jgrasp.org/tutorials200/jGRASP_00_Overview.pdf.
† https://www.jgrasp.org/tutorials200/jGRASP_02_Getting_Started.pdf.
‡ https://www.jgrasp.org/tutorials187/03_Getting_Started_Objects.pdf.

```
Exception in thread "main" java.lang.RuntimeException: Uncompilable source code - Erroneous sym
type: System.out.println
   at com.javaforis.appendixa.AppendixApp.main(AppendixApp.java:9)
Command execution failed.
```

Notice that the error message will often contain the compiler's best guess as to the line number where the error has occurred. In this case, the compiler thinks the error might be on line 9 of our source code in `AppendixApp.java`, and it would be correct, as the syntax for "`System`" has been misspelled in the invocation of `.println()`. You must resolve compiler errors before your program will compile and execute!

Compiler warnings: Often flagged in a color other than red by most IDEs, a compiler warning is somewhat less severe than an error but something the developer should attempt to resolve. For example, figure A.6 shows a warning flagging a variable that is never used in the source listing of an application.

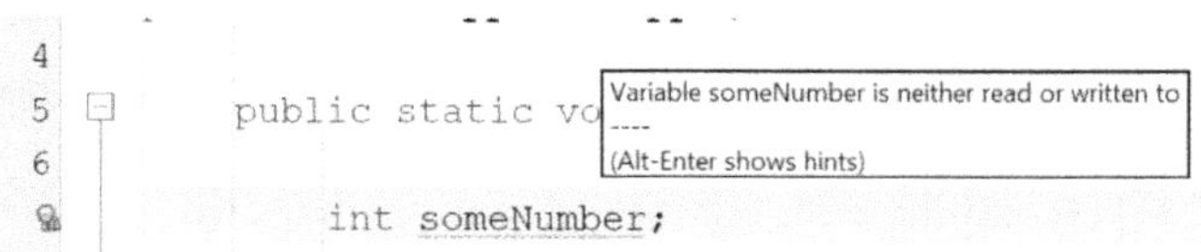

Figure A.6. Unused Variable Flagged by the Apache NetBeans IDE

Logic errors that lead to runtime errors: Errors in your applications are often caused not by syntax issues or misspellings of variable or class names but by mistakes in the way you have structured your logic. Consider the following example, where a developer wishes to change the values of only every **odd**-numbered index position in an `int` array and then print the contents of that array (see chapter 7):

```
int[] anArray = new int[5];
int remainder = 0;
int i = 0;
do
{
    remainder = i % 1;
    if (remainder == 0)
        i += 2;
    anArray[i] = i;

} while (i <= 5);

for (int n : anArray)
{
    System.out.print(n + " ");
}
```

Syntaxwise, there are no errors with this code: no compiler flags are thrown. Also, no warnings seem to be present, as all variables declared are used. When this application is compiled and executed, the following error is received:

```
Exception in thread "main" java.lang.ArrayIndexOutOfBoundsException: Index 6 out of bounds for
length 5
   at com.javaforis.appendixa.AppendixApp.main(AppendixApp.java:16)
Command execution failed.
```

In this case, the error did not occur until the application was executing, a runtime error (as opposed to a compile-time error, discussed earlier). Here an `ArrayIndexOutOfBoundsException` is "thrown" (see chapter 10). The compiler's best guess is that the error is happening on line 16 of the source code for `AppendixApp.java` and is caused by attempting to access an index of "6" for an array that is of length 5. Upon inspection of the code and some thought, you see that you are increasing the value of the variable `i` before accessing an array location, causing the out-of-bounds error. A fix would look like so (changes in **bold**):

```
int[] anArray = new int[5];
int remainder = 0;
int i = 0;
do
{
    remainder = i % 1;
```

```
    anArray[i] = i;
    if (remainder == 0)
        i += 2;

} while (i <= 5);

for (int n : anArray)
{
    System.out.print(n + " ");
}
```

This code will compile and run and when finished will produce output as follows (with changed array elements in **bold** by author):

`0 0 2 0 4`

Notice the output and the changes to the array are not in line with what we wanted! We have changed every even index position in the array instead of the desired odd. So there is a further logic error that is not causing a compiler error but instead causing undesired behavior of the application. Luckily most IDEs have a tool for tracking down these often hard-to-find errors.

Debugging: Using the debuggers of most applications allows you to use what amounts to an "X-ray machine" on your application. You can observe the values of variables as the application executes, pause execution to examine variables, and observe the objects in memory, their structure, and their contents, among other features. This is usually done by placing a **breakpoint** in your source code, which will cause execution to pause at the beginning of that line of code when the application is run in debugging mode. In the Apache NetBeans IDE, for example, a breakpoint can be set by left-clicking on a code-line number, turning that line red, as in figure A.7.

Once a breakpoint is set, you can run the project in "Debug" mode, which will change the UI for most IDEs to provide you with common debugging tools: a frame stack listing, a display of variables in memory and their values/structure, and a highlighting of which line of code the debugger is currently paused at. Notice in figure A.8, the Apache NetBeans IDE has changed to display these debugging tools, and execution is paused at our breakpoint.

Most IDEs allow you to advance the execution of the program one line at a time or continue until the breakpoint is hit again (sometimes if it is placed in a loop) or until the program finishes. Figure A.9 shows execution of our code advanced after a few do…`while` loop iterations have occurred. In most IDEs, you can advance the code execution line by line by using a step-over button (or its equivalent in your IDE of choice). Notice the change in the values of the array and the variable `i` in the debugging tools. Most IDEs will display the variables in memory and allow you to expand them if they are complex data types (see chapter 2) to better view their contents and structure.

Using the debugger, you can see that the use of the modulo operator combined with the `if` statement is causing a logic error of only changing the even-numbered index elements of the array. The developer here has overcomplicated what should be a simple task. A few simple fixes to the code correct this:

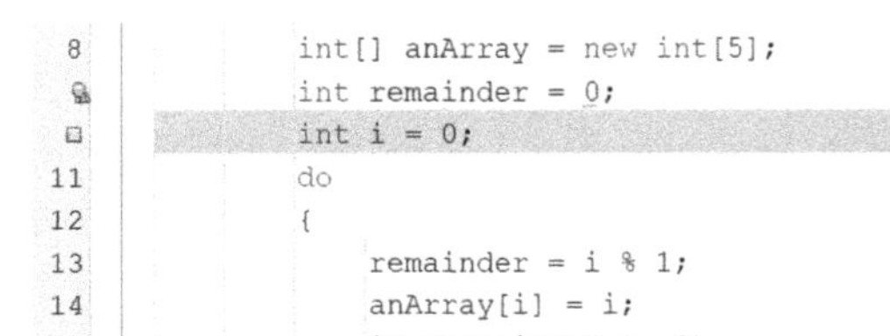

Figure A.7. A Breakpoint Set for a Line of Code in Apache NetBeans IDE

```
int[] anArray = new int[5];
int remainder = 0;
int i = 0;
do
{
    remainder = (i % 2); // i modulo with 2
    if (remainder !=0)   // if there's a remainder
        anArray[i] = i;  // Change anArray at index i
    i++;

} while (i < anArray.length); // Fix the potential out-of-bounds

for (int n : anArray)
```

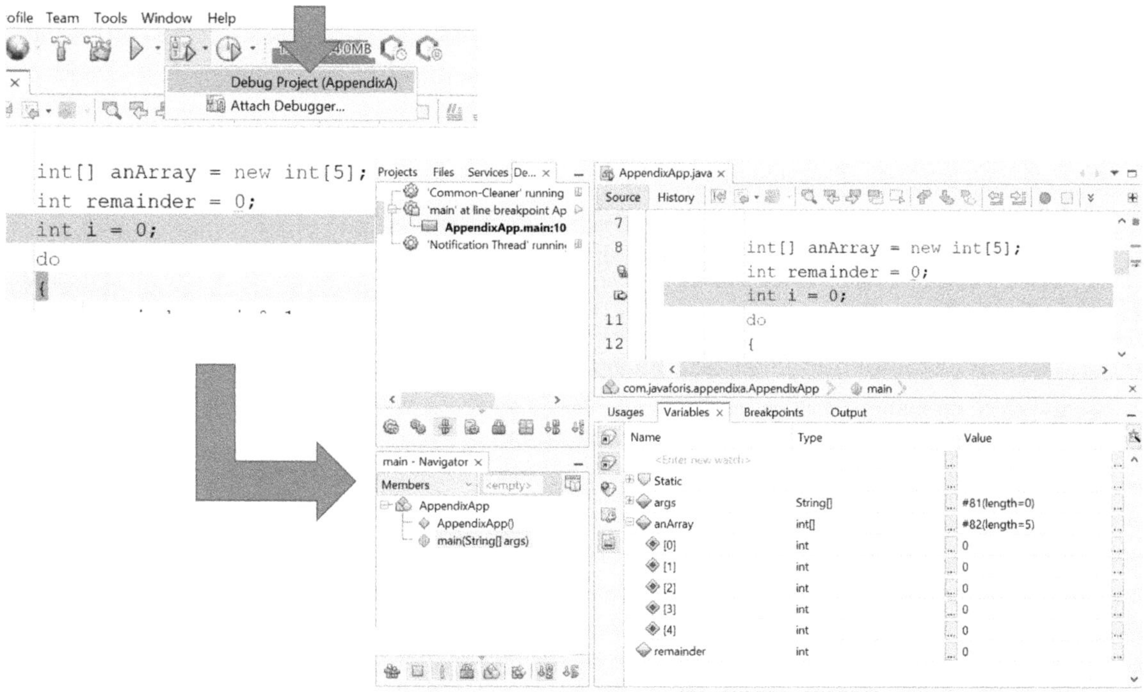

Figure A.8. Apache NetBeans IDE in Debug Mode for a Java Application

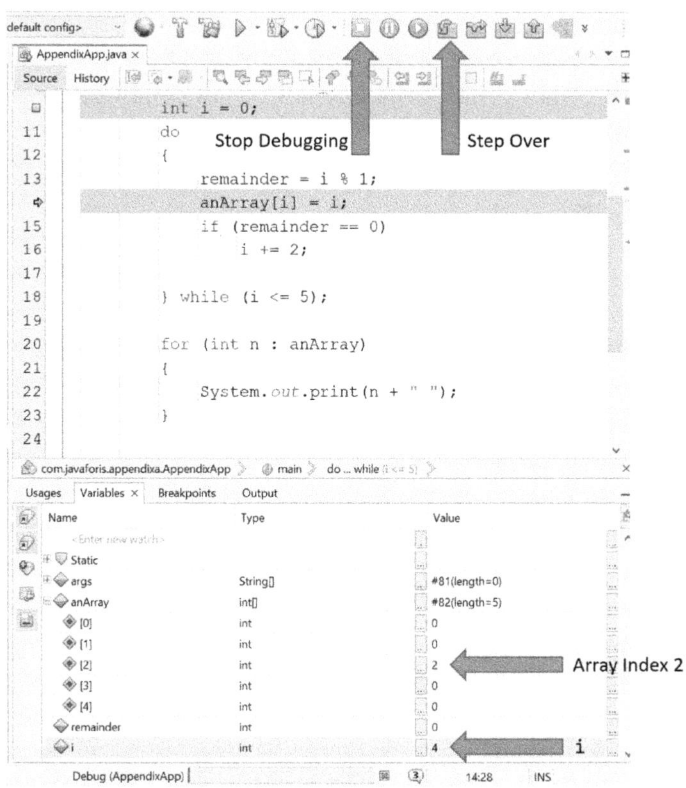

Figure A.9. Apache NetBeans IDE after Advancing Code Execution in the Debugger

```
{
    System.out.print(n + " ");
}
```

This now produces the following output:

```
0 1 0 3 0
```

Practice in using the debugger will pay off dividends as your applications become more complex. Being able to observe both the values of variables in memory and the execution path of code can help the dedicated developer find and fix most issues with the logic in their code.

Description of Some Debugging Controls and Areas in the Apache NetBeans IDE

-  **Finish debugger session:** This will immediately end debugging and execution of the program, taking you back to the code editor.
-  **Pause:** If your application is looping or executing over a long time, pressing this will pause execution and highlight the line of code being executed at the time the button was pressed. Handy for examining variables and memory at select on-the-fly times.
-  **Continue:** This will cause execution to continue, executing the line currently paused on and continuing until either the same breakpoint is encountered again, another breakpoint is used, or the program ends.
-  **Step over:** Advances code execution to the next line of code that will naturally follow if your logic is being executed as written. Can help the developer step through the path of their code's execution to see what is working as expected and what is not.
-  **Step into:** This will cause execution to "descend" into a method or other code that is being invoked instead of just invoking it and moving on. Can allow the developer to examine how code is executing in a method invoked from their application.
-  **Step out:** Causes the code to complete the execution of the current method the debugger is paused in and return to the invoking/calling code.
-  **Run to cursor:** Handy for the developer that wants to skip several lines of code and have the debugger pause at a line of code further along in code execution without tedious, repetitive clicking of the step-over button or setting another breakpoint.
- **Debugging tab:** Shows the method "frame stack" of calls at the breakpoint, with the earliest invoked methods on the bottom (first in, last out order).
- **Variables tab:** Shows the variables that are in memory for the method where the breakpoint is currently located and execution is currently paused at. Double-clicking another method in the "Debugging" tab will change the view of variables to those in that clicked method's memory frame.

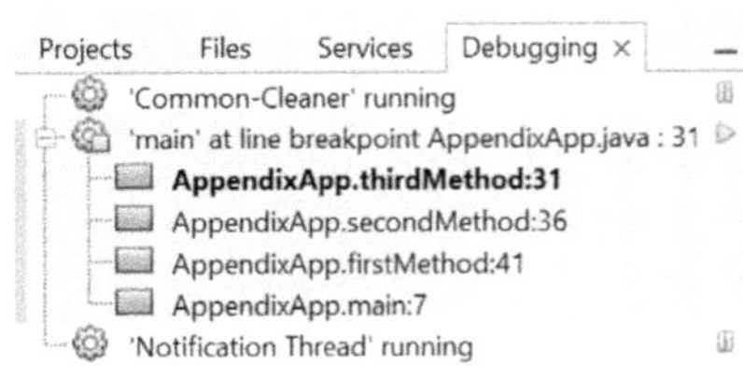

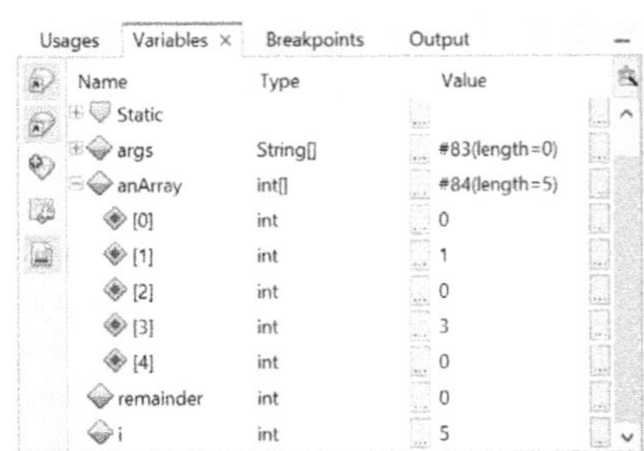

A.2 Installing Oracle Database Express Edition 21c

Java database connectivity (JDBC) drivers have been created to allow Java applications to connect to a variety of both Oracle and third-party database systems: Oracle, MySQL, IBM, Sybase, PostgreSQL, Microsoft SQL, and others. Use of Oracle Express DB 21c is recommended and is used throughout chapter 12. Your learning and/or work environment may use a different database platform intended for connection to your Java application. Follow any installation and/or connection instructions provided to you for those systems. The following installation steps walk you through installing Oracle Database Express 21c Express Edition in order to run the examples given in chapter 12.

Oracle DB Install Instructions (Microsoft Windows OS Only)

1. Download the Oracle DB 21c Express Edition installer:
   Oracle Database 21c Express Edition
   https://www.oracle.com/database/technologies/xe-downloads.html
   Oracle's instructions for installation in the Microsoft Windows Operating System:
   https://docs.oracle.com/en/database/oracle/oracle-database/21/xeinw/index.html
2. The installation file will be compressed/zipped. Create a new empty folder on your desktop or other easy-to-find location, and unzip the contents of the Oracle folder there.
3. In the unzipped files, run the "Setup" installer file.
4. Click "Next" on the initial screen of the installer.
5. Carefully read through the Oracle License Agreement, click the "I accept . . ." button when you are ready, and click "Next" to continue the installation.
6. On the "Destination Folder" screen, click the "Change" button to choose another location to install Oracle to. It is recommended to create an "`oraclexe`" folder on your hard drive at C:\ to install into. Click "Next" when ready.
7. Choose a password for SYS and SYSADMIN accounts. Do not lose this password! Type it carefully, and write it down. Use the password "admin" (without the quotes) for simplicity (never use this in a production environment, of course!).
8. On the Summary screen, verify that the install locations on your hard drive chosen earlier are correct. Click "Install" when ready.
9. During the installation, you might see a pop-up prompt regarding Windows Defender Firewall security. It is recommended to **allow** on public and private networks (check both boxes), but choose the security you are most comfortable with.
10. You might see a second pop-up window titled "Configuring Oracle XE Database"—no action is needed. Let it finish.
11. **Installation could take a few minutes.** Sip some java or another beverage of your choice.
12. When installation has finished, you should see an "Installed Successfully" screen. This screen will also note "Connection Information" for your locally installed database. Typically, the following information will be displayed:
    a. **Multitenant container database:** `localhost:1521`
    b. **Pluggable database:** `localhost:1521/XEPDB1`

    Notice that these detail the network location ("localhost"—your computer) where the Oracle database is located and the port number (1521) where the database "listens" for connections. "XEPDB1" is the name of the database that you will connect to in later steps. Take note of the actual information that your installation screen shows.
13. Click "Finish" to close out the installer.

Setting Up Oracle Database 21c Express Edition for "Local" Use on Your Computer

1. Oracle DB Express runs as a service in Windows with the partial name "XE," which helps identify the specific service. You will need to temporarily stop this service and another in order to edit the configuration file in the next steps. Figure A.10 shows these services.

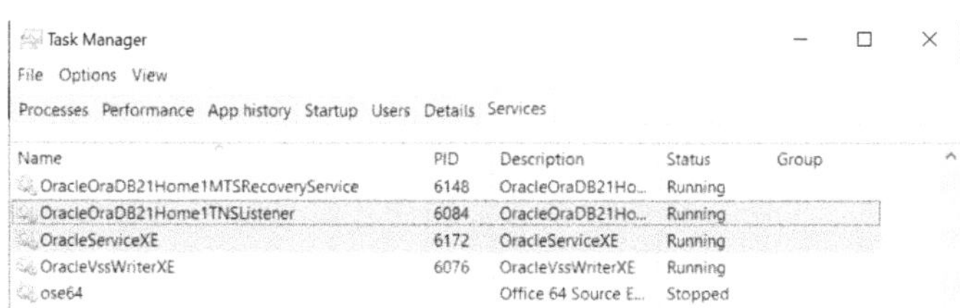

Figure A.10. Two of the Oracle Database 21c Express Edition Services

2. Open the Windows Task Manager by right-clicking on the task bar (where your "Windows" button is located) and clicking "Task Manager."
3. Navigate to the "Services" tab (in Windows 11, this will be a tab on the left side of the window).
4. Scroll down the list until you see the services that begin with the word "Oracle" (as seen in figure A.10).
5. For both the "OracleServiceXE" and the "OracleOraDB21Home1TNSListener" service as highlighted in figure A.10, right-click each, and choose "Stop."
6. **Leave the Task Manager window open to "Services." You will need it later.**
7. In Windows Explorer, navigate to the hard drive location C:**oraclexe**\homes\OraDB21Home1\network\admin.

   (*Note:* Oracle DB was installed in an "oraclexe" folder on C:\\. If you did the same, you can navigate to that location for the file path. If not, navigate to where you installed Oracle DB then the rest of the file path as shown.)
8. In the folder you navigated to, you will find the following two files. One at a time, open each in a text editor (Notepad, etc.):
   - listener.ora
   - tnsnames.ora

   In both files, change the "HOST" address value to "LOCALHOST" (without quotes). See figure A.11 and highlighted areas for the correct configuration in both. **Save changes** in both files and close them out.

Figure A.11. Files listener.ora and tnsnames.ora after Recommended Changes

9. In the same folder, open the file "sqlnet.ora" in a text editor. Place a "#" next to the line that begins "SQLNET.AUTHENTICATION" to comment it out. See figure A.12 for the changes to this file. Save the file and close it.

```
# sqlnet.ora Network Configuration File: C:\oraclexe\homes
\OraDB21Home1\NETWORK\ADMIN\sqlnet.ora
# Generated by Oracle configuration tools.

# This file is actually generated by netca. But if customers
choose to
# install "Software Only", this file wont exist and without the
native
# authentication, they will not be able to connect to the
database on NT.

# SQLNET.AUTHENTICATION_SERVICES= (NTS)

NAMES.DIRECTORY_PATH= (TNSNAMES, EZCONNECT)
```

Figure A.12. File sqlnet.ora after Recommended Changes

10. Back in the Windows Task Manager window, right-click both the " . . . TNSListener" service and the "OracleServiceXE," and choose "Start" for both. Check the "Status" column to make sure that both show "Running" after you do this.
11. Run the application "SQLPlus" on your computer (Start -> "Search for Apps . . ." -> "SQLPlus"). In the window that appears, log in with user "`system`," and use the password that you wrote down earlier during installation.

    Note: For any SQL commands that are listed in the instructions to follow, *do not* copy/paste from this textbook e-book version or from a PDF. Hand-type the listed commands. Copy/pasting may introduce errors in the commands.
12. **Hand-type** (**do not** copy/paste) in the following commands in the listed order (the second command creates the user account for chapter 12's examples in the context of the DB container XEPDB1, not for the overall database server), hitting Enter after each one (do not forget the semicolon at the end of each command):
    - `ALTER SESSION SET CONTAINER = XEPDB1;`
    - `CREATE USER javauser IDENTIFIED BY javapass;`
    - `GRANT CREATE SESSION, ALTER SESSION, CREATE DATABASE LINK, CREATE MATERIALIZED VIEW, CREATE PROCEDURE, CREATE PUBLIC SYNONYM, CREATE ROLE, CREATE SEQUENCE, CREATE SYNONYM, CREATE TABLE, CREATE TRIGGER, CREATE TYPE, CREATE VIEW, UNLIMITED TABLESPACE TO javauser;`
13. Type "Exit," and hit Enter to exit SQLPlus.

Connecting the Apache NetBeans IDE to Oracle Database 21c Express Edition

Most IDEs have a native, built-in UI for interacting with most databases. In the examples in chapter 12, Apache NetBeans IDE is used to connect to the database in addition to allowing our Java application to connect to the same database (two different ways of interacting). To use NetBeans' built-in database GUI, connect it with the following steps:

1. Download the "ojdbc11.jar" driver from Oracle's website at https://www.oracle.com/database/technologies/appdev/jdbc-downloads.html.

    Navigate to and expand the section for Oracle Database 21c. Click to download the file "ojdbc11.jar" into C:**oraclexe** (the Oracle DB installation folder from earlier *or* wherever you chose to install Oracle DB).
2. In Apache NetBeans, click on the "Services" tab, then right-click on "Databases" and choose "New Connection."

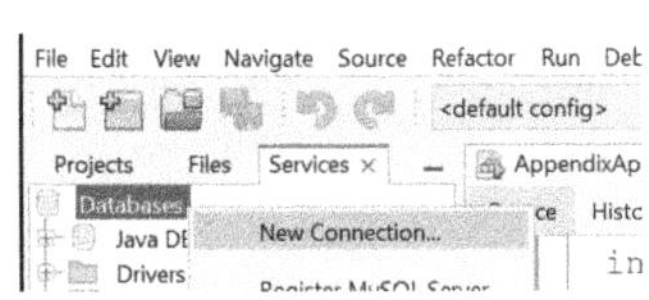

Figure A.13. New Connection Menu Option under "Databases" in NetBeans IDE

3. In the "New Connection Wizard" that appears, choose "Oracle Thin" from the "Driver" drop-down list, and click "Add." Browse to C:\oraclexe (or wherever you downloaded it to), and choose the ojdbc11.jar file copied into that folder from earlier. Click "Next >."

   ***Note:* You might get a warning at the bottom stating, "Selected ojdbc11.jar might cause unexpected problems. Use preferred ojdbc7.jar." You can disregard this warning.**

Figure A.14. New Connection Wizard

4. In the "Customize Connection" window that appears, change the following:
   - For "Driver Name," choose "Oracle Thin (Service Name)." **Make sure to not select "Oracle Thin (Service ID (SID))"!**
   - Make sure that "Host" is set to "localhost" and "Port:" is set to "1521."
   - For "Service," type in "XEPDB1."
   - For "User Name," type in "`javauser`" (from the SQLPlus commands earlier).
   - For "Password," type in "`javapass`" (from the SQLPlus commands earlier).
   - Click the "Remember password" checkbox.
   - Click the "Test Connection" button. You should see a "Connection Succeeded" message. If any errors occur, **retrace your steps above**.

Figure A.15. Connection Details for New Oracle DB Connection in the NetBeans IDE

5. Click "Finish."
6. Back in the Apache NetBeans IDE, you should now see the connection under "Databases," and it should connect automatically. If not, right-click and choose "Connect." Now you can begin creating tables and executing SQL queries. Figure A.13 shows some tables from chapter 12 in the DB once the connection to Oracle DB is made from NetBeans (these will not be automatically created in this installation).

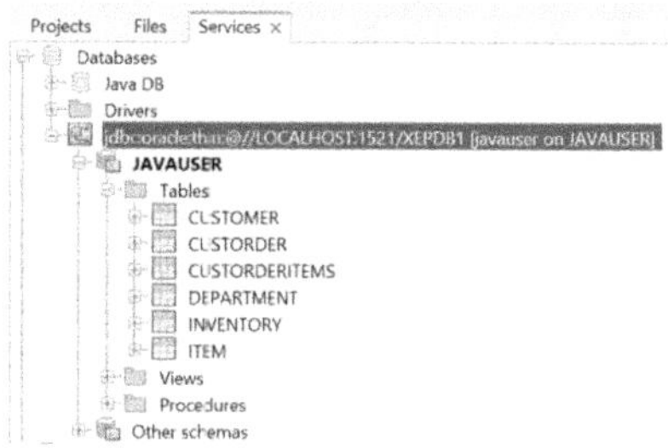

Figure A.16. Connection to the Oracle DB from NetBeans with Tables from Chapter 12 Shown

A.3 Executing SQL Commands in NetBeans

Once you have your connection to the Oracle Database 21c Express Edition set up through your IDE (here, Apache NetBeans), you have a convenient way of creating your database tables and specifying their relationships before writing your Java application that will connect to them.

1. Click on the "Services" tab in NetBeans (if it is not shown, click on the "Window" menu option and click "Services" to display it).
2. Right-click on the connection you created earlier in this appendix, and choose "Connect."

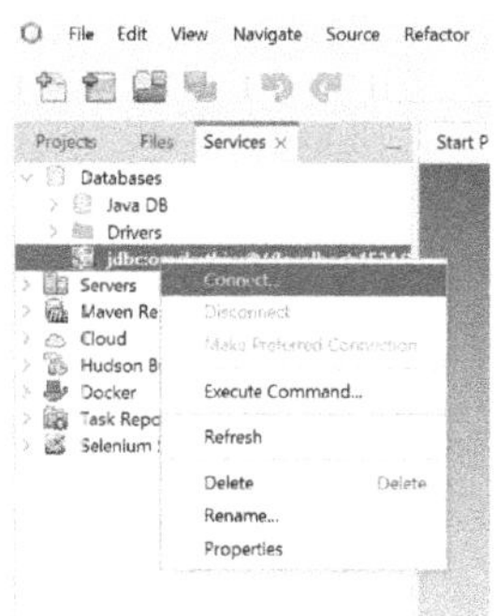

Figure A.17. Connect Option for the DB Connection in NetBeans

3. Once connected, you should see the user ("`javauser`") listed as a schema under the connection, and this expanded will show "Tables," "Views," and so on.

Figure A.18. DB Connection in NetBeans Showing Schema and Views

4. Right-click the connection again, and choose "Execute Command."
5. An editor window will appear to the right. Ensure the "Connection" box shows the appropriate connection (XEPDB1 and `javauser`).

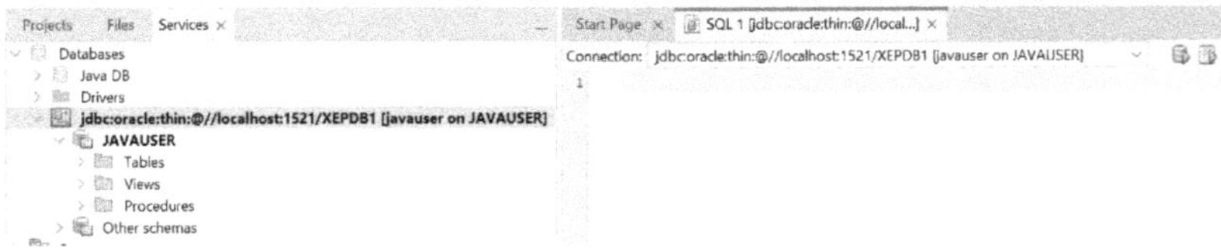

Figure A.19. SQL Command Editor in NetBeans

6. In the SQL command editor, you can use it as you would a normal code editor. You can type in one single SQL command or several.
   a. Select one command, then right-click it and choose "Run Selection" to run one single SQL command.
   b. Click the "Run SQL" button in the editor to run all the SQL commands in the editor. Be sure to end each individual command with a semicolon if there is more than one.

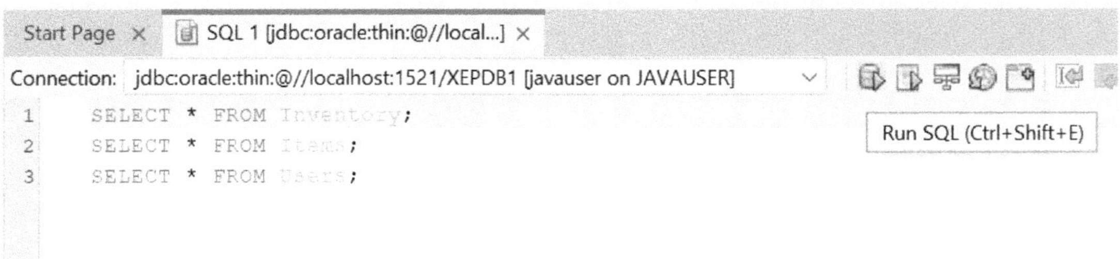

Figure A.20. "Run SQL" Command Button in the SQL Command Editor in NetBeans with Example SQL Statements

A.4 Enabling Database Connections through Your Java Code

This textbook demonstrates how to create Java applications primarily through projects using Maven in NetBeans. Most IDEs (like NetBeans and Eclipse) will allow you to create a Java project using Maven. In all of these, a change has to be made to one of the configuration files of your project to allow your application to talk to the Oracle DB (or any DB). The following instructions are for Java with Maven projects in NetBeans, but the configuration file can be found in projects created in any IDE using Maven.

1. Open your Java project in NetBeans. Under the "Projects" tab, find the section titled "Project Files," and expand it. Double-click the `pom.xml` file within.

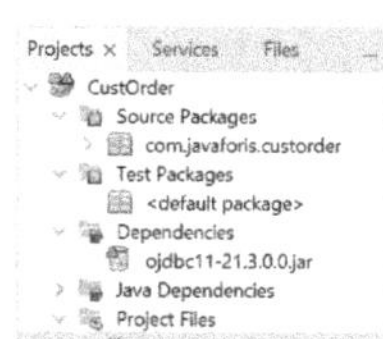

Figure A.21. Java with Maven Project in NetBeans Showing the `pom.xml` Configuration File

2. In `pom.xml`, you may already have a section enclosed by `<dependencies>...</dependencies>` tags. If not, you can add them. Notice in figure A.19 the location of this section, after the `<properties>` tag section.
3. Add the following in between the `<dependencies>` tag section you (may have) added:

```
<dependency>
    <groupId>com.oracle.database.jdbc</groupId>
    <artifactId>ojdbc11</artifactId>
    <version>21.3.0.0</version>
</dependency>
```

Figure A.22. Dependency Information for OJDBC Drivers in `pom.xml`

4. By adding dependency information to `pom.xml`, this will instruct your Java project to download from the Maven repository any needed Java or `.jar` files where various classes and methods used to connect to your DB are defined. You can easily search the Maven repository site at https://mvnrepository.com/. When you search for and click on a framework's or repository's dependency information on the site, you will be given the XML to add to your `pom.xml` file for Maven, Gradle, or whichever type of Java project you are working in.

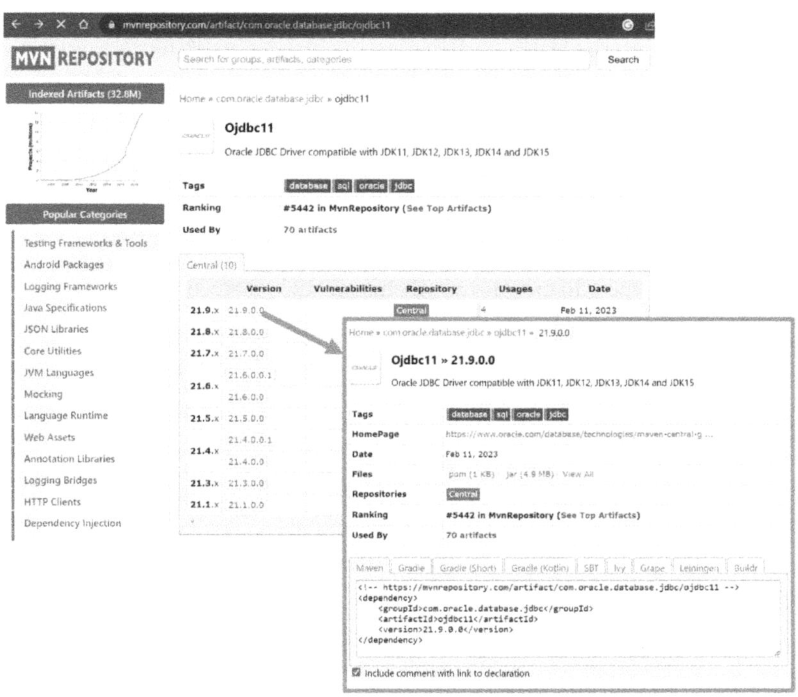

Figure A.23. Screenshot of mvnrepository.com and Search for OJDBC Driver

5. Save `pom.xml`, and close it out. In your project, click the "Build Project" button in NetBeans to have your project download the necessary dependency files for Oracle's OJDBC driver and class definitions. This download will only happen once. If you remove the <dependency> . . . </dependency> section you added to `pom.xml` and then "Build Project" your project, NetBeans will remove the files that were associated with the removed dependency.

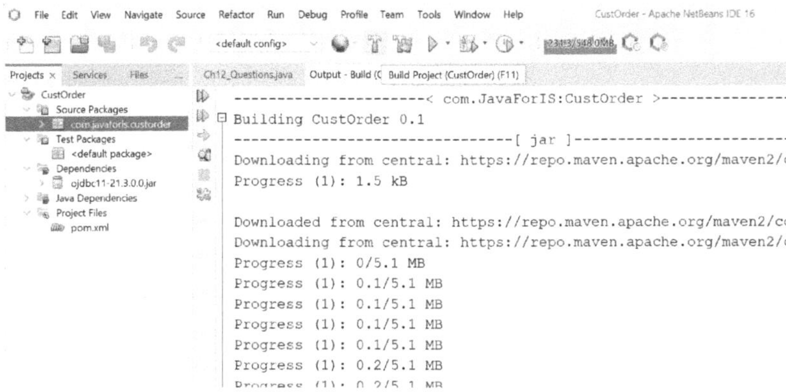

Figure A.24. Downloading Dependencies Automatically While Building a Java Project

Now you are ready to work through the SQL and Oracle DB Integration examples in chapter 12 using the Oracle DB Java classes that make the connections to the DB.

A.5 Running Commands in SQLPlus

Once Oracle DB is installed on your computer and configured correctly, you can run queries the "old-fashioned" way in a command-line window.

1. In Windows, open up a command line (Start Menu -> type "cmd" -> hit the Enter key).
2. The tables and data that are created in chapter 12 are created in the "XEPDB1" pluggable database part of your Oracle DB install. You need to log into Oracle SQL on the command line using the same `javauser` user that you created earlier in these appendix steps (recall the password was "`javapass`"). This same set of credentials is used in chapter 12's instructions as well.
3. On the command line, type in the following to log in as javauser:

   `sqlplus javauser/javapass@LOCALHOST:1521/XEPDB1`

   Note: The "LOCALHOST" part of the command **is case sensitive!** If you type it in as lowercase, the login will not work.
4. You will now be logged into your Oracle DB's pluggable database XEPDB1 and will see the same tables and any data that you will create over in chapter 12.

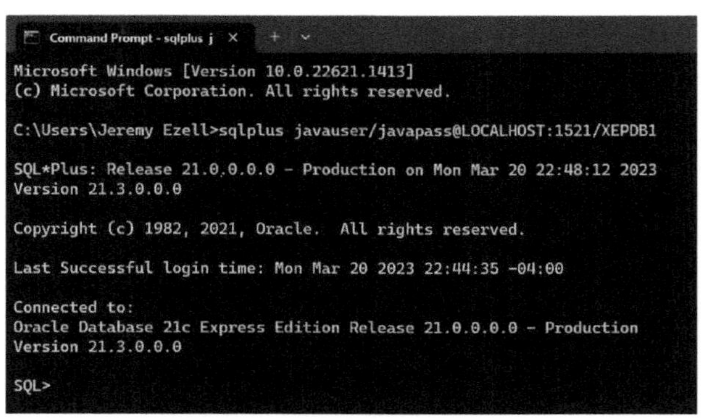

Figure A.25. SQLPlus as the Logged-In "`javauser`" Account to XEPDB1

A.6 Interactive Learning Using `jShell`

Since JDK 9, Oracle has included a tool called jShell that allows you to quickly try out snippets of Java code without the need to write and run a full Java main class. This can be very handy while learning the Java language in many instances, like trying out operators, experimenting with values and decision structures, or understanding order or operator precedence for complicated expressions. You can explore the official Oracle Java Shell documentation (and download it as a PDF) more extensively, but you will cover basic usage and some examples here:*

- Open a command prompt in Windows. In Mac OS X, you may need to add the bin directory for the JDK version you have installed as a PATH variable so that the terminal knows where jShell is located. Some handy instructions that you may need to adapt can be found here.†
- Type `jshell -v`. This will start jShell in verbose mode, letting you see more of what is going on behind the scenes. The version of jShell will also print (this version matches the version of Java installed).
- To exit jShell, simply type `/exit` when done.

Using Variables in a Simple Expression

```
jshell> int firstNum = 4
firstNum ==> 4
|  created variable firstNum : int

jshell> int secondNum = 7
secondNum ==> 7
|  created variable secondNum : int

jshell> firstNum + secondNum
$3 ==> 11
|  created scratch variable $3 : int
```

The "`jshell>`" part is the prompt that is always there while running jShell. You will type your commands to the right of this prompt. To create a variable, you simply need to enter the variable data type and its name and then set it equal to some value using the assignment operator (=). If you leave off the assignment, the variable will be given its default value (see chapter 0). Then type in your expression. Notice that you do not have to invoke `.println()`; because jShell is known as a read-evaluate-print-loop (REPL) tool, it will print out the result automatically.‡

Seeing What Is in Memory

While you are "logged into" jShell, it will keep all these variables in memory. Begin typing a variable name and then press the Tab key on your keyboard to autocomplete the variable name.

If you need to be reminded of what variables jShell has stored in memory currently, type out the following command (in **bold**):

```
jshell> /vars
|    int firstNum = 4
|    int secondNum = 7
|    int $3 = 11
```

Notice that any variables that start with a $ sign are "scratch" variables: just a location automatically created in memory to store a result of your operation. You can use these scratch variables in expressions as well:

```
jshell> firstNum + $3
$4 ==> 15
|  created scratch variable $4 : int

jshell> /vars
```

* https://docs.oracle.com/en/java/javase/17/jshell/index.html.

† https://stackoverflow.com/questions/46371298/how-to-access-java-9-jshell-on-mac.

‡ https://docs.oracle.com/en/java/javase/17/jshell/index.html.

```
|    int firstNum = 4
|    int secondNum = 7
|    int $3 = 11
|    int $4 = 15
```

If you want to see a list of the commands you have already run and a history of the "snippets," use the following:

```
jshell> /list
   1 : int firstNum = 4;
   2 : int secondNum = 7;
   3 : firstNum + secondNum
   4 : firstNum + $3
```

If you want to clear out all the variables and other data in memory, use the /reset command:

```
jshell> /reset
|  Resetting state.

jshell> /list

jshell> /vars
```

Notice that after `/reset`, there are no variables or history remaining in jShell's memory.

Creating a Method Snippet

Creating a method is fairly straightforward (for methods, see chapter 6). You type the header and open up a curly brace, then hit enter. jShell knows that you are not yet done with the definition and will break across multiple lines as you fully define the method. End with a closing curly brace to end the method definition (if you typed /reset earlier, you will have to redefine `firstNum` and `secondNum`):

```
jshell> int addTwoNumbers(int numA, int numB){
   ...>     return numA + numB;
   ...> }
|  created method addTwoNumbers(int,int)

jshell> addTwoNumbers(firstNum, secondNum)
$4 ==> 11
|  created scratch variable $4 : int
```

Once the method is created, you can use any of the variables you have created in memory so far as arguments for the method parameters. If you want to redefine the method, simply type it again with your changes. You can also use the /drop command followed by the method name to delete it (or any variable) from memory.

Testing Out Operators and Expressions

Testing operators and exploring how they work are common learning tasks in jShell. For example, understanding how the modulo operator (chapter 1) works is easy in jShell without a lot of extra code:

```
jshell> 0 % 1
$6 ==> 0
|  created scratch variable $6 : int

jshell> 3 % 1
$7 ==> 0
|  created scratch variable $7 : int

jshell> 1 % 2
$8 ==> 1
|  created scratch variable $8 : int
```

jShell can be handy for testing out boolean operations as well:

```
jshell> boolean boolVar = false
boolVar ==> false
```

```
| created variable boolVar : boolean

jshell> boolean boolVar2 = true
boolVar2 ==> true
| created variable boolVar2 : boolean

jshell> boolVar & boolVar2
$11 ==> false
| created scratch variable $11 : boolean

jshell> (boolVar && boolVar2) || (3 % 5 == 0)
$12 ==> false
| created scratch variable $12 : boolean
```

Testing Out Loops with jShell

Learning loops can be tricky (see chapter 5, which makes it much less tricky to learn!). Using the jShell tool can help with this:

```
jshell> int[] anArray = {1,2,3,4,5,6,7,8,9,10}
anArray ==> int[10] { 1, 2, 3, 4, 5, 6, 7, 8, 9, 10 }
| created variable anArray : int[]


jshell> for (int i=0; i<=10; i++){
   ...>     System.out.print(anArray[i]);
   ...> }
12345678910|  Exception java.lang.ArrayIndexOutOfBoundsException: Index 10 out of bounds for
length 10
|       at (#6:2)


jshell> for (int i=0; i<10; i++){
   ...>     System.out.print(anArray[i]);
   ...> }
12345678910
```

Notice how after creating an array, we make a mistake with the `for` loop header and go beyond the index range of the array. We learn our lesson, and the second `for` loop works perfectly. Note as well that the output from the first `for` loop still occurred; it was followed by the runtime exception.

Using jShell to Test a Class

If you want to test a Java user-defined class out quickly (see chapter 8), you can do so in the jShell tool:

```
jshell> class Person{
   ...>     String name;
   ...>     int age;
   ...>     int heightInInches;
   ...>     String eyeColor;
   ...>
   ...>     public Person(String name, int age, int heightInInches, String eyeColor){
   ...>         this.name = name;
   ...>         this.age = age;
   ...>         this.heightInInches = heightInInches;
   ...>         this.eyeColor = eyeColor;
   ...>     }
   ...>     public String toString(){
   ...>         return this.name + " " + this.age + " " + this.heightInInches + " " +
this.eyeColor;
   ...>     }
   ...> }
```

```
|  created class Person

jshell> Person p = new Person("Sarah",22,70,"Blue")
p ==> Sarah 22 70 Blue
|  created variable p : Person

jshell> p.toString()
$3 ==> "Sarah 22 70 Blue"
|  created scratch variable $3 : String
```

Exploring the rest of the jShell documentation (referenced earlier in this section) is recommended, as this can be a very handy tool for testing out Java code quickly either during learning or during a normal development process.

A.7 Creating a JavaFX Project

PLEASE NOTE: Instructions for creating a JavaFX project can be found at the Student Resources site. The document name is "**Appendix A Supplemental: Creating a JavaFX Project**."

Appendix B

Operator Precedence and Working with Java Expressions

How to Use This Appendix

This appendix details how and in what order the Java language processes operators in expressions. A basic understanding of the Java language (chapter 0) and how operators work, the types of operators, and how they are used in expressions (chapter 1) is recommended. You can practice the examples in section B.2 of this appendix either in a Java main class application or by using `jShell` (appendix A).

B.1 Java Operator Precedence

The Java language imposes an order in which operators in expressions are processed. Operators can be the following, among others (see chapter 1 for details and examples on Java operators):

- Unary (one operand) (i.e., `++` the post-increment operator: `var++`)
- Binary (two operands) (i.e., `+` the addition operator: `var1 + var2`)
- Ternary (three operands). (i.e., `(var > var2) ? resultVar1 : resultVar2;`)
- Of the assignment type (i.e., `=` the assignment operator: `result = var1 + var2`)
- Equality test type (i.e., `==` the equality operator: `booleanResult = (var1 == var2);`)
- Relational type (i.e., `>` the greater-than operator: `booleanResult = (var1 > var2);`)
- Logical type (i.e., `&` the AND operator: `if (boolResult1 && boolResult2) ...`)

Java handles the processing of these operators in two ways: precedence, where some are processed before others, and direction (i.e., "associativity"), either left to right within an expression or right to left within an expression. Table B.1 shows the Java operators and their relationships to one another in terms of precedence and associativity.

Note that in table B.1, some variables (`x`, `y`, and `z`) are used simply as examples when needed to show the nature and use of the operator. Note also that most programmers will commonly use a small subset of these, and expressions will rarely get so complex as to make figuring out operator precedence a difficult task. More commonly used operators are highlighted in **bold** in table B.1. Oracle's documentation provides additional details on operator precedence as well.* Some of these operators, like the unary plus and unary minus (different from the normal "plus" and "minus" operators), have not been covered in this textbook, but you can research them on your own. Operators listed **higher** in the chart are processed **earlier/before** operators that are **lower** in the chart. Operators that are listed on the **same row** are processed at the same time but in directional order of associativity.

* https://docs.oracle.com/javase/tutorial/java/nutsandbolts/operators.html.

Table B.1. Precedence and Associativity of Operators in Java

Precedence	Left-to-right associativity	Right-to-left associativity
(Higher/earlier)	[ ] ( ) .	
	x++ x--	
		+x -x !x ++x --x ~
		(*cast*) new
	* / %	
	+ -	
	<< >> >>>	
	< <= > >=	
	== !=	
	&	
	^	
	|	
	&&	
	||	
		statement ? x : y
(Lower/later)		= += -= *= /= %=

B.2 Examples of Java Expressions

A few examples of expressions using the operators above will help clarify how Java uses operator precedence. Consider the following example:

```
int x = 500;
int y = 100;
System.out.println(x + y / 100);
```

What would you normally expect to print with this? In a normal math expression, you would process this from left to right and add x and y and then divide by 100. You would expect 500 + 100 to be 600, then 600 / 100 to yield 6. But this is not the case here as our output is the following:

```
501
```

Java processes the addition and division operators in the math expression in a different order based on the operator type. Note that in table B.1, the division operator is one precedence level higher than the addition operator. This means it will be processed first. So the first math operation is 100 / 100, giving 1, then the addition operator is processed, and finally 500 + 1 is added, yielding 501. How can you fix this? Use parentheses to change the operator precedence and force parts of the expression to execute first:

```
int x = 500;
int y = 100;
System.out.println((x + y) / 100);
```

Now the result prints as

```
6
```

which is the result ultimately intended. Notice in table B.1 how the parentheses operators are at a higher precedence level than our mathematical operators, and they are processed first. Consider this example:

```
int x = 500;
int y = 100;
int z = 0;

z = (x + y) / 100;

System.out.println(z);
```

Notice again the expression where a value is assigned to the variable z. The assignment operator is at the very bottom of the precedence order in table B.1, and it is processed right to left, meaning that parts of the expression to the right of the operator will be processed first. And indeed this is the case, as the value

```
6
```

prints, showing that the full expression on the right is processed before the final value is assigned to the variable z.

Consider the following example using a mix of int and boolean variables:

```
int x = 5;
int y = 10;
boolean first = false;
boolean second = true;
boolean third = true;
boolean result = false;

result = (x == y) == (first == (second == third));

System.out.println(result);
```

This will print out the value

```
true
```

The parentheses in the expression will be processed in a left-to-right fashion like so:

```
1.      result = (x == y) == (first == (second == third));
2.      result = (false) == (first == (second == third));
3.      result = (false) == (first == (true));
4.      result = (false) == (false);
5.      result = true;
```

Notice that innermost parentheses are always processed first when the parentheses they nest within are up for processing.

Consider this example:

```
int x = 5;
int y = 10;
int z = 0;

z = (x + y++) + y;
System.out.println(z);
System.out.println(y);
```

Notice here we use the post-increment operator on the variable y, which is higher in precedence than the addition operator +. Parentheses are also used here. Recall from chapter 1 that the post-increment operator increases the value of the variable it acts upon by 1, but the prior value is used in the expression until the end of the expression. Here, the parentheses "end" the time frame before the new increased value of y is used. Outside the parentheses, the new value of y is used. The expression is equivalent to this, which demonstrates how the value of y changes inside the expression as it's processed:

```
z = (5 + 10) + 11;
```

Consider this last example using boolean logic operators:

```
boolean first = true;
boolean second = false;
boolean third = false;
boolean result = false;

result = first == second && first == third;

System.out.println(result);
```

Notice that all three operators in this expression are at different precedence levels. The equality operator is higher than the short circuit AND and is processed left to right, so the first boolean comparison is performed. Since it evaluates to `false`, the short circuit AND is processed next, and the expression on the right side of the assignment operator finishes. Finally, the assignment operator is processed, the false value is copied into `result`, and that value prints `false`. If you change the main expression to

```
result = first == (second && first) == third;
```

then the order will change. The parentheses will cause the short circuit AND to process first. Since `second` is `false`, `first` is `true`, and `second` is the left-hand operator, the expression ends and resolves to `true`. Then the boolean equality operators process from left to right and are equivalent to this:

```
1.      result = first == (false) == third;
2.      result = false == third;
3.      result = true;
```

The value `true` will then print to the console.

Appendix C

Working with ASCII Character Codes

How to Use This Appendix

This appendix details how to convert Java characters into their ASCII character code equivalents and back again. A basic understanding of the topics in chapter 3 is recommended in order to use this appendix effectively.

C.1 ASCII Character Codes

The Java language uses the Unicode character set to encode the characters and symbols that are interpreted and compiled by the Java compiler.* Java also provides compatibility with the ASCII (American Standard Code for Information Interchange) character encoding and allows you to convert Java `char` data types back and forth from ASCII.† Both encoding standards allow for easy interchange of data between different languages, systems, and devices. The ASCII character set is typically divided into two categories: characters that control and characters that are visually displayed. Control characters are representative of commands to control a device or the way software displays text. Table C.1 below provides the list of visible ASCII characters and their numeric (i.e., decimal) equivalents. If you are interested in using any of the control characters, you are encouraged to research the full ASCII character table on your own and experiment with the outcomes when you convert them to Java Unicode characters.

* https://docs.oracle.com/javase/specs/jls/se12/html/jls-3.html.

† https://en.wikipedia.org/wiki/ASCII.

Table C.1. Visible ASCII Characters and Their Decimal Equivalents

32: (space)	48: 0	58: :	65: A	91: [	97: a	123: {
33: !	49: 1	59: ;	66: B	92: \	98: b	124: |
34: "	50: 2	60: <	67: C	93:]	99: c	125: }
35: #	51: 3	61: =	68: D	94: ^	100: d	126: ~
36: $	52: 4	62: >	69: E	95: _	101: e	
37: %	53: 5	63: ?	70: F	96: `	102: f	
38: &	54: 6	64: @	71: G		103: g	
39: '	55: 7		72: H		104: h	
40: (	56: 8		73: I		105: i	
41:)	57: 9		74: J		106: j	
42: *			75: K		107: k	
43: +			76: L		108: l	
44: ,			77: M		109: m	
45: -			78: N		110: n	
46: .			79: O		111: o	
47: /			80: P		112: p	
			81: Q		113: q	
			82: R		114: r	
			83: S		115: s	
			84: T		116: t	
			85: U		117: u	
			86: V		118: v	
			87: W		119: w	
			88: X		120: x	
			89: Y		121: y	
			90: Z		122: z	

C.2 Working with `char` and `String` Data Types

Notice that in table C.1, the capital letter "A" is represented by code 65, while its lowercase equivalent "a" is represented by 97. This is handy to know because by adding 32 to any uppercase letter's code, you can yield its equivalent lowercase version. You can subtract 32 from lowercase letters to convert them to uppercase.

The following code uses casting (chapter 1) to demonstrate the conversions between `int` and `char` data types:

```
char letterA = 'A';
System.out.println((int)letterA);
System.out.println((char)65);
```

The output from this would be the following:

```
65
A
```

Consider an example where a lowercase word is converted to uppercase (without using the `.toUpperCase()` method):

```
String name = "caylee";
String converted = "";
char workingChar;
int code = 0;

for (int i=0;i<name.length();i++)
{
    workingChar = name.charAt(i);
    code = ((int)workingChar) - 32;
    converted += (char)code;
}

System.out.println(converted);
```

The output from this would be

```
CAYLEE
```

A simple way (apart from using regular expressions) to check for the validity of an email address might look like the following:

```
String email = "bookauthor@nicebook.net";
int atCount = 0;
int periodCount = 0;
int code = 0;
for (int i=0; i<email.length(); i++)
{
    code = (int)(email.charAt(i));
    switch (code)
    {
        case 64: atCount++;
        break;
        case 46: periodCount++;
        break;
    }
}

if (atCount > 0 & periodCount > 0)
    System.out.println("Email Address Appears Valid");
```

For this example, the following would print to the console:

```
Email Address Appears Valid
```

These examples can be adjusted to check for any sort of business rules (types of characters in a password, for example, or validating other types of user input).

Index

Page numbers followed by *f* and *t* refer to figures and tables, respectively.

Each/
OTHER:
Marie Watt and Cannupa Hanksa Luger

Edited by John P. Lukavic

DENVER art MUSEUM

KOKORO WA
II DESU.
Save Our
Forests
MAKE
Hitched

Table Of Contents

Foreword

Seen in the pristine galleries of museums, works of art tend to become static, divorced from their making, more easily slotted into predetermined stories. What museums tend to elide is the collaborative efforts that go into making the art object—the artist's collaboration with materials, with other artists and craftspeople, and even with the audience. Recovering these multilayered collaborations across space and time seems even more urgent in today's environment. Within the context of a global pandemic, increasing climate catastrophe, and increased attention focused on systemic racial and social injustice, collaboration is essential. Through their creative, collaborative processes and finished works, both Marie Watt (Seneca, Scottish, and German) and Cannupa Hanska Luger (Mandan, Hidatsa, Arikara, Lakota, and European) urge us to reconsider the reasons we prioritize the finished object over its making, to reconsider how museums privilege some stories over others, and they urge us to look into ourselves and question our own place within the systems that subjugate and disenfranchise.

Each/Other: Marie Watt and Cannupa Hanska Luger marks the first time that the two artists have worked with each other. Both artists engage in collaborative methods to create their works and in so doing forge community. Having witnessed Watt's thoughtful community building during her 2013 residency with the museum's Native Arts Artist-in-Residence program, we are excited to present a new community collaboration designed by her and Luger that resulted in a monumental sculpture titled *Each/Other*.

The Denver Art Museum began collecting Indigenous arts of North America in 1925 and has long been commited to exhibiting Indigenous contemporary art. Our late curator Nancy Blomberg made this a major priority over the past three decades, and current curators John Lukavic and Dakota Hoska enthusiastically continue the mission. Exhibitions by their nature are collective endeavors, and I would like to thank our collaborators for their generous support, including Stelo and the Native Arts and Cultures Foundation, as well the Robert Lehman Foundation, the Osage Nation Foundation, and the National Endowment for the Arts for their grants. Our newly constituted Indigenous Community Advisory Council shared their time and insights, and we are grateful to the lenders who were kind enough to share artworks with us: Eiteljorg Museum of American Indians and Western Art; Hood Museum of Art, Dartmouth; Najma and Firoz Lalji; Cannupa Hanska Luger; Portland Art Museum; The Tia Collection; Brian Tschumper; and Marie Watt. We are delighted that the exhibition will travel to the Michael C. Carlos Museum at Emory University in Atlanta, Georgia, and the Peabody Essex Museum in Salem, Massachusetts.

We hope that *Each/Other* sparks conversations, creativity, and discovery—about ourselves, our neighbors, and the world around us. When we open ourselves to collaboration, we forge a greater sense of understanding between people, understanding that is much needed in this contemporary moment.

Christoph Heinrich, Frederick and Jan Mayer Director, Denver Art Museum

Acknowledgments

An exhibition and catalog about collaboration brings into focus the many people who contributed to its success. First, Marie, Cannupa, and I would like to acknowledge the lands where we work and live, as well as the Indigenous people who call these lands home. The Denver Art Museum is located on the homeland of the Arapaho, Cheyenne, and Ute nations as well as the many other Indigenous nations with roots in this place.

I would like to thank Marie and Cannupa for their enthusiasm and willingness to collaborate on this project as well as the catalog contributors Jami Powell and Namita Gupta Wiggers. Marie and Cannupa's collaboration on the new sculpture *Each/Other* would have been unthinkable without the support of Stelo and Camp Colton. From providing space that incorporated families, administrative assistance, childcare, and fabrication support to food, forest, and community, their generosity infuses the sculpture. The artists and I would also like to extend our gratitude to the team workers at Camp Colton, Stelo board members Shir Ly Camin Grisanti and Laurence Grisanti, Native Arts & Culture Foundation, and STTLMNT Indigenous Digital Occupation, in addition to Neal Fegan for fabrication and "nealgineering" and Brit Howard, Beth Malone, and the entire team at the Portland Garment Factory. Along with Marie and Cannupa, we also thank the many hands, hearts, and minds, including those of their families' for their support and contributions.

To Danielle St. Peter, senior interpretive specialist at the Denver Art Museum, I offer my deepest thanks for working hand-in-hand with me throughout every step of the exhibition planning. Museum staff were crucial for pulling together all of the moving parts of the exhibition, including Julia Strunk, Emily Attwool, Lori Iliff, Heather Haldeman, and Renée Miller. Kati Woock, Laura Caruso, and Valerie Hellstein in the Publications department provided project management and editing for the catalog, and Chindo Nkenke-Smith beautifully designed the book. Christina Jackson, along with the artists' studios and galleries, provided photographs for this catalog. Thanks also goes to the staff of The Industry who kindly provided images from *Sweet Land Opera*, to Chip Thomas for helping to reimagine *Return of the Warrior Twins* for the exhibition, and to Ramble Creative for the beautiful and creative graphic design in the exhibition.

We owe a debt of gratitude to Ginger Dunnill, Madalyn Barelle, Stephanie Sun, and Lauren Chacon who helped to manage logistics and provide information from each artist's studio, along with PDX Contemporary Art, Marc Strauss Gallery, Garth Greenan Gallery, and Greg Kucera Gallery who helped to connect us with the collectors of the artists' works.

I would like to thank the staffs of the Michael C. Carlos Museum and the Peabody Essex Museum who partnered with us as venues for the exhibition.

Finally, the ongoing support offered by Christoph Heinrich was crucial to making this project happen.

John P. Lukavic
Andrew W. Mellon Curator of Native Arts

HEALING
RALPH
expecting
a
Massive
Upgrade
CRA
OR
ART?
Hope
Change
Love

Memories of Collaboration

by John P. Lukavic

It was nearly midnight in Manhattan, a city literally built by Haudenosaunee ironworkers.[1] The cool autumn air felt great after piling out of a New York City cab onto the sidewalk in midtown into the rain. At this point, there were only a few of us, but more were on their way. There, along the street, was a descending staircase that led to a nondescript door. Our group walked down this flight of stairs into a place of fear for some and excitement for others: a karaoke bar.[2]

Nearly twenty people packed into a room: a global contingent of Indigenous artists, curators, a program officer from a major arts foundation, and even a radio personality. We travelled from near and far, north (Toronto) and south (Mexico City), and east (Massachusetts) and west (Alaska). This unlikely group came together to share in one thing: singing. Some were amazing. Others were awful, but we didn't care. We were creating something together, and that was all that mattered. One blended voice created a sound that no one of us could create alone. It was against this backdrop, deafened by a verse of Neil Diamond's "Sweet Caroline" (full disclosure: I may have chosen that song), that collaboration and intersectionality reigned. This was where Marie Watt and Cannupa Hanska Luger first met.[3] In this place underground, a place where some creation stories originate, an idea was born.

I recall looking around that room and marveling at the talent surrounding me—not singing talent, but brilliant artistic talent nevertheless. That night a kernel of an idea began to form as I thought of each artist's practice and the common threads that connect them. It took a while for this seed to grow, but that night was what led me to connect Watt and Luger's art conceptually.

Marie Watt was an artist in residence at the Denver Art Museum in the summer of 2013, so I had an opportunity to see how she engages communities of people in a personal way. Visitors to the museum joined Marie in sewing circles (fig. 1) where everyone not only worked together to sew monumental textiles, such as *Butterfly* (2015, cat. 7) and *Trek (Pleiades)* (2014, cat. 6), but also

Fig. 1 Marie Watt and participants at the Sewing Circle, working on *Butterfly*. Denver Art Museum, September 2013.

Fig. 2 *MMIWQT* bead making community engagement with Cannupa Hanska Luger, 2018. Museum of Indian Arts and Culture, Santa Fe, NM.

shared stories. They laughed and learned from one another. Being present in that place and time was powerful. You could feel the connections forming among those who contributed to the projects. It was the time spent together creating that made it special.

Collaboration—with artists and audience alike—is equally integral to Cannupa Hanska Luger's work. Often using short instructional videos, Cannupa teaches a simple act of artmaking—forming a clay bead for *Every One* (2018; fig. 2, cat. 14) or making a mirrored surface for a shield for the *Mirror Shield Project* (2016; fig. 3, cats. 25-27)—and provides instructions on how to send him what was made. These acts bring together the hands of many to create something on a grand scale. Although the collaborators may never meet, each is personally invested in the meaning of the work and dependent on the others to achieve the artist's aims.

In American society today, we place value on the noun "art" and not the verb "to create." When art

Fig. 3 *Mirror Shield* conceived by Cannupa Hanska Luger. Turtle Island direct action, Standing Rock, ND. Thanksgiving Day 2016, police in reflection.

is a verb, and the focus is not on the product, it is neither elitist nor a luxury, nor can it be owned. For much of human history, art was an act of shared creation. Art is a performance that is never truly done alone. The act of artmaking involves collaborating with materials and, by extension (and sometimes directly), with the land or animals that produced them as well as with those who work in the shops or factories that process and sell the materials. When Diné weavers sit at their looms to create textiles, they are collaborating with their families who raised the sheep for wool; with the land that nourished the sheep and produced the natural dyes harvested by their families; and with the generations that preceded them who passed on their knowledge.

Fig. 4 Marie Watt, Sewing Circle, Yale University Art Gallery, September 2019.

Family is an essential part of both Watt's and Luger's practices and is what helped them develop deep bonds with one another, and with me.[4] With family always centered, the artists reinforce the idea that, regardless of what plans we have personally, we also have responsibilities for others (fig. 4). These responsibilities cause us to look at the world around us with a careful eye—seeking to identify harm but also opportunities. Experiences become more meaningful when they are shared, which is why collaborative projects have the potential to have lasting impressions.

In this context, when we talk about art as a verb, for Marie and Cannupa this means that art is a social project where people who participate in the making become invested, relationships are forged, and an exchange happens. The artists recognize that art can also be transformational. It can facilitate learning, maintain mental health, help develop a new way of seeing, and impart new skills. This way of thinking about art is not new, but it is something many of us have forgotten or never had a chance to experience.

Fig. 5 Anna Hawk and family, about 1932-33. Photograph by Reese or Wanda Queenan. Wanda Queenan Collection, Elk City, Oklahoma.

As noted above in the example of Diné weavers, one place we can look to reclaim and share this knowledge of art as a collaborative act is to Indigenous practices. While I was interviewing Cheyenne moccasin makers during my dissertation research, the artists often spoke about how arts in their communities were once communal acts. Intergenerational groups of Cheyenne women would sit together and bead (fig. 5). Art creation was a social act during which Indigenous knowledge was transmitted, stories were told, instructions were given, and lessons were learned. Artmaking was never meant to be a solitary act.[5]

We need each other to ensure our mutual survival—that is to say, the actions required for all of us to survive are beyond the capabilities of any one of us. When art is a collaborative process, it takes on a similar kind of societal importance. We become aware of things outside our limited, individual fields of vision and start to take notice of our neighbors, of the land we share, and of our place as humans in a wider world. These are concepts embedded in Indigenous ways of artmaking that inform both Watt's and Luger's work and which can bring together people from all backgrounds. It is through the artists' work with communities and institutions that they create and amplify platforms for shared experience, new understanding, reframing histories, and neighborly exchange.

When we see collaboration in these broad terms, our eyes are open to the land, animals, and processes with which we sometimes unknowingly collaborate—or even harm. When people come together and share stories and life experiences, something magical can happen: laughter and understanding, things this world needs desperately. Watt and Luger both recognize that humor, gratitude, and connectedness make communities thrive, and those values infuse the projects they lead. Understanding, in turn, is the basis of caring and eventually commitment. We become invested in issues: from challenges faced by our neighbors—from food deserts and environmental racism—to the need to protect clean water on a much larger scale. When we understand, we become truly invested and we feel a sense of responsibility, which then leads to action. In this way, all of Marie's and Cannupa's art is rooted in—and aims to produce—activism and social engagement.

So don't look at the art in this catalog or associated exhibition as a collection of things. Look beyond the noun. Search for signs of the different hands that went into the creation of the artworks here. See the people who sat around a table, making stitches or clay beads, and talking. Ask yourself, again and again as you encounter each piece, "how am I part of this story?" The works presented here are tangible, but they are, more importantly, memories of collaborations that provide us with a model for coming together and taking part in something greater than ourselves.

Notes

[1] For one of many stories supporting this statement, see Stephen Nessen, "Sky Walking: Raising Steel, A Mohawk Ironworker Keeps Tradition Alive," *WNYC News*, March 18, 2012, https://www.wnyc.org/story/192807-sky-walking-raising-steel-mohawk-ironworker-keeps-tradition-alive/. In 2012, 200 out of 2,000 (10 percent) ironworkers in New York City were Mohawk, and in the 1950s, 800 Mohawk ironworkers accounted for 15 percent of all ironworkers. And notably this is just Mohawk people. It doesn't include ironworkers from the other five tribes of the Haudenosaunee Confederacy.

[2] This gathering occurred the night of October 2, 2018, following the opening of the exhibition *Art of Native America: The Charles and Valerie Diker Collection* at the Metropolitan Museum of Art; however, this event only brought a few of us to the city. Cannupa was there for an event at the Museum of Art and Design and others for various other reasons.

[3] Actually, Marie and Cannupa first met at a Native Arts and Cultures Foundation event prior to this night, but both recognize this meeting in New York as the first time they had an opportunity to get to know one another.

[4] When Marie was an artist in residence at the Denver Art Museum in 2013, her family and mine had the opportunity to get to know each other, and over the years, we have fostered those bonds with subsequent visits. Similarly, during their residency at Camp Colton in Oregon, Watt and Luger both brought their children, and they spent time together exploring their surroundings and creating art with each other.

[5] John Lukavic, "Southern Cheyenne Orthodoxy: A Study in Materiality," (PhD diss., University of Oklahoma, 2012), 55-65.

Reclaim
WE

WE ARE
ALL
CONNECTED

In our community, there is no Indigenous word for "art," but works that we would now refer to as "artworks" have been made for a very long time . . . I'm . . . interested in how we can have more cross-disciplinary conversations, and conversations where art isn't institutionalized or segregated from our experience in the world. I . . . think of art as being something that intersects with science, nature, poetry and literature . . . It's integrated in our lives.

– Marie Watt

If art doesn't have a name within the language, it's not an object, it is something else. So, what is that other thing? I started thinking about it within my own practice, and what I realized is an older, more honest interpretation of what art is to human beings in general. Art is a verb, not a noun. Art is a practice, it's an activity. It is an action.

– Cannupa Hanska Luger

Refusal and Generosity: The Work of Marie Watt and Cannupa Hanska Luger

by Jami Powell

The original prompt for this essay was to write about Marie Watt's and Cannupa Hanska Luger's work, situating both artists within Indigenous art history and contemporary art more broadly. While the task seemed easy enough, placing Watt's and Luger's work within any kind of bounded intellectual space was more difficult than I'd anticipated. This, however, is the point. In order to frame Watt's or Luger's work within these predetermined categories, it would have to be flattened and oversimplified. Too often, those of us working within museums, academia, and other institutional spaces are complicit in the distillation of Indigenous art. Why? Because it is too hard not to be. It is incredibly difficult to talk about the entangled histories of colonial violence and Indigenous resilience and all of the messy moments and exchanges in between, particularly to a general audience. Ask any Indigenous artist what the most exhausting part of their work is, and I would be willing to bet most of them would answer: trying to explain it in a way that is digestible for mainstream audiences.

Therefore, institutions insist we limit and homogenize Indigenous art and experiences, obliging us to warp and force amorphous, dynamic, and complex ideas and works into particular boxes aligned with preconceived

Fig. 1 T. C. Cannon (Kiowa/Caddo, 1946–1978), *Beef Issue at Fort Sill*, 1973. Acrylic paint on canvas, 71½ × 55¾ in. Denver Art Museum: Native Arts acquisition funds, 2017.94.

expectations. The problem with these boxes or categories, however, is they are based on Eurocentric and colonial, and therefore patriarchal and heteronormative, ways of understanding and organizing, and thereby controlling, the world. Entrenched within Watt's and Luger's work—and more specifically within the materiality and social collaboration of their practice—is a refusal to conform to this type of categorization. This defiance emerges from the centrality of Indigenous epistemologies and aesthetics within their individual artistic practices. However, this refusal also grows from a space that was created by the artists, cultural workers, ancestors, and others who preceded them.

For the past several decades, there have been movements to decolonize institutions and to dismantle the ideological structures that continue to maintain white supremacy within museums and academia. Black, Indigenous, and people of color (BIPOC) have led the charge, with artists playing a key role and using their work as a means to critique museums while also creating space for more meaningful and multiple self-representations and knowledges. Fritz Scholder, T. C. Cannon (fig. 1), Betye Saar, El Anatsui, Yayoi Kusama, Faith Ringgold, Ruth Asawa, George Morrison, James Luna, Truman Lowe, Jaune

By grounding their work within Indigenous understandings of place, relationality, and materiality, Watt and Luger refuse Western art historical categorization and argue for a consideration of art as inseparable from our humanity.

Quick-to-See Smith, Anita Fields, Shan Goshorn, and numerous others created the space in which Watt and her contemporaries—artists such as Jeffrey Gibson, Kent Monkman, Glenn Ligon, Alison Saar, Roxanne Swentzell, Will Wilson, Alan Michelson, and Rebecca Belmore, to name a few—work and continue to push boundaries and expectations. Even though their work is being shown alongside one another in this exhibition, it is important to note that Luger's practice also benefits from space Watt and her generation imagined and created.

Watt (b. 1967) and Luger (b. 1979), alongside other BIPOC artists, are not only occupying but also growing this space, helping future generations of artists and their audiences imagine what is possible within and outside of museum spaces. Instead of trying to fit their work inside the prescribed and established categories of the Western art historical canon, or even pushing against the museum as an institution, Watt and Luger situate their work within complex webs informed by Indigenous knowledges and understandings of place, community, and material resonance. Their work is predicated on long-held understandings that art is inseparable from our lives and experiences. It is also a continuation of the experimentation, adaptation, innovation, and the avant-garde that have always been a part of Indigenous creative expression.

Embedded within Watt's and Luger's work is an intellectual and interpersonal generosity, an entry point into these complex spaces where we as the audience can enter into a dialogue with the work, learn to sit with ambiguity, and imagine possible futures. Therefore, in order to dig a bit deeper into their work, I'll begin with a closer look at the ways placemaking influences their artistic practices. From this stems a conversation about the ways space and place cannot be created or considered without the relationships from which they emerge and those which they create. Here, relationality, a concept grounded in Indigenous knowledges, represents a foundational element of their individual practices and a shared concept that is woven throughout their works and the works of many Indigenous artists today. Lastly, I'll look at the materiality of Watt's and Luger's practices and how the cultural resonance and specificity of materials shape and inform their work in ways that grapple with the complexity of Indigenous art and experiences while also forming connections with larger audiences.

Fig. 2 Marie Watt, *Skywalker/Skyscraper (Axis Mundi)*, 2012, and *Skywalker/Skyscraper (Babel)*, 2012. Installed at PDX Contemporary Art, 2012.

Place & Space

Although people tend to assume that the majority of Native Americans live on reservations, nearly eighty percent of us do not.[1] This statistic reflects the ongoing and enduring history of Indigenous diaspora, not to mention extensive trade networks, which preceded the arrival of Europeans to this continent. However, it also points to the legacies of dispossession and displacement that characterize the history, creation, and expansion of what we now call the United States. Many, but not all, American

Indian nations were removed from ancestral homelands, which included places of cultural, spiritual, and material nourishment. Through Euro-American understandings of nationhood as based in territory, tribal sovereignty also became inextricably tied to place and land ownership.

These complex understandings of place, and more, are integrated within Watt's and Luger's work, which often includes site-specific references and examinations of our relationships to particular places. For example, Watt created her *Skywalker/Skyscraper* series after living in Brooklyn and learning more about the history of Haudenosaunee (Iroquois) "skywalkers," highly skilled ironworkers who built several bridges and buildings in New York City and other metropolitan areas throughout what we now call the United States and Canada. In *Skywalker/Skyscraper (Babel)* (2012; fig. 2, cat. 1), the stack of wool blankets is pierced with a steel I beam, the most direct aesthetic reference to the built environment within the series. In other works from the series, Watt stitches wool blankets into circular or semicircular forms that mimic Haudenosaunee architectural forms and oral histories. In describing these forms, she states:

> ***My mom says that circles expand and contract to include everyone, and it is in a circle where peoples' voices are equal. I am interested in how circles connect us through space and time, while being wary of how circles [are] used by corporate retailers. I am mindful that my circles intersect with others, ancient and modern. My circle is a shield, a flag, and a talisman.***[2]

For Watt, this series not only emerges from the diaspora of Seneca and other Haudenosaunee skywalkers and their impact on the built environment but also a deeper examination of place as physical and metaphysical. This example also refers to the specificity of Watt's engagement with Indigenous knowledge as a Seneca proto-feminist in the images articulated through the works but also through the sewing circles that are integral to her practice.[3]

Both Watt and Luger engage in placemaking through social collaboration. For Luger, much of this collaboration happens through video calls shared via social media, inviting folks to create an object (or several) that will contribute to a larger work of art. In 2018, Luger released an instructional video as a call for collaboration from communities across what we now call the United States and Canada. Over the next few months, Indigenous and non-Indigenous participants sent thousands of hand-shaped, two-inch clay beads, which Luger fired, painted, and strung to re-create the image of a tintype photograph taken by Kali Spitzer (Kaska Dena). The more than 4,000 beads that compose *Every One (#MMIWQT Bead Project)* (2018; fig. 3, cat. 14) visualize and acknowledge the more than 4,000 cases of missing and murdered Indigenous women and girls in Canada, based on data

Fig. 3 Cannupa Hanska Luger, *Every One*, 2018 (cat. 14).

collected by the Native Women's Association of Canada. Within its title, #MMIWQT (Missing and Murdered Indigenous Women/Girls, Queer and Trans people) recognizes the LGBTQ+ and Two-Spirit community members not reflected in available data. This work brings light to the lack of data currently available on similar violence in what is currently known as the United States.

The call for this project resulted in over thirty gatherings and workshops—some of which Luger attended—during which participants created beads for the project. In places where people were unfamiliar with the MMIWQT crisis, the bead-making workshops were often accompanied by supplementary lectures or informational pamphlets created for participants. *Every One* was first installed as the centerpiece for the *Lazy Stitch* exhibition organized by Luger in 2018. When asked about the title, he said:

> ***The term "lazy stitch" describes a sewing methodology often used in Indigenous beadwork. Individual multicolored beads are threaded and sewn, one row at a time, eventually revealing a complex image when all rows are complete. The lazy stitch is an approach to craft-making but also represents a value system in which each individual is important to the whole. Lazy Stitch uses this metaphor as a way to explore contemporary issues through collaborative practice, while revealing the potential for collective social agency.***[4]

Here, Luger describes the practical importance of including many participants to create such a large-scale work, but also the impact of coming together in a particular place and the potential to manifest understanding, healing, and even change within such a space.

Relationality

The social collaborative aspect of Luger's and Watt's practices is certainly practical, but also emerges from long-held communal practices of creating within Indigenous communities and among women. Watt has described how "this type of multigenerational and cross-disciplinary gathering approximates the way knowledge is traditionally shared and passed down in Indigenous communities."[5] Watt's social collaboration exists in her sewing circles, which often take place in museums, universities, and community centers. For these events, Watt has had the same invitation for over a decade (fig. 4): "I will trade a print for your time; and feed you when circumstances permit. No sewing experience necessary. Come and go as your schedule permits. Bring a friend."[6]

Fig. 4 Marie Watt, Sewing Circle Invitation, Peabody Essex Museum, November 2019.

For Watt, social collaboration and place-based engagement are rarely one-time events, but rather, projects that are ongoing. Sustaining the relationships created and discussions that emerge from these spaces is integral to her work. By creating a space for engagement and dialogue, Watt and Luger also create the possibility of relating to one another on a deeper, more human, level. The material and dialogic exchange are intrinsic to the work, not a means to an end. Other Indigenous artists like Will Wilson (Diné/Navajo), through his *Critical Indigenous Photographic Exchange*, and Gina Adams (Ojibwe descent), through her *Broken Treaty Quilt Letter Cutting Sessions*, also emphasize intellectual and physical exchange within their practice (figs. 5 and 6). Through an emphasis on reciprocity, these artists center equitability and sustainability

Fig. 5 Gina Adams, *Broken Treaty* letter cutting session at Dartmouth College, 2018.

Fig. 6 Gina Adams, *Broken Treaty* letter cutting session at Dartmouth College, 2018.

within their social collaboration, something that sets their work apart from other artists engaging in social practice.[7] For these artists, social practice doesn't emerge from neoliberal understandings but is grounded in established and enduring community-based practices of creating.

Fig. 7 Cannupa Hanska Luger, *(Be)Longing*, 2019. Ceramic, steel, ribbon, fiber; 42 × 80 × 80 in.

In addition to providing a space for us to consider our relationships and responsibilities to one another as humans, Watt and Luger both interrogate our relationships to place and nonhuman beings. Luger's *(Be)Longing*—a lifesize ceramic buffalo (American bison) skeleton—reflects on the symbiotic relationships that sustain an environment (fig. 7). The buffalo, grasses, and people of the Plains in particular share a long history of nourishing one another. This ecosystem was drastically altered during the mid-to-late 1800s, when the United States and settlers engaged in a campaign of dispossession in the region. As part of the broader project of westward expansion, settlers were encouraged to slaughter buffalo to collect bounty, ultimately reducing the estimated population of between 30 and 60 million buffalo to just 1,500 by 1895. Luger explains:

> ***This loss of species not only affected my ancestors but also the land. Running down the center of North America, the Great Plains are one of the most endangered environments; many Indigenous grasses are dependent on the buffalo to thrive and have therefore also degenerated. In fact, there can be no true restoration without roaming herds of buffalo.*** **(Be)Longing** ***explores the cascading effects of a decimated species on our precious and interconnected environment.***[8]

Here, Luger speaks to the deep connections between humans and our environments, relationships that have been strained through the imposition and internalization of Western understandings of land ownership and extractive capitalism. Luger addresses these ideas in other bodies of work including *Mirror Shield Project*, *This Is Not A Snake*, *The One Who Checks*, and *The One Who Balances* (cats. 21–23). Within these works, Luger centers Indigenous ways of knowing and being in the world as a response to crises facing the global community. In doing so, he is in conversation with painters such as Jaune Quick-to-See Smith, Christi Belcourt, and Kent Monkman who have each created large-scale works addressing issues of global climate change and Indigenous ecological knowledge. In Quick-to-See Smith's *Trade Canoe: Forty Days and Forty Nights* (fig. 8), she draws on imagery from the Christian Bible, Salish creation stories and homelands,

Fig. 8 Jaune Quick-to-See Smith, Trade Canoe: *Forty Days and Forty Nights*, 2015. Acrylic paint, paper collage, crayon, and marker on canvas; 60 × 160 in. Hood Museum of Art, Dartmouth: Loan of Judith Liff Barker and Joseph N. Barker, Class of 1966, and The Judy and Noah Liff Foundation.

art historical references, and pop culture, creating a cacophonous visual narrative, signaling the possible future of mass flooding as a result of rising sea levels. Luger and photographers like Will Wilson (fig. 9), Cara Romero, and Michael Namingha demonstrate the deep entanglements between colonialism and capitalism, particularly as it relates to issues of extraction. In 2015, Romero created a series of photographs addressing the histories of

Fig. 9 Will Wilson, *Auto Immune Response no. 5*, 2004. Archival pigment print; 44 × 110 in. Hood Museum of Art, Dartmouth: Purchased through the William S. Rubin Fund.

resource extraction and flooding of tribal lands. Romero asked Luger—whose own community has experienced massive changes to their social, economic, and physical lanscape due to the discovery of the Bakken oil field in the 1950s—to serve as a model for *Oil Boom* (fig. 10).[9] In the image, Luger is suspended in a sea of oil, arms outstretched, with a horde of pumpjacks forming a dystopic landscape above him. The sepia color of this underwater photograph thickens its appearance and creates a sense of murkiness, a possible metaphor of the difficulties we face in navigating the waters of our current moment.

Fig. 10 Cara Romero, *Oil Boom*, 2015. Archival pigment print; 43³⁄₁₆ × 44⅛ in. Hood Museum of Art, Dartmouth: Purchased through the Sondra and Charles Gilman, Jr. Foundation Fund.

Watt, who is also part of these conversations—alongside other artists such as Roxanne Swentzell, Courtney M. Leonard, and Rose B. Simpson—

draws on Indigenous knowledges to explore our relationships to place and nonhuman beings. In her *Companion Species* series (cat. 8–13), Watt poses the question, "What would the world look like if we thought of ourselves as companion species?" In this body of work, Watt draws on the Seneca creation story in which Sky Woman sees a hole in the sky and falls to the Earth, where her landing is softened by birds and four-legged animals.[10] As a result, animals become the first teachers, informing a different kind of relationship between humans and animals. In talking about these relationships and teachings that inform her practice, she comments:

> ***There's also the Iroquois teaching of the Seven Generations—what we do affects not just the next generation but the next seven. Animals and the environment are . . . important parts of that belief system. It teaches that we have a responsibility to them, but I also think that our relationship with animals and the natural world is deeply reciprocal. In Western culture, people can enter into this conversation with some familiarity in respect to their companion animals—dogs in particular.***[11]

In these examples, the intellectual and interpersonal generosity of Watt's and Luger's practices and Indigenous epistemologies more broadly are front and center. The centering of Iroquois (Haudenosaunee) oral histories or Mandan, Hidatsa, and Arikara experiences does not exclude non-Indigenous peoples from the conversation, but, rather, provides an invitation for audiences to think about our interactions to our environments and nonhuman beings as relational, not extractive. They are helping us imagine a possible future where we all live in good relation with the lands, waters, and the beings within them.

Materiality

The generosity embedded within Luger's and Watt's work is also related to the myriad of materials used within their practices. Wool blankets, for example, have particular meanings and cultural resonance within Indigenous communities. However, blankets are also meaningful in our daily lives and experiences. As Watt explains, "Blankets, one of my primary materials, are everyday objects that can carry extraordinary histories of use. In my tribe and other Indigenous communities, we give blankets away to honor those who are witness to important life events. In working with blankets, my process is both solitary and collaborative."[12] For many Indigenous peoples, blankets are markers of memory and stories, objects that carry knowledge. For nearly all of us, however, blankets are objects of comfort and can hold deep personal meaning and importance.

Although Luger also uses fiber in his artwork, within his large-scale, collaborative projects, he often uses clay. Clay also exists at the intersection of cultural specificity and broader material resonance. *Every One* exemplifies this through the individual beads made by hundreds of people—each of them leaving their fingerprints and unique forms on the project—but when put together to create the image, those differences are less noticeable. This is not to say that they are unimportant or erased but rather that each bead and its unique qualities inform and contribute in significant ways to the larger work (fig. 11).

In speaking about this within her own practice, Watt often discusses how the "no sewing experience necessary" part of her invitation is sincere: "I love people without sewing experience, because their stitches are so expressive."[13] Similar to the thumbprints on the clay beads, each person's stitch represents a unique contribution and imprint on the larger work. Although Watt maps out the larger composition with tape for

Fig. 11 *MMIWQT* bead making community engagement with Cannupa Hanska Luger. Tewa Women United, Espanola, NM. 2018.

Fig. 12 Marie Watt, *Companion Species (Speech Bubble)* (detail), 2019. Reclaimed wool blankets, embroidery floss, and thread; 136 × 198½ in. Collection of Crystal Bridges Museum of American Art, Bentonville, AR.

participants to use as a guide, the expressive stitches provide an opportunity for Watt to respond to as she brings the individual pieces of fabric back together in the final composition (fig. 12).

The materiality of the blankets and the entangled histories of colonialism and exchange woven into them contribute to the intellectual generosity of Watt's practice. In Watt's work, the simplicity of the line stands out from the complex and overlapping background, as if to remind us of what is important. The complexity of our histories and the violence that have informed our current moment play a foundational role in the composition. However, the line, singular at first, but upon closer inspection clearly a constellation of multiple efforts, reminds us of what we can accomplish and overcome when we join together and collaborate in meaningful ways.

Concluding Thoughts

Marie Watt and Cannupa Hanska Luger are pushing the boundaries of collaborative practice and what sustained engagement in art and museums looks like. Building on the legacy of artists and ancestors who came before them, their practices are helping to create space for complexity and ambiguity in a way that invites dialogue and participation from multiple audiences. By grounding their work within Indigenous understandings of place, relationality, and materiality, Watt and Luger refuse Western art historical categorization and argue for a consideration of art as inseparable from our humanity. Through it all, their work and practice are characterized by a deep intellectual and interpersonal generosity, something that we should all strive to embody, now more than ever.

Notes

Marie Watt interviewed by Caoimhe Morgan-Feir, "Marie Watt Returns to the National Gallery of Canada," *canadianart*, March 3, 2015. https://canadianart.ca/features/marie-watt-returns-national-gallery-canada/; Cannupa Hanska Luger, "Social Engineer, The Artist as Bridge Builder," lecture, Power Talk series, Art/Toronto, October 26, 2018, https://vimeo.com/304437840.

1 "2010 Census Shows Nearly Half of American Indians and Alaska Natives Report Multiple Races," January 25, 2012, https://www.census.gov/newsroom/releases/archives/2010_census/cb12-cn06.html.

2 Marie Watt, *Skywalker/Skyscraper (Allegory)*, 2012. Pennsylvania Academy of the Fine Arts, pafa.org/museum/collection/item/skywalker/skyscraper-allegory.

3 Proto-feminism refers to feminism that preceded the first wave Euro-American feminism that began in the mid-1800s. In Watt's case, this is a recognition of women's power, knowledge, and authority within aspects of Haudenosaunee, and specifically Seneca, social organization.

4 Cannupa Hanska Luger, "*Lazy Stitch* Exhibition," 2018, www.cannupahanska.com/lazy-stitch-exhibition.

5 Marie Watt, "In Conversation with Marie Watt: A New Coyote Tale," *Art Journal* 76, no. 2 (Summer 2017), artjournal.collegeart.org/?p=9492.

6 Ibid.

7 Manuel Arturo Abreu, "We Need to Talk About Social Practice," *Art Practical*, March 6, 2019. https://www.artpractical.com/column/we-need-to-talk-about-social-practice/.

8 Cannupa Hanska Luger, "Artwork Statement," 2019 cannupahanska.com/belonging.

9 Gary Braasch, "North Dakota's Lanscape Energized," *Scientific American, The Daily Climate*, February 21, 2014, https://www.scientificamerican.com/article/north-dakotas-landscape-energized-photos/.

10 Marie Watt, "First Teachers Balance the Universe," lecture at Yale University Art Gallery, November 2, 2019, https://www.youtube.com/watch?v=9V8Vl6Kjw7s.

11 Watt, "In Conversation with Marie Watt."

12 Marie Watt, "Artist Statement," *Posit* 21 (May 2019), http://positjournal.com/2019/05/19/marie-watt/.

13 Watt, "First Teachers Balance the Universe."

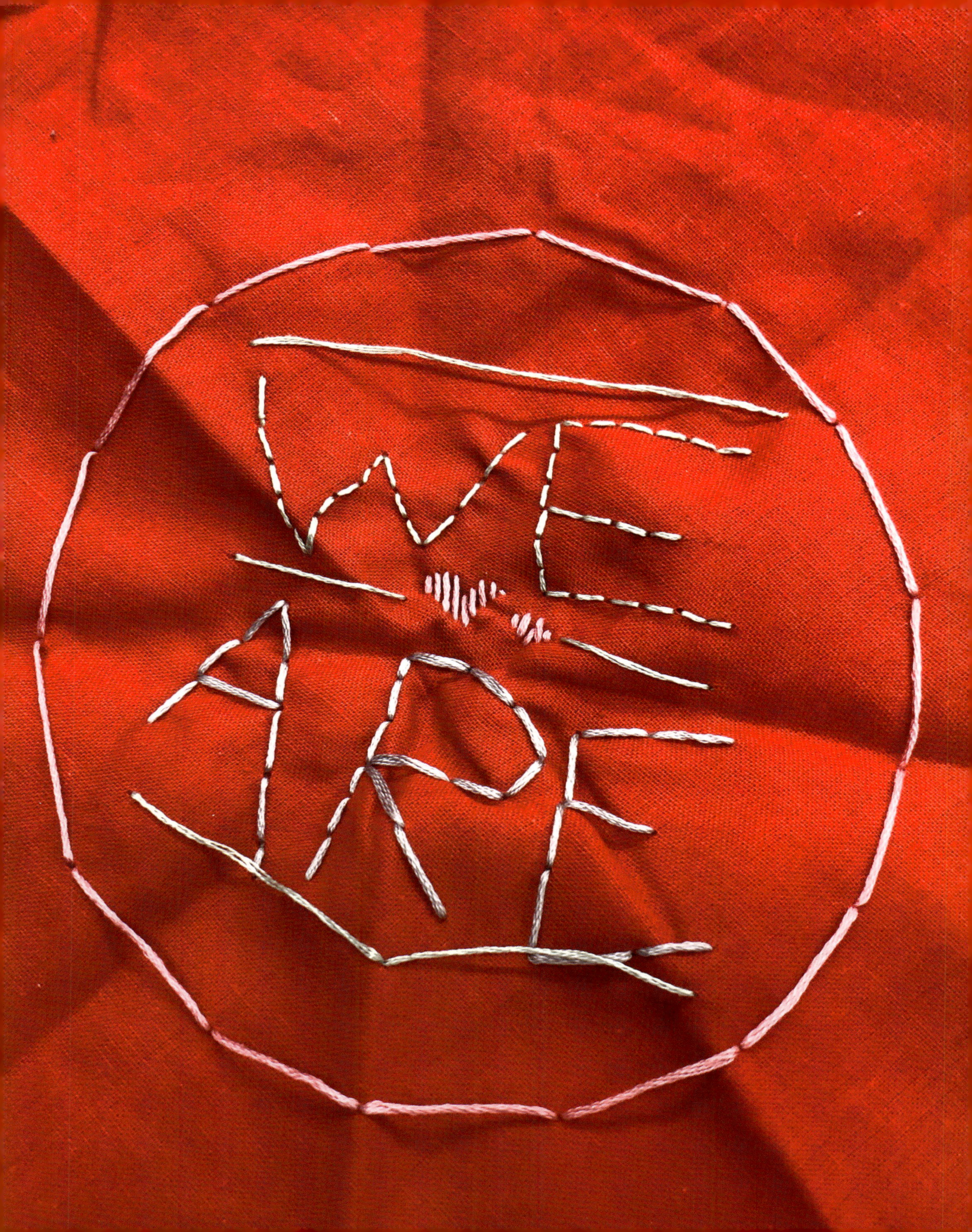
WE
ARE

RECLAIM

Cannupa Hanska Luger and Marie Watt in conversation

with Namita Gupta Wiggers

Namita: How well did you know one another before this project? Had you worked together before?

Cannupa: Indian country is small and you end up running into each other at different functions and things like that. But we never really got to sit down and make something together. The interesting thing is that we set out to develop an idea of an exhibition and started the process of moving forward, but all of a sudden we had to halt in the wake of a global pandemic. How do you collaborate when you are socially distanced?

Namita: How, then, are you working around COVID-19?

Cannupa: It's been challenging because we haven't gotten any time together in the studio to physically make art with one another. Something that we have in common, Marie and I, is that we are makers. We're craftspeople. And we like material. We like working with material and the physicality of it. The conceptual part is only a fragment of it. The material is also a participant in the collaboration. Understanding the edge of that material is a big part of both of our practices.

Marie: What does it mean to make things when you work with community, but then community is existing in a different way? I'm really looking forward to this collaboration with Cannupa because in collaborating we are learning from

Marie Watt, *Blanket Stories: Confluence, Heirloom, and Tenth Mountain Division*, 2013 (cat. 3).

We're craftspeople. And we like material. We like working with material and the physicality of it. –Cannupa

each other's processes. One thing I really admire about the way Cannupa works is how he does these prompts and uses the Internet and all the various tools that are accessible to us. My experience has been different. In some ways, I've looked at sewing circles as almost a remedy for the way technology distances us from one another.

I love the intimacy of sitting next to somebody and not having to talk, but then when your hands are stitching, the stories flow. And for people who might not otherwise meet to share a table and leave having made a connection. Maybe that connection is to something within themselves or to another story, or maybe it involves exchanging a phone number. Or maybe it means that you start your own sewing circle on a project that's important to you.

I've been doing sewing circles for almost twenty years, and I remember when they used to be more intimate and assembled through word of mouth or email because Instagram and Facebook didn't really exist. And then when I was invited to the University of Washington to work with a class and host a sewing circle, I realized I needed a way to do sewing circles that didn't involve everybody around a table working on one piece. So then the work became panels that could be put together, and the sewing circles could accommodate not just sixty students but several hundred participants over the course of three hours.

It wasn't about just dropping in but also having an ongoing relationship, bringing this back into communities. I think that's an aspect of your work, Cannupa, because even though you're using technology—what I referred to as a distancing tool—you actually do create meaningful relationships for people who participate in making something with you.

Cannupa: More often than not I get invited into university settings or craft groups that use a

Marie: We can't have this conversation without talking about culture workers in a broader way because things are slowly changing. There are more people of color in institutions, and undergraduate and graduate school programs are changing. [Schools are] being forced to shift the way they've taught art history. Institutions are having to look at themselves differently because of who they serve, right? But it's been a super-slow process, and I feel like anybody who's gone through those institutions knows it is so much work to bring yourself to a table where the dominant conversation is not something that's reflective of our own experiences.

Namita: What are some of those experiences, Marie?

Marie: I go through periods of feeling frustrated that I don't fit easily into anybody's box. Why do I have to be in this box? I feel like culturally I come from a place where there are no boxes, right? There's not a word for art. There's not the word for craft, probably, in most Indigenous languages. Making things, making things in community, making things that have aesthetic beauty but also utility . . . , yet in school we're trying to understand how we fit into a Western educational context.

Namita: Marie, you've talked about this before, that there is no word for art in Indigenous languages. Language is key for both of you. Cannupa, can you talk about this for a bit?

Cannupa: Recognizing art as a process rather than as a product . . . how do you share art if it's a verb and not a noun? How do you share the verb of art as making and not the thing-because you end up with an object, you know? You end up with something that's kind of like an echo of the art [that is, the verb form], and that's usually what is celebrated in institutions because the infrastructure is built for that. It's a box for boxing things. The act of turning things into nouns, into objects, into things that can be categorized is the epitome of the museum of any sort, of the cabinet of curiosities. [Creating] an exhibition [like *Each/ Other*], turns [the art] into something that can be categorized and held and witnessed; it's no longer what it was. It's a facsimile of what it was at that moment.

All of the work that we have going into this exhibition is collaborative in one way, shape, or form. I work with clay. The material itself is a partner that I have to work with and informs me quite a bit. We are all in collaboration [in all that we do]. We are always participating in one way or another, so showing the variety of that under this umbrella of a collaborative art exhibition, I think, will help challenge people to understand what collaboration means.

Marie: One thing that's so important is really doing just what you said, Cannupa, and exploding this idea of what collaboration is.

Cannupa: The art is the process of people [and materials] coming together and creating. When people come together and create together, they also share ideas and they share practices. And that act of sharing is the maintenance of culture. Marie and I both recognize that, I think, in our effort to do socially collaborative work, because that's the art. And so, trying to make a location for it—it has to be a noun. It has to be static in order for that to happen. But the moment you think you have it in your hands, it slips through and becomes something else. The act of trying to confine it changes it. And that's why the museum needs us more than we need it because we are actually the process of culture. Not the location of it, but the maintenance of it. Trying to define culture and reduce that to a simpler, distilled version undermines all of the complexity that is within culture and the varieties of culture that exist.

Marie: Western institutions are accustomed to the business of sanctioning art as a noun, right? But it's the process that is the art; although I'm a

PHER
Sharpie

You can't invite communities into your institutions without engaging with communities in their spaces as well, if your intentions are authentic. –Marie

Marie Watt and participant at the Sewing Circle, working on *Butterfly*. Denver Art Museum, September 2013.

little hesitant of calling it that because "process" sounds like it's a means to an end, whereas the connections are meaningful events unto themselves that amplify the work—they're what the participants walk away with. When you look at a work, if you participated in it, then you can't separate those two things. That's the tricky part with exhibitions: people see this thing on a wall.

Cannupa: We are object makers, you know? We literally produce nouns [objects] all the time, but the noun is celebrated, the object is celebrated—that's what transfers and moves through these spaces. By turning it [art] into a noun, you put all that has happened and is happening into a moment so that it can be scrutinized and labeled and isolated and put aside. But what we miss is that these are human beings. These are people.

I haven't completely figured out what to do with the role of [my work] living in an institution—being a part of a collection or something along those lines when hundreds of people participated in it. If I'm the one being paid for it, how does that justify the labor of so many people involved in the process? It's tricky, sticky work. For example, the project *Every One*. Stewarding that work has been super hard. It's taxing traveling that piece to different spaces to be exhibited. I think it is important because it amplifies the story of missing and murdered Indigenous women. But what's really difficult for me is each one of the beads represents a life, and now they are stuck as an object. And it kills me to watch these institutions with their white cotton gloves, being so careful with these beads when nobody was careful with the bodies that they represent. And so every time I exhibit that I have that same thing just well up inside of me, and I'm like, "I fucking hate this place." I hate how important this is to you when the people that these beads represent didn't mean shit.

Namita: I feel the weight of those beads and that piece from how you're talking about it. I don't like how I've seen it installed—it is presented in a way that is about the image and not about the individuals.

Cannupa: Yes, and the presentation of that piece has less to do with what that piece is—as an object it is already removed. So put it in the basement, that would be fine by me at this point because all of the people who made that work together, it's in them. That object lives in the hearts of those hundreds of people who participated in it.

Namita: So what is driving you to do this kind of work in institutional contexts? Why bring it into the museum context? What does that do?

Marie: For one, it challenges what the institution has historically presented, and it presents what I think should be part of the narrative.

Cannupa: When we put this sort of work into these spaces, yes, on one hand, it becomes a noun. It becomes the object. But there's a whole story and narrative that happens that we're not a part of within those spaces. Maybe somebody didn't get to participate in the project. Maybe they didn't have the courage or the access to know that this was happening but then they go and see it there—that's also a part of that effort.

Marie: We're also bringing people who might not have envisioned their hand, and labor, and conversation, and stories and things that they've shaped into an institution as well. There's excitement in gathering with other people and seeing yourself in an institution where you've historically not seen yourself or you didn't even know it was possible. I think that that also becomes another reason why it's important to have these works in there because it opens up a space that's maybe felt closed off to us or not representative of us or our communities.

Cannupa: I totally agree with Marie that when you are allowed to be within those spaces, that gives you this incredible privilege. But to be allowed into those spaces also undermines the exclusivity of the institution. These are tiny efforts that we make. They're like eighty-grit sandpaper —it's abrasive and it smooths out corners and edges and allows flow into those spaces a little bit at a time. We can sand it and sand it and sand it, slowly working toward it becoming hopefully obsolete.

Marie: Cannupa, your sandpaper reference reminds me of one of my favorite objects in our family, a Seneca mortar and pestle. What's beautiful about this pestle is its four feet, and it's kind of baton-like and then it tapers. You use it to grind hominy for traditional corn soup. But the tapered part of pestle is just so soft and really smooth, and I always think that's because of all these hands working with the same tool.

Namita: You're [both] using different strategies to create scenarios where that kind of possibility—of conversation and dialogue—can happen.

Cannupa: The reality is none of this stuff is for the institution. They benefit from it greatly, but it's not for them. Best-case scenario, they just get out of the way and allow this stuff to happen.

Edited and condensed from conversations between Namita Gupta Wiggers and Marie Watt and Cannupa Hanska Luger held July 6, July 7, and July 10, 2020.

Namita Gupta Wiggers thanks Cannupa Hanska Luger and Marie Watt for the time and conversations, Laura Caruso for editing, and John Lukavic for the opportunity to participate in this project.

do your best

Catalog Entries

Skywalker & Antipodes

When Marie Watt brings together different blankets in her works, she connects their related stories, histories, and memories. Her blanket columns also connect the sky and ground, and this relationship is intentional. In her work, sky is a mythic and magical space. When tall buildings are constructed in cities, they occupy this sky space as well as remaining rooted to the ground. These ideas are woven into her blanket columns but are even more clearly articulated in works like *Skywalker/Skyscraper (Babel)* (2012). "I moved from the Brooklyn neighborhood in Portland, Oregon, to the Brooklyn borough of New York City," Watt wrote in her artist statement for this work. "The conifers and totem poles of my Pacific Northwest upbringing have been replaced by skyscrapers and scaffolds. One interesting coincidence in moving to Brooklyn is that the border of Cobble Hill . . . and Gowanus (where I keep my studio), is where Iroquois ironworkers and their families settled in the 1950s, when most of Manhattan's skyscrapers were being built. These Iroquois were called 'skywalkers' due to their ability to work on the high steel without safety harnesses."[1] In this work, Watt asks us to think about how we as humans seek to reach the sky and the actions we take to achieve this dream.

Notes

[1] Marie Watt, Artist Statement, *Skywalker/Skyscraper*, October 2, 2012–October 27, 2012, PDX Contemporary Art, https://pdxcontemporaryart.com/skywalkerskyscraper.

Cat. 1 ***Skywalker/Skyscraper (Babel)*, 2012**

Cat. 2a ***Antipodes*** **(detail), 2020**

Cat. 2b ***Antipodes*** **(detail), 2020**

Blanket Stories

While Marie Watt creates much of her work through sewing circles where stories are shared in person, other works, such as *Blanket Stories: Confluence, Heirloom, and Tenth Mountain Division* (2013), are the result of asking people near and far to contribute treasured blankets that hold meaningful stories. These blankets and associated stories are brought together to form giant columns that reference the verticality of trees in her current home in the Pacific Northwest, story poles made by Indigenous carvers in that region, and the Seneca creation story of Sky Woman, whose plunge from the sky to earth connects the two realms. It takes many blankets to reach such heights, and by extension it takes many stories that people are willing to share.

Cat. 3 ***Blanket Stories: Confluence, Heirloom, and Tenth Mountain Division***, 2013

Cat. 4 ***Blanket Stories: Talking Stick, Works Progress, Steward** (**White Pine**)*, **2016**

Blanket Stories: Indian Territory, Round Dance, Grandmother, 2016

Trek (Pleiades)

Inspiration can come from near and far (and even the final frontiers of space). Marie Watt's recognition of the sources of inspiration adds a nuance to our understanding of collaboration. Those who came before us, the stories that are passed down through generations, and those who we come to know within our lives connect us to others in many ways. When these connections manifest themselves in an artwork, the artist engages in a form of collaboration.

In *Trek (Pleiades)* (2014), Watt acknowledges a variety of sources that she brought together from seemingly unconnected elements—geometric forms from basket designs by an unrecorded artist along the Pacific coast; the positioning of design elements to form the constellation Pleiades to represent a friendship she formed with Alma Nungarrayi Granites, a Warlpiri Aboriginal woman; and the starship Enterprise from the television series *Star Trek*—to blend together history which, in her words, "underscores [the] intersection of the historical and contemporary, the real and mythical."[1]

Each of these sources of inspiration connect in some way to storytelling. "Whether that is through astronomy and specific constellations or through science fiction, all are ways of explaining our existence, and for me, all are giving voice to material objects—baskets and blankets—that still have significance in our time," Watt says. "Stars are the source of so many stories and teachings for Indigenous people; but also when you look at Greek and Roman myths, a lot of those stories are referenced in astronomy and space science as well as our contemporary science fiction. I'm interested in revealing and understanding these connections between the ancient and modern and how the threads intersect."[2]

Notes

[1] "In Conversation with Marie Watt: A New Coyote Tale," *Art Journal* 76, no. 2 (Summer 2017), http://artjournal.collegeart.org/?p=9492.

[2] Ibid.

Cat. 6 ***Trek (Pleiades)*,** **2014**

Butterfly

When people sit down together in Marie Watt's sewing circles, they open up and share personal stories. They ask questions and give answers. While in residence at the Denver Art Museum in 2013, Watt had an opportunity to visit with two young Indigenous girls who told her about their experiences as powwow dancers. She asked them about what style dance they liked: one was a fancy shawl dancer and the other a jingle dress dancer. The fancy shawl dancer shared that when she dances she feels like she is floating like a butterfly, and the jingle dress dancer told the origin story of that style of dress and its ties to healing. Inspired by this conversation, Watt went home and later returned to the museum for a final sewing circle during the museum's annual powwow, where *Butterfly* (2015) began to take shape. This work blends the colorful frenzy of movement of the fancy shawl dance with a large field of shiny metal cones used on contemporary jingle dresses. While some of the cones came pre-rolled, Watt had flat discs available at the powwow on which collaborators were invited to write wishes before they were rolled into cones and incorporated into the work. The sharing of stories, feelings, and experiences, such as what Watt heard from those two young girls, leads to beautiful things. In this case, a captivating work of art that holds a community's collective wishes.

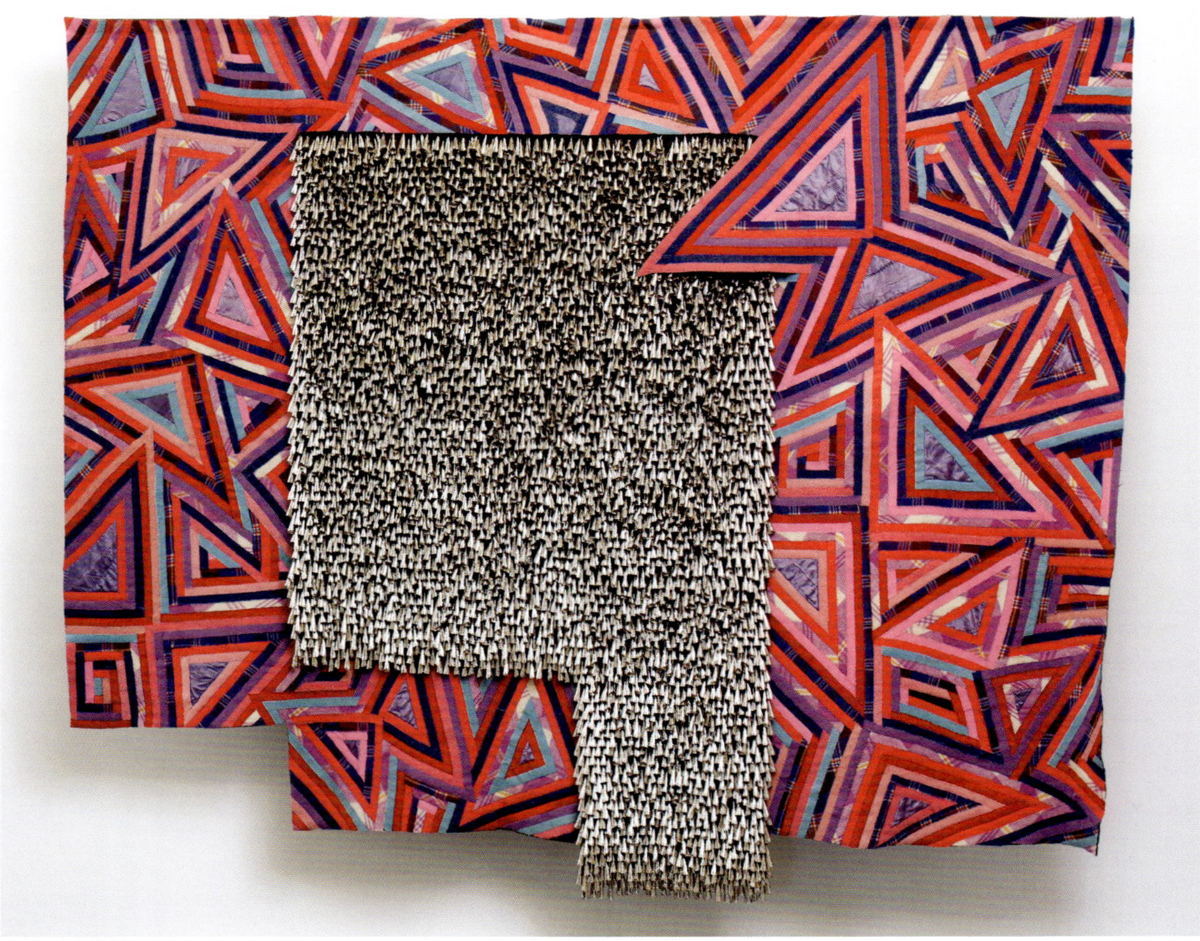

Cat. 7 ***Butterfly*, 2015**

Companion Species

When Marie Watt brings people together for sewing circles, such as she did with over 140 participants at the Block Museum at Northwestern University in 2017 when creating *Companion Species: Ferocious Mother and Canis Familiaris* (2017), conversations organically grow—sometimes riffing off a theme and at other times without any prompts. At the Block, conversations circulated around the theme of equity.[1] This sewing circle was part of the programming related to the exhibition, *If You Remember, I'll Remember*, which invited visitors to "reflect on the past while contemplating the present through works of art exploring themes of love, mourning, war, relocation, internment, resistance, and civil rights in 19th- and 20th-century North America."[2] Knowing the prompt that drove conversations along with the themes of the related exhibition, we can glean the deep meaning of the words stitched into this work-Equity, Love, Shelter, Solidarity, and Voice. What we see here are visual thoughts brought to life by many hands, unified by a single shared experience (the sewing circle) and diverse life experiences (what each person brought to the conversations).

Watt's repeated use of canine forms and subjects represents our symbiotic relationship with the natural world. She explains, "Seneca and Haudenosaunee (People of the Long House) people believe animals to be our First Teachers. From this viewpoint, it is interesting to consider how other cultures hold their relationship to animals, and by extension the greater natural world."[3] The series *Companion Species* "addresses the reciprocal relationship humans have with nature, and our responsibilities as responsive stewards."[4] If we all acknowledge we are companion species with other animals, would our actions towards them and the environment change? "[W]hen one is raised to think of animals as teachers and also as extensions of us—our relatives or relations—you're less likely to be able to separate how our actions affect the environment, animals, and the natural world," Watt says.[5]

Notes

[1] For more information on the program, including video, see "Marie Watt (2017)," The Block Museum of Art, https://blockmuseum.northwestern.edu/projects/marie-watt.html.

[2] *If You Remember, I'll Remember* exhibition description, February 4–June 8, 2017, The Block Museum of Art, https://blockmuseum.northwestern.edu/exhibitions/2017/if-you-remember,-ill-remember.html.

[3] Marie Watt, "Statement," *Companion Species*, August 31–September 30, 2017, PDX Contemporary Art, https://pdxcontemporaryart.com/companion-species.

[4] Ibid.

[5] "In Conversation with Marie Watt: A New Coyote Tale," *Art Journal* 76, no. 2 (Summer 2017), http://artjournal.collegeart.org/?p=9492.

Cat. 8 ***Companion Species (Canopy)*, 2016**

TRICKSTER
touchstone
HEALER
Ancient
milk
guide
negotiator
Home
VOICE
guardian
NEIGHBOR
ACCOMPLICE
TEACHER
WILD
legacy
CUSTODIAN
All My Relations
FEMINIST
Companion
MEDICINE
AGENCY
FRIEND
SHELTER
MAKER
EQUITY
community
HUMANITY
love
WANDERER

Cat. 9 ***Companion Species: Ferocious Mother and Canis Familiaris*, 2017**

Cat. 10 ***Companion Species: Assembly (Auntie)*, 2020**

Cat. 11 ***Companion Species: Assembly (Guardian Tree)*, 2020**

Cat. 12 ***Companion Species (Is this a pipe?)*, 2020**

Cat. 13 ***Companion Species (Radiant)*, 2017**

Every One

For the work *Every One* (2018), Luger began with a dataset with numbers of missing and murdered Indigenous women, girls, and transgender people in Canada. His intention was to make over 4,000 clay beads to interpret a photographic portrait titled *Sister* (2016) taken by First Nations artist Kali Spitzer, while standing in solidarity with those impacted by this crisis; however, as he began to make the beads, he began to think of the individuals and what they had been through. This rumination led him to think about the troubling connection between the missing and murdered and the increased number of laborers living and working in so-called "man camps" established by extractive industries such as lumber, oil, and gas companies.[1] Recognizing this connection led Luger to consider how his own use of these resources implicated him in this exploitation and violence. Each clay bead he formed alone added to the pain he felt. It was at this time that he created a short video to teach people how to make a clay bead for inclusion in the work he aimed to create. "These engagement techniques combine technology and handwork to mobilize and even heal the communities who are facing immeasurable trauma from colonization," says Luger.[2] It took the collective efforts of many to shoulder a bit of culpability in the processes that lead to such violence, the responsibility to bring these issues to light, and to work to realize this project, leading to shared healing.

Notes

[1] Avery Zingle, "Study Gendered Impacts of Resource Development: MMIWG Inquiry," *CBC News*, July 2, 2019, https://www.cbc.ca/news/canada/north/gendered-impacts-resource-extraction-mmiwg-1.5195580.

[2] Cannupa Hanska Luger, "Artist Statement," http://www.cannupahanska.com/artist-statement, accessed October 16, 2020.

Cat. 14 ***Every One*, 2018**

Emergent

In *Emergent* (2021) by Cannupa Hanska Luger, ash black (ceramic) bones emerge from the floor like those exposed in an eroded riverbank. In the 1800s, non-Native settlers and military forces undertook the intentional slaughter of bison herds, driving the species to near extinction. This deliberate, destructive act destroyed the economies, food sources, and lifeways of Plains Tribes. *Emergent* draws attention to how the loss of a single species has impacts on communities and the environment over 150 years later. "[T]he Great Plains are one of the most endangered environments; many Indigenous grasses are dependent on the buffalo to thrive and have therefore also degenerated," says Luger.[1] Ecosystems need balance to survive. A single disruption to a system destroys the entire system. Through this work, Luger brings attention to the bones of the past to raise awareness of our actions today, for our actions today will continue to impact the ecosystem 150 years from now.[2]

Notes

[1] Cannupa Hanska Luger, *(Be)Longing*, http://www.cannupahanska.com/belonging, accessed October 28, 2020.

[2] For more information on the ecological interdependence of bison, the soil, and grasses, see "The Great Plains," Carnegie Museum of Natural History, https://nsew.carnegiemnh.org/lakota-nation-of-the-plains/the-great-plains/, accessed September 3, 2020.

Cat. 15 ***Emergent*, 2021**

Sweet Land

Histories of place and colonial impacts are central as well to the *Sweet Land Opera* (2020), which Cannupa Hanska Luger codirected (he was also one of two costume designers). In this opera, narratives of violence and erasure replace the popular tales of early colonization, the rise of the United States, and its expansion into the West. The Industry, an independent, artist-driven opera company in Los Angeles, describes the plot and structure of *Sweet Land*: "The Arrivals wash up on the shore. They make contact with another civilization they call 'the Hosts.' And from there, the story splinters, following diverging perspectives. Starting as a procession through the LA State Historic Park, *Sweet Land* becomes an opera that erases itself."[1] Of his role in sharing these often silenced histories, Luger acknowledges, "I didn't do this alone, I did it on the shoulders of giants with a pile of bones under each foot."[2] His collaborators included other producers, directors, designers, composers, and performers who brought this opera to life, making it, at once, a collaboration with others but also a collaboration with the land, exposing the incomplete narratives too often told of colonial experiences.

Notes

[1] *Sweet Land*, February 29–March 22, 2020, The Industry, https://theindustryla.org/projects/sweet-land/.

[2] Cannupa Hanska Luger, quoted in Kathy Hereford, "Cannupa Hanska Luger Wins Museum of Arts and Design's Burke Prize," LiveLearnNona, November 8, 2018, http://www.livelearnnona.com/2018/11/08/cannupa-hanska-luger-wins-museum-of-arts-and-designs-burke-prize/.

Sweet Land Opera, 2020

Cats. 16–18 ***Coyote, Wiindigo,* and *Coyote***
from *Sweet Land Opera*, 2020

Sweet Land Opera, 2020

Nature, This Is Not A Snake, The One Who Checks, and The One Who Balances

When these four works, *Nature* (2015), *This Is Not A Snake* (2017), *The One Who Checks* (2018), and *The One Who Balances* (2018), are brought together, Luger effectively models how we might rise up to act against forces, corporations, and attitudes that impact the world around us. He has exhibited the last three together in the past, but in the present exhibition the scene is complete with the addition of *Nature*. Together, we see the warrior twins, figures in Mandan oral stories, protecting nature from environmental disaster through "industrial exploitation of Indigenous land and its minerals."[1] The newly realized *Return of the Warrior Twins*, a large-scale, photographic living mural video loop installation created by Luger in collaboration with Chip Thomas (A Luta Continua) and based on a mural installation by Thomas for Luger's exhibition *Lazy Stitch, UCCS GOCA* (2018), pictures the Warrior Twin characters witnessing and responding to the destruction of the Navajo Generating Station in Arizona, as documented by Ramble Creative. While the twins tell us to act to protect nature, Luger acknowledges that nature is endless. "No matter how much you take and take and take, they are just going to keep going . . . They are a part of everything . . . They are open and protected. Animal and human. Not existing in any certain time or place other than right now," he says.[2]

Notes

[1] Cannupa Hanska Luger, *This is Not a Snake*, http://www.cannupahanska.com/this-is-not-a-snake, accessed October 28, 2020.

[2] Cannupa Hanska Luger, *Nature*, http://www.cannupahanska.com/nature-nurture-2015/qhfpusigzo7uit5fv40jprb4cmach5, accessed October 28, 2020.

Cat. 20 ***Nature*****, 2015**

Cats. 21–23 ***One Who Checks, This is Not a Snake, One Who Balances,*** 2018

Cat. 24 ***Return of the Warrior Twins*, 2021**

Mirror Shield

Cannupa Hanska Luger's work often takes on specific social issues, and some, like the *Mirror Shield Project* (2016), are not only site specific but also have a sense of contemporary urgency. This work was a collaborative performance and political act created to support and make visible the Indigenous water protectors in their standoff with militarized police during the attempted construction of the Dakota Access Pipeline. Through an online call for collaborators and planned workshops, a large number of people from across the country created mirrored, shield-like forms for the water protectors. Holding these up while on the front lines of the standoff, the water protectors forced the police officers to see their own reflection in the mirrored surfaces, reflecting their own humanity back at them. These shields were also used in a performance, *Mirror Shield Project: Water Serpent Action* (2016), at the Oceti Sakowin camp near Standing Rock, which was organized in collaboration with and filmed from above by a drone-mounted camera by Anishinabe contemporary artist Rory Wakemup. Speaking of his work more generally, Luger explains that it "has become inherently social and requires engagement. I aim to craft richly symbolic objects, but moreover, I want to lay groundwork, to establish connections, to mobilize action. I want to make real impact and this motivation increasingly pulls me out of the studio and into the world, to collectively challenge the systemic conditions of capitalism while claiming space for urgent and emergent Indigenous narratives."[1] The *Mirror Shield Project* continues to bring visibility not only to the problematic militarization of the police but also to the necessity of and right to clean water and land and treaty rights. Here the collaborative process of artmaking led to collective social action. By bringing attention to an issue and engaging people through art, Luger and his collaborators established understanding and responsibility.

Notes

[1] Cannupa Hanska Luger, *Artist Statement*, http://www.cannupahanska.com/artist-statement, accessed October 28, 2020.

Cats. 25–27 ***Mirror Shield Project*, 2016**

Each/ Other

As part of the exhibition *Each/Other*, Marie Watt and Cannupa Hanska Luger have merged their practices to create a participatory sculpture, also titled *Each/Other* (2021). Both artists were awarded the Stelo Arts & Culture Foundation c3:core residency (2020–21), which supported the artists coming together with their families at Camp Colton in Oregon for two sessions of concept building and construction of this large-scale, she-wolf sculpture. The two artists filmed a video call for submissions for this new work. Instructing viewers to take a bandana-sized square of fabric, fold it once into a triangle, embroider a word, message, or visual sentiment that is meaningful to them during this time of the COVID-19 pandemic, and mail their creation to the artists. The triangles of fabric were then stitched together into a giant animal pelt by the Portland Garment Factory, a woman-owned and environmentally conscious fabrication studio. This pelt was then draped over a steel armature of the body constructed by Neal Fegan from the artists' design. Onsite Watt and Luger then welded the head, hand-stitched the bandana submissions onto the she-wolf's body, and embedded ceramic eyes, bringing this monumental canine figure to life.

This collaborative artwork is, as both Watt and Luger described in conversations during the work's planning, "the echo of collaborative handwork, bringing audiences into a tactile encounter with critically relevant issues of protection, shelter, reciprocity, sustenance, exchange, power, stewardship, wildness, homelessness, kinship, vulnerability, and ferocity."[1] And when installed in a gallery or museum, its shelter-like form becomes a place for gathering, healing, and sharing (pending COVID protocols, of course). When engaging with this work, the artists ask viewers to contemplate "how acts of collaboration may help heal broken bonds with the environment and with each other."[2]

Notes

[1] "Participate in a monumental artwork: *Each/ Other: Marie Watt & Cannupa Hanska Luger*," http://cannupahanska.com/eachother, accessed October 28, 2020.

[2] Ibid.

Next Page: Cat. 28 ***Each/Other*, 2021**

Each/Other, 2021

Each/Other, 2021

Each/Other, 2021

Each/Other, 2021

KOKORO WA
II DESU.
Save Our
Forests
MAKE
We are
Hitched

WAVES
RECLAIM

Artist & Contributor Biographies

Marie Watt is an American artist and citizen of the Seneca Nation with German-Scot ancestry. Her interdisciplinary work draws from history, biography, Iroquois protofeminism, and Indigenous teachings; in it, she explores the intersection of history, community, and storytelling. Through collaborative actions she instigates multigenerational and cross-disciplinary conversations that might create a lens and conversation for understanding connectedness to place, one another, and the universe. Watt holds an MFA in painting and printmaking from Yale University; she also has degrees from Willamette University and the Institute of American Indian Arts; and in 2016, she was awarded an honorary doctorate from Willamette University. She has received fellowships from Anonymous Was a Woman, the Joan Mitchell Foundation, the Harpo Foundation, The Ford Family Foundation, and the Native Arts and Culture Foundation. Watt serves on the board for VoCA (Voices in Contemporary Art) and on the Native Advisory Committee at the Portland Art Museum. In 2020, she became a member of the Board of Trustees at the Portland Art Museum. Selected collections include the Denver Art Museum, the Seattle Art Museum, the Whitney Museum of American Art, Crystal Bridges Museum, the Smithsonian National Museum of the American Indian, the National Gallery of Canada, the Metropolitan Museum of Art, the Albright-Knox Art Gallery, the Peabody Essex Museum, the Eiteljorg Museum of American Indians and Western Art, and the Portland Art Museum.

Cannupa Hanska Luger is a New Mexico-based multidisciplinary artist who uses social collaboration in response to timely and site-specific issues. Raised on the Standing Rock Reservation in North Dakota, he is of Mandan, Hidatsa, Arikara, Lakota, and European descent. Luger produces multipronged projects that take many forms—through monumental installations that incorporate ceramics, video, sound, fiber, steel, and repurposed materials, interweaving performance and political action to communicate stories about twenty-first-century Indigeneity. Luger is a recipient of a 2021 United States Artists award, a 2020 Creative Capital Fellow, a 2020 Smithsonian Artist Research Fellow, the recipient of the 2020 A Blade Of Grass Artist Fellowship for Socially Engaged Art, and the recipient of the Center For Crafts inaugural Craft Research Fund Artist Fellowship for 2020. He is the recipient of a 2019 Joan Mitchell Foundation Painters & Sculptors Grant, a 2019 Yerba Buena Center for the Arts Honoree, and the recipient of the Museum of Arts and Design's 2018 inaugural Burke Prize. Luger has exhibited internationally in venues such as the Gardiner Museum, Washington Project for the Arts, Art Mûr, Crystal Bridges Museum of American Art, and the National Center for Civil and Human Rights, among others. He lectures, participates in residencies and large-scale projects around the globe, and his work is in many public collections. Luger holds a BFA in studio arts from the Institute of American Indian Arts.

Contributors

John P. Lukavic is the Andrew W. Mellon Curator of Native Arts at the Denver Art Museum, where he conducts and presents scholarly research, develops exhibitions, collects Native arts, and disseminates knowledge of the museum's American Indian, African, and Oceanic collections. He has curated several exhibitions, including *Each/Other: Marie Watt and Cannupa Hanska Luger* (2021), *Jeffrey Gibson: Like a Hammer* (2018), *Super Indian: Fritz Scholder, 1967–1980* (2015), and *Revolt 1680/2180: Virgil Ortiz* (2015), and was the lead curator for *Stampede: Animals in Art* (2017). Lukavic received his PhD in Cultural Anthropology at the University of Oklahoma (2012) and his MA in Museum Science from Texas Tech University (1999). In 2018, he was selected for the Getty Leadership Institute at Claremont Graduate University's NextGen program for emerging top talent in the museum field. In 2019, he received an Award for Excellence from the Association of Art Museum Curators for his essay in the *Jeffrey Gibson: Like a Hammer* exhibition catalog. He serves on the Board of Directors for the Native American Art Studies Association as well as for the Denver Indian Center, Inc.

Jami Powell is the Hood Museum's first associate curator of Native American art and was recently appointed as a lecturer in Native American Studies at Dartmouth. Powell is a citizen of the Osage Nation and has a PhD in anthropology from the University of North Carolina at Chapel Hill. Prior to working at the Hood, she was a faculty lecturer at Tufts University. She has also worked as a research assistant at the Denver Museum of Nature and Science, was a Mellon Fellow at the Peabody Essex Museum, and has conducted research projects at the Field Museum of Natural History and the Denver Art Museum. Powell's research examines the representations of Indigenous peoples in museums as well as the interventions contemporary Indigenous artists make through creative acts of self-representation. Powell is currently working on a book manuscript titled *Stitching an Osage Future: Aesthetic Resistance and Self-Representation*. She has also published articles in *Museum Anthropology, Panorama, Museum Management and Curatorship* and is an editorial advisor for *First American Art Magazine*. Powell has served on curatorial advisory boards for the Philadelphia Museum of Art, Yale University Art Gallery, and the Smithsonian Museum of American Art. She is a recipient of the 2020 New Leadership Award from ArtTable, the foremost professional organization dedicated to advancing the leadership of women in the visual arts.

Namita Gupta Wiggers is an educator, curator, and writer based in Portland, OR. She is the Director of the MA in Critical Craft Studies at Warren Wilson College, North Carolina, the first low-residency graduate program to focus on this field. She is the Director and Co-Founder of Critical Craft Forum. From 2014 to 2017, Wiggers lectured, juried, and curated exhibitions, conducted research, and taught workshops across the United States and in Denmark, France, New Zealand, Norway, South Africa, South Korea, and Sweden. During this time, she taught in the MFA Applied Craft + Design, coadministered by Oregon College of Art + Craft and Pacific Northwest College of Art, at Portland State University, and at Oregon College of Art + Craft. From 2004 to 2014, she served as the Director and Chief Curator at the Museum of Contemporary Craft in Portland, OR. She contributes to online and print journals and books and served on the Editorial Board of *Garland* and *Norwegian Crafts*, and the Editorial Advisory Board of *The Journal of Modern Craft*. Her current projects include serving as the inaugural Writer-in-Residence, Center for Art Research, University of Oregon and as a member of the Creative Time Think Tank; a forthcoming craft anthology; and an ongoing research project with Benjamin Lignel on gender and adornment. She serves on the Board of Trustees for Haystack Mountain School of Crafts.

WHOSE
LAND
R U
ON

Exhibition Checklist

Marie Watt (Seneca and German-Scots, born 1967)

Cat. 1
***Skywalker/ Skyscraper* (*Babel*), 2012**
Reclaimed wool blankets and steel
96 × 20 × 22 in.
Lent by Brian A. Tschumper

Cat. 2a & 2b
***Antipodes*, 2020**
Vintage Venetian glass beads, thread, cotton twill tape, industrial felt, and steel
Skywalker: 54 × 63¼ × ¼ in.
Skyscraper: 53½ × 59½ × ¼ in.
Courtesy of the artist, Marc Straus Gallery, PDX Contemporary Art, and Greg Kucera Gallery

Cat. 3
***Blanket Stories: Confluence, Heirloom, and Tenth Mountain Division*, 2013**
Wool and cotton blankets and reclaimed cedar
243½ × 24 × 24 in.
Denver Art Museum: Native Arts acquisition funds, 2013.75

Cat. 4
***Blanket Stories: Talking Stick, Works Progress, Steward* (*White Pine*), 2016**
Salvaged white pine from High Desert Museum property
144 × 11¼ × 11¼ in.
Lent by Firoz and Najma Lalji

Cat. 5
Blanket Stories: Great Grandmother, Pandemic, Daybreak, 2021
Blankets, manilla tags, and cedar base
10 ft. × 27 in. × 27 in.
Courtesy of the artist

Cat. 6
***Trek* (*Pleiades*), 2014**
Reclaimed wool blankets, satin binding, embroidery floss, and thread
74 × 123½ in.
Tia Collection, Santa Fe, NM

Cat. 7
***Butterfly*, 2015**
Reclaimed wool blankets, satin binding, thread, cotton twill tape, and tin jingles
96 × 126 in.
Denver Art Museum: Funds from Loren G. Lipson, M.D., Vicki and Kent Logan, with additional funds from Brian Tschumper, Nancy Benson, Jan and Mike Tansey, and JoAnn and Bob Balzer, 2016.1

Cat. 8
***Companion Species (Canopy)*, 2016**
Reclaimed wool blankets, thread, and embroidery floss
99 × 94 in. (part A), 96 × 156 in. (part B)
Loan from the Eiteljorg Museum of American Indians and Western Art, Indianapolis, Indiana, USA

Cat. 9
***Companion Species: Ferocious Mother and Canis Familiaris*, 2017**
Reclaimed wool blankets, thread, and embroidery floss
108 × 217¾in.
Portland Art Museum

Cat. 10 & 11
***Companion Species: Assembly (Auntie) / Companion Species: Assembly (Guardian Tree)*, 2020**
Reclaimed wool blankets, embroidery floss, thread, cotton twill, tape, and tin jingles
121½ × 90 in; 118¼ × 92 in.
Tia Collection, Santa Fe, NM, Courtesy of Marc Straus Gallery, New York

Cat.12
***Companion Species (Is this a pipe?)*, 2020**
Reclaimed wool blankets, embroidery floss, and thread
55½ × 148 in.
Hood Museum of Art, Dartmouth: Purchased through the Miriam H. and S. Sidney Stoneman Acquisition Fund and the Acquisition and Preservation of Native American Art Fund; 2021.4

Cat. 13
***Companion Species (Radiant)*, 2017**
Crystal with western maple base
8 × 16 × 27 in.
Made in collaboration with Jeff Mack, Lead Gaffer at the Corning Museum of Glass and the Rockwell Museum
Courtesy of the artist, Marc Straus Gallery, PDX Contemporary Art, and Greg Kucera Gallery

Cannupa Hanska Luger (Mandan, Hidatsa, Arikara, Lakota, and European, born 1979)

Cat. 14
***Every One*, 2018**
Ceramic and collaboration
144 × 144 × 2 in.
Courtesy of the artist

Cat. 15
***Emergent*, 2021**
Ceramic
24 × 84 × 60 in.
Courtesy of the artist

Cat. 16
***Coyote*, 2020**
Mixed media
6½ ft. × 12 in. × 8 in. (approximate)
Courtesy of the artist

Cat. 17
***Wiindigo*, 2020**
Mixed media
6½ ft. × 12 in. × 8 in. (approximate)
Courtesy of the artist

Cat. 18
***Coyote*, 2020**
Mixed media
6½ ft. × 12 in. × 8 in. (approximate)
Courtesy of the artist

Cat. 19
***Bone*, 2020**
Mixed media
6½ ft. × 12 in. × 8 in. (approximate)
Courtesy of the artist

Cat. 20
***Nature,* 2016**
Clay, steel, and wool
103 × 48 × 40 in.
Gift from Vicki and Kent Logan to the Collection of the Denver Art Museum, 2016.31

Cat. 21
***The One Who Checks,* 2018**
Ceramic, riot gear, afghan, wool surplus industrial felt, and beads
6½ ft. × 12 in. × 8 in. (approximate)
Beadwork by Kathy Elkwoman Whitman
Courtesy of the artist

Cat. 22
***This Is Not A Snake,* 2017–20**
Ceramic, fiber, steel, oil drums, ammunition cans, trash, and found objects
78 × 36 × 600 in.
Courtesy of the artist

Cat. 23
***The One Who Balances,* 2018**
Ceramic, riot gear, afghan, wool surplus industrial felt, and beads
6½ ft. × 12 in. × 8 in. (approximate)
Beadwork by Kathy Elkwoman Whitman
Courtesy of the artist

Cat. 24
***Return Of The Warrior Twins,* 2021**
In collaboration with Chip Thomas (A Luta Contnua) & Ramble Creative
Single channel video
Approximately 1 min. loop
Courtesy of the artist

Cat. 25
***Mirror Shields,* 2016**
Masonite, mirror adhesive foil, paracord, and social collaboration
48 × 16 in.
Courtesy of the artist

Cat. 26
Onsite field recording, Standing Rock, ND, September 2016
Courtesy of the artist

Cat. 27
Still from *River (The Water Serpent)*, 2016
Mirror Shield Project concept by Cannupa Hanska Luger
Water serpent performance organization and drone operation by Rory Wakemup
Film editing by Dylan McLaughlin
Field recording and sound mastering by Ginger Dunnill
Audio: Oceti Sakowin main camp announcer, prayer song
Courtesy of the artist

Marie Watt and Cannupa Hanska Luger

Cat. 28
***Each/Other*, 2020–21**
Steel, wool, bandanas, and embroidery thread
12 × 20 × 9 ft. (approximately)
Courtesy of the artists

Image Credits

Pages 4, 8, 13, 14, 25 (fig. 12), 27-8, 38, 77, 80-6, 92 Photographs by Kevin McConnell

Pages 10 (fig. 1), 36, 51 & 69 Photographs by Christina Jackson

Page 10 (fig. 2) Photograph by Robert Mesa

Page 11 (fig. 3) Rob Wilson Photography

Page 11 (fig. 4) & p. 31 Photograph by Jessica Smolinski, courtesy of Marie Watt Studio

Page 19 (fig. 2) Photograph by Aaron Johanson

Pages 20 (fig. 3) & 61 Marie Walsh Sharpe Gallery of Contemporary Art at Ent Center for the Arts, UCCS

Page 21 (fig. 4) Courtesy of the Peabody Essex Museum, Salem, MA. Photography by Kathy Tarantola

Page 22 (figs. 5 & 6) Courtesy Gina Adams artist and Edie Fuertas photography

Page 22 (fig. 7) Kate Russell Photography

Pages 23 (fig. 8) Photograph by Brian Wagner. Courtesy the artist and Garth Greenan Gallery, New York

Page 23 (fig. 9) Courtesy the artist

Page 23 (fig. 10) © Cara Romero. All rights reserved

Page 25 (fig. 11) Photograph by Tewa Women United

Pages 34-35 Marie Watt and Cannupa Hanska Luger at Camp Colton, Oregon, August 2020. Photograph by Barbara Soulé

Pages 41 & 49 Courtesy of PDX Contemporary Art

Pages 42-3 & 58-9 Courtesy of Marc Straus Gallery

Page 46 Courtesy of Greg Kucera Gallery

Page 47 Courtesy of Marc Straus Gallery. *Blanket Stories: Indian Territories, Round Dance, Grandmother* (2016), collection of Autry Museum of the American West, Los Angeles, photographed at Kasmin Gallery, New York

Page 63-5 Casey Kringlen for The Industry

Page 80 Marie Watt, photograph by Sam Gehrke

Page 81 Cannupa Hanska Luger, photograph by Brendan George Ko, 2019

Published on the occasion of ***Each/Other: Marie Watt and Cannupa Hanska Luger***

Organized by the Denver Art Museum
May 23, 2021–August 22, 2021

Michael C. Carlos Museum, Emory University, Atlanta, Georgia
September 25, 2021–December 12, 2021

Peabody Essex Museum, Salem, Massachusetts
January 29, 2022–May 8, 2022

This exhibition is made possible with generous support from the National Endowment for the Arts, the Robert Lehman Foundation, the donors to the Annual Fund Leadership Campaign, Stelo, Native Arts and Culture Foundation, Osage Nation Foundation, and the residents who support the Scientific and Cultural Facilities District (SCFD).

Copyright © 2021 Denver Art Museum

Denver Art Museum
100 West 14th Avenue Parkway
Denver, CO 80204
denverartmuseum.org

Distributed by University of Washington Press
4333 Brooklyn Avenue NE
Seattle, WA 98105
uwapress.uw.edu

All rights reserved. This book may not be reproduced, in whole or in part, including illustrations, in any form or by any means electronic or mechanical, including photocopy, recording, or other information storage and retrieval systems, without written permission the publisher.

ISBN 978-1-945483-09-7
Library of Congress Cataloging-in-Publication Data
Names: Lukavic, John. | Powell, Jami C. | Wiggers, Namita Gupta, interviewer. | Denver Art Museum, organizer, host institution. | Michael C. Carlos Museum, host institution. | Peabody Essex Museum, host institution.
Title: Each/Other : Marie Watt and Cannupa Hanska Luger.
Other titles: Each/Other (Denver Art Museum) | Each Other
Description: Denver, CO : Denver Art Museum, [2021] | "Published on the occasion of Each/Other: Marie Watt and Cannupa Hanska Luger, curated by John P. Lukavic, Andrew W. Mellon Curator of Native Arts"--Colophon. | Includes bibliographical references. | Summary: "Exhibition catalog on the work of Marie Watt and Cannupa Hanska Luger with an interview with the artists"-- Provided by publisher.
Identifiers: LCCN 2021010076 | ISBN 9781945483097 (hardback)
Subjects: LCSH: Watt, Marie, 1967---Exhibitions. | Luger, Cannupa Hanska, 1979---Exhibitions. | Artists and community--United States--Exhibitions.
Classification: LCC N6537.W297 A4 2021 | DDC 700.1/03--dc23
LC record available at https://lccn.loc.gov/2021010076

Cover: Marie Watt, *Trek (Pleiades)* (detail), cat. 6, and Cannupa Hanska Luger, *Every One* (detail), cat. 14

Editing and project management by Laura Caruso, Valerie Hellstein, and Kati Woock
Design: Chindo Nkenke-Smith, OC Studio
Printed and bound in Canada by Friesens

MÉLANIE WENGER

MARIE-CLAUDE

ACTES SUD | PRIX HSBC POUR LA PHOTOGRAPHIE

Pour défendre une cause,
un avocat met sa robe.
La femme ... l'enlève.

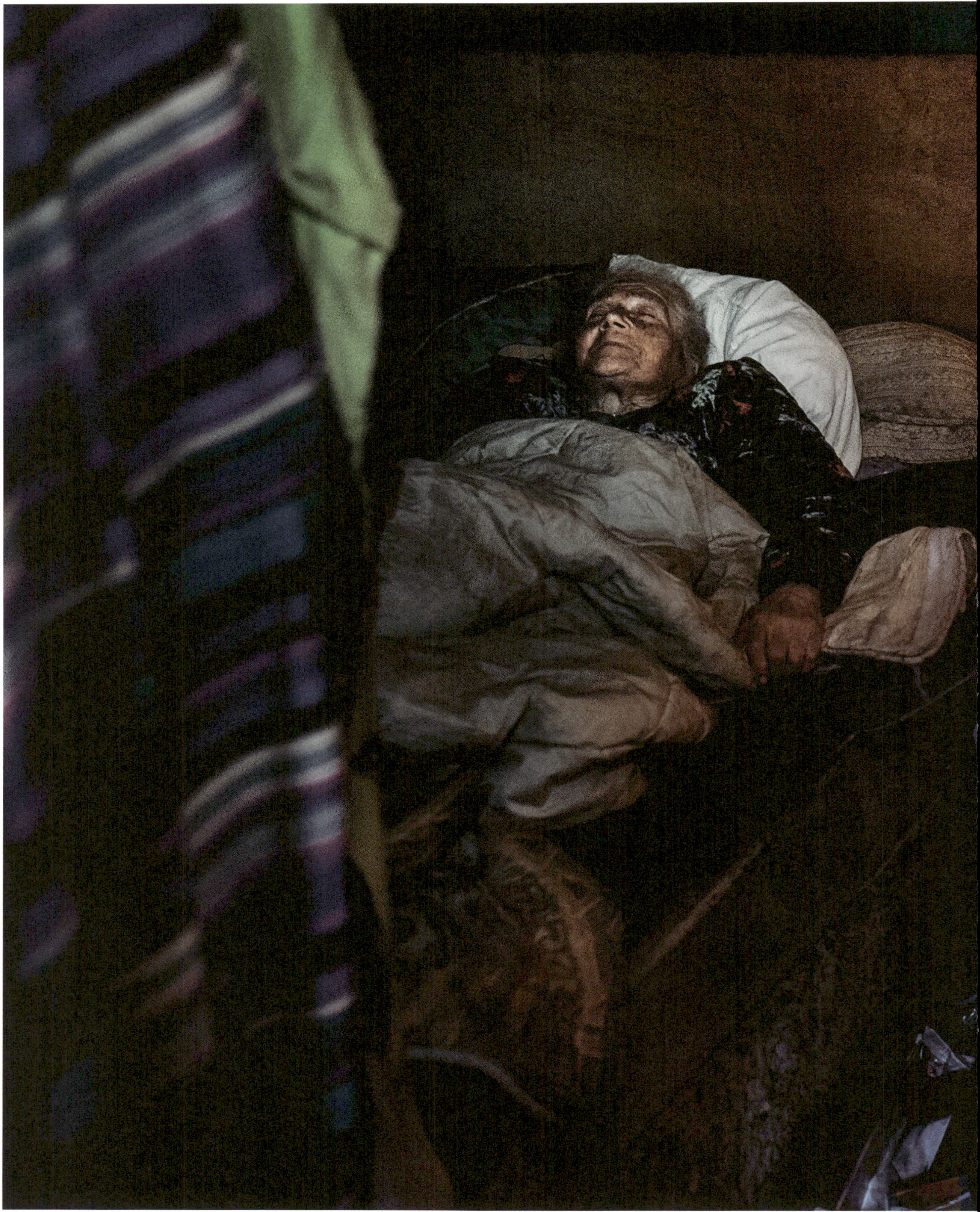

VIEUX MOULIN
FRUIT

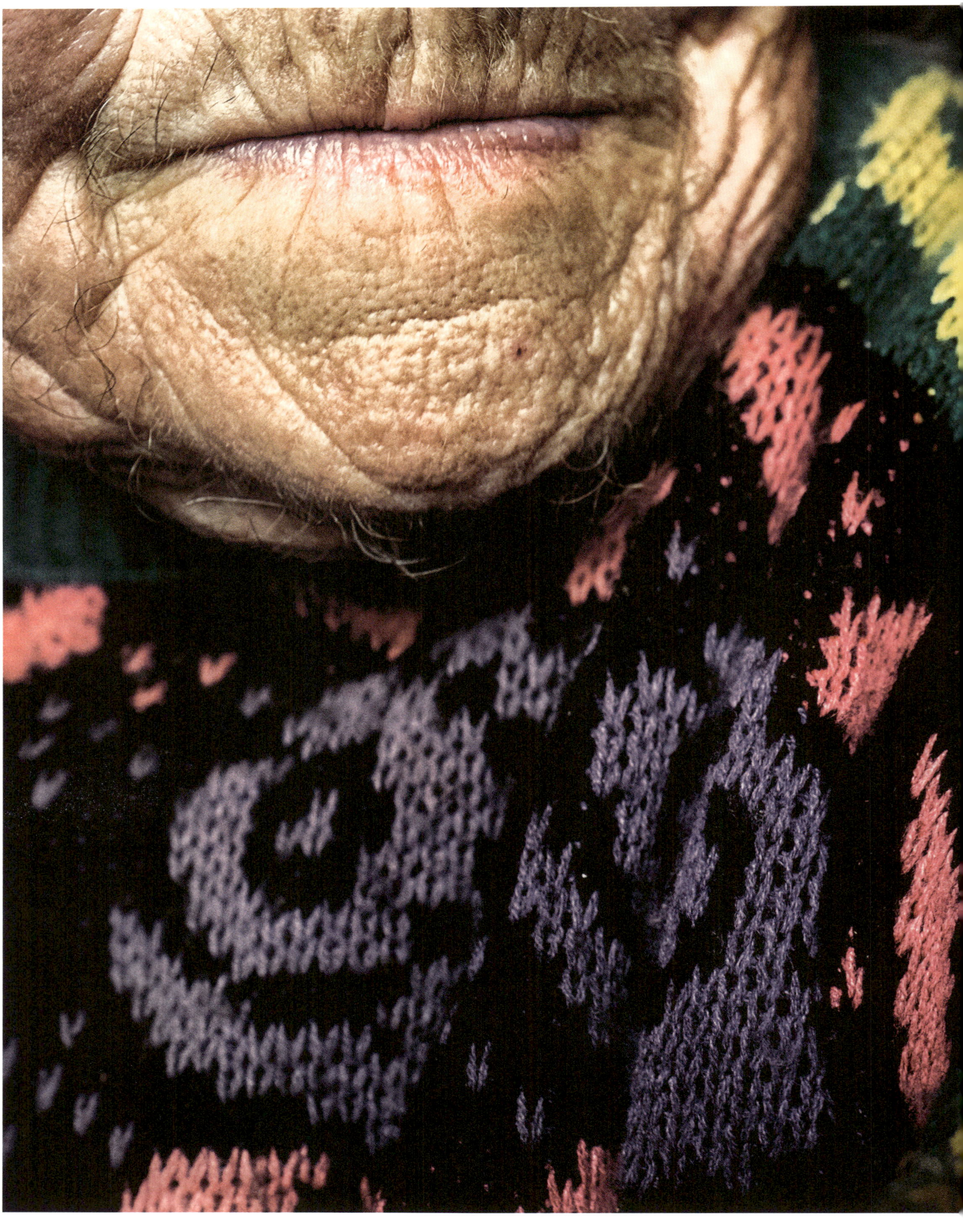

Pour défendre une cause,
un avocat met sa robe.
La femme... l'enlève.

MARIE-CLAUDE // LA DAME AUX POUPÉES

CONTE PHOTOGRAPHIQUE DE MÉLANIE WENGER

J'ai craint qu'elle ne soit plus là. Qu'elle nous ait quittés. Peut-être n'a-t-elle pas perdu la tête autant qu'elle voudrait me le faire croire. Peut-être veut-elle simplement me raconter une autre vie. Celle qu'elle aurait voulu avoir, vivre. Tout ce dont elle a rêvé. Elle m'en parle, chaque jour. Son histoire change, toujours. Chaque fois. Entre la vérité, ce qu'elle aurait voulu vivre, ce qu'elle a interprété, ses histoires évoluent, varient, changent. Elle est ces histoires, c'est tout ce qui importe. Qu'elles soient vraies n'est pas la question. Mais en tant que photographe, ce qui importe est de savoir ce que l'on va voir, ou ne jamais voir. Ces histoires, faut-il les rêver ? Faut-il les créer ? Faut-il les oublier ?
Ces belles histoires, comme quand elle prenait son bain dans son bateau. Celle où elle teignait ses cheveux seule dans le seau. Celle où le chat dormait dans son lit, propre. Faut-il les attendre ? Peut-être ne vont-elles jamais se produire. Se reproduire ? Celles qu'elle-même attend peut-être toujours... Attend-elle autant que moi que quelque chose se passe ?

Je suis tombée sur Marie-Claude en rentrant de Libye, au bout d'un chemin sans issue dans un lieu-dit perdu des monts d'Arrée bretons en avril 2014. "Tu viens voir mes poupées ?" me lança-t-elle, en m'indiquant mon chemin. Dans sa maison de bric et de broc, je découvre un monde que je ne quitterai plus. Qui me hante et m'emplit de joie à la fois. Cette vieille dame de soixante-quinze ans, cette ancienne bûcheronne, pêcheuse et couturière attachante et effrayante me touche, me parle de moi, de ma mère, de ce que je suis aujourd'hui et de ce que je crains de devenir. Elle interroge la rébellion qui est en moi et qui ne veut pas s'éteindre. Elle me montre que tout persiste et que rien ne s'éteint. Comme ma grand-mère, vieille mais rebelle. Elle n'a jamais eu d'enfants et me fascine pour cela, moi qui en ai perdu ou chassé, qui résiste (peut-être) à l'appel de la féminité. Est-elle femme ? Est-elle enfant ? Est-elle folle ? Suis-je folle ? Autour d'elle, tous la fuient. Sa particularité, son caractère. Elle n'a jamais suivi les rails, les règles de la communauté. Une marginale. Un peu comme moi, parfois. Un peu comme nous tous en fait, sauf que certains n'osent pas.

À dix-huit ans, elle épouse Albert, dix-sept ans de plus qu'elle. Elle emménage dans la maison de son mari, qu'elle ne quittera plus jamais. Ils sont sans le sou, elle vole ses parents, sa sœur, pour lui. Il la bat, la séquestre et la prive de tout contact extérieur. À sa mort en 1999, elle se retrouve seule avec une maigre retraite. Marie-Claude est une accumulatrice compulsive, solitaire, sénile, mais elle a un caractère bien trempé. Elle n'a pas de famille mais un bon millier de poupées. Elle a perdu la mémoire, une bonne partie de sa tête, mais elle est fascinante. Tous les trois mois, je prends ma voiture, de Bruxelles ou d'ailleurs, et vais la voir en Bretagne. Je passe plusieurs jours avec elle, la photographie. Elle ne se souvient parfois plus de moi, elle m'ouvre sa maison. À l'aide de petits papiers et de photos, je lui remémore chaque fois qui je suis et ce que nous faisons ensemble.

Mais que fait-elle toute la sainte journée ? Je ne l'ai vue que se balader, chercher des racines, se perdre. Pisser dans le café, manger des crêpes n'importe quand... Que fait-elle ? Elle-même ne veut pas répondre à cette question. Comme si je devais rester dans le coin pour le savoir. Ou peut-être aussi pour qu'elle arrête de le savoir. Suis-je simplement celle qui arrive dans sa vie ? Ne puis-je donc jamais être celle qui observe ? Suis-je arrivée trop tard ? Vit-elle ces histoires qu'elle me raconte, assise dans son salon ? Ou en vit-elle d'autres ? Se souvient-elle parfois ? Sait-elle qui elle est, qui elle fut ; ce qu'elle est devenue ? Ermite, sorcière, vieille folle, korrigan ou petite grand-mère. La voici.

MARIE-CLAUDE – THE DOLL LADY

PHOTOGRAPHIC TALE OF MÉLANIE WENGER

I met Marie-Claude in the dead end of a country road in the Monts d'Arrée, Brittany, France, in April 2014. "Do you want to see my dolls?," she offered, waving to help me find my way back. In her home, filled with mountains of junk, I discovered a world I will never leave. It haunts me and fills me with joy at the same time. This seventy-five-year-old lady, woodcutter, fisherwoman and seamstress, is endearing and frightening at the same time. She moves me, waking parts of me. She looks a little bit like my mother sometimes, and a lot like me.

At eighteen years old, she married Albert, seventeen years older than her. She moved to his house, two kilometres away, with his mother. He beat her, kept her inside, deprived her of any contact with the world, including her family, for thirty years. When he died, in 1999, she found herself alone with a very tiny pension of 600 euros a month, in a little house with no friends and no family. Marie-Claude still has some trauma from this life. She accumulates things, compulsively, feels lonely a lot, is losing her mind, her memory and has a very strong temper. No children, no family, no trips, no car. Dementia has taken a large part of her mind but she is fascinating. She never takes a shower, does not have a bathroom and hates watching television. For three years now I have been spending hours, day and night, at her place. Taking pictures. It is sometimes disgusting and almost always freezing and smelly, but also very interesting. At first she agreed to my presence. Now she does not always remember me, but always opens her door, kisses me, calls me "ma chérie". She has the same way to speak to me, and is a little bit more confident and open every time, as if something was still happening behind the curtains of memory. Every time I bring pictures of her I made, I write notes to her that I leave all around her home. Despite the fact that she always forgets to read, or reads and then just forgets, sometimes, when I come, and I wrote I would come, somewhere, on white paper, the door is open when I arrive, and she is ready.

I feared she would not be here anymore. That she had left us. Maybe she has not lost her mind as much as she would like me to believe. Maybe she simply wants to tell me about another life. The one she would have had. All she has dreamt of. She talks about it, every day. Her story changes, all the time. Every time. Between the truth, what she would have wanted to live, her stories are changing, evolving, mutating. All that matters is that these stories are hers, her. Whether they are true is not the point. Should you dream it? Should you create it? Should you forget it? These beautiful stories, where she would take her bath in her little fishing boat. Where she dyed her hair alone in a bucket. Where the cat had his own bottle to drink milk. Should you wait for it?

What is she doing all bloody day ? I have seen her walk, look for tree roots, get lost, in the trees … Pee in the coffee during the night, eat crêpes in the middle of the afternoon. … Hermit, witch, old crazy woman, gnome or just a grandma. Here she is.

Over three years I saw her grow old, loose her short-term memory more and more, forget to heat, wash, eat ...
Marie-Claude is about this slice of old age, a single woman's fight against solitude and dementia, eating her, slowly.
A fight between shadows and light until the end, before darkness takes it all.

LÉGENDES / *CAPTIONS*

p. 8-9
Décembre sur la montagne, pendant une semaine la brume est restée. Enfin nous partons nous balader, doucement. La montée est rude, elle a du mal à respirer.
December on the mountain; for a whole week the fog did not let up. Finally we can go for a walk, slowly. The hike is rough; she is having trouble breathing.

p. 10-11
Décembre. Sur la route, en allant chercher le pain au village.
December. On her way to fetch some bread in the village.

p. 12 (haut)
Dans la cour. Petite toilette du matin. La seule arrivée d'eau est celle-ci, dans la cour, il n'y en a aucune dans la maison. Pas de robinet, pas de salle de bain.
In the courtyard. Small morning wash. This is the only water inlet in the courtyard. There are none in the house. No tap, no bathroom.

p. 12 (bas)
Sur la route vers le village. C'est la Toussaint. Il fait encore doux. Mais la marche dans la montée de la route est difficile et elle s'essouffle très vite. "C'est la boule dans l'estomac", me dit-elle.
On the road. It is All Saints' Day. It is still a little warm. But the walk is difficult and she gets out of breath very fast. "It is the ball in my stomach," she tells me.

p.13
À table, un après-midi. Elle est incapable de me dire ce qu'elle a fait. D'ailleurs elle ne me reconnaît pas. "On se connaît ?" me dit-elle en ouvrant la porte. Alors je lui montre nos photos prises ensemble la dernière fois. J'écoute les mêmes histoires, celles du chat, celles de son mari, celles de Jean-Claude. La confiance revient.
In the kitchen, one afternoon. This time, I find her in very bad shape. She is unable to tell me what happened. Moreover she does not recognize me. "Do we know each other?" She asks me, opening the gate. Then I show her our photos taken together last time. I listen to the same stories, those with the cat, those of her husband, those of Jean-Claude. The trust comes back slowly.

p. 14-15
Dans la cuisine, à midi. Le fourneau ne démarre toujours pas, nous sommes en plein hiver. La maison est froide, le sol en terre battue humide, et l'odeur nauséabonde. Marie-Claude ne cuisine pas ce midi. Elle oublie, je crois. Elle dit avoir déjà mangé. Mais je suis là depuis le matin, ce n'est pas le cas.
In the kitchen, at noon. The wood stove still won't start; it's the middle of the winter. The house is cold, the ground is wet hard-packed surface, and there is a very bad smell. Marie-Claude does not cook today. She forgets, I believe. She says she has already eaten. But I have been there since the morning, and have not seen her eat.

p. 16-17
Dans la maison, Marie-Claude porte trois pulls, il ne fait pas très chaud, elle ne se découvre jamais. Le pull du dessus, je le vois dépérir, mois après mois, jusqu'à ce qu'on lui en offre un autre. Un pull égal cinq mois minimum.
In the house, Marie-Claude wears three pullovers; it is never very hot, she never undresses. The pullover on top, I see it eroding further, month after month, until someone gives her another. One pullover = Five months, minimum.

p. 18-19
Dans le salon, toujours les mêmes poupées bigoudènes. Sauf qu'elles bougent, parfois.
In the living room, always the same "bigoudene" dolls. Except that they move, sometimes.

p.21
Devant le fourneau du salon. Les souris ont pris leurs quartiers dans la pièce principale, les placards crépitent, les papiers d'aliments sont déchirés. Petites et grandes défilent à gauche, à droite. "On va mettre un piège", dit-elle, puis, quelques minutes plus tard, s'étonne à nouveau de voir une souris.
In front of the living room's stove. Mice are everywhere in the main room; you can hear them in the cupboards and the wrappers of the food have all been chewed open. Little mice and some much bigger mice are walking fearlessly around the place. "We will set up a trap," she says, but then, a few minutes later, is astonished again to see a mouse inside...

p. 22-23
Marie-Claude joue avec sa poupée préférée dans son salon. "Elle est belle hein", me dit-elle. Elle la cajole, lui caresse le visage, puis elle la repose sur son promontoire, juste derrière la télé, et lui ordonne de ne pas bouger.
Marie-Claude is playing with her favourite doll in her living room. "She is so beautiful, right?" she says. She coddles her, caresses her face, puts her back in her place, behind the TV, and orders her not to move.

p. 24-25
Marie-Claude dans son salon. De petits sentiers entre les montagnes de bibelots, de journaux et de poupées permettent encore l'accès au buffet, à la gazinière et à la porte d'entrée.
Marie-Claude in her living room. Narrow paths between mountains of knick-knacks, newspapers and dolls let us reach the cupboard, the stove and the door.

p. 26-27
Marie-Claude aussi fait des photos. Plein. Il paraît. Dans un instant de confusion, elle me raconte un moment passé ensemble, pendant lequel elle prenait des photos. Les miennes, dont les tirages ornent ses montagnes de bibelots.
Marie-Claude takes a lot of photos, she says. In a moment of confusion, she tells me all about a time we spent together, while she was taking pictures. The very pictures I took and that are displayed around her home.

p. 28-29
Dans le salon, un après-midi de pluie. En fouillant dans son fatras, avant mon arrivée, elle a retrouvé une tiare. Elle se trimballe avec partout dans la maison. Elle avait d'ailleurs oublié que je venais, le portail était fermé.
In her living room, a rainy afternoon. By searching her big pile of junk, before my arrival, she found a tiara. She lugs it around everywhere in the house, her tiara on her head. She had forgotten that I was coming; the gate was closed.

p. 30-31
Dans le salon, au milieu des amas de poupées, il y a une télé… Mais je ne l'ai jamais vue allumée. Trop d'humidité, elle ne démarre plus.
In the living room, in the midst of the dolls, there is a TV... She has never turned it on. Too damp it does not work anymore.

p. 32-33
Avec la nouvelle collection de pipes, des vieux polaroïds de Marie-Claude jeune avec son chat sont apparus. “Essuie tes petites pattes, mais pas dans le lit à maman” : elle raconte comment elle a élevé son chat pour qu'il soit propre, que le chat buvait le biberon tout seul. “Ah, elle en a eu des fessées !”
With the new collection of pipes, some old Polaroids of young Marie-Claude with her cat appeared. “Wipe your little feet, but not in mama's bed.” She tells about how she raised her cat for it to be clean, that the cat would drink her bottle on its own, “Ah she had a lot of spankings”.

p. 34-35
... Chat sur la fenêtre du salon. Chat trouvé. Chat cassé.
... Cat on the living room window. Found cat. Broken cat.

p. 36-37
Dans le salon. Elle est un peu une accumulatrice compulsive, elle cherche des poupées dans les décharges ou brocantes des villages voisins et confectionne elle-même leurs costumes.
Elle les considère comme ses enfants.
In the living room. One might say she has a compulsive hoarding disorder; she searches for dolls in rubbish dumps or flea markets in the surrounding villages and makes their costumes herself. She considers them a little like her children.

p. 38-39
Dans la chambre. Elle y emporte chaque nuit l'une de ses poupées, pour lui tenir compagnie. Marie-Claude ne jette rien et récupère tout. Tout ce qu'elle n'avait pas le droit de rapporter quand son mari était encore vivant.
In her room. Every night she takes one of her dolls with her, to keep her company. Marie-Claude throws nothing away. Everything that when her husband was alive he didn't allow her to own.

p. 40-41
La maison le matin à l'aube.
Marie-Claude's house, at dawn.

p. 42-43
Sur la route. Une seule route dans le village, un cul-de-sac dont on ne part qu'à reculons. Marie-Claude m'accompagne, je la quitte pour quelques semaines.
On the road. A single road in the village, a cul-de-sac which I have to reverse out of. Marie-Claude comes with me; I'm leaving her for a few weeks.

p. 44-45
Noël dans la chapelle de la montagne Saint-Michel.
Marie-Claude ne fait rien à Noël. Jean-Claude est avec sa fille et son fils. En même temps, elle ne sait plus trop quand c'est. Elle me raconte qu'elle a offert un pantalon à Jean-Claude et que c'était bien le repas de Noël, mais nous ne sommes que le 22...
Christmas at Mont Saint-Michel chapel. Marie-Claude does not share Christmas with anyone. Jean-Claude spends it with his daughter and son. And she does not really know when it is. She tells me she offered pants to Jean-Claude and that Christmas Eve was great, but we are only the 22nd.

p. 46-47
Crépuscule d'hiver breton, dans la cour.
Brittany's winter twilight, in the courtyard.

p. 48-49
Dans le salon. Marie-Claude remet du bois dans le fourneau. Jean-Claude l'a trouvé à la fin de l'hiver dernier, d'occasion. Elle avait passé l'hiver dans le froid.
In the living room. Marie-Claude is feeding the stove. Jean-Claude found a used one last winter; she had spent all the rough months in the cold.

p. 50-51
Je débarque en plein après-midi. Dans le salon, vaisselle ? Lessive ?
I arrive in the middle of the afernoon, in the living room, dish washing? Laundry? Who knows?

p. 52 (haut)
Marie-Claude, coquette, parfois.
Marie-Claude, appearence conscious, sometimes.

p. 52 (bas)
Marie-Claude est une femme de la campagne, elle n'est jamais sortie d'un périmètre de trente kilomètres autour de sa maison. Avec son mari, ils vendaient le bois à domicile et pêchaient des vairons.
Marie-Claude is a country woman. She has never left her area. With her husband, they used to sell wood to the neighboring villages and fish minnows.

p. 53
Marie-Claude n'a jamais eu d'enfants mais, depuis la mort de son mari, un paquet de poupées.
Marie-Claude, never had children but since her husband died, a bunch of dolls.

p. 54-55
À table, un mardi, au petit-déjeuner. Au lever, elle vide d'abord le pot de chambre, une simple bassine qu'elle met dans une poubelle. Puis elle réchauffe le café, dans la cafetière gardée au pied du lit. Elle a dû confondre le pot de chambre et la cafetière dans la nuit. “Marie-Claude, t'as pissé dans le café ?!”
In the kitchen, at breakfast, on a Tuesday. At sunrise, she first empties the chamber pot, which is nothing more than a basin which she puts in a bin. Then she warms up the coffee, in the coffeepot, kept at the end of the bed. She must have confused the chamber pot and the coffeepot last night. Pfffrrrffff. “Marie-Claude, you peed in the coffee?!”

p. 56 (haut)
Marie-Claude compte ses sous sur la table de la salle à manger. Bûcheron, pêcheur, épicier à la campagne, son mari ne lui a laissé qu'une petite retraite : 600 euros.
Marie-Claude is counting her money on the dining-room table. As a lumberjack, fisherman and itinerant grocer, her husband did not leave her a big pension. She lives with 600 euros a month.

p. 56 (bas)
Dans la salle à manger à midi. Je ne la vois plus manger que des morceaux de pain. Elle me raconte avoir mangé des “collettes et des ponnes' terre” à midi, mais il n'y a jamais eu de côtelettes dans le panier de courses...
In the living room, at noon. I see her eating only bread. She tells me she has been eating meat and potatoes for lunch, but I have never seen any meat in the groceries...

p. 57
Dans la chambre, c'est le bordel. Il y a aussi le frigo et un amoncellement de fringues.
In the bedroom, it's a mess. You'll also find the fridge and a mountain of clothes.

p. 58-59
Dans la maison de Marie-Claude. C'est une femme isolée. Son mari, mort en 1999, l'a coupée du monde extérieur pendant trente ans. La seule personne qu'elle voit, Jean-Claude, le meilleur ami de son mari, lui apporte ses courses tous les vendredis. À sa mort, son mari lui a fait promettre qu'il s'occuperait de sa femme.
In Marie-Claude's house. She is an isolated woman. Her husband, who died in 1999, had been cutting her off the outside life for thirty years. The only person she sees is Jean-Claude, her husband's best friend, who brings her groceries every Friday. On his death bed, her husband made Jean-Claude promise to take care of his wife.

p. 60-61
À table pour le goûter. La petite dame a un caractère bien trempé. Ce n'est pas parce qu'elle vit seule qu'on peut venir l'"emmerder" ! Elle me raconte que des personnes se faisant passer pour des aides ménagères lui ont volé son argent. Une histoire corroborée par Jean-Claude. Depuis, plus personne ne rentre.
In the kitchen. The small lady has a sturdy temper. It is not because she lives alone that we can come "to annoy" her! She tells me that people pretending to be home helpers stole her money, in her house. A story confirmed by Jean-Claude, actually. Since then, nobody comes in anymore.

p. 63
À table, pour le quatre-heures. On se mange une crêpe artisanale achetée à la boulangerie du village voisin. Ses préférées.
Snack time. We are eating a traditional crêpe bought in the bakery of the neighboring village. Her favorites.

p. 64-65
Le soir, vers 20 heures, dans le salon. C'est le moment d'aller se coucher. Elle n'enlève son pull que pour dormir. Elle dort en pantalon et sous-pull. Il ne fait pas très chaud ce soir mais Marie-Claude éteint le fourneau pour la nuit.
The evening, at about 8:00 pm, in the living room. It is time to go to bed. She removes her pullover only to sleep. She sleeps in her pants and her polo-neck jumper. It's not very hot this evening, but Marie-Claude puts off the stove for the night.

p. 67
Dans le salon de Marie-Claude, le matin. Elle se peigne et se fait une petite couette. Elle me dit se teindre les cheveux. J'ai bien vu quelque part le carton d'une nouvelle teinture, mais les cheveux jaunissent depuis un an et demi, et la teinture est toujours dans sa boîte.
In Marie-Claude's living room, one morning. She is combing her hair and makes a small braid. She tells me she dyes her hair herself. I did see somewhere the box of a new dye treatment, though her hair has been turning yellow grey eighteen months now and the dye is still in its box.

p. 68-69
Dans le salon, le matin, après le petit-déjeuner. Marie-Claude danse sur Tino Rossi avec son voile de mariée sur la tête. Elle me raconte que son mari était "méchant", qu'il ne la laissait pas sortir, parce qu'il croyait qu'elle voyait d'autres hommes.
In the living room, in the morning, after breakfast. Marie-Claude dances to Tino Rossi with her bridal veil on her head. She tells me that her husband was "nasty", that he did not let her go out, because he believed that she was unfaithfull to him.

p. 70-71
Dans l'entrée, le matin au réveil. Elle se met à papoter, du chat qui boit seul son biberon de lait, qui l'appelle maman... comment elle faisait l'amour dans les champs avec Jean-Claude (l'ami de son mari, je la soupçonne de mélanger les prénoms, il ne me semble pas qu'ils aient été amants) et qu'il ne voulait pas salir son pantalon…
In the entrance, the morning, waking up. She is chatty today, she talks about the cat that drinks by itself from its bottle of milk, that calls her "mum"; she speaks in a loop. Of how she made love in the fields with Jean-Claude (the friend of her husband. I suspect her of mixing up the names; it does not seem to me that they were lovers before) and that he did not want to make his pants dirty …

p. 72-73
L'électricité a disjoncté à la tombée de la nuit dans la salle à manger.
In the dining room the electricity cut at dusk.

p. 74-75
Dans la cour-jardin. Elle et son mari avaient créé une forteresse de tôle pour protéger la maison. Au centre, elle a fait placer un menhir dont on ne voit que la moitié. À gauche le garage avec tous les outils de son mari, à droite un rangement pour le bois, qui fuit.
In the courtyard/garden. She and her husband had created a fortress of sheet metal to protect the house. In the centre, she set up a menhir. On the left, the garage and all her husband's tools, on the right a storage space for wood, which sometimes floods.

p. 76-77
Dans son jardin, devant la grange à bois faite en tôle, Marie-Claude pisse. Comme dans sa maison, il n'y a pas de toilettes… C'est toujours mieux que de pisser dans le café !
In her garden, in front of the wood barn, Marie-Claude is peeing. As she does not have a toilet in her house… it is always better than peeing in the coffee.

p. 78-79
Je quitte Marie-Claude un petit moment. Je reviendrai en janvier, je pars en Belgique, pour elle "c'est trop loin, ouf".
Leaving Marie-Claude for a while. I'll be back in January; I'm going back to Belgium, for her "It is too far, ouf".

p. 80-81
Après avoir coupé son petit bois, Marie-Claude le rapporte dans le salon pour le placer près du fourneau.
After cutting the kindling, Marie-Claude brings it back to the living room near the stove.

p. 82-83
Elle saigne encore, elle s'est pris un j'ton. En faisant quoi ? On ne le saura pas, en tombant du toit, dit-elle, en se levant. On ne saura pas. Elle est dans un sale état. C'est récent, le sang est à peine sec. Elle a déjà oublié pour son nez. "Du sang ? D'où ça sort ça encore !"
She is bleeding again, she has taken a blow. Doing what? We will never know, falling from the roof, she might say, waking up, she might say. She is in a bad shape. It happened not so long ago, blood is not yet dry. She has already forgotten. "Blood? Where is that coming from?"

p. 84-85
Marie-Claude ne retrouve plus le chemin de sa maison, en rentrant du lac.
Marie-Claude does not find her way back home from the lake.

p. 86-87
Au cimetière, devant la tombe de son mari. Il est mort brutalement d'une maladie en 1999. Le maire accuse Marie-Claude d'avoir piqué des fleurs sur une tombe voisine pour fleurir celle de son mari.
In the cemetery, at the grave of her husband. He died after a short disease in 1999. The mayor accused Marie-Claude of having stolen flowers from a nearby grave to decorate that of her husband.

p. 88-89
Autour du lac qui borde la vieille centrale nucléaire à l'arrêt. Marie-Claude a soixante-quinze ans. Elle vit dans une zone reculée, où le vieillissement de la population est l'un des gros problèmes.
Around the lake skirting the old power plant. Marie-Claude is seventy-five years old; she lives in a remote area where the ageing of the population is one of the biggest problems.

p. 91
Marie-Claude, au-dessous de la chapelle de la montagne Saint-Michel.
Marie-Claude, just under the chapel of the Mont Saint-Michel.

LE PRIX HSBC POUR LA PHOTOGRAPHIE

Créé en avril 1995[1], le Prix HSBC pour la Photographie accompagne depuis 22 ans la génération émergente de la photographie et s'engage à soutenir de manière encore plus forte le travail de ses lauréats, en créant une cinquième étape dans l'itinérance et en leur offrant une aide à la production d'œuvres présentées lors de cette dernière exposition, insufflant ainsi un nouvel élan aux lauréats. Un concours annuel est ouvert de septembre à novembre à tout photographe n'ayant jamais édité de monographie, sans critère d'âge ni de nationalité.
Chaque année, un conseiller artistique désigné pour apporter un nouveau regard présélectionne une dizaine de candidats. Il présente alors ses choix au Comité exécutif, qui élit les deux lauréats. María García Yelo[2], conseillère artistique 2017, témoigne : "Beauté, surréalisme, ébahissement et douleur : tous font partie intégrante des projets sélectionnés pour l'édition 2017 du Prix HSBC pour la Photographie. Leurs auteurs, à l'imagerie visuelle très riche, nous incitent à lire des significations multiples et superposées. Nous passons ainsi de l'étonnement à l'accablement, de la reconnaissance au désarroi… Et quand nous finissons par comprendre, une profonde mélancolie nous envahit."

Accompagnement des deux artistes :
– publication de la première monographie de chaque artiste avec Actes Sud, dans la "Collection du Prix HSBC pour la Photographie";
– création et organisation de l'exposition itinérante de leurs œuvres dans cinq lieux culturels en France et/ou à l'étranger ;
– aide à la production, durant l'année de promotion, de nouvelles œuvres, présentées lors de la cinquième étape ;
– acquisition par HSBC France de six œuvres par lauréat pour son fonds photographique.

1. Sous l'égide de la Fondation de France. / 2. María García Yelo est directrice de PHotoEspaña à Madrid.

Created in April 1995[1], the Prix HSBC pour la Photographie has been supporting emerging photographers for 22 years. It undertakes to help its award winners, by creating a fifth stage in the travelling exhibition and by helping to produce the works presented in this latest exhibition, thus providing winners with a fresh impetus. An annual competition, it is open from September to November to any photographer who has never had a monograph published, with no age or nationality criteria.
Each year an artistic advisor is nominated to give a fresh outlook and to preselect around ten candidates who are then presented to the Executive Committee who select the two award winners. María García Yelo[2], 2017 artistic advisor, says:
"Beauty, surrealism, amazement and pain are all present in the selected projects of the 2017 edition of the Prix HSBC pour la Photographie. These photographers, with very rich visual imageries, force us to read several layers of meanings. We go from astonishment to overwhelm, from recognition to disconcert... When we finally understand, a deep melancholy invades us."

The HSBC Prize supports the two photographers by:
- Publishing each artist's first monograph in association with the publisher Actes Sud in the Prix HSBC pour la Photographie Collection;
- Creating and organizing the travelling exhibition of their works at five cultural venues in France and/or abroad;
- Help in promoting new works throughout the year, presented during the fifth stage;
- Guaranteeing HSBC France's acquisition of six works by each award winner for its photography collection.

1. Under the eagis of the Fondation de France. / 2. María García Yelo is the director of PHotoEspaña in Madrid.

LIVRES PARUS DANS LA COLLECTION / PREVIOUSLY PUBLISHED IN THE COLLECTION

2016
Marta Zgierska
Post

Christian Vium
Ville nomade

2015
Maïa Flore
Rememories

Guillaume Martial
Slap-stick

2014
Dephine Burtin
Encouble

Akiko Takizawa
Where We Belong

2013
Noémie Goudal
The Geometrical Determination of the Sunrise

Cerise Doucède
Liens intimes

2012
Leonora Hamill
Art in Progress

Éric Pillot,
In situ

2011
Alinka Echeverriá
Sur le chemin de Tepeyac

Zhang Xiao
Coastline

2010
Laurent Hopp
Sublunaire

Lucie & Simon
Vertiges du quotidien

2009
Grégoire Alexandre

Matthieu Gafsou
Surfaces

2008
Aurore Valade
Grand miroir

Guillaume Lemarchal
Paysages de l'après

2007
Julia Fullerton-Batten
Teenage Stories

Matthew Pillsbury
Time Frame

2006
Clark et Pougnaud

Marina Gadonneix
Paysages sur commande

2005
Éric Baudelaire
États imaginés

Birgitta Lund
In Transit

2004
Malala Andrialavidrazana
D'outre-monde

Patrick Taberna
Au fil des jours

2003
Mathieu Bernard-Reymond
Vous êtes ici

Laurence Leblanc
Rithy, Chéa, Kim Sour et les autres

2002
Laurence Demaison

Rip Hopkins
Tadjikistan Tissages

2001
Franck Christen

Jo Lansley & Helen Bendon

2000
Valérie Belin

Carole Fékété

1999
Catherine Gfeller
Urban Rituals

Yoshiko Murakami
Les Mains pour voir

1998
Milomir Kovacevic
La Part de l'ombre

Seton Smith
Without Warning

1997
Jean-François Campos
Après la pluie…

Bertrand Desprez
Pour quelques étoiles…

1996
Éric Prinvault
C'est où la maison ?

Henry Ray †
Amazonia

MÉLANIE WENGER

Mélanie Wenger est photographe documentaire, représentée par l'agence Cosmos basée à Bruxelles. Diplômée de lettres et d'un master en journalisme, elle a choisi de raconter des histoires d'Hommes, de héros de l'ordinaire, de révéler leur profondeur au travers de l'immédiateté permanente de la photographie. Sans oublier les aspérités, surtout, qui les rendent si uniques.
En 2011, elle commence à travailler sur la série *Wasted Young Libya (L'Enfance brisée de la Libye libre)*, qui lui prendra trois ans.
Entre 2014 et 2016, elle travaille sur les migrations entre la Libye, Malte et la Belgique. Pour sa série *Lost in Migration*, elle passe six mois en immersion dans un centre d'accueil pour demandeurs d'asile en souffrance mentale.
En parallèle, elle travaille sur le trafic d'ivoire et le braconnage au Cameroun et au Zimbabwe pendant deux ans. Elle suit des anti-braconniers dans la forêt comme dans la brousse, et photographie des chasseurs d'éléphants et des pisteurs bakas à la traque.
Depuis 2014, elle développe une série documentaire au long cours dans l'intimité d'une personne âgée isolée en Bretagne : *Marie-Claude, la dame aux poupées.*

Mélanie Wenger is a documentary photographer based in Brussels and represented by Cosmos agency. A graduate in Literature and with a master's in journalism, she has chosen to tell stories about human beings, heros of the ordinary, to reveal their depth through the permanent immediacy of photography. Without forgetting the harshness that makes them so unique.
In 2011 she started work on the series Wasted Young Libya, *which would take her three years.*
Between 2014 and 2016 she focused on migrations between Libya, Malta and Belgium, for the serie Lost in Migration. *She also spent six months in the psychiatric asylum seekers center CARDA in Bierset. In parallel she works on ivory trafficking and poaching in Africa and follows anti-poaching teams, poachers, trackers and hunters in the forest and the bush in Cameroon and Zimbabwe. Since 2014 she has been developing a long-term documentary series in the intimacy of an elderly isolated person in Brittany:* Marie-Claude, the Doll Lady.

REMERCIEMENTS / *ACKNOWLEDGEMENTS*

Je souhaite remercier toute l'équipe du Prix HSBC, Christine Raoult en particulier, María García Yelo, Christian Caujolle et Actes Sud. La DRAC Alsace grâce à son aide à la création, et tout particulièrement Bernard Goy. Il y a aussi l'agence Cosmos, Annie Boulat, Fanny Merrien, Victor Point, sans oublier Julie Caudan pour son soutien et sa confiance, et Cédric Gerbehaye pour son regard.
PICTO et François George pour les tirages de lecture.

Jef Bonifacino, qui m'accompagne, sans qui ce livre ne serait pas, Soizick Roulinat, pour son accueil, mes parents et mes amis.

Et finalement Marie-Claude pour sa beauté d'âme et son franc-parler. Pour avoir partagé sa fantaisie comme ses aspérités. Elle m'a tout montré, sans choisir un côté. Mais surtout je voudrais la remercier d'avoir arrêté de pisser dans le café !

À ma mère. À ma grand-mère.

I would like to thank the team from the Prix HSBC, particularly Christine Raoult, María García Yelo, Christian Caujolle and Actes Sud. The DRAC Alsace for their creation support, especially Bernard Goy. Also Cosmos agency, Annie Boulat, Fanny Merrien, Victor Point, without forgetting Julie Caudan for her support and confidence, and Cédric Gerbehaye for his eye.
PICTO and François George for the proofs.

Jef Bonifacino, who acompanies me, without whom this book would not be, my parents and my friends.

And finally, Marie-Claude, for her trust, the beauty of her soul and her directness. For having shared her fantasies and her acerbity. She showed me everything, without choosing a side. But above all, I would like to thank her for stopping to pee in the coffee!

To my mother. To my grandmother.

Graphisme : Anne-Laure Exbrayat
Fabrication : Géraldine Lay
Photogravure : Terre Neuve

Reproduit et achevé d'imprimer en avril 2017
par l'imprimerie Graphius, à Gand, Belgique
pour le compte des éditions Actes Sud,
Le Méjan, place Nina-Berberova,
13200 Arles.

Dépôt légal 1re édition : mai 2017